CRITICAL SURVEY
OF
DRAMA

CRITICAL SURVEY

OF

DRAMA

REVISED EDITION

Jon-Mil

4

Edited by
FRANK N. MAGILL

SALEM PRESS
Pasadena, California   Englewood Cliffs, New Jersey

∞ The paper used in these volumes conforms to
the American National Standard for Permanence of
Paper for Printed Library Materials, Z39.48-1984.

**Library of Congress Cataloging-in-Publication
Data**
  Critical survey of drama. English language series/
edited by Frank N. Magill.—Rev. ed.
      p.   cm.
  Includes bibliographical references and index.
  1. English drama—Dictionaries. 2. American
drama—Dictionaries. 3. English drama—Bio-
bibliography. 4. American drama—Bio-bibliography.
5. Commonwealth drama (English)—Dictionaries.
6. Dramatists, English—Biography—Dictionaries.
7. Dramatists, American—Biography—Dictionaries. 8. Commonwealth drama (English)—Bio-
bibliography.
I. Magill, Frank Northen, 1907-   .
PR623.C75   1994
822.009′03—dc20   93-41618
ISBN 0-89356-851-1 (set)   CIP
ISBN 0-89356-855-4 (volume 4)

PRINTED IN THE UNITED STATES OF AMERICA

LIST OF AUTHORS IN VOLUME 4

CRITICAL SURVEY
OF
DRAMA

HENRY ARTHUR JONES

Born: Grandborough, England; September 20, 1851
Died: London, England; January 7, 1929

Principal drama

Hearts of Oak, pr. 1879, pb. 1885 (also known as *Honour Bright*); *A Clerical Error*, pr. 1879, pb. 1904; *The Silver King*, pr. 1882, pb. 1907 (with Henry Herman); *Saints and Sinners*, pr. 1884, pb. 1891; *Wealth*, pr. 1889; *The Middleman*, pr. 1889, pb. 1907; *Judah*, pr. 1890, pb. 1894; *The Crusaders*, pr. 1891, pb. 1893; *The Dancing Girl*, pr. 1891, pb. 1907; *The Bauble Shop*, pr. 1893, pb. 1893(?); *The Tempter*, pr. 1893, pb. 1898; *The Masqueraders*, pr. 1894, pb. 1899; *The Case of Rebellious Susan*, pr. 1894, pb. 1897; *The Triumph of the Philistines*, pr. 1895, pb. 1899; *Michael and His Lost Angel*, pr., pb. 1896; *The Liars*, pr. 1897, pb. 1901; *The Physician*, pr. 1897, pb. 1899; *Carnac Sahib*, pr., pb. 1899; *Mrs. Dane's Defence*, pr. 1900, pb. 1905; *The Lackey's Carnival*, pr., pb. 1900; *The Princess's Nose*, pr., pb. 1902; *Whitewashing Julia*, pr. 1903, pb. 1905; *The Hypocrites*, pr. 1906, pb. 1907; *The Evangelist*, pr. 1907, pb. 1908(?) (also known as *The Galilean's Victory*); *The Lie*, pr. 1914, pb. 1915; *Plays by Henry Arthur Jones*, pb. 1982 (includes *The Silver King*, *The Case of Rebellious Susan*, and *The Liars*).

Other literary forms

Henry Arthur Jones, a prolific dramatist, was also an energetic theatrical critic and polemicist. His prose writings include *The Renascence of the English Drama* (1895), *The Foundations of a National Drama* (1913), and *The Theatre of Ideas* (1915). Jones's polemics are found in his attacks on H. G. Wells and George Bernard Shaw in *Patriotism and Popular Education* (1919) and *My Dear Wells: A Manual for the Haters of England; Being a Series of Letters upon Bolshevism, Collectivism, Internationalism and the Distribution of Wealth, Addressed to Mr. H. G. Wells* (1921, 1922). Jones actively campaigned for the abolition of theatrical censorship. *The Renascence of the English Drama* brings together the essays in which he argues that drama has definite artistic forms, that it is a serious literary genre, and that a national theater should be established. He calls for copyright laws to be reformed and plays printed—at the time, radical ideas meeting with much opposition. *The Foundations of a National Drama* continues Jones's advocacy for the establishment of a national theater, argues for a more intelligent theater, and attacks contemporary theatrical frivolity. Jones believed that art has a social value—that the theater should educate audiences and bring beauty and culture to otherwise impoverished ordinary lives.

Achievements

Jones is regarded as one of the most important English dramatists and men of the theater during the last decades of the nineteenth century. *The Silver King*, hailed as a masterpiece of melodramatic stage craftsmanship, ran for 289 performances—a lengthy run by the standards of the time. In subsequent plays, Jones turned his attention to such serious themes as the exposure of hypocrisy and deceit and the depiction of the emerging "new woman." At his best, Jones was a master craftsman, a superb manipulator of theatrical dialogue and writer of problem plays. After the turn of the century and the success of *Mrs. Dane's Defence* in 1900, Jones, while continuing to write prolifically, began merely to rework well-tried formulas and melodramatic successes. Repetitious melodrama, social comedy, and problem plays made him a theatrical back-number. His energies turned to the attempt to influence the course of subsequent theatrical literature through the dissemination of his ideas in books, pamphlets, and lectures. The 1982 publication by the Cambridge University Press of three of Jones's plays— *The Silver King*, *The Case of Rebellious Susan*, and *The Liars*—demonstrates that he is not an obscure late-Victorian dramatist of merely historical interest. Jones's reputation as a consummate dramatic craftsman stands secure, as does his place in the English theatrical renaissance of the last decades of the nineteenth century.

Biography

Henry Arthur Jones was born on September 20, 1851, in Grandborough, Buckinghamshire. His background was Nonconformist; his father was a farmer, and his mother was a farmer's daughter. Jones's formal education seems to have stopped at the age of twelve, when he was sent to work for his uncle, who had a draper's shop on the Kentish coast at Ramsgate. Jones stayed for three and a half years in Ramsgate before moving to Gravesend, which was nearer to London, and to another draper's shop. In 1869, he moved into London, where he was to remain for most of his life. Self-educated, he read widely; his favorite authors were John Milton, Herbert Spencer, and Samuel Butler, and his favorite works were about scientific advancements. From Milton—a lifetime obsession—Jones learned verse drama techniques and the interweaving of biblical quotation into the texture of his plays. Scientists, explorers, and doctors often appear in his plays, and he makes frequent use of Spencerian and Butlerian ideas. In his first year in London, Jones wrote several unstaged one-act plays and an unpublished novel. *Hearts of Oak*, the first of his plays to be produced, premiered at the Theatre Royal, Exeter, on May 29, 1879, and the production encouraged Jones to devote his whole energies to drama. *A Clerical Error*, his first London play, was performed in October, 1879. Jones's reputation was secured by *The Silver King*, which opened at the Princess's Theatre on November 16, 1882. The success of this play provoked a dispute over its authorship, which Wilson Barrett, an actor-manager, claimed to share with Jones and Henry Herman. A 1905 legal settlement denied Barrett's claim. *The Silver King* gave Jones some degree of financial security. His experience with Barrett soured Jones's attitude toward the prevailing actor-manager theatrical hierarchy of his day, but *The Crusaders*, his self-financed effort, which was produced in November, 1891, proved to be a disastrous financial failure.

In the 1890's Jones's work met with mixed fortune. *The Masqueraders*, *The Tempter*, *The Bauble Shop*, and *The Liars* succeeded, whereas *The Triumph of the Philistines*, *Michael and His Lost Angel*, *Carnac Sahib*, and *The Lackey's Carnival* aroused controversy and lost money. *Mrs. Dane's Defence*, first performed at Wyndham's in October, 1900, was his last real theatrical success. George Bernard Shaw, writing in his regular *Saturday Review* column, denounced *The Princess's Nose* as morally bankrupt, and another hostile critic, Arthur B. Walkley of *The Times* of London, was barred from attending the opening of *Whitewashing Julia* in 1903. *The Hypocrites* was warmly received in America, but Jones's subsequent American theatrical venture, *The Evangelist*, failed. Deeply troubled by World War I, as were so many of his contemporaries, Jones wasted much energy in publically feuding with H. G. Wells and Shaw. He opposed what he regarded as their lack of patriotism in their opposition to the war. The fledgling film industry purchased and produced several of Jones's plays, but he disapproved of the end products. In 1923, he achieved a modest theatrical success in London with *The Lie* (originally produced nearly a decade before in the United States); this drama was prematurely replaced at Wyndham's by Shaw's *Saint Joan*.

Jones's private life is an enigma. With failing health and lack of success in his late years, he retreated from the theatrical world he loved so much. Jones had married Jane Eliza Seeley, the daughter of an artificial flower manufacturer, in 1875; she died in 1924. They had seven children, three sons and four daughters, one of whom, Doris Arthur Jones, produced in 1930 the official biography of her father, *The Life and Letters of Henry Arthur Jones*. A recurring leitmotif in Jones's drama is the conflict among sexual passion, social duty, and respectability. Such a conflict may well have had a foundation in the secrets of his own carefully guarded private life.

Analysis

In 1894, Henry Arthur Jones called for "a school of plays of serious intention, plays that implicitly assert the value and dignity of human life, that it has great passions and great aims, and is full of meaning and importance." He set out to gain respect for the theater as a serious art form, rejecting the sensational melodrama so prevalent on the English stage. In

The Old Drama and the New (1923), William Archer, a distinguished, perceptive critic, looked back at the theatrical world of late-Victorian and Edwardian England. For Archer, Jones was a natural dramatist whose chief aim was to criticize life as he saw it and especially to expose philistinism. Jones's chief weakness, in Archer's view, was his inability to free himself from the melodramatic traditions in which he served his theatrical apprenticeship. Jones's work largely falls into two categories: melodrama and comedy of intrigue. "The pity is" writes Archer, "that the world of his imagination is not sunlit but limelit."

The plot of *The Silver King*, Jones's first major success, provides a good illustration of his manipulation of melodramatic form. The play contains dialogue that is natural without being artificial (a quality of Jones's drama at its best), real passion, and some elements of genuine comedy (a quality sometimes lacking in Jones). *The Silver King* has a wronged hero, a persecuted heroine, a ruthless landlord, a snobbish aristocrat, a faithful family servant, a detective, and a Cockney comic. Wilfred Denver loses his money at the races and, while drowning his sorrows in a London pub, is taunted by his wife's former admirer, Henry Ware. Denver publicly swears to kill Ware. Ware's house is broken into by a gang led by the aristocrat Captain Skinner; Denver is chloroformed. Skinner, using Denver's gun, kills Ware, and Denver, believing that he is the murderer, takes a train north from London—the dramatist not missing the opportunity to throw in a scenically lavish but costly railway scene. Denver gets out at the first station and subsequently discovers that the train he was on has crashed. The police believe him to be dead. Going to the United States, he makes a fortune in the Montana silver mines. Returning to England, Denver discovers that his starving, ailing wife and child are to be ejected from Skinner's land without a roof over their heads. Secretly he gives them money and, in the disguise of an idiot, infiltrates Skinner's gang in order to find out what really happened. Justice triumphs in the end. All the ingredients of classic melodrama are here: an exciting plot, a great deal of action, violence, intrigue, a wronged hero and a suffering heroine, a malignant and devious villain of aristocratic origins, asinine police officers, and the triumph of good over evil. Even Matthew Arnold (not an easy critic to please), writing in the *Pall Mall Gazette*, December 6, 1882, thought that Jones had managed to transcend the limitations of his chosen genre: "throughout the piece the diction and sentiments are natural, they have sobriety, they are literature." In spite of Jones's subsequent attempts to free himself from the shackles of melodrama and to write serious theatrical literature, he is still remembered for *The Silver King*, with its masterly use of well-tried formulas and its invigorating theatricality.

Saints and Sinners is an example of Jones's early attempts to render contemporary social problems dramatically, to write "plays of serious intention." The plot revolves around a village girl's seduction by a handsome, worldly villain—the Little Emily syndrome. The honest fiancé is forced abroad, returning to claim his girl. Jones's aim in *Saints and Sinners*, as stated in his preface to the published text (in which Jones changed his original ending to a happy one), was to expose the "ludicrous want of harmony, or apparently of even the most distant relation of any sort between a man's religious professions and his actions." Letty, the seduced, is the daughter of a pastor in conflict with his materialistic congregation. Pastor Fletcher opposes the attempt of his deacon, a tanner, to throw the widow of his former partner out of his home. The tanner, Hoggard, makes public Letty's seduction, and Fletcher is forced by his congregation to resign. The 1884 theater audience found Jones's exposure of the congregation's hypocrisy too much and strongly reacted to the play, which had a long but controversial London run. After *Saints and Sinners*, Jones had a reputation as an unconventional dramatist who daringly exposed folly. *Saints and Sinners* began his fight for theatrical freedom of expression, and he published the play in book form—not standard practice at the time—in order to give its ideas permanence as serious literature. In the following year, 1885, his one-act play "Welcome Little Stranger" was turned down by the Lord Chamberlain on the grounds that its opening hinted at the mysteries of childbirth. From the viewpoint of the late twentieth century, Jones's depiction in *Saints and Sinners* of seduction, hypocrisy, and the dichotomy between religious belief and private conduct may appear tame and the Victorian public's outcry surprising. "Welcome Little Stranger" provides insight into Victorian attitudes concerning what was permissible onstage and what was not. Two plays of 1889, *Wealth* and *The Middleman*, demonstrate Jones's theatrical attempt to develop serious themes. *Wealth* revolves around the refusal of its heroine to obey her father and marry the wealthy man he has chosen for her. Turned out into the streets for her disobedience, she marries for love and finally is reconciled with her father on his deathbed. In *Wealth*, Jones deals with the conflict between love and wealth, emotion and filial duty. He was tackling a subject which was increasingly to occupy the attention of his fellow dramatists Arthur Wing Pinero, Oscar Wilde, and Shaw: the emerging modern woman and her aspirations. As theater, however, *Wealth* was not a success—it was believed to lack wit, William Archer's "sunlight." By contrast, *The Middleman* was a stage success and is a very witty play. Humor, love, and social comment are inextricably interwoven into its plot, which has as its focal point a dreamy, exploited porcelain worker turning the tables on his ruthless master. The subplot unites the worker's daughter and the master's son. In terms of the development of Jones's stagecraft, *The Middleman* paved the way for his success with *Judah*; it is with *Judah* that Jones threw off the shackles of melodrama and wrote a genuine problem play.

Reviewing *Judah* in the *Saturday Review*, Shaw objected to it on the ground that it failed to tackle the issues it raised, merely skirting around them. The play, Shaw wrote, "consists of clever preliminaries; and when the real play begins with the matrimonial experiment of Judah and Vashti, down comes the curtain as usual." *Judah*, with its pervasive biblical allusions, its use of allegory, and its hereditary motif, proved to be too ambitious for its author. The plot is not complicated and centers upon a low-church clergyman, Judah, who holds extreme religious beliefs. Judah falls passionately in love with Vashti, a faith healer manipulated by her father into practicing public deceit. Vashti, true to the origin of her name, is torn between loyalty to her father and love. Judah helps her to free herself from her father's deception, and in the final act, after public confession, he resigns his ministry. There appear to be Ibsenite influences at work in the play's treatment of remorse and conscience, even though Jones vigorously denied that he had been influenced by Henrik Ibsen. Contemporary theatergoers were moved by powerful performances in the leading role, but *Judah* is essentially a closet play, more suited to reading than to theatrical performance.

Jones regarded *The Tempter* as one of his finest efforts. A verse play of ideas in five acts, *The Tempter* concentrates on the conflict between duty and passion. The blank verse drama is set in the fourteenth century, with the Devil setting traps for the other characters, especially for a religious man who, despite himself, falls deeply in love with a rebellious, unhappily married girl. The setting is too ambitious and the play too full of Shakespearean and Miltonic echoes and associations to be successful. Jones returned to the theme of the struggle against temptation in *The Masqueraders*, in which one of the leading characters is a scientist, presented as a high-principled but tempted man, devoted to his work and endeavoring to expand the frontiers of knowledge. One woman (a role played for all its worth by one of the leading ladies of the day, Mrs. Patrick Campbell), is caught between two men: her dissolute feckless husband and the scientist. Eventually, the latter chooses the path of research and goes to Africa, but not before he has given the heroine, who has thrown in her lot with him, financial security. The play's attempt to reveal the unhappiness behind the glitter of seemingly successful lives is interesting, but theatrically it does not succeed.

Jones's next play, *The Case of Rebellious Susan*, was a box-office success. Set in high society and wittily focusing upon the new woman and sexual repression, it tackled adultery and sexual discrimination. The play demonstrates in the character of its heroine, Susan, Jones's remarkable ability to create a character whose ideas are basically not in sympathy with his own. *The Case of Rebellious Susan* and *The Triumph of the Philistines* were partly reactions to Shaw's counsel that Jones should write detailed comedies of manners. In *The Triumph of the Philistines*, Jones returned to his earlier theme of attacking English philistinism and resistance to change, while in *The Liars*, he returned to social comedy, the comedy residing in each character's frantic attempts to cover up the "truth" from the others. Lady Jessica Napean weaves a tangled web in order to divert her jealous husband's suspicion concerning what in effect was an innocent meeting. Edward Falkner, a young explorer in love with Lady Jessica, plans an elaborate and complicated elopement, stopped at the last moment by Sir Christopher Deering. Sir Christopher upholds the traditional social conventions and the wisdom that, in English society, pretenses have to be maintained at all costs. Marriage cannot be destroyed. The young explorer goes on an expedition to Africa. Particularly noticeable in *The Liars* is the superb craftsmanship exhibited in the plotting, which reaches a crescendo of Jamesian elaborateness of deceit in the third act. In the brilliant dialogue of *The Liars*, Jones captures the upper-class spirit of his milieu. Even Shaw remarked, when reviewing the play, that Jones gave a "very keen and accurate picture of smart society." Unfortunately, Jones's play ultimately accepts the very conservative values which it seems to have set out to attack.

Today, *Mrs. Dane's Defence* is regarded as Jones's masterpiece. It has been praised for its tightness and economy of construction, its strength of characterization, and its superb dialogue—especially in the third act's cross-examination scene between Sir Daniel (Mr. Justice) Carteret and Mrs. Dane. The ending is not without power. Mrs. Dane is forced into exile to Devonshire, "outside the palings." She and Jones accept that "the world is very hard on a woman," but that is the way of the world. There is no attempt at a happy ending. The dramatist accepts what he regards as inexorable social laws. Jones was a superb craftsman, and his skill reached its consummate height in *Mrs. Dane's Defence*. After this play, he churned out another twenty-six full-length plays, variations on anachronistic themes with settings in a time gone forever. *The Lie*, produced in London in 1923 but written and produced in New York nearly a decade before, became a West End hit. Jones tapped his old melodramatic techniques to produce a drama which revolves around two sisters in love with the same man and which deals with illegitimacy and deceit.

Jones remained a dramatist of the last decades of the nineteenth century, a superb craftsman, the author of a melodrama to outdo all the others, *The Silver King*, and of two brilliantly constructed plays, *The Liars* and *Mrs. Dane's Defence*. He is remembered as a champion of the serious theater, of the theater of ideas, and as an advocate of theatrical freedom. Jones was largely antagonistic toward contemporary theatrical developments, finding, for example, Anton Chekhov's *The Cherry Orchard* (pr. 1904) to be the product of "someone who had visited a lunatic asylum." Even though Jones was eclipsed by Pinero, Shaw, and Wilde, his best plays are still appreciated. After all, as Shaw pointed out, Jones possessed "creative imagination, curious observation, inventive humour, originality, sympathy, and sincerity."

Other major works

NONFICTION: *The Renascence of the English Drama*, 1895; *The Foundations of a National Drama*, 1913; *The Theatre of Ideas*, 1915; *Patriotism and Popular Education*, 1919; *My Dear Wells: A Manual for the Haters of England; Being a Series of Letters upon Bolshevism, Collectivism, Internationalism and the Distribution of Wealth, Addressed to Mr. H. G. Wells*, 1921, 1922.

Bibliography

Booth, Michael R. *Theatre in the Victorian Age.* Cambridge, England: Cambridge University Press, 1991. Jones, one of the two most popular writers of melodrama (the other being Arthur Wing Pinero, with whom he is always linked), was deeply interested in the themes of the exploitation of the working class and the conflict between capital and labor. He was also concerned with religious subjects and the struggle between faith and doubt, and he was a mortal enemy of hypocrisy, causing his plays to sound somewhat preachy. At the same time, he seemed ambivalent in his attitude toward socially risky themes; as a result, his ideas proved bolder than his execution of them. Illustrations.

Eaton, Walter Prichard. *The Drama in English.* New York: Charles Scribner's Sons, 1930. An account of the playwright's attempts to introduce more realism into the English theater, despite initial audience hostility. Although Jones began his career by writing melodramas that were heavy on plot and short on credibility, as he progressed he became more interested in "holding the mirror up to nature." Ironically, although his temperament drove him in the direction of serious drama, Eaton believes that he was more successful in writing such comedies of manners as *The Liars.*

Jones, Doris Arthur. *The Life and Letters of Henry Arthur Jones.* London: Victor Gollancz, 1930. This biography, written by the playwright's daughter, consists of a compilation of letters to friends and family. It gives the reader a vivid picture of both the public and the private man, his kindness, his generosity, and his dedication to the theater. It also provides a vivid account of the London of his day, with a delightful introductory letter by critic-artist Max Beerbohm. Illustrations, chronology, appendices.

Trewin, J. C. *The Edwardian Theatre.* Oxford, England: Basil Blackwell, 1976. Trewin views Jones as a playwright who never lost an opportunity to preach his messages; although skillful at dialogue, Jones lacked gloss and sophistication, and he continued throughout his career to use the same people and the same themes in his dramas. Contains an interesting account of his working methods and his aims at reaching his audience. Although interested in ideas, he rejected Henrik Ibsen's dramas, finding them too radical for his taste.

Wearing, J. P. "Henry Arthur Jones: An Annotated Bibliography of Writings About Him." *English Literature in Transition, 1880-1920* 22, no. 3 (1979): 160-228. A useful collection of critical reviews, ranging from an appreciation of Jones's contributions to the theater to a dismissal of his work as hopelessly out of fashion. Some critics note that one or two of his plays, however, have enjoyed successful revivals.

William Baker
(Updated by *Mildred C. Kuner*)

PRESTON JONES

Born: Albuquerque, New Mexico; April 7, 1936
Died: Dallas, Texas; September 19, 1979

Principal drama

The Last Meeting of the Knights of the White Magnolia, pr. 1973, pb. 1976; *Lu Ann Hampton Laverty Oberlander*, pr. 1974, pb. 1976; *The Oldest Living Graduate*, pr. 1974, pb. 1976; *A Texas Trilogy*, pr. 1974, pb. 1976 (includes *The Last Meeting of the Knights of the White Magnolia*, *Lu Ann Hampton Laverty Oberlander*, *The Oldest Living Graduate*); *A Place on the Magdalena Flats*, pr. 1976, pb. 1984; *Santa Fe Sunshine*, pr., pb. 1977 (one act); *Juneteenth*, pr. 1979 (one act); *Remember*, pr. 1979.

Other literary forms

Preston Jones is known only for his plays.

Achievements

Preston Jones is often labeled a regional playwright, and certainly one of his achievements was his treatment of the American Southwest as a setting for serious drama. His plays capture the idiosyncratic characters, regional language, and unique experience of the rural Southwest at a time of transition for the land and its people. The significance of Jones's work, however, is not limited to his recording of the life of a specific community. The plays are significant commentaries on the way people deal with fundamental human problems: the pain of loneliness, the fear of failure, the effects of time. Like Anton Chekhov, Jones chronicles the passing of a way of life, and he does so with much of the gentle criticism and humorous affection of the Russian playwright. Jones's work also contains an exuberance and rough energy, however, which are uniquely his and which are rooted in the language and energy of his characters. Indeed, Jones's discovery of the value to be found in the lives and troubles of the most ordinary of people and of the lyric poetry embedded in their native idiom constitutes his most important theatrical achievement.

Biography

Preston St. Vrain Jones was born in Albuquerque, New Mexico, on April 7, 1936. His father, a former lieutenant governor of New Mexico, had been a professional military man who at one time had hoped for a career writing Western novels. Jones grew up in New Mexico, attending a Catholic boarding school for boys for a short time before he was graduated from high school in Albuquerque. After a brief period of military service, Jones entered the University of New Mexico, from which he received a bachelor of science degree in speech in 1960. He taught one semester in a high school in Tucumcari, New Mexico, before returning to the University of New Mexico to study drama for a year. During this period, he also spent some time working with the State Highway Department in and around Colorado City, Texas, which later became the model for Bradleyville, Texas, the setting of *A Texas Trilogy*.

In 1961, Jones enrolled in the drama department of Baylor University in Waco, Texas, where he studied with Paul Baker, nationally known as an innovative force in Southwestern theater. Baker quickly became, and remained, a major influence on Jones's life and career; he asked Jones to join the Dallas Theater Center, where Jones continued his studies and worked with the theater's professional company. While there, he married Mary Sue Birkhead, an actress and designer and then assistant director of the Dallas Theater Center. In 1963, the Dallas Theater Center transferred its academic affiliation from Baylor to Trinity University in San Antonio, Texas, from which Jones received a master of arts in drama in 1966. Jones remained in Dallas as a member of the Dallas Theater Center's resident professional company, accumulating experience in all phases of theater, which served him well when he began to develop his interest in playwriting.

Although interested in writing for much of his life, Jones did not emerge as a serious playwright until 1973, with the premiere of *The Last Meeting of the Knights of the White Magnolia*. The previous year, Jones had been appointed producer of the Dallas Theater Center's small, experimental theater. Dissatisfied with the scripts available, particularly with the lack of good regional drama, Jones decided to write something himself, drawing on his knowledge of the Southwest and especially on his experiences in Colorado City. He completed *Lu Ann Hampton Laverty Oberlander* first, following quickly with *The Last Meeting of the Knights of the White Magnolia* and *The Oldest Living Graduate*. In 1974, the three plays were performed in repertory at the Dallas Theater Center. *The Last Meeting of the Knights of the White Magnolia* was selected as the offering of the American Playwright's Theater the following year, and in 1976, the three plays broke all box-office records at the Kennedy Center in Washington and opened on Broadway. Although the reviews of the New York production were mixed, the popular and critical success of the plays across the United States established Jones as a major new American playwright.

Following *A Texas Trilogy*, Jones wrote three more full-length plays and a short one-act. All but one of the works premiered at the Dallas Theater Center, where Jones continued to work as an actor and director as well as resident playwright. While the later plays have not received the widespread production and recognition of the first three plays, they show Jones's growing maturity as a writer as well as his continuing interest in the major themes of the trilogy. Unfortunately, Jones's career was cut short when he died unexpectedly on September 19, 1979, following surgery for a bleeding ulcer. The seven plays which he finished, a remarkable feat for the relatively brief span of his writing career, represent an important contribution to American dramatic literature.

Analysis

The plays of Preston Jones are remarkably consistent in their concentration on character over plot, in their exploration of the poetry inherent in ordinary speech, and in their emphasis on certain prominent themes. From the beginning of his literary career, Jones's central theme was time. He explored—sometimes seriously, sometimes humorously, but always sympathetically—the effects of the inexorable march of time on people never quite prepared for the changes it will bring. His characters are usually lonely, isolated, cut off from the mainstream of the world by social changes, by geography, by ghosts from their past. They are often people who would be considered failures by normal standards but in whom Jones finds strength and emotional depth which mitigate their lack of the usual hallmarks of success.

Jones's concerns with the fear of failure, the pain of loneliness, and the effects of time are presented principally through character. Jones's great strength as a dramatist lies in his depiction of original and distinct characters who are able to engage the audience's emotions in a profound way. Like the plays of Chekhov, Jones's theater is often singularly undramatic. If his plotting is sometimes weak or contrived, however, his language never is, and it is primarily through dialogue that his characters are rendered. Jones possessed a sure ear for dialogue, an ability to capture the idiosyncratic phrases, the natural rhythms, the inherent poetry of everyday language. If that language is often rough and profane, it is just as often lyrically beautiful, reverberating with a poetry that transcends its common origins.

Jones is best known for the three plays which make up *A Texas Trilogy*: *The Last Meeting of the Knights of the White Magnolia*, *Lu Ann Hampton Laverty Oberlander*, and *The Oldest Living Graduate*. These plays are not unified by consecutive events, as is typical in dramatic trilogies, but by a single setting, shared characters, and common themes. The action of each play is separate and independent of the others, but each deals in its own way with Jones's themes of failure, isolation, and time. The town of Bradleyville, of which Jones created a map with the locations of various characters' homes and other important landmarks carefully noted, is isolated from the present and the future, bypassed by the new highway, and its people are isolated from one another by racial prejudices, past events, and present needs. The town is a relic of a past way of life, in which most of its characters are trapped by their own pasts: Lu Ann by her marriages, the Colonel by his war experiences, Skip Hampton by his failures and his alcoholism. In the three plays, Jones examines different aspects of the passing rural way of life that Bradleyville represents.

The first of the plays to be produced was *The Last Meeting of the Knights of the White Magnolia*. The plot of the play is very simple: The members of a social lodge gather for their monthly meeting, expecting the usual evening of drinking and playing dominoes, only to find the last remnants of the dying fraternal order disintegrate during the evening as they attempt to initiate their first new member in more than five years. Neither the individual members nor the lodge itself, with its basic ideals of white supremacy and unquestioning patriotism, has been able to adjust to the social changes of the late 1950's and early 1960's.

While Jones ridicules the ludicrous aspects of such fraternal orders—the mystical ceremonies, the pointless rules and regulations—and while he never excuses his characters' basic ignorance and bigotry, he presents sympathetically their need for companionship and sense of community and their fears and confusions at the potential loss of these values. The play is uproariously funny, but it never loses sight of the basic humanity of the characters, each of which is etched with depth and precision. The most memorable figure is that of Colonel J. C. Kinkaid, a shell-shocked veteran of World War I whose physical and mental deterioration during the course of the evening graphically parallels the dissolution of the group and, in a broader sense, of the Bradleyville way of life.

While *The Last Meeting of the Knights of the White Magnolia* presents a general view of Bradleyville, Jones's second play concentrates more closely on a single character. *Lu Ann Hampton Laverty Oberlander* begins in 1953, when its title character is a bubbly but dissatisfied eighteen-year-old cheerleader, and traces her life over a twenty-year period. Eager to leave her hometown and see the world, Lu Ann never gets any farther than a trailer park in a nearby town, but she survives a divorce, her second husband's death, her brother's alcoholism, and her mother's debilitating illness, and she achieves a kind of quiet dignity through her acceptance of her fate. A failure by most standards, Lu Ann is seen by Jones as a survivor, worthy of sympathy and praise. *Lu Ann Hampton Laverty Oberlander* also traces the life of Skip Hampton, a character introduced in *The Last Meeting of the Knights of the White Magnolia*. As Lu Ann grows in strength and dignity, her brother degenerates from an optimistic but ineffectual schemer to a painfully dependent alcoholic. The plot of *Lu Ann Hampton Laverty Oberlander*, with its careful symmetry, is perhaps too contrived, but the characters are memorable and the dialogue compares well with that of Jones's other plays. In a typically realistic and poignant sample of Jones's language, Skip notes how ironic it is "when all that stands between a man and the by-God loony bin is his sister's tab down to the Dixie Dinette."

The last play of the trilogy, *The Oldest Living Graduate*, focuses on

Colonel Kinkaid, who, as he did in *The Last Meeting of the Knights of the White Magnolia*, reflects the values and attitudes of the past. His distrust of business, his love for the land, and his insistence on salvaging a small part of his past from the ravages of time place him in conflict with his son Floyd, the forward-looking local entrepreneur. The play looks with humor at the foibles and prejudices of Bradleyville's country-club set and its small-town morality, at academic and military folderol, at the values of a lost way of life, at the conflicts between generations, and at death itself. *The Oldest Living Graduate* is the most sophisticated and finely crafted of the three plays which make up the trilogy. In it, Jones combines his skill at characterization with a more complex plot and achieves a level of poetry, particularly in the Colonel's dialogue, that is unmatched in any of the earlier plays. The character of the Colonel is perhaps Jones's finest achievement; it is a portrait that evokes sentiment without being sentimental, a feat achieved principally through the clarity and complexity of the Colonel's language.

While each of the plays of *A Texas Trilogy* stands as a completely independent unit, the three plays have been produced as a single work. In such a production, the events in the three stories are arranged chronologically, beginning with the first act of *Lu Ann Hampton Laverty Oberlander*. *The Last Meeting of the Knights of the White Magnolia* is played after the first half of *The Oldest Living Graduate*. The performance concludes with the rest of the Colonel's story and the last two acts of *Lu Ann Hampton Laverty Oberlander*. Combining the plays in this way makes clear the intimate connection between the three works, which runs much deeper than the shared locale and characters, and reveals the novelistic aspect of Jones's vision. The details of place and characters give the plays a solid basis in realism which becomes even clearer when the plays are seen together. The town of Bradleyville takes on a level of dense reality akin to that of William Faulkner's Yoknapatawpha County: The lives of the characters interweave with and reflect one another, as they often do in Faulkner's fiction. Lu Ann and Colonel Kinkaid, in particular, take on new nuances as their stories are told together; the Colonel, who left Bradleyville and was destroyed by a war he never fully understood, is paralleled by Lu Ann, who remained at home and grew strong and forgiving by facing her troubles there. *A Texas Trilogy*, as a whole, has an import beyond the significance of any of the plays individually.

Jones's later plays have not achieved the success of *A Texas Trilogy*; they share, however, the qualities which characterize that work. *A Place on the Magdalena Flats* was first produced in Dallas in 1976. It underwent substantial revision during later productions in New Mexico and Wisconsin in 1976 and 1979, respectively. The principal changes in the script were alterations in the plot which focused the play more clearly on the older brother,

Carl. While improved, the final version is not completely satisfactory, because of the lack of resolution of the younger brother's story. Although it contains rich humor, *A Place on the Magdalena Flats* is more restrained in mood than any of the trilogy plays. Again, characters deal in isolation with ghosts from their past, this time in the drought-stricken cattle country of New Mexico. The language of the play is particularly rich in poetic imagery and metaphor, marking a growing maturity in Jones's writing.

With *Santa Fe Sunshine* and *Juneteenth*, the latter commissioned by the Actors' Theatre of Louisville as one of a series of one-act plays on American holidays, Jones turned to pure comedy. *Juneteenth* is a rather thin play; the plot is weak, and the one-act form does not allow Jones time to develop his characters fully. *Santa Fe Sunshine* is actually an earlier work to which Jones returned after the success of *A Texas Trilogy*. It lacks the depth of Jones's other plays, but it contains some delightfully eccentric characters and very witty dialogue. Set in Santa Fe, New Mexico, during the 1950's, when the city was a growing artist colony, the play gently ridicules the local beatniks, the patrons who know little about art, and the artists themselves, who are all in the business of making art for money's sake, although they like to pretend otherwise.

While Jones drew on his own experiences for all of his plays, his last play, *Remember*, contains the most obviously autobiographical material. Jones, like his leading character Adrian Blair, was graduated from high school in 1954, after spending some time at a Catholic boarding school. Also like Adrian, he began to reexamine his religious roots as he reached middle age. Adrian is a second-rate actor who finds himself playing a dinner theater in his hometown on his fortieth birthday. He has avoided the town, and his past, for twenty years. Now he finds that little of what he remembers is left: His old home is gone, his friends have changed, his former teacher, Brother Anthony, has left the order and become a real-estate salesman. As Adrian tries to go back in time and rediscover values he has lost—religion, friendship, love—he finds that the world he once knew exists, in fact, only in his memory. When his former sweetheart offers the possibility of renewing their love, he rejects her, preferring the past to the present with its shifting values and lack of continuity.

While *Remember* clearly deals with the themes that preoccupied Jones in all of his plays, it also represents a new direction in Jones's writing. Although the geographical location of the play remains the Southwest, the characters are better educated and more self-aware than the inhabitants of Bradleyville. This shift allows Jones a use of literary allusion and metaphor which the more limited experience of his earlier characters prohibited, and his dialogue becomes even richer and more lyric with this addition. This enhanced language, combined with Jones's usual depth of character and his engaging wit, places *Remember* among his finest achievements.

Preston Jones represented a new and important force in American theater. As a successful playwright who lived and worked entirely outside New York, he helped to establish a new acceptance of the work of regional theaters and writers around the country. The weaknesses of his plays, his often thin or contrived plots and an overreliance on the Southwestern setting, are more than balanced by the strength and originality of his characters, the realistic density of his imaginative world, and the natural poetry of his dialogue. His plays grew out of the life of the American Southwest, but they deal with more universal and immediate human problems. In a very short span of time, he created a body of work that should secure his place among the best American playwrights.

Bibliography

Busby, Mark. *Preston Jones.* Idaho: Boise State University Press, 1983. Although many theses and dissertations have been written providing background on, and analysis of, Jones's plays, this slim volume (fifty-two pages) is one of very few books published on the playwright and his works. Busby's book, part of the Western Writers series of Boise State University, offers readers valuable criticism and interpretation of the playwright's drama.

Clurman, Harold. Review of *A Texas Trilogy*. *The Nation*, October 9, 1976, 348-350. Compares Jones's *A Texas Trilogy* to a farce of Eugene O'Neill's projected cycle, *A Tale of Possessors, Self-Dispossessed*, based on O'Neill's belief that "the greatest failure in history" was the United States, which, in its race for materialism, "lost all valid faith." Clurman points out that Jones's Bradleyville is a "microcosm" representing "domains beyond Texas or the South."

Cook, Bruce. "Preston Jones: Playwright on the Range." *Saturday Review* 3 (May 15, 1976): 40-42. Written three years before the playwright's death, this article provides an informative look at the man, the artist, and the intellectual. Cook calls Jones "an original, a walking bundle of contradictions," and the "most promising American playwright to come along in two or three decades." Includes brief comments by critic Audrey Wood. Contains a photograph of Jones and another of a scene from *A Place on the Magdalena Flats.*

Kroll, Jack. "Branch Water." Review of *A Texas Trilogy*. *Newsweek*, October 4, 1976, 97. Kroll includes a brief discussion of the reasons for the mixed reviews and ambiguity that followed the trilogy's Broadway opening. His comments on the three plays that form the trilogy help show the playwright's depiction of the "emptiness, despair and absurdity of small-town life." Contains a photograph of actress Diane Ladd in *Lu Ann Hampton Laverty Oberlander.*

_____. "Texas Marksmanship." Review of *A Texas Trilogy*. *News-*

week, May 17, 1976, 95-96. Although the word "regionalism" has become outmoded in American culture, Kroll explains that regionalism, which is found in Jones's drama, may be coming back, as "more and more Americans seek their identity close to home." Kroll says that region extends beyond a physical area to become a "psychic and spiritual locale." Photographs.

Prideaux, Tom. "The Classic Family Drama Is Revived in *A Texas Trilogy.*" *Smithsonian* 7 (October, 1976): 49-54. This six-page essay, strewn with photographs, contains brief biographical information, traces the playwright's career, and provides summaries of the three plays in *A Texas Trilogy.* Includes quotations from a conversation with Jones, in which the author reminisced about his youth, his high school days, and his college friends.

Kathleen Latimer

BEN JONSON

Born: London, England; June 11, 1573
Died: London, England; August 6, 1637

Principal drama
The Isle of Dogs, pr. 1597 (with Thomas Nashe; no longer extant); *The Case Is Altered*, pr. 1597, pb. 1609; *Every Man in His Humour*, pr. 1598 (revised 1605), pb. 1601 (revised 1616); *Hot Anger Soon Cold*, pr. 1598 (with Henry Chettle and Henry Porter; no longer extant); *Every Man out of His Humour*, pr. 1599, pb. 1600; *The Page of Plymouth*, pr. 1599 (with Thomas Dekker; no longer extant); *Robert the Second, King of Scots*, pr. 1599 (with Henry Chettle and Thomas Dekker; no longer extant); *Cynthia's Revels: Or, The Fountain of Self-Love*, pr. c. 1600-1601, pb. 1601; *Poetaster: Or, His Arraignment*, pr. 1601, pb. 1602; *Sejanus His Fall*, pr. 1603, pb. 1605 (commonly known as *Sejanus*); *Eastward Ho!*, pr., pb. 1605 (with George Chapman and John Marston); *Volpone: Or, The Fox*, pr. 1605, pb. 1607; *Epicœne: Or, The Silent Woman*, pr. 1609, pb. 1616; *The Alchemist*, pr. 1610, pb. 1612; *Catiline His Conspiracy*, pr., pb. 1611 (commonly known as *Catiline*); *Bartholomew Fair*, pr. 1614, pb. 1631; *The Devil Is an Ass*, pr. 1616, pb. 1631; *The Staple of News*, pr. 1626, pb. 1631; *The New Inn: Or, The Light Heart*, pr. 1629, pb. 1631; *The Magnetic Lady: Or, Humours Reconciled*, pr. 1632, pb. 1640; *A Tale of a Tub*, pr. 1633, pb. 1640; *The Sad Shepherd: Or, A Tale of Robin Hood*, pb. 1640 (fragment).

Other literary forms
Ben Jonson was a masterful poet as well as a dramatist. His poetry, with some justification, has the reputation of being remote from modern readers. A dedicated classicist, Jonson emphasized clarity of form and phrase over expression of emotion, and many of his poems seem to be exercises in cleverness and wit rather than attempts to express an idea or image well. Other of his poems, however, retain their power and vision: "To Celia," for example, has given the English language the phrase "Drink to me only with thine eyes."

The difficulty of Jonson's poetry originates in large part in his very mastery of poetic form. Jonson was a student of literature; he was a man of letters with few equals in any era. He studied the poetic forms of classical Greek and Latin literature as well as those of later European literature, and he used what he learned in his own work. The result is a body of poetry that is very diverse, including salutations and love poems, homilies and satires, epigrams and lyrics. Much of the poetry appeal primarily to academics because of its experimental qualities and its displays of technical virtuosity. Yet those who allow themselves to be put off by Jonson's prodigious intellectualism miss some of the finest verse in English.

Jonson was also a prodigious writer of masques—dramatic allegorical entertainments, usually prepared to celebrate special occasions and presented at court. Jonson's masques have in common with his poetry technical achievement and with much of his occasional verse a focus on the virtues, real and reputed, of nobility and royalty. Although the emphasis was on spectacle and celebration of the aristocracy, Jonson tried to make his masques legitimate works of literature, and they have enjoyed increasing critical attention in recent years.

Achievements

Ben Jonson was the foremost man of letters of his time. His knowledge of literature was combined with a passionate personality and a desire to be respected; the combination resulted in his efforts to elevate authors in the estimation of society. He endeavored to demonstrate the importance of literature in the lives of people and in their culture. Although he regarded his dramatic work as merely one facet of his literary life, he was determined that the playwright should receive the esteemed title of "poet." In the Elizabethan era, plays were regarded as unimportant public amusements; satires, sonnets, and narrative verse were expected to carry the heavy freight of ideas and art. Jonson worked to establish drama as a legitimate literary form by showing that it could be a conscious art with rules of organization that were as valid as those of more esteemed literary genres.

In 1616, Jonson published *The Workes of Benjamin Jonson*, including in the volume nine of his plays in addition to other writings. Never before had any author dared to give his plays the title "Works." The term "works" was usually reserved for profound philosophical treatises. Jonson was derided by some writers for being conceited and for trying to make plays seem important; even after his death, some traditionalists found his title difficult to accept. Further, Jonson promoted the cause of drama as high art by devoting much care to the publishing of the texts of his plays, thereby establishing a higher standard for published texts of dramas than had existed before. The publication of *The Workes of Benjamin Jonson* led at least indirectly to the important First Folio edition of William Shakespeare's plays.

Jonson's reputation as a dramatist is inextricably bound with that of Shakespeare. Although Jonson was esteemed above Shakespeare by most of his contemporaries, subsequent eras have elevated Shakespeare at Jonson's expense. Thus, although Jonson's comedies are wonderful and are well received by modern audiences, they are rarely performed. Shakespeare's poetry is better than Jonson's; his tragedies are more moving; his comedies are more diverse and have superior characterizations. To acknowledge Shakespeare's superiority is not to derogate Jonson's achievement; Shakespeare is alone atop the world's authors, but Jonson is not far below. In addition, Jonson's plays are superior to Shakespeare's in consistency of plot and structure. Had there been no William Shakespeare, there might today be Jonson festivals, and *Volpone* and *The Alchemist* might be the revered standards for college drama productions.

Biography

Tradition has it that Benjamin Jonson was born in 1572; literary historians put his birth in 1573, probably on June 11. His father, an Anglican minister, died about a month before Jonson was born. His mother married a master bricklayer in 1574; the family lived in Westminster. While growing up, Jonson attended Westminster School and became a student of William Camden, who was perhaps the greatest classicist and antiquarian of the Elizabethan and Jacobean ages. Jonson's interest in classical literature, his care in constructing what he wrote, and his respect for learning all have their origins in the teachings of Camden. Techniques for writing that Jonson used throughout his life were first learned from Camden, including the practice of writing out a prospective poem first in prose and then converting the prose to verse.

In about 1588, Jonson became an apprentice bricklayer. This part of his life became the subject of jokes and gibes in his later years, but he seems to have taken pride in his humble origins. His respect for achievement and general lack of respect for claims of importance based solely on heredity or accident may have had their roots in his own struggles as a lower-class laborer. He left his bricklaying work to join the army in its war against the Spanish in the Lowlands in 1591 or 1592. During his tenure in the army, he apparently served with some distinction; he claimed that he was the English champion in single combat against a Spanish champion and that he slew his opponent while the assembled armies watched. He was handy with swords and knives and was, when young, quite combative and physically intimidating.

Jonson eventually returned to England. Little is known of his activities until 1597, save that he married Anne Lewis on November 14, 1594. The marriage seems to have been unhappy. Before 1597, Jonson might have been an actor with a traveling troupe, many of whose members eked out marginal livings in the towns and hamlets of England. He was imprisoned in 1597 for having finished a play begun by Thomas Nashe; *The Isle of Dogs* was declared seditious by the Privy Council of the queen. The play, like most of Jonson's collaborations, has not been preserved. After a few weeks, Jonson was released from prison.

Jonson's career as a playwright began in earnest in 1598 after the production of *The Case Is Altered*, which was performed by a troupe of boys from the Chapel Royal. In that same year, *Every Man in His Humour*, the first of Jonson's important plays, was performed by William Shakespeare's company, the Lord Chamberlain's Men. Tradition has it that Shakespeare recognized Jonson's talent and persuaded the Lord Chamberlain's Men to stage the play. Although he admired Shakespeare, Jonson never regarded himself as principally a playwright, and thus he never became a permanent shareholder in an acting company, as did Shakespeare. This enabled Jonson to maintain his artistic freedom but prevented him from earning the good living that Shakespeare and other shareholders enjoyed.

The year 1598 was a busy one for Jonson; he was again imprisoned, this time for killing an actor, Gabriel Spencer, in a duel on September 22. Jonson's property was confiscated, he was branded on the thumb, and he was to be executed, but he saved his life by pleading benefit of clergy, which he could do under ancient English law because he could read. While in prison, he was converted to Roman Catholicism, a faith he practiced until about 1608. In 1606, he was charged with seducing young people into Roman Catholicism; the charges were dropped when he converted back to Anglicanism.

Jonson pursued an active life as an author of plays, poetry, and treatises. His comedies were successful, but his tragedies were badly received. In 1603, Queen Elizabeth died and King James assumed the English throne. Jonson's *Entertainment at Athorpe* helped to launch him on a long career as a court poet. Also that year, his son Benjamin died at the age of six. Though Jonson was finding public acclaim and honor, his private life was miserable. He and his wife lived apart from 1602 to 1607, he lost his namesake son, and he grew obese. In 1605, he collaborated with John Marston and George Chapman on the rollicking comedy *Eastward Ho!* and was again imprisoned for a supposed slight to King James; the play made fun of Scots.

Jonson's plays *Volpone*, *Epicœne*, and *The Alchemist* enhanced his reputation among his literary peers; his court poetry and masques enhanced his status with King James. In 1616, he published *The Workes of Benjamin Jonson* and was awarded a pension by the king. The pension and Jonson's position as the leading literary figure in England in 1616 have encouraged many historians to call him an unofficial poet laureate, and he is usually honored as the first to fill that role in England. Until the death of King James in 1625, Jonson enjoyed his role as a favorite of the king and a respected author; his honors included a master of arts degree from the University of Oxford.

When Charles I assumed the throne, Jonson's status at court declined. The pension of wine and money was haphazardly delivered, and Jonson had difficulty pursuing his scholarly career because his lodgings burned down in 1623, and his books and papers were destroyed. He returned to playwriting with *The Staple of News* in 1626; the play was not as well received as his earlier comedies. In 1628, he suffered a stroke and was partially paralyzed. In 1629, his play *The New Inn* was staged by the King's Men and was a disaster. He continued to write until his death on August 6, 1637. He left unfinishèd the play *The Sad Shepherd*, which some critics admire. Although cranky, egotistical, and homely, Jonson retained much of his hold on the leading literary people of his time and was esteemed by younger authors even after his death. He is one of literature's most colorful figures. Combative, robust, and dedicated to his art, Jonson made major contributions to the development of English literature.

Analysis

Ben Jonson's dramatic canon is large, and most of the plays in it are worthy of long and careful study. He is best remembered for his comedies, which influenced comedy-writing well into the eighteenth century and which remain entertaining. Jonson took Horace's maxim to heart—that to teach, a writer must first entertain—and he followed literary rules only so far as they enabled him to instruct and entertain his audience. By observing the neoclassical unities of time and space in his plays, Jonson gave his works a coherence often lacking in the comedies of his contemporaries: Loose ends are resolved, subplot and main plot are interwoven so that each enhances the other, and the conclusion of each play resolves the basic issues brought up during the action. Jonson's concern with entertaining makes most of his comedies delightful and attractive to modern audiences; his effort to instruct makes his plays substantial and meaningful.

From the beginning of his career as a playwright, Jonson was successful with comedy. His two attempts at tragedies are interesting as experiments but are unlikely to be successful with general audiences. His comedies are varied, ranging from the city to the countryside and including satires, comedies of manners, and farces. He was most successful when writing about city life, moralizing with good-natured humor.

Of his early comedies, *Every Man in His Humour* is the most important. Jonson's first significant popular success, it best represents those qualities that make some of his later plays great works of literature. Typical of a Jonsonian comedy, *Every Man in His Humour* has a complex interweaving of plots that creates an atmosphere of comic frenzy. Fools are duped, husbands fear cuckolding, wives suspect their husbands of having mistresses, fathers spy on sons, a servant plays tricks on everyone, and myriad disguises and social games confuse the characters. The audience is not left in confusion, but is carefully let in on the nuances of the various plots.

The plot features Edward Knowell, who journeys to London to visit Wellbred, a wit whose devil-may-care behavior might get Edward into trouble. Old Knowell, Edward's father, follows his son to London in order to spy on him; his servant Brainworm connives and plays tricks—as much to amuse himself as to gain anything. Subplots involve Captain Bobadill, a braggart soldier; Cob and Tib, the landlords of Bobadill; Kitely, a merchant; and Downright, Wellbred's plainspoken brother. The almost bewildering multiplicity of characters is typical of many of Jonson's plays. He borrows the plot of unwarranted suspicions from classical dramatists. Captain Bobadill is the miles gloriosus, the braggart soldier (usually a coward), a stock character in classical comedies. Brainworm is the conniving servant, another stock figure from classical comedies. Other characters also serve specific purposes: Downright is a shatterer of illusions—he points out the falseness in others. Edward Knowell is the romantic lead—a hero who retains his innocence in the middle of the turmoil of the plot. Kitely, Dame Kitely, Cob, and Tib provide much of the low comedy and serve to reflect the ridiculousness of the behavior of the main characters.

Although it shares many of the characteristics that typify Jonson's later comedies, *Every Man in His Humour* shows the dramatist still in the process of forging his mature style. He is still trying to reconcile his classical models to the traditions of English drama and to the tastes of his audience. The plot is loose, almost chaotic, and not as tightly controlled as those of *The Alchemist* and *Volpone*.

"What a rare punishment/ Is avarice to itself," declares Volpone. At the heart of the complex play *Volpone* is the straightforward moral judgment that the evil one commits brings with it a suitable punishment. In *Volpone*, Jonson satirizes human nature and the baser impulses of humanity.

The play's characters pursue basely materialistic ideals, and in attaining their goals, they ensure their own downfall. Volpone begins the play with a monologue that is in itself a classic: "Good morning to the day; and next, my gold!/ Open the shrine that I may see my saint." His servant and partner in crime, Mosca, draws open a curtain and reveals piles of gold. Volpone has called the repository a "shrine" and the gold a "saint." As the rest of the monologue reveals, Volpone regards wealth with a religious fervor; gold, he asserts, is the "son of Sol"; it "giv'st all men tongues"; it "mak'st men do all things."

Volpone is not merely a clever faker, nor is his servant, Mosca. He is a devotee of an ideal, and as such he is at once more likable and more dangerous than an ordinary thief. He has the excuse that confidence men traditionally have had: that the greed of his victims is their undoing; if they were good people, he would be unable to cheat them. As long as he sticks to victimizing greedy people, he is spectacularly successful; the victims eagerly give him gold and jewels in the hope of gaining his fortune by having it left to them when he dies. When he seeks to "bed" innocent Celia, however, his empire of gold and deceit begins to crumble into its component parts of venality, lust, and spiritual morbidity.

Volpone is a captivating character. He is capable of wonderful flights of language and of clever intrigue, and he is a consummate actor; his strength is his knowledge of how much he can manipulate people into doing what he wants done; his weakness is his overweening pride—he revels too much in his ability to dupe his victims. By pretending to be an old, dying man, he helps convince his victims of his imminent death and of the possibility that one of them will inherit his wealth. They give him expensive gifts in order to ingratiate themselves with him. His accomplice, Mosca, is also a skilled actor, who can be obsequious one moment, gallant the next—all things to all people. Mosca convinces each victim that he is favored above all others in Volpone's will. The scheme is very successful, and there is much hilarity in the gulling of the lawyer Voltore (the vulture), the elderly Corbaccio (the crow), and the merchant and husband of Celia, Corvino (the raven). The actors should resemble their roles: Voltore is craven and menacing; Corbaccio is thin and leggy; and Corvino is quick-eyed and aggressive. There is exuberance in Volpone's shifts from boisterous and athletic man to bedridden old cripple, in Mosca's cheerful conniving, and in the duping of three socially prominent and nasty men. The subplot of Lord and Lady Politic Would-be heightens the comedy as Volpone, in his guise as cripple, endures Lady Would-be's endless talking and her willingness to surrender her virtue for his favor. Volpone's gold-centered world would be thoroughly jolly if he were not right about gold's ability to influence people. His victims include innocents, such as Bonario, who is disinherited by his father, Corbaccio, so that Corbaccio can leave his wealth to Volpone in the hope that Volpone will reciprocate. Corvino values wealth above all else; he is a fitting worshiper at the shrine of gold, and he would sacrifice anything to the high priest Volpone in exchange for the promise of acquiring more wealth: Corvino even gives his jealously guarded and naïve wife, Celia, to the supposedly impotent Volpone; she is expected to sleep with him.

Underlying the gold-centered world is ugliness; under Volpone's dashing personality is bestiality; under Mosca's wit is spiritual paucity. Jonson shows this graphically. Volpone must pretend to be physically degenerated, yet the pretense mirrors the spiritual reality. As the play progresses, his performance becomes more extreme; eventually, he pretends to be nearly a corpse. The more complex his scheming becomes, the more wretched he must show himself to be. He is trapped in his world of gold; when he wants to leave his home to see what Celia looks like, he must disguise himself as a lowly mountebank. The physically vibrant Volpone is restricted to his gold and Mosca. When he reveals himself as ardent lover to the trapped Celia, his feigned physical degeneration emerges in his spiritual self, and he is doomed.

Volpone is a great play because it is a nearly perfect meshing of comedy, symbolism, suspense, and moralizing. Each change in any of its aspects is matched by changes in all. Its satiric targets are universals, including greed, moral idiocy, and the replacement of spiritual ideals with materialistic ones. Greed brings down most of the principal characters, including Mosca. Pride brings down Volpone; he cannot resist one more chance to display his brilliance. He pretends to be dead and to have left his fortune to Mosca, simply for the sake of seeing how his victims respond when they learn that he has left them nothing. Mosca, loyal only to the money, wants to keep all for himself. Gold turns the world upside down when made the focus of human endeavor: A husband gives his wife to another man; a father displaces his son; the just are made to look false; and a servant becomes master. Gold should serve its owner, and when Volpone enshrines it, he upsets the proper order of society.

The carnality of Volpone is discovered by Bonario, who was accidentally present during Volpone's near-rape of Celia because of one of Mosca's plots involving Corbaccio. In the ensuing trial, Volpone is presented to the court as a nearly dead old man who is incapable of molesting anyone. Voltore puts on his public mask of respectability and argues to the court that Bonario and Celia are liars and worse, and that those accused by them are honest and innocent. An important theme in the play is that of performance versus reality. Corbaccio properly *acts* the part of the kindly old gentleman. Corvino *plays* the honest merchant. Both are respected members of society. Yet, just as the exuberant exterior of Volpone covers a decayed spirit, so, too, do the public personalities of Corbaccio, Corvino, and Voltore belie their evil. In a world where gold is of paramount importance, such people can seem good; likewise, the truly honest and chaste Bonario and Celia can be made to seem conniving, greedy, and concupiscent.

Mosca almost gets the money. Corbaccio and Corvino almost escape with their reputations intact. Voltore almost wins a false case with his skillful arguments. Volpone cannot stand to lose his gold and cannot stand to see his victims succeed where he has failed. He reveals all to the court. The conclusion seems contrived—after all, the clever Volpone could start over and find new victims to gull—but it is thematically apt. No matter how often Volpone were to start over, his plotting would end the same way, because he worships a base and false god that cannot enrich his soul. The ending reveals the falseness in the principal characters and lays bare the emptiness of Volpone's world.

The use of the villain as protagonist can be found in the tragedies of Jonson's contemporaries. Shakespeare's Macbeth, for example, remains one of literature's most interesting villainous heroes. The use of a villain as protagonist in a comedy was more rare and may have come from classical comedies, in which conniving servants were often the most entertaining characters. Jonson created for himself a distinctive literary voice by using villains such as Volpone to carry his moral ideas; in *The Alchemist*, he exploited the same tension with equal success.

Samuel Taylor Coleridge ranked the plot of *The Alchemist* among the three best in literature, along with those of Sophocles' *Oedipus Tyrannus* (c. 429 B.C.) and Henry Fielding's *Tom Jones* (1749). Like *Volpone*, the play is about people pretending to be what they are not. *The Alchemist*, however, goes a step further: Its characters seek to be transformed, to be made over into new people. The three characters who gull the others operate out of a house, and as in *Volpone*, the victims are brought to the house for fleecing. In contrast to the action of *Volpone*, however, the action of *The Alchemist* remains tightly focused on the house; society at large comes to the Blackfriars house to be duped and cheated. Jeremy, the butler, goes by various names—usually Face, the conspirator. When his master leaves on a trip, he takes in Subtle, a down-on-his-luck swindler, and Doll Common, a prostitute. There is little pretense of a noble alliance, as in *Volpone*; these are criminals whose ignoble characters are never in doubt, although they, like their victims, aspire to become what they are not.

Part of the genius of the play is the fooling of the victimizers even as they prey upon their victims. Doll Common plays the Queen of Faery for the stupid Dapper and a noblewoman for Sir Epicure Mammon; she throws herself into her roles with the hope that she will become—not simply pretend to be—a lady of noble character. Subtle forgets his recent destitution and begins to believe in his ability to transmute human character, even if his alchemical tricks cannot change matter. Face retains some sense of proportion as he shifts from one role to another, but even he hopes to become the important man in society that he cannot be while he remains a butler. These three quarrelsome rogues are laughable, but they also carry Jonson's moral freight: One must know oneself before a change in character is possible. All except the house's master, Lovewit, hope to be what they are not yet cannot change because they do not know themselves.

Dapper is a clerk who hopes to be a successful gambler; he hopes that Subtle, who poses as an alchemist, will be able to guarantee him good luck. Drugger is a silly shopkeeper who wants a guarantee of good business. Kastril is a country squire who wishes to become an urban wit. His sister, Dame Pliant, is an empty-headed, wealthy widow whose beautiful body hides an almost nonexistent personality. Tribulation, Wholesome, and Ananias are hypocritical Puritans who hope that Subtle will give them the philosophers' stone—which is reputed to have great alchemical powers to transmute—so that they will be able to rule the world. Sir Epicure Mammon (regarded by many critics as one of Jonson's greatest dramatic creations), egotistical and blind to his own weaknesses, wants the philosophers' stone so that he can become a kind of Volpone, ruling a materialistic realm in which he would be wonderful in his generosity and terrible in his appetites. Mammon is already living a fantasy, and he needs little encouragement from Subtle, Face, and Doll Common. The victims are motivated by greed and lust; their desires dictate the nature of their cozening.

The fun is in the increasingly complex machinations of the resourceful schemers. The satire is in the social roles of the victims, who range from clerk and shopkeeper to religious leader and gentleman. By the play's end, Surly, the friend of Mammon, has tried to reveal the schemers for what they are, but only Pliant believes him, and she believes whatever she is told. Mammon is in ardent pursuit of a prostitute in whom he sees noble ancestry; Wholesome and his aide Ananias are fearful of losing their chance to transform the world; Dapper is bound, gagged, and locked in a closet; and Subtle and Face are hopping from one deceit to another in order to keep their schemes balanced. Their small world is based on false understandings of self; no one understands who he really is. The hilarious confusion ends when Lovewit returns home and refuses to be fooled by Face's explanations.

Some critics argue that Lovewit is every bit as deluded as the other characters. They argue that the world of *The Alchemist* remains disordered at the play's finish. Yet Lovewit seems to see through Face's lies and games; he seems to know perfectly well what he is doing when he takes Pliant and her fortune for himself. While his remark to Face, "I will be rul'd by thee in any thing," can be taken to mean that master has yielded to servant, which would be a representation of disorder, it is more likely that Lovewit is expressing gratitude for the deliverance to him of Pliant, as his subsequent remarks suggest. He puts Face back in his place as servant; he puts Kastril in his proper place as his brother-in-law; and he handles the officers of the law and Tribulation and Mammon with confidence. He is in command of the problems created by Face, Subtle, and Doll Common almost from the moment he enters his home. Given the moral themes of the play, Lovewit's commanding presence provides a satisfying conclusion by showing a character who knows himself bringing order to the chaos brought on by fools.

Between *Volpone* and *The Alchemist*, Jonson wrote *Epicœne*, and after *The Alchemist* he wrote *Bartholomew Fair* and *The Devil Is an Ass*. The last-named work is an amusing play but not one of Jonson's best. The other two, however, rank among his most successful comedies. Unlike *Volpone* and *The Alchemist*, they involve broad social milieus. *Volpone* and *The Alchemist* present tight little worlds that parody reality; Volpone and Mosca rule theirs at the shrine of gold; Subtle, Face, and Doll Common are minor deities in the world encompassed by their house. In both plays, the outer world intrudes only to resolve their plots. In *Epicœne* and *Bartholomew Fair*, the larger world of Jacobean society appears on the stage.

Epicœne was written for a theatrical company made up entirely of boys, and the central conceit of the play turns on that aspect of its first performance, much as Shakespeare's *As You Like It* (pr. c. 1599-1600) has the young man playing Rosalind, a woman, pretend to be a woman pretending to be a man pretending to be a woman. Jonson's trick is to have Epicœne, played by a boy, turn out at play's end to be a boy. As in his other great comedies, false pretenses form one of the play's major themes. The duping of Morose, who loathes noise, draws in braggarts, pretentious women, and urbane wits. Coarse language, persistent lying, and brutality are revealed as the underlying traits of the supposedly refined and sophisticated members of polite society. In addition, Jonson calls into question the validity of sexual roles; Epicœne is called everything from the ideal woman to an Amazon—the boy who plays her fits easily into the society of women and is readily accepted by women until revealed as a boy.

Bartholomew Fair also deals in disguises and confused identities, but is more cheerful than Jonson's other great comedies. The setting of a fair encourages varied action and characters, and Jonson evokes the robust nature of the fair by providing vigorous action and scenes that would be typical of the fairs of his day. The character Ursula is representative of the fair: She is the pig-woman, the operator of a stall that sells roast pig. Big, loud, and sweaty, she embodies the earthiness of the fair, which is noisy and hot with crowding people. The language of the characters is coarse, and they often use vulgarities. The effect is one of down-to-earth good humor and the happy-ending plot. This effect contrasts with *Epicœne*, which also features grossly vulgar language; its characters are supposedly refined, but they reflect their gutter minds in gutter language. Instead of being down-to-earth, much of the humor seems dirty.

Jonson's stature as a playwright is greater than popular knowledge of him would indicate. Had Shakespeare lived at another time, Jonson would be the dramatic giant of his era. His comedies deserve to be performed more often than they are; his masterpieces play well before modern audiences, and even his minor plays have wit and ideas to recommend them. Jonson is a dramatist of the first rank.

Other major works

POETRY: *Poems*, 1601; *Epigrams*, 1616; *The Forest*, 1616; *Underwoods*, 1640.

NONFICTION: *The English Grammar*, 1640; *Horace His Art of Poetry*, 1640; *Timber: Or, Discoveries Made upon Men and Matter*, 1641.

MISCELLANEOUS: *The Workes of Benjamin Jonson*, 1616; *The Works of Benjamin Jonson*, 1640-1641 (2 volumes).

Bibliography

Barish, Jonas A. *Ben Jonson and the Language of Prose Comedy*. Cambridge, Mass.: Harvard University Press, 1960. This seminal study of

Jonson's comedy goes beyond the scope suggested by the title and examines virtually every aspect of his comedy. Some important discoveries that are now standard assumptions in Jonson criticism (such as the role of subplots) were first made here. Barish's bibliography is helpful.

Barton, Anne. *Ben Jonson, Dramatist.* Cambridge, England: Cambridge University Press, 1984. The only major work dealing with Jonson's few tragedies as well as his more successful comedies, Barton's book updates the seminal works of Jonas A. Barish (above) and Edward B. Partridge (below). The biographical background rounds out this book, providing a study of every aspect of Jonson's career in theater, distinguishing popular from courtly forms.

Bloom, Harold, ed. *Ben Jonson.* New York: Chelsea House, 1987. A selection of what Bloom considers the most important scholarly articles on Jonson from the second half of the twentieth century. Some articles focus on Jonson's poetic work as well, but several deal exclusively with Jonson's major comedies and his "humors" theory of comedy.

Partridge, Edward B. *The Broken Compass: A Study of the Major Comedies of Ben Jonson.* New York: Columbia University Press, 1958. This important study of Jonson's comedy influenced everything that followed. The language and tone is quite scholarly but accessible to a beginner. Partridge does not ignore Jonson's works that are not "major comedies" but touches on poetry and tragedy only insofar as they affect the comedies that made Jonson's reputation.

Summers, Claude J., and Ted-Larry Pebworth. *Ben Jonson.* Boston: Twayne, 1979. Though this book covers Jonson's nondramatic writings as well as his plays, it is an excellent starting point for understanding his drama. Each major play receives a full analysis, and Jonson's entire canon is placed in the context of its time. The excellent annotated bibliography offers helpful evaluations.

Kirk H. Beetz
(Updated by *John R. Holmes*)

GEORGE S. KAUFMAN

Born: Pittsburgh, Pennsylvania; November 16, 1889
Died: New York, New York; June 2, 1961

Principal drama

Someone in the House, pr. 1918 (with Larry Evans and Walter Percival; originally as *Among Those Present*, pr. 1917); *Dulcy*, pr., pb. 1921 (with Marc Connelly); *To the Ladies*, pr. 1922, pb. 1923 (with Connelly); *Merton of the Movies*, pr. 1922, pb. 1925 (with Connelly; based on Harry Leon Wilson's novel); *Helen of Troy, N.Y.*, pr. 1923 (musical comedy with Connelly; music and lyrics by Bert Kalmar and Harry Ruby); *The Deep Tangled Wildwood*, pr. 1923 (with Connelly); *Beggar on Horseback*, pr. 1924, pb. 1925 (with Connelly); *Be Yourself*, pr. 1924 (musical comedy with Connelly; music by Lewis Gensler and Milton Schwartzwald); *Minick*, pr., pb. 1924 (with Edna Ferber); *The Butter and Egg Man*, pr., pb. 1925; *The Cocoanuts*, pr. 1925 (musical comedy; music and lyrics by Irving Berlin); *The Good Fellow*, pr. 1926, pb. 1931 (with Herman J. Mankiewicz); *If Men Played Cards as Women Do*, pr., pb. 1926; *The Royal Family*, pr. 1927, pb. 1928 (with Ferber); *Animal Crackers*, pr. 1928 (musical comedy with Morrie Ryskind; music and lyrics by Kalmar and Ruby); *June Moon*, pr. 1929, pb. 1931 (with Ring Lardner); *The Channel Road*, pr. 1929 (with Alexander Woollcott); *Strike Up the Band*, pr. 1930 (musical comedy with Morrie Ryskind; music by George Gershwin and lyrics by Ira Gershwin); *Once in a Lifetime*, pr., pb. 1930 (with Moss Hart); *The Band Wagon*, pr. 1931 (musical revue with Howard Dietz; music by Arthur Schwartz and lyrics by Dietz); *Of Thee I Sing*, pr. 1931, pb. 1932 (musical comedy with Ryskind; music by George Gershwin and lyrics by Ira Gershwin); *Dinner at Eight*, pr., pb. 1932 (with Ferber); *Let 'em Eat Cake*, pr., pb. 1933 (musical comedy with Ryskind; music by George Gershwin and lyrics by Ira Gershwin); *The Dark Tower*, pr. 1933, pb,. 1934 (with Woollcott; based on Guy de Maupassant's story "Boule de suif"); *Merrily We Roll Along*, pr., pb. 1934 (with Moss Hart); *First Lady*, pr. 1935, pb. 1936 (with Katherine Dayton); *Stage Door*, pr., pb. 1936 (with Ferber); *You Can't Take It with You*, pr. 1936, pb. 1937 (with Moss Hart); *I'd Rather Be Right*, pr., pb. 1937 (musical revue with Moss Hart; music by Richard Rodgers and lyrics by Lorenz Hart); *The Fabulous Invalid*, pr., pb. 1938 (with Moss Hart); *The American Way*, pr., pb. 1939 (with Moss Hart); *The Man Who Came to Dinner*, pr., pb. 1939 (with Moss Hart); *George Washington Slept Here*, pr., pb. 1940 (with Moss Hart); *The Land Is Bright*, pr., pb. 1941 (with Ferber); *The Late George Apley*, pr. 1944, pb. 1946 (with John P. Marquand; based on Marquand's novel); *Park Avenue*, pr. 1946 (musical comedy with Nunnally Johnson; music by Arthur Schwartz and lyrics by

Ira Gershwin); *Bravo!*, pr. 1948, pb. 1949 (with Ferber); *The Small Hours*, pr., pb. 1951 (with Leueen MacGrath); *The Solid Gold Cadillac*, pb. 1951, pr. 1953 (with Howard Teichmann); *Fancy Meeting You Again*, pr., pb. 1952 (with MacGrath); *Silk Stockings*, pr. 1955 (musical comedy with MacGrath and Abe Burrows; music and lyrics by Cole Porter; based on Menyhért Lengyel's film *Ninotchka*).

Other literary forms

George S. Kaufman began his literary career by voluntarily writing humorous verse and prose for Franklin P. Adams' column in the New York *Evening Mail*. Later, he was hired to write his own column in the Washington *Times*. Kaufman then replaced Adams at the *Evening Mail* for a short time, was fired, and took a job as a reporter on the New York *Tribune*. Shortly thereafter, he was made drama editor, only to leave the *Tribune* in 1917 for the same position at *The New York Times*. He held on to his relationship with *The New York Times*, despite his success as a playwright, until 1930, when he was asked to resign because his career as a playwright was taking too much of his time. Throughout his life he contributed short sketches, prose humor, and light verse to such magazines as *Saturday Review*, *The Nation*, *Life*, *Theatre* magazine, *Playbill*, and *The New Yorker* (founded by his friend Harold Ross), as well as various newspapers.

Kaufman also wrote several screenplays, although he disliked Hollywood and, as a rule, avoided long-term relationships with the film industry. The Marx Brothers' films *The Cocoanuts* (1929) and *Animal Crackers* (1931), which Kaufman wrote in collaboration with Morrie Ryskind, were adapted from their plays and filmed in New York. Later, Samuel Goldwyn hired Kaufman and Robert E. Sherwood to write the screenplay for *Roman Scandals* (1933); a disagreement with star Eddie Cantor caused Kaufman to invoke the clause of his contract which stipulated that he would not have to work with Cantor. In 1935, Irving Thalberg of Metro-Goldwyn-Mayer guaranteed Kaufman $100,000 to write (with Ryskind) the Marx Brothers' classic *A Night at the Opera* (1935). By 1936, his distaste for Hollywood was such that he refused to adapt his and Moss Hart's Pulitzer Prize-winning play *You Can't Take It with You* for the screen. Ironically, the film later won the 1938 Academy Award for Best Picture.

Achievements

Although George S. Kaufman is generally considered to be one of the greatest geniuses of the Broadway theater, it is difficult to assess his individual talents because he wrote nearly all of his plays in collaboration. *The Butter and Egg Man*, his only full-length comedy written solo, was composed early in his career and shows his talent; nevertheless, apparently never fully confident of his talent even after dozens of successful plays, he continued, until his death, to work with collaborators, some of whom were among the major literary figures of his period. From 1918 to 1955, Kaufman's name appeared as author or coauthor on more than forty productions, some of which were unsuccessful and many of which were successful. Forty-eight full-length motion pictures from 1920 to 1961 were based on plays Kaufman had either written or directed. He directed some forty-five plays, many by notable authors other than himself. As a result, perhaps no one had more influence on the shape and direction of popular drama in the 1920's through the 1950's than Kaufman. He was considered a master of stage technique, an incomparable wit, and an extraordinary satirist. His record of success on the Broadway stage is without equal.

Biography

George Simon Kaufman was born to Joseph S. Kaufman and Henrietta Myers, both members of the German-Jewish community of Pittsburgh. Joseph Kaufman had once worked as a deputy sheriff in Leadville, Colorado, and participated in one of the Ute Indian wars, but returned to Pittsburgh poorer than when he had left. Marrying the wealthiest woman in his social circle was no help, as he soon brought his family to the brink of poverty. Mrs. Kaufman was a hypochondriac, and young George, who had been overprotected because of the infant death of his older brother, became an introverted, skinny adolescent who read adventure stories in *Argosy* magazine. (He even attempted to write for *Argosy* but had nothing accepted.) His father determined to toughen him up by sending him to an old family friend's ranch in Idaho, but the boy was only confirmed in his reclusive tendencies.

In his teens, Kaufman became interested in theater. Encouraged by a rabbi, he first acted the part of a Scotsman in a religious production, and thereafter he was hooked for life. He collaborated on a play in 1903 with another boy, Irving Pichel, who would later become a Hollywood actor-director. The play was entitled *The Failure*, and both boys acted in it.

Kaufman studied law for three months, then gave it up, and on the advice of a physician took a job on a surveying team in West Virginia. That job did not last either, and other jobs followed. He went to secretarial school and became a stenographer for the Pittsburgh Coal Company. He became a window clerk for the Allegheny County tax office. In 1909, Joseph Kaufman got a job with the Columbia Ribbon Manufacturing Company in Paterson, New Jersey, and George became a traveling salesman for the company. It was in Paterson and on his trips into New York City selling ribbons that Kaufman began reading Franklin P. Adams' column "Always in Good Humor" in the New York *Evening Mail*. The column consisted of humorous contributions from throughout the area, as well as Adams' witticisms, and Kaufman began submitting pieces under the initials "G.S.K." to mimic Adams' use of "F.P.A." (only later in his life did Kaufman, who did not have a middle name, decide that the "S" represented "Simon," his grandfather's name.)

Adams recognized Kaufman's talent and urged him to take acting lessons at the Alveine School of Dramatic Art, as well as a playwriting course at Columbia University. In 1912, Adams maneuvered Kaufman into a position on the Washington *Times*, where he wrote a column entitled "This & That," similar to Adams'. He became familiar with the works of Mark Twain while there and honed his staccato writing style and ability to play poker. Within a year, however, the owner of the paper, who had never seen Kaufman face-to-face, noticed him in the office and remarked, "What is that Jew doing in my city room?" After several words were exchanged, Kaufman was fired and returned to New York, where he succeeded Adams at the *Evening Mail*, only to be dismissed. Adams then got him a job on the *Tribune*, where he covered local news. While reporting on incoming ships and other insignificant events, he began cadging free admission into the theaters, and eventually got himself assigned to the drama desk. In 1914, he became the drama editor. Three years later, after losing out to Heywood Broun for the position of top drama critic, he became drama editor of *The New York Times*.

In March of 1917, Kaufman married Beatrice Bakrow, whose ambitions and contacts helped thrust him into the theatrical world. She provided emotional support and critical and social guidance for the always uncertain Kaufman for most of his long career, despite the deterioration of their marital relationship after the stillbirth of a deformed child. They later adopted a daughter, Anne, but, as part of their "arrangement" sought sexual relationships outside the marriage. They remained married until Beatrice's death in 1945.

In 1917, John Peter Toohey noticed a play submitted by Kaufman to the Joseph W. Stern Music Company. The play was never produced, but Toohey introduced Kaufman to impresario George C. Tyler, who offered Kaufman the task of revising a play by Larry Evans and Walter Percival. Though produced, *Among Those Present*, which finally reached Broadway after still more revisions as *Someone in the House*, was never a success. Kaufman next tried to adapt Hans Miller's *Jacques Duval*, a European hit. Although George Arliss played the lead, it, too, failed. Tyler, however, continued to have faith in Kaufman, and put him to work on *Dulcy* with Marc Connelly. Based on a character, Dulcinea, created by Kaufman's friend Adams, the play opened in New York on August 13, 1921, and became an immediate hit.

Connelly and Kaufman worked together until 1924, when each decided to write a play on his own. Connelly became successful on his own and would eventually write the remarkable *The Green Pastures* (pb. 1929).

After the breakup, Kaufman did write *The Butter and Egg Man*, a rare solo effort, but working alone was not to his liking, and he spent most of the rest of his life collaborating. Through the rest of his career, his collaborators included some of the most successful writers of the time, including Edna Ferber, Alexander Woollcott, Herman J. Mankiewicz, Ring Lardner, John P. Marquand, Moss Hart, and Abe Burrows. He also collaborated with Morrie Ryskind; Howard Dietz; Katherine Dayton; Nunnally Johnson; his second wife, Leueen MacGrath; and his biographer, Howard Teichmann. Although he was never much interested in music, Kaufman was associated with George and Ira Gershwin and Cole Porter, and he rewrote Gilbert and Sullivan's *H.M.S. Pinafore*. He served as a "play doctor" for an unknown number of plays for which he got no credit, and he advised John Steinbeck on adapting *Of Mice and Men* for the stage.

After having codirected *The Good Fellow* with Howard Lindsay in 1926, Kaufman was persuaded by producer Jed Harris in 1928 to direct *The Front Page* by Ben Hecht and Charles MacArthur. After he had overcome his shy way of sending notes to the stage, Kaufman also had a remarkable career as a director. Besides his own plays, which he felt might be botched by another director, Kaufman directed *Joseph* (pr. 1930) by Bertram Bloch, *Here Today* (pr. 1932) by George Oppenheimer, *Of Mice and Men* (pr. 1937) by John Steinbeck, *My Sister Eileen* (pr. 1940) by Jerome Chodorov and Joseph Fields, *Mr. Big* (pr. 1941) by Arthur Sheekman and Margaret Shane, *The Naked Genius* (1943) by Gypsy Rose Lee, *Over Twenty-One* (1944) by Ruth Gordon, *While the Sun Shines* (pr. 1943) by Terence Rattigan, *The Next Half Hour* (pr. 1945) by Mary Chase, *Town House* (pr. 1948) by Gertrude Tonkonogy (based on short stories by John Cheever), *Metropole* (pr. 1949) by William Walden, *The Enchanted* (pr. 1950) by Jean Giraudoux, *Guys and Dolls* (pr. 1950) by Abe Burrows and Jo Swerling, and *Romanoff and Juliet* (pr. 1957) by Peter Ustinov. This extraordinary list ought to have been more than enough for one man's lifetime, but when one includes the list of plays he wrote, one sees exactly how inexhaustible Kaufman was.

Yet the anxieties of Kaufman's childhood drove him to do even more. He adapted two of his plays (with Ryskind) for the Marx Brothers for the screen, and then (also with Ryskind) wrote *A Night at the Opera* for them. He directed the movie *The Senator Was Indiscreet* with William Powell and Ella Raines in 1947, but—basically uninterested in the mechanics of filmmaking and disappointed with the way Hollywood was handling McCarthyism—he returned to the theater. He also acted in productions of *Once in a Lifetime* and *The Man Who Came to Dinner* and served as a panelist on an early television show, *This Is Show Business*. Given his extraordinarily productive working life, the legends portraying Kaufman as an incessant womanizer, a skilled poker player, and a regular member of the Algonquin

Round Table may seem exaggerated, but the sheer number of these stories testifies to their probable basis in fact, to his incredible capacity for unceasing activity, and perhaps to a neurotic inability to relax.

The least productive period of Kaufman's life followed the death of Beatrice in October, 1945, and lasted until he married actress Leueen Emily MacGrath in May, 1949. The disparity in their ages led to an eventual separation in 1957, but even after their divorce, Leueen spent much time helping him in various ways as his health declined. Small strokes hindered his ability to work, so much so that he was a mere shadow of himself when directing *Romanoff and Juliet*. In the last few years of his life, his mind deteriorated, and, among other things, he would wander onto Park and Madison Avenues in his nightshirt. After he fell against a radiator in 1961 and was badly burned, he rarely left his bed, and he died peacefully in June, 1961.

Analysis

As a practical man of the theater, George S. Kaufman concerned himself with the meticulous details of whatever project he was working on and gave little consideration to his place in the literary world or posterity. If he was writing, he would badger his collaborators to write better exit lines, to add more humor, to refine every sentence. When directing, he acidly chastized the slightest carelessness of an actor. As a literary figure, though, he was peculiarly unconcerned with plays or productions he had done in the past, eschewing the role of an author of drama, ignoring the possibility that what he had written with his collaborators had literary merit. Only once was he active in the revival of one of his plays, *Of Thee I Sing*. Indeed, his own attitude toward his art has contributed to the critical neglect of his work.

Primary among Kaufman's talents was his wit. The only weapon of a slim, shy boy and honed by his association with Adams, Woollcott, Dorothy Parker, Groucho Marx, and others of the Algonquin Round Table, "wisecracks" became characteristic of a Kaufman play and are obvious in every play on which he worked, from *Dulcy*, his first success, to *The Solid Gold Cadillac*. After three failures on Broadway, the success of *Dulcy*, with Lynn Fontanne in the title role, surprised Kaufman as much as anyone else (he always seemed to see his success as undeserved and always expected a disaster). As Malcolm Goldstein observes, *Dulcy* was basically a rehash of materials used by dozens of writers; what made it different from other plays was its flow of wit.

Although Kaufman would use any form of humor or stage technique to achieve his desired effect—in his plays there are many examples of slapstick, parody, nonsense, and various levels of verbal humor—satire is a recurring element. Ironically, one of the most famous quotations of Kaufman is "Satire is what closes Saturday night," as if he wished to ignore his own use of it. His wit could be quite vicious, particularly toward those who he felt had crossed him in some way. Even Dorothy Parker, the master of the acid quip, was severely wounded by Kaufman's barbs on more than one occasion. Earl Wilson once commented that Kaufman had been "blasting away at somebody or something all his life." It was only natural that such wit would be turned to satiric purpose against the pompous, the pretentious, the rich, and the powerful.

Little in society escaped his satire. *Beggar on Horseback* (written with Marc Connelly), the only commercially successful American expressionist play, satirized the American obsession with success, as if Kaufman were trying to exorcise the ghosts of failure from his own childhood. *Merton of the Movies* (also with Connelly) and *Once in a Lifetime* (with Hart) mocked Hollywood. *June Moon* (with Ring Lardner) satirized Tin Pan Alley. *I'd Rather Be Right* (with Hart) satirized Franklin D. Roosevelt, while *Of Thee I Sing* (with Ryskind) took on the presidential election process and vice-presidency. *The Solid Gold Cadillac* (with Teichmann) poked fun at big business. One of his more curious satiric vehicles is *The Man Who Came to Dinner* (with Hart), in which the major character was based on Kaufman's pompous friend Alexander Woollcott, who even good-humoredly agreed to play the title role in one production. It was perhaps convenient, even wise, for Kaufman to deny that he had satiric intent, particularly when he was more concerned with giving an audience a pleasant evening, but the moral outrage, sarcasm, and derision that is characteristic of satire is present to an extraordinary degree in his work.

Yet another element which can be observed in many of Kaufman's plays is the struggle and eventual triumph of the "little man" against the forces which oppress him, particularly big government and big business. In play after play, regardless of his collaborators, people in low social positions turn the tables on their social superiors. In his early plays, there is usually a relatively innocent young man who is ambitious but not intelligent enough to carry out his plans for advancement without the help of a more intelligent, maternal young woman in love with him. In Kaufman's play *The Solid Gold Cadillac*, an old woman triumphs over the executives of General Motors. It is a pattern observed in many of the plays and films of the 1920's and 1930's, such as in Frank Capra's *Mr. Deeds Goes to Town*. Such plays, particularly in the Depression, seemed to draw much of their appeal from the general feeling that the titans of business and their governmental allies had let down or betrayed the common person.

Despite the popularity of Kaufman's plays and their nearly predictable success, only two of his works were taken seriously enough to win the Pulitzer Prize. The first play to win was *Of Thee I Sing*, written with Morrie Ryskind, with music and lyrics by George and Ira Gershwin. Although Kaufman had been forced to soften the satire of *Strike Up the Band* only a few years previously, he believed that the country was weary of the Depression and the Republican platitudes of prosperity being "just around the corner," and might just be serious-minded enough to accept a play that satirized American politics, especially presidential elections. He invited Ryskind to join him on the project. Ryskind, who never believed such a scathing play would ever be produced, thought it might be fun to write. They began with the working title "Tweedledee" to refer to two virtually indistinguishable parties, and the plot of a presidential election hinging on the selection of a national anthem ("The Star-Spangled Banner" was not made the official national anthem until March 3, 1931). The Gershwins, who were attracted by the musical possibilities, were immediately interested and quickly began composing.

Ryskind and Kaufman soon realized the abstractness of their plot and decided to put a romantic interest into it, even though Kaufman maintained an absolute abhorrence of romantic scenes and generally refused to write them, leaving them to his collaborators. In the play, presidential candidate John P. Wintergreen uses the notion of marriage to a "typical American girl" as a device to win votes: He agrees to marry the winner of an Atlantic City beauty contest arranged by his managers. Once elected, however, he rejects the winner, marries his secretary, and causes international turmoil (she is of French descent). Facing impeachment, he is finally saved by his wife's delivery of twins and by a curious interpretation of the Constitution which forces the Vice President to marry the contest winner.

In August, 1931, over a period of seventeen days, the collaborators completed the book, turning the harmless fluff of their plot into withering satire. It opened to rave reviews in Boston and became an extraordinary hit on its opening in New York, when George Gershwin conducted the orchestra and the audience was filled with such luminaries as Mayor Jimmy Walker, ex-presidential candidate Al Smith, Florenz Ziegfeld, Beatrice Lillie, Ethel Barrymore, Condé Nast, and Samuel Goldwyn. The play was praised in every way possible, although critic Robert Benchley dissented. It was compared to Gilbert and Sullivan's *Iolanthe* (pr. 1882) and called a new departure from the musical comedy style. The songs were considered so well integrated that some critics went to the extreme of calling *Of Thee I Sing* more an "operetta" than a "musical," particularly ironic praise, since Kaufman would later do an unsuccessful updating of *H.M.S. Pinafore* called *Hollywood Pinafore* (pr. 1945); he was not much interested in music and often resented the intrusions of songs into his comic plots. In 1932, when the Pulitzer Prize committee astounded the theater world by awarding the prize to a musical for the first time in its history, it caused much controversy, because such plays as *Mourning Becomes Electra* by Eugene O'Neill and Robert E. Sherwood's *Reunion in Vienna* were passed over. The critic of *Commonweal* defended the decision, however, when he wrote that *Of Thee I Sing* ". . . is much closer to Aristophanes than O'Neill ever came to Euripides."

The remark was particularly well-founded. A. Cleveland Harrison has commented extensively on what he perceives as the revival of Aristophanic Old Comedy in the Kaufman-Ryskind play, noting how the episodes of the plot are linked less by a cause-effect relationship than by the development of aspects of the central topic. Extreme characters and situations are used to put ideals into conflict. The ideal of democracy, for example, is in conflict with the reality of it, where politicians use side issues to get themselves elected. The stereotyped characters themselves are less important than the allegorical concepts they represented. Furthermore a wide range of societal types is represented, from Irish and Jewish power-brokers, to newspapermen and Southern pork-barrel senators, each using their particular slang, with many of society's institutions, such as the beauty contest and the vice presidency, subjected to ridicule. The satire was sufficiently irreverent to lead Victor Moore, who played Vice President Throttlebottom, to wonder if he would be arrested on opening night. Today, however, *Of Thee I Sing*, like many of Kaufman's works, seems somewhat dated. The Aristophanic nature of most of his comedies may indeed contribute to the general current impression of them as extremely amusing, cleverly written, brilliantly constructed period pieces.

Other major works

SCREENPLAYS: *Business Is Business*, 1925 (with Dorothy Parker); *The Cocoanuts*, 1929 (with Morrie Ryskind); *Animal Crackers*, 1931 (with Ryskind); *Roman Scandals*, 1933 (with Robert E. Sherwood, George Oppenheimer, Arthur Sheekman, Nat Perrin, and W. A. McGuire); *A Night at the Opera*, 1935 (with Ryskind); *Star-Spangled Rhythm*, 1943.

Bibliography

Goldstein, Malcolm. *George S. Kaufman: His Life, His Theater.* New York: Oxford University Press, 1979. This volume is considered the standard biography of the prolific man who wrote or collaborated on more than forty Broadway plays.

Hart, Moss. *Act One.* New York: New American Library, 1959. *Act One* is a witty memoir written by the great American dramatist who was Kaufman's longtime collaborator.

Meredith, Scott. *George S. Kaufman and His Friends.* Garden City, N.Y.: Doubleday, 1974. This useful biography offers much Broadway local color and theater lore. It is also available in abridged form under the title *George S. Kaufman and the Algonquin Round Table.*

Pollack, Rhoda-Gale. *George S. Kaufman.* Boston: Twayne, 1988. Pollack has written a concise but useful biography on the playwright. Supplemented by a short bibliography.

Teichmann, Howard. *George S. Kaufman: An Intimate Portrait.* New York: Athenum, 1982. Although dated, this volume is still useful, especially in its discussion of Kaufman's origins in Pittsburgh and his early career. It is exhaustive and carefully illustrated.

J. Madison Davis
(Updated by *Peter C. Holloran*)

ADRIENNE KENNEDY

Born: Pittsburgh, Pennsylvania; September 13, 1931

Principal drama

Funnyhouse of a Negro, pr. 1962, pb. 1969; *The Owl Answers*, pr. 1963, pb. 1969; *A Rat's Mass*, pr. 1966, pb. 1968; *The Lennon Play: In His Own Write*, pr. 1967, pb. 1969 (with John Lennon and Victor Spinetti); *A Lesson in Dead Language*, pr., pb. 1968; *Sun: A Poem for Malcolm X Inspired by His Murder*, pr. 1968, pb. 1971; *A Beast's Story*, pr., pb. 1969; *Boats*, pr. 1969; *Cities in Bezique: Two One Act Plays*, pb. 1969; *An Evening with Dead Essex*, pr. 1973; *A Movie Star Has to Star in Black and White*, pr. 1976, pb. 1984; *A Lancashire Lad*, pr. 1980; *Orestes and Electra*, pr. 1980; *Black Children's Day*, pr. 1980; *The Alexander Plays*, pb. 1992; *The Ohio State Murders*, pr., pb. 1992.

Other literary forms

In addition to her plays, Adrienne Kennedy has published a wide-ranging memoir, *People Who Led to My Plays* (1987). In 1988, she published *Adrienne Kennedy in One Act* and followed it two years later with *Deadly Triplets: A Theatre Mystery and Journal* (1990).

Achievements

Kennedy departs from the theatrical naturalism used by other African-American playwrights in favor of a surrealistic and expressionistic form. Her plays capture the irrational quality of dreams while offering insight into the nature of the self and being. Most of her works are complex character studies in which a given figure may have several selves or roles. In this multi-dimensional presentation lies Kennedy's forte—the unraveling of the individual consciousness.

The playwright received an Obie Award in 1964 for *Funnyhouse of a Negro*, her best-known play; held a Guggenheim Fellowship in 1967; and received grants from the Rockefeller Foundation, the New England Theatre Conference, the National Endowment for the Arts, and the Creative Artists Public Service. She was a lecturer at Yale University from 1972 to 1974 and a Yale Fellow from 1974 to 1975. In addition to lecturing at Yale, Kennedy has taught playwriting at Princeton and Brown universities.

Biography

Adrienne Kennedy was born on September 13, 1931, in Pittsburgh, Pennsylvania, the daughter of Cornell Wallace Hawkins, a social worker, and the former Etta Haugabook, a teacher. She grew up in Cleveland, Ohio, and attended Ohio State University, where she received a bachelor's degree in education in 1953. A few years later, she moved to New York and enrolled in creative writing classes at Columbia University and the New School for Social Research. In 1962, she joined Edward Albee's Playwrights' Workshop in New York City's Circle in the Square. She wrote *Funnyhouse of a Negro* for Albee's workshop. A decade later she became a founder of the Women's Theater Council. In 1953, the playwright married Joseph C. Kennedy, whom she divorced in 1966. She has two sons.

Kennedy settled in New York, where she divided her time between writing and teaching. She continued to receive awards and recognition for her writing. On March 7, 1992, the opening date of her play *The Ohio State Murders*, the mayor of Cleveland proclaimed the day Adrienne Kennedy Day in Cleveland.

Analysis

Adrienne Kennedy's plays are consistent in their exploration of the double consciousness of African Americans who are themselves inheritors of both African and European American culture and tradition. Symbolically represented by the split in the head of Patrice Lumumba, one of the selves in *Funnyhouse of a Negro*, this double identity frequently results in a schizophrenic division in which a character's selves or roles are at odds with one another. Typically it is the African identity with which the protagonist—who is often a sensitive, well-read young woman—is unable to come to grips. By using a surrealistic form to treat such a complex subject, Kennedy is able to suggest that truth can be arrived at only through the unraveling of distortion. Indeed, what Kennedy's protagonist knows of Africa and of blacks has come to her filtered through the consciousness of others who are eager to label Africans and their descendants "bestial" or "deranged." This seems to be what theater critic Clive Barnes means when he says that Kennedy "thinks black, but she remembers white." For this reason, animal imagery, as well as black and white color contrasts, dominates Kennedy's plays.

Kennedy's concerns with isolationism, identity conflict, and consciousness are presented primarily through character. She has called her plays "states of mind," in which she attempts to bring the subconscious to the level of consciousness. She achieves this essentially by decoding her dreams. Indeed, many of the plays were actually dreams that she later translated into theatrical form. This surrealistic or dreamlike quality of her work has been compared to August Strindberg's dream plays, in that both dramatists render reality through the presentation of distortion. Extracting what is real from what is a distortion as one would with a dream is the puzzle Kennedy establishes for her characters, as well as for her audience, to unravel in each of her major plays: *Funnyhouse of a Negro*, *The Owl Answers*, *A Rat's Mass*, and *A Movie Star Has to Star in Black and White*.

As in life, truth in Kennedy's plays is frequently a matter of subjectivity, and one character's version of it is often brought into question by another's. This is the case in *Funnyhouse of a Negro*, Kennedy's most critically acclaimed play. From the moment a somnambulist woman walks across the stage "as if in a dream" at the beginning of the play, the audience is aware that it is not viewing a realistic performance. Such figures onstage as the woman sleepwalker, women with "wild, straight black hair," a "hunchbacked yellow-skinned dwarf," and objects such as the monumental ebony bed, which resembles a tomb, suggest a nightmarish setting. The action of the play takes place in four settings: Queen Victoria's chamber, the Duchess of Hapsburg's chamber, a Harlem hotel room, and the jungle. Nevertheless, it is not implausible to suggest that the real setting of *Funnyhouse of a Negro* takes place inside the head of Sarah, Kennedy's protagonist. As Sarah tells the theater audience in her opening speech, the four rooms onstage are "[her] rooms."

As with the four sets that are really one room, Sarah has four "selves" who help to reveal the complexity of her character. At first, Sarah appears to be a version of the kindhearted prostitute, or perhaps a reverse Electra who hates rather than loves her father. Kennedy builds upon these types to show Sarah's preoccupation with imagination and dreams, as well as her divided consciousness as a partaker of two cultures. Queen Victoria and the Duchess of Hapsburg are identified with Sarah's mother, or with her white European identity. The other two personalities, Jesus and Patrice Lumumba, the Congolese leader and martyr, on the other hand, are identified with Sarah's father, or with her black African heritage. Significantly, Sarah's four personalities tell the story of the parents' marriage and subsequent trip to Africa and the rape of the mother, which results in the conception of Sarah, each of which events can be called into question by the dreamlike atmosphere of the play and by the mother's insanity. One by one, the four alter egos add details to the story which allow the picture of Sarah's family to build through accretion. Even so, this story is undermined by the final conversation between the landlady and Sarah's boyfriend, Raymond. Doubling as "the Funnyman" to the landlady's "Funnylady," Raymond comes onstage after Sarah's suicide to tell the audience the truth about Sarah's father in the epilogue to the play. Although Sarah claimed to have killed her father, Raymond tells the audience that the father is not dead but rather "liv[ing] in the city in a room with European antiques, photographs of Roman ruins, walls of books and oriental carpets."

The same eschewal of linear progression in *Funnyhouse of a Negro* occurs in *The Owl Answers*, the first of two one-act plays appearing with *A Beast's Story* in the collection titled *Cities in Bezique*. Clara Passmore, the protagonist in *The Owl Answers*, like Sarah in *Funnyhouse of a Negro*, is a sensitive, educated young woman torn between the two cultures of which she is a part.

Riveted by her fascination for a culture which seems to want no part of her, Clara, a mulatto English teacher from Savannah, Georgia, learns from her mother that her father, "the richest white man in town," is of English ancestry. She comes to London to give him a fitting burial at Saint Paul's Cathedral, among the "lovely English." Once there, she has a breakdown and is imprisoned in the Tower of London by William Shakespeare, Geoffrey Chaucer, and William the Conquerer, who taunt her by denying her English heritage. Clara, who is both the daughter of the deceased William Mattheson and the Reverend Mr. Passmore (who, with his wife, adopted Clara when she was a child), is as firm in her claim to English ancestry as she is in her plans to bury her father in London. Like Sarah in *Funnyhouse of a Negro*, Clara's true prison exists in her mind. Ironically, Clara Passmore, whose name suggests racial passing, passes only from human into animal form. In a final, violent scene in which the third movement of Haydn's Concerto for Horn in D accentuates the mental anguish of Clara and her mother, Clara's mother stabs herself on an altar of owl feathers. Clara, in the meantime, fends off an attack from a man whom she calls "God," who has assumed that the love she seeks from him is merely sexual. Sarah, who has grown increasingly more owl-like as the play has progressed, utters a final "Ow... oww." In this play, as in *Funnyhouse of a Negro*, Kennedy leaves the audience with questions about the nature of spiritual faith in a world in which one calls upon God, yet in which the only answer heard comes from the owl.

Similar preoccupations with the clash of African and European culture in *Funnyhouse of a Negro* and *The Owl Answers* can be seen in *A Rat's Mass*, a one-act play set in the time of the marching of the Nazi armies. Brother and Sister Rat, who have a rat's head and a rat's belly, respectively, are both in love with Rosemary, a descendant of "the Pope, Julius Caesar, and the Virgin Mary." The two rat siblings struggle to atone for the dark, secret sin they committed when they "went on the slide together," which has forced them into hiding in the attic of their home. Alone together in their misery, Kay and Blake, the sister and brother, remember a time when they "lived in a Holy Chapel with parents and Jesus, Joseph, and Mary, our wise men and our shepherd." Now they can only hear the gnawing of rats in the attic. In desperation, they turn to Rosemary to help them atone for their sins. Rosemary refuses, stating that only through their deaths will there be a way of atonement. The way comes when Jesus, Joseph, Mary, two wise men, and the shepherd return as the Nazi army to open fire on the rats, leaving only Rosemary, like the evergreen shrub for which she is named, to remain standing.

The animal motif employed in *The Owl Answers* and *A Rat's Mass* is less apparent in *A Movie Star Has to Star in Black and White*. Clara Passmore of *The Owl Answers* returns for a "bit role" in which she reads from several of Kennedy's plays. The English literary tradition highly esteemed by the protagonist in *Funnyhouse of a Negro* and *The Owl Answers* is replaced by the American film tradition. Reinforcing the theme of illusion versus reality begun in *Funnyhouse of a Negro*, *A Movie Star Has to Star in Black and White* is actually a series of plays-within-a-play in which scenes from the films *Now, Voyager*, *Viva Zapata*, and *A Place in the Sun* take place in a hospital lobby, Clara's brother's room, and in Clara's old room, respectively. As the title of the play indicates—as well as a stage note directing that all the colors be shades of black and white—Kennedy continues her experimentation with black and white color contrasts onstage. As in other plays by Kennedy, linear progression is eschewed and the illusion of cinema merges with the reality of the life of Clara, a writer and daughter to the Mother and Father, the wife of Eddie, the mother of Eddie Jr., and the alter ego to the film actresses.

Through lines spoken in the first scene by Bette Davis to Paul Henreid, the audience learns of Clara's parents' dream of success in the North, which ends in disappointment when they learn that racial oppression is not confined to the South. The scene takes place simultaneously in an ocean liner from *Now, Voyager* and a hospital lobby where Clara and her mother have come to ascertain the condition of Wally, Clara's brother, who lies in a coma.

Scene 2 moves to Wally's room, while Jean Peters and Marlon Brando enact lines from *Viva Zapata*. History repeats itself when it is revealed that Clara, like her mother before her, is having marital problems with her husband, Eddie. In the meantime, Marlon Brando's character changes the bed sheets onto which Jean Peters' character has bled, reminding the audience of Clara's miscarriage while Eddie was away in the armed services.

In the following scene, Shelley Winters and Montgomery Clift appear onstage in a small rowboat from the film *A Place in the Sun*. In this scene, Clara reveals her frustration as a writer who is black and a woman. She says that her husband thinks that her life is "one of my black and white movies that I love so . . . with me playing a bit part." The play ends with the news that Wally will live, but with brain damage. In the interim, Shelley Winters' character drowns as Montgomery Clift's character looks on, suggesting a connection between Clara's fantasy life in motion pictures and the real world, from which she struggles to escape.

Kennedy's other plays deal with themes similar to those in the works discussed. The animal motif, coupled with the theme of sexuality, is continued in *A Beast's Story* and *A Lesson in Dead Language*. In *A Beast's Story*, Beast Girl kills her child with quinine and whiskey and then kills her husband with an ax after he attempts to make love to her. Her parents, Beast Man and Beast Woman, preside over the dark course of events as shamans anxious for their daughter to rid the household of the "intruder" whose presence has caused a black sun to hover above them. Animal imagery is paired with the rite-of-passage motif in *A Lesson in Dead Language*. In this play, a schoolteacher who is a white dog "from the waist up" instructs seven young girls about menstruation. Similarly, the dreamlike quality of earlier plays continues in *Sun*, a play-poem written about the death of Malcolm X, and in *An Evening with Dead Essex*, based on the assassination of black sniper Mark James Essex.

With the 1980's, Kennedy branched out into the writing of children's plays on commission. Among these plays are *A Lancashire Lad*, *Orestes and Electra*, and *Black Children's Day*. Kennedy was a prolific writer in the late 1980's and early 1990's, with her esteemed "scrapbook of memories" *People Who Led to My Plays*, *Deadly Triplets: A Theatre Mystery and Journal*, and *The Alexander Plays*, the latter centering on the protagonist Suzanne Alexander and including such pieces as *The Ohio State Murders*, *She Talks to Beethoven*, *The Dramatic Circle*, and *The Film Club*.

Notable among her later works is her play *The Ohio State Murders*, the source of which was Kennedy's emotionally scarring experience as an undergraduate at Ohio State University. According to dramaturge Scott T. Cummings, "the play reflects [Kennedy's] abiding feeling that 'nothing has changed for American blacks,' that 'American blacks would have been better off leaving this country.'"

Kennedy dares to be innovative both in her subject matter and in theatrical form. She writes difficult plays that raise questions rather than provide answers. From *Funnyhouse of a Negro* onward, Kennedy chose a subjective form that she has retained throughout her literary career. Her plays grow out of her own experiences as a sensitive and gifted black American who grew up in the American Midwest. There may be little plot in Kennedy's plays, but there is, to be sure, a wealth of symbolism concerning the inherent tensions of the African-American experience.

Other major work

NONFICTION: *People Who Led to My Plays*, 1987; *Adrienne Kennedy in One Act*, 1988.

MISCELLANEOUS: *Deadly Triplets: A Theatre Mystery and Journal*, 1990.

Bibliography
Benston, Kimberly W. "Cities in Bezique: Adrienne Kennedy's Expressionistic Vision." *College Language Association Journal* 20 (1976): 235-244. In this essay on *The Owl Answers* and *A Beast's Story*, Benston delineates Kennedy's skillful use of expressionism. Sees part of Kennedy's richly symbolic form as having been borrowed from both the folktale and August Strindberg's dream plays.

Blau, Herbert. "The American Dream in American Gothic: The Plays of Sam Shepard and Adrienne Kennedy." *Modern Drama* 27 (1984): 520-539. Blau examines three plays by Shepard and three by Kennedy. Combines personal reflections on his work with Kennedy with sociological, psychological, and thematic approaches to her plays. Sees her as having been "out of place in the emergence of Black Power" and views powerlessness and death as obsessions in her oeuvre.

Bryant-Jackson, Paul, and Lois More Overbeck, eds. *Intersecting Boundaries.* Minneapolis: University of Minnesota Press, 1992. An anthology of essays on Kennedy's work, this volume consists of four parts, including interviews and critical analyses of her work by various scholars. The first of its sort on Kennedy's plays, it makes a substantial contribution to Kennedy scholarship.

Curb, Rosemary. "Fragmented Selves in Adrienne Kennedy's *Funnyhouse of a Negro* and *The Owl Answers.*" *Theater Journal* 32 (1980): 180-195. Curb argues that Kennedy eschews linear narrative progression to portray "the fragmented mental states of her characters," with the central conflict occurring inside the main character's mind. Suggests that Kennedy is a "poet-playwright," examines Kennedy's central images alongside her theme of death, and compares her work to that of Ntozake Shange.

Kennedy, Adrienne. "A Growth of Images." *Tulane Drama Review* 21 (1977): 41-47. Kennedy discusses her reasons for selecting autobiographical materials for her plays and states that most of them grow out of her dreams. Provides sources for Clara Passmore in *The Owl Answers.*

Meigs, Susan. "No Place but the Funnyhouse: The Struggle for Identity in Three Adrienne Kennedy Plays." In *Modern Drama: The Female Canon*, edited by June Schlueter. Rutherford, N.J.: Fairleigh Dickinson University Press, 1990. Meigs begins her discussion of *Funnyhouse of a Negro*, *The Owl Answers*, and *A Movie Star Has to Star in Black and White* by noting the significance of Kennedy's trip to Africa in 1960, which had a substantial impact on her worldview. Believes that the conflict between Western and African tradition and culture undergirds the major theme of Kennedy's "complex, surrealistic psychodramas."

Sollors, Werner. "Owls and Rats in the American Funnyhouse: Adrienne Kennedy's Drama." *American Literature: A Journal of Literary History, Criticism, and Bibliography* 63 (1991): 507-532. States that Kennedy's oeuvre is best seen as "a full-fledged modern American attempt at rewriting family tragedy." Examines seven plays against the background of her autobiography, *People Who Led to My Plays.*

Zinman, Toby Silverman. "'In the Presence of Mine Enemies': Adrienne Kennedy's *An Evening with Dead Essex.*" *Studies in American Drama, 1945-Present* 6 (1991): 3-13. Notes that unlike most of Kennedy's plays, this one "is based on a newspaper account, and is mostly male, apparently realistic, and raggedly structured." Concludes that Kennedy has enormous enemies in mind, including the American government and American society.

P. Jane Splawn

SIDNEY KINGSLEY
Sidney Kirshner

Born: New York, New York; October 22, 1906

Principal drama

Men in White, pr., pb. 1933; *Dead End*, pr. 1935, pb. 1936; *Ten Million Ghosts*, pr. 1936; *The World We Make*, pr., pb. 1939 (adaptation of Millen Brand's novel *The Outward Room*); *The Patriots*, pr., pb. 1943; *Detective Story*, pr., pb. 1949; *Darkness at Noon*, pr., pb. 1951 (adaptation of Arthur Koestler's novel); *Lunatics and Lovers*, pr. 1954; *Night Life*, pr. 1962, pb. 1964.

Other literary forms

Sidney Kingsley is known exclusively for his plays.

Achievements

Kingsley is generally regarded as a social dramatist, one who made the social and political problems of his age the subject matter of his plays. Because his early work was done in the 1930's, a time of economic depression and of a crisis for capitalism, there are strong liberal (at times leftist) perspectives in his dramas. Invariably his characters struggle with a fate not simply personal but, in a very explicit sense, social as well. George Ferguson in *Men in White*, Thomas Jefferson in *The Patriots*, Nicolai Rubashov in *Darkness at Noon*, and Will Kazar in *Night Life* are very different as characters, yet all of them, in Kingsley's plays, must weigh their personal desires and private dreams against their social responsibilities and public ambitions.

Kingsley's plays demonstrate his interaction with the world of his day: its politics, its institutions, its social issues, its technologies. The movies inspired by three of his plays—*Men in White* (1934), *Dead End* (1937), *Detective Story* (1951)—expanded his already strong influence on the popular culture of his day.

By concentrating on the interaction between the idealist and the community in which he functions, Kingsley was able to project the tensions and dynamics of society in the midst of industrial transformation. Although the actions in Kingsley's plays are often melodramatic, they serve to illuminate the struggle between materialism and idealism, between the structures of a society and the people trying to adjust to their social institutions. Few twentieth century writers have been more thorough in examining the dedicated professional and the meaning of work to those whose work is the property of others.

Kingsley is also significant because he has interacted with many of the major talents of his age. The varied list of prominent theatrical people associated with his productions is impressive in itself: Luther Adler, Morris Carnovsky, Elia Kazan, Clifford Odets, Lee Strasberg, Norman Bel Geddes, the Dead End Kids, Lee Grant, Ralph Bellamy, Orson Welles, Howard Lindsay, Russel Crouse, Claude Rains, Jack Palance, Kim Hunter, Buddy Hackett, and Kingsley's wife, Madge Evans. In addition to pursuing his own active career as a creative artist, Kingsley has attempted to encourage the creativity of others, particularly in his work with the Dramatists Guild. Playing many different roles, Sidney Kingsley has been a major figure in American theatrical history.

Kingsley has received extensive recognition for his accomplishments. He received a Pulitzer Prize for *Men in White* as well as New York Theatre Club Medals for it, for *Dead End*, and for *The Patriots*. Kingsley also received New York Drama Critics Circle Awards for *The Patriots* and for *Durkness at Noon*. *The Patriots* also earned for him the New York Newspaper Guild Front Page Award, and for *Detective Story*, he earned a Newspaper Guild Page One Citation and an Edgar Allan Poe Award. *Darkness at Noon* also won a Donaldson Award for Outstanding Achievement and an American Academy of Arts and Letters Award of Merit Medal. Finally, Kingsley has received a Yeshiva University Award for Achievement in the Theatre (1965), a doctor of letters degree from Monmouth College (1978), and an induction into the Theatre Hall of Fame (1983).

Biography

Sidney Kingsley was born Sidney Kirshner on October 22, 1906, in New York City; he has spent most of his life in the New York area. Involved in the drama from an early age, he was already writing, directing, and acting in one-act plays at Townsend Harris Hall in New York City. After he was graduated from high school in 1924, Kingsley attended Cornell University, where he was a member of the Dramatic Club and acted with Franchot Tone. At Cornell, he continued to write plays: His play "Wonder-Dark Epilogue" won a prize for the best one-act play written by a student. After receiving his bachelor of arts degree in 1928, Kingsley did some acting with the Tremont Stock Company in the Bronx. Although he had a role in the 1929 Broadway production *Subway Express*, he decided at that time that acting was not the career for him.

That year, Kingsley went to California where he worked for Columbia Pictures as a play reader and scenario writer, but he soon returned to New York. At this time he was working on his own play, originally entitled "Crisis," later to be *Men in White*. During the writing he began to research the subject matter systematically, a procedure he would employ during the composition of several other plays. Since his play was to be about doctors, he visited various hospitals in the New York City area—Bellevue, Beth Israel, Lebanon—to gather material and to render as accurate a social picture as he could. (One story has it that he once masqueraded as an intern.) While several would-be producers had options on the play, it was finally presented by the soon-to-be-famous Group Theatre. It was their first major success, and the play established Kingsley as a prominent American playwright, winning for him the Pulitzer Prize (in a controversial decision) and the Theatre Club Award. It was also a financial success; Kingsley reportedly received forty-six thousand dollars for the motion-picture rights. Kingsley had become a principal figure in the theatrical community of New York.

Kingsley has directed all of his plays except *The Patriots*. Perhaps because he is himself an amateur painter and sculptor, he has shown great concern throughout his career for the physical appearance of his plays onstage. His second drama, *Dead End*, owed its immediate impact in no small part to a spectacular New York setting created by Bel Geddes. Animated by the energetic argot of his New York boys, the Dead End Kids, Kingsley's second play was even more popular and critically acclaimed than his first effort. Although the next two plays, *Ten Million Ghosts* and *The World We Make*, were not the popular hits his first two had been, they also featured memorable visual effects. By this time, Kingsley was regarded as a dramatist of social realism and spectacular staging effects, one whose plots inclined to melodrama and whose sympathies were clearly with the less fortunate.

In July, 1939, Kingsley married actress Madge Evans, a marriage that would last until her death in 1981. She retired from her film career soon after the marriage and assisted Kingsley in the historical research for his new play, tentatively entitled "Thomas Jefferson." She later appeared in the 1943 production version, *The Patriots*. Kingsley found himself inducted into the United States Army in March, 1941, about the time he finished the first version. He spent his free time polishing the play and was rewarded by largely favorable notices, most of which found Sergeant Kingsley's dramatization of the precarious nature of freedom in the early republic pertinent to the contemporary struggle of the United States in World War II. Later in 1943, Kingsley was promoted to lieutenant.

After his discharge from the army, Kingsley spent some time working for Metro-Goldwyn-Mayer on the movie scripts for *Cass Timberlane* (1947) and *Homecoming* (1946). Much of the time in the late 1940's, however, he was back in New York, haunting detective squad rooms to gather material for his new production, *Detective Story*. Even though it did not win the great awards some of his earlier efforts received, *Detective Story*, with its harsh, intense drama and convincing factual setting, is considered by many critics to be Kingsley's best play. Like *Men in White* and *Dead End*, it was made into a successful motion picture.

Kingsley's next drama, *Darkness at Noon*, was based on Arthur Koestler's 1941 novel of the same title. The production, featuring Claude Rains, Jack Palance, and Kim Hunter, was successful enough to win for Kingsley the Donaldson Award and the New York Drama Critics Circle Award. Kingsley and Koestler, however, quarreled publicly about the play; indeed, Koestler threatened to take Kingsley to court for what he thought were distortions of his text. In addition, Brooks Atkinson, the reviewer for *The New York Times*, raised similar unfavorable comparisons between the novel and the play. Produced in 1951, a time of strong anti-Communist feeling (and of reaction against that feeling), the play may have been a victim of its era. In spite of inspiring some harsh criticism, the play ran for almost two hundred performances.

For his next effort, *Lunatics and Lovers*, Kingsley shifted to totally different dramatic material, presenting the mid-1950's in a farce complete with lots of noise, various con games, and a plethora of sexual comedy. Although most critics were not fond of the play, it had a respectable run of more than three hundred performances. *Night Life*, presented in 1962, focuses on a labor racketeer, but in its frenzied surreal quality it reflects an era's growing emphasis on style rather than on social or political issues, an emphasis not suited to Kingsley's talents.

Since *Night Life*, much of Kingsley's creative energy has gone into the writing of a dramatic trilogy, "The Art Scene," which would examine the phenomenon of radical change in the contemporary world as reflected in graphic arts, modern dance, and the theater. Kingsley finished the first part, "Man with a Corpse on His Back," in the early 1970's.

When not involved with his own work, Kingsley has been concerned with encouraging and improving the artistic endeavors of others. Convinced that television was going to set the intellectual and spiritual climate of the age, he was briefly in the 1950's a television consultant to the Columbia Broadcasting System. As president of the Dramatists Guild from 1961 to 1969, he was active in efforts to help young playwrights and to preserve Off-Broadway theater. In the late 1970's, as chairman of New Jersey's Motion Picture and TV Authority, he was able to encourage film companies to shoot movies in the New Jersey area.

In recognition of his many contributions to the cultural scene, Kingsley was inducted into the Theatre Hall of Fame in May, 1983. He was awarded the Gold Medal for Drama by the American Academy and Institute of Arts and Letters in 1986 and won the William Inge Award for Lifetime Achievement in 1988.

Analysis

As a dramatist, Sidney Kingsley is noted for being a theater technician—not a surprising reputation, since he has spent all of his life in the theater and has directed all of his plays except *The Patriots*. Typically, the characters in his plays represent a social spectrum and dramatize sharp, overt ideological differences. Within this pattern there are also more subtly contrasting pairs of individuals: Gimpty and "Baby-Face," former members of the same youth gang in *Dead End*; the two proletarian brothers in *The World We Make*; the two women who love George Ferguson in *Men in White*; Rubashov and his inquisitor in *Darkness at Noon*.

Kingsley's plays have invariably displayed his fondness for spectacle. His settings are obviously the result of studied decisions, and they appear in virtually every production to be an indispensable element in the play. Bel Geddes' stunning set for *Dead End* articulated the social contrasts at the heart of the play as much as did its plot. The prison set in *Darkness at Noon*, with its spectacular tapping out of communication from one cell to another, starkly defined Soviet Russia for Kingsley's audience. The operating room in *Men in White* and the squad room of *Detective Story* anticipated in their powerful immediacy the television series of a later era. Indeed, Kingsley's sets have sometimes been disproportionately powerful: The expressionistic set of *Ten Million Ghosts* may in fact have been too heavy for the play, and the first two settings in *The World We Make* convey such a sharp, deterministic insistence that the rest of the play, set in John's room, seems too sequestered.

Dr. Schiller's statement in *The World We Make*, that no normal human being lives alone in the world, is a basic truth for Kingsley's plays, which stress the working out of the necessary difficulties in social existence. His characters tend to be types, figures who seem vibrantly alive only when struggling with the idea of their social duties. In this respect, it is society which animates them. Like other social realists, Kingsley has the gift of evoking a sense of community, the feeling that his characters are bound, for better or worse, by a system of deeply felt values. When this system breaks down, as it does in Kingsley's later work, the basic unity of the plays begins to fragment.

The title of Kingsley's first play, *Men in White*, indicates the play's focus on the profession of medicine itself. Throughout, Kingsley is concerned with what a doctor's life is and what it should be, examining the ethics, economics, and the dedication of the medical community. The entire play is confined to various parts of St. George's Hospital, and in one of the most crucial scenes, Kingsley takes the audience into the operating room, where the real and the melodramatic mingle. As Laura prepares to witness her fiancé operating, she suddenly discovers that the case, a botched abortion, is the result of her fiancé's affair. As this is happening, the visual dimension of the play emphasizes the ritual, the impersonal element, of medicine, so much so that the scene becomes an ironic comment on the plot and the action, a measure of the personal frustrations of the characters. The efficiency and sterility of the operating room conveys an atmosphere of professional mystery: The putting on of the gloves, the scrubbing, and the masks all blend to suggest the distinct, new nature of this community and the people in it, and the scientific impersonality of its activities.

Two doctors, one mature and one at the beginning of his career, are at the center of the action. The older man, Dr. Hochberg, is a model for those around him. While he seems casual in his initial appearance, it is soon apparent that he is a very disciplined, confident practitioner, the expert to whom everyone turns for advice and direction. He is a man of principle, informing the rich Mr. Hudson that doctors are more interested in working and learning than in making money, yet he is practical enough at board meetings to realize that the hospital's economy requires wealthy friends. In explaining his profession, he states that success in medicine is essentially a kind of glory, that one lifetime is not long enough to get at all the problems that confront medicine.

The younger man, Dr. George Ferguson, is more dynamically involved in the plot. At a position in life where he must make many crucial career decisions, George finds himself torn between Hochberg's demand for dedication—ten more years of hard work—and the insistence of Laura that he devote more time to her and to his personal life. Despite George's genuine respect for the master professional, Hochberg, his fiancée's request does not seem unreasonable. The conflict here defined between the responsibilities and ambitions inherent in public life and the demands of private life is a recurrent situation in Kingsley's drama.

George seems to acquiesce to Laura's wishes, though he wants to compromise with Hochberg rather than reject him. At this point, the plot is complicated by the botched abortion, a problem, the play suggests, resulting from a thoughtless moment between George and a sympathetic nurse. When Laura discovers the situation, she rejects George, saying that there is no excuse for what he did. Hochberg is much more tolerant and objective, noting that human bodies are human bodies and that the pregnancy was an accident. George seems about to marry the nurse, but she conveniently dies. In the conclusion, George explains to a more forgiving Laura that the hospital is where he belongs and where she ought to leave him. In terms of what the play has presented, he seems to be right.

Kingsley's most popular play, *Dead End*, owed its success to its theatrical boldness and to its projection of the mood of the 1930's. The spectacular set by Bel Geddes emphasized the contrasts of a New York neighborhood by placing a tenement house opposite the exclusive East River Terrace Apartment. For the river, a play area for the boys of the neighborhood, Bel Geddes flooded the orchestra pit. To give the flavor of the working city, a huge, red sand hopper stood prominently in the right center of the stage and a Caterpillar steam shovel stood farther back, up the street.

The boys of the neighborhood—later to be known in motion pictures as the Dead End Kids—carry much of the action of the play. Eager and energetic, they project vividly the communal intimacy of the neighborhood and define the kind of life that is nurtured by such surroundings. Kingsley's transcription of the lower-class New York dialect ("Howza wawda?"— "How's the water?") and his ethnic mixing add local color to his cultural portrait.

Insistent in its emphasis on economic desperation, *Dead End* is one of the representative literary documents of the 1930's. Like other literary works that examine the social problems of the era, it romanticizes the inner goodness of the poor and treats the rich with contempt. The play is a grim speculation about the power of social conditions to define the fate of the individual.

Two former residents of the neighborhood, Gimpty and "Baby-Face" Martin, have been marked by growing up in this environment, each in his own way. Gimpty, a lame but resourceful slum-boy who has become an architect but cannot find work in the barren economy of the day, suggests the inability of his generation to build a new world, having been deprived of the chance to make its own future; his physical disability symbolizes his socially disadvantaged state. Gimpty is in love with Kay, who has overcome poverty by becoming a rich man's mistress.

Martin, a criminal on the run, serves to trace a more disastrous path for a tenement boy, from the ranks of the underprivileged to the criminal class. He advises the kids to become more violent in their gang wars, to forget about fighting fair. His corruption is certified when even his mother rejects him. Gimpty turns Martin in just when he seems on the verge of hatching a kidnaping scheme, and the G-men kill Martin. In one sense, Gimpty's action is a betrayal of a neighborhood code—indeed he is filled with anguish over his part in Martin's death, but by this time Martin can be seen as one who has gone too far to be saved. In the end, Kay declares her love for Gimpty but will not give up her luxurious life for him.

In the subplot, a Dead End Kid, Tommy, gets into trouble when he plays a trick on a rich boy and then stabs the boy's father in a struggle. This situation opens the possibility that he will go Martin's way. The boys enthusiastically point out that he can pick up all kinds of criminal know-how in reform school; in contrast, his sister Drina is horrified by what seems an inevitable direction for his life. Her plea for the forgiveness of Tommy proves not a strong argument with the rich, but because Gimpty now has the reward money he got from turning in Baby-Face, the two can hire a good lawyer and work to make the social system operate for their benefit.

The conclusion of the play moves back, appropriately, to focus on the rest of the Dead End Kids and their innocent (and ignorant) energy. As they play around with the song "If I Had the Wings of an Angel," the audience is reminded that the boys must fly over the walls of a social prison if they are to have a chance in life.

As a play, *The Patriots* is a skillfully crafted historical drama centered on the conflict in early American history between Jeffersonian democracy and Hamiltonian conservatism. It is also Kingsley's warning about the precarious nature of freedom, a warning that prompted many reviewers to call attention to the play's relevance to World War II and the struggle to preserve democratic institutions. The action begins with Thomas Jefferson's return from France to accept, albeit reluctantly, President George Washington's offer to make him his secretary of state and concludes with Jefferson's election as president. Throughout the play, the three historical giants—Washington, Jefferson, and Hamilton—dominate the stage. Kingsley did extensive research for the play, and he succeeded in introducing much material from original documents, but the strength of *The Patriots* lies in Kingsley's talent for endowing these historical characters with believable personalities.

Throughout the conflict between Jefferson and Hamilton, Washington represents a middle ground, the understanding of two American political extremes. In his concise portrait of the first president, Kingsley brings out a struggle between Washington's weariness with politics and his sense of public responsibility. It is this conflict treated on a larger dramatic scale that animates, as well, the character of Jefferson. Kingsley's Jefferson is a private doer, an inventor and architect who would rather retire to the comforts of private life than deal with Hamilton's petty political intrigues.

Hamilton is more completely the politician, one who will connive but who is also statesman enough to compromise for the better candidate when his side cannot win. The play treats neither Hamilton's ambitions nor his ideas kindly; in fact, Kingsley seems to have gone out of his way to bring in a nasty case involving Hamilton's philandering, perhaps to contrast Hamilton's sense of private pleasures with Jefferson's pastoralism. Although Hamilton is not simply a villain in this version of American history, there is no question that Kingsley's sympathies are with Jefferson, the man who trusts the people. At the end, it is Jefferson who has come to be in the middle, standing between the extremes of anarchy (the excesses of the French Revolution) and monarchy (Hamilton's desire for an aristocratic America). The conclusion places Jefferson's election in the context of progressive history. Hamilton laments that he lacks Jefferson's faith in the people, and both he and Jefferson conclude finally that their particular portion of American history has been fashioned by an irresistible destiny, the people's need for freedom.

In preparation for the writing of *Detective Story*, Kingsley spent two years haunting detective squad rooms in Manhattan, gathering the naturalistic details which would give his dramatization of New York police work a searing authenticity. The resulting production featured a combination of the contemporary and the timeless, a blending of the texture of realism with a structure drawn from dramatic tradition.

The opening of the play features a symphonic blending of the varied characters of the police world and suggests immediately the richness and flexibility of the social interaction in this place of emerging good and evil. The initial dialogue presents the quotidian nature of police work—even its monotony. More idiosyncratic elements appear with Keogh, the singing policeman, and the paranoid Mrs. Farragut. These elements help to sketch out the varied nature of humanity's furtive desperations, an idea basic to Kingsley's vision.

The play focuses on the character of Detective James McLeod and the series of events that combine to destroy him. Although he seems a good man, committed to justice and integrity, McLeod's cruelty and his tendency to make absolute judgments are his tragic flaws. His understandable impatience with the criminal justice system lures him into a false confidence in his own instinctive sense of the evil in people. Although his superior tells him that he has a messianic complex, McLeod sees himself as a man of principle fighting both criminals, whom he believes are a separate species, and the justice system, which he sees as hopelessly flawed by loopholes for criminals. The plot centers on his search for evidence to convict an abortionist, the notorious Dr. Schneider. McLeod is also interrogating a shoplifter and a burglar, Arthur, who is a young first offender. Even though the complainant is willing to drop the charges against Arthur, McLeod refuses to release him, and he also beats Schneider severely during questioning, seriously injuring him. Ironically, McLeod's relentless quest for truth leads to the discovery that his own wife, Mary, whom he has idealized, has had an abortion performed by Dr. Schneider.

Kingsley's stage directions refer to the squad room as "ghost-ridden," and the play reveals McLeod as a prisoner of an unexamined past. His wife's accusation that he is cruel and vengeful, like the father he has despised, rings true: Though torn by his love for Mary, McLeod cannot help but condemn her. For him, forgiveness is too great a price to pay to a flawed world. His whole existence is at stake, yet he is unable to take the action—the act of forgiveness—that would save him. Indeed, his inflexibility is so inherent in his character that when, dying from wounds he received when the burglar tried to escape, he relents—letting young Arthur go and forgiving his wife—this final insistence on the possibility of change seems implausible and melodramatic.

Because McLeod's attitudes are tied to the social system, tragic form and cultural realism blend rather smoothly. The other characters contribute to the tragic dimension as well. The uncooperative attitude of the suborned witness, Miss Hatch, gives credence to McLeod's view that his instincts are more reliable than the system of courts and juries. Both Schneider's lawyer and McLeod's own lieutenant warn him not to act as judge and jury, and Joe Feinson, a journalist, advises him to humble himself before he digs his own grave. Arthur represents the essential goodness McLeod would deny, and Pritchett's willingness to forgive Arthur stands out as one alternative for the detective-accuser. Detective Brody, who has been humanized by the death of his son, makes the strongest case for a belief in the fundamental goodness of human beings.

Few dramatists have more consistently articulated in their works the liberal political philosophy than has Kingsley. Keenly attentive to the social and political events of his day, Kingsley's plays demonstrate his faith in the essential goodness of people, his suspicion of authority and power, his belief in progress, and his admiration for the life of reason. Thomas Jefferson, the hero of *The Patriots*, is Kingsley's ideal intellectual; those who work with dedication and integrity are the cornerstones of his hope for the future. At times, Kingsley tends to be sentimental about the working class, and frequently his idealism and his belief in the value of work for its own sake lead him into melodramatic conflicts and facile resolutions. At his best, however, he powerfully embodies the virtues of liberal humanism.

Bibliography

Atkinson, Brooks. "Darkness at Noon." Review of *Darkness at Noon*. *The New York Times*, January 15, 1951, p. 13. Finds the acting of Claude Rains, as Rubashov, to be effective but believes that Kingsley, "less a writer than a showman in this theatre piece," does not do justice to Arthur Koestler's novel: "His melodrama comes with elements of the glib propaganda play that we find so distasteful when it is on the other side." Also finds fault with Kingsley's "cumbersome and diffuse" scenes. Kingsley directed this play, as he did all of his Broadway plays except *The Patriots*.

_____. "Detective Story." Review of *Detective Story*. *The New York Times*, March 24, 1949, p. 34. This review of Kingsley's "vivid drama with a disturbing idea" cites Kingsley's reputation as a responsible playwright, finding this play of intolerance in "the day's grist of crime in a New York precinct police station . . . often pithy and graphic," especially in the minor characters. Kingsley "has the saving grace of being thorough and sincere; and he makes quite a play of it in the end." The play marked the beginning of Kingsley's reputation as an artist and a technician, rather than a visionary.

Clurman, Harold. "Theatre: Good Show." Review of *Detective Story*. *The New Republic* 120 (April 11, 1949): 25-26. Favors the premiere production of *Detective Story* for "its entertainment value" and the theme of "the superiority of our legal system . . . over the type of summary justice that fanatics demand." Kingsley manages the material well, and "bad moments . . . serve as convenient resting places."

Gassner, John. *Theatre at the Crossroads: Plays and Playwrights of the Mid-Century American Stage.* New York: Holt, Rinehart and Winston, 1960. An overview of Kingsley's work from the Group Theatre days to *Darkness at Noon*, of which Gassner opines: "more workmanlike than inspired, more melodramatic than tragic, more denunciatory than psychologically and intellectually explorative."

Krutch, Joseph Wood. "An Event." *The Nation* 137 (October 11, 1933): 419-420. One of the first to praise *Men in White* (the Group Theatre effort), Krutch was one of drama's most distinguished critics and scholars. The play "stands firmly on its merits" despite its experimental label and "moves with a seemingly effortless inevitability."

Morphos, Evangeline. "Sidney Kingsley's *Men in White.*" *Tisch Drama Review* 28 (Winter, 1984): 13-22. A full and thorough study of the Group Theatre's production of *Men in White*, offering several insights into the selection, rehearsal, and performance processes. Particularly valuable is the discussion of the Lee Strasberg/Sidney Kingsley partnership. Includes many comments by Kingsley about the process, production history, and actors' methods. This issue is devoted entirely to Group Theatre productions. Photographs throughout.

Walter Shear
(Revised by *Thomas J. Taylor*)

JACK KIRKLAND

Born: St. Louis, Missouri; July 25, 1901(?)
Died: New York, New York; February 22, 1969

Principal drama

Frankie and Johnnie, pr. 1928; *Tobacco Road*, pr. 1933, pb. 1934 (adaptation of Erskine Caldwell's novel); *Tortilla Flat*, pr. 1938 (adaptation of John Steinbeck's novel); *I Must Love Somebody*, pr. 1939 (with Leyla George); *Suds in Your Eye*, pr., pb. 1944 (adaptation of Mary Lasswell's novel); *Georgia Boy*, pr. 1945 (with Haila Stoddard; adaptation of Caldwell's novel); *Mr. Adam*, pr. 1949 (adaptation of Pat Frank's novel); *The Man with the Golden Arm*, pr. 1956 (adaptation of Nelson Algren's novel); *Mandingo*, pr. 1961 (adaptation of Kyle Onstott's novel).

Other literary forms

Although Jack Kirkland wrote or worked on a number of screenplays, he is best known for his stage plays.

Achievements

Kirkland is remembered less for the literary or dramatic quality of his plays than for their social impact. From his first play, *Frankie and Johnnie*, to his last, *Mandingo*, he challenged the accepted standards of the American stage. His plays never won awards and were often castigated by critics for their perceived crudeness, artlessness, and obscenity. Kirkland, in fact, consistently received some of the worst reviews accorded to any major playwright. Nevertheless, his dramatization of Erskine Caldwell's *Tobacco Road*, which premiered on December 4, 1933, became at the time the longest-running play in the history of the Broadway stage, a veritable institution for seven and a half years in the New York theaters. Deplored by most first-night critics, it won influential fans and supporters, who rallied to it as something more than a shocking, brutal (though often humorous) portrait of poor Georgian sharecroppers. Over the years, the play earned a grudging admiration for its frankness, vitality, and dramatic power. From a social standpoint, it led the battle against outdated, unfair, often arbitrary and conflicting censorship laws across the country. None of Kirkland's other works achieved such success (nor did they deserve it), although they did provoke similar indignation and outrage (often justified). Thus, Kirkland's fame rests primarily on the reputation of *Tobacco Road*, which forever changed the state of modern drama.

Biography

Jack Kirkland was a member of the hard-living, no-nonsense school of professional writers (as opposed to artists) epitomized by such figures as Ben Hecht and Charles MacArthur. Like them, he began his career as a reporter, working for such papers as *The Detroit News*, the *St. Louis Times*, and the *New York Daily News*, and like them, he turned his talents to both film and stage. From this background, he brought to his drama a scorn for sentimentality, a tendency toward sensationalism, and a penchant for a kind of vulgar, black comedy which seems to have characterized his view of the world. He was not so much interested in art as in effect, and the subjects he chose often came from the demimonde familiar to any streetwise reporter.

Kirkland was born in St. Louis, Missouri, on July 25, 1901 (or possibly 1902, since there was no official birth record and other sources conflict on these dates); he was the son of William Thomas and Julia Woodward Kirkland. In his teens, he roamed about the country, working from state to state at odd jobs and often living with and observing the kind of people about whom he would later write. He claimed to have developed a kinship with the poor and homeless which enabled him to understand and sympathize with them in such works as *Tobacco Road*. Soon thereafter he began his newspaper career and made his way to New York, where he attended Columbia University and worked at the *New York Daily News*. In 1924, he married Nancy Carroll, the first of his five wives. (His subsequent wives were Jayne Shadduck, Julia Laird, Haila Stoddard, and Nancy Hoadley.) Carroll was a noted Broadway chorine, and when she was called to Hollywood, Kirkland accompanied her and began to write films, among them *Fast and Loose* (1930), with Miriam Hopkins, and *Now and Forever* (1934), with Gary Cooper, Shirley Temple, and Carole Lombard. Nancy Carroll became one of the most popular stars of the 1930's and was nominated for an Academy Award for her performance in *The Devil's Holiday* in 1930. She and Kirkland were divorced in 1935.

Kirkland's main interest, however, lay in the theater. His first play was *Frankie and Johnnie*, which he wrote in 1928. In 1929, during its Chicago performance, it was attacked as obscene and was closed. Kirkland brought the play to New York in 1930 where, once again, it was closed on charges of obscenity, and Kirkland was arrested. He and the theater owners took the case to court, and in 1932, in a landmark ruling, the play was judged not to be obscene. Kirkland would be involved in many such court cases throughout his career.

In 1931, while in Hollywood, Kirkland was given a copy of Erskine Caldwell's scandalous new novel *Tobacco Road*, which dealt with the almost subhuman existence of a family of Georgian sharecroppers. In the spring of 1933, Kirkland (having spent much of his film earnings on the legal battles surrounding *Frankie and Johnnie*) retreated to the island of Majorca to write a dramatic treatment of the book. He took the play to New

York, where it was turned down by every Broadway producer whom Kirkland approached. Finally, producer Harry Oshrin agreed to cosponsor the play. Kirkland put up his last six thousand dollars as investment and went into partnership with Oshrin and Sam H. Grisman, who became his lawyer and personal representative. The play, directed by Anthony Brown, opened at the Masque Theatre in New York on December 4, 1933, the day Prohibition ended. Despite praise of the acting, initial reviews were generally negative (although not as awful as theater lore has it), and the play lost thirty-eight hundred dollars in the first five weeks. To keep the play alive, ticket prices were reduced, the cast took pay cuts, and Kirkland and the others (except Caldwell) waived their royalties. "I had a hunch after that first night at the Masque that the show would click," Kirkland later remembered. "It left me all in a heap." After this shaky start, *Tobacco Road* established itself as a crowd-pleaser, and its popularity continued largely unabated during its record run of 3,180 performances. Since Kirkland held more than half ownership (approximately sixty-six percent) and sold the film rights to Twentieth Century-Fox for $200,000 plus a percentage of the earnings (Kirkland and Oshrin were listed as associate producers of the film, which was directed by John Ford), he became a rich man. "I hate to think how much money I made," he said shortly before his death, "because so much isn't there any more."

Kirkland never repeated the success he achieved with *Tobacco Road*, but he remained active on the New York theater scene for the next thirty years. In 1936, he coproduced two unsuccessful plays, *Forbidden Melody* and *Bright Hour*. In 1938, he adapted and coproduced John Steinbeck's short novel *Tortilla Flat* (1935) for the stage, but the play quickly failed. Kirkland, furious at the reviews, threw a punch at the New York *Herald Tribune* drama critic Dick Watts, causing *The New York Times* critic Brooks Atkinson to call him "Killer" Kirkland in his review of Kirkland's next play, *I Must Love Somebody*, which Kirkland cowrote (with Leyla George) and produced in 1939. *I Must Love Somebody* proved to be Kirkland's second hit, although its run of 191 performances did not challenge the success of *Tobacco Road*. From 1940 to 1943, Kirkland produced three other plays—*Suzanna and the Elders* (1940), *Tanyard Street* (1941), and *The Moon Vine* (1943)—but the longest run of any was only thirty performances.

In 1944, Kirkland wrote *Suds in Your Eye*, based on Mary Lasswell's popular 1942 novel about the American homefront during World War II. The play was an inoffensive comedy, but it failed to equal the success of the book and closed after thirty-seven performances. The following year, Kirkland returned to the work of Erskine Caldwell with a dramatization of Caldwell's 1943 novel *Georgia Boy*, which Kirkland cowrote with his third wife, Haila Stoddard. He also directed and coproduced this effort, which opened and closed in Boston. In 1949, he wrote, produced, and directed *Mr. Adam*, based on a novel by Pat Frank concerning life after a nuclear explosion. It was savaged by every critic who bothered to review it, was called the worst play of the year, and quickly disappeared. *The Man with the Golden Arm*, taken from Nelson Algren's novel about drug addiction, met with more favorable reviews and ran for seventy-three performances, but Kirkland's last play, *Mandingo*, inspired by Kyle Onstott's pulp novel of slavery in the antebellum South, was howled off the stage after only eight performances.

When Kirkland died of heart trouble, he was remembered primarily for *Tobacco Road*. Indeed, he never wrote anything as good, and he returned to the material at various times in his career, through revivals (in 1950 it was revived with an all-black cast) or revisions (at his death he had recently completed a musical version called "Jeeter").

Analysis

Most of Jack Kirkland's work was derived from other sources, usually popular novels, and it would probably be pushing matters to discuss too intently the overriding themes or concerns in his plays. His works reflected not so much a personal philosophy as a desire to entertain. Kirkland did speak of the social significance of *Tobacco Road*, noting that the play realistically illustrated the plight of poor Southern sharecroppers caught in an economic and cultural dead end. He also spoke of Jeeter Lester, his most enduring character, in terms of his universal qualities, stating that his "tolerance for the sins and beliefs of others makes him a man apart, a man whose one great virtue is more important than his lack of lesser ones. . . . " In his other plays, Kirkland dealt with such problems as nuclear war, slavery, and drug addiction, but rarely did he aim for more than a superficial treatment of complex issues. In *Mr. Adam*, for example, the bomb is nothing more than a pretext for a series of dirty jokes, and *Mandingo* uses its historical setting as an excuse to indulge in sexual titillation and sadistic violence. Kirkland was a competent playwright who, with *Tobacco Road*, did achieve a dramatic power above the average, but who all too often appealed to the lowest common denominator among his audiences.

As a professional man of the theater, Kirkland believed strongly in the need for artistic freedom. His willingness to challenge, through lengthy and costly legal battles, the prevailing concepts of obscenity changed the standards of what could be presented on the legitimate stage. For example, Kirkland's first play, *Frankie and Johnnie*, was based on the popular and racy American folk song, which told of love, betrayal, and murder. Kirkland's drama was set in 1849, in the red-light district of St. Louis among the waterfront dens and gambling houses. Like the couple of the song, Frankie is a prostitute and Johnnie a gambler. When Johnnie has a run of luck, he is secretly stolen from Frankie by a rival prostitute, Nellie Bly, on whom he spends all of his money. Meanwhile, to maintain his life-style, Johnnie acts as pimp for Frankie, who works for him out of love. When Frankie discovers that Johnnie has "done her wrong," she shoots and kills him.

Reviewers of the play found it to be coarse, vulgar, and clumsy. As Atkinson put it, "A gaudy lithograph, dramatizing literally the song . . . it has moments of theatrical effectiveness, split seconds of amusement. But it does not sustain itself or what it attempts in the way that Mae West did in *Diamond Lil.* . . . " When first performed, the play was ruled obscene and closed in Chicago, only the second time the city had taken such action. When it opened Off-Broadway at the Carlton Theatre in New York in September of 1930, it was raided following the third performance by plainclothes police officers who arrested Kirkland, the cast, and others connected with the play. Found guilty of obscenity, Kirkland fought for the next two years to have the judgment overturned. In a landmark decision made in March, 1932, Judge Cuthbert W. Pound of the New York Court of Appeals wrote that although the play was "indecent" and "degrades the stage," it "does not counsel or invite to vice or voluptuousness" and, therefore, could not be considered obscene. The play itself had opened on Broadway at the Republic Theatre on September 25, 1930, where it ran for sixty-one performances. By the time of the court ruling, the play was long forgotten.

The *Frankie and Johnnie* ruling, however, set the precedent for the legal maneuverings surrounding Kirkland's second play, *Tobacco Road*, which became a *cause célèbre* for the defenders of free speech and a public event which reached beyond the merits of the play itself. When the play was accepted by the Masque Theatre in New York, its acceptance was contingent on a special clause which allowed either party to break the contract at the end of the first three weeks. Rehearsals started without an actress to play Jeeter's wife Ada (Fay Bainter, Jessie Royce Landis, and Dorothy and Lillian Gish had all refused the role, which was finally taken by Margaret Wycherly). The initial reviews praised the acting of Henry Hull as Jeeter Lester, but they found the play offensive, although infused with a kind of brutal realism. As *The New York Times* review put it, "Although *Tobacco Road* reels around the stage like a drunken stranger to the theatre, it has spasmodic moments of merciless power when truth is flung into your face with all the slime that truth contains." When, after poor business, the Masque Theatre owners exercised their option, the play moved to the Forty-eighth Street Theatre, where it was nursed along with cut-rate prices until it had built an audience largely through word-of-mouth. In the summer, Henry Hull left the show to try his luck in films. As a result, the play was once again asked to move. The owners leased the Forrest Theatre, where, in September of 1934 (with James Barton as Jeeter), the play settled in for its record-setting run. There would be five Broadway Jeeters in all (James Bell, Eddie Garr, and Will Geer all played the role, which became known as "the American Hamlet") in addition to other Jeeters in the three road-show companies that traversed the country.

When the play opened, it was considered a serious portrayal of social dehumanization. *Theatre Arts Monthly* called it "one of the bitterest plays ever produced in New York, but one of the most compelling." Most thought it too brutal for the average audience. Like Caldwell's novel, the play deals with the Lesters, a family of impoverished sharecroppers abandoned on a worn-out farm, which had once belonged to Jeeter's people. Kirkland focused the play on Jeeter's sincere love of the land and, conversely, his basic shiftlessness and immorality. In truth, Kirkland had toned down the more outrageous and shocking episodes found in the book. For example, he had Ada tell Jeeter that Pearl (the daughter Jeeter sold in marriage to Lov Bensey for seven dollars) was not really his child, thus diluting the incestuous nature of Jeeter's desire for her. Grandmother Lester simply disappears in the woods rather than being run over and left to die while the family ignores her, as occurs in the book. Jeeter and Ada are no longer burned to death at the story's end; instead, it is Ada who is killed by Sister Bessie's car as she tries to help Pearl escape to a better life in Augusta. The play thus ends with Jeeter facing an uncertain future, alone but still alive.

Moreover, the longer the play ran, the more its tone began to shift, and soon it was staged more for its comedy than for its supposed realism. Caldwell's novel, to be sure, has many moments of dark humor throughout, but overriding them is a sense of intense outrage. When James Barton, a former vaudevillian, took over the role of Jeeter, he played the character as a reprobate and rascal; lost was the sense of despair and doom which Caldwell's characterization of Jeeter evokes. By the end of its run, the play had become a rollicking and bawdy good time, having long since lost its original seriousness.

Despite its shocking nature, *Tobacco Road* aroused little legal opposition until it began to tour the country. In October of 1935, after it had played for seven weeks without protest in Chicago, its license was suddenly revoked by Mayor Edward H. Kelly, who proclaimed the play "an insult to decent people." Kirkland immediately responded. "I am opposed to arbitrary censorship, particularly when it affects something which has been accepted nationally and possesses a definite social purpose," he said, asking for an injunction against the mayor's ban. Following Chicago's lead, other cities, such as Detroit, Boston, St. Paul, Tulsa, Albany, and even New Orleans, also stopped production of the play, while still other cities allowed only expurgated versions to be performed. In each case, Kirkland and his co-owners went to court. A permanent legal staff was kept busy following the road shows from place to place. By 1939, Kirkland had won thirty-two out of thirty-five court cases. Many celebrities and advocates of free speech had spoken out in favor of the work; even Eleanor Roosevelt defended it as a play of fundamental seriousness and social importance.

By the time *Tobacco Road* closed, it had permanently changed the American stage. *The New York Times* ran an article on May 31, 1941, which colorfully captured the effect of the play: "*Tobacco Road* Retires Tonight Undefeated; Champ of All Plays Beat Critics 3,180 Rounds." More important, it had altered the acceptable moral standards of the stage throughout the country. Cities that had originally banned the play during its first tour accepted it without protest in following years. The play itself was reevaluated as well. As George R. Kernodle observed in a 1947 retrospective article, "The Audience Was Right," in *Theatre Arts Monthly*, the play illustrated people's ability to endure and thus offered reassurance during the Depression years of its run. Kirkland himself believed that the play was an "American classic," as, in fact, it has proved to be.

In his next play, *Tortilla Flat*, Kirkland tried once again to adapt a book by a leading American writer, but John Steinbeck's short episodic novel of Danny and the other *paisanos* living on the outskirts of Monterey, California, had less substance than Caldwell's work, and none of the characters was as original or fascinating as Jeeter Lester. Moreover, whereas *Tobacco Road* had starkly portrayed the grinding effects of poverty on the human will, *Tortilla Flat* tried to make its impoverished inhabitants seem comic and charming free spirits in rebellion against the soul-killing inducements of the materialistic world. As long as Danny and his companions are poor, they are happy, but when Danny inherits two shacks, the responsibility of ownership comes between him and the others. Only by burning down the shacks in an act of deliberate repudiation can Danny recapture the good and easy life. Compared to *Tobacco Road* (however burlesque the play had become), *Tortilla Flat* seemed an abrupt turnabout for Kirkland, and the play lasted only five performances after its premiere on January 12, 1938.

With his next play, *I Must Love Somebody*, Kirkland returned to sexually suggestive material and to the legal arena. He coauthored the play with Leyla George, a former actress who had originated the role of Charmaine in Maxwell Anderson's *What Price Glory?* (pr. 1924). *I Must Love Somebody* is a fictionalized account of the Florodora Girls, six chorines who had appeared in the play *Florodora*, a musical imported from London to the Broadway stage in 1900, where it ran for 505 performances (only the second musical to break the five-hundred-performances mark). The girls, according to legend, all married millionaires. Kirkland and George's version concentrates on the backstage affairs of these high-living women and their top-hatted stagedoor Johnnies, with scenes in the dressing rooms of the Casino Theatre, in private rooms of Canfield's gambling establishment, and in the girls' apartments. Like *Frankie and Johnnie*, the play emphasizes atmosphere more than story. One of the girls, Birdie Carr, falls in love and decides to give up the fast life. Another of the girls, Ann Gibson, discovers that her "protector" has infected her with a venereal disease and kills him. While Birdie and her friends try to keep Ann out of jail, Birdie learns that her lover, Bob Goesling, has no intention of marrying her as he has promised but plans only to set her up as his mistress. The play was judged poorly written and poorly acted when it opened on February 7, 1939, at the Longacre Theatre in New York. It moved, on April 24, from the Longacre to the Vanderbilt Theatre. There, the owners claimed that Kirkland had added salacious material to the show and demanded that it vacate by May 6. Kirkland asked for an injunction against the owners but lost. Nevertheless, the play ran for 191 performances, making it Kirkland's second most successful show.

Kirkland's next work (which he both wrote and directed) was *Suds in Your Eye*, an inoffensive and rather frothy comedy based on a popular novel by Mary Lasswell. When Kirkland adapted it to the stage, the book had sold more than seventy thousand copies since its publication in 1942. Like the book, the play relies heavily on the Irish charm of the main character, Mrs. Nora Feeley (portrayed by Jane Darwell, famed as Ma Joad in the film version of John Steinbeck's *The Grapes of Wrath*). Mrs. Feeley, a type of Tugboat Annie in drydock, owns a junkyard in San Diego, California, during World War II. Living with her is a small Oriental boy named Chinatown, who actually runs the business; Miss Tinkham, a refined, retired music teacher; and Mrs. Rasmussen, a neighbor who can no longer abide to stay with her daughter and her daughter's crass husband. What plot there is revolves around the efforts of this unusual group to save the junkyard from the tax collector and to fix up Mrs. Feeley's nephew, a sailor home from the war, with a local teacher. The play is pure escapism, sweet, sentimental, and silly enough to make it an anomaly among Kirkland's works. It closed on February 12, 1944, after thirty-seven performances.

With *Mr. Adam*, which Kirkland wrote and directed in 1949, he reached the nadir of his career. The play was inspired by a novel by Pat Frank concerning the last sexually competent male on earth after an atomic explosion has left all other men sterile. Homer Adam (who was in a lead mine at the time of the accident) is called upon by the National Refertilization Program to perpetuate the race with a number of desperately willing women. The play was set to premiere at the Lobero Theatre in Santa Barbara, California, on March 12, 1949, but was banned by the city council. After playing in San Francisco, Chicago, and Detroit, *Mr. Adam* opened at the Royale Theatre in New York on May 25, 1949, to the most devastating reviews received by any of Kirkland's works. Both *The New York Times* and *Theatre Arts Monthly* deemed it the worst play of the year. Words such as "gruesome," "loathsome," "tasteless," and "stupid" were used to de-scribe it, and *Mr. Adam* closed after five performances, much to Kirkland's anger and bafflement.

Kirkland's next play was a redemption of sorts and remains one of his most interesting works. *The Man with the Golden Arm*, based on the novel by Nelson Algren, opened at the Cherry Lane Theatre on May 21, 1956. The book had been made into a hit film by Otto Preminger during the pre-vious year, and the film had provided Frank Sinatra with one of his best dramatic roles as Frankie, the small-time Chicago gambler who becomes addicted to drugs. In the opening run of Kirkland's play, Frankie was com-pellingly portrayed by Robert Loggia. His downfall, leading to murder and suicide, is dispassionately shown through a series of short episodes, chrono-logically arranged, making the play more impressionistic than realistic. In one sense, the play was a return to the underworld that Kirkland had romantically portrayed in *Frankie and Johnnie*, but in *The Man with the Golden Arm*, the tone is stark and darkly shaded. The dialogue is rough and accurate, and Frankie's doom is inevitable. It is a hard play to like, one that challenges an audience, but it enjoyed a first run of seventy-three performances.

Kirkland's last play was *Mandingo*, a ludicrous and sensationalized reworking of a ludicrous and sensationalized novel by Kyle Onstott. Osten-sibly a study of the evils of slavery in antebellum Alabama, the play (like the book and the later film) revels in violence, racism, and sexual perver-sity. *Mandingo* opened at the Lyceum Theatre on May 22, 1961, with Franchot Tone as the vile plantation owner Warren Maxwell, Dennis Hop-per as his crippled son Hammond, Brooke Hayward as Hammond's wife Blanche, and Rockne Tarkington as the Mandingo slave Mede. The play uses every racial and sexual stereotype imaginable: the alcoholic Warren Maxwell beats his slaves, breeds them to sell, and keeps a special one as his mistress. His son, who believes in more humane treatment of slaves, marries a Southern belle who has been her brother's lover and who devel-ops an insatiable craving for the proud slave Mede. Disgusted by his wife, Hammond Maxwell falls in love with a beautiful octoroon, much to his father's outrage. The play ends with Blanche flogging the pregnant oc-toroon to death and the elder Maxwell shooting his son and the Mandingo in order to preserve the old Southern way of life. A critic in the July, 1961, issue of *Theatre Arts* aptly put it, "The play is so offensively ill-written, wantonly violent, pointless and immoral that everyone connected with it should be ashamed." It closed after eight performances.

Of Kirkland's plays, only *Tobacco Road* is likely to be remembered. It is a better work than its reputation suggests, more important than is sug-gested by the popular hoopla and controversy which surrounded it. In its original form, before it became a parody of itself, it was a brave dramatization of a serious novel. It affected its audiences (both in this country and abroad) because it acknowledged human beings' universal suffering and celebrated their ability to endure. In Jeeter Lester, Kirkland (although greatly indebted to Caldwell) gave the modern stage one of its classic roles. Finally, through his willingness to defend his work against censorship, Kirkland expanded the range and depth to which other and better artists could explore the human condition. For these reasons, Kirkland deserves to be remembered as an important figure of twentieth century American drama.

Other major works

NONFICTION: "How Long *Tobacco Road,*" 1939 (in *The New York Times*).
SCREENPLAYS: *Fast and Loose*, 1930; *Zoo in Budapest*, 1933; *Now and Forever*, 1934; *Adventures in Manhattan*, 1936, *Sutter's Gold*, 1936.

Bibliography

Caldwell, Erskine. Introduction to *Tobacco Road: A Three Act Play.* New York: Duell, Sloan and Pearce, 1952. Caldwell's introduction to Kirkland's adaptation recalls *Tobacco Road*'s origins, reception, and ultimate success. Beginning as "an unwelcome intruder in the American theater" and often censored or banned in performances throughout the United States, the play nevertheless captured the imagination of the American people and the world.

_____. "Two Years on the Road." *The New York Times*, December 1, 1935, p. K7. Written near the third anniversary of *Tobacco Road*'s opening on Broadway, Caldwell's article recounts the origins of the story and describes the Eastern Georgia of his memory. Attributing the play's popularity and the controversy surrounding it to the "constant search for something we can like a lot, or hate a lot," Caldwell maintains that negative criticism of the play stemmed from the United States' refusal to recognize the existence of its indigent and degraded citizens.

Howard, William L. "Caldwell on Stage and Screen." In *Erskine Caldwell Reconsidered*, edited by Edwin T. Arnold. Jackson: University Press of Mississippi, 1990. In this article about adaptations made of Caldwell's novels, Kirkland's interpretation of *Tobacco Road* is compared unfavorably to the original novel. Howard believes that the play distorted Caldwell's intentions, turning sympathetic understanding and a respect for the social realities of poor whites into slapstick comedy and sentimentality.

"Jack Kirkland Is Dead at Sixty-six; Was *Tobacco Road* Adapter." *The New York Times*, February 23, 1969, p. A73. This obituary is a good source of biographical facts and includes a list of the most notable writings. Kirkland was predisposed to *Tobacco Road* because his family's roots extended to a part of South Carolina very near tobacco-road country.

Krutch, Joseph Wood. "Poor White." Review of *Tobacco Road. The Nation* 137 (December 20, 1933): 718. This review by a distinguished critic is a probing analysis of *Tobacco Road*'s mood of "grotesque and horrible humor." Noting that the "emotional meaning" of the work is ambiguous, Krutch nevertheless categorizes it as a comedy, explaining that the spectator's detachment from the characters is a necessary ingredient of the comic mode.

Rigdon, Walter. *The Biographical Encyclopaedia and Who's Who of American Theatre.* New York: J. H. Heineman, 1965. A compilation of basic facts about Kirkland's life, including information about his family, marriages, education, career as a journalist, service in the military, and the conflict surrounding his birthdate. Lists the plays and work for the film industry.

Edwin T. Arnold
(Updated by *William L. Howard*)

JAMES SHERIDAN KNOWLES

Born: Cork, Ireland; May 12, 1784
Died: Torquay, England; November 30, 1862

Principal drama

Leo: Or, The Gypsy, pr. 1810, pb. 1873; *Caius Gracchus*, pr. 1815, pb. 1823; *Virginius: Or, The Liberation of Rome*, pr., pb. 1820; *William Tell*, pr., pb. 1825 (based on Friedrich Schiller's play); *The Beggar's Daughter of Bethnel Green*, pr., pb. 1828 (revised as *The Beggar of Bethnel Green*, pr., pb. 1834); *Alfred the Great: Or, The Patriot King*, pr., pb. 1831; *The Hunchback*, pr., pb. 1832; *The Vision of the Bard*, pr., pb. 1832; *The Wife: A Tale of Mantua*, pr., pb. 1833; *The Daughter*, pr. 1836, pb. 1837; *The Love Chase*, pr., pb. 1837; *Woman's Wit: Or, Love's Disguises*, pr., pb. 1838; *Love*, pr. 1839, pb. 1840; *John of Procida: Or, The Bridals of Messina*, pr., pb. 1840; *Old Maids*, pr., pb. 1841; *The Secretary*, pr., pb. 1843.

Other literary forms

Though James Sheridan Knowles is now remembered almost exclusively for his drama, he wrote several other works which were highly regarded in his own time. At the beginning of his literary career, he wrote a popular ballad, *The Welch Harper* (1796), which the critic William Hazlitt praised in his critical volume *The Spirit of the Age* (1825). In 1810, Knowles published (by subscription) a collection of his best early verses entitled *Fugitive Pieces*; this work received little acclaim, and Knowles subsequently wrote little nondramatic poetry.

Knowles's most significant nondramatic writings concerned oratory and theater. The most famous and influential of these was *The Elocutionist* (1823), a textbook on debate that he wrote for his students while teaching at Belfast. This book expresses Knowles's view that the effective speaker must avoid artificiality and be in earnest, and it contains one of his most popular model debates, "Was Julius Caesar a Great Man?" *The Elocutionist* became a very popular textbook in both English and American schools and went through many editions during Knowles's lifetime. His writings and lectures on poetry were also well received by his contemporaries, and his *Lectures on Oratory, Gesture and Poetry*, published posthumously in 1873, considered the adaptability of poetry for elocutionary purposes. Though these discourses often concerned poetry by important writers, such as Sir Walter Scott and Lord Byron, they were neither profound nor influential as literary criticism.

Knowles's *Lectures on Dramatic Literature*, also posthumously published in 1873, reveals the depth of his practical knowledge of stagecraft. These discourses consider important dramatic subjects, such as Greek drama and William Shakespeare's plays, and address significant technical questions of unity, plot, and characterization. Typically, Knowles concentrated more on issues relating to acting than to literary criticism, but his critical judgments were often sound. For example, his view that the unity of action is more essential to successful drama than are the unities of time and place reflects a significant departure from neoclassical dramatic theories. Knowles realized how much his audience valued carefully developed climactic action and powerful characterizations.

Knowles was not a sophisticated theologian, and the religious writings he produced after 1843 were zealous but unsophisticated. These tracts, such as *The Rock of Rome: Or, The Arch Heresy* (1849), were published during a period of great religious controversy in England involving the Oxford Movement, which sought to ally the Anglican Church with Roman Catholicism. In an age during which religious inquiry occupied some of England's greatest minds, Knowles's contribution was negligible. As a preacher, his elocutionary training served him well, but, though he could keep his congregation's attention, his published sermons were undistinguished.

In his youth, Knowles wrote several operas and adaptations of plays written by others, but these are of little significance. His two novels, *Fortesque* (1846) and *George Lovell* (1847), though somewhat more successful in the United States than in England, have now been largely forgotten. Knowles's fame rests primarily on his plays.

Achievements

During the course of the nineteenth century, England's population quadrupled, and the nation became increasingly democratic. The rapidly growing theater audience of the time was largely uneducated; they had little use for either the poetry of Shakespeare or the numerous imitations of Jacobean drama which writers such as Samuel Taylor Coleridge—and a host of lesser talents—inflicted upon them. Instead, they favored the melodrama, with its sentimentalized faith in justice and moral purity and its thrilling, often spectacularly staged, plots.

Though Knowles followed the traditional Aristotelian model in writing his tragedies, he consciously tried to write a less ornate poetic language that would be more appealing to his audience. The critic Hazlitt praised Knowles's avoidance of artificial poetic language, and a reviewer in *The London Magazine* wrote in June, 1820, that the diction of his play *Virginius* was "colloquial and high-spirited; in short it is the true language of life." Though Knowles's attempt to write tragedy in a more realistic style was not always so well received by more conservative critics, his prosaic blank verse was the product of a conscious attempt to reconceive drama in the realistic terms required by his audience. Furthermore, Knowles's concern for English domestic, patriarchal values, a theme which recurs frequently in his plays, touched the lives of his audience and contributed significantly to the success of *Virginius* and that of many of his later dramas. Though critics have complained that Knowles's anachronisms and stilted verse result in inferior tragedy, his attempt to make his drama more realistic and contemporary suited the tastes of his audience. It also can be seen as a significant transition between the obsolete pseudo-Elizabethan style of the late eighteenth and early nineteenth century tragedies and Gothic dramas and the more carefully crafted, satiric, and socially conscious dramas of W. S. Gilbert, Arthur Wing Pinero, and Henry Arthur Jones.

A further ground of Knowles's achievement lay in his collaborations with the greatest actor of his day, William Charles Macready, who played the title role in Knowles's *Virginius*. The great success of *Virginius* launched Knowles's career as a playwright; at the same time, the success of *Virginius* also helped establish Macready as, in Harry M. Ritchie's words, "the leading actor in England, confirming the supremacy of a new [acting] style based on 'domesticity' and 'humanity.'" Until this time, Edmund Kean, another of Knowles's acquaintances, had been the most celebrated actor in England, largely praised for his declamatory—some would say ranting—portrayals of Shakespeare's tragic heroes. When Kean opened in his own version of the Virginius story a few days after the first performance of Knowles's play, he failed completely.

This was Kean's first London defeat, and as such it can be considered the beginning of the decline of the exaggerated, romantic acting style for which he was so famous. From this point on, Kean's acting career declined, while Macready's flourished. *Virginius* not only established Macready as a powerful figure in the London theater but also marked his debut as the leading practitioner of a more natural style of tragic acting. More than one-third of Knowles's subsequent plays were written for Macready or at his suggestion, and their symbiotic relationship enabled both to achieve considerable success and to influence the development of nineteenth century English drama.

Though Knowles was an actor as well as a playwright, his own performances were generally not very successful in England. He lacked the physical stature and intensity required of a great performer, and he had an Irish brogue which many English critics found objectionable. Nevertheless, in September, 1833, he was elected an honorary member of the Cambridge Garrick Club. Knowles's English audience recognized him primarily for his playwriting, but when he toured America in 1834, he was phenomenally successful as an actor and as a lecturer with the less sophisticated American audiences.

Perhaps the most eloquent testimony to the English public's esteem of

Knowles as a playwright is the fact that, in 1850, he was one of four writers nominated to succeed William Wordsworth as poet laureate of England. The other nominees were John Wilson, Sir Henry Taylor, and Alfred, Lord Tennyson; the latter was finally chosen by Queen Victoria, largely because of Prince Albert's liking for Tennyson's great elegy *In Memoriam* (1850). The fact that a writer of Knowles's limited poetic talents could be seriously considered for such an honor might now seem peculiar—even ludicrous— but it shows how highly Knowles's contemporaries regarded his dramas.

Biography

James Sheridan Knowles was born on May 12, 1784, in the city of Cork, Ireland. His father, James Knowles, a somewhat well-known Protestant schoolmaster and lexicographer, was also a first cousin of the great playwright Richard Brinsley Sheridan, for whom he named his son. Knowles was such a frail child that his parents frequently feared for his life, until he finally recovered his health at about the age of six. When he was twelve years old, he made his first visit to the theater; it was at that point that he resolved to be a dramatist.

Knowles's parents had originally intended that he study medicine, but, when his mother died in 1800, his father remarried, and young James, who disliked his stepmother, left home. When he finally did begin to study medicine in 1806, his heart was not in it. Instead, he became interested in the ministry and spent considerable time listening to sermons and yearning to preach to vagrants in the streets of London. Knowles still longed to be a dramatist, and the moral and didactic fervor which he had inherited from his father found expression in the plays which he soon began to write. After receiving his medical degree and practicing for three years, Knowles abandoned his medical career and joined a professional acting company in 1808.

Knowles's acting debut, in which he ill-advisedly attempted the demanding role of Hamlet, was a total failure, and he soon joined another company at Wexford. There, in July of 1809, he met Catherine Charteris, a young Edinburgh actress, whom he married, after a rather tempestuous courtship, on October 15 of the same year. The newlyweds moved to Waterford and joined Cherry's acting company. At Waterford, Knowles first met the as yet unknown actor Edmund Kean, who encouraged him to complete a play entitled *Leo: Or, The Gypsy*, which became a minor hit. Knowles was also improving as an actor, and by the time he and his wife moved to Swansea in 1811, he had acted successfully in operas, comedies, and tragedies. His first child, James, was born the same year, and the young family moved to Belfast.

At this point, Knowles's budding stage career was temporarily halted when his depleted finances forced him to accept a teaching position.

Knowles enjoyed teaching, and his love of oratory made him so successful at it that he opened his own school in Belfast. A short time later he joined his father, who was then headmaster at the Belfast Academical Institution, as his assistant. When the two quarreled violently over the son's theory of elocution, the father was fired and the son resigned his post. Then, in 1815, the success of Knowles's first mature play, the tragedy *Caius Gracchus*, rekindled his theatrical ambitions, and the family moved to Glasgow, where Knowles was teaching in 1820 when the success of *Virginius* made him famous.

Following the triumph of *Virginius*, Knowles established a Whig newspaper, *The Free Press*, in Glasgow, but the enterprise collapsed after three years. In 1825, Knowles was rescued from financial problems by the success of his historical drama *William Tell*, but his first comedy, *The Beggar's Daughter of Bethnel Green*, performed in 1828, failed miserably. Beset again by financial problems, Knowles lectured publicly to supplement his income. His lectures on poetry, elocution, and drama were generally admired, and his financial situation improved accordingly.

In 1832, Knowles presented a petition to Parliament which sought greater protection for author's rights through a copyright bill. In 1833, he supported an actors' movement which opposed the monopoly theaters. Neither enterprise produced results, and Knowles continued to increase his acting roles both in his own dramas and in productions of Shakespeare's plays. Because his stage activities had become full-time, the Knowles family had settled in London, but by that time Knowles had ten children, and, when an acting tour of Ireland in April and May of 1834 was unsuccessful, he resolved to travel to the United States, where his dramas had been much more widely acclaimed than in England.

When Knowles arrived in New York on September 6, 1834, he was hailed as the greatest living English playwright. The tour was a resounding success; Knowles himself was thoroughly surprised by the warmth and praise of the American audiences. He captivated them with dramatic performances in his own plays, lectures, and readings from his poems; indeed, so great was his American success that he formed a lasting friendship with President Andrew Jackson, and, as a farewell gesture, a huge dramatic festival was held in his honor on April 8, 1835. Knowles understandably retained a warm regard for the United States until his death and continued to correspond with his many American friends.

During the eight years following his return to England in 1835, Knowles continued to act in his own plays and wrote several more dramas. He toured Dublin and Edinburgh in 1836 and acted in *William Tell*, *The Hunchback*, *The Wife*, *Virginius*, *The Beggar of Bethnel Green* (his revised version of the earlier, failed effort), and *Alfred the Great*; later that year, he performed in several plays by Shakespeare. Though he announced in

November, 1837, that he would retire from acting, he continued to perform from time to time and to manage his own plays until as late as 1849. *The Secretary* was produced in 1843, but he continued to write plays until 1846. Nevertheless, by 1843, Knowles, for all practical purposes, was no longer actively involved with the stage.

Knowles's retirement from the stage and his subsequent ordination as a Baptist minister can be at least partly explained by certain character traits which he had always possessed. Throughout his life, he had been a man of strong moral principles, and his plays often reflected his convictions. His love of oratory and elocution, combined with his concern with matters of conscience, had almost turned him to preaching in the streets earlier in his life, so Knowles's conversion from the boards to the pulpit was not so radical a change as it might at first appear. Knowles himself was not comfortable preaching against acting and drama, as his new calling required him to do; in fact, he wrote two novels after being ordained and continued to present friends with copies of his plays.

Though his American tour had made him wealthy, Knowles was both generous and careless with his earnings. He continued to realize some income from his popular plays, but not nearly what he would have received if copyright laws had been more stringent. His financial state, therefore, became so critical that in 1846 a group of his friends tried to obtain a pension for him, finally succeeding in establishing a fund for his benefit in 1848. Knowles himself succeeded in securing a pension of two hundred pounds a year. This, with his earnings as curator of Shakespeare's house at Stratford—a post he was awarded in 1848—enabled him to support himself until his death on November 30, 1862.

Analysis

Though critics have maintained that James Sheridan Knowles's tragedy *Virginius* is his greatest play, many of Knowles's most characteristic themes find their earliest expression in his first mature and original play, the tragedy *Caius Gracchus*. *Caius Gracchus* is not a great play, but in spite of its flaws, it is in some respects both intense and compelling. Knowles's radical political attitudes were crudely but vividly presented in some of the title character's speeches, and the prosaic quality of the blank verse reflects Knowles's intention of writing dialogue in a language that would be more accessible to his audience. The play also seeks to combine elements of the popular melodrama with the more traditional themes of political intrigue and ambition which characterize Shakespearean and Jacobean tragedy. *Caius Gracchus* is, in fact, modeled on Shakespeare's *Coriolanus*, and Knowles's title character closely resembles Shakespeare's protagonist, particularly in his self-destructive devotion to the state. *Caius Gracchus* was Knowles's first attempt to synthesize different dramatic influences into a popular form, the domestic tragedy. The later success of *Virginius* can largely be attributed to the fact that in that play Knowles achieved a more natural synthesis of these disparate influences than he did in *Caius Gracchus*. Therefore, the earlier play is interesting as a precursor of the values and techniques which Knowles tried to refine in his later tragedies.

Part of the problem with *Caius Gracchus* was that Knowles had selected an inappropriate story on which to graft his rather mundane and sentimental values. His choice of the traditional and popular story of Virginius, the noble Roman who kills his own daughter, Virginia, rather than allow her to be defiled by the tyrant Appius, was a much more appropriate vehicle to express his ideals of virtue, honor, and liberty. Knowles probably based his tragedy on the version of the story told by Livy, the Roman historian, though he often departs significantly from that model. In *Virginius*, as in his other tragedies, Knowles used the classical five-act structure and em phasized many of the themes he had developed in *Caius Gracchus*: oppression of the common people, the purity of familial (domestic) love, and the importance of justice and liberty.

The villain, Appius, is a deceitful Roman senator who has turned against the citizens who elected him, and Knowles's characterization of him is effective. Appius' evil machinations, though somewhat improbable, are cleverly conceived, and the audience certainly appreciated the malice, if not the psychological subtlety, of his character. Appius is reminiscent of Shakespeare's Richard III, and, though he lacks Richard's complexity, his absolute depravity generates an exciting plot. Appius' character was clearly conceived in the tradition of the "fall of princes" tragedy, and Knowles obviously intended his audience to rejoice loudly at his demise. In fact, the playwright seems consciously to have sacrificed psychological complexity for moral effect.

Virginius, on the other hand, is as noble as Appius is evil. In act 4, Virginius reviles Appius for his treachery and incites the crowd to attack him. After leading the charge, Virginius is deserted by the cowardly citizens; realizing that he can no longer save his daughter from Appius, Virginius stabs her to death and races, mad with grief, from the Forum. Knowles conceived the daughter's character along typically sentimental Victorian lines. She is beautiful and pathetic in her innocence and vulnerability, but she lacks any deeper qualities. Thus, her death has no real tragic impact. Though it is Virginia who dies, Knowles directs our real pity toward her father, forced by circumstances to kill his only child.

Like *Caius Gracchus* and *Virginius*, Knowles's next tragedy, *William Tell*, has civic liberty as its main theme. *William Tell* is based on a play by the great German playwright, Friedrich Schiller, but it lacks the philosophical depth of its model. By modern standards it also suffers considerably from the excessive ranting of the protagonist. Knowles was probably influenced by the work of Lord Byron in this regard, but while the Byronic hero is driven by some mysterious obsession, the emotions of Knowles's hero are superficial. The addition of humorous episodes and lyrics also tends to detract from the play's unity, and it was later revised from five to three acts, which improved it greatly. Next to *Virginius*, *William Tell* was Knowles's most popular tragedy. Its romantic excesses and volatile speeches were well suited to Macready's acting style and thus made it successful onstage.

Knowles's comedies are somewhat less competent than are his tragedies. Though his tragedies frequently suffered from shallow characterizations and unimpressive poetry, they often succeeded in terms of presenting an exciting plot that could keep an audience involved. Furthermore, both *Caius Gracchus* and *Virginius* combine contemporary, Renaissance, and classical dramatic influences into a compelling whole. In his comedies, however, Knowles's characters are often poorly conceived, while the complex plots and subplots, inspired by Elizabethan comedies, are poorly integrated. Knowles's penchant for the five-act structure caused him to include considerable extraneous material in his comedies. In fact, one of his best comedies, *The Beggar of Bethnel Green*, is a three-act revision of the earlier, unsuccessful five-act play *The Beggar's Daughter of Bethnel Green*. Knowles's most popular comedy, *The Hunchback*, was also much improved by revision from five to three acts. None of his comedies, however, showed the artistic consistency of *Virginius*.

As a dramatist, Knowles was trying to achieve two conflicting goals. He wanted to reach his audience by banishing artificiality from dramatic poetry and by using more natural cadences of speech, yet he could not help but aspire to the traditional poetic standards of the greatest Renaissance writers. Both Knowles's tragedies and his comedies reflected the taste of his time as well as the limitations of his creative abilities. Nevertheless, they are often superior to the dramas of his contemporaries, many of whom gave themselves up to writing facile and sensationalized melodramas. Knowles's drama has its share of such elements, but their presence is always counterbalanced by the playwright's attempt to restore the grandeur of the Renaissance tradition to the nineteenth century stage.

Other major works

NOVELS: *Fortesque*, 1846; *George Lovell*, 1847 (3 volumes).

SHORT FICTION: *The Magdalen and Other Tales*, 1832; *The Letter-de-Cachet*, 1835; *Tales and Novelettes*, 1874.

POETRY: *The Welch Harper*, 1796; *Fugitive Pieces*, 1810.

NONFICTION: *The Senate: Or, Social Villagers of a Kentish Town*, 1817; *The Elocutionist*, 1823; *The Rock of Rome: Or, The Arch Heresy*, 1849; *The Idol Demolished by Its Own Priest*, 1851; *The Gospel Attributed to Matthew Is the Record of the Whole Original Apostlehood*, 1855; *A Debate upon the Character of Julius Caesar*, 1856; *Lectures on Dramatic Literature*, 1873; *Lectures on Oratory, Gesture and Poetry*, 1873; *Lectures on Dramatic Literature: Macbeth*, 1875; *Sheridan Knowles' Conception and Mrs. Irving's Performance of Macbeth*, 1876.

Bibliography

Davies, Robertson. "Playwrights and Plays." In *The Revels History of Drama in English, 1750-1880*. Vol. 6. London: Methuen, 1975. Davies describes and evaluates each of Knowles's plays in chronological order. He draws attention to the recurring theme of "fatherhood" and focuses on Knowles's artistic development.

Fletcher, Richard M. *English Romantic Drama: 1795-1843*. New York: Exposition Press, 1966. Based on previously unavailable materials, Fletcher seeks to correct evaluations previously made about English Romantic drama. He concludes that it is more vibrant, vital, and artistic than has been generally acknowledged in the past. Fletcher, however, decries Knowles's popularity while lauding William Wordsworth, Samuel Taylor Coleridge, and Richard Lalor Sheil as the innovators of the age. He recognizes Knowles's success and original approach but laments his lack of savoir faire. Extensive bibliography.

Horne, Richard Hengist. *A New Spirit of the Age*. New York: Oxford University Press, 1907. Horne introduces and critiques the works of approximately forty contemporary literary figures. He describes Knowles as the only eminent playwright of the day, personifying the age's "domestic feeling," and critically examines his major works.

Knowles, Richard Brinsley. *The Life of James Sheridan Knowles*. London: James McHenry, 1872. Written by his son, this volume is the standard biography and primary authority on Knowles's life.

Meeks, Leslie Howard. *Sheridan Knowles and the Theatre of His Time*. Bloomington, Ind.: The Principia Press, 1933. This standard introduction to Knowles's plays is based mainly on primary sources. Meeks places the works into historical and literary context and provides a thorough analysis of *Virginius*, *The Hunchback*, and *William Tell*. The other plays are examined only briefly. He concludes that Knowles, alone, tried to preserve the high tradition of the English stage in a time of "dying English drama." Bibliography and index.

Nicoll, Allardyce. *A History of Early Nineteenth Century Drama, 1800-1850*. Vol. 1. Cambridge, England: University Press, 1930. Knowles tended to be melodramatic, but he was far ahead of his contemporaries in treating themes in a vivid manner. Nicoll briefly describes and evaluates the plays. Index.

Michael McCully
(Updated by *Gerald S. Argetsinger*)

ARTHUR KOPIT

Born: New York, New York; May 10, 1937

Principal drama

The Questioning of Nick, pr. 1957 (staged), pr. 1959 (televised), pb. 1965 (one act); *Gemini*, pr. 1957; *Don Juan in Texas*, pr. 1957 (with Wally Lawrence); *On the Runway of Life, You Never Know What's Coming Off Next*, pr. 1957; *Across the River and into the Jungle*, pr. 1958; *Aubade*, pr. 1959; *Sing to Me Through Open Windows*, pr. 1959, pr. 1965 (revised), pb. 1965; *To Dwell in a Palace of Strangers*, pb. 1959; *Oh Dad, Poor Dad, Mamma's Hung You in the Closet and I'm Feelin' So Sad: A Pseudoclassical Tragifarce in a Bastard French Tradition*, pr., pb. 1960; *Mhil'daiim*, pr. 1963 (one act); *Asylum: Or, What the Gentlemen Are Up To, Not to Mention the Ladies*, pr. 1963 (also as *Chamber Music*, pb. 1965, pr. 1971); *The Conquest of Everest*, pr. 1964, pb. 1965; *The Hero*, pr. 1964, pb. 1965; *The Day the Whores Came Out to Play Tennis*, pr., pb. 1965 (one act); *The Day the Whores Came Out to Play Tennis and Other Plays*, pb. 1965 (includes *Sing to Me Through Open Windows, Chamber Music, The Conquest of Everest, The Hero, The Questioning of Nick*; reissued as *Chamber Music and Other Plays*, pb. 1969); *An Incident in the Park*, pb. 1967; *Indians*, pr. 1968, pb. 1969; *What Happened to the Thorne's House*, pr. 1972; *Louisiana Territory*, pr. 1975; *Secrets of the Rich*, pr. 1976, pb. 1978; *Wings*, pr. 1977 (radio play), pr., pb. 1978 (staged), pr. 1983 (televised); *Good Help Is Hard to Find*, pb. 1982 (one act); *Nine*, pr. 1982, pb. 1983 (music, libretto, and lyrics by Maury Yeston; adaptation of Federico Fellini's film *8½*); *End of the World*, pr., pb. 1984; *Bone-the-Fish*, pr. 1989 (also as *Road to Nirvana*, pr. 1990, pb. 1991); *Phantom of the Opera*, pr. 1991 (music and lyrics by Yeston; adaptation of Gaston Leroux's novel); *Success*, pr. 1991, pb. 1992; *Discovery in America*, pr. 1992.

Other literary forms

Arthur Kopit has written *The Conquest of Television* (1966) and *Promontory Point Revisited* (1969) for television. In addition, an article by Kopit entitled "The Vital Matter of Environment" was published in *Theatre Arts* in April, 1961. His television miniseries, *Phantom of the Opera*, based on Gaston Leroux's novel, was aired in 1990.

Achievements

Critics have applied labels to Kopit based on his first successful work, *Oh Dad, Poor Dad, Mamma's Hung You in the Closet and I'm Feelin' So Sad*, and while his work has continued to evolve, the labels have stuck.

Reviewers called the play an unsuccessful example of the Theater of the Absurd and Kopit an Absurdist whose extraordinary titles have been far more enticing than his plays. In spite of these charges, *Oh Dad, Poor Dad, Mamma's Hung You in the Closet and I'm Feelin' So Sad* won the Vernon Rice Award and the Outer Circle Award in 1962 and was popular enough to be made into a motion picture (directed by Richard Quine and Alexander Mackendrick) in 1967.

While Kopit's titles certainly attract attention, he is more than a clever deviser of titles. *Indians*, for example, must be considered one of the major American plays written in the 1960's, and *Wings*, one of the major dramas of the 1970's. Furthermore, he has displayed a diversity of style and a range of theme uncommon among his contemporaries. Kopit has publicly criticized the American theatrical tradition, especially as embodied by Broadway—a stance which may in part account for his lack of critical recognition. Subsidized by a Harvard University Shaw Traveling Fellowship, Kopit toured Europe and studied continental theater in 1959, and his essay "The Vital Matter of Environment" summed up his feelings about the mediocrity and lack of vitality of the American theater in comparison to European drama. "One can never wholly dissociate a work of art from its creative environment," he wrote, "Tradition has always been the basis of all innovation. . . . Style is related to tradition to the extent that it is representative of a cultural or social characteristic of its creative environment, and is itself characteristic to the extent that it has evolved from or rebelled against any of these." Consequently, Kopit charged, the lack of tradition in the American theater forces American playwrights to rely on European dramatic innovations. Clearly, Kopit has used his knowledge of European traditions to bring innovations to the American stage. Although some of his work is obviously and even consciously derivative, he has gone beyond his models to produce distinctive plays of great strength.

In 1964, Tyrone Guthrie, with the help of a Rockefeller Foundation grant of seventy thousand dollars, offered to mount Kopit's one-act plays *The Day the Whores Came Out to Play Tennis* and *Mhil'daiim* in connection with the University of Minnesota, but a problem arose with university officials. The university's position was that the intent of the grant was to provide playwrights with an opportunity to revise scripts under experimental conditions, and that the plays were not meant to be performed publicly, in spite of Kopit's assumption to the contrary. Kopit withdrew his plays from rehearsal, and in a scathing interview in the January 13, 1964, issue of *The New York Times*, he accused the university of "deceit" and "censorship in its most insidious form" in denying him the benefit of an audience.

Like all successful playwrights, Kopit roots his plays in performance. His recognition of the importance of producing an effect on his audience is central to his writing, yet his intellectual approach to his themes keeps his dramas from degenerating into melodramas. The combination of powerfully emotional theatrical moments and significant subject matter is a staple in Kopit's drama.

Kopit is sensitive both to the dignity of humankind and to the absurdity of the human condition. To explore this tension between dignity and absurdity, Kopit has utilized a number of different formats and techniques; *The Questioning of Nick* is realistic, *Oh Dad, Poor Dad, Mamma's Hung You in the Closet and I'm Feelin' So Sad* contains Absurdist elements, *Indians* owes some of its structure to Bertolt Brecht's concept of epic theater, and *Wings* is surreal, impressionistic, psychological realism. Kopit's musical books for *Nine* and *Phantom of the Opera* have demonstrated his flexibility in form. The combination of mythic elements with almost hyperrealistic dialogue in *Bone-the-Fish* (its working title, which parodies David Mamet's 1988 *Speed-the-Plow*, also about Hollywood, was changed to *Road to Nirvana* when the play reached New York) points up Kopit's humor and seriousness at the same time. With *Discovery in America*, Kopit continued to fulfill the promise of his earlier experimental work.

Biography

Arthur Lee Kopit was born in New York City, New York, on May 10, 1937, the son of George Kopit, a jeweler, and Maxine (née Dubkin) Kopit. He married Leslie Ann Garis, a concert pianist from Amherst, Massachusetts, on March 14, 1968; they have three children: Alex, Ben, and Kathleen.

During an "uneventful" childhood, living in a prosperous suburb in which he found himself to be the "victim of a healthy family life," Kopit demonstrated an interest in dramatics by entertaining his friends with puppet shows. Radio was an important element in his development; he says, "It's a much more exciting medium than TV because it involves your creative faculties." Although he wrote for the school newspaper while attending Lawrence (Long Island) High School, Kopit showed little inclination toward a career in the arts when he was graduated in 1955, and he entered Harvard University with a scholarship to study electrical engineering. After taking some creative writing courses, however, he decided that he wanted to become a playwright, and he was graduated cum laude and Phi Beta Kappa with a bachelor of arts degree in June, 1959.

Kopit's first theatrical experiences at Harvard took place during his sophomore year; as he reports in the introduction to *The Day the Whores Came Out to Play Tennis and Other Plays*, "My career was determined." His class work with Robert Chapman and his success under the tutelage of Gaynor Bradish, a tutor in Dunster House who was in charge of its Drama Workshop, stimulated Kopit's interest in the stage and introduced him to the fundamentals of playwriting. Over a period of three or four days during his spring vacation, the aspiring dramatist wrote *The Questioning of Nick*, a one-act play which won a collegewide playwriting contest the following fall; it was subsequently performed on television in New Haven, Connecticut, in June, 1959. The seven other dramas that Kopit wrote while studying at Harvard include *Don Juan in Texas*, written in collaboration with Wally Lawrence; *On the Runway of Life, You Never Know What's Coming Off Next*; *Across the River and into the Jungle*; "Through a Labyrinth"; and the productions of his senior year, *Aubade, Sing to Me Through Open Windows*, and *To Dwell in a Palace of Strangers*, the first act of a projected three-act drama that was published in the *Harvard Advocate* in May, 1959. A revised version of *Sing to Me Through Open Windows* was produced Off-Broadway in New York in 1965 and in London in 1976.

During a tour of Western Europe in 1959, Kopit wrote *Oh Dad, Poor Dad, Mamma's Hung You in the Closet and I'm Feelin' So Sad* "to enter [in another] playwriting contest at Harvard," this time in the Adams House competition. Again Kopit's work won a prize, and the reaction when the play was mounted as a major undergraduate production was so overwhelming that, with the aid of a Ford Foundation grant, it was moved to the Agassiz Theatre in Cambridge, Massachusetts, in January, 1960. Kopit had cast a young woman from Radcliffe College in one of his Harvard productions, and through his friendship with her, he was introduced to the Broadway producer Roger L. Stevens. *Oh Dad, Poor Dad, Mamma's Hung You in the Closet and I'm Feelin' So Sad* opened at the Phoenix Theatre in New York City on February 26, 1962, as part of their repertory offerings, produced by Stevens and directed by famed choreographer Jerome Robbins. The play ran for 454 performances before it closed on March 31, 1963, and it then toured for eleven weeks. On August 27, 1963, it returned to the Morosco Theatre in New York for a brief revival (forty-seven performances). *Oh Dad, Poor Dad, Mamma's Hung You in the Closet and I'm Feelin' So Sad* was the first of Kopit's plays to be published by a major house, Hill and Wang, and it has been performed in London, Paris, Australia, Belgium, Canada, Italy, Mexico, the Scandinavian countries, Turkey, and West Berlin. Kopit also received the Vernon Rice Award and the Outer Circle Award in 1962, and a film version was released by Paramount in 1967. The motion picture did not repeat the success of the stage play.

Asylum: Or, What the Gentlemen Are Up To, Not to Mention the Ladies, was scheduled to open at the Off-Broadway Theatre de Lys in March, 1963, but after five preview performances, Kopit decided to cancel the production. The dramatist reports that the bill was actually composed of two one-act plays, *Chamber Music* and a companion piece that he intended to expand into a three-act play later. The concept for *Chamber Music* occurred to Kopit sometime in 1959, though he did not begin writing the play until late in the spring of 1962, finishing it that summer. The author withdrew the plays because he "wanted to do more work on them." *Chamber Music* was revised and rewritten during the summer of 1964 and staged in London in 1971. With *The Day the Whores Came Out to Play Tennis*, *Sing to Me Through Open Windows*, *The Hero*, *The Conquest of Everest*, and *The Questioning of Nick*, it was collected in *The Day the Whores Came Out to Play and Other Plays*, the second of Kopit's five volumes to be published by Hill and Wang. The collection was published under the title *Chamber Music and Other Plays* in England four years later.

The *Hero* and *The Conquest of Everest* were both written in March, 1964. Kopit explains that *The Hero* contains no dialogue because he was "struck dumb by the prospect of writing two plays in a single day." *The Conquest of Everest* was produced in New York in 1964 and in London in 1980; *The Hero* was produced in New York in 1964 and in London in 1972.

As part of a Rockefeller Foundation grant, two other one-act plays, *The Day the Whores Came Out to Play Tennis* and *Mhil'daiim*, were to be staged at the Tyrone Guthrie Theatre in Minneapolis, Minnesota, in February, 1964, but, as mentioned above, Kopit withdrew the plays because of a disagreement with the University of Minnesota. On March 15, 1965, director Gerald Freeman opened *The Day the Whores Came Out to Play Tennis* on a double bill with *Sing to Me Through Open Windows* (directed by Joseph Chaikin) at the Player's Theatre in Greenwich Village. *Sing to Me Through Open Windows*, written while Kopit was at Harvard, had actually served as a curtain raiser for *Oh Dad, Poor Dad, Mamma's Hung You in the Closet and I'm Feelin' So Sad* in the New York previews in 1962, but because of production difficulties, it, too, had been canceled before opening night. The revised version also played in London in 1976. Next came *An Incident in the Park*, published in Bob Booker and George Foster's *Pardon Me, Sir, but Is My Eye Hurting Your Elbow?* in 1968; in 1969, one of his television plays, *Promontory Point Revisited*, a segment of the series *Foul* on the New York Television Theatre, followed.

Kopit's next major play, *Indians*, was written with the aid of a Rockefeller Foundation grant. It premiered as part of the Royal Shakespeare Company's repertory at the Aldwych Theatre in London under Jack Gelber's direction on July 4, 1968, a symbolically appropriate date for this play. On May 6, 1969, the play was transferred to the Arena Stage in Washington, D.C., and on October 13 of the same year, it was moved again to the Brooks Atkinson Theatre in New York under the direction of Gene Frankel (ninety-six performances). High production costs were blamed when the play, cited by Otis L. Guernsey, Jr., as one of the "best plays of 1969-1970," closed on January 3, 1970. *Indians* was met with critical acclaim and has been performed in France, Germany, Japan, and the Scandinavian countries. In 1976, Robert Altman, working from a script suggested by Kopit's play, directed a film entitled *Buffalo Bill and the Indians:*

Or, Sitting Bull's History Lesson. Kopit received $500,000 for the screen rights to *Indians*.

Between 1969 and 1977, Kopit's output diminished, and he wrote nothing of great significance for the stage. The Impossible Time Theatre held a Kopit Festival in 1977; in the same year, Kopit wrote *Wings*, which had been commissioned in the fall of 1976 by Earplay, the drama project of National Public Radio. John Madden directed the version of *Wings* broadcast on National Public Radio in 1977, and when Kopit, at the urging of Robert Brustein, then dean of the Yale School of Drama, rewrote the work for a stage presentation during the Yale Repertory Theatre's 1978 season, Madden again served as director. *Wings* was produced at the New York Shakespeare Festival in 1978 (sixteen performances at the Public/ Newman Theatre), at the Lyceum Theatre in 1979 (113 performances), and in London in 1979; it was published simultaneously in the United States and Canada in 1978, with British publication coming the following year. *Wings* was televised on the Public Broadcasting System in 1983. *Wings* marked the return to productivity for Kopit, with his musical books for *Nine* and *Phantom of the Opera* (but whose libretto he wrote as early as 1984, a project shelved when Andrew Lloyd Webber produced his version in 1985) and his full-length works, developed in regional theaters such as the Actors Theatre of Louisville, the Circle Repertory Theatre, the Actors Repertory Theatre, and the Mark Taper Forum.

Like many contemporary American playwrights, Kopit has subsisted at least in part through the support of foundation grants, supplemented by academic positions. He was awarded a Guggenheim Fellowship in 1967 and a Rockefeller grant in 1968; he was a National Endowment for the Arts grantee and a Fellow at the Center for the Humanities at Wesleyan University from 1974 to 1975; he served as playwright-in-residence at Wesleyan from 1975 to 1976; he was a CBS fellow at Yale University from 1976 to 1977; and in 1979 he became an adjunct professor of playwriting at the Yale School of Drama.

In addition to the awards already noted, Kopit was the recipient of a National Institute of Arts and Letters Award and was elected to the American Academy of Arts and Letters in 1971; in 1979, he won both the Italia Prize for his radio version of *Wings* and the Pulitzer Prize for the stage version.

Kopit, who settled in Connecticut, prefers to live and work away from people ("any holiday resort in the off-season . . . Majorca . . . [in] a huge hotel almost empty"). A man of the theater, he has also directed some of his own works, including the 1959 television production of *The Questioning of Nick*, and the stage productions of *Oh Dad, Poor Dad, Mamma's Hung You in the Closet and I'm Feelin' So Sad* in Paris, in 1963, and of *Louisiana Territory* in Middletown, Connecticut, in 1975.

Analysis

There has been relatively little scholarly attention paid to the works of playwright Arthur Kopit, with almost nothing written about his entire canon, and most of the criticism that has been published is not very impressive. Furthermore, those critics who attempt an overview of the plays usually devote a fair amount of time to discussing the plays that he wrote as an undergraduate at Harvard. While Sherwood Anderson, Robert Sherwood, Eugene O'Neill, and other playwrights have moved from Harvard to Broadway in the past, critical studies of their works have focused on what they wrote as professional playwrights. There are three related reasons that justify a different approach to Kopit. First, the Harvard plays represent nearly half of the author's output; second, the majority of his twelve later plays have been short and relatively insignificant; and third, as a result of these first two points combined with the reputation established by his major plays, several of the Harvard pieces have been published and are thus easily accessible.

The best of Kopit's early plays is *Sing to Me Through Open Windows*. Clearly not meant to be realistic (the set is a bare stage hung with black curtains), the drama is in the tradition of Theater of the Absurd and shows the influence of Samuel Beckett in its setting, language, pauses, minimal plot, and mysterious characters. In spite of Kopit's statement that Beckett "has had no influence on me as far as I know," critics have pointed out structural and linguistic resemblances between this play and Beckett's *Endgame* (pr. 1957).

The protagonist of the play is a boy, Andrew Linden, who visits the home of a magician, Ottoman Jud, and his helper, Loveless the Clown, in the middle of a dark forest. Ottoman and the Clown have entertained Andrew on the first day of spring every year for five years. This year, however, Ottoman's illusions fail, and Andrew is exposed to the games that Ottoman and the Clown play, mysterious games that also prove unsuccessful. This year, too, Andrew announces that he wants to stay with Ottoman, but the announcement is made in the third person, answering a "Distant Voice of Ottoman," as though the event is being recalled even while the present action continues: "And although I say them, some time later I will ask myself, Now what was it again that you said to him . . . back there? . . . And the boy said yes, he wanted to stay there. . . . I love you, Mr. Jud." The play ends with Ottoman apparently dead and Andrew gone.

The format of the work combines with its symbolism to depict a transitional moment in life. Memory and the present intermix as Andrew must leave the unworried, love-filled, exciting, circuslike atmosphere of his childhood and move into manhood. Ottoman, a symbolic father figure, is failing, certainly growing old and perhaps even dying (another transition), and while he can put his arm around the boy's shoulder to encourage him, the youngster must continue his journey through life alone. Symbolically, the time of year during which the action takes place represents hope, birth, and renewal, but it is cold, and snow is falling as the play ends, negating the positive aspects of spring and suggesting the fear that both old man and young man feel as they approach the unknown. Kopit has said that *Sing to Me Through Open Windows* is "about the necessity of certain things dying to enable certain things to live. It deals with memory and time. . . . "

Oh Dad, Poor Dad, Mamma's Hung You in the Closet and I'm Feelin' So Sad caught theatergoing audiences in America by surprise, and a summary of the action provides a clue as to why this happened. The three-scene production, subtitled *A Pseudoclassical Tragifarce in a Bastard French Tradition*, is set in a Caribbean island hotel where Madame Rosepettle, her son Jonathan, two large Venus flytraps, and a cat-eating, talking piranha fish named Rosalinda (after Rosepettle's husband's former secretary) are in transit. Also traveling with the family is the stuffed body of Rosepettle's husband, which is kept in a coffin when traveling and hangs from a hook in Rosepettle's bedroom closet the rest of the time: "He's my favorite trophy. I take him with me wherever I go," she chortles. In scene 1, Rosepettle harangues the bellboys and dominates her son. Scene 2, set two weeks later, brings Jonathan together with a young governess, Rosalie, who tries to seduce him, but who is run off by his mother. One week later, in scene 3, Rosepettle is courted by elderly Commodore Roseabove, but her story of how she brought about her husband's death (a description that paints men as bestial and women as virginal) unnerves him. She proclaims that her goal in life is to protect her son (he was delivered after a twelve-month term, so she obviously began her campaign early): "My son shall have only Light!" Later, while Rosepettle is out on her habitual round, searching for couples making love on the beach so she can kick sand in their faces, Rosalie returns to try to persuade Jonathan to run off with her, but she is so self-centered and insensitive that her sexual desire arouses only terror in Jonathan. When his father's corpse falls on them, Rosalie commands, "Forget about your father. Drop your pants on top of him, then you won't see his face." The play concludes when Rosepettle returns to find that Jonathan has killed the girl by smothering her.

There are many Freudian and Oedipal overtones to *Oh Dad, Poor Dad, Mamma's Hung You in the Closet and I'm Feelin' So Sad*, with its theme of a domineering mother and Milquetoast son. The theme is not a new one, having been dealt with in Sidney Howard's *The Silver Cord* (pr. 1926) and later in Harold Pinter's *A Night Out* (pr. 1960) and Philip Roth's *Portnoy's Complaint* (1969) yet Kopit's embroidering of the theme with man-eating plants (symbolic of the emasculating wife/mother), maniacal cuckoo clocks, uncontrollable tape recorders (as in Arthur Miller's *Death of a Salesman*, pr. 1949), and self-propelled chairs, spiced with a loved one's body (as in

Joe Orton's *Loot*, pr. 1965), results in a unique creation.

Some critics claim that Kopit is metaphorically portraying the neurosis brought about by the tensions of the nuclear age. This reading is certainly reinforced by the dramatist's use of Absurdist techniques, though this interpretation is not completely convincing. The play is not really an Absurdist play, in spite of Kopit's use of Absurdist techniques—a careful examination of Rosepettle's dialogue, for example, reveals the psychological realism which underlies the bizarre surface of the action. There are flashes of brilliance in the grotesque humor, but they are not sustained throughout the play. Some critics called the work a satire that mimics avant-garde conventions, while others dismissed it as an unsuccessful example of the Theater of the Absurd. In any case, the play conclusively established Kopit's theatrical talent.

After a series of lesser works, Kopit surprised audiences again with *Indians*, his second major play. *Indians* fuses the principal themes and techniques of Kopit's previous works. The conception of the play dates to March, 1966, when Kopit read a statement made by General William Westmoreland, the commander-in-chief of American forces in Vietnam, regarding incidents in which American soldiers had killed Vietnamese civilians: "Of course innocent people have been killed. In war they always are. And of course our hearts go out to the innocent victims of this." Realizing that this sentiment could be traced throughout American history, Kopit put Westmoreland's exact words in the mouth of a character in *Indians*, Colonel Forsythe, who speaks them while looking over the site on which a group of Indians have been massacred the day before. The casual dismissal of the action is overwhelming. At the moment that he read Westmoreland's quote, Kopit has recalled, he "was listening to Charles Ives' Fourth Symphony. There are two orchestras playing counterpoint. The orchestras play completely opposing pieces of music based on American Folk songs— 'Shenendoah,' 'Columbia the Gem of the Ocean.' . . . You have this serene, seraphic music based on these folk songs, and then the violent opposition of a marching band drowning it out." The dramatist admits that when the Westmoreland quote was juxtaposed to the music, "I just sort of went berserk."

Another ingredient that contributed to the play's success was the tempering influence of Kopit's intellectual approach to his material. In both *Don Juan in Texas* and *Across the River and into the Jungle*, he had touched on the source of mythic heroes. In *Indians*, he complemented this interest with research. The emotional content and the research came together in the composition process to create interwoven subtexts: "Most of the scenes in the play are based on real incidents that were then distorted." For example, Kopit notes, "The scene on the Plains is based upon a famous expedition of the Grand Duke Alexis. Spotted Tail was not killed then, but he could have been." He goes on to observe that "in a way he was killed; he was made to play the stage Indian for the Grand Duke."

The play is composed of thirteen scenes, alternating between Buffalo Bill's Wild West Show and an 1886 Indian Commission hearing. The extravagant Wild West Show segments illustrate American prejudices, reveal Buffalo Bill's character, comment on historical events, and develop Kopit's theme that Americans create heroes through a mythmaking process that lets their society justify the destruction of other less powerful societies. The commission scenes demonstrate how alien the white and Indian societies appear to each other. The whites do not understand why Indians will neither abide by their treaties nor recognize the innate inferiority of their race. The Indians do not understand how the treaties can be valid, since land cannot be owned, and also why, if there are treaties, the whites do not abide by the agreed-upon terms. Neither side understands, respects, or grants dignity to the opposing side.

The conflict between basic cultural instincts is emphasized by the tension between the alternating scenes and epitomized by the contrast between Westmoreland's words and the noble, moving surrender speech given by Chief Joseph in 1877, which Kopit incorporates into the play twice, the second time as the concluding speech in the play:

> . . . I am tired of fighting. Our chiefs have been killed. . . . The old men are all dead. It is cold and we have no blankets. The children are freezing. My people, some of them, have fled to the hills and have no food. . . . No one knows where they are—perhaps frozen. I want to have time to look for my children and see how many of them I can find. Maybe I shall find them among the dead. Hear me, my chiefs. I am tired. My heart is sick and sad! From where the sun now stands, I will fight no more, forever.

For his part, Buffalo Bill is trapped by his own nature, by historical events, and by America's need to create heroes. He is instrumental in destroying a people and a way of life he admires.

Kopit does not intend his play to be taken on a literal level. The chronology (referred to as a "Chronology for a Dreamer") that is supplied in the printed version of the play is not the chronology followed in the drama. Spotted Tail rises after his death to make a speech. The opening, in which the figures of Buffalo Bill and Sitting Bull are seen as though they are in museum cases, is intended to alert the viewer immediately that the play is not to be taken realistically. Instead, Kopit offers an emotional gestalt, an impressionistic, surreal representation of his theme. By means of a deliberately confusing Brechtian production through which the spectators are made aware of historical processes, the playwright forces them to realize that those processes are man-made, not natural elements, and that they are alterable. The play gets off to a weak start, but after the first three or four scenes, the cumulative effect of Kopit's dramatic structure begins to build, and the play gathers power as it progresses, each scene taking its strength from the scenes that precede it while simultaneously adding to their impact.

As impressive as *Indians* was, *Wings* was the product of an even more mature dramatist and is probably Kopit's finest work. Again he combined a strong emotional expression with an intellectual context, and again he relied on the themes and techniques that had served him well in the past, but he explored new material as well. Stylistically there is an impressive distance between the realism of *The Questioning of Nick* and the impressionism of *Wings*; there is also an interesting thematic progression from the commonplace subject matter of the early plays to the public, social impulse behind *Indians* and then to the personal, individual content of *Wings*.

In the spring of 1976, Kopit's father suffered a massive stroke that rendered him incapable of speech. This event became the source of *Wings*'s emotional content. During his visits to the Burke Rehabilitation Center in White Plains, New York, as he explains in a Shavian preface to the published script, Kopit formulated what became the operative or controlling questions for the play, going beyond a mere exploration of the problems of communication and of the nature of language: "To what extent was [his father] still intact? To what extent was he aware of what had befallen him? *What was it like inside?*" In addition to his father, the dramatist observed several other patients, upon whom the protagonist, Emily Stilson, was to be modeled. Kopit not only became involved in trying to convey what it would be like to undergo the personal and terrifying catastrophe of a stroke but also began examining the nature of identity and of reality itself, for to the disoriented victim, reality is confused and unverifiable, and the resultant terror must be faced in virtual isolation.

To supplement his own observations, Kopit once more turned to exhaustive research. The published text of the play has an epigraph from Charles Lindbergh's *The Spirit of St. Louis* (1953), which describes the pilot's feeling of being cut off and unsure of what is real; ironically, the feeling is similar to that experienced by a stroke victim, and Lindbergh's words are later echoed in Emily's dialogue. Kopit also drew on two books concerning brain damage, Howard Gardner's *The Shattered Mind* (1975) and A. R. Luria's *The Man with a Shattered World* (1972), and on the experience of the center's therapist, Jacqueline Doolittle, herself a former stroke victim.

The effective representation of the mind of the victim is what sets this drama apart from most of its contemporaries and supplies a strength that would be missing if the playwright had adopted a documentary approach. The ninety-minute play moves from fragmentation to integration, a movement synchronized with stage effects—live and recorded sound, colored and flashing lights, shifting points of view, a minimal set conveying a sense of limbo, overlapping dialogue, loudspeakers situated throughout the theater, and other such devices, which exercise the potential of the theater to the maximum.

The play is open-ended in that it comes to no climax or conclusion. Performed without intermission, it is composed of four segments. In "Prelude," Emily suffers her stroke. In "Catastrophe," she realizes that something has happened, but she cannot determine what or identify her status. "Awakening" traces Emily's transition from a total lack of understanding to the dawning of understanding. In "Explorations," the final segment, she begins to sort out her identity and starts to appreciate the significance of her condition. Although these states of being are distinct, the person progressively experiencing them cannot perceive either edge of the transition, a condition that Kopit reproduces nicely while still managing to maintain a sense of Emily's gradual reconstruction of her personality and of reality itself.

The dramatist's careful combination of logic and nonsense, of articulate speech and babble, parallels his stage effects to depict an extraordinary, nonverbal sequence of events. There is not much action in *Wings*, and what there is seems confusing and unstructured. The audience, however, soon becomes deeply involved with Emily; tension is created not by dramatic action, but by the audience's effort to decipher what is happening in the play and what is real, and by their concern for Emily. The charge that *Wings* is not interesting because it lacks sufficient rising action is similar to the criticism leveled against Eugene O'Neill's *Long Day's Journey into Night* (pb. 1955) and is equally invalid. *Wings* is not meant to entertain superficially in the way that Lanford Wilson's *Talley's Folley* (pr. 1979), or Neil Simon's plays do; like *Long Day's Journey into Night*, it sheds light on the perennial human condition.

Kopit's reputation no longer rests solely on *Oh Dad, Poor Dad, Mamma's Hung You in the Closet and I'm Feelin' So Sad* despite its continued popularity among college students. With *Indians* and *Wings*, he proved his early promise; with his later work, especially *Road to Nirvana* and *Discovery in America*, his technical skills (in several genres) have served his personal voice to present strong dramatic statements on significant topics. After David Mamet, Sam Shepard, and Edward Albee, Kopit belongs among the major American playwrights of the late twentieth century.

Other major works

NONFICTION: *"The Vital Matter of Environment,"* pb. 1961 (in *Theatre Arts*).

TELEPLAYS: *The Conquest of Television*, 1966; *Promontory Point Revisited*, 1969; *Hands of a Stranger*, 1987; *Phantom of the Opera*, 1990 (based on Gaston Leroux's novel).

TRANSLATION: *Ghosts*, 1984 (by Henrik Ibsen).

Bibliography

Dieckman, Suzanne Burgoyne, and Richard Brayshaw. "Wings, Watchers, and Windows: Imprisonment in the Plays of Arthur Kopit." *Theatre Journal* 35 (May, 1983): 195-212. Concentrates on *Wings* and earlier short plays but speaks intelligently of *Indians* and *Nine* as well. The authors find that Kopit's later work "explores the process of transformation, a process which involves the interplay between freedom and limitations." Imprisonments are mental and political, and Kopit dramatizes "the process of transcending those limitations."

Kauffmann, Stanley. *Persons of the Drama: Theater Criticism and Comment.* New York: Harper & Row, 1976. A collection of reviews that includes a long look at *Indians*, in which Kauffmann sees more intention than fulfillment. Pointing to some awkward moments in the work, he comments that "the playwright who could sink to such depths has a foggy conception of the heights." Speaks well of Stacy Keach, Jr., as Buffalo Bill, and Oliver Smith's design.

Kelley, Margot Anne. "Order Within Fragmentation: Postmodernism and the Stroke Victim's World." *Modern Drama* 34 (September, 1991): 383-391. A study of *Wings*, written for radio in 1976 and revised for the stage in 1978. Kopit, in addition to examining the character possibilities, also "manipulates contemporary cultural ideas from the sciences and literature through his disability metaphor," a change from earlier treatments of this disorder. Notes point to other semiotic and psychological studies.

Rich, Frank. "Art Imitates Art (and Artists)." Review of *Bone-the-Fish.* *The New York Times*, March 8, 1991, p. C1. This review demonstrates what is wrong with the New York theater criticism system: Rich did not like the play but in the act of damning it points out its strengths. The fullness and insight of Kopit's parody of David Mamet is not the weakness, but the strength of this play. The review analyzes Kopit's comic voice, but without appreciating its subtleties.

Szilassy, Zoltan. *American Theater of the 1960s.* Carbondale: Southern Illinois University Press, 1986. Discusses Kopit's works throughout, especially *Indians*, but also covers the one-acts surrounding *The Day the Whores Came Out to Play Tennis.* Szilassy speaks well of these "one-acters, improvisations, and trifles" and discusses *Chamber Music* at some length. Index.

Westarp, Karl-Heinz. "Myth in Peter Shaffer's *The Royal Hunt of the Sun* and in Arthur Kopit's *Indians.*" *English Studies: A Journal of English Language and Literature* 65 (April, 1984): 120-128. A good introduction to the vocabulary of myth criticism, and a strong source of comparison between *Indians* and Shaffer's own examination of the fall of the Incas at the hands of the Spanish. Kopit is seen here as a "demystifier" rather than a mythmaker, an important distinction for understanding his later work, especially *Road to Nirvana.*

Steven H. Gale
(Revised by *Thomas J. Taylor*)

BERNARD KOPS

Born: London, England; November 28, 1926

Principal drama

The Hamlet of Stepney Green, pr. 1957, pb. 1959; *Good-Bye World*, pr.
1959; *Change for the Angel*, pr. 1960; *The Dream of Peter Mann*, pr., pb.
1960; *Enter Solly Gold*, pb. 1961, pr. 1962 (music by Stanley Myers); *Stray
Cats and Empty Bottles*, pr. 1964 (televised), pr. 1967 (staged); *The Boy
Who Wouldn't Play Jesus*, pr., pb. 1965 (children's play); *David, It Is Getting Dark*, pr., pb. 1970; *It's a Lovely Day Tomorrow*, pr. 1975 (televised),
pr. 1976 (staged) (with John Goldschmidt); *More Out than In*, pr. 1980;
Ezra, pb. 1980, pr. 1981; *Simon at Midnight*, pr. 1982 (radio play), pr. 1985
(staged).

Other literary forms

Bernard Kops is a prolific writer. He has published numerous novels,
including *Awake for Mourning* (1958), *Motorbike* (1962), *Yes from No-
Man's Land* (1965), *The Dissent of Dominick Shapiro* (1966), *By the Waters
of Whitechapel* (1969), *The Passionate Past of Gloria Gaye* (1971), *Settle
Down Simon Katz* (1973), *Partners* (1975), and *On Margate Sands* (1978).
His books of poetry include *Poems* (1955), *Poems and Songs* (1958), *An
Anemone for Antigone* (1959), *Erica, I Want to Read You Something*
(1967), and *For the Record* (1971). Kops's powerful autobiography, *The
World Is a Wedding*, was published in 1963. His dramatic writing includes
work for television and radio as well as for the stage.

Achievements

First and foremost, Kops is a lyric poet who uses the theater, television,
and radio as vehicles for poetry. Theatrically, he is an innovator in his use
of music and songs and in his often successful attempts to restore vitality to
hackneyed themes. Kops's exploration of fantasy, of inner states of being,
and of schizophrenia is juxtaposed to the presentation of realistic, sordid
surroundings. His handling of dream logic is superb and explains why he is
so attracted to the radio as a dramatic form. Radio drama depends upon
pauses, sounds, words, silences, and the intimate relationship between the
listeners (the unseen audience) and the unseen performers in the studio.
Such a form is ideally suited to Kops's synthesis of past and present, actual-
ity and fantasy.

Kops's plays have been hailed as triumphs of sordid realism much in the
kitchen-sink mold, as imaginative explorations of psychic worlds, and as

politically charged allegories. Kops was at first bracketed with Harold Pinter and Arnold Wesker, two other East End Jewish dramatists who emerged in the new wave of British drama heralded by the 1956 Royal Court Theatre performance of John Osborne's *Look Back in Anger*. Each has since gone his own way, the differences being greater than the similarities. Unlike Pinter's work, Kops's theater is frequently overtly Jewish. While hostility in Pinter is characterized by innuendo and body movement sometimes erupting into violence, hostility in Kops is overt; it does not simmer. Unlike Wesker, Kops does not preach. Most of Kops's drama, even when focusing upon old age and death, has a vitality, an instinctive sense of life, and often a coarse humor which are lacking in Wesker.

The relative critical neglect of Kops may result in part from his extensive work in nontheatrical dramatic forms such as radio and television; his prolific activity as a novelist may have further distracted attention from his dramatic achievements. Nevertheless, following the widespread publicity given to his brilliant evocation of Ezra Pound's insanity in *Ezra*, Kops is beginning to be recognized in England as a supreme master of dramatic dream poetry.

Biography

Bernard Kops's work is intensely autobiographical. Details of his early life may be found in *The World Is a Wedding*. He was born in Stepney in the East End of London in 1926. His father was a Dutch Jewish immigrant cobbler who came to London's East End in 1904, and his mother was born in London of Dutch Jewish parents. Kops was the youngest of a family of four sisters and two brothers. Although his family was very poor, Kops grew up in an intense, colorful, and cosmopolitan environment. The English Fascist demonstrations and counterdemonstrations of the late 1930's in the East End of London provided a personal background for the awareness of anti-Semitism which pervades Kops's work.

Kops left school when he was only thirteen to earn a living as best he could—as a docker, chef, salesman, waiter, liftman, and barrow boy, selling books in street markets. Already writing and reading intensely, he was particularly moved by Eugene O'Neill's *Mourning Becomes Electra* and its depiction of family conflicts and fantasy states. T. S. Eliot was another early literary influence, from whom Kops gained insight into the theatrical use of popular songs. The foundations for Kops's dramatic methodology were formed at the evening drama classes he attended at Toynbee Hall in London's East End.

During World War II, Kops's family moved around England in frequent evacuations and return trips to the badly blitzed East End. The postwar years saw Kops acting in repertory theater; traveling through France, Spain, and Tangier; living in a caravan in Camden Town, North London;

and taking drugs. Following the death of his mother in 1951, Kops was committed to a psychiatric hospital. Kops has twice been institutionalized; the concern with extreme mental states in his work clearly has a personal genesis. Kops's meeting with and marriage in 1956 to Erica Gordon, a doctor's daughter, eased his bereavement and transformed his life, giving him the support he so desperately needed. They had four children, and, beginning in the late 1950's, he earned his living as a professional writer.

Kops's first play, *The Hamlet of Stepney Green*, was produced by Frank Hauser at the Oxford Playhouse in 1957, subsequently moving to London's Lyric Theatre and then to New York. With the success of this play, Kops arrived on the theatrical scene. Kops was the first person to be awarded the C. Day Lewis fellowship (1980), was the recipient of several Arts Council bursaries, and has been writer-in-residence in Bristol and the London Borough of Hounslow.

Kops settled in London, where he continued to write frequently on the artistic life, especially in retrospect from his earlier days in SoHo. His play *Ezra*, based on the life of Ezra Pound, is often performed in colleges; *Simon at Midnight* was broadcast on radio in 1982 and was made into a stage play in 1985.

Analysis

Much of Bernard Kops's work revolves around family situations, the basic conflict he sees in such situations, and the individual's doomed attempt to free himself from the family and its nets. He is obsessed with family themes, with people tied together in intense love-hate relationships. Like O'Neill, Kops uses the theater to express the inner life of human beings. All of his plays are shadowed by the streets and sounds of the London of his childhood, by his Jewishness, by his family, and by his wild, anarchic, surrealistic inner life.

The plot of *The Hamlet of Stepney Green* provides a good illustration of the nature of Kops's drama. Kops transforms William Shakespeare's *Hamlet* into an East End London Jewish lyric fantasy. Hamlet becomes David Levy, twenty-two years old, tall, and intelligent, who wants to be a singer like Frank Sinatra. He refuses to see his future in terms of inheriting his aging father's small pickled-herring street stall. Kops describes two ways in which David Levy can be played—as someone who can sing, or as someone who cannot: "The crucial thing about David is that although he is bored with the life around him he is waiting for something to happen." Hava Segal, the daughter of Solly Segal, David's father's best friend, becomes Ophelia and dotes on David. Throughout the first act, Sam, David's father, is dying; the curtain to the first act falls as he dies. At the moment of death, father and son are united. Like so many of Kops's subsequent creations, the old man is unwilling to relinquish his hold on life. He is sad because there is a gulf between him and his son and because there is no love in his relationship with Bessy, his young and still quite attractive wife.

In the second act, Sam returns to the stage as a ghostly figment of his son's imagination, calling upon David to avenge his death. In David's heightened imagination, his mother has poisoned his father. Bessy is going to marry Solly Segal. David, imitating Hamlet, dresses in black and is treated as though he were insane by relatives and a chorus of salesmen. Meanwhile the ghost attempts to dampen David's vengeful desires. Sam, aware that only good can come through Bessy's marriage to Solly, arranges, through a séance, for the marriage to take place.

In the final act, the ghost persuades David to mix a seemingly deadly potion to be used on the wedding day, but the potion is actually life-giving. The drama concludes on a frenzied note of love and reconciliation, and the ghosts haunting David's mind are liberated and disappear into nothingness.

Throughout *The Hamlet of Stepney Green*, realism and fantasy interweave. The play, like much of Kops's work, is rooted in the East End of London (the equivalent of New York's Lower East Side)—its characters, noise, bustle, rhythms, and songs. Music is used to great effect by Kops, to re-create the East End ambience, to evoke nostalgia, and to provide a sad, ironic commentary on the action. During the mourning period at the end of the first scene of the second act, for example, Sam's family and friends gather around the home in the traditional Jewish way to remember him. David, in black, disrupts tradition by singing "My Yiddisher Father" to the tune of Sophie Tucker's famous "My Yiddishe Mamma." The "shiva" rituals (for mourning the dead) are parodied by transforming the gender of popular song lyrics. Reviewers noted that the play was far too long, especially when it indulged in lyric fantasies concerning the past—a reflection of Kops's lack of discipline. Kops often forgets his plot, forgets the limitations of the stage, and even forgets the patience of an audience; Sam takes a long time to die. In spite of these defects, the play generates a tremendous sense of life and bustle, brilliantly rendering ordinary London Jewish existence with its hopes, fears, music, and tears.

Good-Bye World, performed in Guildford Surrey in 1959, has long, rambling dream sequences which make it theatrically unsatisfactory. Kops enjoys conveying the details of low-life London. His setting is a Paddington boardinghouse, and the protagonist is a thuggish, obsessive dreamer, a hardened criminal of twenty-two who breaks out of prison because his mother has committed suicide. The play contains three of Kops's basic dramatic ingredients: London rhythms and atmosphere, dreams and fantasies, and mothers and their influence upon their sons. The protagonist, John, has two objectives: to find out if his mother left him a message, and to give her a decent burial. In his room, the characters who knew his mother—a landlady, a drunken Irishman, and a blind circus clown—come and talk to him. While John listens, the police wait outside to recapture him. The long personal monologues of each character reveal Kops's fascination with the poetry of the inner mind, his handling of dream logic, his sudden switches of mood and tone, and his exploration of schizophrenia. These dramatic elements achieve their summit in his mature drama, *Ezra*.

Kops's next play, *Change for the Angel*, which had a limited run at the Arts Theatre in London in March, 1960, develops many of the ideas introduced in *The Hamlet of Stepney Green* and *Good-Bye World*. Paul Jones is a teenager in search of a meaningful life; his sister, Helen, is a machinist; and his brother, Martin, is the leader of a local gang of Fascist youths. Paul's father, Joe, is a baker whose business has been adversely affected by a supermarket. He takes to drinking in the pub to escape from work and the family. Paul wants to be a writer and resists his father's efforts to turn him into an engineer. By the end of the first act, Paul is praying for his father's death, and Helen has been seduced by an American serviceman.

The second act introduces the first of a long line of Kopsian characters, just released from mental institutions, who have to face a hostile world. In this instance, the former mental patient is the victim of Joe's attempted rape.

In the third act, Paul hates his father so much that he invokes the Angel of Death, who takes the wrong life—his mother's instead of his father's. The audience is treated to a very lengthy deathbed scene and to frenetic, hysterical reactions. Paul leaves home and, in a manner reminiscent of the ending of D. H. Lawrence's *Sons and Lovers*, goes into a hostile world after his beloved mother, rather than the detested father, dies.

The name of the family in *Change for the Angel* may be Jenkins, but the cadences are those of East End Jewish family life. The play contains Kops's recurrent ingredients, but there is also an overt political conviction not so evident in his earlier plays. The threat of nuclear disaster dominates the play, as does the continual fear of anti-Semitism.

Oedipal elements, the bomb, and lyric fantasy are the essential ingredients of *The Dream of Peter Mann*, which suffered the insult, on its Edinburgh Festival premiere early in September, 1960, of having half the first-night audience walk out. The play proved to be too expensive to perform satisfactorily and too much goes on in it; nevertheless, it remains one of Kops's most interesting works. The author reflected in a personal communication that he "wanted to write a play about a man who was up with progress but got mixed up in power and in so doing helped to create the destruction of the world." The protagonist, Peter Mann, dominated by his strong Jewish mother, has grown up in a London street of run-down small shops. A small, cunning tramp named Alex persuades Peter to travel the world to make his fortune. After he robs his mother's safe, Peter's fantasies take over most of the remainder of the play. The people in the street become robots compulsively digging for uranium, then change into savages prepared to lynch Peter on his return from his travels, into slaves working twenty-four hours a day preparing shrouds for the next war, into rebels, and finally back into themselves. During the action of the play, Peter is defeated, victorious, penniless, and enormously wealthy. Clearly, Peter Mann is Everyman, a leader and a victim, hopeful and despairing, generous and selfish, shrewd and simple. The fantasy is an enlargement of reality, another dimension of the everyday. Kops keeps the play in control by grounding its frenetic fantasy in the sounds of London Jewish life, conveyed through colloquial dialogue, Cockney backchat, dance-hall rhythms, catchy songs, and contemporary political references.

Superficially, *Enter Solly Gold* may appear to be different from Kops's earlier working-class-oriented plays; nevertheless, it has much in common with them. It won a competition organized by Centre 42, an early 1960's movement designed to bring the theater to people outside London and to factory districts where little if any theater had been performed. The hero of the drama is a carpetbagger, Solly Gold, who informs the audience within the first few minutes that "work is all right for workers . . . but for Solly Gold?" Solly is scavenging in London's East End, trying to get enough money to emigrate to America, his "spiritual home," where he believes "dog eats dog" and ". . . that's the way [he] like[s] it."

The opening scene is Rabelaisian. Solly fiddles money out of a tailor, carries on with the tailor's wife, sleeps with a hard-bitten prostitute, and dons the clothes of a widow's deceased husband, a rabbi, in order to cheat her out of a bunch of large chickens.

In the second scene, Solly, still disguised as a rabbi, has gate-crashed a wealthy home where a wedding is taking place. Solly announces the start of "Rabbinical Chicken Sunday" and gradually takes over the household, making himself indispensable to Morry Swartz, head of the house and king of a shoe business, a melancholy millionaire. Solly sets about making Morry the Messiah so that Morry will find the peace of mind he lacks and Solly will get the cash he needs.

In the course of the drama, Kops lashes out at Bar Mitzvahs, weddings, and big business, writing some of his most sustained and brilliant comic lines. Many of these reflect the love-hate attitude he has toward his own Anglo-Jewish background. The play's warm reception in non-Jewish communities is evidence, however, of its universality: Carpetbaggers exist everywhere, and Kops's depiction of greed and hypocrisy speaks to audiences of all kinds, as does his blend of slapstick comedy and exuberant verbal wit.

David, It Is Getting Dark, produced and performed in France in 1970 by the distinguished French actor Laurent Terzieff, depicts the conflict between a right-wing English writer and a Socialist English Jewish writer. In this play, Kops tackles an issue which has continued to absorb him: how to reconcile great writing with inhuman political theories. The play also examines the relationship between victim and victor. While *David, It Is Getting Dark* can be viewed as a trial run for *Ezra*, it is a valuable work in its own right. Success and failure, the need to love and be loved, loneliness and the need to communicate, Jewishness and anti-Semitism, the need for God, the way human beings use and are used in turn by one another, sterility, and creativity, the dark forces within the self transcending political conviction—all these themes swirl together in the play. The long final scene, which depicts David, the Jewish poet, returning to his room and dancing with his mistress, Bella, while Edward, the reactionary artist, pleads with him to look at his manuscript, is made unforgettable by Kops's powerful, haunting, and evocative poetry.

David, It Is Getting Dark is intensely autobiographical: David's sense of failure is Kops's. There is superb irony in the fact that nearly a decade after its composition, Kops decided to restore Ezra Pound to life. A seemingly failed English Jewish writer uses a great anti-Semitic writer's last, sad years to show how human that writer was and, in the process, achieves fame for himself. In *David, It Is Getting Dark*, Edward Nichols appropriates David's autobiography; Kops transforms Pound's last years in *Ezra*.

Ezra explores the relationship between insanity, political extremism, and poetic power. Kops has long been obsessed with the question of how great poetry can be written by a man holding vicious political opinions and insidious economic ideas. At the same time, *Ezra* continues his exploration of extreme mental states. Kops gets inside Pound's mind by creating a world in which all things coexist at the same time: the past and the present, the living and the dead, fact and fantasy, truth and illusion. Once again, Kops's drama inhabits the territory of fantastic juxtapositions. Benito Mussolini and Antonio Vivaldi are as real for Pound as his wife, his mistress, and the officials who put him into a cage and then into a Washington, D.C., asylum. Kops's Pound is sensitive, learned, egotistical, and eccentric. Onstage he is exhibited as a gorilla in a large cage, all the while producing poetry for his seminal work, *The Cantos*. Kops intertwines snatches of poetry, dialogue, ranting, animal sounds, contemporary popular songs, and fragments of great lyric insight. The effect is profoundly moving—the summit of Kops's theatrical achievement. Using stream-of-consciousness techniques, Kops enters Pound's mind, developing surreal scenic juxtapositions to structure the text and convey the howling sounds of genius at bay. *Ezra* encapsulates all of Kops's recurring themes and techniques: his social and political awareness, his obsession with down-and-outs, with the antisocial and the insane, with the victim-predator relationship, and with the family. Pound is caught in a love-hate relationship with his wife, his mistress, his country—and himself. Theatrically, the power of the play lies in the visual presentation of entrapment. Kops uses a wooden set with protruding nails. The prison and the cage are projections of the entangled web of Pound's mind. Ian McDiarmid played Pound in the London performance. His long white hair hung from his head like that of an Old Testament prophet. Accompanied by the music of Antonio Vivaldi and Richard Wagner in the background, McDiarmid switched in mood from King Lear to his Fool in less than a second.

Simon at Midnight, which was produced as a BBC radio play before being staged in 1985, recalls the playwright's childhood in a Jewish section of London. Kops described the play as being about "political and emotional bankruptcy."

Kops is a supreme dramatist of frenetic states. The distinguished English theater critic Irving Wardle, in a 1980 review in *The Times* (London), wrote that "no other living playwright matches" Kops "in the virtuoso handling of dream logic." Kops has progressed from the often undisciplined rendering of Oedipal fantasies and dreamy young poetic rebels and confidence tricksters to the exploration of the subconscious mind, where reality and illusion intertwine and provide the vehicle for richly resonant dramatic poetry. Kops is a writer aware of the drama inherent in the sudden shifts in perception and changes of mood he has always found so natural. In *Ezra*, the London working-class Jewish poet has found his métier: *Ezra* places Kops in stature and achievement with the best dramatists of his generation.

Other major works

NOVELS: *Awake for Mourning*, 1958; *Motorbike*, 1962; *Yes from No-Man's Land*, 1965; *The Dissent of Dominick Shapiro*, 1966; *By the Waters of Whitechapel*, 1969; *The Passionate Past of Gloria Gaye*, 1971; *Settle Down Simon Katz*, 1973; *Partners*, 1975; *On Margate Sands*, 1978.

POETRY: *Poems*, 1955; *Poems and Songs*, 1958; *An Anemone for Antigone*, 1959; *Erica, I Want to Read You Something*, 1967; *For the Record*, 1971; *Barricades in West Hampstead*, 1988.

NONFICTION: *The World Is a Wedding*, 1963; *Neither Your Honey Nor Your Sting: An Offbeat History of the Jews*, 1985.

TELEPLAYS: *I Want to Go Home*, 1963; *The Last Years of Brian Hooper*, 1967; *Alexander the Greatest*, 1971; *Moss*, 1975; *Rocky Marciano Is Dead*, 1976; *Night Kids*, 1983.

RADIO PLAYS: *Home Sweet Honeycomb*, 1962; *The Lemmings*, 1963; *The Dark Ages*, 1964; *Bournemouth Nights*, 1979; *Over the Rainbow*, 1980; *Trotsky Was My Father*, 1984.

Bibliography

Cohn, Ruby. *Modern Shakespeare Offshoots.* Princeton, N.J.: Princeton University Press, 1976. Kops wrote *The Hamlet of Stepney Green* in 1957, here discussed in the context of modern interpretations of the univeral Hamlet character in "the life of Jewish immigrants in London's East End—[Kops's] own background." Cohn sees Kops's work as essentially a melodrama in which "everyone else [but Hamlet] lives happily ever after."

Glanville, Brian. "The Anglo-Jewish Writer." *Encounter* 14 (January, 1960): 62-64. Glanville, in this overview of the Anglo-Jewish writer, refers to Kops as "a young playwright [who] has written plays in the . . . romantic genre." He discusses the scarcity of important Anglo-Jewish writers and their avoidance of Jewish life as a topic. Mentions Peter Shaffer's *Five Finger Exercise* (pr., pb. 1958) and several novelists as well.

Kops, Bernard. "The Modest Muse." Interview by Sue Limb. *Listener* 107 (April 29, 1982): 32. An interview with Kops on the occasion of the radio broadcast of *Simon at Midnight.* Kops's life "pours through" the play, in "the surges of emotion; the all-powerful mother still laying down the law long after her death. . . ." Kops views radio as "a close-up medium . . . intensely personal." He mentions his large family, his writer-in-residence post at Hounslow, and his commissions for television and film scripts. Includes a photograph of the playwright.

_____. "Oasis for Misfits." *New Statesman Society* 3 (June 1, 1990): 40-41. Kops remembers the SoHo life-style from the late 1940's to the mid-1950's, when he was living on Arts Council awards and finding his creative voice, "talking, taking drugs, women, reading *Finnegan's Wake* at 3 a.m." A good self-sketch.

Taylor, John Russell. *The Angry Theatre: New British Drama.* Rev. ed. New York: Hill & Wang, 1969. A fairly long description of Kops's start at the Oxford Playhouse and Centre 42, and his contribution to British theater, especially *The Hamlet of Stepney Green*, *The Dream of Peter Mann*, and *Enter Solly Gold.*

Wellwarth, George E. *The Theater of Protest and Paradox.* Rev. ed. New York: New York University Press, 1972. A chapter on Kops entitled "The Jew as 'Everyman'" deals with *The Hamlet of Stepney Green*, *The Dream of Peter Mann*, and *Enter Solly Gold*, all set in London but "modeled on the type of Jewish folk literature written by Sholom Aleichem or Isaac Babel." The first two plays, says Wellwarth, are "sophomoric philosophy," but *Enter Solly Gold* is "gay and witty," and thus will not be taken seriously by "English critics who are fostering the new movement."

William Baker
(Updated by *Thomas J. Taylor*)

THOMAS KYD

Born: London, England; November 6, 1558 (baptized)
Died: London, England; August, 1594

Principal drama

The Spanish Tragedy, pr. c. 1585-1589, pb. 1594(?); *Soliman and Perseda*, pr. c. 1588-1592, pb. 1599; *Cornelia*, pr. c. 1593, pb. 1594 (translation of Robert Garnier's *Cornélie*; also known as *Pompey the Great: His Fair Cornelia's Tragedy*, pb. 1595).

Other literary forms

Although Thomas Kyd was cited by Francis Meres for commendation not only for tragedy but also for poetry, no verse remains that can with certainty be ascribed to him. The translation of Torquato Tasso's *Il padre di famiglia* (pr. 1583), published in English in 1588 as *The Householder's Philosophy*, is the only nondramatic work now generally attributed to Kyd.

Achievements

Probably no one questions Kyd's historical importance in the development of Elizabethan English drama, and few who read *The Spanish Tragedy* doubt his power to move audiences even today. Though he has, inevitably, been damned for his failure to be William Shakespeare, modern critics and historians have generally regarded Kyd, along with Christopher Marlowe, as one of Shakespeare's most important forerunners. Kyd entered the theatrical world of Elizabethan London at a time when medieval popular drama had run its course and classical drama, though influencing such plays as Thomas Norton and Thomas Sackville's *Gorboduc* (pr. 1562), had not effected a reshaping of contemporary English drama. Kyd brought the traditions together in *The Spanish Tragedy*, probably the most famous play of the sixteenth century. He combined an intrigue plot worthy of the comic machinations of Plautus or Terence with the revenge motif and violence suggested by Seneca's closet dramas and presented it all with spectacular theatricality. He rescued blank verse from the boredom of discourse and used it to create the excitement of psychological realism. He exploited the possibilities of the theater by employing imaginative staging techniques. Although his reputation rests safely on *The Spanish Tragedy* alone, the fact that scholars have so easily believed through the years that Kyd may be responsible for a pre-Shakespearean version of *Hamlet* suggests the imaginative power most readers attribute to him.

Biography

What is known of Thomas Kyd is based on a very few public documents and a handful of allusions and references to him, most of them occurring after his death. Contemporary biographical accounts of Kyd, including this one, are indebted to Arthur Freeman's careful investigation of Kyd's life in *Thomas Kyd: Facts and Problems* (1967). Records show that Kyd was baptized in London on November 6, 1558. Though there is no documentary identification of his parentage, scholars generally believe that his father was Francis Kyd the scrivener. If one may judge by other scriveners (John Milton's father was a scrivener), Francis Kyd was educated and reasonably well-to-do. Records also show that Kyd was enrolled at the Merchant Taylors' School in October, 1565. There—like Edmund Spenser, who was an older pupil in the school when Kyd entered—Kyd came under the influence of the school's well-known headmaster, the Humanist Richard Mulcaster. The date of Kyd's leaving the Merchant Taylors' School is not recorded; indeed, nothing is known "for fact," Freeman says, about Kyd for the decade after he should have left school. Although some have conjectured that Kyd may have entered a university or traveled abroad, there is no evidence for either. The curriculum of the Merchant Taylors' School was sufficient to have taught him the Latin he used in *The Spanish Tragedy* and in the translations he made.

In a tantalizing allusion that most scholars have interpreted as a reference to Kyd, Thomas Nashe, in his preface to Robert Greene's *Menaphon* (1589), complains of someone who has left the trade of scrivener, to which he was born, and is busying himself with the "indevors of Art," apparently writing imitations of Senecan tragedy and dabbling in translations. Though much has been made of this passage, especially in an effort to link Kyd with an early version of *Hamlet* (also mentioned in the passage), the allusion, if it does in fact refer to Kyd, yields very little biographical information other than that Kyd was active in the theater by, and probably before, 1589. T. W. Baldwin has shown in "Thomas Kyd's Early Company Connections" (1927) that a reference by Thomas Dekker in a 1607 pamphlet to "industrious Kyd" and his associates at that time indicates clearly that Kyd was writing for the theater as early as 1585. It was probably during these years, 1583 to 1589, that he wrote *The Spanish Tragedy* as well as *Soliman and Perseda* and translated a dialogue by Tasso, *Il padre di famiglia*, as *The Householder's Philosophy*. If he was truly "industrious Kyd," as Dekker labeled him, and if he was of real concern to Nashe, it must be assumed that he wrote, or had a hand in, many other plays.

Kyd's career came to an inglorious end; he died, apparently abject and desolate, in 1594 after a period of imprisonment and a seemingly unsuccessful effort to stage a comeback. In a letter to Sir John Puckering, an important member of the Privy Council, Kyd recounts some of the circumstances surrounding his arrest, defends himself against the charges, and pleads for assistance in regaining the favor of his former patron. Since the letter was written shortly after Kyd's release from prison and refers to Marlowe as already dead, it was probably written in the summer of 1593. Kyd was arrested earlier that year under suspicion of having written some libelous attacks on foreign residents of London. A search of his quarters revealed even more incriminating papers, containing "vile hereticall Conceiptes." Kyd was jailed and tortured, although the papers were not written by him and belonged, he said, to Marlowe, having by mistake been mixed with some of his own when they were "wrytinge in one chambere twoe yeares synce."

After his release, Kyd apparently hoped to regain favor with his former lord; when he was not reinstated to that service, he wrote to Puckering asking for help. From the letter it is clear that Kyd had been for some years in the service of a patron, that he at one time had shared quarters— or at least had written in the same chamber—with Marlowe, that he had been arrested, imprisoned, and released, and that he found life after imprisonment difficult without assistance from his patron. A reference to "bitter times and privie broken passions" in the dedication to *Cornelia*, published early the next year, suggests that his suit was unsuccessful and that he had resumed his writing in an effort to regain favor. In only a few months, however, Thomas Kyd was dead. The parish register of St. Mary Colchurch, London, records his burial on August 15, 1594. The final public document relating to Kyd is a formal renunciation by Anna and Francis Kyd of the administration of their son's estate, a legal means of dissociating themselves not from their son but from his debts.

Analysis

Thomas Kyd is best known for a play not specifically attributed to him during his lifetime. Although the early editions of *The Spanish Tragedy* are anonymous, few readers have seriously disputed Kyd's authorship, since the play was first attributed to him by Thomas Heywood (in his *An Apology for Actors*) in 1612. Most readers of *Cornelia*, ascribed to Kyd in the original edition, and of *Soliman and Perseda*, presumed by most to be by Kyd, point to similarities which suggest common authorship with *The Spanish Tragedy*. The play has traditionally been dated between 1582 (when a work by Thomas Watson, which it seems to echo, was published) and 1592, the date the play was first entered in the Stationers' Register. Modern biographers do not agree when they attempt to narrow the limits, but the lack of any reference in the play to the famous English victory over the Spanish Armada and the suggestion in Ben Jonson's *Bartholomew Fair* (pr. 1614) that the play had been around for twenty-five or thirty years make the period from 1585 to 1589 more likely. Kyd's influence on the development of Elizabethan drama could be more surely assessed if the date of *The Spanish Tragedy* were certain, but, whether it or Marlowe's *Tamburlaine the Great* (pr. c. 1587) came first, *The Spanish Tragedy* holds a place of high importance in English dramatic history.

Critical assessment of *The Spanish Tragedy* has been made difficult by a perplexing textual problem. Scholars who have sorted out the extant texts from the 1590's are able to agree that the authoritative text is the unique copy of the undated octavo printed by Edward Allde for Edward White. What has baffled researchers, however, is the presence of about 320 lines of additions deriving from a quarto of 1602. Most editors, though they assume that the lines are by a later hand, include them nevertheless, set in a different typeface, within the text of the play, so that the additions have, in effect, become a part of most modern readers' experience of the play. It is possible, as Andrew S. Cairncross notes in his Regents edition of the play (1967), that the so-called additions were originally written by Kyd, later cut, and still later restored as "additions." Much scholarly effort has gone into trying to identify the author of the additions. *Henslowe's Diary* records payment in 1601 and 1602 to Ben Jonson for "adicyons" to "Jeronymo." If the reference is to *The Spanish Tragedy*, Jonson was employed to rework to some degree a play which he ridiculed in other places. Without further evidence, modern readers have no way of knowing who wrote the additions. It is probably safest to believe that they were not written by Kyd and to attempt to see the play whole without them, in spite of the fact that some of them, especially the "Painter Scene," are interesting both in their own right and as they are integrated into the play.

Coming at the outset of Elizabethan drama, *The Spanish Tragedy* is inevitably seen in historical perspective, but what is remarkable about the play is its own interest apart from historical considerations. Although it is clear that Kyd is doing some things either for the first time or quite crudely in comparison to later dramas, it is possible to understand how *The Spanish Tragedy* enthralled audiences in Kyd's day and to read it with pleasure even today.

The play opens with a long speech by the Ghost of Andrea, but if there is little that is dramatic in that technique, the vividly descriptive speech illustrates the theatricality that characterizes this play from start to finish. From "dreadful shades of ever-glooming night," Revenge and the Ghost of Andrea have come to witness the working out of vengeance for Andrea's death at the hand of Balthazar on the battlefield. They remain to "serve for Chorus in this tragedy" and return after each act to reestablish this infernal atmosphere and to comment on the progress—or the apparent lack of progress—toward the goal of revenge.

Kyd plants the seeds of a psychological conflict between Andrea's friend Horatio and Lorenzo, son of the Duke of Castile and brother of Horatio's beloved Bel-imperia, in scene 1, when Lorenzo claims credit for capturing Balthazar and when the King of Spain, Lorenzo's uncle, rewards him with the captive prince's horse and weapons. Because Horatio had bested Balthazar in single combat, he feels cheated of spoils and honor that should have been his. When he submits to the king's decision, a spectator might wonder how the conflict, here seemingly prepared for, is going to effect Andrea's revenge. In truth, the play shifts even more radically in the next act to reveal not Horatio but his father, Hieronimo, as the inheritor of his son's conflict and as the chief character in the developing tragedy. Though Kyd does not fully develop the psychological conflict he sets up here, it is characteristic of *The Spanish Tragedy* to get beneath the surface of events to that psychological level, and it is this tendency to get at the heart of human action that sets Kyd's work apart from the plays of the previous two decades which he might have chosen to follow as models.

The following scene has proved a problem for critics. The action shifts abruptly to the Portuguese court, where the nobleman Villuppo forges a tale about how his enemy Alexandro (another nobleman) shot Balthazar in the back and caused Portugal to lose the battle. Some readers believe that Kyd introduces essentially extraneous material in this second plot line. The similarity of the situations, however—each turning on a vicious man's deception of his ruler to the hurt of another—suggests that Kyd may have intended that the subplot amplify and comment on the main plot. If so, the Portuguese viceroy's decision to investigate before taking action against Villuppo may suggest to the audience that Hieronimo, who will soon have cause to act, must also be sure before he moves.

At this point, there is still no hint of how Andrea's revenge is to be effected. To make Horatio, and ultimately Hieronimo, the instrument of Andrea's revenge, Kyd must provide a greater reason for the involvement of Horatio with Bel-imperia. In the next scene, without very much regard for consistency in Bel-imperia's character, Kyd reveals that she has chosen Horatio not only as the agent of her revenge but also as her "second love." The action has come back to the subject announced by the Ghost and Revenge, but the real subject of the play has not yet been broached. Though spectators are reminded at the end of each act that Andrea's revenge is the true concern of the tragedy, the play takes a turn in the next act that puts Hieronimo at the center. As yet, this central figure has appeared in only a minor role. His next appearance is in scene 5, where—again with no suggestion of his later importance—he presents at court a dumb show depicting England's conquest of Portugal and Spain. Remarkably, this spectacle pleases both the Spanish king and the Portuguese ambassador (and doubtless appealed to the patriotism of Kyd's English audience as well). The first act ends with the Ghost of Andrea complaining bitterly about this "league, love, and banqueting" between the Spanish and the Portuguese. He wants vengeance. Revenge promises to turn it all sour in due time. Essentially that is what happens: It all turns sour, and Andrea is revenged after a fashion, but Andrea is never the focus of the play. In the second act, Hieronimo assumes that position.

A new cry of revenge is heard as act 2 begins. Upon learning that Bel-imperia loves Horatio, Balthazar vows to take revenge against this man who first took his body captive and now would "captivate" his soul. He is encouraged by Lorenzo, who—without an apparent motive for his evil deeds—manipulates much of the action in the second act. Kyd's early development of a character reflecting the popular notion of a Machiavellian villain suggests once again his importance as a forerunner of the creator of Iago. As manipulator of the action, Lorenzo arranges for Balthazar to spy on Horatio and Bel-imperia as they make an assignation to meet in her father's "pleasant bower." The staging of this scene reveals Kyd's skill in using several levels of the stage at once. Balthazar and Lorenzo observe the conversation between Horatio and Bel-imperia from "above," while the Ghost of Andrea and Revenge, from their vantage point, watch the couple being watched.

When in the third scene a state marriage is arranged for Balthazar and Bel-imperia (the Spanish king's niece), it seems certain that the direction of the play is fixed: Bel-imperia has succeeded in involving Horatio so intimately in her life that this announced marriage will be the spark that triggers Horatio's anger toward Balthazar, and Andrea, through that anger, will be revenged. The play, however, here moves structurally, as a Roman comedy might, and introduces a significant bit of action that will provide a basis for the intrigue worked out in the double-length third act. When Horatio and Bel-imperia meet and wage a poetic "war" of love, they are surprised by Lorenzo, Balthazar, and his servant Serberine. Horatio is hanged and stabbed, and Bel-imperia is taken away as their captive. Hieronimo hears Bel-imperia's cry and finds Horatio's body; the play now becomes the story of Hieronimo's revenge. In what surely must have been both visually and aurally a spectacular moment, Hieronimo, in fourteen lines of Latin and with a dramatic sword-to-breast gesture, vows revenge. Modern critics, following Alfred Harbage's observation in his essay "Intrigue in Elizabethan Tragedy" (1962), recognize the significance of Kyd's innovation in this development of tragic materials with comic methods and within a comic structure.

It is not surprising that the Ghost of Andrea renews his complaint that events are not moving very directly toward his revenge: His friend, not his enemy, has been slain. Telling him that he must not expect harvest "when the corn is green" and promising to please him, Revenge allows act 3 to begin. The sudden reappearance, after seven scenes, of the matter of Alexandro and Villuppo is doubtless the reason some critics regard this "subplot" as an intrusion. Others, calling attention to the parallel between the Portuguese viceroy and Hieronimo, see this scene as a warning to

Hieronimo not to be too hasty in reacting to his son's murder. The intrigue plot that feeds Hieronimo's delay is set in motion when a letter written in blood (the stage direction specifies "red ink") falls into Hieronimo's hands. It is a message from Bel-imperia revealing that Lorenzo and Balthazar are Horatio's murderers. Lorenzo suspects that Serberine has talked. One intrigue leads to another: He hires Pedringano to kill Serberine and then sets up a time for them to meet when the watch, whom he has alerted, will be able to catch Pedringano in the act of murder. Serberine will be murdered, Pedringano will be executed, and Lorenzo will be rid of them both. When, after Pedringano is arrested, he sends to Lorenzo for help, the action—in keeping with the structure—becomes darkly comic. Lorenzo plays a cruel joke on Pedringano; he sends him word that he will save him and then sends a page to him bearing a box that supposedly contains a pardon. Despite instructions to the contrary, the page opens the box and sees that it is empty, but he decides to go along with the deception. The comedy with the cloud of death louring over it continues as Pedringano, certain that he will be saved, confesses recklessly in Hieronimo's court of justice and jests with the hangman even as he is turned off the scaffold.

With this third death onstage, spectators may begin to suspect that Kyd is exploiting in action the horrors only reported in Seneca. Neither the horror nor the comedy of the situation can obscure the painful irony of Hieronimo's position as minister of justice, himself crying out for justice. This theme, introduced near the midpoint of the long third act, grows to major significance in the second half. When in scene 7 the hangman brings to Hieronimo Pedringano's letter, written to reveal all in death if Lorenzo has failed to deliver him, Hieronimo has the evidence he needs to confirm Bel-imperia's identification of Horatio's murderers. Still able to believe that justice exists, he resolves to "go plain me to my lord the king,/ And cry aloud for justice, through the court...."

This theme of justice, placed for development in close juxtaposition to the darkly comic, promises to shift the play from a mere revenge intrigue to an exploration of a genuinely tragic experience. Not all critics agree that Kyd is successful in bringing the play from mere sensational display of horror and intrigue into the realm of tragedy, but most readers will agree that the play takes on that potential at this point. The revenge theme that has informed the play up to this point will inevitably clash with the theme of justice. Hieronimo will cry out for both. Critics lament that Kyd's control of this conflict is uncertain. It is not clear exactly what Kyd intends when he has a minister of justice desert his own quest for justice and resort to private revenge, as Hieronimo does in the final act. Perhaps Kyd—among the first to attempt to reconcile this pagan theme of revenge, which he and his contemporaries found so attractive in Seneca, with the Christian conscience of his audience—was not careful enough with the consistent development of his central character. Modern readers, at least, are left unsure of his intent. Perhaps Kyd was also.

The remainder of this long third act is given over to two things: taking care of plot necessities in order to set up Hieronimo's revenge in act 4 and exhibiting Hieronimo in various states of calm or distraction, always searching for justice. The plans for the marriage of Balthazar and Bel-imperia proceed; the Portuguese viceroy arrives and announces that he intends to give his son Balthazar his crown upon Balthazar's marriage to Bel-imperia. It is this royal wedding which later provides the occasion, in act 4, for Hieronimo's revenge. Hieronimo, meanwhile, confronts the Spanish king and demands justice, but his wild manner of doing so makes it easy for Lorenzo to persuade the king that he is "helplessly distract." An entire scene is given to exhibiting Hieronimo distraught and to underscoring the reason: his failure to find justice in his own cause. The man who had been the best advocate in Spain is now so distracted by his own frustrated efforts to find justice for himself that he is incapable of doing his duty. In the final scene of act 3, Kyd—his eye always on the theatrical—has Lorenzo's father demand to know why the relationship between Lorenzo and Hieronimo is so strained. The Duke of Castile accepts his son's explanation and requires the two to embrace. Hieronimo, on the verge of executing his revenge, accedes, and the Ghost of Andrea labors the irony by his furious reaction to seeing "Hieronimo with Lorenzo ... joined in league." To calm Andrea down, Revenge shows him an ominous dumb show—another Kyd spectacular—revealing two bearing nuptial torches burning brightly, followed by a sable-clad Hymen, who puts them out.

In act 4, Hieronimo moves swiftly to act on his plan for revenge. He confides his plan to Bel-imperia and asks her to cooperate in whatever way he asks. When Hieronimo is asked for an entertainment for the court on the first night of the wedding feast, he agrees, provided the courtiers themselves consent to act in his tragedy of Soliman and Perseda. They agree also to the strange request that they speak their lines in different languages. Hieronimo promises to explain all in a final speech and "wondrous show" which he will have concealed behind the curtain. Before the entertainment can begin, Isabella cuts down the arbor in which Horatio was hanged and stabs herself. Her death, the fourth in this tragedy, is only the beginning. With all locked in the room and with the keys securely in Hieronimo's possession, the play begins. What seems to be a play within a play, which is itself being watched by two who have been an onstage audience throughout, turns out to be all too real for those who think they are acting. The Bashaw (Hieronimo) stabs Erasto (Lorenzo); Perseda (Bel-imperia) stabs Soliman (Balthazar) and herself. Hieronimo reveals the "wondrous show" behind the curtain (his dead son) and explains his "play" as revenge for Horatio. He then runs off to hang himself but is stopped.

Though it is not perfectly clear what more they want to know, the king and Castile try to force Hieronimo to give further explanation. Kyd's taste for the spectacular is not yet satiated: Hieronimo bites out his tongue rather than talk. Then, calling for a knife to mend his pen in order to write an answer, he stabs Castile and finally himself.

A dead march ends the action except for the chorus. Finally, the Ghost of Andrea is happy, though his own death is avenged only in the fact that Balthazar has died in Hieronimo's revenge for Horatio. The final chorus, like all the others, recalls the ostensible subject of the play, but even more it points up the fact that Andrea's primary function has been to provide atmosphere. If spectators have come to accept him and Revenge as a touch of atmosphere, they are not shocked to hear him say that "these were spectacles to please my soul." To be pleased by these "spectacles," which include the death of his lover, his best friend, and his friend's father and mother, is certainly to go beyond his function as a real character. As a bit of spectacle, however, and as a means of providing both atmosphere and obvious structural links for the various revenges in the play, the chorus serves well.

The ambiguity of Hieronimo's portrayal precludes the possibility of a confident assessment of the meaning of the play. A more certain hand might have drawn Hieronimo clearly as one who tragically fails to wait for God's justice and destroys himself in the process or, alternatively, as one who seeks diligently and finds the world void of justice and in despair seeks his own redress. Hieronimo is probably best understood as a person destroyed by the tragic dilemma of being a minister of justice who is forced—or feels that he is forced—to take justice into his own hands. On reflection, this looks very much like private revenge, but there is little doubt that even Kyd's first audience, constantly reminded from the pulpit that God claims vengeance for his own, would fail to make allowances for a man so sorely abused and so faithful in his own administration of justice to others. The tragedy is that he destroys himself and his own faith in justice in the process.

Kyd's other works are of lesser interest. The only play ascribed to Kyd in the first edition is *Cornelia*, his translation of Robert Garnier's *Cornélie* (pb. 1574), which had appeared in a collected edition of Garnier's works in 1585. Kyd was trying to recover from the disgrace of imprisonment by offering to a potential patron this translation, done under the influence of an earlier translation by the Countess of Pembroke (*Antonius*, 1592) of Garnier's *Marc Antoine* (pr. 1578). He excuses the flaws in his translation by reference to "those bitter times and privie broken passions that I endured in the writing of it." To read *Cornelia* after reading *The Spanish Tragedy* is to understand the originality of the latter. One coming to *Cornelia* from *The Spanish Tragedy* would be surprised to find a play filled with talk rather than action—talk voiced in rather uninspired blank verse. *Cornelia* preserves Garnier's brand of French Senecanism in its quiet, reflective, and very long speeches. Act 1, for example, consists of one long speech by Cicero, lamenting Rome's war-torn state, followed by further lamentation and reflection by the chorus. In act 2, Cornelia debates with Cicero whether she should take her own life; having lost two husbands, she believes that she is a plague on any who love her. Much of the middle part of the play is about Caesar's tyranny; the focus returns to Cornelia in act 5 when a messenger, in a speech of nearly three hundred lines, provides a detailed account of the defeat of her father, Scipio, and his decision to take his own life rather than submit to captivity. Lamenting, Cornelia, who has longed for death throughout the play, wonders if the time has now come for her to die. She decides against suicide, however, because no one would be left to provide proper burial and tombs for Scipio and her husband, Pompey. The play ends with her quiet resolve to live. For all of its quiet manner, however, *Cornelia* was, as Freeman notes, Kyd's "most celebrated work for nearly two centuries."

Soliman and Perseda, published anonymously in 1599 by the same publisher who issued *The Spanish Tragedy*, is ascribed to Kyd by most literary historians because of the plot relationship to Hieronimo's final "entertainment" in *The Spanish Tragedy* as well as other parallels, echoes, and stylistic considerations. If it is indeed Kyd's, he probably wrote it during the same period when he was writing *The Spanish Tragedy* and Marlowe was writing *Tamburlaine the Great*, another play of death and destruction set in the Near East. Critics have paid little attention to *Soliman and Perseda*, but Kyd's mingling of the comic and tragic, evident in *The Spanish Tragedy*, is given such full development here that *Soliman and Perseda* should surely be seen as a forerunner of a long line of Elizabethan plays which integrate the two modes. Freeman believes that Kyd may have been the first to effect a "true confrontation of comic and tragic themes within mixed scenes," a confrontation which goes beyond the mere mixing of tragic matter with unrelated buffoonery. Like *The Spanish Tragedy, Soliman and Perseda* employs a chorus to preside over a bloody story. Love, Fortune, and Death vie for position as chorus, each claiming a major role in causing the story. In the end, Death lists twelve dead, brutally murdered onstage, as evidence of his power. (At that, Death must have lost count, for the toll is even larger.) The play also offers the beautiful love of Erastus and Perseda, the comic pursuit of Perseda by the boastful but cowardly Basilisco, and the murderous obsession of Soliman for Perseda—a desire so strong that he is persuaded to kill Erastus, whom he loves and admires, for her. In the final scene, Soliman kills Perseda herself. Having disguised herself as a man and vowed to defend Rhodes against Soliman's attack, Perseda challenges Soliman to single combat, promising to yield

Perseda to him if he wins the duel. When she is mortally wounded, she reveals herself, and Soliman asks for a kiss before she dies. Perseda, having earlier poisoned her lips, grants his request, and Soliman dies giving orders that his soldiers take Rhodes ("Spoil all, kill all. . . .") but that he and Perseda be buried with his friend and her husband, Erastus.

Of several other plays that have been attributed to Kyd, the most difficult attribution to prove or refute is that of the *Ur-Hamlet*. Assuming that Nashe was referring to Kyd as the "English Seneca" who would, "if you intreate him faire in a frostie morning, . . . affoord you whole *Hamlets,*" many scholars have concluded that there was some pre-Shakespearean dramatic version of *Hamlet* and that Kyd was probably the author of it. Kyd's obvious interest in the revenge theme has fed this suspicion. No such play is extant, however, and it seems fruitless to try to reconstruct the lost play—if one ever existed—unless further evidence comes to light. *The First Part of Jeronimo* (pb. 1605), though it has been advanced as a first part of *The Spanish Tragedy,* was probably not by Kyd but, like the *Spanish Comedy* (mentioned in *Henslowe's Diary*), a spin-off from Kyd's extremely popular play.

Whatever is said of Kyd's other works, *The Spanish Tragedy* is an enduring achievement. Kyd adapted to his own purposes the horrors, the theme of revenge, the trappings of ghosts and chorus, the long speeches, and the rhetoric of Senecan drama. He pointed the way to a new form merging the impulses of the popular drama with the structure and methods of classical drama—both tragedy and comedy. He demonstrated that what gives life to a play is not argument or idea so much as psychological reality—characters that develop naturally out of the action of the play. He brought together in one play, perhaps not with perfect success, a variety of styles ranging from the sententiousness of his Senecan models to the lyric love combat between Bel-imperia and Horatio and the anguished cries of a distraught father. The extravagance Kyd permitted himself in Hieronimo's raving ("O eyes! no eyes, but fountains fraught with tears. . . .") made the play a byword in Ben Jonson's day, but Kyd's sense of dramatic propriety helped rescue blank verse from monotony for use in genuine dramatic expression. Kyd's flair for the theatrical allowed him to pave the way for an exciting and meaningful use of the stage; later developments in stagecraft may have proved more subtle, but few have surpassed the power of the final scene of *The Spanish Tragedy.* If the play could be dated with exactness, *The Spanish Tragedy* might well prove to be historically the most important play written before Shakespeare's. Even without exact dating, however, the play makes Kyd, with Marlowe, one of the two most significant predecessors of Shakespeare. Whatever its historical importance, the play retains, even today, its own intrinsic power.

Other major works

TRANSLATION: *The Householder's Philosophy*, 1588 (of Torquato Tasso's *Il padre di famiglia*).

MISCELLANEOUS: *The Works of Thomas Kyd*, 1901 (Frederick S. Boas, editor).

Bibliography

Ardolino, Frank R. *Thomas Kyd's Mystery Play: Myth and Ritual in "The Spanish Tragedy."* New York: Peter Lang, 1985. Though somewhat specialized in focusing on a specific aspect of a particular play, this book places Kyd's best-known tragedy in the context of previous, not subsequent, plays, looking at allegorical and mystery-play elements in *The Spanish Tragedy.* Ardolino's scholarly language may be daunting, but the work is short (189 pages).

Boas, Frederick S. *The Works of Thomas Kyd.* Oxford, England: Clarendon Press, 1901. Though the commentary is dated, the general introduction to this still-standard edition of Kyd's works remains a valuable resource, and the introductions to individual plays are in some cases the best starting point. Explanatory notes provide valuable help to the reader unfamiliar with Kyd's works.

Edwards, Philip. *Thomas Kyd and Early Elizabethan Tragedy.* London: Longmans, Green, 1966. The brevity of this booklet makes it an ideal first source for students, for its scope is general enough. Edwards identifies imagery and idea patterns essentially classical and pagan and argues against overt Christian interpretation of Kyd's dramas. Includes an illustrated title page from a Kyd play.

Freeman, Arthur. *Thomas Kyd: Facts and Problems.* Oxford, England: Clarendon Press, 1967. As its title suggests, this book concerns itself mostly with the factual matters of dating, biography, and authorship, yet it contains some limited analysis of structure, style, and performance history of Kyd's plays. Though there are more problems than facts in determining what Kyd wrote, Freeman never presents scholarly guesses as fact.

Murray, Peter B. *Thomas Kyd.* Boston: Twayne, 1969. Of all the full-length works on Kyd, this volume is perhaps the easiest for the beginner to digest. Piecing together what little biographical information is available on Kyd, this study proceeds to an analysis of each of the dramatic works attributed to Kyd. Includes a well-annotated bibliography.

E. Bryan Gillespie
(Updated by *John R. Holmes*)

ARTHUR LAURENTS

Born: Brooklyn, New York; July 14, 1918

Principal drama

Home of the Brave, pr. 1945, pb. 1946; *The Bird Cage*, pr., pb. 1950; *The Time of the Cuckoo*, pr. 1952, pb. 1953; *A Clearing in the Woods*, pr., pb. 1957; *West Side Story*, pr. 1957, pb. 1958 (libretto; lyrics by Stephen Sondheim, music by Leonard Bernstein); *Gypsy*, pr. 1959, pb. 1960 (libretto; adaptation of Gypsy Rose Lee's autobiography; lyrics by Stephen Sondheim, music by Jule Styne); *Invitation to a March*, pr. 1960, pb. 1961; *Anyone Can Whistle*, pr. 1964, pb. 1965 (music by Stephen Sondheim); *Do I Hear a Waltz?*, pr. 1965, pb. 1966 (libretto; lyrics by Stephen Sondheim, music by Richard Rodgers); *Hallelujah, Baby!*, pr., pb. 1967 (libretto; lyrics and music by Styne, Betty Comden, and Adolph Green); *The Enclave*, pr. 1973, pb. 1974; *A Loss of Memory*, pr. 1981, pb. 1983; *Nick and Nora*, pr. 1991 (libretto; lyrics by Richard Maltby, Jr., music by Charles Strouse).

Other literary forms

Although primarily a playwright and author of librettos for several musicals, Arthur Laurents has also written for both radio and the movies. Shortly after his first Broadway success, he began writing screenplays as well, producing eight over the next thirty years: *The Snake Pit* (1948, with Frank Partos and Millen Brand), *Rope* (1948, with Hume Cronyn), *Caught* (1949), *Anna Lucasta* (1949, with Philip Yordan), *Anastasia* (1956), *Bonjour Tristesse* (1958), *The Way We Were* (1973), and *The Turning Point* (1977). Because of their wide popularity with moviegoers, Laurents wrote novelizations of both *The Way We Were* and *The Turning Point.* His foray into work for television came in 1967, with the script for *The Light Fantastic: How to Tell Your Past, Present, and Future Through Social Dancing.*

Achievements

Among American dramatists of his generation, Laurents certainly stands out as one of the more versatile: He is the author of plays that have received New York productions, as well as of Broadway musicals, several radio plays and one-act plays, Hollywood screenplays, novels based on screenplays, and a teleplay. Other plays or musicals have been given minor productions—all this while Laurents himself has become involved in directing, both his own works and those of others, and even in coproducing a film. A few of his radio plays, including *Western Electric Communicade* (1944) and *The Face* (1945), have been selected for inclusion in collections of "best" one-act plays. His first Broadway success, *Home of the Brave,* won for him the Sidney Howard Memorial Award in 1946; this was followed in the next decade by three additional Broadway productions: *The Bird Cage*, *The Time of the Cuckoo*, and *A Clearing in the Woods*.

In the mid-1950's, Laurents began his collaboration with Stephen Sondheim, writing the librettos for a series of musicals—an association that would last a decade and result in two of the most important works in the genre, *West Side Story* and *Gypsy*. The libretto for the latter work is so strong that it could almost stand on its own, without the songs, as a serious play, making it both the culmination and the epitome of a long line of book musicals. Little wonder that Sondheim singled out Laurents as one of the best book writers in the musical theater, or that he collaborated with him on two further works, the original *Anyone Can Whistle* and the book, *Hallelujah, Baby!*, which won the Tony Award as Best Musical of 1967. Sandwiched in between the musicals with Sondheim was Laurents' last Broadway play *Invitation to a March*, although his full-length work *The Enclave* did receive an Off-Broadway production in 1973.

Ever since the late 1940's, Laurents has lent variety to his writing career by work in film, providing screenplays for a number of well-received movies, including *Anastasia*, *Bonjour Tristesse*, *The Way We Were*, and *The Turning Point*, the last of which he coproduced and which won the Writers Guild of America Award, the Golden Globe Award, and the National Board of Review Best Picture Award. The 1960's and 1970's saw Laurents extend his expertise to yet another area of theatrical activity when he began to direct a number of his own works, including the highly successful London and New York revival of *Gypsy* during the 1973-1974 season. He also directed the Broadway blockbuster *La Cage aux Folles*, which won the 1984 Tony Award for Best Musical.

Biography

The son of a lawyer (Irving) and a schoolteacher (Ada), Arthur Laurents was born in Brooklyn on July 14, 1918. A summer camp gave him his first theater experience when he was cast in a play, *The Crow's Nest*, for his ability to climb up a ship's mast and remember his lines at the same time. "Theatre is fantasy, and you can make it all come true," he remarked in a later interview, when asked of his love for theater. He was graduated from Erasmus Hall High School and continued his education at Cornell University, earning a B.A. degree in English in 1937. He wrote radio plays until World War II, when he enlisted in the U.S. Army and eventually worked in films that helped train the troops. *The Face*, a short radio play from that period, appeared in *The Best One-act Plays of 1945-1946*.

After a few partially successful plays (such as *Home of the Brave* in 1945) and failed dramatic efforts, Laurents found Hollywood and his flair for writing mysteries and thrillers, such as *Rope* and *The Snake Pit*. He tried Broadway once again with *The Bird Cage* in 1950, and in 1965 he collaborated on the more successful *Do I Hear a Waltz?* with Richard Rodgers and Sondheim. His play *A Clearing in the Woods* was praised by critics as "ambitious and original." Laurents visited the musical genre once more in 1957 and wrote the book for Sondheim's and Leonard Bernstein's *West Side Story*, finally experiencing all the joys of a full Broadway hit; the film version (1961) earned eleven Academy Awards. The next musical success, *Gypsy*, was a collaboration with Sondheim and Jule Styne. It has been revived several times, including in 1989, with Laurents directing and Tyne Daly in the role of Rose, a role that had been played by Ethel Merman in the original and by Angela Lansbury in the 1974 revival.

The 1970's saw Laurents' most successful film work: the screenplays for both *The Way We Were* (1973, with Barbra Streisand and Robert Redford) and *The Turning Point* (1977, with Anne Bancroft and Shirley MacLaine). In 1983, he directed *La Cage aux Folles*. Returning to writing Broadway musical theater after some years, Laurents pinned his hopes on *Nick and Nora* (a musical version of the novel and film series *The Thin Man*), which opened in December of 1991, and which he directed. *Nick and Nora* closed after one week to depressingly negative but apparently well-aimed reviews.

Analysis

If Arthur Laurents can be said to belong to any group of post-World War II American dramatists, his closest affinity is surely with those who might be called psychological realists and who came into maturity in the late 1940's and early 1950's, especially William Inge and Robert Anderson. Like them, Laurents is primarily a playwright who focuses upon character. He often, though not always, portrays women caught up in the age of anxiety, beset by self-doubt or even self-loathing. Yet unlike either Inge or Anderson, Laurents reveals a solid measure of Thornton Wilder's influence, both in the generally optimistic philosophy as well as in the nonrealistic stylistic techniques of some of his later plays and musical books. Although he has, like Anderson, decried those playwrights, particularly of the late 1960's and 1970's, who value experiments in form and style over content, who make the manner rather than the matter count most, Laurents will depart from strict realism and from a linear method of dramatizing his story when a legitimate reason exists for doing so, as he does in his use of narrators in *Invitation to a March* and *Anyone Can Whistle*, in his use of characters to change sets in *The Enclave*, and in his use of variations on the flashback technique in *Home of the Brave* and *A Clearing in the Woods*. As he says in the preface to *A Clearing in the Woods*, he willingly embraces greater theatricality if it brings with it a greater ability to illuminate the truth.

In that same preface, Laurents provides perhaps his clearest statement of the central insight into the human condition that pervades all of his writing for the theater: If men and women are lonely, and they are, it is because they cannot accept themselves for the flawed, imperfect creatures that they are; and until they achieve such self-acceptance, they will be unable to feel sufficiently, or to give of themselves sufficiently, to experience a sense of completion and fulfillment. When Laurents' characters are unhappy in this way, when they are hurting within themselves, they lash out and, attempting to deflect their own misery, hurt others. The pattern is as applicable to Peter Coen (*Home of the Brave*), Leona Samish (*Time of the Cuckoo*), and Virginia (*Clearing in the Woods*) as it is to Wally Williams (*The Bird Cage*), Mama Rose (*Gypsy*), or Ben (*The Enclave*). Wally, for example, is a sexually disturbed egomaniac who destroys others and eventually himself, while Ben has been hurting for so long from having to keep his homosexuality hidden that he finally decides to hurt his friends back by shocking them into recognition, if not acceptance, of his lover Wyman. Rose is the archetypal stage mother, seeking in her daughter's accomplishments a substitute for the success she never had. (The influence of parents in Laurents' work, it should be noted, is not invariably restrictive; for every Rose who uses a child to gain something for herself, there is a Camilla Jablonski—*Invitation to a March*—who, by example and urging, liberates the child.)

The diminished sense of self-worth exemplified by so many of Laurents' characters has an individual psychological basis, but it can also be greatly exacerbated by social forces, such as prejudicial attitudes and the drive to conform. The prejudice may be racial, as in *Home of the Brave*, *West Side Story*, and *Hallelujah, Baby!*, or sexual, as in *The Enclave*, while the conformity may be either in the area of perpetuating the success syndrome through seeking a comfortable economic status, as in *A Clearing in the Woods* and *Invitation to a March*, or in the inability to break free of repressive sexual mores and conventions, as in *The Time of the Cuckoo* and *Invitation to a March*. Finally, Laurents' characters are often plagued by an impossible dream, by a desire to find magic in their lives. Sometimes the magic is short-lived, as it is for Leona in *The Time of the Cuckoo* or for the young lovers in *West Side Story*; at other times, it endures, as it does for Camilla, Norma, and Aaron in *Invitation to a March* or for Fay Apple in *Anyone Can Whistle*. Indeed, characters such as Camilla and Fay (complicated women who need and, luckily, find heroes) come closest to embodying Laurents' ideal of being free and wholly alive, of enjoying each and every moment, an ideal that he seems to have inherited from Wilder. If Laurents' upbeat endings sometimes seem slightly forced, and if his sentiment once in a while veers over into sentimentality, he remains an intelligent, sensitive, and thoroughly professional man of the theater.

A taut drama about prejudice during World War II, Arthur Laurents' *Home of the Brave* dramatizes how the experience of being condemned as an outsider, being made to feel different from others, affects the victim. Although not as theatrically elaborate as Peter Shaffer's *Equus* (pr. 1973) three decades later, *Home of the Brave* employs a surprisingly similar dramatic strategy: A doctor attempts to uncover the cause of a patient's symptoms by having the patient, under the influence of drugs, abreact, or therapeutically act out traumatic events from the past; what might appear to be flashbacks, then, are more accurately considered as deeply embedded memories now reenacted. Private first class Peter Coen (nicknamed "Coney") suffers from paralysis and amnesia brought on when, of necessity, he left behind his friend Finch during a dangerous reconnaissance mission on a Japanese island. For a long time, the sensitive Finch (he retches after having to kill an enemy soldier) had been one of the few to refrain from— and even physically defend Coney against—the anti-Semitic remarks rampant among the other soldiers. Especially guilty is Colonel T. J. Everitt, a former company vice-president who makes Coney the butt of his resentment over finding himself at war, not seeing any connection between his attitudes and those of the enemy.

Coney has been on the receiving end of such hatred ever since grade school, and Doctor Bitterger counsels that for his own good Coney must, to a degree, become desensitized to such unthinking prejudice. Under the pressure of their fatal wartime mission, Finch had hesitatingly called him a "lousy yellow . . . jerk," and Coney sensed then that Finch had caught himself just in time to prevent "Jew bastard" from slipping out. When Finch died and Coney's gut reaction was to be glad that it was not he who was killed, he felt shame and guilt, and he continues to imagine that there was some connection between the momentary hatred he experienced for Finch and his not staying behind and dying with him. Although Bitterger helps his patient understand intellectually that he acted in much the same way in which anyone else might have under the same circumstances, this realization does not sink into Coney's heart until another soldier, Mingo, recounts a similar experience.

Coney is not the only soldier whom Mingo tutors. Their commander, Major Robinson, though—like Mingo and Finch—essentially free of judging others in terms of racial distinctions, still experiences some difficulty in knowing how to command a group of men. Younger than some of the soldiers under him, Robinson attempts to compensate for lack of experience through an excess of enthusiasm, seeing war metaphorically as a game to be won. He cannot easily admit that his men might instinctively know more than he does—he fails, for example, to see T. J. for the bigot he is—nor does he fully understand that they deserve respect as men just as much as he does as an officer. Mingo, already overly sensitive to the fact that his poet-wife is better educated than he, has recently received a "Dear John" letter telling him she is leaving him for another man. When, as a result of the mission on which Finch was killed, Mingo loses an arm, he feels doubly afraid to return home, since as a cripple he will now be one of society's outsiders.

When Coney discovers that Mingo, too, despite his crippling injury, felt glad to be alive when he saw comrades die, he has a vision of his communion with all of humanity: Despite differences, all men are fundamentally the same. Two frightened individuals can now go home from the war brave enough to start life again. Together Coney and Mingo will open the bar that Coney had originally planned to run with Finch. The land they will return to is not yet free of the prejudice that wounds men like Coney and Mingo, and this helps keep Laurents' ending from being too saccharine. If the revelation that Coney receives seems perhaps too meager to effect much in the way of a permanent cure, Laurents' play is for that very reason both honest and understated.

Perhaps because of the perennially popular 1955 Katharine Hepburn movie *Summertime* that was adapted from it, *The Time of the Cuckoo* will probably remain the best remembered of Laurents' plays. This bittersweet romance concerns a clash of cultures, of life-styles, that occurs when Leona Samish, a thirtyish American spinster, has a brief affair in Venice with the somewhat older and attractively silver-haired Renato Di Rossi. As Leona remarks, Americans abroad carry with them "more than a suitcase": They bring a whole trunk load of attitudes and values, manners and mores. New World brashness confronts Old World charm; money—in the person of the boorish Lloyd McIlhenny on a hop-skip-and-a-jump tour with his wife—meets culture; and puritan guilt and repression come up against an instinctive lust for life. Partly under the tutelage of Signora Fioria, at whose pensione the action occurs, Leona can overcome her initial qualms and experience her night of love with Di Rossi, a devoted father enduring a now loveless marriage.

Signora Fioria and Di Rossi both serve as foils to the American tourist in matters of sexual morality. Di Rossi, regarding himself as a kind of spokesman for Mediterranean culture, believes that abstract notions of right and wrong simply do not exist; to live life fully and to make contact with others is the only good, and so he bemoans the tendency of Americans to always "feel bad" and wallow in sexual guilt. Signora Fioria, who had an affair while her husband was alive and is having another now, also deems as "impractical" any morality except discretion, urging others to live life as it is, being certain only to leave it a little "sweeter" than they found it by entering a giving relationship from which they do not necessarily get anything in return. The values of these two Italians gain added weight when Laurents shows the shortcomings of the traditional notions of sexual morality by which another American couple, the young, beautiful, blond Yaegers, live and love. Eddie Yaeger, an artist whose later work has never measured up to his first exhibit, suffers from painter's block; his wife June, earlier married to a musician, suffers from something even less tangible but equally destructive: the romantic ideal that a wife must be her husband's complete life. She attributes Eddie's infidelities with Signora Fioria to his temporary inability to create, and she reconciles with him—albeit in an uneasy truce—only after he comes around to her strict notion that love cannot be love without complete fidelity. Into this subplot, Laurents introduces as well a staple theme of the 1950's, lack of communication, through Eddie's comment that language is often a method of "excommunication" and June's observation that people without the ability to talk might feel less alone.

What finally prevents Leona and Di Rossi from achieving even a shaky truce is not so much their differing attitudes toward sexual morality and the need for love as a failure within Leona herself. A woman who prides herself on independence but who is increasingly hiding her insecurities behind drink, she underestimates her attractiveness to Di Rossi; if she at first acts insulted by his forwardness, she later thinks he must want her only for her money. What finally brings her around to Di Rossi is not, however, his and Signora Fioria's accusations that she actually insults herself by having so little self-esteem, but rather his gift of a garnet necklace, a gesture so overwhelming that she—together with the audience— hears a waltz. When it appears that he has made money off her by exchanging her dollars for counterfeit on the black market, however, she rejects him. Emotionally bruised herself, she must hurt others by telling June about Eddie and Signora Fioria. The "wonderful mystical magical miracle," the impossibly romantic ideal she had hoped to and did fleetingly meet in Italy, evaporates quickly, yet it leaves Leona with a new awareness of her limitations: her inability to love herself; her need for someone outside herself to confirm her value and self-worth by wanting her.

Her souvenirs of Venice—two wine-red eighteenth century goblets that she buys in Di Rossi's shop and the longed-for garnet necklace which he gives her—suggest by their color her long repressed passion. That she insists on keeping the necklace, that she must take something tangible home with her, indicates her insecurity, her need for things as a proof of feelings. Leona has not yet outgrown her inability to give of herself without getting something in return, and she finds it difficult to believe that others can either: When the street urchin Mauro, who has been trying to swindle her all along, offers a souvenir for free, she still instinctively wonders why, rather than simply saying thank you. It is not clear whether she will return to America any the wiser, but at least she stays in Venice to complete her vacation rather than fleeing further experiences that might test her conventional moral code.

A Clearing in the Woods concerns a woman who must confront the past in order to move into the future, thus continuing Laurents' exploration of the need for psychological wholeness. The most theatrically intricate—and, according to the playwright's own testimony, the most difficult yet satisfying of his plays to write—it does not lend itself to simple categorization. Laurents himself discounts all the formulas—flashback, dream, nightmare, hallucination, psychoanalysis, psychodrama—that might readily describe this play in which not only the woman Virginia but also her three former selves all appear onstage. Even stream of consciousness does not seem an accurate enough classification; perhaps nonrealistic fantasy, with a dose of Expressionism, comes closest. Each of Virginia's three earlier selves is seen mainly in the way she interacts with a man—father, teenage "lover," husband—in acted out fragments of her past experience.

Jigee, Virginia as a little girl of nine or ten, rebels against both the restraints and lack of attention of her father Barney; she feels, in fact, cut off from both her parents—distant from a mother too absorbed in her father, as well as jealous of her mother's hold over him. In a plea that he pay attention to her, she cuts off his necktie, wishing it were the tongue that had lashed out. Virginia's initiation into sexuality is seen through Nora, her seventeen-year-old self who goes off with a woodchopper, as, simultaneously in the present, Virginia enters the cottage for an abortive assignation with George, a suspect homespun philosopher who counsels enjoying the pleasures of today that lead to pleasant memories tomorrow while he advocates a belief in "Nothing," for then there can be no risk of disappointment and disillusionment. Virginia's lack of success in marriage is seen through twenty-six-year-old Ginna's relationship with Pete. The big man on campus, he had married her thinking she was pregnant; he never reaches his potential, and his life seems to have peaked at twenty. No longer sexually excited by her and believing not only that she has given up on him but also that she actually feels glad when he fails, Pete is temporarily impotent, effectively emasculated by Ginna.

Like Virginia now, neither Nora nor Ginna wanted to be ordinary; each wanted a life somehow special and set apart from that of ordinary people. This same desire stands in the way of Virginia's marrying Andy. Two years before the present time of the play, she called off their engagement on their wedding day, knowing that he would always be simply a competent researcher rather than a brilliant discoverer. Virginia now invites him to cross over the magic circle and enter the fantasy world of the clearing in the woods with her, hoping to erase that day as if it never happened, but, like Ginna with Pete, Virginia demands that Andy live up to her goals for him, and will be angry if he fails, while he is happier accepting and living within his limitations. Because Virginia has never been satisfied with herself, she has placed unhealthy, destructive expectations upon others. As Bitterger does for Coney in *Home of the Brave*, Andy acts as a kind of therapist for

Virginia, helping her see that she has never really loved anyone, even herself, and that she has consequently destroyed the men in her life. Yet as each of the men returns in the present, she discovers that her impact upon them has not been wholly negative: The boy in the woods, who actually thought Nora pretty and not ordinary, surreptitiously left a bouquet of flowers behind; Pete, now remarried, reveals that Ginna actually provided color and excitement in his rather ordinary existence; and Barney, now on the wagon, can be reconciled with his adult daughter by their mutual understanding that a parent sometimes needs more love than a resentful child is willing to offer. Virginia, by becoming content with herself as she is rather than seeking a false image that could never be, can finally accommodate her former selves rather than deny their existence. By accepting them for what they can teach her about herself, she can reach integration and move freely and with hope into the future.

Invitation to a March is a charming romantic comedy about people's need to march to no drummer at all, even to break out and dance. Deedee and Tucker Grogan have come East to the Long Island coast to see their son Schuyler married to Norma Brown. Deedee and Norma's mother, Lily, the widow of a General who starts each day with a flag ceremony complete with toy bugle, are conventional, status-happy women: Deedee has wealth, Lily, social position, and both are morally proper; yet their limited lives are dull, dreary, without adventure, and it annoys them even to think that others might have something more. The bride-to-be's one peculiarity is her propensity to fall asleep for no apparent reason; this odd habit is her quiet revolt against the conformity and complacency that surround her. She sleeps because life is not worth staying awake for—that is, until Aaron Jablonski, riding on a horse in the rose-colored light, arrives to fix the plumbing and wakes her with a kiss. If Schuyler's mother, Deedee, is literary cousin to Lloyd McIlhenny from *The Time of the Cuckoo*, Aaron's mother, Camilla, is drawn in the same mold as Signora Fioria and Renato Di Rossi.

Although many of the characters in *Invitation to a March* at times face front and unselfconsciously and ingratiatingly address the audience, taking them into their confidence and interpreting for them, Camilla is the chief of these narrators—and the playwright's mouthpiece. There is more than a little of the down-to-earth philosophizing of Wilder's Stage Manager about her, and more than a bit of Wilder's point of view within the play. A wacky individualist, a free spirit who treasures the adventures life offers, Camilla knows that one can deaden life by not living it the way one wants to; since time passes and one does not have many chances, one must take the opportunities that present themselves, as she did twenty years earlier during a summer romance with Aaron's father—who turns out to be Tucker Grogan and thus will be the father of the groom no matter what. Tucker had made Camilla feel attractive simply by wanting her, and for all these years the memory of that time, nurtured by imagination, has sustained her so that she has wanted no other man. She found her magic.

Norma's similarity to Camilla reveals itself in her penchant for tearing up calendar pages, an act symbolic of her desire to break free from the restrictions of a confined, regimented life. In the play's title passage, Camilla warns about all the marchers in the world who try to take away one's individuality, who want one to toe the line, to move in lockstep, as do those in the military. It is easier and safer to submit than to assert one's difference, but it is finally deadly dull to do so. Although Norma feels no guilt after her first night with Aaron, it takes some time before she can break free and dance by giving up the prospects of a secure and success-oriented life in suburbia with a lawyer-husband and replace that goal with her love for Aaron. Eventually, though, they do hear their waltz, and they do dance off.

Camilla makes no excuses for her conduct; what she did was right for her. If she has any guilt, it stems from her selfishness in letting Aaron love her so much that he finds it temporarily difficult to love another. Tucker is not perfect either; finding it awkward to communicate with other men, he has never made enough effort until now to reach out to Schuyler. Although Schuyler, so much the prisoner of conventionality that he cannot respond to feelings, finds the shoe Norma kicks off before she dances away, he is no Prince Charming—in fact, he confesses to not believing in princes anymore—and so he symbolically falls asleep, a victim of the march, while his fully awakened and alive beauty waltzes off with another.

Since Laurents has turned increasingly from writing to directing, it appears that his career as a dramatist is virtually complete and that his position among American dramatists is now open to some overall assessment. No one would claim that Laurents belongs among the indisputably first rank (with Eugene O'Neill and Tennessee Williams, for example). Still, he has produced, along with librettos for two of the best works of the musical theater—*West Side Story* and *Gypsy*—one or two memorable plays that readers will return to and little theaters will revive: *The Time of the Cuckoo* and *Invitation to a March*. The latter work, in fact, with its deft handling of tone and comfortable assimilation of Wilder's philosophical outlook and stage techniques to Laurents' own purpose, may finally be seen as his most significant play.

Because Laurents' major efforts are so varied in form and structure, he remains difficult to categorize. He resembles both Lillian Hellman and Arthur Miller in his hatred of prejudice and his compassion for those who must hide a facet of themselves, whether racial or sexual, to avoid rejection. In Laurents, however, it is not only, or even primarily, the other person or society which seeks to limit his characters' world; rather, the central characters themselves, through their psychological inhibitions and moral or sexual repression, circumscribe their own existence. Like several other playwrights from the decade immediately following World War II, Laurents has not always escaped criticism for his "group therapy session" or "pop psychologizing" plays, which have, admittedly, sometimes ended with victories too contrived or too easily won: Simply recognizing one's own frailties does not always assure a newfound freedom and integration and maturity. Laurents' accurate reading of modern human beings' injured psyches, awash in the anxiety and self-doubt that inevitably accompany any search for an ethical system running counter to traditional social and sexual mores, remains in somewhat uneasy balance with his innately positive view that the individual can win through to a sense of personal wholeness. Yet Laurents dramatizes this tension with such honesty and in such understated terms that Coney's and Leona's and Norma's victories seem to be the audience's own; the illusion complete, they, too, at least momentarily hear a waltz. Like his spokeswoman Camilla in *Invitation to a March*, Laurents at his best can be an adroit stage manager, gently pulling the strings that have always moved audiences in the theater.

Other major works

NOVELS: *The Way We Were*, 1972 (novelization of his screenplay); *The Turning Point*, 1977 (novelization of his screenplay).

SCREENPLAYS: *The Snake Pit*, 1948 (with Frank Partos and Millen Brand); *Rope*, 1948 (with Hume Cronyn); *Caught*, 1949; *Anna Lucasta*, 1949 (with Philip Yordan); *Anastasia*, 1956; *Bonjour Tristesse*, 1958; *The Way We Were*, 1973; *The Turning Point*, 1977.

TELEPLAY: *The Light Fantastic: How to Tell Your Past, Present, and Future Through Social Dancing*, 1967.

RADIO PLAYS: *Now Playing Tomorrow*, 1939; *Western Electric Communicade*, 1944; *The Face*, 1945; *The Last Day of the War*, 1945.

Bibliography

Barnes, Clive. "Bad Idea Kills *Nick and Nora.*" Review of *Nick and Nora. Post* (New York), December 9, 1991. According to Barnes, "a bad idea turned sour." He points at Laurents' multiple contribution as the main reason for the show's failure: "This is not a musical. It is a 'bookical'— a book with songs rather than a songbook." Unromantic in his criticism but kind to the actors.

Guernsey, Otis L., Jr., ed. "An Ad Lib for Four Playwrights." In *Playwrights, Lyricists, Composers on Theater*. New York: Dodd, Mead, 1974. A conversation among Laurents, Sidney "Paddy" Chayefsky, Israel Horovitz, and Leonard Melfi, in which Laurents proves the most insightful regarding playwright expectations of directors and actors in production.

Pacheco, Patrick. *"Nick and Nora*: Inside the Bunker." *Los Angeles Times*, December 8, 1991, p. E1. After another month's delay, the show is ready to open, and Pacheco reviews the controversy and problems that plagued the preparations. Mostly an interview with lead player Barry Bostwick, with insights into Laurents' approach to the libretto and his directing style: "It's Arthur Laurents' circus. He's the puppeteer and I'm just one of the puppets," Bostwick remarks.

Post (New York). *"Gypsy* Stripped of Spirit." Review of *Gypsy* (November 17, 1989). This revival of *Gypsy*, with Tyne Daly in the role of Gypsy Rose Lee, was the second (a 1974 revival starred Angela Lansbury, and the original 1959 production starred Ethel Merman). Laurents directed this version and is here credited, with some reservations, for its success.

Rousuck, J. Wynn. "Promoting *Nick and Nora." Baltimore Sun*, May 22, 1991. The planned out-of-town run at the Mechanic Theatre in September, some two months before the show's scheduled Broadway opening, occasioned this piece. It is a report of a half-hour talk by Charles Strouse and Richard Maltby, performing seven of the show's songs for three hundred "group sales leaders." (The show eventually skipped the Baltimore tryout in an economizing move.)

Thomas P. Adler
(Updated by *Thomas J. Taylor*)

RAY LAWLER

Born: Melbourne, Australia; May 23, 1921

Principal drama

Cradle of Thunder, pr. 1949; *Summer of the Seventeenth Doll*, pr. 1955, pb. 1957 (commonly known as *The Doll*); *The Piccadilly Bushman*, pr. 1959, pb. 1961; *The Unshaven Cheek*, pr. 1963; *The Man Who Shot the Albatross*, pr. 1971; *Kid Stakes*, pr. 1975, pb. 1978; *Other Times*, pr. 1976, pb. 1978; *The Doll Trilogy*, pr. 1977, pb. 1978 (includes *Kid Stakes*, *Other Times*, *Summer of the Seventeenth Doll*); *Godsend*, pr. 1982.

Other literary forms

Although Ray Lawler has written and adapted works for the British Broadcasting Corporation, he is known primarily for his playwriting.

Achievements

Lawler won first prize in a minor play competition in Melbourne, Australia, for his *Cradle of Thunder* and wrote nine plays before becoming internationally famous with *Summer of the Seventeenth Doll*. He shared first prize, worth about two hundred dollars, for *Summer of the Seventeenth Doll* in a competition sponsored by the Playwrights Advisory Board in 1955. *The Doll*, as it is known among Australian theater aficionados, was one of 130 plays submitted for judging. It shared first prize with a play by Oriel Gray, *The Torrents*, and served as Lawler's catapult to fame. With this play, he almost single-handedly revolutionized Australian theater, bringing it out of its previous lethargy.

Prior to the production of *Summer of the Seventeenth Doll*, there had been a feeling in Australia that the homegrown dramatic product was inferior to foreign drama. It was largely because of the unparalleled international success of *Summer of the Seventeenth Doll* that Australian theater enjoyed a spectacular period of growth throughout the late 1950's and during the next two decades. Today, Australian theater is produced throughout the English-speaking world, and even in non-English-speaking countries. With his play, which won the *Evening Standard* Award for Best Play in 1957, Lawler helped to stimulate Australians to a fuller appreciation of their own culture, not only in terms of theater but also in other fields of artistic endeavor, such as literature, music, and the plastic arts.

Biography

Raymond Evenor Lawler was one of eight children born to a tradesman in Melbourne, Australia. At the age of thirteen, Lawler started work in an engineering plant and took lessons in acting in his spare time. When he was twenty-three, he sold his first play, which was never produced, to J. C. Williamson's theatrical company, known in Australia simply as "the Firm." Lawler acted and wrote pantomimes and scripts for revues, and when he was in his mid-thirties, he became manager and director of the Union Theatre Repertory Company. While in that position, he worked on the script of his masterpiece, *Summer of the Seventeenth Doll*, in which he had written a part for himself, that of Barney.

Lawler appeared in the original Australian production and in both the London West End and New York Broadway productions, and his work as an actor received high praise. After the early closing of the Broadway production, he moved to Denmark; later, he returned to London, then moved to Ireland in 1966. These moves were indirectly prompted by the success of *Summer of the Seventeenth Doll*: Lawler could not return to Australia, nor could he live in London or New York, because of a tax situation resulting from productions of his play and the sale of film rights. He took up residence in Ireland after learning that he could obtain an income exemption granted to writers in that country. Lawler is of Irish descent and admires Irish writers. Lawler's wife, Jacqueline Kelleher, is an actress originally from Brisbane; they have twin sons, born in 1957, and a daughter, Kylie, born in 1959.

Lawler returned briefly to Australia in 1971, after a lengthy absence, to assist with the production of *The Man Who Shot the Albatross*, a play about Captain William Bligh's rule as Governor of New South Wales. He moved back to Australia in 1975, and in 1977 assisted with the production of *The Doll Trilogy*, comprising *Kid Stakes*, *Other Times*, and *Summer of the Seventeenth Doll*. *The Doll Trilogy* relates the history of the protagonists of *Summer of the Seventeenth Doll* in the sixteen years prior to the time frame of that play. Both *Kid Stakes* and *Other Times* were written in the 1970's, some twenty years after Lawler's success with *Summer of the Seventeenth Doll*.

Analysis

Summer of the Seventeenth Doll is by far Ray Lawler's most important work. His early plays have not been published, and his subsequent plays do not have the same verve, although two of them, *The Piccadilly Bushman* and *The Man Who Shot the Albatross*, have both received critical acclaim.

Summer of the Seventeenth Doll is a seminal play in the development of contemporary Australian drama. It was written at a time when Australia was emerging from the domination of Great Britain and the United States, although both countries have retained a strong influence on the Australian way of life. Australia was subjected to a veritable invasion of British immigrants after World War II. By the time the play was written, more than one million Britons had moved to Australia. British and American films dominated the Australian market, and the most popular stage productions were from the West End or Broadway, often with second-rate British or American actors in the main roles and Australians in the secondary roles.

This problem had been recognized in Australia since at least 1938, when a number of Australians joined together to start the Playwrights Advisory Board (PAB), with a view to promoting the work of indigenous playwrights. The PAB was to have a lasting effect on Australian theater. One of its aims was to circulate plays among Australian producers, thereby seeking outlets for the playwrights, and it was responsible, during its existence from 1938 to 1963, for nurturing a great number of Australian playwrights. One of its methods for encouraging Australian writers was to develop competitions for Australian works. It was in one of these competitions that Lawler won first prize in 1955.

While Lawler was writing *Summer of the Seventeenth Doll*, the Australian Elizabethan Theatre Trust—"the Trust," for short—was being formed. This organization was begun at the instigation of H. C. Coombs, Governor of the Commonwealth Bank of Australia. The Trust was to be formed as a private enterprise, with the support of the public in the form of subscriptions. As Coombs wrote in 1954, in the literary magazine *Meanjin*, "The ultimate aims must be to establish a native drama, opera and ballet which will give professional employment to Australian actors, singers and dancers and furnish opportunities for those such as writers, composers and artists whose creative work is related to the theatre." The Trust was to encourage such activities by offering financial support and guarantees to those producing Australian works. The initial appeal was for $200,000, and it was hoped that, once the Trust was established, the Australian federal government would lend its support to the cause of theater subsidies—which is precisely what happened. The federal government matched grants on a one-to-three basis, contributing one dollar for every three dollars raised by the Trust.

Both the PAB and the Trust played immensely important roles in Lawler's career. His sharing of first prize in the 1955 PAB-sponsored competition was a turning point for all involved. By 1954, the Trust had its own home, a former theater in the industrial Sydney suburb of Newtown, converted to a movie house and then restored to a theater. In January, 1955, it produced its first play, and then three more, not one of which was Australian. This was contrary to its founders' philosophy. On January 11, 1955, however, according to the official publication of the Australian Elizabethan Theatre Trust, *The First Year*, "a new page of theatrical history was written. . . . An Australian play by an Australian author, with an all-Australian cast, achieved at once a complete and resounding success." *Summer of the Seventeenth Doll* was the play, and with that success, Lawler's career was launched.

On November 28, 1955, Lawler's play opened at the Union Theatre at the University of Melbourne, where he was director. Although Lawler had felt somewhat diffident about having his play produced in the theater in which he was employed, fearing the production would lead to charges of favoritism, both the PAB and the executive director of the Trust prevailed on the vice-chancellor of the University of Melbourne to encourage the production.

The play opened to critical acclaim in Melbourne newspapers, as well as in other Australian and even British papers. It played for three weeks at the Union, earning for that theater the princely sum of $3,735.50, probably more money than the theater had hitherto made from any one play.

Once the play had gone through its tryout period as an experimental, university-produced play and had proved a success, the Trust was confronted with the problem of where to stage it in Sydney. The Trust owned the theater in Newtown, newly opened and renamed The Elizabethan. It was an immense barn of a theater, with some fifteen hundred seats, and it was almost solidly booked for its first year of operation. There was, however, a three-week gap in its bookings, starting in mid-January: This period falls right in the middle of Australian summer, and the theater had no air-conditioning. Lawler's play was booked for this slot and once again received universal praise; Lawler's pioneering work was compared to that of Eugene O'Neill in the United States and John Millington Synge in Ireland, establishing a first-rate national theater.

After it completed its three-week booking at the Elizabethan, *Summer of the Seventeenth Doll* was taken on tour throughout New South Wales by the Arts Council of Australia. Other touring companies were formed, and some amusing anecdotes relate to those tours. Australia has vast distances, and the play was touring the Northern Territory. One playgoer saw the production and thought that his wife should see it also. The following night, however, it had moved some six hundred miles, to the "neighboring" community. The man took his wife to that community for the production and then returned home—a trip of twelve hundred miles to see a play.

After eighteen months, negotiations were under way to present the play in London, where Sir Laurence Olivier, who had read the script, became involved. It opened on the West End in April, 1957, with most of its original Australian cast from The Elizabethan, after tryouts in Edinburgh, Nottingham, and Newcastle. Lawler made a curtain speech in which he said: "The first play was produced in Australia in 1789. It was a convict production—and, need I add, it had an all-English cast. It has taken 168 years for an Australian company to pay a return visit."

During its run at the New Theatre in London, the film rights for the play were sold to an American company. Lawler shared in the profits, together with the Trust, Olivier, and a Broadway management firm. Arrangements were also made for a Broadway production, and after seven months at the New Theatre, the play was moved to New York. On opening night, there were seven curtain calls, but the press reviews were largely negative, and the production closed after three and a half weeks. Nevertheless, *Summer of the Seventeenth Doll* did find American success: Ernest Borgnine played the part of Roo in the film adaptation, and the play was very popular with summer stock companies. It was also presented in translation in Germany and Finland and was even translated into Russian.

Summer of the Seventeenth Doll relates the story of two sugarcane cutters, Roo and Barney, who work seven months of the year in the Australian north and then have a five-month summer layoff in Melbourne, in the Australian south. Thus, they follow the sun. For the previous sixteen years, during their Melbourne sojourns, Roo and Barney have stayed in a boardinghouse, where they have taken up with Olive and Nancy, two barmaids whom they have known for the entire sixteen years. The play derives its title from Roo's habit of bringing Olive a Kewpie doll each time he arrives for the layoff. Olive has collected and kept all of these dolls as symbols of the good times the foursome have had during the sixteen previous years.

This summer, the seventeenth, Nancy is no longer at the boardinghouse. She has decided to marry, and Olive has tried to replace her with a fellow barmaid, Pearl. Unfortunately, Pearl does not have the same disposition as Nancy, and Barney and Pearl do not hit it off. Matters are further complicated by the fact that Roo and Barney are getting old. Roo had a disastrous season and left the cane cutting early, being supplanted as the chief of his gang (the "ganger" in Australian idiom) by a younger man, Johnny Dowd. For his part, Barney has always had the reputation of being a "lady's man," having sired a number of illegitimate children, yet halfway into the play, the audience discovers that he had a disappointing season with women up north. This discovery is reinforced by his singular lack of success with Pearl.

Because Roo left the cane fields early, he was forced to seek employment in Melbourne, where he found work in a nearby paint factory. This is a vital point, for it is a complete loss of face for Roo to have to work in the city during the layoff. Barney brings Johnny, the new ganger, to the house and they discover Roo asleep in his paint-spattered clothes after a hard day's work. Roo is humiliated into making peace with Johnny but cannot forgive Barney for the humiliation, and this eventually leads to a fight between the two old friends.

Olive, meanwhile, has realized that the layoff romance has come to an end. Her "eagle, flying out of the sun to mate," has feet of clay. Still, she resists this realization, and when Roo offers to marry her, she has a tantrum and rages against the inevitability of the situation.

Summer of the Seventeenth Doll is a play about ordinary people. It is very simple in its construction. Its language is plain, studded with everyday expressions; it is not strained, and does not strive for eloquence. The play develops in the customary three-act manner: exposition, development, a second-act climax, and a third-act resolution. There are no earth-shattering events, nothing startlingly out of the ordinary. It is a play that examines an Australian situation—a play that depends for its universality on the inter-relations of men and women, ordinary working people who choose to live in a somewhat unorthodox manner but who have all the same needs and desires as the rest of the world: friendship, love, comfort, companionship.

Lawler recognizes Olive's need when Roo offers her marriage. Roo says tenderly: "Look, I know this is seventeen years too late, and what I'm offering is not much chop, but... I want to marry you, Ol." Olive responds emphatically: "No!" She says: "You can't get out of it like that—I won't let you." Roo is appalled. "Olive, what the hell's wrong?" Olive replies: "You've got to go back [to cane cutting]. It's the only hope we've got." "Give me back what you've taken," she says, to which Roo replies: "It's gone—can't you understand? Every little scrap of it—gone. No more flyin' down out of the sun—no more eagles.... This is the dust we're in and we're gunna walk through it like everyone else for the rest of our lives." Olive stumbles out of the house, and Roo, too inarticulate to weep, sees the seventeenth doll lying on a piano and crushes it. Barney leads him out of the house, their friendship perhaps restored, and the curtain falls.

Summer of the Seventeenth Doll is a truly indigenous play, firmly rooted in the Australian ethos, and it illustrates a world that was disappearing, even as the play was being written. The "mateship" that it espouses was eroding as rapidly as Australia was becoming an urban society, and it is this realization, more than any other, that shocks Roo into offering to marry Olive. Still, Lawler does indicate that life is cyclical. Johnny Dowd is introduced to Bubba, a neighbor in her twenties who has been friendly with Olive and Nancy all of her life. Bubba is determined to follow the same lifestyle, except that "things will be different"; she is sure that she will not suffer the same fate as Roo, Olive, Barney, and Nancy.

Lawler's mastery of the Australian vernacular was certainly responsible in part for the play's instant success with Australian audiences. Before the triumph of this play, most Australian playwrights had been careful to use a "cultured" or "refined" dialogue, with very few slang terms and little cursing. With one or two notable exceptions, such as Sumner Locke-Elliott's play *Rusty Bugles* (pr. 1948), which had audiences shocked by its use of the word "bloody," playwrights had eschewed the strong language so characteristic of everyday Australian speech. This caution was a reflection of the power wielded by the various State Chief Secretaries, analogous to the British Lord Chamberlain, with the right to remove plays from the stage because of perceived immoralities or offenses to public decency. Thus, Lawler's use of street language—which is employed in the play in the most natural way, not intrusively—had a great impact on Australian drama. Indeed, it has been suggested that the play failed on Broadway because of its use of Australian vernacular and dialect: The reviewer in the *New York Daily News* spoke of a "great invisible barrier of language between the United States and Australia."

Lawler's next play was *The Piccadilly Bushman*. The term "Piccadilly Bushman" is a derogatory one and refers to a wealthy Australian who lives in the West End of London, in Earl's Court, known as "Kangaroo Court," not in the judicial sense but because of the large numbers of Australians ("kangaroos") living there. It was presented in 1959 in Melbourne, and in 1961 in Adelaide.

A savage portrait of a bitter man who has been unable to find his place in his homeland, the play examines the Australian feeling of inferiority that was instilled while Australia was a British colony. Australia was settled at the close of the eighteenth century as a substitute for the American colonies, at a time when Great Britain needed an outlet for the hundreds of convicts imprisoned in rotting hulks on British rivers. There were two classes of settler: On the one hand, there was the convict, and on the other, his supervisors and those who, for one reason or another, believed that they would have a better chance at a new life in a new land. These two classes, the penal and the free, maintained a certain distance from each other for nearly two hundred years, and both classes always referred to Great Britain as "home." The supervisory and free-settler class looked down on the emancipists, and British visitors looked down on the free settlers as colonials. By the end of the nineteenth century, when wealthier Australians began visiting Great Britain, they were lumped together with the descendants of the convicts and patronized by the British.

It was only in 1901, upon federation, that Australia became independent, although retaining the status of membership in the British Commonwealth of Nations and recognizing the British monarch as titular head of the nation. The feeling of inferiority was pervasive in Australia, and it manifested itself in many different ways. Typical Australians referred to a British person as a "bloody Pommie," but they still regarded themselves as of British stock. It was only with the vast postwar immigration to Australia, at which time two million Britons as well as many hundreds of thousands of European migrants were attracted to the vastness of Australia from their own war-ravaged countries, that Australian attitudes began to change, and Australia began to come to terms with its own national ethos.

Lawler, who was himself an expatriate at the time of writing *The Piccadilly Bushman*, examines the motivations and feelings of an expatriate film actor who returns to Australia to star in a film and to try to save his marriage, or, if that is not possible, to take his son back to England with him. The play is written in three acts and is set in Sydney, in a spacious house overlooking Sydney Harbour. Alec, the protagonist, left Australia at the age of twenty-five, and he considers that his life up to that time had been a prison sentence. He has become successful and famous in Britain but has never overcome his sense of inferiority.

One of the secondary characters, O'Shea, is the writer of the film in which Alec is to star, and he is the foil to the expatriate. He realizes that Meg, Alec's wife, must stay with Alec. Meg has had a history of alcoholism and infidelity in England. It emerges that the men with whom she has been having affairs are the type categorized by O'Shea as misfits, that type of person who goes overseas but does not succeed in his chosen field. Meg does not understand that, while Alec is successful, he, too, is a misfit, and she consoles these other men rather than her husband. O'Shea points out to her that it is Alec who is the greatest misfit of all.

Lawler tries, without much success, to address a number of questions in *The Piccadilly Bushman*. The play's central themes—the patronizing attitude of the British toward "colonials," homesickness, and the ambivalent attitudes of Australians toward Britain—were aimed at a rather small audience, and while the play attracted some praise, it was largely a failure, critically as well as financially.

Neither Alec nor O'Shea is drawn with great sympathy. Alec is shown to be something of an opportunist; he has used his wife as a stepping-stone in his career, and his attitudes throughout the play are essentially negative. O'Shea, supposedly the voice of reason, is long-winded and unpretentious almost to the point of naïveté.

Of greater interest are the first two plays of *The Doll Trilogy*: *Kid Stakes* and *Other Times*. Though written many years after *Summer of the Seventeenth Doll*, as noted above, these two plays precede it in the internal chronology of the trilogy. Interestingly enough, the three plays worked very well together when first performed as a trilogy. After having been written separately and produced as self-contained plays, they were presented in repertory for two weeks in February, 1977, with two Saturdays devoted to productions in which all three plays were presented in sequence. The general slide from the joyous youth of *Kid Stakes* into the disillusionment of postwar Australia in *Other Times* and thence into the devastating finale of *Summer of the Seventeenth Doll* was accomplished with style and great success.

Kid Stakes had been presented for the first time in Melbourne in November of 1975. Reviews were not encouraging, and the play probably suffered because of comparisons with, and distant memories of, *Summer of the Seventeenth Doll*. Nevertheless, Lawler was encouraged to proceed with *Other Times* while *Kid Stakes* toured Australia. *Other Times* opened in

December, 1976, at the Russell Street Theatre, to favorable reviews.

Kid Stakes begins immediately after the Depression. Barney and Roo have arrived in Melbourne for their first layoff, and they meet Olive and Nancy at the Aquarium. Also appearing is Bubba, here five years old, and the stage is set for the following sixteen years. Olive and Nancy quit their jobs as milliners to become barmaids, and Roo and Barney establish the pattern of the years to come. Olive's mother, Emma, is the owner of the boardinghouse where Olive and Nancy live. Emma is a crusty, middle-aged woman who accepts her daughter's life-style with some misgivings, feeling herself powerless to change things.

The setting for *Other Times* is the same boardinghouse, at the end of World War II. Barney and Roo have served in the Australian Army and are about to be demobilized. They are waiting to return north to resume their jobs as cane cutters, and they look forward to continuing their relationships with Olive and Nancy during layoffs. *Other Times* is the pivotal play in the series. In it, the characters become mature adults, whereas in *Kid Stakes* they were in their early twenties. Life is portrayed as no longer a game; Barney's practical jokes backfire for the first time during a poignant scene in which Emma's dreams of black-market profiteering are ridiculed.

Indeed, probably the turning point of the entire trilogy is the scene at the end of the second act of *Other Times*, which foreshadows the eventual breakup of the foursome. Nancy points out to Olive exactly what it has meant for Roo to stay together with Barney throughout the war. Roo rejected promotions, first, so that he and Barney would not be separated, and, second, so that he and Barney could go on leaves together and visit the girls. The audience understands that Nancy has outgrown the good-times philosophy of the layoffs and needs to put down more permanent roots. At the close of the play, her departure seems inevitable. *Other Times* is a melancholy and somber play, dramatizing a process of disillusionment that is thoroughly Australian in its particulars but universal in its import.

Bibliography

Bartholomeuz, Dennis. "Theme and Symbol in Contemporary Australian Drama: Ray Lawler to Louis Nowra." In *Drama and Symbolism*, edited by James Redmond. Cambridge, England: Cambridge University Press, 1982. The author believes that "the pronounced anti-intellectual strain in Australian life" is glamorized in *Summer of the Seventeenth Doll*; images of flying eagles are incongruous with the "drab necessities of urban employment." Cites Lawler's own comments on the deemphasis of plot in favor of characterization. Sees the play as "the tragedy of those who are made inarticulate by words." Judges it to be still [in 1982] the most perfect machine devised for the Australian stage."

Brisbane, Katharine. "Beyond the Backyard." In *Australia Plays.* London: Walker Books, 1989. An anthology of five new Australian plays, all of which owe a debt, according to Brisbane's introductory essay, to Lawler's *"The Doll*, as it came to be called." Brisbane sees an irony that "the backbone of Australian drama is its Irish sensibility to language, rhythm, humour and logic." The play "is an almost perfect example of the conventional three-act form."

Fitzpatrick, Peter. *After "The Doll": Australian Drama Since 1955.* Melbourne: Edward Arnold, 1979. A strong chapter on Lawler sets out the argument for a decline in quality from *The Doll* to the two plays completing the trilogy, *Kid Stakes* and *Other Times.* While *The Doll* was precedent setting, it was not altogether "helpful," as it "left an inheritance which had partly to be lived down."

Hooton, Joy. "Lawler's Demythologizing of *The Doll*: *Kid Stakes* and *Other Times."* *Australian Literary Studies* 12 (May, 1986): 335-346. Examines the "retrospective" plays following *The Doll* and finds that the ambiguities of *The Doll* have been reconciled in the sequels. "Reformed text is much more thematically consistent, although far less richly suggestive" than the earlier play, the author states. Finds it less concerned with outback values, more a psychological than "a universally relevant study of the effects of time."

Rees, Leslie. *The Making of Australian Drama: A Historical and Critical Survey from the 1830s to the 1970s.* London: Angus and Robertson, 1973. In a chapter called "The Trust, *The Doll*, and the Break-through," the history of Lawler's relationship with the theater world is told, "a long and exciting history" at that. It gave Australian actors their opportunity "to present images of their own people in a natural, indigenous way, and to do this not only before Australians but before audiences abroad." Photographs including ones of Lawler as Barney. Index and bibliography.

Peter Goslett
(Updated by *Thomas J. Taylor*)

NATHANIEL LEE

Born: Hatfield (?), England; c. 1653
Died: London, England; May, 1692

Principal drama

The Tragedy of Nero, Emperor of Rome, pr. 1674, pb. 1675; *Sophonisba: Or, Hannibal's Overthrow*, pr., pb. 1675; *Gloriana: Or, The Court of Augustus Caesar*, pr., pb. 1676; *The Rival Queens: Or, The Death of Alexander the Great*, pr., pb. 1677; *Mithridates, King of Pontus*, pr., pb. 1678; *Oedipus*, pr. 1678, pb. 1679 (with John Dryden); *The Massacre of Paris*, wr. 1679, pr., pb. 1689; *Caesar Borgia: Son of Pope Alexander the Sixth*, pr. 1679, pb. 1680; *The Princess of Cleve*, pr. 1680 (?), pb. 1689 (based on Madame de La Fayette's romance *La Princesse de Clèves*); *Theodosius: Or, The Force of Love*, pr., pb. 1680; *Lucius Junius Brutus: Father of His Country*, pr. 1680, pb. 1681; *The Duke of Guise*, pr. 1682, pb. 1683 (with Dryden); *Constantine the Great*, pr. 1683, pb. 1684.

Other literary forms

While Nathaniel Lee published a few occasional poems, he is known primarily for his drama.

Achievements

Nathaniel Lee was an extremely popular dramatist of his time; many of his plays, including *Sophonisba*, *The Rival Queens*, *Theodosius*, *Oedipus* (written with John Dryden), and *Mithridates, King of Pontus* were frequently revived and reprinted. These plays, five of the most popular Restoration dramas, were produced through the seventeenth century and occasionally revived in the next.

Lee wrote primarily heroic tragedy, characterized by superhuman heroes torn between passion and honor, a struggle that usually results in the hero's death. Spectacle, battles, processions, and bombastic language in rhymed couplets are common to this form. Moreover, along with Dryden, with whom he collaborated on two plays, *Oedipus* and *The Duke of Guise*, Lee abandoned the use of rhymed couplets and employed blank verse, which allowed for greater expressiveness, realism, and emotive force.

Like the quality of his work, critical estimation of Lee as a dramatist varies. Lee has been criticized for his lack of balance and control, for allowing his scenes to degenerate into mere spectacle and his dialogue, into rant. Nevertheless, he created individual scenes of great effect and passages of compelling beauty and dramatic power. Many critics and historians of English drama have placed him in the first rank of English dramatists and some have called him great. Unfortunately, very little attention has been paid to his work, which, according to the famous critic George Saintsbury, has been "shamefully neglected."

Biography

Little is known about the early life of Nathaniel Lee. The playwright was born to Richard and Elizabeth Lee about 1653. A minister thoroughly engaged in the religious and political issues of the day, Richard Lee tended to the intellectual development of his children, sending five of his six surviving sons to Oxford or Cambridge University. Thus, Lee was educated at the Charterhouse School in preparation for Trinity College, Cambridge, where he received his bachelor of arts degree in 1668-1669.

At the beginning of the next decade, Lee became an actor, playing the Captain of the Watch in Nevil Payne's *Fatal Jealousie* (pr. 1672) and Duncan in Sir William Davenant's *Macbeth* (pr. 1663). Although Lee was handsome and had a powerful voice, he apparently suffered from stage fright, so he retired and began playwriting. Lee's first play, *The Tragedy of Nero, Emperor of Rome*, failed, but *Sophonisba* was a success. *Gloriana* also failed, but Lee recovered with *The Rival Queens*, which achieved a popularity that lasted into the eighteenth century. In the next few years, Lee saw plays such as *Oedipus*, *Theodosius*, and *Mithridates, King of Pontus* become successes.

Lee's last three plays did not match the success of *Theodosius*, and on November 11, 1684, he was admitted to the Bethlehem Royal Hospital, the insane asylum popularly known as Bedlam. The reasons for Lee's "distraction," as it was called, are not clear. He was evidently a heavy drinker and had a rather mercurial temperament; it is possible that, at the time of his confinement, he was suffering from the effects of poverty. Whatever the origins of his illness, Lee spent the next four years in Bedlam. He was discharged from the hospital in 1688, taking up residence on Duke Street. There is no solid evidence that Lee wrote any plays either during or after his stay at Bedlam, although he did compose some poetry. In the spring of 1692, he was found dead in the street and was buried on May 6, 1692, in an unmarked grave.

Analysis

Nathaniel Lee consistently used historical figures and events as his dramatic subjects. In *The Rival Queens*, Lee dramatized the fall of Alexander the Great, a larger-than-life figure who succumbs to his own passions and to the plots of others. His fall is truly tragic. When the play opens, Alexander is returning from his most recent exploits and is about to enter Babylon. Having committed some personal and political indiscretions, Alexander may not be warmly received by everyone. He has executed some of his most respected generals, imagining that they were trying to stage a coup. He publicly insulted Polyperchon, commander of the Phalanx, and Cassander, son the the Macedonian governor, Antipater. Breaking a promise to his devoted Babylonian queen, Statira, he has returned to the bed of his hot-blooded first wife, Roxana. Finally, he has sanctioned the match between Parisatis, sister to Statira, and Hephestion, an unctuous courtier. Parisatis, however, is the lover of Lysimachus, a fearless soldier loyal to Alexander. Lysimachus believes that he is more deserving than Hephestion of Alexander's favor, as does Clytus, the conqueror's old and faithful adviser, who also served under Philip of Macedonia, Alexander's father.

Alexander enters Babylon triumphantly, but he is soon embroiled in the conflict between Hephestion and Lysimachus. Alexander tries to settle the issue by having Lysimachus thrown to a lion. The doughty warrior slays the lion with his bare hands, however, and Alexander, who cannot overlook such a marvelous feat, lets Lysimachus compete for the hand of Parisatis, deciding that the woman will go to the soldier who serves most impressively in battle.

At the same time, the rival queens are contending for Alexander's affections. Upon hearing that Alexander had bedded Roxana, Statira decides to remove herself from him. By this ploy, however, she risks losing him to Roxana, so she later entertains his impassioned lovemaking and forgives his recent intrigue with Roxana. Roxana witnesses the reunion and seeks revenge. Cassander convinces her to murder Statira as she awaits the conqueror's return from the banquet. Cassander, however, has arranged for Alexander to be poisoned at the feast.

At the banquet, a drunken Alexander becomes enraged at Clytus for his satiric barbs, and he kills the old man on the spot. Alexander's maudlin remorse for the impulsive deed is cut short by the news that Roxana and her band of thugs are threatening Statira. Alexander arrives just in time to see Roxana stab the queen. As she dies, Statira begs Alexander not to kill Roxana; he resists taking revenge, but only because his first wife is pregnant. The audience now discovers that Hephestion drank himself to death at the banquet. Alexander then begins to stagger from the poison poured into his drink. After hallucinating about his heroic past, the conqueror dies, leaving Lysimachus to apprehend the assassins and to claim, at last, Parisatis.

This play dramatizes the story and spectacle of a great man brought down by his own failures. If Alexander were merely the victim of an unfortunate series of events, as are many heroes of the Restoration's serious drama, the audience would not care about his fate, but Lee's Alexander is a tragic figure because he had the power to save himself. Poor judgment, not inescapable fate, causes him to fall. The play is made even more tragic because the audience can see his fall coming. The audience has more information than Alexander and knows that, by the conventions of tragedy, seemingly small lapses in judgment at the beginning of a play have large and damnable consequences toward the end.

Alexander's mistakes result from his letting passion overrule reason. Throughout the play, Alexander increasingly becomes the tool of his own passions. One of his first acts is to favor Hephestion by supporting his suit for Parisatis over that of Lysimachus. Like King Lear, Alexander elevates those who flatter him the most, rather than those who display quiet virtue: The glib court favorite is preferred over the silent but dutiful soldier. As the play continues, mistakes become misdeeds: At the banquet, Clytus is not merely ignored, he is slain. In the last scene of the play, Alexander loses his reason entirely and goes mad under the poison's influence.

The tension between Alexander's affective and intellectual faculties is dramatized by opposing pairs of characters. Roxana is a lusty, sensuous woman, intent on satisfying her sexual desires; Statira, in contrast, is a model of selfless devotion, ethereal, rather than earthy. On the side of passion is Hephestion, the sot; on the side of reason, Lysimachus, the soldier. Cassander is a scheming, sinister malcontent, willing to say what Alexander wants to hear, while he plots the conqueror's destruction; Clytus is a blunt, stoical adviser, who risks Alexander's wrath to criticize his indulgence in Persian luxuries. Lee polarizes the selfish character and the selfless, the scheming, and the honest. The spiritual land of the first group is Babylon, the lap of decadent luxury; the spiritual land of the second group is Macedonia, the seat of austerity and other martial virtues. Thus, the characterization and the very structure of the play reflect Alexander's inner conflict.

If *The Rival Queens* is quite clearly a tragedy, *The Princess of Cleve* defies precise generic description; Lee himself called the play "Farce, Comedy, Tragedy or meer Play." Set in Paris, the play focuses on the amorous exploits of Duke Nemours, a nobleman with a penchant and talent for seducing the wives of his compatriots. Despite his appetite for sexual sport, Nemours is betrothed to Marguerite, Princess of Jainville. Queen Catherine de Medici, however, wants to end the match so that the princess can marry the Dauphin, soon to be King Francis II.

To achieve her political ends, Catherine, who never appears in the play, persuades one of her ladies, Tournon, to sleep with Nemours and to find him other women to bed as well. Presumably, Marguerite will discover Nemours' faithlessness and welcome the Dauphin's attentions. In her campaign, Tournon first suggests to Marguerite that an amorous letter from a whore to her anonymous lover belongs to Nemours. She next attempts to involve Nemours with Celia and Elianor, the lusty wives of two fops, St. Andre and Poltrot. Tournon then spreads the news that the newly married Princess of Cleve is accepting Nemours' adulterous advances.

The action involving the two fops and their wives soon takes off without Nemours. St. Andre and Poltrot try intensely to be in style—which, by

Restoration standards, meant betraying one's wife in a cavalier, offhand manner. Celia and Elianor, for their part, also engage in flirtations. All receive their proper reward: Celia and Elianor run off with Nemours (under the eye of Marguerite) and are eventually debauched by his cronies, Bellamore and Vidam; the husbands are unsuccessful in their own attempts, in effect receiving no compensation for the privilege of being cuckolded.

When the Prince notes a certain malaise in his wife, he implores her to reveal the origin of her low spirits, suspecting that she has taken a lover. She reluctantly confesses her passion for Nemours—a confession which eventually causes the Prince to die from heartbreak.

Nemours' association with the wives of the fops and with the Princess of Cleve arouses Marguerite's suspicion that he has not been faithful. She attends the ball in disguise and tries to arouse Nemours' passions as another woman. She succeeds, and when she doffs her disguise, Nemours can hardly deny his infidelity. Nemours, then, has presumably lost Marguerite, whose last words are "Monster of a Man," and he has lost the Princess of Cleve as well, even though she is now technically available: She has given him up forever. No sooner has she left the stage, however, when Nemours predicts that "I Bed her eighteen months three weeks hence, at half an hour past two in the Morning."

Nemours' prediction suggests the sleazy atmosphere and ethos of the play. He does not believe that the Princess of Cleve is as good as her word, but he does believe in his own sexual prowess. Indeed, any kind of oath in the universe of this play is meaningless. The Princess, Celia, Elianor, St. Andre, and Poltrot all do their best to violate their marriage vows. Since no character in the play is untainted by sin, the audience tends to judge them not by ethical standards but by sheer performance. Since there are no saints and no sinners, only winners and losers, the most impressive performer is Nemours.

Lee wanted to show his audience sexual libertinism unvarnished by witty rationalizations. When this play was composed, in about 1680, sexual promiscuity was almost a way of life for the English courtiers and their king, Charles II; George Villiers, the second Duke of Buckingham and John Wilmot, the Earl of Rochester, in particular, were infamous for their sexual adventures. The English court's rakish ways were reflected in plays such as John Dryden's *Marriage à la Mode* (pr. 1672), William Wycherley's *The Country Wife* (pr. 1675), and Sir George Etherege's *The Man of Mode: Or, Sir Fopling Flutter* (pr. 1676). Lee's intention in *The Princess of Cleve* was to provide a corrective to the tacit acceptance of promiscuity often found in such works, whatever their explicit moral.

The plays of Nathaniel Lee are, for Allardyce Nicoll, "of inestimable importance in any attempt to divine the quality of tragedy of his age."

From this glimpse into Lee's tragedy we can perhaps see at work a serious search for a more comprehensive ethical perspective, despite staginess, special effects, and sensational events.

Other major works

POETRY: "On the Death of the Duke of Albemarle," 1670; "To Mr. Dryden, on His Poem of Paradice," 1677; "To the Prince and Princess of Orange, upon Their Marriage," 1677; *To the Duke on His Return*, 1682; *On Their Majesties Coronation*, 1689; *On the Death of Mrs. Behn*, 1689.

Bibliography

Armistead, J. M. *Nathaniel Lee.* Boston: Twayne, 1979. The best introduction to a study of Lee. After presenting the playwright and his milieu, Armistead marches straight through the plays, summarizing and identifying their themes. In a chapter entitled "Lee's Artistry," Armistead identifies Lee's "distinctive" style. Complemented by a genealogy tree and an excellent bibliography.

Cooke, A. L., and Thomas B. Stroup. "The Political Implications in Lee's *Constantine the Great.*" *Journal of English and Germanic Philology* 49 (1950): 506-515. Earlier scholars are indecisive about the political references in *Constantine the Great*, but Cooke and Stroup analyze the play thoroughly. They find "a remarkable number of allusions and analogies to political personages and their intrigues, especially to the Popish Plot and subsequent political scandals."

Ham, Roswell Gray. *Otway and Lee: Biography from a Baroque Age.* New Haven, Conn.: Yale University Press, 1931. Lee and Thomas Otway both enlivened the English Restoration stage, and this fluent study follows the various contretemps of their careers. Ham's chapter "So Noble a Pleasure" discusses the exaggerated heroics of *Sophonisba* and the genre's relationship to the "ornate" baroque French novels of the period. A fine study.

Knight, George Wilson. *The Golden Labyrinth: A Study of British Drama.* New York: W. W. Norton, 1962. Knight discusses *The Tragedy of Nero, Emperor of Rome*; *Sophonisba*; *Gloriana*; *The Rival Queens*; *Mithridates, King of Pontus*; *Constantine the Great*; and *Lucius Junius Brutus.* Lee is judged "an expert in the pathology of tyranny" and the "psychology of power."

Lee, Nathaniel. *Works.* Edited by Thomas B. Stroup and Arthur L. Cooke. 2 vols. New Brunswick, N.J.: Scarecrow Press, 1954. Reprint. Metuchen, N.J.: Scarecrow Reprints, 1968. A good scholarly edition with a sketch of Lee's life and copious informative notes on the texts. Each play has its separate introduction, giving dates, stage history, sources, criticism, and textual history.

Marshall, Geoffrey. *Restoration Serious Drama.* Norman: University of Oklahoma Press, 1975. Marshall discusses Restoration drama and Lee's plays in chapters entitled "The Seriousness of Restoration Serious Drama," "The Dimensions of Serious Drama," "The Paradox of Manners and Decorum," "Diction," and "Comedy and Tragedy, the Sentimental, and a Critical Crux." His model for his comments on diction is Lee's *Lucius Junius Brutus,* and in varying contexts he also comments on *The Duke of Guise, Oedipus, The Rival Queens, Sophonisba,* and *Theodosius.*

Douglas R. Butler
(Updated by *Frank Day*)

HUGH LEONARD
John Keyes Byrne

Born: Dublin, Ireland; November 9, 1926

Principal drama

The Italian Road, pr. 1954; *The Big Birthday*, pr. 1956; *A Leap in the Dark*, pr. 1957; *Madigan's Lock*, pr. 1958, pb. 1987; *A Walk on the Water*, pr. 1960; *The Passion of Peter McGinty*, pr. 1961; *Stephen D*, pr., pb. 1962 (adaptation of James Joyce's novels *A Portrait of the Artist as a Young Man* and *Stephen Hero*); *The Poker Session*, pr., pb. 1963; *Dublin One*, pr. 1963 (adaptation of Joyce's short-story collection *Dubliners*); *The Saints Go Cycling In*, pr. 1965 (adaptation of Flann O'Brien's novel *The Dalkey Archives*); *Mick and Mick*, pr. 1966, pb. as *All the Nice People*, 1966; *The Au Pair Man*, pr., pb. 1968; *The Patrick Pearse Motel*, pr., pb. 1971; *Da*, pr., pb. 1973; *Summer*, pr. 1974, pb. 1979; *Irishmen: A Suburb of Babylon*, pr. 1975, pb. 1983 (includes *Irishmen*, *Nothing Personal*, and *The Last of the Mohicans*); *Liam Liar*, pr. 1976 (adaptation of Keith Waterhouse and Willis Hall's play *Billy Liar*); *Time Was*, pr. 1976, pb. 1980; *A Life*, pr. 1979, pb. 1981; *Kill*, pr. 1982; *Scorpions*, pr. 1983; *Pizzazz*, pr. 1984, pb. 1987; *The Mask of Moriarty*, pr. 1985, pb. 1987.

Other literary forms

Home Before Night: Memoirs of an Irish Time and Place by the Author of "Da" (1979) is a charming, humorous memoir, which includes many of the characters, incidents, conversations, and witticisms in *Da*. *Out After Dark* (1989) is a sequel to his autobiography. Hugh Leonard has been a regular contributor of amusing topical commentaries in such Irish newspapers as *Hibernia*, the *Sunday Independent*, and the *Sunday Tribune*. He has also reviewed theater for *Plays and Players*. In 1991, he published a novel, *Parnell and the Englishwoman*.

Achievements

Leonard is among the most widely produced of contemporary Irish dramatists. His plays have achieved commercial success in Ireland, Great Britain, and the United States. Exceptionally prolific and yet polished, Leonard has been a good journeyman author in various media. He honed his dramatic skills by writing extensively not only for the stage but also for radio, television, film, and newspapers, always with entertainment as a prime consideration. (His television play *Silent Song*, 1966, received the Italia Award.)

Leonard's reputation as an Irish Neil Simon suggests the aspects for which he has been both admired and criticized. His greatest asset as a playwright is essential to any commercially successful dramatist: He knows how to keep an audience entertained with humorous dialogue and situations. Conversely, his detractors have usually complained that his main weakness is a facile, glib superficiality. His best plays combine a theatrical flair for clever language and situation comedy with thoughtful depth of human understanding.

For example, his greatest achievement on the stage has been *Da*, which in 1978 won the Tony Award, New York Drama Critics Circle Award, Outer Critics Circle Award, and Drama Desk Award for Best Play. Mel Gussow of *The New York Times* claimed that *Da* is "in a class with the best of [Sean] O'Casey." Even the fastidious John Simon of *New York* magazine found it "complex and graceful" and "entertaining, endearing and gently moving."

A new play by Leonard has often been a highlight of the Dublin Theatre Festival. At the same time, the theatrical facility and universal accessibility of his plays allow them to be transplanted with ease from Dublin's Abbey or Olympia theaters to London's West End and America's Broadway or regional companies.

Biography

Hugh Leonard is the pen name of John Keyes Byrne, who was born on November 9, 1926, in Dublin, Ireland. Leonard was adopted and reared by a couple in Dalkey, in south County Dublin, who were the prototypes for the foster parents in *Da*.

In 1945, at age eighteen, Leonard started work in the Land Commission for five pounds per week. He was always expecting to leave soon but remained for fourteen years, by which time his salary was ten pounds, eight shillings. In 1955, he married Paule Jacquet, a Belgian who lived in Moscow and Los Angeles during World War II. They had a daughter, Danielle.

To escape from the drudgery of his civil service job, Leonard joined a dramatic society. Amateur theater has been the seedbed for some of Ireland's best playwrights, and this was true for Leonard as well. *The Italian Road* was given an amateur production but was turned down by the Abbey Theatre. Then Leonard submitted *The Big Birthday* (which had an amateur production as *Nightingale in the Branches* in 1954), taking his pseudonym from the psychopath Hughie Leonard in the rejected play. *The Big Birthday* was produced in 1956 by the Abbey. He also wrote serial radio dramas, including the daily *The Kennedys of Castleross*, which was the main dramatic experience for the non-theatergoing, pretelevision majority in Ireland. He resigned from the Land Commission in 1959 to become a full-time professional writer.

Leonard wrote for Granada television in Manchester, England, and then moved there, and he later lived in London from 1963 until 1970, writing adaptations and original scripts for television. His numerous adaptations for television have included *The Hound of the Baskervilles* (1968), *Dombey and Son* (1969), *Great Expectations* (1967), *The Moonstone* (1972), *Nicholas Nickleby* (1968), *The Possessed* (1969), *A Sentimental Education* (1970), and

Wuthering Heights (1967). He claimed that he could write an original television play in six to eight weeks or an episode of adaptation in two days. Leonard wrote the script for a major Irish television production in 1966, *Insurrection*, for the commemorations of the 1916 Easter Rising. He also wrote for film, including *Great Catherine* (starring and coproduced by Peter O'Toole) and *Interlude* (both 1968). Leonard's first play to open in London's West End was *Stephen D*, his adaptation of fellow Dubliner James Joyce's *A Portrait of the Artist as a Young Man* (1916) and *Stephen Hero* (1944). Before *Stephen D* was produced in New York in 1967, it had its American premiere at the Olney Theater, near Washington, D.C., which has often introduced Leonard plays to the United States, with James Waring as the director, working closely with the playwright.

In 1970, Leonard returned with his family to Dalkey in south Dublin. Productions of *The Patrick Pearse Motel, Da, Summer, Irishmen, Time Was, A Life, Kill, Scorpions*, and *The Mask of Moriarty* attracted large audiences and generally favorable reviews. He continued to write for television, including the adaptation of *Strumpet City* (1981) for Radio Telefís Eireann with Peter O'Toole and Peter Ustinov featured in a major Irish production.

Leonard has been quite successful financially, and he especially benefited from a 1970's Irish tax law regarding artistic income as nontaxable. A segment of the television program *Sixty Minutes*, focusing on the Irish tax law, revealed that Leonard's large royalties from *Da* were not taxable whereas actors in Irish productions of Leonard's plays were taxed as usual. An article in the *Sunday Independent* entitled "Leonard's 'Da' Gives Him £4,000 a Week!" quoted Leonard as saying that the Broadway production of *Da* was grossing eighty thousand dollars a week, of which he got ten percent, amounting to £200,000 a year tax-free. He expected another two thousand pounds per week from United States touring productions. Moreover, he claimed to have sold the film rights for $150,000 with an extra $100,000 for writing the screenplay.

Some of his compatriots may have seen the prolific writer as a prodigal son, returned yet rich and unrepentant. Leonard has lived out much of his life in the public eye, particularly in the Irish newspapers. Whereas his new plays often appeared annually, his essays often appeared weekly, covering similar material in a different genre but containing what could be scenarios, scenes, themes, or quips from plays-in-progress. Leonard's humorous columns in Irish periodicals, such as *Hibernia*, the *Sunday Independent*, and the *Sunday Tribune*, have given his opinions high visibility, even notoriety. In his articles, private reminiscences have mingled with public declarations, winning him praise and blame as a wise man and a foolish egotist. He has used such extratheatrical forums to sound off wittily and sometimes bitterly on diverse subjects, including Irish provinciality or modishness, contraception, narrow nationalism, prudery or vulgarity, Abbey Theatre policy, inefficient services, political shibboleths, demagoguery and skulduggery, and the violence of the Irish Republican Army, a daring target for ridicule. Indeed, few issues in Irish public life have gone unnoticed in Leonard's satirical essays. Allusions to "my present wife" in a country without divorce teased those who might regard this cosmopolitan author as a jet-set Don Juan contaminated by alien life-styles and ideas. He has been among the celebrities that some Irish love to hate. While some would praise him as a brave clear voice with sharp barbs against deserving enemies, others would blame him for cheap, cynical, glib wisecracks. For example, his review of events in the year 1986 in the *Sunday Independent* (January 4, 1987) included sardonic put-downs of both God and an Irish prime minister in the same paragraph: "The Gobshite of the Year Award goes to God, for having His chance and missing it." Such comments, direct from the author rather than filtered through a mouthpiece in a play, add to Leonard's vivid public persona in Holy Ireland.

Leonard, whose work is better known in other parts of the world than the United States (although *Da* received considerable attention among American theater audiences and was made into a film starring Jack Lemmon), is less involved with political questions and more concerned with the family and small social groups of typical urban Irish life. His memoirs, the last installment of which, *Out After Dark*, was published in 1989, are rather more typical of his laconic humor and sometimes distancing technique.

Leonard remained with his wife and daughter in his home village of Dalkey, now an upscale suburb of Dublin City, writing weekly humorous and satirical columns for various newspapers, according to Cóilín D. Owens, "with scathing wit, denouncing political violence, extreme nationalism, provinciality, inefficiency, and the mores of Irish suburban social climbers."

Analysis

As a playwright, Hugh Leonard is a dependable professional. He may not be of the first rank (few are), but unlike many a would-be dramatist, he can hold an audience. His plays are usually of some interest if not always of great depth. In short, his plays show great talent but no genius, which is perhaps all an audience requires for the price of admission. In adapting Joyce's novels for the stage as *Stephen D*, Leonard showed a command over the special demands of theater as a genre. His play *The Poker Session* used a little humor, a staple of much of his work, but held the audience's attention with a Pinteresque menace, as a patient from a mental asylum takes revenge on his family with both method and madness. *The Au Pair Man* was an interesting allegory about the relationship between a dying British Empire and an emerging Ireland. *Summer* and *Irishmen* showed both Leonard's compassion for, and critique of, his compatriots. *Time Was* stretched Leonard's theatrical powers but did not really amount to a satisfying work. *The Mask of Moriarty* was a clever and original Sherlock Holmes story but did nothing more than tell a detective yarn with slick theatrical aplomb. Three plays that stand out among Leonard's large oeuvre and that will be examined in this analysis are *The Patrick Pearse Motel*, *Da*, and *A Life*.

The Patrick Pearse Motel is a hilarious two-act farce meticulously constructed and cleverly written. This bedroom farce is in the style of a Georges Feydeau, Eugène Labiche, or Alan Ayckbourn, with the unusual distinction that it is set in Ireland. It is not only an amusing sex romp but also an outrageous satire ridiculing the Dublin nouveau riche anxious to get more money and to forget their humble pasts. Set after the 1966 commemorations of the 1916 Easter Rising, the play portrays a new Ireland with a confused identity, invoking the pieties of nationalistic heroism while scrambling to assimilate with the worst of Anglo-American culture. The very title of *The Patrick Pearse Motel* suggests the contradictions of the new Ireland willing to peddle its devalued cultural icons as it enters the Common Market of international mediocrity and homogeneity.

Such a theme may seem rather heavy for a farce, but Leonard handles all aspects of his play with a light, sure touch. The setting is the upscale suburb of Foxrock in Dublin's "vodka-and-bitter-lemon belt," but the names of the characters are from Irish myths. There are three couples: Dermod and Grainne, Fintan and Niamh, and James Usheen and Venetia Manning. Usheen is obsessed with the English Miss Manning but is too full of self-love to share himself with any one woman. A talk-show host on British television, he is an outrageous parody of the modern celebrity whose character is profoundly shallow.

Dermod is a get-rich-quick businessman and social climber who, with Fintan, is opening the Patrick Pearse Motel in the Dublin mountains and the Michael Collins Motel in Cork. He and his beautiful wife, Grainne, have risen from a working-class housing estate to a Foxrock home with all the material goods that a *parvenu* couple could want. There is still something more, however, that Grainne desires: one "night of harmless innocent adultery." The man she is luring is Usheen, and the site for the consummation is to be the Patrick Pearse Motel, the setting for act 2.

The set for the motel is two bedrooms, which are mirror images of each other, with a corridor between. Nearly all the eighty-four rooms in the motel are identical (the Manchester Martyrs' room has three single beds), and all are named after the pantheon of Irish patriots, including Brian Boru, Thomas Davis, Michael Davitt, O'Donovan Rossa, and Bernadette Devlin. The action takes place in the Charles Stewart Parnell room (appropriate for adultery), where Grainne intends to have Usheen, and the Robert Emmet room, where her husband is being seduced by Venetia Manning.

Moreover, Fintan, who madly desires only his plain wife Niamh and wrongly suspects her of adultery, is trying to kill her as she hides in a wardrobe. The characters are not aware of the proximity of the other characters, because as one enters a space, another exits with split-second timing. A letter, wet trousers, a negligee, a fur coat, a shillelagh, and brandy, as well as husbands and wives, go astray and lead to all kinds of comic confusion. Despite the complications, the dramatist, like a master puppeteer, never loses control of the characters or the action, and as a social satirist, never loses sight of the thrust of the comedy to ridicule and correct human folly.

Da is Leonard's most successful play both commercially and artistically. As much as in any other Leonard play, entertaining humorous dialogue and situations are mingled with a depth of compassion. In this autobiographical memory play, the humor is mirthful without malice and moves toward forgiveness. *Da* was conceived and premiered at the Olney Theater near Washington, D.C. Leonard's program notes for the 1973 world premiere at Olney said that during rehearsals for *The Patrick Pearse Motel* at Olney in 1972, someone (perhaps James Waring, the longtime American director of Leonard's plays) suggested that Leonard's stories about his father could be the basis for an amusing play. Within a year, Leonard had turned the suggestion into perhaps his best play. The original production, with John McGiver in the title role, was a success at Olney, in Chicago, and at the 1973 Dublin Theatre Festival. In 1978, *Da* featured Barnard Hughes in the successful Broadway production at the Morosco Theater and won many awards, including a Tony for best play.

"Da, in my part of the world, means father," writes Samuel Beckett in *Molloy* (1951; English translation, 1955). Leonard is also from Beckett's part of the world, south Dublin, but his treatment of his da is quite different from Beckett's stark, mordant style. Leonard's coming to terms with his dead father is bathed in a nostalgic, almost sentimental, glow. The tone of Charlie, the narrator, may indeed be resentful throughout the drama, but the overall tone of the play is light, generous, and forgiving. John Keyes Byrne the man may indeed have drawn on bittersweet personal experiences for this memory play, but Hugh Leonard the entertainer refined and altered that autobiographical material for the sake of a good yarn.

Charlie is a playwright in his early forties who has returned from London to Dalkey for his father's funeral in present time May, 1968. In the play as well as in Leonard's life, his "Da" and "Ma" were not his real parents but a couple who adopted him as a baby. As he is straightening up in the house in which he was reared, he has flashbacks to his childhood and is haunted by the memories of his (foster) parents and by his own younger selves (played by a second actor). Unlike Thornton Wilder's *Our Town* (1938), in which the dead observe the living and cannot communicate with them, Charlie observes those now dead and even argues with them. He quarrels even with his younger self.

The theatrical device of Charlie Now and Charlie Then, played by two actors, two decades apart but in lively debate, is more than a gimmick and is very effective for both humor and insight. It is interesting to note that Irish playwrights Brian Friel and Thomas Murphy have used similar anti-naturalistic techniques in plays dealing with similar subjects. In *Philadelphia, Here I Come!* (1964), Friel split his main character into public and private selves played by two actors. In *A Crucial Week in the Life of a Grocer's Assistant* (1967), Murphy's protagonist slips from present time into fantasies of what might be. Such antinaturalistic techniques can use entertaining devices to reveal insight into interior life.

Another theatrical dimension that gives the play fluidity to move in time and place is the set. The main playing area in *Da* is the kitchen ("the womb of the play"), but this play is not the mere "kitchen-sink" realism of the stereotypical early Abbey drama, as there are several playing spaces. Moreover, as most of the characters now supposedly exist in the haunted mind of Charlie, they break the conventions of literal realism by walking through walls and crossing boundaries of playing areas, as well as moving forward and backward in their ages. The areas include a seafront and a hilltop. "On the other side of the stage is a neutral area, defined by lighting," to signify various locales.

In the opening scene, as Charlie Now meets his old friend Oliver (who can be played by the same actor who will play Oliver at a younger age), a remark about the dead father is the cue for Da to pass through the kitchen and contradict the remark. When Charlie is again alone, Da nonchalantly returns to comment on his own funeral. He disregards his son's order to "Piss off." About one of his catch phrases, "Yis, the angels'll be having a pee," Da says, "You ought to put that down in one of your plays." The protagonist playwright replies, "I'll die first." This irony is typical of how this reflexive play makes the playwright figure a target of humor, whereas Da, the "ignorant man," "lop-sided liar," "an old thick, a zombie, a mastodon," "a sheep," is the life of the drama. Charlie is learning that "love turned upside down is love for all that."

The dramatic conflict is not only between father and son but also within the son himself. In the fine scene that opens act 2, Charlie is berated by his younger self for not properly taking care of Da: "All the dirty bits over with when you got here." In fact, young Charlie finds the man he is to become "jizzless" and "a bit of a disappointment." In return, Charlie finds his younger self naïve and self-righteous.

An important theme in *Da* as in other Leonard plays is class differences. Having worked as a gardener for the upper-class Prynne family for fifty-four years, Da received a mere twenty-five pounds as severance pay. Charlie castigates Da for being so obsequious in accepting the mean, condescending patronage of the rich. In order to help his son, Da works for another four years for "Catholics with money, letting on they're the Quality." Charlie's debt to

Da goes beyond the grave: The allowance that Charlie had been sending Da was saved as an inheritance. Da proclaims, "I didn't die with the arse out of me trousers like the rest of them—I left money!" The curtain falls as Da's ghost follows Charlie back to England.

Da's 1978 American success was followed by a 1979 sequel, *A Life*, premiered at the Abbey for the Dublin Theatre Festival and featuring Cyril Cusack. From *Da*, Leonard takes the thin, acerbic Mr. Drumm, the man who gets Charlie into the Irish civil service, the foil to Da, and makes him the central character of *A Life*. In the bittersweet *Da*, the sweetness of the title character gave the play its warm, even sentimental quality, triumphing over the bitter aspects of Charlie and Mr. Drumm. So it was a daring move to make the testy Drumm the chief protagonist of a sequel and yet retain the audience's interest in and sympathy for him. Mr. Drumm's attempts at humor are his cold caustic quips against his wife and few friends, and yet the play engages an audience's compassion for the dying central character despite his life of nastiness.

Desmond Drumm is described at various ages as "prickly," "a dry stick," "a nun," "a bitter old pill," with "a face on you like a plateful of mortal sins" (an Irishism also used by James Joyce and Brendan Behan). Foils to Mr. Drumm are his dotty wife, Dolly; exuberant, teasing Mary ("Mims"), whom Des loves when young but with whom he seems to be incompatible because she had "a mind like a mayfly"; and the man whom Mary marries instead, "feckless, good-humored" Lar Kearns. All four characters (Mr. Drumm, Dolly, Mary, and Kearns) are about sixty and have corresponding selves about forty years younger (Desmond, Dorothy, Mibs, and Lar) played by four other actors.

Like *Da*, *A Life* is set in May, but the mood is more autumnal and melancholy. Instead of looking forward to a well-earned retirement, Mr. Drumm is facing death and looking back on his life, with a sad realization of what was and what might have been. He visits Mary and Lar Kearns in order to redeem the time, perhaps not only the previous six years of silence but also a lifetime of opportunities for love wasted by selfish righteousness. As in *Da*, the set is inventively designed and lighted with various spaces to accommodate flashbacks to youth. As two older characters cross from a parlor into a kitchen, the scene jumps back forty years to their younger selves.

There are beautiful symmetries of comparison and contrast among the characters, the time periods, the stage areas, and various other mirror images. Such techniques are not only clever in themselves, but also, by distilling time and space, they reveal to the audience the importance of using well a life's short precious time. Drumm has such an epiphany in the play's last minutes: "Three hundred days a year for forty years . . . I've spent twelve thousand days doing work I despise. Instead of friends, I've had standards . . . Well, *I* failed."

Other major works

NOVEL: *Parnell and the Englishwoman*, 1991.

NONFICTION: *Home Before Night: Memoirs of an Irish Time and Place by the Author of "Da,"* 1979; *Leonard's Year*, 1987; *Out After Dark*, 1989 (autobiography).

SCREENPLAYS: *Great Catherine*, 1968; *Interlude*, 1968.

TELEPLAYS: *Insurrection*, 1966; *Silent Song*, 1966; *Great Expectations*, 1967 (based on Charles Dickens' novel); *Wuthering Heights*, 1967 (based on Emily Brontë's novel); *Nicholas Nickleby*, 1968 (based on Dickens' novel); *The Hound of the Baskervilles*, 1968 (based on Arthur Conan Doyle's story); *The Possessed*, 1969 (based on Fyodor Dostoevski's novel); *Dombey and Son*, 1969 (based on Dickens' novel); *A Sentimental Education*, 1970 (based on Gustave Flaubert's novel); *The Moonstone*, 1972 (based on Wilkie Collins' novel); *Strumpet City*, 1981 (based on James Plunkett's novel).

Bibliography

Hogan, Robert. *After the Irish Renaissance: A Critical History of the Irish Drama Since "The Plough and the Stars."* Minneapolis: University of Minnesota Press, 1967. In a long chapter on the Dublin Theatre Festival, Hogan cites Leonard as "the most produced, most commercially successful playwright of the Festival." Contains a biographical sketch, followed by overviews of several plays, including *The Poker Session*, *Mick and Mick* (with a new title, *All the Nice People*, given it after its 1966 Festival opening), and *A Walk on the Water*.

Leonard, Hugh. *Out After Dark.* London: Andre Deutsch, 1989. Not only an autobiographical reminiscence of Leonard's beginnings in the theater (as an actor before a playwright), but also a full-length portrait of the life and energies of twentieth century Ireland, especially the Dalkey village life from which Leonard's humor and charming hardheadedness emerged. Leonard's first short pieces, such as "The Man on Platform Two" and "Nightingale in the Branches" (renamed *The Big Birthday*), were the seeds from which his successes grew.

Morrison, Bill. "Father Who Wouldn't Die." Review of *Da. News and Observer* (Raleigh, N.C.), November 12, 1991. A revival of *Da* prompted this review of the "universal story of pain and suffering" with a comic twist. The two main characters, Charlie and "Da," share the day, "reliving the past and once again doing battle with Mother," who "suffers anew, because that's what she was put on this earth to do—suffer."

Owens, Coilín D., and Joan N. Radner, eds. *Irish Drama, 1900-1980.* Washington, D.C.: Catholic University of America Press, 1990. This preface to Leonard's *Da* offers a biographical overview, covering the early plays, Irish radio, and television free-lance writing. The authors quote Leonard on *Da* as "a monument to my father." Includes a select bibliography, a biography, criticism, and a good update on Leonard's journalistic endeavors and "upscale" suburban life in Dalkey.

Rollins, Ronald Gene. *Divided Ireland: Bifocal Vision in Modern Irish Drama.* New York: Lanham, 1985. Rollins pairs Brian Friel and Leonard in a "Fathers and Sons" chapter, whose thesis is that both focus on "the always awkward and ambivalent father-son relationship"; *Da*, like Friel's *Philadelphia, Here I Come* (pr. 1964, pb. 1965), moves from objectivity to subjective memory and back.

Christopher Griffin
(Updated by *Thomas J. Taylor*)

MATTHEW GREGORY LEWIS

Born: London, England; July 9, 1775
Died: At sea, near Jamaica; May 14, 1818

Principal drama

Village Virtues, pb. 1796; *The Minister*, pb. 1797 (translation of Friedrich Schiller's play *Kabale und Liebe*); *The Castle Spectre*, pr. 1797, pb. 1798; *Rolla: Or, The Peruvian Hero*, pb. 1799 (translation of August von Kotzebue's play *Die Spanier in Peru: Oder, Rollas Tod*); *The Twins: Or, Is It He or His Brother?*, pr. 1799, pb. 1962 (adaptation of Jean François Regnard's *Les Ménechmes: Ou, Les Jumeaux*); *The East Indian*, pr. 1799, pb. 1800; *Adelmorn the Outlaw*, pr., pb. 1801; *Alfonso, King of Castile*, pb. 1801, pr. 1802; *The Captive*, pr. 1803 (dramatic monologue); *The Harper's Daughter: Or, Love and Ambition*, pr. 1803 (adaptation of Lewis' play *The Minister*); *Rugantino: Or, The Bravo of Venice*, pr., pb. 1805 (two acts; adaptation of Lewis' *The Bravo of Venice*); *Adelgitha: Or, The Fruits of a Single Error*, pb. 1806, pr. 1807; *The Wood Daemon: Or, "The Clock Has Struck,"* pr. 1807; *Venoni: Or, The Novice of St. Mark's*, pr. 1808, pb. 1809 (adaptation of Jacques Marie de Monvel's play *Les Victimes cloîtrées*); *Temper: Or, The Domestic Tyrant*, pr. 1809 (adaptation of Sir Charles Sedley's translation, *The Grumbler*, of David Augustin Brueys and Jean Palaprat's play *Le Grondeur*); *Timour the Tartar*, pr., pb. 1811; *One O'Clock: Or, The Knight and the Wood Daemon*, pr., pb. 1811 (music by Michael Kelly and Matthew Peter King; adaptation of Lewis' *The Wood Daemon*); *Rich and Poor*, pr., pb. 1812 (music by Charles Edward Horn; adaptation of Lewis' *The East Indian*).

Other literary forms

Although Matthew Gregory Lewis was one of the most successful British dramatists of the Romantic era, his primary claim to fame today is his authorship of that most extravagant of Gothic novels, *The Monk: A Romance*, which was originally published, in 1796, as *Ambrosio: Or, The Monk*. This was Lewis' first significant published work, and it created such a sensation among his contemporaries that he is still referred to more often by his nickname of "Monk" Lewis than by his given name. Despite the objections of moralists and literary critics alike, this lurid tale of human perversity, with its seductive demons and bleeding ghosts, sold prodigiously during Lewis' lifetime and remains standard reading for anyone studying the development of the English novel.

Two of Lewis' nondramatic publications were *The Love of Gain* (1799), written in imitation of the Thirteenth Satire of Juvenal, and *Tales of Wonder* (1801), an anthology of horror poems. The former, an insignificant throwback to the subject matter and the style of the Age of Johnson, attracted little attention, but the latter stirred considerable interest, some of it admiring but much of it amused. *Tales of Wonder* was compiled in response to a vogue for Gothic ballads which occurred after the publication in the 1790's of several translations of G. A. Bürger's *Lenore* (1773). Unfortunately, the vogue had begun to wane by the time the anthology appeared, and it was unmercifully parodied during the months following its publication. Nevertheless, it remains a work of considerable historical interest because of its inclusion of some of the early poetry of Robert Southey and Sir Walter Scott and because of its influence throughout the nineteenth century on poetic Gothicism.

Much of Lewis' work was derived from or was influenced by German sources, and in 1805 and 1806, he published translations of a pair of German romances, one of which he subsequently dramatized. The first, *The Bravo of Venice*, was based on J. H. D. Zschokke's *Aballino der Grosse Bandit*, and the second, *Feudal Tyrants: Or, The Counts of Carlsheim and Sargans*, was a somewhat freer rendering of Christiane Benedicte Eugénie Naubert's *Elisabeth, Erbin von Toggenburg: Oder, Geschichte der Frauen in der Schweiz*. Suffice it to say of these works that they again show Lewis' fascination with the sensational and that both, especially *The Bravo of Venice*, achieved popular success.

Lewis was also an important writer of popular songs, many of which appeared first in his plays and a number of which were Lewis' original contributions to the works of his fellow playwrights. His nondramatic poetry, too, was sometimes set to music, and, collaborating with such people as Charles Edward Horn, Michael Kelly, and Harriet Abrams, Lewis was frequently able to catch the public's musical fancy. Such songs as "The Banks of Allan Water" (from *Rich and Poor*), "The Wind It Blows Cold" (from *Adelmorn the Outlaw*—both words and music by Lewis), "The Wife's Farewell: Or, Oh No My Love No!" and "The Orphan's Prayer" are unknown today, but in the early nineteenth century they were sung *ad nauseam*. Lewis himself was a reasonably skillful melodist, and as the title of his most substantial song collection, *Twelve Ballads, the Words and Music by M. G. Lewis* (1808), indicates, he occasionally composed his own tunes.

Lewis published a mixed collection of poetry and prose, *Romantic Tales*, in 1808. This four-volume work contained one long narrative poem, five short stories, and seven ballads. Much of the material was translated or adapted from Continental originals, some of it again from the German. Although *Romantic Tales* shows frequent Gothic touches reminiscent of much of Lewis' other work, the individual works vary considerably in tone and subject matter and belie the usual exclusive association of Lewis' name with the wondrous and the horrifying. Two other publications, *Monody on* the Death of Sir John Moore (1809) and Poems (1812), are even more remote from Gothic extravagance and exhibit a neoclassical polish that would startle those who know Lewis only through The Monk, Tales of Wonder, and The Castle Spectre.

Poems was the last volume of Lewis' work to be published during his lifetime, but two others appeared posthumously, The Isle of Devils: A Metrical Tale (1827) and Journal of a West India Proprietor (1834). The former is a narrative poem in heroic couplets concerning a young woman who is pursued and victimized by monsters after a shipwreck. Critics have not treated it well. Journal of a West India Proprietor, on the other hand, has been praised more consistently than any of Lewis' other writings. It gives an engaging and unpretentious account of Lewis' two voyages to his estates in the West Indies, an account which Samuel Taylor Coleridge, generally one of Lewis' severest critics, found impressively well written.

Also of interest are Lewis' letters, many of which appeared in Margaret Baron-Wilson's The Life and Correspondence of M. G. Lewis (1839). Although he was not an important epistolary stylist, Lewis wrote letters which exhibit considerable charm and which, because of his extensive acquaintance with prominent persons, are sometimes of significance to the literary biographer and the historian.

Achievements

Lewis is one of those delightful literary figures whose ability to appeal to the bad taste of the public brings them immense popularity during their own day and critical damnation forever after. In an age when most of Britain's greatest writers found themselves incapable of pleasing London audiences, Lewis brought immense sums into the coffers of the Drury Lane and Covent Garden theaters. He was a master of the sentimental and the sensational, and sentiment and sensation were what London audiences clamored for. Although not all of his plays, referred to by his biographer Louis F. Peck as "brainless stories," were popular successes, enough of them were to make Lewis the darling of the theater managers.

As one might expect of the author of The Monk, Lewis is primarily important for his contributions to dramatic Gothicism. Indeed, Bertrand Evans, author of Gothic Drama from Walpole to Shelley (1947), writes that "the name of Matthew Gregory Lewis is perhaps the most important in the history of Gothic drama." Lewis, Evans observes, drew together the "materials of his predecessors and contemporaries, English and German, and out-Gothicized them all." He did this most triumphantly in The Castle Spectre, which was an immediate and overwhelming theatrical sensation. According to Evans, its forty-seven performances made it "the most successful play of its time," a success achieved by ruthlessly sacrificing "consistency of character, probability of action, and forward movement of plot . . .

to immediate sensational effect."

In order to appraise Lewis' approach fairly, however, it is necessary to know what was considered to be the height of fashion and of entertainment in his day—just at the beginning of the Regency period. The royal establishments at Blenheim and Bath set the tone for outrageous combinations of exaggerated Oriental borrowings mixed with every new fad that the empire builders had brought home from around the world. People went to playhouses more to see and be seen by others than to pay attention to the story line of any play. The audiences in general were so preoccupied with finery and social scandals and made so blasé by experience at places such as Astley's Amphitheatre with fireworks, lakes filled with boats on which naval engagements were reenacted, and the like that it took a lot to get even a moment of their attention.

A man well suited to his time, Lewis was more skillful as an entertainer than as a dramatic artist, and his theatrical creations were so well attended because he had the capacity of engaging his audience's interest, often through unsubtle means. Whether by means of music, melodrama, or shameless spectacle, Lewis made his works impossible to ignore.

Biography

Matthew Gregory Lewis, the first child of Matthew Lewis and the former Frances Maria Sewell, was born in London, England, on July 9, 1775. His father served for a number of years as both Chief Clerk in the War Office and as Deputy-Secretary at War, positions whose salaries, in combination with the revenues from estates owned by the elder Lewis in Jamaica, rendered the Lewis household financially prosperous. Prosperity did not assure marital harmony, however, and his parents agreed to a permanent separation when young Matthew Gregory was seven or eight years old. According to a bill of divorcement which was never brought to enactment, the primary cause of his parents' estrangement was an adulterous affair carried on by Mrs. Lewis, which resulted in her giving birth to a child.

In addition to this illegitimate sibling, Lewis had two sisters, Maria and Sophia, and a brother, Barrington, all of whom lived with their father. Young Matthew Gregory, who had begun his education at Marylebone Seminary, resided at Westminster College and Christ Church College, Oxford, during much of his childhood and adolescence and maintained affectionate contact with both of his parents. Throughout his lifetime, in fact, whatever slight cohesiveness existed within the Lewis family was largely the result of Matthew Gregory's efforts.

Although young Lewis was not a systematic, self-disciplined scholar, he did exhibit considerable talent in foreign languages, music, and literature, and by age sixteen, largely through the stimulation of a summer spent in Paris, he was busily at work as both writer and translator. His earliest efforts, about which he carried on a regular correspondence with his mother, who also had literary ambitions, were refused publication. Of the works which eventually made Lewis famous, however, a surprising number were completed, or at least begun, during his teens—a genesis that goes far to explain the adolescent feverishness of many of his most characteristic productions.

In Paris, Lewis became familiar with French drama, and there he may also have encountered translations of contemporary German literature. At any rate, he became thoroughly imbued with the spirit of the German *Sturm und Drang* movement during a stay in Weimar which began in July of 1792 when Lewis was seventeen. His father had sent him there to learn German so that he might enter the diplomatic service, and during his stay, he met Johann Wolfgang von Goethe and Christoph Martin Wieland, spent many hours translating German literary works, and continued to fashion a literary style of his own, a style heavily influenced by his experiences in both Paris and Weimar.

Lewis returned to Oxford in the early months of 1793 and was graduated in the spring of 1794, shortly before his nineteenth birthday. Between May and December of 1794, he held a minor diplomatic post at The Hague, where he found ample time to complete the novel which was to assure his fame. That novel, *The Monk*, was published in 1796 and made Lewis an immediate, and slightly infamous, celebrity. His presence was very much in demand at London social gatherings, a fact which delighted the gregarious young author.

In this same eventful year, Lewis became the parliamentary representative for Hindon in Wiltshire, a position he retained until 1802. His parliamentary duties and his literary fame brought him the acquaintance, during these and subsequent years, of many of the prominent men of England, a number of whom mention Lewis in their correspondence and other writings. The impression which these accounts give of Lewis is of a physically unattractive, dreadfully nearsighted man, whose kindliness and affability made him difficult to dislike but whose boring garrulousness often made his company difficult to enjoy. A tone of amused, sometimes exasperated, affection suffuses many of these verbal portraits, especially those by Lord Byron.

As he had at The Hague, Lewis found sufficient time while a Member of Parliament to carry forward his literary projects. He was occasionally instrumental, too, in advancing the careers of other literary men, the most important of whom was Sir Walter Scott. In addition to inviting Scott, whom he had met in 1798, to contribute to *Tales of Wonder*, Lewis helped to arrange for the publication of Scott's 1799 translation of Goethe's *Goetz von Berlichingen*. It is amusing to read Scott's account of the deference with which he, then almost entirely unknown as a writer, received Lewis' often imperious pronouncements concerning literary style.

During this same period, Lewis' talents as a playwright came to the public's attention, with *The Castle Spectre*, the third of his plays to be published but the first to be staged. *Village Virtues*, a social farce, and *The Minister*, a translation of Friedrich Schiller's *Kabale und Liebe*, had attracted little attention to Lewis' dramatic skills, but *The Castle Spectre*, which opened on December 14, 1797, earned eighteen thousand pounds for Drury Lane Theater in less than three months.

Lewis' next dramatic project, a translation of August von Kotzebue's 1794 play *Die Spanier in Peru*, appears originally to have been intended as a collaboration with Richard Brinsley Sheridan, but the pair found it impossible to work together, and Sheridan turned to another translator for assistance. Sheridan's version of the play, *Pizarro: A Tragedy in Five Acts*, opened in May, 1799, without acknowledgment of Lewis' initial contributions to the production, and achieved spectacular success. Lewis' version, *Rolla*, was published but not performed, and the ill will generated by this incident and by various other difficulties experienced by Lewis at Drury Lane eventually led to a temporary shift of his loyalties to Covent Garden.

Before this occurred, however, three more of his plays were presented at Drury Lane, *The Twins* and *The East Indian* in 1799 and *Adelmorn the Outlaw* in 1801, but none achieved any extraordinary success. The first two, a social farce and a sentimental comedy, were originally acted as benefit presentations for a pair of Drury Lane's veteran performers; although they served that purpose adequately, the critical and popular reception of the plays was at best lukewarm. Like his other attempts at comedy, they were neither great triumphs nor notable catastrophes. *Adelmorn the Outlaw* on the other hand, threatened to become an embarrassment of the first order. The stage set and the incidental music were well received, but the play itself was a critical failure. *Adelmorn the Outlaw* included many of the same melodramatic plot elements and Gothic flourishes that had attracted enthusiastic audiences to *The Castle Spectre*, but *Adelmorn the Outlaw* was so absurdly and, at times, so tastelessly constructed that Lewis' utmost exertions were able to sustain it through a first run of only nine performances.

The reviewers treated Lewis' first Covent Garden production, *Alfonso, King of Castile*, with considerably more kindness. Although praise was not universal, some reviewers thought *Alfonso, King of Castile* the greatest tragic play of its age, and it was certainly Lewis' most concerted attempt at high dramatic art. The play is written in blank verse, occasionally with impressive poetic effect, but the plot is marred by a melodramatic intensity that makes it difficult for a twentieth century reader to take seriously. *Alfonso, King of Castile* was published several weeks before its January 15, 1802, premiere, and though its first run of only ten performances suggests that it was a very modest popular success, it remained the play in which

Lewis took the greatest artistic pride.

During 1803, Lewis' only new theatrical productions were *The Captive*, a dramatic monologue, and *The Harper's Daughter*, a shortened version of *The Minister*. They both appeared at Covent Garden, on March 22 and May 4, respectively, and each was successful after its own fashion. *The Harper's Daughter* was a benefit presentation and drew a large enough audience to provide a tidy sum. *The Captive*, billed as a "mono-drama," was an extended speech by a young wife who had been consigned to a madhouse by her cruel husband. So effective was its presentation of the wife's gradual loss of sanity that several spectators experienced hysterical fits during and after the performance and the drama was withdrawn in order to preserve the mental health of Covent Garden's customers.

Lewis' next play, a melodrama in two acts entitled *Rugantino*, opened at Covent Garden on October 18, 1805, and was performed thirty times before enthusiastic houses. Lewis again caught the public's fancy by relying on spectacle rather than subtle art, and though an occasional viewer might complain of headaches brought on by the play's many pistol shots and thunderclaps, most were enthralled, nor did the dazzling costume changes and the gorgeous Venice scenery hurt the play's attendance. Lewis knew his audience well and gave it what it wanted.

Rugantino was followed on April 1, 1807, this time at Drury Lane, by the even more spectacular *The Wood Daemon*. Full of more Gothic paraphernalia than any of Lewis' previous dramatic creations, *The Wood Daemon* is more truly a play of special effects than of plot and dialogue, and it was judged in such terms by contemporary reviewers: There was considerable praise for the production's visual impact but very little positive comment on the play as literary art. The visual impact was enough, however, to assure *The Wood Daemon* a first run of thirty-four performances.

Lewis' next three productions met with a more modest reception. *Adelgitha*, a play which Lewis had published in 1806, opened at Drury Lane in April of 1807 to favorable reviews. Centering on a character whose tragic life was meant to illustrate the fatal consequences of youthful sin, the play relies for its effect on melodramatic plot complication rather than visual spectacle, and although its nine first-run performances compare unfavorably with the thirty-four of *The Wood Daemon*, it was not nearly so ambitious a theatrical project and seems fully to have satisfied the expectations of those involved in its staging.

Venoni did not, at first, fare so well. The play, whose plot Lewis adapted from a French original, premiered at Drury Lane on December 1, 1808, and was immediately attacked by the reviewers. One scene in particular, in which a pair of lovers, unaware of each other's presence, speak alternating soliloquies from their adjoining dungeon cells, was judged especially ludicrous. The play required extensive rewriting, which Lewis undertook with some success, and *Venoni* had reached its eighteenth performance when a fire destroyed the theater. Lewis then provided the Drury Lane troupe, temporarily housed at the Lyceum Theater, with a farce entitled *Temper*, which opened on May 1, 1809, attracting so little attention that it was lost from Lewis' dramatic canon until 1942.

At this point, Lewis announced that he would write no more plays, a decision which, if he had adhered to it, would have denied posterity his most dubious contribution to British theater, the grand equestrian drama *Timour the Tartar*. *Timour the Tartar* was not the first play to introduce horses onto the British stage; that honor belongs to *Blue Beard*, whose cast of characters was horseless until February 18, 1811. On that date, the Covent Garden management made its initial test of the public's readiness to accept equestrian performers. The popular response was gratifying, and *Timour the Tartar*, whose equestrian elements were not extraneous interpolations but integral parts of the plot, was awaited with considerable anticipation. The play opened on April 29, 1811, to the howls of the critics and the applause of the paying customers. In the ensuing months, parodies and imitations abounded, one featuring a performing elephant, and *Timour the Tartar* itself was staged a profitable forty-four times.

Lewis' final two theatrical offerings were reworkings of old material. They do, however, illustrate Lewis' frequent use of songs to increase the entertainment value of his plays. Working with Michael Kelly and Matthew Peter King, Lewis transformed *The Wood Daemon* into "a grand musical romance" with the slightly altered title, *One O'Clock: Or, The Knight and the Wood Daemon*; collaborating with Charles Edward Horn, he extensively revised *The East Indian*, turning it into a comic opera entitled *Rich and Poor*. The musical romance premiered on August 1, 1811, and was performed twenty-five times during its first season by the company of the English Opera House; the comic opera opened on July 22, 1812, and was performed twenty-seven times by the same organization.

Lewis' literary endeavors had been made possible largely by a yearly allowance of a thousand pounds granted him by his father. This allowance was reduced for a time as a result of an argument between father and son over a sexual affair in which the elder Lewis had become involved, but the two managed to reconcile their differences before the father's death in May of 1812, and Lewis inherited all of his father's considerable wealth. Very soon thereafter, he used a portion of the money to purchase a permanent home for his mother.

Another consequence of the inheritance was the first of Lewis' two voyages to Jamaica to inspect his island properties. The primary purpose of his visit, which occurred during the first three months of 1816, was to ascertain that slaves on his plantations were properly treated. Although Lewis made no provision for the freeing of these slaves, he did establish strict rules intended to make their lives more bearable. Also, to prevent a deterioration in their living conditions after his death, he added a codicil to his will insisting that any future heir to his estates visit the plantations every third year for the purpose of looking after the slaves' welfare. In addition, no slaves were to be put up for sale.

The alterations in Lewis' will were witnessed on August 20, 1816, by Lord Byron, Percy Bysshe Shelley, and Dr. John W. Polidori during a trip Lewis took to the Continent, a trip which lasted for more than a year. The most noteworthy literary events of that tour were his oral translation of Goethe's *Faust* (1808, 1833) for Byron, the latter's first direct experience with that work, and Lewis' telling ghost stories for the entertainment of Byron and the Shelleys. Although Lewis cannot be claimed to have inspired Mary Shelley's *Frankenstein* (1818), since she had begun her novel several weeks before Lewis' arrival in Geneva, his enthusiasm for the Gothic is likely to have encouraged her to continue the project.

After a short stay in England following his wanderings on the Continent, Lewis again set sail for Jamaica on November 5, 1817. During this second visit, he introduced further reforms to improve the plight of his slaves, and having assured himself that he had done what he could for them, he embarked for England on May 4, 1818. He was ill with yellow fever when the voyage began, and within two weeks, he was dead.

Analysis

Despite considerable diversity in style and content, Matthew Gregory Lewis' plays are generally characterized by a melodramatic intensity that is often reinforced by visual spectacle. Dramatic subtlety was difficult to achieve in the huge theaters for which Lewis wrote, and Lewis' unsubtle ways were peculiarly suited to the physical environment in which his plays were performed. This is not to say, however, that Lewis presents no unified dramatic vision, that he has nothing to say about the state of human beings. On the contrary, his plays are surprisingly consistent in their expression of one particular theme—that the sanctity of human relationships should not and must not be violated.

The Castle Spectre, for example, relates the tale of the villainous Earl Osmond, who has sinned against the bonds of love at every opportunity and who pays the ultimate price for his crimes. Long before the action of the play begins, Osmond has already launched his egocentric career by overthrowing his own brother, the benevolent Earl Reginald, and inadvertently killing Lady Evelina, the woman whom he had hoped to marry but who had married his brother instead. Evelina has martyred herself to love by throwing her body in the path of a dagger-thrust which Osmond intended for Reginald. Her sacrifice has not prevented the usurpation of her husband's power, but it has, as the audience is eventually informed, preserved her husband's life.

As one might expect of such a man, Osmond has shown no more respect for the relationship between a ruler and his subjects than he has for the ties of blood, and though he conceals the guilty secret of his rise to power, Osmond is universally hated as a tyrant. He surrounds himself with brutal henchmen who deal efficiently and savagely with any who would oppose their master. At the beginning of the play, there are no obvious threats to Osmond's continued dominion, but the isolation and loneliness which his actions have brought upon him are soon to lead to his downfall.

Appropriately enough, the undoing of this sinner against the bonds of affection is the direct result of his falling in love. The unwilling object of his amorous attentions is his niece, the beautiful and virtuous Angela, daughter of Reginald and Evelina. To minimize Angela's threat to his power (as heir to the rightful lord), Osmond has placed her with a peasant couple who have reared her as their own child. He makes the fateful decision to call her back to the court, however, when her resemblance to Evelina inspires his passion. To legitimate Evelina's sudden change in status, Osmond invents a story affirming her noble birth while concealing her actual parentage.

Like his obsession with Evelina, though, his interest in Angela is doomed to failure—again because the woman he has chosen has already selected a worthier man. During the last weeks of her peasant existence, she has fallen in love with the lowly Edric, whom she had met while she was living as a peasant, and even the opportunity to marry an earl is not temptation enough to shake her fidelity to this humble swain. Neither sweet words nor threats of imprisonment are sufficient to win her consent to become Osmond's wife.

As the audience soon discovers, Angela has chosen more wisely than she knows, because Edric is actually Percy, Earl of Northumberland, whose benevolent rule has earned for him the respect and affection of his people and whose purity of heart is suggested by the circumstances of his falling in love. Neither Percy nor Angela had been aware of the other's noble birth, but each has recognized the other's nobility of character. Percy and Osmond are spiritual opposites, and their rivalry for Angela is a clash between codes of behavior, between the ways of sentiment and the ways of selfishness.

One manifestation of this opposition is the method each uses to form alliances. Osmond surrounds himself with men who are motivated by fear and hatred or by self-interest. He enslaves his henchmen and awes them with his power, or he entices them with the hope of illusory rewards. His black slaves, like Hassan, have been stolen from their homelands and welcome every opportunity to wreak vengeance on the race which separated them from their loved ones. Others, like Kenric, have been promised worldly wealth and release from service in exchange for their fidelity, only to discover Osmond's intention to betray them. Percy's followers, on the other hand, eagerly join his effort to rescue Angela; they are motivated by love and remain faithful to their master at moments when Osmond's followers are most likely to become undependable. One in particular, Gilbert the Knave, has been the object of Percy's generosity during a period of personal crisis and shows his gratitude through his courageous support of his master at several key points in the play. As Percy himself says, "Instead of looking with scorn on those whom a smile would attract, and a favor bind forever, how many firm friends might our nobles gain, if they would but reflect that their vassals are men as they are, and have hearts whose feelings can be grateful as their own."

Osmond refuses to recognize this sentimental truth, and as a result, he loses the loyalty of a man who is in a position to reveal more about Osmond's perfidious nature than that noble cares for the world to know. When Kenric discovers that his master is plotting to kill him, he tells Angela the secret of her birth and that her father Reginald is alive, hidden away in a dungeon by Kenric himself so that he might blackmail Osmond if the need should ever arise. Unfortunately, Osmond overhears this conversation and goes in search of his hated brother, intending to carry to completion the fratricide which he had thought he had already committed.

Before the climactic arrival of the principal characters at Reginald's dungeon, the sympathy of the supernatural with the defenders of sentiment has been implied by the spectacular appearance to Angela of her mother's ghost. The specter of Evelina blesses Angela and directs her to rescue her father; elements in this scene suggest the triumph of love over hatred, a triumph which occurs in the play's busy final moments. Osmond and Angela come upon her father's darkened cell at almost the same time, and Osmond uses the occasion to threaten her with Reginald's death unless she acquiesces to their immediate marriage. This she is about to do when Reginald stops her by saying that he will take his own life rather than see his daughter dishonored. Enraged by this declaration and by news that Percy's forces have taken the castle, Osmond prepares to kill his brother but falls back in horror when Evelina's ghost repeats the self-sacrificing gesture of the living Evelina. Angela then strikes Osmond with the same dagger with which her mother had been stabbed, and the sinner against sentiment is carried away to die.

As one might imagine, despite the extraordinary commercial success of *The Castle Spectre*, it was not a universal favorite of the critics. This fact seems not to have concerned Lewis, however, who was especially cavalier in his response to one very particular objection to his play. When the critics pointed out that his inclusion of black slaves in the cast of characters of a Gothic story was a patent absurdity, he defended himself by saying that he had done it to "give a pleasing variety to the characters and dresses" and that if he could "have produced the same effect by making my heroine blue, blue I should have made her."

Obviously, Lewis did not take *The Castle Spectre* seriously as a work of art, but he did feel considerable artistic pride in *Alfonso, King of Castile.* Nevertheless, the two plays have essentially the same theme: The forces of sentiment are pitted against the forces of selfish ambition, and after the moral superiority of sentiment has been clearly displayed, ambition is defeated. In *Alfonso, King of Castile*, however, there are surprising twists of plot and characterization which create a greater sense of dramatic sophistication than is evident in the earlier play.

The curtain rises on a narrative situation that is already quite complex. Alfonso has been a good king, but he has been duped into committing one act of injustice. He has imprisoned his best friend, Orsino, on the basis of evidence fabricated by Orsino's enemies. As a result, Orsino's wife, Victoria, has died in poverty-stricken exile after swearing her son, Caesario, to avenge his father. Concealing his identity, Caesario has insinuated his way into the good graces of the king and has so successfully encouraged the rebellious spirit of the king's son that the son has defected to the king's foes. Caesario has also secretly won the love of and married the king's daughter, Amelrosa, but he has not managed, as the play begins, to break the filial bond between Alfonso and his daughter.

Ironically, it is love—for his parents—that causes Caesario to become filled with hatred. His hatred is directed against a man whose only fault is gullibility, and he attempts to make use of the innocent love of a virtuous woman to further his despicable ends. Like Osmond, Caesario is a sinner against the dictates of sentiment, and he, too, will pay with his life for his crimes.

That Caesario's actions are crimes is made clear in a number of ways. First, while courting Amelrosa, Caesario has shown his duplicitous nature by carrying on an illicit liaison with Ottilia, the vicious wife of Marquis Guzman, the man primarily responsible for his father's fall from grace. The difficulties of this situation cause him to weave a web of lies which suggest that his feelings toward neither woman are genuine. Furthermore, as the moment of Caesario's final vengeance against Alfonso approaches, it becomes increasingly obvious that a desire for personal power is at least as important in motivating Caesario as any wish to punish his father's persecutor. In fact, the killing of Alfonso is to be carried out in a way intended to alert any English audience to his murderer's villainy; a cache of explosives is to be detonated beneath Alfonso's palace, an obvious allusion to the infamous Gunpowder Plot.

During the course of the play, Orsino is discovered to be alive, and, despite his bitterness over the sufferings of himself and his family, he condemns Caesario's plans for the overthrow of Alfonso. When Alfonso has come to beg his forgiveness, his resentment has been too great to allow a reconciliation to occur, but when his son reveals his dastardly plotting, Orsino affirms the basic goodness of his former friend and allies himself with Alfonso rather than with Caesario. In a speech which summarizes the central idea of the play, he tries to draw his son back to the paths of virtue:

> True glory
> Is not to wear a crown but to *deserve* one.
> The peasant swain who leads a good man's life,
> And dies at last a good man's death, obtains
> In Wisdom's eye wreaths of far brighter splendour
> Than he whose wanton pride and thirst for empire
> Make kings his captives, and lay waste a world.

Unfortunately, Caesario's hatred and ambition blind him to the truth of his father's statement.

As they generally are in a Lewis play, the final scenes of *Alfonso, King of Castile* are almost overburdened with action. When the play ends, all the principals, with the exception of Alfonso himself, are either dead or dying, and Orsino, mortally wounded, has been forced to choose between killing his vicious son and watching the flawed but virtuous Alfonso be murdered. He chooses, in an odd affirmation of the laws of sentiment, to save the friend who had once betrayed him and to sacrifice the son.

Although it does call for the simulated detonation of a cache of gunpowder, *Alfonso, King of Castile* is less dependent for its success on sensational stage effects than are most of Lewis' plays. *Timour the Tartar*, for example, is unashamed stage spectacle from beginning to end. A play in which live horses take part in elaborate battle scenes and in which one particular equine performer leaps with its rider over a parapet into the sea could hardly be anything else. Nevertheless, the same thematic material which gives *Alfonso, King of Castile* some semblance of high seriousness is also to be found in *Timour the Tartar*, another tale of the triumph of sentimental virtue over egocentric vice.

Timour himself is the ruthless villain whose selfishness threatens the very existence of those whose actions are motivated by selfless love. Even his father, Oglou, fears for his life when in Timour's presence. As the code of sentiment dictates, however, he loves his son despite being afraid of him. Throughout the play, Oglou struggles to act in accordance with this love for his son while at the same time behaving properly toward two of his dearest friends, Agib and Zorilda, the most dangerous of Timour's enemies.

Agib is the son and Zorilda the widow of the murdered Prince of Mingrelia, and when the play opens, Agib is Timour's captive. Fortunately, Agib's jailer is the kindly Oglou, whose life was once saved by Zorilda.

Oglou will protect Agib as best he can, but he lacks the courage to defy his son by setting Agib free. In a display of the deepest maternal fortitude, that task is undertaken instead by Zorilda.

Zorilda boldly enters Timour's palace disguised as his fiancée, the Princess of Georgia, a woman to whom Timour has become engaged without having met her. Her intention is to demand that Agib, a threat to their united power, be placed with her compatriots for safekeeping. Unfortunately, just as this plot is about to succeed, Oglou is forced to reveal Zorilda's true identity because he anticipates a similar revelation by Octar, Timour's messenger to the Georgian court.

In defiance of every rule of sentiment and decency, Timour proceeds to demand that the spirited Zorilda become his bride despite her obvious distaste for her husband's barbaric murderer; her son, Agib, is to be killed if she refuses. The necessity of making such a choice is obviated, however, when the faithful Oglou assists in getting Agib out of the palace. He asks only, as paternal sentiment demands, that mercy be shown to Timour if Agib and his allies succeed in overthrowing the tyrant. Out of respect for their friend's fatherly feelings, Zorilda and Agib agree.

By this point in the play, there have been illustrations of the sentiments appropriate to a number of human relationships: widow to deceased husband, son to deceased father, mother to son, father to son, and friend to friend. The play's final scene portrays, in rather spectacular fashion, the courageous love of a son for his mother. As Agib and his troops gather for their attack on Timour's stronghold, Timour, in full sight of the massed armies, attempts to kill the captive Zorilda. She flees and is forced to leap into the sea, at which point Agib spurs his horse over a parapet and rescues his mother from a death by drowning. The stage then becomes a battleground where the forces of virtuous sentiment defeat the forces of self-serving oppression with convincing finality.

For his next theatrical effort, Lewis turned from the comparatively new equestrian drama to the more familiar Gothic drama. He transformed his earlier *The Wood Daemon* into *One O'Clock: Or, The Knight and the Wood Daemon*, advertising this extraordinary concoction as "a grand musical romance." In keeping with this designation, it contains considerable singing and dancing, and its costumes, sets, and stage machinery are more extravagant than anything used in Lewis' previous productions. Nevertheless, *One O'Clock* is thematically consistent with Lewis' other plays in that it deals with the corrupting influence of egocentric ambition and the saving grace of sentimental virtue.

The power-mad villain of this particular piece is Hardyknute, a former peasant who has become the Count of Holstein by forming a pact with Sangrida, the Wood Daemon. Sangrida has granted him wealth, beauty, eternal youth, and invulnerability in battle in exchange for an annual sacrifice of a child. Each year, on the seventh of August, Hardyknute must spill innocent blood or become the Wood Daemon's perpetual slave. If he fails to accomplish his hideous task before Sangrida's clock strikes one in the morning, he will be subjected to everlasting torment. The play centers on Hardyknute's attempt to sacrifice a ninth child, Leolyn, and take possession of his reward, the beautiful peasant girl Una.

The representatives of virtuous innocence within the play are Leolyn, Clotilda, Oswy, and Una. Leolyn is the long-lost son of the former count, Ruric, whom Hardyknute clandestinely murdered in order to seize power. Leolyn, who had been entrusted to Una's sister, Clotilda, was stolen by marauding Gypsies and reappears as the play opens, struck dumb and recognizable only by a birthmark on his wrist. Una, whose name suggests (among other things) the dreaded hour of sacrifice, is a young peasant maiden who has been so confounded by the magic of Sangrida that she is on the brink of marrying Hardyknute; her heart, however, belongs to Oswy. Oswy is the poor but faithful peasant who loves Una to distraction and would unhesitatingly lay down his life for her.

To an even greater extent than usual, Lewis concentrates the significant action of the play in the final scenes. The first two acts contain a painfully slow exposition of the plot, the introduction of sentimental subplots which are never satisfactorily integrated with the main plot, and the insertion of various entertainments and spectacles that are obviously intended to dazzle and divert the audience. Storms, secret passages, disappearing statues, and a miraculous bed are only a few of the special effects, with other diversions including a chorus of spirits, a procession of Gypsies, a triumphal march of troops leading a captured giant and dwarfs, a prophetic dream, and a ballet of the seasons, as well as intermittent outbursts of ballad-singing and guitar-playing. By the end of act 2, however, Hardyknute has come to realize, through the venerable device of the birthmark, that his predecessor's son is within the castle and that he must act if he is to preserve his power. He has also been reminded, by the terrifying voice of Sangrida, that only a few hours remain before he must make his annual sacrifice.

In the final act, the allegiance of the central characters to the laws of sentiment is tested, and only Hardyknute is found wanting. Clotilda, suspicious of Hardyknute's murderous intentions, guards Leolyn's bedchamber and is foiled in her vigilance only by a treacherous mechanism that lowers Leolyn's bed into a subterranean dungeon. At this point, Oswy is called upon to seek help from the King of Denmark, a task he undertakes despite his worries concerning the wavering fidelity of his beloved Una. Una herself is tried most severely of all. After gaining access to the dungeon into which Leolyn has been caged and releasing him from his chains, she is confronted by Hardyknute, who reveals his dreadful secret and makes clear that he will spill her blood in place of Leolyn's if he can save himself from

Sangrida in no other way. His love for her will make the murder difficult, but his self-love, being greater, will steel him to commit the crime. Faced with the choice of becoming Hardyknute's accomplice by revealing Leolyn's hiding place or of jeopardizing her own life, Una hesitates for a moment but then chooses to save the innocent young boy. Leolyn, in turn, proves himself worthy of Una's courageous selflessness by remaining in the dungeon and by finding a means of preventing her death. In full sight of Hardyknute, he climbs to Sangrida's clock and pushes the hands forward to the hour of one, thereby calling up the demon before Una can be killed. Sangrida appears immediately and, in a scene that is reminiscent of the conclusion of *The Monk*, four fiends drag Hardyknute away to his eternal punishment.

Although the artistic merit of Lewis' plays is minimal, his contemporaries enjoyed them. The sensationalism and the melodramatic moralizing of his dramatic works are symptomatic of the bad taste which produced one of the most sterile periods in British theatrical history, and if Lewis cannot be accused of creating this bad taste, he can justly be said to have been the most adept playwright of his age at exploiting it.

Other major works

NOVEL: *Ambrosio: Or, The Monk*, 1796 (also as *The Monk: A Romance*).

POETRY: *The Love of Gain: A Poem Imitated from Juvenal*, 1799; *Monody on the Death of Sir John Moore*, 1809; *Poems*, 1812; *The Isle of Devils: A Metrical Tale*, 1827.

NONFICTION: *Journal of a West India Proprietor, Kept During a Residence in the Island of Jamaica*, 1834 (also as *Journal of a Residence Among the Negroes in the West Indies*, 1861).

ANTHOLOGIES: *Tales of Terror*, 1799 (also as *An Apology for Tales of Terror*; includes work by Sir Walter Scott and Robert Southey); *Tales of Wonder*, 1801 (2 volumes; includes work by Scott, Southey, Robert Burns, Thomas Gray, John Dryden, and others).

TRANSLATIONS: *The Bravo of Venice: A Romance*, 1805 (of J. H. D. Zschokke's novel *Aballino der Grosse Bandit*); *Feudal Tyrants: Or, The Counts of Carlsheim and Sargans: A Romance, Taken from the German*, 1806 (4 volumes; of Christiane Benedicte Eugénie Naubert's novel *Elisabeth, Erbin von Toggenburg: Oder, Geschichte der Frauen in der Schweiz*).

MISCELLANEOUS: *Romantic Tales*, 1808 (4 volumes; includes poem, short stories, and ballads); *Twelve Ballads, the Words and Music by M. G. Lewis*, 1808; *The Life and Correspondence of M. G. Lewis, with Many Pieces Never Before Published*, 1839 (2 volumes; Margaret Baron-Wilson, editor).

Bibliography
Evans, Bertrand. "Lewis and Gothic Drama." In *Gothic Drama from Walpole to Shelley*. Berkeley: University of California Press, 1947. Evans' pioneering volume remains the definitive study of Gothic drama in England and is among the best sources for gaining a sense of Lewis' peculiar niche in British dramatic history. Evans labels Lewis the preeminent Gothic dramatist and analyzes three of his plays in considerable detail: *The Castle Spectre*, *Adelmorn the Outlaw*, and *The Wood Daemon*. Several other of Lewis' plays are discussed less thoroughly.
Frank, Frederick S. "The Gothic Romance: 1762-1820." In *Horror Literature: A Core Collection and Reference Guide*, edited by Marshall B. Tymn. New York: R. R. Bowker, 1981. Although Frank's primary concern is the Gothic novel, with Lewis' *The Monk* mentioned prominently, he also gives accounts of several Gothic plays, including Lewis' *The Castle Spectre*, *Adelmorn the Outlaw*, and *The Wood Daemon*. The difficulty of finding copies of Lewis' plays outside the rare-book rooms of major university libraries considerably increases the value of Frank's plot summaries and limited critical commentary.
Irwin, Joseph James. "Success and Failure in the Theater." In *M. G. "Monk" Lewis*. Boston: Twayne, 1976. Concentrating on the essential information needed by a first-time reader of Lewis' works, Irwin's book is an excellent introduction to both the life and the literary career. The chapter dedicated to Lewis' plays includes pertinent biographical facts, comments on the place of each drama in theatrical history, analyses of plots and themes, and accounts of the plays' popular and critical receptions.
Nicoll, Allardyce. *A History of Late Eighteenth Century Drama, 1750-1800*. Cambridge, England: Cambridge University Press, 1937.
_____. *A History of Early Nineteenth Century Drama, 1800-1850*. Vols. 1 and 2. Cambridge, England: Cambridge University Press, 1930. Nicoll's remarks about Lewis emphasize his contributions to Gothic drama and melodrama and his mastery of those elements of spectacular stage effect, which contributed to his popular appeal and detracted substantially from his literary reputation. Nicoll's handlists of plays add a further useful dimension to this standard stage history.
Peck, Louis F. "Dramas." *A Life of Matthew G. Lewis*. Cambridge, Mass.: Harvard University Press, 1961. Peck's study is the standard critical biography of Lewis, despite its date of publication. Although Peck expresses disdain for Lewis' plays, he dedicates a meticulous chapter to discussing the circumstances of their composition and production and to analyzing them as indicators of contemporary theatrical taste. Especially noteworthy are Peck's comments on Lewis' dramatic technique.

Robert H. O'Connor

GEORGE LILLO

Born: London, England; February 4, 1693
Died: London, England; September 3, 1739

Principal drama

Silvia: Or, The Country Burial, pr., pb. 1730; *The London Merchant: Or, The History of George Barnwell*, pr., pb. 1731; *The Christian Hero*, pr., pb. 1735; *Guilt Its Own Punishment: Or, Fatal Curiosity*, pr. 1736, pb. 1737 (commonly known as *Fatal Curiosity*); *Marina*, pr., pb. 1738; *Britannia and Batavia*, pb. 1740 (masque); *Elmerick: Or, Justice Triumphant*, pr., pb. 1740; *Arden of Feversham*, pr. 1759, pb. 1762 (with John Hoadly); *The Works of Mr. George Lillo*, pb. 1775 (2 volumes; Thomas Davies, editor).

Other literary forms

George Lillo is known only for his plays.

Achievements

Of George Lillo's seven plays, only *The London Merchant* was both a popular and critical success when first presented, and only it and *Fatal Curiosity* continued to be performed long after most plays of their period had been forgotten. These homiletic domestic tragedies, which reflect their author's creed as a Dissenter, had a profound effect upon the Continental drama of the late eighteenth century and early nineteenth century.

During a playwriting career that spanned less than a decade, Lillo tried his hand at most popular dramatic forms: ballad opera, heroic drama, masque, prose tragedy, blank-verse tragedy, even adaptations of Elizabethan domestic tragedy (*Arden of Feversham*) and Shakespearean romance (*Marina*, a reworking of the last two acts of William Shakespeare's *Pericles*). Lillo worked within the bounds of tradition but at the same time went beyond past practice. For example, his first play, *Silvia*, is a ballad opera of the sort that had become popular in the wake of John Gay's success with *The Beggar's Opera* in 1728. In it, Lillo follows Gay's pattern of punctuating the action with dozens of familiar tunes, and he includes burlesque and seriocomic elements. The pastoral motif dominates, however, and Lillo's announced intention—"to inculcate the love of truth and virtue and a hatred of vice and falsehood"—foreshadows the strong didacticism and sentimentalism of his two major plays which were to follow.

Lillo was a relatively inexperienced playwright when he offered *The London Merchant* to Theophilus Cibber, manager of a summer company acting at the Drury Lane. Though the famous actor David Garrick credited Lillo with "the invention of a new species of dramatic poetry, which may properly be termed the inferior or lesser tragedy," the drama of hapless George Barnwell is actually in the tradition of such Elizabethan domestic tragedies as the anonymously authored *Arden of Feversham* (1592) and *A Yorkshire Tragedy* (c. 1606). Further, earlier in the eighteenth century there were such middle-class forebears as Lewis Theobald's *The Perfidious Brothers* (pb. 1715) and Aaron Hill's *The Fatal Extravagance* (pb. 1720), the latter based on *A Yorkshire Tragedy*; Thomas Otway during the Restoration and Nicholas Rowe early in the eighteenth century also wrote plays whose sentimentalism and pathos verged on the melodramatic. Despite these predecessors, Lillo's achievement in *The London Merchant* is notable, for it is a realistic prose drama that consciously celebrates the virtues of middle-class life. It offered theatergoers (in its day, and for more than a century thereafter, as a Christmas and Easter entertainment for London apprentices) not a tale of "prinses distrest and scenes of royal woe," but the story of an honest merchant, his errant apprentice, and a conniving woman, characters with whom middle-class Londoners could identify and whose emotions they could share. Eschewing blank verse, Lillo chose to write in "artless strains," which emphasized both the realism and the bourgeois subject matter of the play and successfully accommodated his work "to the circumstances of the generality of mankind." Young men about town came to the first performance ready to scoff (having purchased from street hawkers copies of the Elizabethan ballad on which the play was based), but they soon "were drawn in to drop their ballads and pull out their handkerchiefs." Alexander Pope was at the first performance and reacted favorably; Queen Caroline asked for a copy of the play, and the royal family went to see it; and both *The Weekly Register* and *The Gentleman's Magazine* defended it enthusiastically against charges that its characters, "so low and familiar in Life," were therefore "too low for the Stage."

Enduringly popular as the play was, it did not start a trend on the London stage; there were some imitations, but only Edward Moore's *The Gamester* (pr. 1753) is noteworthy. On the Continent, however, it was both popular and influential. It was translated into French, German, and Dutch, and it was praised by Denis Diderot and Gotthold Ephraim Lessing, the latter of whom wrote, "I should infinitely prefer to be the creator of *The London Merchant* than the creator of *Der sterbende Cato*." Indeed, Lillo's play is a clear ancestor of Lessing's *Miss Sara Samson* (pr. 1755), an early *Schicksaltragödie*, or German domestic drama.

Fatal Curiosity, another mercantile domestic drama but in blank verse, has been described by Allardyce Nicoll as the only tragic masterpiece produced between 1700 and 1750 and by William H. McBurney as a landmark play: "at once a climax to Restoration tragedy written according to 'the rules,' and a dramatic protest against the 'frigid caution' of an age in which 'Declamation roar'd whilst Passion slept.'" When first presented in 1736 at

Henry Fielding's theater, it ran only seven nights, but when it was revived the following March as a curtain raiser for Fielding's *The Historical Register for the Year 1736*, it lasted for eleven nights. The play was revived again in 1741, 1742, and 1755; George Colman's pre-Romantic version was done in 1782; and Henry MacKenzie's reworking (called *The Shipwreck*) was presented in 1784. *Fatal Curiosity* clearly had continuing appeal to eighteenth century audiences, and its characterizations, moral sentiments, and theatricality withstood changing dramatic fashions. (Mrs. Elizabeth Inchbald, in *The British Theatre*, 1808, described a performance of Colman's version at which "a certain horror seized the audience, and was manifested by a kind of stifled scream.") In addition to its continuing presence on the English stage, the play was widely read, particularly in the aftermath of James Harris' enthusiastic comparison (in *Philological Inquiries*, 1781) of it to Sophocles' *Oedipus Rex*, to Shakespeare's *Othello* and *King Lear*, and to John Milton's *Samson Agonistes*, and his description of it as "the model of a Perfect Fable." As in the case of *The London Merchant*, however, the enduring popularity of the play had very little effect on subsequent English tragedy. In Germany, however, where imitations, adaptations, and translations abounded between 1781 and 1817, it was as influential a forerunner of the *Schicksaltragödie* as was *The London Merchant*.

Though Lillo's other works were failures on the stage, and even though *The London Merchant* and *Fatal Curiosity* sometimes are dismissed as little more than sentimental melodramas, both are of lasting interest not only because they obviously addressed a need felt by audiences in England and on the Continent but also because they significantly influenced the course of German tragic drama.

Biography

George Lillo was born in London near Moorgate on February 4, 1693; his father was Dutch, his mother English. He was reared as a Puritan Dissenter. Lillo learned his father's trade as a jeweler, and the two were partners in London for some years until the son decided to become a playwright. Little else is known about Lillo's life; contemporary accounts by Thomas Davies and Theophilus Cibber are still the primary sources.

Davies says that though Lillo was a Dissenter, he was "not of that sour cast which distinguishes some of our sectaries." He further describes him as being "lusty, but not tall, of a pleasing aspect, though unhappily deprived of the sight of one eye." Of a meeting with Lillo during a rehearsal of *Fatal Curiosity* in 1736, Davies recalls:

> Plain and simple as he was in his address, his manner of conversing was modest, affable and engaging. When invited to give his opinion of how a particular sentiment should be uttered by the actor, he exprest himself in the gentlest and most obliging terms, and conveyed instruction and conviction with good nature and good manners.

Soon after the death of Lillo, Fielding wrote in tribute to him the following words of eulogy:

> He had the gentlest and honestest Manners, and, at the same Time, the most friendly and obliging. He had a perfect Knowledge of Human Nature, though his Contempt for all base Means of Application, which are the necessary Steps to great Acquaintance, restrained his Conversation within very narrow Bounds. He had the Spirit of an old Roman, joined to the Innocence of a primitive Christian.

On the evidence of these statements, one can conclude that Lillo patterned the character Thorowgood in *The London Merchant* after himself.

The prologue to *Elmerick*, his last completed play, suggests that near the close of his life Lillo was "Deprest by want, afflicted by disease . . . ," and the third performance of the play, at Drury Lane on February 26, 1740, was said to be "for the benefit of the author's poor relations. . . ." The evidence of his will, however, indicates otherwise (his primary beneficiary was a nephew, John Underwood, also a jeweler), and Davies reports that Lillo had accumulated a considerable estate from productions of his plays (*The London Merchant* alone was done seventy times between 1731 and his death) and through their publication by his friend John Gray, a London bookseller to whom Lillo sold the rights to all of his works.

Lillo died on September 3, 1739, and was buried three days later in the vault of St. Leonard's Church, in London's Shoreditch.

Analysis

"The Ballad of George Barnwell" (which was sung to the tune of "The Merchant"), the late Elizabethan song which became the source of George Lillo's masterpiece, *The London Merchant*, was said to have been inspired by an actual murder case in Shropshire. The case concerned an apprentice who was seduced by an unscrupulous woman, embezzled funds from his master and gave them to the seductress, and then murdered an uncle in order to rob him. The authors of Elizabethan domestic tragedies often turned to accounts of murder cases for their sources, and Lillo was familiar with these sixteenth and seventeenth century middle-class plays (he wrote his own version of one, *Arden of Feversham*), so it is easy to understand the appeal of such a moralistic ballad to a young playwright who had been a shopkeeper and was a Calvinist Dissenter. It provided him with a substantive basis for a dramatized sermon on loyalty, honor, greed, and sexual morality—all of which he had touched upon in his first play, *Silvia*.

Allusions early in *The London Merchant* date the action prior to the defeat of the Spanish Armada, but there is nothing else to detract from its contemporary realism (its original title included the words "A True History"), and Lillo's addition of the characters of Maria, Trueman, and Millwood's servants to the four in his source increased the possibilities for thematic development as well as dramatic conflict. He also made Millwood, the seductress, into a tragic figure through passages that recall Cleopatra and Lady Macbeth and by focusing upon the reasons for her misanthropy.

The play opens with a dialogue between Thorowgood, the merchant, and Trueman, an apprentice, in which the master praises his country, its queen, and his fellow merchants, who "sometimes contribute to the safety of their country as they do at all times to its happiness." Thorowgood warns Trueman that if he "should be tempted to any action that has the appearance of vice or meanness in it," he should reflect "on the dignity of our profession," and then "may with honest scorn reject whatever is unworthy of it." When his only child, Maria, enters, the merchant recalls her many suitors, but she discounts "high birth and titles"; her melancholia, one suspects, is the result of unrequited love (for Barnwell, as it turns out).

The scene shifts to the home of Millwood, a malcontent who labels men "selfish hypocrites," hates other women, and supports herself by taking advantage "only of the young and innocent part of the sex who, having never injured women, apprehend no injury from them." Eighteen-year-old Barnwell, whom she has observed in financial transactions, is her latest intended victim, and Lillo prepares the audience well for his naïveté and easy distraction in the face of her advances. When she asks what he thinks about love, he talks about "the general love we owe to mankind" and his attachment for his uncle, master, and fellow apprentices. First addled and then smitten, Barnwell almost as quickly is miserable, having bought "a moment's pleasure with an age of pain." Conscience-stricken, he returns home, unable to reveal his transgression even to Trueman, his fellow apprentice and closest friend, but he is convinced that Millwood loves him. Thorowgood confronts but quickly pardons Barnwell for his unexplained absence ("That modest blush, the confusion so visible in your face, speak grief and shame") and then warns his charge: "Now, when the sense of pleasure's quick and passion high, the voluptuous appetites, raging and fierce, demand the strongest curb." Barnwell, though, is tempted anew, this time by Millwood's story of poverty. He seals his fate by giving her money taken from Thorowgood, but again is immediately tormented by remorse.

Asides and soliloquies are the means by which Lillo reveals Barnwell's recurring bouts of conscience, and they serve not only to develop his character but also to advance Lillo's didactic purposes, for almost all such speeches are brief exempla, parts of a play that Stephen L. Trainor, Jr., describes as structured "according to the prescribed format for a Dissenting sermon."

Trueman, not present in Lillo's source, is a moral counterpart of the fallen Barnwell. He remains Thorowgood's willing student and loyal apprentice and illustrates the highest ideals of lasting friendship. Shaken as he is by Barnwell's flight and confession of embezzlement in a letter to him, Trueman plans with Maria to make up the losses and thus conceal all from her father. During their plotting, Maria turns to the audience: "In attempting to save from shame one whom we hope may yet return to virtue, to Heaven and you, the judges of this action, I appeal whether I have done anything misbecoming my sex and character." Lillo apparently wanted theatergoers to wrestle with the moral implications of the action not only after a play but also during it. Millwood's servants, like Trueman and Maria creations of Lillo, are the traditional helpmates and coconspirators of their mistress at the start, but they quickly become disillusioned and decide that " 'Tis time the world was rid of such a monster" when Millwood convinces Barnwell to kill his uncle, for "there is something so horrid in murder that all other crimes seem nothing when compared to that." They resolve, therefore, to prevent the crime. The four characters Lillo has created thus dedicate themselves to saving a soul and eradicating evil. Representing several walks of life—apprentice, servants, daughter of a well-to-do merchant—they are role models for Lillo's audience, a substantial portion of which had been sent to the theater by masters and elders for edification as well as for entertainment.

The longest speech in the play is Barnwell's third-act soliloquy prior to the murder. Aware as he is of the "impiety" of his "bloody purpose" and sensing that nature itself trembles because of his "accursed design," he cannot fail to do Millwood's bidding: "She's got such firm possession of my heart and governs there with such despotic sway. . . . In vain does nature, reason, conscience, all oppose it." Hesitant to act, he finally stabs his uncle, who in his dying words asks the "choicest blessings" for his "dearest nephew" and forgiveness for his murderer. Barnwell's self-serving laments over the body have led many to echo Millwood's characterization of him as a "whining, preposterous, canting villain" who fails to evoke sympathy and lacks tragic stature. Lillo, however, was not influenced solely by classical tradition; his Calvinistic background also was likely a determining force in Barnwell's course of action. When he is seized as a result of Millwood's treachery, Barnwell complains: "The hand of Heaven is in it. . . . Yet Heaven, that justly cuts me off, still suffers her to live, perhaps to punish others. Tremendous mercy!" On the other hand, he recognizes the heinous nature of his crime ("This execrable act of mine's without a parallel") and accepts responsibility for what he has done: "I now am—what I've made myself." He also warns youths in the audience to "Avoid lewd women, false as they are fair. . . . By my example, learn to shun my fate. . . ." Such statements support Trainor's thesis that "Lillo seeks to bring the theatregoer to a sentient realization of the evil that exists within him for the purposes of confession and correction of that evil" and that this tragic concept evolved "from Puritan homiletic theory, which also seeks to achieve reformation by affective means. . . ."

The play as first presented and published has Millwood make her final appearance at the end of the fourth act as she is taken to prison, having been denounced by her servants. She lashes out at "men of all degrees and all professions ... alike wicked to the utmost of their power," and as for religion, "War, plague, and famine have not destroyed so many of the human race as this pretended piety has done. . . ." Warped though her self-justification may be, she sees herself as a victim of society and is utterly unrepentant, as bitterly and uncompromisingly defiant as she was earlier in the play. There is not even a last expression of despair in the manner of Macbeth or Faustus.

Lillo originally had reunited Barnwell and Millwood at the gallows in a closing scene, "but by the advice of some friends it was left out in the representation," and not until the fifth edition (1735) was it included with the rest of the text. In addition to the highly charged drama of a meeting at the scaffold, the scene also softens a bit the sharp edges of Millwood's character, since she laments the end of her "flattering hopes," admits to having "sinned beyond the reach of mercy," echoes Barnwell's Calvinism with her statement "And I was doomed before the world began to endless pains . . .," and tells Barnwell that his prayers for her "are lost in air, or else returned perhaps with double blessing to your bosom, but they help me not." Her plaintive final cry recalls Christopher Marlowe's Faustus: "Encompassed with horror, whither must I go? I would not live—nor die! That I could cease to be—or ne'er had been!" These expressed doubts notwithstanding, Millwood remains unrepentant at the end, and as McBurney notes, "Millwood, rather than Barnwell, enacts the 'tragic' role of the Christian drama by dying in blasphemous despair."

The London Merchant is a play that must be considered from several vantage points. While the primary reason for its contemporary success was its middle-class realism and bourgeois morality, its newness was primarily a matter of degree and style, for Elizabethan domestic tragedies were equally homiletic and journalistically true to life. Lillo's occasional rhetorical excesses, however, tie it to the classical tradition, and his background as a Dissenter also is apparent.

His only other noteworthy play is *Guilt Its Own Punishment: Or, Fatal Curiosity*, which was first presented in 1736 (when printed by Gray in 1737, its title was given as *Fatal Curiosity: A True Tragedy*). On this occasion as in 1731, Lillo based his domestic tragedy upon an Elizabethan crime. Originally reported in a 1618 pamphlet, *Newes from Perin in Cornwall of a most Bloody and un-exampled Murther very lately committed by a Father on his owne Sonne (who was lately returned from the Indyes) at the Instigation of a mercilesse Step-mother . . .*, the event was later recounted in Sir William Sanderson's *Compleat History of the Lives and Reigns of Mary Queen of Scotland, And of Her Son and Successor, James the Sixth, King of Scot-*

land . . . (1656), and this condensation of the pamphlet was included in *The Annals of King James and King Charles the First* (1681), known as *Frankland's Annals*. Lillo probably did not use the pamphlet as his source; he likely was familiar with one or both of the compendiums. In each of them, the wicked stepmother of the original has become the real mother of the victim, and preceding the murder account in each there is a discussion of Sir Walter Raleigh's fall from grace. In *Fatal Curiosity*, the real mother is the murderer, and early in the play, Old Wilmot and Randal, his young servant, discuss Raleigh's arrest.

Fielding's prologue spoken at the first performance was intended to justify this tragedy of "lower life," which also stood apart from most other plays of the period in that it had only three acts. Its pervasive didacticism, with love for country and the honorable nature of commerce again expressed, recalls *The London Merchant*. Loyalty to one's master and selfless love are also portrayed.

The action opens at the Cornwall home of Old Wilmot. Ruined by poverty and saddened by his son's failure to return from a voyage to India, the old man moves to discharge his loyal servant Randal from his "unprofitable service." Randal objects, but to no avail, and Old Wilmot suggests that he renounce "books and the unprofitable search/ Of wisdom there, and study humankind," for doing so will teach him how to "wear the face of probity and honor" as he proceeds to deceive people in order to take advantage of them for his own ends. The old man cynically instructs Randal: "Be a knave and prosper!" His own ruin, he says, has come about through his failure to treat mankind as they deserve; the world, he claims, "is all a scene of deep deceit," and the man "who deals with mankind on the square/ Is his own bubble and undoes himself." The lesson in villainy concluded, Randal bemoans the fall of his "High-minded . . . pitiful and generous" master, who once had honor as his idol. At the same time, though, Randal refers to Wilmot as improvident and pleasure-loving, the first of several such inconsistent and conflicting views of the protagonist of the play, whose tragic flaw is his misguided and untempered reason. The scene shifts to the home of Charlot, who is engaged to the missing Young Wilmot. Charlot rejects overtures by other men and supports his parents, whom Maria, Charlot's maid, describes as gloomy, proud, and impatient. When Agnes, the mother, enters, Maria says that the old lady's "pride seems to increase with her misfortunes" and also refers to "her haughty, swelling heart." Thus, one is prepared for the emergence of Agnes as a villain who is destroyed by hubris and greed. Further, in conversation with Charlot, Agnes is scornful of "the common herd," to whose level she has been reduced by poverty. She is equally disdainful of her "wretched husband," whose "fixed love for me" is all that "withholds his hand" from "foul self-murder," a blasphemous desire that reveals the old man's loss of faith. Charlot attempts to counter Agnes' miseries by telling of a possibly prescient dream she had the night before in which Patience and Contemplation were joined by Young Wilmot and his parents. In the first two scenes, then, Lillo sets the stage for the return of the long-lost son and sows the seeds of the catastrophes to come.

Young Wilmot's appearance in the next scene is punctuated by a patriotic paean to England and a tedious speech of devotion to Charlot, to whose home he then repairs. Their reunion is marked by rhetorical bombast that the blank verse fails to ameliorate. Charlot, though a sentimental heroine in the tradition of Otway's Belvidera, is the most fully realized and believable person in *Fatal Curiosity*.

Soon after his reunion with Charlot, Young Wilmot has a chance meeting with Randal, and they scheme to hide the son's identity from his parents (his features having sufficiently changed during his long absence so they would not recognize him) to enable him to satisfy his curiosity by first meeting with them as a stranger. Lillo thus portrays him not only as a virtuous, loving, brave, and successful merchant but also as a self-indulgent adventurer who is very much his parents' son and is as much his own victim as he is Agnes'. He arrives at their home just as Agnes is leaving to sell a volume of Seneca to get money for bread. He gives them a letter of introduction ostensibly from Charlot, and they welcome him, talking of their lost son and listening to an account of his adventures. Fearful that his emotions will betray him into revealing his identity before Charlot arrives, he feigns a need for sleep and retires, giving into Agnes' care a casket with "contents of value." Alone, she is overtaken by curiosity and opens the box, which is filled with jewels, treasures that would end their "Base poverty and all its abject train. . . ." Old Wilmot enters; she shows him the jewels; and he senses her purpose: "Th' inhospitable murder of our guest!" What ensues is the most exciting dialogue in the play, as wife urges husband on, first gaining his tacit assent and eventually convincing him to commit the act. Her determination, persistence, and success are reminiscent of Lady Macbeth, while his reluctance and malleability recall Macbeth himself. No sooner is the deed committed than Agnes reacts in a manner that also recalls Shakespeare's play: "Inconstant, wretched woman!/ What, doth my heart recoil and bleed with him/ Whose murder you contrived?" When Charlot and Randal arrive in the wake of the stabbing, the parents learn the full horror of their act, and Wilmot resolves that "Our guilt and desolation must be told/ From age to age to teach desponding mortals/ How far beyond the reach of human thought/ Heaven, when incensed, can punish." He then stabs Agnes, who asks forgiveness from her son and vows: "Had I ten thousand lives/ I'd give them all to speak my penitence,/ Deep, and sincere, and equal to my crime." Wilmot stabs himself, and before he dies proclaims that he and Agnes brought their ruin upon themselves with their pride and impatience. "Mankind may learn . . .," he says as he dies.

However serious the weaknesses of the first two acts may be, the tragic intensity of the third is overwhelming. While the action of the entire play spans a period no greater than the time of presentation, there is a startling rapidity to the final progression toward the terrible catastrophes. This classical compression of time is as important to the effect as is Lillo's decision to have the murder done offstage, with Young Wilmot's muted "Oh, Father! Father!" and Agnes' reports and urgings providing all the immediacy that is needed. To avoid diluting the emotional impact, Lillo wisely brings the play to a rapid close after the father dies, while Randal delivers a choruslike coda: "Let us at least be wiser, nor complain/ Of Heaven's mysterious ways and awful reign."

Largely because of *The London Merchant*, George Lillo is a playwright to be reckoned with in any consideration of middle-class or domestic trag cdy, not only in England but also on the Continent, where his influence was more generally felt. He demonstrated once and for all that tragedy was not the exclusive province of princes, but that middle-class men and women possessed the necessary stature for tragic action. While his plays are not of the first rank, they are worthy progenitors of a large body of later drama.

Bibliography

Faller, Lincoln B. *The Popularity of Addison's "Cato" and Lillo's "The London Merchant," 1700-1776.* New York: Garland, 1988. Faller attempts to explain why *The London Merchant*, which seems awkward and didactic to modern readers, achieved such success in the eighteenth century. He finds that the balance of sentimentalism, realism, and tragedy that went into establishing this domestic drama appealed to its contemporary audience. The play was also politically relevant, it flattered its audience, and it established a moral authority.

Havens, Raymond D. "The Sentimentalism of *The London Merchant.*" *Journal of English Literary History* 12 (1945): 183-187. Havens refutes George Bush Rodman's arguments (below), contending that sentimentalism in *The London Merchant* is found in the separation in the moral code of action from feeling and in valuing feeling above action. Sentimentalism reduces the play from a tragedy to a diversion.

Hudson, William Henry. "George Lillo and *The London Merchant.*" In *A Quiet Corner in a Library.* Chicago: Rand McNally, 1915. This essay is the foundation for twentieth century critical evaluations of Lillo and *The London Merchant.* Hudson gives a brief account of Lillo's life and career as well as a synopsis of the play, which he condemns as didactic and unconvincing. Hudson then expounds the play's historical significance resulting from its initial popularity and its literary impact as the first significant domestic tragedy. He shows it as the precursor to both modern melodrama and social realism.

Nicoll, Allardyce. *British Drama.* 6th ed. New York: Harper & Row, 1978. Chapter 5, "Drama in the Eighteenth Century," of this standard introduction to the British drama places Lillo's *The London Merchant* into literary perspective. Nicoll shows how the play marked the downfall of classical tragedy, establishing domestic drama and melodrama as the new aesthetics. Illustrations, bibliography, and index.

Rodman, George Bush. "Sentimentalism in Lillo's *The London Merchant.*" *Journal of English Literary History* 12 (1945): 45-61. Rodman argues that *The London Merchant* is not representative of eighteenth century sentimentalism and that it was not Lillo's intent for it to be so. The play does not strike against the orthodox view of life, nor does it reveal confidence in human nature or emotions. Rather, it shows that ordinary people are subject to the same tragic weaknesses as kings.

Gerald H. Strauss
(Updated by *Gerald S. Argetsinger*)

ROMULUS LINNEY

Born: Philadelphia, Pennsylvania; September 21, 1930

Principal drama

The Sorrows of Frederick, pb. 1966, pr. 1967; *Goodbye Howard*, pr. 1970; *The Love Suicide at Schofield Barracks*, pr. 1972, pb. 1973; *Democracy and Esther*, pb. 1973 (adaptation of Henry Adams' novels *Democracy* and *Esther*; revised as *Democracy*, pr. 1974, pb. 1975); *Holy Ghosts*, pr. 1974, pb. 1977; *The Seasons, Man's Estate*, pr. 1974; *Appalachia Sounding*, pr. 1975; *Old Man Joseph and His Family: A Play in Two Acts*, pr. 1977, pb. 1978; *Childe Byron*, pr. 1977, pb. 1981; *Just Folks*, pr. 1978; *The Death of King Philip*, pr. 1979; *Tennessee*, pr. 1979, pb. 1980; *The Captivity of Pixie Shedman*, pb. 1980, pr. 1981; *El Hermano*, pr., pb. 1981; *Laughing Stock*, pr., pb. 1984 (includes *Tennessee, Goodbye Howard*, and *F.M.*); *Why the Lord Come to Sand Mountain*, pr., pb. 1984; *The Soul of a Tree*, pr. 1984; *Sand Mountain*, pr., pb. 1985 (includes *Why the Lord Come to Sand Mountain* and *Sand Mountain Matchmaking*); *A Woman Without a Name*, pr. 1985, pb. 1986; *Pops*, pr. 1986, pb. 1987 (six short plays); *Heathen Valley*, pr. 1987 (adapted from his novel); *April Snow*, pr. 1987; *Juliet*, pr. 1988; *Three Poets*, pr. 1989; *Unchanging Love*, pr. 1989; *Two*, pr. 1990; *Can Can*, pr., pb. 1991; *Ambrosio*, pr. 1992.

Other literary forms

Romulus Linney is the author of novels—*Heathen Valley* (1962), *Slowly, by Thy Hand Unfurled* (1965), and *Jesus Tales* (1980)—as well as innumerable articles, reviews, poems, and short fiction, published in *The New York Times Sunday Book Review, New York Quarterly*, and elsewhere.

Achievements

Linney's dramatic achievements are in two areas: historical biography and Appalachian mountain tales. He is ranked high among the few American playwrights writing historical drama for the contemporary theater. Without sacrificing theatricality, Linney brings to the stage the soaring language and large ideas that have been attributed to other great dramatic eras. In addition, through his folk plays dealing with Appalachian areas, he has become a voice for the rural life-styles in danger of extinction in America. Like John Millington Synge in Ireland and Federico García Lorca in Spain, Linney captures the unique features of the speech of the rural areas of the Carolinas, Virginias, and Tennessee.

The much-produced Linney has been the recipient of virtually every major playwriting award and fellowship in the United States, including those of the

National Endowment for the Arts (1974), the Guggenheim Foundation (1980), and an Obie Award (1980). In 1984, he was honored with an Award in Literature from the American Academy and Institute of Arts and Letters. While his plays have been performed all over the United States and Europe, he has a special relationship with the Whole Theatre in New Jersey and the Philadelphia Festival Theatre.

Biography

Romulus Linney was born in Philadelphia and reared in Madison, Tennessee. His father, a doctor and an avid outdoorsman, greatly influenced Linney's life but died when Linney was thirteen. He and his mother moved to Washington, where she taught public speaking. After he was graduated from Oberlin College in 1953, Linney attended the Yale School of Drama, where he received an M.F.A. degree in directing in 1958. He began his writing career as a novelist, writing *Heathen Valley* in 1962 and *Slowly, by Thy Hand Unfurled* in 1965. After some struggling, he wrote his first play, *The Sorrows of Frederick*, and found his true voice. After that time, Linney wrote many plays. He was a member of New Dramatists for seven years, and he continued to write, lecture, and conduct workshops at several colleges in the New York area, where he settled.

Linney's first attempt at Broadway, *The Love Suicide at Schofield Barracks*, while beautifully acted and staged, did not receive the necessary rave reviews to keep it running. Clive Barnes, in particular, complained of the script's improbability: "The play could not . . . ever make a particularly convincing or satisfying evening in the theater." Its subject matter, the double suicide of a general and his wife, was not palpable to the typical Broadway audience.

A prolific and imaginative writer, Linney writes from two usually distinct points of view: the Tennessee-born background of such plays as *Sand Mountain* and *A Woman Without a Name*, and the cultured, historical perspective found in such works as *Childe Byron* and *Pops*, the latter being a series of short plays based on musical themes and reaching back in history to Hrosvitha, the tenth century German nun. *Sand Mountain*, actually two plays about the rural mountain life of Linney's youth, contains a Christmas celebration, *Why the Lord Come to Sand Mountain*, in which Jesus returns to earth to hear a mountain storyteller recount the story of the Nativity.

Linney has succeeded tremendously well in the regional theaters, where his plays are well received by non-New York audiences; in New York, his plays get fine reviews when produced on the League of Resident Theatres (LORT) stages, in workshop and showcase productions, and Off-Broadway. Returning to Oberlin College as a guest speaker in 1990, Linney read from several of his works. *A Woman Without a Name*, a diary play in which the main character's control of the English language improves as the play moves forward, was successful after various workshop productions. His play *Three Poets*, three one-act plays centered on three female poets (Hrosvitha, Ono no Komachi, and Anna Akhmatova), was extremely successful in New York. In Louisville, at the Actors Theatre of Louisville, his play *Two*, about the second-in-command under Adolf Hitler, was well received in 1990; his six short plays gathered under the title *Pops*, and each having a musical theme, continued to be performed all over the United States in various venues.

Analysis

Despite his rural childhood, Romulus Linney is a sophisticated and very well-read author, drawing on his education and scholarly research as much as on his personal experiences to bring a surprisingly simple but authentic worldview to his work. Fascinated by the storytelling traditions of Appalachia, Linney finds a gold mine of material in the folktales of that region. Yet what separates his work from the anthropologist's is his ability to exploit the inherent dramatic qualities of the storytellers themselves. In Linney's mountain plays, he makes use of the natural storytelling power of the stage to spin fascinating yarns about simple folk whose intuitive understanding of human relationships is expressed in superstitious old wives' tales. The action is often the dramatization of a story to witnesses—a play-within-a-play device that works well because the characters are natural storytellers. Linney's own storytelling powers are enhanced by this format, because the characters, by their attitudes toward the value of tall tales, reinforce for the audience the magical qualities of theatrical reenactment. Yet Linney's work never descends to simple recitation; the personality of the storyteller, the reactions of the character-listener, and the presence of "something at stake" for both always keep the dramatic tension intact.

The best illustration of the texture of Linney's mountain plays is the one-act play *Why the Lord Come to Sand Mountain*, which, together with *Sand Mountain Matchmaking*, constitutes the evening of drama *Sand Mountain*. An old mountain woman named Sang Picker (she gathers ginseng root for a living) asks the audience if they know any good "Smoky Mountain head benders," and proceeds to tell one of her own, a story which comes alive before her as the Lord and Peter enter, looking for Sand Mountain. When they find Jack, Jean, and Fourteen Children (played by one actor), the Lord and Peter are treated to another story: a reenactment of the conception, birth, and childhood of Jesus, reared by Joseph (acted by Jack) and Mary (acted by Jean), embellished with apocryphal details. "He'd come to Sand Mountain," Sang Picker tells the audience, "to hear tell about his Daddy, and Mary and hisself as a child, and he had." Jean supplies the moral (a favorite of Linney): "Hit ain't the ending whut's important. Hit's the beginning."

One early success, which has been re-created in many regional theaters, is

Holy Ghosts, about a primitive Fundamentalist sect that uses snakes in its worship services. A convert to this religion, Nancy Shedman, leaves her husband, Colman, to marry the old father of the religion, Obediah Buckhorn; Colman follows her to the church and debunks her quasi-religious conversion. At the play's climax, however, Nancy chooses neither her husband nor her "savior"; she exercises a newfound independence from both and leaves for business school. Thematically, Linney deals with the shortcomings of unquestioning obedience (implied in Obediah's name), but Nancy's decision is a typical Linney signature: women turning their backs on men, the weaker sex. *Sand Mountain Matchmaking* pursues the dramatic potential of the courtship ritual. The widow Rebecca listens patiently to three suitors (in the traditional folktale format), then follows the bizarre but effective advice ("Cure a cold sore—kiss a dog") of an old mountain woman. The final match is an equal partnership based on mutual honesty. In *A Woman Without a Name* (based on Linney's novel *Slowly, by Thy Hand Unfurled*), serious in theme and tone, the nameless central figure keeps a journal, clumsily at first, but more and more articulately as the years pass. In the journal, she collects her feelings about the loss of her children one by one, the guilt she feels because she believes that she has somehow caused their deaths, and the indifference of the men in her life to her longing to express herself and to live a full life. The outcome of the play, partially drawing on historical fact, finds her the leader of a temperance society: "Anneal, Journal, Standard Dictionary: to put to the fire, then to freezing cold. To temper. To toughen. To make enduring. That is the word I understand now." The play bears a resemblance to *The Captivity of Pixie Shedman*, in which a young man reads the diary of his grandmother and learns of her exploitation by the men in her life, who treated her like property.

Linney's erudition and penchant for scholarly research are most clearly seen in his historical dramas, which in his hands become dramatic expressions of the chasm between the conceived ideal and the practical application of that ideal in an imperfect world. Frederick II, in *The Sorrows of Frederick*, abandons an important battle to attend the funeral of his dog; his greatest military triumphs are always marred by a personal loss. In Linney's portrait, Frederick is forceful, clearheaded, and single-minded in public affairs but almost pathetically inept in dealing with his personal life. His friendship with Voltaire, his unconsummated marriage to Elizabeth Christine, and especially his love for Fredersdorf, a childhood comrade, are all clumsily handled, while his military victories often come fortuitously, without effort. Linney dramatizes the complex career of Frederick through a series of time changes, moving backward and forward from pivotal public events to the significant personal events that exacerbate or ameliorate them.

Democracy and Esther, later titled simply *Democracy*, is a dramatic combination of two Henry Adams novels. As in *Holy Ghosts*, the women in the play prove to be the strongest characters, declining offers of marriage from seemingly eligible men whose strength of character does not fulfill the women's expectations. Another historical drama, *Childe Byron*, deals with an imaginary meeting of Lord Byron and his estranged daughter, Ada, who challenges her father to justify his wretched life, in a mock trial at the moment of her death. One of the most complex storytelling devices Linney has ever employed is used in the essentially antiwar play *The Love Suicide at Schofield Barracks*. Here, by the specific instructions of the General of Schofield Barracks, his own public suicide, along with his wife's, is reenacted by the officers and witnesses to the tragedy on the morning after the deaths. By means of disparate testimonies, which give a multiple perspective of the General's personality, the complex motives of his act are examined.

Linney is perhaps most comfortable in the short-play format, where his storytelling abilities transform human relationships into entertaining yarns with warm-hearted morals. *Laughing Stock* consists of three fairly short pieces, at the same time comic and touching. *Tennessee* tells the story of a woman whose husband promised to take her to Tennessee, only to drive in circles until she was only seven miles from her childhood home. *Goodbye, Howard*, despite its hospital setting, is a comedy in which three elderly sisters prematurely announce the death of their brother, only to discover that they have simply got off the elevator on the wrong floor. In *F.M.*, which takes place in a college writing class, a Faulkner-like novelist pours out his heart in the classroom, incidentally reminding the teacher of her own sidetracked talent and writing career. The most ambitious collection of short plays, however, is *Pops*, a series of six short plays on the theme of love, designed to be performed by the ideal company of actors: juvenile, ingenue, leading man, leading lady, character man, and character woman. Sometimes working with historical material (as in "Ave Maria") and sometimes with the present (as in the delightful "Tonight We Love"), Linney finds the universal question in all love stories: whether two people fall in love through fate or through their own efforts.

Music, virtually always present in his work, is Linney's universal metaphor for the harmonies and cadences of human interaction. *Childe Byron*, for example, calls for some fourteen distinct musical pieces as accompaniment to the action. Linney has stated that, because his plays are often episodic, they fall into a natural structural rhythm, like music. His words are musical as well; Linney's works reveal his fine ear for dialogue, especially for the regionalisms embedded in folktales, old saws and sayings, and figurative language born of the mountain life. An authenticity of expression, along with a sensitivity to linguistic rhythms, characterizes Linney's dialogue. From a position of healthy skepticism rather than cynicism, Linney sees a world of humor and warmth, in which the search for relationships based on mutual respect is never-ending.

Other major works

NOVELS: *Heathen Valley*, 1962; *Slowly, by Thy Hand Unfurled*, 1965; *Jesus Tales*, 1980.

TELEPLAY: *The Thirty-fourth Star*, 1976.

Bibliography

DiGaetani, John L. *A Search for a Postmodern Theater: Interviews with Contemporary Playwrights.* New York: Greenwood Press, 1991. This interview with Linney (with photograph) concentrates on his influences (Pär Lagerkvist, the Swedish playwright and novelist among them) and on the relationship between language and writing for the theater. Includes good discussions of several works, including *Childe Byron.*

Disch, Thomas M. "Holy Ghosts." *The Nation* 245 (September 19, 1987): 282-283. Disch is much impressed with virtually all Linney's New York work; here, he claims that *Holy Ghosts* should be a standard, "like *Glass Menagerie* . . . [l]ike prime Ibsen . . . flawlessly put together." The essay provides an overview of Linney's work and addresses Linney's Broadway problems and Clive Barnes's unfavorable review of *The Love Suicide at Schofield Barracks.* Disch notes that the wonderful thing about Linney "is that he did soldier on to write dramas of the same high and unfashionable ambition for Off Broadway and regional theaters."

_____. "Theater." *The Nation* 252 (March 18, 1991): 355-356. When Linney's play *Unchanging Love* moved from its premiere performance in Milwaukee in 1989, at the Milwaukee Repertory Theater, to its New York premiere at the Triangle Theatre Company, with the same director (John Dillon), Disch once again took the opportunity to speak highly of Linney's whole canon: "Linney's play has attracted a [high] caliber of acting talent . . . because Linney creates the kind of roles in which actors shine."

Rich, Frank. "Theater: *Holy Ghosts* Salvation for the Lonely." Review of *Holy Ghosts. The New York Times*, August 12, 1987, p. C17. The Off-Broadway Theater 890 saw this production of *Holy Ghosts*, after two Off-Off Broadway productions in the 1970's. In this visiting production of the San Diego Repertory Theatre, Rich finds that Linney "unfurls an arresting sensibility closer to that of Eudora Welty than Sinclair Lewis." He notes the script's shortcomings and the director's (Douglas Jacobs) failure to surmount them, but says that "we find ourselves unexpectedly moved by the grace of lost souls who risk everything."

Seligsohn, Leo. "Fervent Rural Souls Handling Snakes." Review of *Holy Ghosts. New York Newsday*, August 12, 1987. This review of *Holy Ghosts* speaks well of the mood, "established as soon as one enters the theater and walks across deep, caked soil between the in-the-round stage and the audience." The characters are "walking caricatures [who] ingratiate themselves," and the plot, "though serviceable, is far less worthy than what it's wrapped in."

Thomas J. Taylor

HENRY LIVINGS

Born: Prestwich, England; September 20, 1929

Principal drama

Stop It, Whoever You Are, pr. 1961, pb. 1962; *Big Soft Nellie*, pr. 1961, pb. 1964; *Nil Carborundum*, pr. 1962, pb. 1963; *Kelly's Eye*, pr. 1963, pb. 1964; *The Day Dumbfounded Got His Pylon*, pr. 1963 (radio play), pr. 1965 (staged), pb. 1967; *Kelly's Eye and Other Plays* (includes *Big Soft Nellie*), pb. 1964; *Eh?*, pr. 1964, pb. 1965; *The Little Mrs. Foster Show*, pr. 1966, pb 1969; *Good Grief!*, pr. 1967, pb. 1968 (one acts and sketches: *After the Last Lamp, You're Free, Variable Lengths, Pie-eating Contest, Does It Make Your Cheeks Ache?, The Reasons for Flying*); *Honour and Offer*, pr. 1968, pb. 1969; *The Gamecock*, pr. 1969, pb. 1971; *Rattel*, pr. 1969, pb. 1971; *Variable Lengths and Longer: An Hour of Embarrassment*, pr. 1969 (includes *The Reasons for Flying, Does It Make Your Cheeks Ache?*); *The Boggart*, pr. 1970, pb. 1971; *Conciliation*, pr. 1970, pb. 1971; *The Rifle Volunteer*, pr. 1970, pb. 1971; *Beewine*, pr. 1970, pb. 1971; *The ffinest ffamily in the Land*, pr. 1970, pb. 1973; *You're Free*, pr. 1970; *Mushrooms and Toadstools*, pr. 1970, pb. 1974; *Tiddles*, pr. 1970, pb. 1974; *Pongo Plays 1-6*, pb. 1971 (includes *The Gamecock, Rattel, The Boggart, Beewine, The Rifle Volunteer, Conciliation*); *This Jockey Drives Late Nights*, pr. 1972, pb. 1972, 1976 (adaptation of Leo Tolstoy's play *The Power of Darkness*); *Draft Sam*, pr. 1972 (televised), pb. 1974, pr. 1976 (staged); *The Rent Man*, pr. 1972, pb. 1974; *Cinderella: A Likely Tale*, pr. 1972, pb. 1976 (adaptation of Charles Perrault's story); *The Tailor's Britches*, pr. 1973, pb. 1974; *Glorious Miles*, pr. 1973 (televised), pr. 1975 (staged); *Jonah*, pr. 1974, pb. 1975; *Six More Pongo Plays Including Two for Children*, pb. 1974 (includes *Tiddles, The Rent Man, The Ink-Smeared Lady, The Tailor's Britches, Daft Sam, Mushrooms and Toadstools*); *Jack and the Beanstalk*, pr. 1974 (music by Alan Glasgow); *Jug*, pr. 1975 (adaptation of Heinrich von Kleist's play *The Broken Jug*); *The Astounding Adventures of Tom Thumb*, pr. 1979 (children's play); *Don't Touch Him, He Might Resent It*, pr. 1984 (adaptation of a play by Nikolai Gogol); *This Is My Dream: The Life and Times of Josephine Baker*, pr. 1987.

Other literary forms

In addition to his plays for the stage, Henry Livings is known for his 1968 screenplay adaptation of *Eh?*, entitled *Work Is a Four-Letter Word*, and for his work as a television writer. He has also been a prolific writer of television and radio drama, and in the 1980's he published two short-story collections, *Penine Tales* (1983) and *Flying Eggs and Things: More Penine Tales* (1986).

Achievements

Usually clustered uncomfortably with the post-Osborne playwrights of Great Britain, Livings is perhaps more popular in the regional theaters than in London itself. An actor influenced by Joan Littlewood and her presentational approach to theater, Livings first confounded London audiences with *Stop It, Whoever You Are*, especially the industrial lavatory scene, the beginning of Livings' career-long interest in the workingman *in situ*. Along with successes at the Royal Court Theatre, London, Livings' plays have been successful in Stratford, Manchester, Oxford, Lincoln, Birmingham, and Stoke-on-Trent. This appeal to the less sophisticated audience is what separates Livings from both critical approval and big-name notoriety in London theatrical circles. As for American productions, only the Cincinnati Playhouse in the Park has shown continuing interest in Livings' work, having produced *Honour and Offer* as well as *Eh?*, his best-known play in America, which won a 1966 Obie Award for its production at New York's Circle in the Square Theatre. The value of Livings' contribution lies in his concentration on the fairly short entertainment segment, appealing directly to the working-class audience of every age, without concessions to more traditional dramatic considerations such as structure and psychological character studies. Combining the vaudevillian *lazzi* (the stock-in-trade of the British comic actor) with an uncanny insight into the real problems and delights of the British working class, Livings manages to make an evening at the theater the robust, titillating, hugely entertaining experience it was meant to be. His work adds humor and linguistic virtuosity to the otherwise sober, even whining, "kitchen sink" school of British drama.

Biography

Born in Prestwich, Lancashire, on September 20, 1929, Henry Livings was not, as might be suspected from his work, reared in a working-class family, but in a white-collar family. Perhaps from visits to his father's place of work (George Livings was a shop manager), he began to look carefully at the lives of people at work. Livings' grammar-school years at Park View Primary School (1935-1939) and Stand Grammar School (1940-1945) put him in contact with the lives of his sturdy public-school classmates from Lancashire during the war years. After a brief enrollment (on scholarship) at Liverpool University (1945-1947), where he concentrated on Hispanic studies, Livings served as a cook in the Royal Air Force until 1950, when a series of jobs finally brought him to an acting career with the Century Mobile Theatre, in Leicestershire. Livings' association with Joan Littlewood's company at the Theatre Royal, Stratford East, London, began with a role in Brendan Behan's *The Quare Fellow* (pr. 1954). It was Joan Littlewood who encouraged Livings to continue writing, and, having married Fanny Carter, an actress with the company, in 1957, he wrote his first successful play, *Stop It, Whoever You Are*, produced at the Arts Theatre in London in 1961. Despite the furor it raised, and encouraged by the *Evening Standard* Award in 1961, Livings wrote busily during the next five years, a period which produced *Eh?*, *The Little Mrs. Foster Show*, *Kelly's Eye*, and several other plays. His audience, he found, was not in London but in the shires, where a more solidly working-class audience understood the world Livings was creating onstage, the language with which the characters communicated and failed to communicate, and the special defeats and triumphs of their social class. The anti-intellectual bias of Livings' vision naturally led him to radio and television; he was associated with the British Broadcasting Corporation's program *Northern Drift* and wrote several short radio works collected and published under the title *Worth a Hearing* (1967). After 1970, Livings worked in shorter forms, writing short sketches centering largely on a picaresque but British working-class Scapin named Pongo. The Pongo plays have been collected in two volumes (1971 and 1974); the latter contains two plays for children, an important part of Livings' work, Livings finds his voice in the gathering places of the common worker, the lodge halls and Rotary clubs that recognize the veracity of his imagination and comprehend the language and life of his characters. Livings continued to write for the working class and children, with *Flying Eggs and Things* (1986) and the more serious *This Is My Dream: The Life and Times of Josephine Baker* (1987).

Analysis

Quite a few of Henry Livings' plays begin with the entrance of a man at work or just from it, who addresses the audience directly, setting up the first confrontation, either with his environment or with the scabrous social system that put him somehow beneath the station he deserves, if wit and perception were the criteria. Henry Cash, beekeeper and bookkeeper in *Honour and Offer*, is typical: "HENRY (*sombre and intense, to us*): This is where I contemplate. Later in the day, the bees murmur, and I'm able to contemplate even better." This kind of opening, which violates traditional rules against addressing the audience directly, typifies the nature of Livings' relationship with the theater: It is a place where he goes to present himself in various disguises, to discuss in theatrical and humorous ways the dilemma of being in this world and happy at the same time. The signature of Livings' characters is whatever is opposite passivity, helplessness, anguish, and defeat. What separates the workingman from his pitiable superiors is that he works, while they merely swot at the free enterprise system as it is oddly practiced in England. Stanley, the lisping hero in *Big Soft Nellie*, defends his entire existence with the simple statement, "I am a man and I do a job."

The corollary to the dignity of work is the sanctity of the workplace. In

Livings' world, a man's shop is his castle, and no interfering foreman or supervisor is going to taint it. Livings' best-known play, *Eh?*, takes place in the boiler-room of a mammoth dye factory, where someone upstairs shovels coal into the boiler while the hero, Valentine Brose, watches the gauges, at least in theory. Instead, Val commands his fortress like a baron, growing hallucinogenic mushrooms in the moist heat; bedding his new bride in the double bunk; confounding the works manager, the personnel officer, and the local environmentalist with startling vigor. Winning them over with his mushrooms does not save his castle, however, which is destroyed from within by a vigor of its own. "Once upon a time. There was a boiler. Once upon a time," recites Val as the boiler explodes, making the connection between children's tales and working-class life that Livings has claimed as his own invention.

For exploding or confounding, the best tool available to Livings' characters is the language. Just as Federico García Lorca captures the naturally poetic diction of the Spanish peasant and John Millington Synge re-creates the rhythms and cadences inherent in the Western Irish tongue, Livings reproduces the amazing language patterns of the working-class families of Liverpool, Yorkshire, Manchester, and Birmingham. It is a difficult tangle of near-communication, lost threads, subjective references, internal arguments going on underneath the normative conversation, subtexts overpowering the superficially civil correspondences, vague antecedents, and private vocabularies hinting at metaphoric connections long lost to logic. Miraculously, they understand each other—in fact, they are bonded by the commonality of their language, so that an argument shouted in the presence of strangers has all the secrecy of a family code. The reader may wish for more signposts through the labyrinth of utterances that seem to be attacks and ripostes but whose meaning is just out of reach; the signposts are there, but they are obscured by the lush undergrowth of Livings' imagination. If his characters are rather more loquacious than those of Harold Pinter, David Mamet, or Samuel Beckett, they share the same uneasy distrust of oversimplified exposition.

The comparison with Beckett does not end with the language. Livings finds great resources in the vaudeville skits and sight gags that find their way into Beckett's *Waiting for Godot* (pb. 1952). In the opening scene of Livings' *The ffinest ffamily in the Land*, Mr. Harris spends a good five minutes at the elevator looking for his key in every possible nook and cranny of his outfit, while his wife and son look on. When Mrs. Harris takes a try, her hand goes through a hole in Mr. Harris' pocket and her wedding ring gets caught in the hair on his leg. Trapped in this ridiculous position, the Harrises take several elevator rides trying to avoid being seen by their lodger and her male companion. The short sketches collected as the Pongo plays (1971 and 1974) are essentially music-hall skits, featuring such visual tricks as walking in place, miming puddles and other impediments, exaggerated playing at saber and pistols, and mugging reactions. The broad appeal of this kind of humor calls upon the talents of the actor, who must do considerably more than memorize his lines in order to bring the theatrical moment to life. Songs often introduce the plays, sung by a "Musician" visible onstage who often takes a small part in the stage business as well, as though the fictive stage intrudes on the real world at every turn. When, in *The Boggart*, the monster succeeds in scaring Pongo into wrestling with his daughter, the Musician joins in the fun with a song sung in harmony with the Boggart. In *Beewine*, however, an angry master, foiled in his pursuit of Pongo, takes out his wrath on the Musician, who must flee for his life as the skit ends.

While critics generally acknowledge Livings' debt to vaudeville and other popular forms, they find fault with his dramatic structure. Plots moving in one direction suddenly shift; pieces of business elaborately constructed are abandoned; characters introduced are left behind. Livings explains that he writes in short bursts, keyed to the attention span he perceives in the theater, and otherwise gives little attention to structure. A case in point is his first success, *Stop It, Whoever You Are*, actually a five-scene vehicle for a series of slapstick routines involving Perkin Warbeck and his attempts at simple survival. The play begins with a harmless flirtation between Warbeck (recently retired) and a buxom fourteen-year-old, and ends, after several visits to the factory lavatory, with the explosion of the leaking gas in the Warbeck household, peopled with Warbeck's ghost and Mrs. Harbuckle, medium extraordinaire, now bald and looking "like Warbeck in drag." The play resembles a meandering Sunday drive; it steps from point to point, and the sights are worth the trip.

More serious in tone and more structurally sound is *The Little Mrs. Foster Show*, a nightmarish look not only at the decolonialization of Africa but also at the madness of war without zeal. Presented in the format of a touring lecture-with-slides on the adventures of Mrs. Foster's missionary work in Africa, the play deals with her relationship to a mercenary, Hook, who has been abandoned by his comrade, Orara, after his leg has been injured in a grenade blast. Stumbling on Hook in the jungle, Mrs. Foster submits to his charms but denounces him on their return to civilization, to save her reputation as a maiden. Orara imprisons and tortures Hook, but when an enterprising Mr. Clive convinces Mrs. Foster to take her story on the lecture circuit, they need Hook to help them dramatize those months together. Now sporting an artificial leg (but keeping the original one in a handy package on his lap), Hook joins the show. In an attempt to avoid the smell of the leg, Mrs. Foster splits her dress in half; now exposed, she "abandons the ruined dress and takes her place, brave and breathless, by HOOK, to wave to us." Thus, her earlier modesty and refusal to face her own sensuality, which began Hook's troubles, now are abandoned in favor of a more honest admission of her complicity in the seduction. For critics who seek thematic consistency and structural integrity in Livings' work, this play provides a sufficiency of both.

The Hook-Mrs. Foster seduction contains a kind of vigor that typifies all the romances in Livings' work, especially those between husband and wife. Women here are demonstrative, even aggressive; they like to be tickled and chased; any sort of terrain will do, whether garden or workshop, and vows must be renewed and reinforced with deeds. Perhaps Livings' only purely serious full-length play, *Kelly's Eye*, is at base a love story. Fleeing the automobile of a young seducer, Anna finds the beach hut of Kelly, fugitive from the law for the murder of his best friend. Responding to their sudden attraction for each other, but not wanting to reduce it to a simple sexual one, they agree to sleep apart, Kelly protecting Anna while she reexamines her values. When Anna's father, Brierly, a typical Livings antagonist from the world of high finance, tries to return Anna to her country-club life, Kelly takes her away to a small seaside room, giving up his own anonymity and obscurity. A prying landlady and a nosy reporter ruin Kelly and Anna's substitute "honeymoon" by showing Brierly where they are hidden, and, in one of the most gruesome scenes in Livings' generally optimistic theater, Kelly swallows disinfectant and dies. Reminiscent of Eugene O'Neill or D. H. Lawrence, the play confused critics who expected the same kind of farce that Livings had produced before, and it did not receive favorable reviews. The starkness of the landscape in which this bizarre but honest love affair grows and the suddenness of the characters' willingness to expose themselves to one another mark this play as a significant work waiting only to be refound by a sensitive director.

For the reader, however, the delights of Livings' plays lie in their humor. This humor is almost always subtle when embedded in the language, but it is broad in the action. There is a kind of tension set up between the obvious, even childish, silliness of the stage business and the droll and obtuse humor of the dialogue, often understated, sardonic, in the ironic mode, and consequently available only to the careful reader. A particular habit of Livings is the elaborate stage direction, not unlike George Bernard Shaw's: Highly literate prose is inserted into the dialogue not only as a signal to the actor but also as a parenthetical comment by the playwright to the reader. As is always the case with irony, the sense of the line is apparent not necessarily in the words but in the tone, and Livings sees fit to assist the reader or actor in those moments. In a scene of conjugal bliss *al fresco*, from *Honour and Offer*, Livings prescribes this stage direction: "Doris shrieks with shocked glee, claps her hand to her mouth, glances toward the bench, and flees on tiptoe. They tiptoe hazardously round the savage bee-hive, excited as much by the need for silence and the danger of the malignant bees as by the prospect of one catching hold of the other." This sort of rhetorical insertion is not meant to get in the way of the director's task but to help the reader grasp the texture of the scene.

Conversely, Livings' ostensibly prose works contain the same theatrical flair that identifies his stage pieces. His work for the British Broadcasting Corporation, some of which is gathered in the collection entitled *Pennine Tales*, straddles the boundary between prose and drama; their personal style and their obviously autobiographical content render them a sort of continuation of Livings' dramatic work, but reduced to words without pictures. "Twice-Nightly, Thursday Off to Learn It." "Fit-Up Touring, Also to Help in Kitchen," and "Will the Demon King Please Wear the Hat Provided?" all reflect Livings' early struggles as an actor. While it is a mistake to take these short radio pieces as pure autobiography, it can be said, as a narrator admits in one of the stories about childhood, "The boy was me."

The 1986 volume *Flying Eggs and Things: More Penine Tales* continued in the same vein. The 1987 production of *This Is My Dream: The Life and Times of Josephine Baker*, however, examined the career of the celebrated expatriate African American singer and actress in more serious fashion.

Taken together, Livings' plays constitute something more than just a variation on the "kitchen sink" or "dustbin" drama of the 1960's and 1970's. Livings' distinct contribution is a heartiness in the people dramatized in that era. They are harder-working, prouder, more robust than their counterparts in the hands of John Osborne, Arnold Wesker, or John Arden. They are more loving, more open, and more insistent that life give them their share. And, like Livings himself, they are more content with being themselves and less charmed with the prospect of trying to be something they are not.

Other major works

SHORT FICTION: *Penine Tales*, 1983; *Flying Eggs and Things: More Penine Tales*, 1986.

NONFICTION: *That the Medals and the Baton Be Put on View: The Story of a Village Band, 1875-1975*, 1975.

SCREENPLAY: *Work Is a Four-Letter Word*, 1968 (adaptation of *Eh?*).

TELEPLAYS: *The Arson Squad*, 1961; *Jack's Horrible Luck*, 1961; *There's No Room for You Here for a Start*, 1963; *A Right Crusader*, 1963; *Brainscrew*, 1966; *GRUP*, 1970; *Shuttlecock*, 1976; *The Game*, 1977 (adaptation of Harold Brighouse's play); *The Mayor's Charity*, 1977; *Two Days That Shook the Branch*, 1978; *We Had Some Happy Hours*, 1981; *Another Part of the Jungle*, 1985; *I Met a Man Who Wasn't There*, 1985.

RADIO PLAYS: *Worth a Hearing: A Collection of Radio Plays*, 1967; *A Most Wonderful Thing*, 1976; *Crab Training*, 1979; *Urn*, 1981; *The Moorcock*, 1981.

Bibliography

Giannetti, Louis D. "Henry Livings: A Neglected Voice in the New Drama." *Modern Drama* 12 (May, 1969): 38-48. Giannetti finds that Livings draws "heavily on his working-class background, like Arnold Wesker and John Osborne," and that his plays "incorporate the imagery of popular culture." He judges *Eh?* to be Chaplinesque: "Little man pitted against the Machine." Provides a good discussion of *Kelly's Eye*, a dramatization of the battle "between the life force [and] the forces of death, alienation and fragmentation."

Goorney, Howard. *The Theatre Workshop Story*. London: Methuen, 1981. Livings discusses his warm relationship with Joan Littlewood and her Theatre Workshop, where he worked and acted in the mid-1950's, "after an odd audition during which I was required to scythe hay across the stage." On his plays, Livings remarks, "I should like to think one play of mine could catch, just once, the rich texture and the tough purpose she displays again and again."

Hunt, Hugh, Kenneth Richards, and John Russell Taylor. *The Revels History of Drama in English: 1880 to the Present Day*. Vol. 7. London: Methuen, 1978. Livings took his place in modern drama "by virtue of the power and variety of his output, the striking individuality of his means of dramatic expression, alongside the major figures of the heroic days." Short but informative overview, from *Stop It, Whoever You Are* to *Honour and Offer*.

Rusinko, Susan. *British Drama 1950 to the Present: A Critical History*. Boston: Twayne, 1989. Rusinko discusses Livings under the heading "Working Class Writers." She provides a brief biographical sketch, followed by informative outlines of *Stop It, Whoever You Are*, *Nil Carborundum*, and *Eh?*. Discusses words and Livings' detailed instructions about how certain words are pronounced.

Taylor, John Russell. *The Angry Theatre: New British Drama*. Rev. ed. New York: Hill & Wang, 1969. An essential starting place for the study of Livings. Some critics, says Taylor, find his work "both profound and riotously funny [while] others determinedly find it neither." The important difference, he says, is that not only "does he come from the working class, but he writes principally for the working class." Good long discussions of several works, including *Jack's Horrible Luck* and more popular plays.

Thomson, Peter. "Henry Livings and the Accessible Theatre." In *Western Popular Theatre*, edited by David Mayer and Kenneth Richards. London: Methuen, 1977. An appreciation of the common appeal of Livings' work to the British housewife, "the bawdy mockery of respectable middle-class avarice." Considers the primacy of language, the convention of direct address, and other aspects of Livings' craft. Thomson says that Livings is "a man with a lot of plays in him, and hardly anywhere to put them."

Thomas J. Taylor

THOMAS LODGE

Born: London(?), England; 1558(?)
Died: London, England; September, 1625

Principal drama

The Wounds of Civill War, pr. c. 1586, pb. 1594; *A Looking Glass for London and England*, pr. c. 1588-1589, pb. 1594 (with Robert Greene).

Other literary forms

Thomas Lodge is best known for his prose romances, which are among the precursors of the novel. The most famous of these prose romances, *Rosalynde: Or, Euphues Golden Legacy* (1590), was William Shakespeare's major source for *As You Like It* (pr. c. 1599-1600). Lodge also published several collections of poetry, a volume of poetic satire (*A Fig for Momus*, 1595), translations of Josephus (1602) and Seneca (1614), and a commentary on du Bartas (1621). Most of Lodge's works are available in the four-volume *The Complete Works of Thomas Lodge* (1883).

Achievements

Although Thomas Lodge is better known for his lyric poetry and his romances than for his drama, his two extant plays have an important place in the history of the English drama. Lodge was a competent if not a brilliant writer, and, more important, he was an innovative one. *The Wounds of Civill War* is one of the earliest dramas to be written principally in blank verse and may be the earliest extant example of an English drama based on classical history, a mode which became very popular with later Elizabethan playwrights. *A Looking Glass for London and England* provides almost a summary of the various strands of drama being woven together by Lodge and his contemporaries to form the framework of the drama of the Elizabethan period. Elements from both of the plays were borrowed by more successful playwrights whose works eventually overshadowed Lodge's. Lodge's drama remains important, however, from a historical standpoint and for its influence on his more brilliant contemporaries.

Biography

Because of the wide range of his abilities and interests, Thomas Lodge's biography is often offered as an example of the life of a typical Elizabethan gentleman and man of letters. Neither the date nor the place of his birth is known definitely, but he was probably born in 1558. He was the second son of a Lord Mayor of London. Lodge studied at the Merchant Taylors' School in London and entered Trinity College, Oxford, in 1573, completing his bachelor's degree in 1577. In April of 1578, he was admitted to study law at Lincoln's Inn, London.

Lodge's early years in London were marked by personal problems, the exact nature of which is unknown, but which led to an appearance in court and a brief period of imprisonment. He may have had some problems with debts, which may have led to the criticism of usury that appears in some of his works, including *A Looking Glass for London and England*, but it is unlikely that he was ever truly profligate. More likely, his personal difficulties resulted from his leanings toward and eventual conversion to Catholicism. Lodge's literary career began in 1579 with the publication of an epitaph for his mother. The next year, he became widely known for his reply to Stephen Gosson's *School of Abuse* (1579), a pamphlet attacking the arts on moral grounds. The quarrel between Lodge and Gosson continued for some years, with Lodge's final reply appearing in an epistle published with his *An Alarum Against Usurers* (1584).

Around 1585, Lodge made a voyage to the Canaries, during which he wrote his famous romance *Rosalynde*. Little is known of his activities during the next four years, but it is likely that he spent part of his time writing for the theater and that his two extant plays date from this period. He seems to have renounced the theater about 1589. In August of 1591, Lodge sailed to South America with Sir Thomas Cavendish. The expedition was plagued by misfortune, and Lodge was one of the few survivors to return safely to England.

Lodge continued to produce and publish a variety of nondramatic literature until 1596, when he turned to the study of medicine, receiving a degree from Avignon in 1598; the degree was recognized by Oxford in 1602. After studying law, enjoying a modestly successful literary career, and experiencing a brief stint as an adventurer, Lodge seems to have found his place in life as a physician. He married about 1601 and apparently developed a large practice in London, particularly among the Catholic population. Although the date of his conversion is unknown, he was definitely a professed Catholic by this time and had some difficulties with the law over his recusancy. He died in September, 1625, perhaps of the plague, which he may have caught while attending the poor in London.

Analysis

Despite attempts to credit him with a number of early Elizabethan plays, especially the highly successful *Mucedorus* (pr. 1598), Thomas Lodge can be definitely identified as the author of only two extant plays, *The Wounds of Civill War* and *A Looking Glass for London and England*, the latter written with Robert Greene. Neither play has received much critical attention, nor has either play remained a living part of the English theatrical repertory. Lodge had considerable talent as a lyric poet, a gift that can be glimpsed in the verse of his plays. His sense of dramatic structure was unsure, but his works were innovative, breaking new ground for the English theater. Lodge's plays are important as examples of early stages in the development of the drama and as plays that had a strong influence on his contemporaries.

Neither of Lodge's plays can be dated with any precision, but both were probably written between 1585, when he made his first voyage to the Americas, and 1589, when he seems to have given up writing for the theater. Both *A Looking Glass for London and England* and *The Wounds of Civill War* were first published in 1594. Although published slightly later, *The Wounds of Civill War* is believed to be the earlier of the two. Little is known of the stage history of either play. The title page of *The Wounds of Civill War* indicates that the play was performed by the Admiral's Men, but the records of the company do not mention the play. The early history of *A Looking Glass for London and England* is similarly blank, but there are records of a revival in 1592 and other indications that the play was successful. Allusions to Jonah and the whale and the story of Nineveh became popular on the puppet stage, and the influence of the play may have reached as far as Germany.

The exact date of Lodge's first play, *The Wounds of Civill War*, is matter of considerable critical discussion, principally because of its possible relationship with Christopher Marlowe's *Tamburlaine the Great*, Parts I and II (pr. c. 1587). *The Wounds of Civill War* has traditionally been dated later than Marlowe's tragedy. The two plays show a number of striking similarities, but while it seems probable that one play influenced the other, it is impossible to determine in which direction the influence moved. The argument for dating *The Wounds of Civill War* after 1587 is based primarily on the questionable assumption that the weaker playwright, Lodge, must have been influenced by the stronger writer, Marlowe. This assumption has been challenged by critics who offer strong evidence for an earlier date for Lodge's play. In his *Thomas Lodge: The History of an Elizabethan* (1931), N. Burton Paradise notes that similar scenes which have been noted in the two plays could easily have begun with Lodge rather than with Marlowe, or could have been borrowed by both playwrights from other sources. The often-mentioned chariot scene in each play, for example—in which the hero enters in a chariot pulled by men—could have been derived from a similar scene in *Jocasta* (pr. 1566), an earlier play that is a translation by George Gascoigne and Francis Kinwelmershe, which might have been familiar to both writers. It has also been noted that there are no verbal parallels between the two plays. It seems unlikely that Lodge, who shows in his other works a particularly sensitive ear for language, would have borrowed details from Marlowe's drama without picking up some of Marlowe's dynamic verse style. The verse in *The Wounds of Civill War* tends to be monotonous, with little flexibility or variety; most of the lines are end-stopped, with few feminine endings, suggesting that the play was written before Marlowe's important advances in the handling of dramatic blank verse. Finally, Lodge's play shows no influence of *The Spanish Tragedy* (pr. c. 1585-1589) by Thomas Kyd. Kyd's bloody tragedy seems to have initiated the Elizabethan interest in spectacular and often brutal special effects and had an immediate impact on the developing English drama. *The Wounds of Civill War* contains many possibilities for such action. Had Lodge's chronicle been written after *The Spanish Tragedy*, one would expect its influence to appear in the staging of the battle scenes, at least, but Lodge's play makes little use of such sensational effects. The available evidence, then, suggests that *The Wounds of Civill War* might have been written about 1586, soon after Lodge's return from the Canaries but before the productions of Marlowe's and Kyd's popular and highly influential works.

If *The Wounds of Civill War* was written this early, it is the earliest English play based in classical history still extant. Even if it was written a few years later, it remains one of the first of a long series of history plays that were popular during the last years of Queen Elizabeth's reign. Lodge apparently used at least two sources for his chronicle: Appian's *Roman History* (second century A.D.), translated in 1578, and Sir Thomas North's translation (1579) of the *Parallel Lives* (105-115), by Plutarch. In turning to the latter work, Lodge pointed the way for Shakespeare, who later used Plutarch as his major source for his Roman plays.

Although the title page of the first edition of *The Wounds of Civill War* identifies it as a tragedy, the play is more properly described as a chronicle or history play. It concerns the continuing conflict between Marius and Sulla during the Roman Civil Wars, beginning in 88 B.C. The story is episodic, covering a ten-year period of Roman history, and the play lacks unity, chiefly because Lodge followed his sources too closely. Although Lodge concentrates on the clash of personal ambitions between the major characters, the incidents are never quite drawn together with a central dramatic focus. The central conflict is one of ambition rather than of character, and the play lacks psychological depth, a fact that is particularly clear in the final act, when Sulla's remorse and subsequent death seem sudden and unmotivated. Despite numerous battle scenes, Lodge's chronicle remains rather static; its emphasis is on language rather than action. Fortunately, Lodge was a talented poet, and the verse, though often monotonous, is well-crafted and sometimes melodious.

The Wounds of Civill War, while imperfect, represents an important step in English dramatic history. The play is innovative and experimental rather than a polished achievement, and it should be judged accordingly. Lodge's writing tended to be better when he followed an established form, as in his prose romances. Lodge's experimentation with classical history may have produced a somewhat flawed work, but it provided other writers with an indication of the dramatic potential of the material.

A Looking Glass for London and England is similarly experimental and similarly flawed, but it is, for the most part, a tighter and more interesting drama than *The Wounds of Civill War*. Whether this is at all attributable to the influence of Lodge's collaborator, Robert Greene, is impossible to determine. The styles of the two writers are very similar, and in this play, they blend so smoothly that it is impossible to identify the authorship of the various parts.

The date of composition of *A Looking Glass for London and England* is most frequently given as 1588 or 1589. The play shows some influence of *Tamburlaine the Great* and *The Spanish Tragedy*, which suggests that it was written after 1587. The greater variety and flexibility of the verse suggests the influence of Marlowe, while the spectacular effects may have been designed to appeal to the taste for sensationalism primed by Kyd's tragedy. Lodge's renouncement of the theater in 1589 sets the latest possible date for the play, but it is likely that it was composed earlier, since despite frequent references to contemporary events, it makes no mention of the Spanish Armada. This fact suggests that the play could have been written as early as 1587, just after the appearance of Marlowe's tragedy but before the threat of invasion by Spain.

A Looking Glass for London and England is a highly didactic work based loosely on the Old Testament book of Jonah. Lodge and Greene also probably used Josephus' history of the Jews, a work Lodge later translated. The authors exercised considerable freedom in expanding the story, particularly in the development of the character of Rasni, the King of Nineveh, who does not appear in the sources, and in the addition and elaboration of a clown plot involving a smith and his servant.

Like *The Wounds of Civill War*, *A Looking Glass for London and England* is episodic, but it is held together by a clearer sense of dramatic purpose. Although the play's moralizing often seems naïve, it provides a central focus that holds the many disparate elements of the drama together. The final turn toward romantic comedy at the end is sudden, but it is prepared for by the biblical story and the basic moral stance of the work. *A Looking Glass for London and England* is innovative and traditional at the same time, blending together a variety of theatrical traditions into an original work. Its heavy didacticism suggests the influence of morality interludes. The basic story of the conversion of Nineveh is reminiscent of the plays of the mystery cycles, while the clown plot, with its devils, echoes the vice episodes of the morality plays. John Lyly's euphuistic style, which Lodge used quite seriously in his romances, is parodied in one scene. The characterization of the despot Rasni may be derived from Marlowe's *Tamburlaine the Great*, and the spectacular and sometimes violent effects suggest a debt to Kyd's *The Spanish Tragedy* as well as to the elaborate stage machinery of the mystery cycles. All of these elements are brought together in a kaleidoscopic form which possesses a surprising degree of unity and a distinct charm.

Both of Lodge's dramatic works are experimental, which is at once their strength and their weakness. Like the other University Wits, Lodge was a dramatic pioneer, experimenting with new forms or with new uses for old theatrical materials. Unfortunately, he does not seem to have had the sense of dramatic form that allowed other writers, such as Shakespeare, to take the basic idea of the history play and create from it a much tighter and richer drama. Lodge's chief talent seems to have been as a lyric poet, but the verse of his plays shows his full lyric genius only rarely. Written at a time when blank verse first began to appear on the stage, Lodge's lines tend to be monotonous. He depends heavily on long set speeches rather than on true dialogue, which makes the plays seem rather stiff and sometimes unemotional. The plays also suffer from Lodge's tendency to moralize rather than let the action carry his moral concerns.

Many of these weaknesses come from the experimental nature of Lodge's work, however, and he should not be judged too harshly. While he was not a Shakespeare or a Marlowe, Lodge was a competent and sometimes daring dramatist. Despite his weaknesses, his influence on the English theater is significant and undeniable. *The Wounds of Civill War* and *A Looking Glass for London and England* remain important texts, the first for its pioneering role in the development of the history play and the second for its sophisticated combination of widely diverse literary elements, providing almost a summary of the most significant influences on the early English theater.

Other major works

NOVELS: *The Delectable History of Forbonius and Prisceria*, 1584; *Rosalynde: Or, Euphues Golden Legacy*, 1590; *Euphues Shadow*, 1592; *A Margarite of America*, 1596.

POETRY: *Scillaes Metamorphosis*, 1589; *Phillis with the Tragical Complaynt of Elstred*, 1593; *A Spider's Webbe*, 1594; *A Fig for Momus*, 1595.

NONFICTION: *A Defence of Poetry, Music, and Stage Plays*, c. 1579; *An Alarum Against Usurers*, 1584; *The Famous, True, and Historical Life of Robert Second Duke of Normandy*, 1591; *Catharos*, 1591; *The Life and Death of William Long Beard*, 1593; *The Diuel Coniured*, 1596; *Prosopopeia*, 1596; *Wits Miserie and Worlds Madnesse*, 1596; *The Flowers of Lodowicke of Granado*, 1601 (translation); *The Famous and Memorable Works of Josephus*, 1602 (translation); *A Treatise on the Plague*, 1603; *The Works, both Morall and Natural, of Lucius Annaeus Seneca*, 1614 (translation); *The Poore Mans Talentt*, 1621; *A Learned Summary upon the Famous Poem of William of Saluste, Lord of Bartas*, 1625 (translation).

MISCELLANEOUS: *The Complete Works of Thomas Lodge*, 1883 (Sir Edmund Gosse, editor; 4 volumes).

Bibliography

Paradise, N. Burton. *Thomas Lodge: The History of an Elizabethan.* New Haven, Conn.: Yale University Press, 1931. A substantial biography with a lengthy discussion of Lodge's two plays and of *Rosalynde: Or, Euphues Golden Legacy*, the source of Shakespeare's *As You Like It* (pr. c. 1599-1600). Notes similarities between *The Wounds of Civill War* and George Gascoigne's *Jocasta* (pr. 1566, pb. 1573). Claims that Lodge's most notable characteristic is the "sensitiveness with which he responded to new developments in the techniques of versification," a claim used to support the contention that Lodge was not influenced by Thomas Kyd's *The Spanish Tragedy* (pr. c. 1585-1589), for Lodge's plays lack many of the elements notable in Kyd's work.

Rae, Wesley D. *Thomas Lodge.* New York: Twayne, 1967. Covers the life and works and stresses the variety of Lodge's literary production. Finds *The Wounds of Civill War* weak in plot but acceptable for style and judges the collaboration with Robert Greene successful, producing *A Looking Glass for London and England*, a play heavy in its moral judgments. The play compares the evils of Nineveh, which were castigated by Hosea and Jonah, with such London evils as usury, corrupt justices, and drunken husbands and fathers who fail to care properly for their families. Bibliography, index.

Ryan, P. M. *Thomas Lodge, Gentleman.* Hamden, Conn.: Shoe String Press, 1958. This critical biography contains a separate section on Lodge as dramatist, where such aspects of *The Wounds of Civill War* as its imagery and heavy repetition are noted. Finds *A Looking Glass for London and England* to contain "trenchant contemporary satire," discusses dates and sources at length, and is critical of previous biographies and bibliographies of Lodge. Poor proofreading.

Tenney, Edward A. *Thomas Lodge.* Ithaca, N.Y.: Cornell University Press, 1935. This biography considers all the works published about Lodge in the early 1930's. Discusses Lodge's literary work at length in chapters 5 and 7 but pays little attention to his plays. Bibliography, index.

Walker, Alice. *The Life of Thomas Lodge.* London: Sidgwick and Jackson, 1933. A brief account of the writer's life, with information about other members of his family, gleaned from examination of various Elizabethan documents. Expands the information found in other biographical accounts, such as N. Burton Paradise's study above.

Kathleen Latimer
(Updated by *Howard L. Ford*)

FREDERICK LONSDALE
Lionel Frederick Leonard

Born: St. Helier, Jersey, Channel Islands; February 5, 1881
Died: London, England; April 4, 1954

Principal drama

Who's Hamilton?, pr. 1903; *The Early Worm*, pr. 1908; *The King of Cadonia*, pr. 1908 (libretto; music by Sidney Jones; based on Anthony Hope's novel *The Prisoner of Zenda*); *The Best People*, pr. 1909; *The Balkan Princess*, pr. 1910 (libretto, with Frank Curzon; music by Paul Rubens); *Betty*, pr. 1914 (libretto, with Gladys Unger; music by Rubens); *The Patriot*, pr. 1915; *High Jinks*, pr. 1916 (libretto; music by Rudolph Friml); *Waiting at the Church*, pr. 1916; *The Maid of the Mountains*, pr. 1917, pb. 1949 (libretto; music by Harold Fraser-Simson, lyrics by Harry Graham); *Monsieur Beaucaire*, pr. 1919 (libretto; music by André Messager, based on a French libretto); *The Lady of the Rose*, pr. 1921, pb. 1922 (libretto; music by Jean Gilbert, lyrics by Graham; adaptation of Rudolph Schanzer and Ernst Welisch's libretto); *Aren't We All?*, pr. 1923, pb. 1924 (originally as *The Best People*); *Spring Cleaning*, pr. 1923, pb. 1925; *The Fake*, pr. 1924, pb. 1927; *Katja the Dancer*, pr. 1924 (libretto, with Graham; music by Gilbert); *The Street Singer*, pr., pb. 1924 (libretto; music by Fraser-Simson); *The Last of Mrs. Cheyney*, pr., pb. 1925; *On Approval*, pr. 1926 (staged), pb. 1927, pr. 1982 (televised) (originally as "The Follies of the Foolish"); *The High Road*, pr., pb. 1927; *Lady Mary*, pr. 1928 (libretto, with John Hastings Turner; music by Albert Sirmay and Philip Craig); *Canaries Sometimes Sing*, pr., pb. 1929; *Never Come Back*, pr. 1932; *Once Is Enough*, pr., pb. 1938 (originally as *Half a Loaf*, wr. 1937, pr. 1958); *The Foreigners*, pr. 1939; *Another Love Story*, pr. 1943, pb. 1948; *But for the Grace of God*, pr. 1946; *The Way Things Go*, pr. 1950, pb. 1951 (revised as *Day After Tomorrow*, pr. 1950); *Let Them Eat Cake*, pr., pb. 1959 (revision of *Once Is Enough*).

Other literary forms

Frederick Lonsdale's success as a librettist for musical comedies and operettas was equal to his success as a playwright. His libretto for *The King of Cadonia* was clearly inspired by Anthony Hope's novel *The Prisoner of Zenda* (1894) and in its turn influenced Ivor Novello's operetta *King's Rhapsody* (pr. 1950). Lonsdale's most popular work in this vein was *The Maid of the Mountains*, which ran at Daly's Theatre, London, for a total of 1,352 performances. Lonsdale collaborated with other leading musical theater composers of the early twentieth century English stage, including Paul Rubens, who did the music for *The Balkan Princess* (written with Frank Curzon) and *Betty* (written with Gladys Unger). He also had a hand in a number of adaptations of European successes, such as *The Lady of the Rose* and *Katja the Dancer*, both with music by the German composer Jean Gilbert (pseudonym of Max Winterfield); *High Jinks*, with a score by the Hungarian-born Rudolf Friml; and *Monsieur Beaucaire*, with music composed by André Messager, the last major writer of French operetta. Lonsdale's last effort as a librettist was *Lady Mary*, which he coauthored with John Hastings Turner to a score by Albert Sirmay and Philip Craig.

Generally, Lonsdale seems to have been sought out by the impresarios of musical theater for his ability to supply sprightly, well-constructed books which blended wit and sentimentality. The most convincing testimony to his skill in this area is *The Maid of the Mountains*, which was second only to Oscar Asche and Frederic Norton's *Chu Chin Chow* (pr. 1916) as the major musical success of London's West End theater during World War I.

After his major drawing-room comedies had achieved success in New York, Lonsdale's talents were also recognized and recruited by the film industry. He wrote, or had a hand in, several screenplays, including Alexander Korda's vehicle for Douglas Fairbanks, *The Private Life of Don Juan* (1934; with Lajos Biro), and Metro-Goldwyn-Mayer's episodic World War II tribute to British patriotism, *Forever and a Day* (1943; with Charles Bennett, C. S. Forester, John Van Druten, Christopher Isherwood, R. C. Sherriff, and many others too numerous to mention). That he wrote so little for the screen can be attributed partly to his dislike of Hollywood ("I could never live in a film city because there is no conversation") and partly to his habit of breaking contracts.

Achievements

Lonsdale reached his peak of acclaim in the 1920's and early 1930's, when his name was closely associated with sophisticated drawing-room comedies, such as those of Noël Coward, S. N. Behrman, and Philip Barry. During Lonsdale's long career as a playwright, which extended from the staging of *Who's Hamilton?* at the New Theatre, Ealing, in 1903, to the posthumous production of *Let Them Eat Cake* at the Cambridge Theatre, London, in 1959, his work was praised by such diverse theater critics as Henrik Ibsen's archenemy Clement Scott of *The Daily Telegraph*, Arthur B. Walkley of *The Times* (London), *The Sunday Times'* convivial James Agate, Heywood Broun of *New York World*, *The New Yorker's* resident wit, Robert Benchley, and the British eccentric, Hannen Swaffer of the *Daily Express*. Typical of such critics' comments was Benchley's on *Spring Cleaning's* New York production in 1923: "It is written with a respect for the audience's intelligence and has an easy humor which brought a pleasant glow to this sin-hardened heart." In the same vein, Agate, reviewing a revival of *On Approval* in London in 1933, observed that "time is powerless against true wit and diversion."

Lonsdale's reputation declined in the 1940's and 1950's, and indeed, in 1953, almost at the end of his life, he experienced the bitterness of an old established author being goaded by a critical wunderkind when Kenneth Tynan, writing in the *Evening Standard* about a revival of *Aren't We All?*, said: "Frederick Lonsdale's comedy, first produced thirty years ago, is what some would call gentle, others toothless: where Somerset Maugham chews and digests his characters, Lonsdale merely mumbles them." More recently, however, there has been an upsurge of interest in Lonsdale's work. A successful revival of *The Last of Mrs. Cheyney* was presented at the Chichester Festival in 1980, and in 1982, a polished and hard-edged British Broadcasting Corporation television production of *On Approval* with Jeremy Brett and Penelope Keith proved that the years have not eroded its quality. Though no innovator, Lonsdale was one of those artists who take a particular form and handle it with consummate skill and flair.

Biography

Unlike the heroes and heroines of his own plays, Frederick Lonsdale came from a decidedly humble background. Lonsdale was born Lionel Frederick Leonard on February 5, 1881, in St. Helier, the capital of Jersey in the Channel Islands. The third son of a local tobacconist and his wife, Frederick and Susan Leonard, Lonsdale was an unruly child who disappointed his family by refusing to attend school and by running off to Canada in his late teens on a romantic impulse. There he seems to have lived by his wits and, according to his own account, was not above perpetrating fraud to finance his passage back to England. On his return, he worked for some time on the Southampton docks and wrote plays in his spare time. When he moved back to Jersey in 1903, his first play had already been produced at a suburban London theater and had been noticed favorably by one of the leading British critics, Clement Scott, who had entered the theater by chance to shelter himself from the rain. The producing company brought the play to St. Helier that same year, and from that point Lonsdale began to be accepted into the more elevated reaches of Jersey society. His transformation from the "villainous and undisciplined child" of a small-town shopkeeper into an international celebrity whose smallest sartorial innovations made instant newspaper copy seems to have begun at about this time. Lonsdale was obviously a keen observer and a gifted mimic, and he rapidly assumed the manners and accent of the upper class, about which he was to spend much of his life writing.

In 1904, Lonsdale—still known in private life as Frederick Leonard—married Leslie Hoggan, the daughter of a retired colonel. For the first four years of their marriage, the young couple spent much of their time apart. Lonsdale had returned to England to pursue his career as a playwright and was not making sufficient income to provide a home for both of them there. Finally, however, he attracted the attention of a London impresario, Frank Curzon, who staged Lonsdale's first successful work, *The King of Cadonia*, at the Prince of Wales Theatre in September, 1908. The young couple were reunited and soon afterward changed their names by deed poll from Mr. and Mrs. Frederick Leonard to Mr. and Mrs. Frederick Lonsdale, the name which the playwright had adopted as his nom de plume. From that time onward, Lonsdale's success was assured, and with *The Maid of the Mountains* in 1917, he achieved sufficient financial security to enable him to play the man-about-town for the next two decades.

By the mid-1920's, Lonsdale was equally celebrated in England and the United States. His marriage had failed, and he had separated from his wife and family. In the 1930's, he was invited to Hollywood to write screenplays, chiefly for Metro-Goldwyn-Mayer. In that decade, his productivity as a playwright declined, and only three new works were staged between 1930 and 1940. With the advent of World War II, Lonsdale's criticism of the war effort and his voluntary exile in the United States lost him the respect of many of his compatriots. Nevertheless, when the war ended, he returned to England and resumed his career as a West End playwright. From 1950 onward, he spent much of his time in France, but by that time, his particular brand of witty drawing-room comedy had begun to fall out of favor, and his income declined steeply. Furthermore, age brought with it an increasing uncertainty of temper which made him unpopular with many members of the theatrical profession. Lonsdale died in London in 1954. He was survived by his wife, Leslie, and three daughters.

Analysis

Frederick Lonsdale's plays were the product of an almost fatally facile talent. He wrote so easily and on the whole so successfully that he seems to have begun to regard his achievement as a species of confidence trick, similar to the one he claimed to have perpetrated as an adolescent in Canada. Peter Daubeney, the English director who staged *But for the Grace of God* in 1946, has spoken of Lonsdale's "Olympian contempt for the theatre," calling him "an outstanding example of a man who despises the very medium where he excels." Clearly, though Lonsdale rivaled both Coward and Maugham in his ability to devise effective and amusing drawing-room comedies, he rarely attempted to extend his range. When he did—as in *The Fake* and *The Foreigners*—the result was invariably one of his rare failures at the box office. Maugham, on the other hand, though best in such high comedy as *The Circle* (pr. 1921) and *The Constant Wife* (pr. 1926), was able to write sardonic domestic comedies such as *The Breadwinner* (pr. 1930) and effective melodramas such as *The Letter* (pr. 1927). Coward, in whom sentimentality and romantic patriotism coexisted with cynicism and outrageousness, also stretched his talents to encompass not only the comedy of manners of *Private Lives* (pr. 1930) but also the lower-class realism of *This Happy Breed* (pr. 1942), the suburban pathos of *Still Life* (pr. 1936), and the epic social history of *Cavalcade* (pr. 1931). In itself, to be sure, such a narrow social range does not invalidate Lonsdale's work, any more than it does the work of Jane Austen, Henry James, Ivy Compton-Burnett, or, for that matter, of William Congreve, Marivaux, or Anton Chekhov. The question that remains is how far Lonsdale succeeded in using the essentially atypical milieu of the English upper class to reflect something beyond itself.

A close examination of Lonsdale's plays reveals not merely a fascination with the lives and manners of members of the English upper class but also a deeply divided attitude toward them. On the one hand, there is the apparent disdain for certain types who do not belong to the charmed circle—as in his occasional disparaging references to shop girls, Socialist politicians who never bathe, and illiterate Jewish theater managers; on the other hand, there is a moralizing tone in several of the plays in which the palms of honesty and worthiness are awarded to ex-chorus girls and women who live by their wits rather than to the aristocrats who patronize or exclude them. Another theme which emerges almost as consistently is that of the pleasures and perils of disguise. It is difficult to resist the temptation to speculate that both of these themes attracted Lonsdale so powerfully because he had emerged from a world of shop girls, advanced by living on his wits, succeeded finally in making London society accept him by adopting an upper-class persona, and ever after feared that some day he would be unmasked.

Lonsdale's love-hate relationship with the aristocracy and his preoccupation with disguise predate his first successful West End comedies. They go back, indeed, to his days as the librettist of such works as *The King of Cadonia* and *The Balkan Princess*. *Monsieur Beaucaire*, though an adaptation of a French libretto based on Booth Tarkington's novella (1900), illustrates the point almost perfectly. Lonsdale must have found it an appealing project, since it attacks the hypocrisy and snobbishness of the upper class by unfolding the tale of a mysterious young French nobleman, the Marquis de Chateaurien, who is in love with an English noblewoman, Lady Mary Carlisle. His rival for Lady Mary's love, Lord Winterset, unmasks him as Monsieur Beaucaire, a common barber. Lady Mary then rejects him, only to discover to her chagrin that the common barber is, in reality, under the multiplicity of disguises, Louis XV's cousin, the Duc d'Orléans. Translated into the idiom of Lonsdale's later work, its message becomes that it is unwise to snub a shop girl, for she may turn out to have the soul of a duchess. Other possible propositions which might spring from this—that a duchess may turn out to have the soul of a shop girl, or that the souls of both duchesses and shop girls could be equally worthy of consideration—

seem not to have interested Lonsdale to the same degree.

In his first really successful West End comedy, *Aren't We All?*, Lonsdale was still in his first flush of infatuation with the peerage. His depiction of Lord Grenham and his heir, Willie Tatham, of Lady Frinton, and of such representatives of the *jeunesse dorée* as Arthur Wells and Martin Steele is on the whole benign. Quite untypically, in fact, Lonsdale reserves his sharpest barbs for a Church of England clergyman who is married to Grenham's sister, Angela. Pompous, narrow-minded, hypocritical, and defensive, the Reverend Ernest Lynton is not so much a character as a caricature from *Punch*, and he clearly belongs to a world about which Lonsdale shows little knowledge or interest. His presence in the play, like that of his wife, is not essential to the main plot; he is there to provide an easily shocked target for Grenham's worldly cynicism and to set up the curtain line, which is also the title of the play:

> VICAR: . . . In answer to a simple remark I made last night, Grenham, you called me
> a bloody old fool! (*Puts his head in his hands as if crying.*)
> LORD GRENHAM: (*Puts his arm around his shoulder.*) But aren't we all, old friend?

To the degree that they are unable to separate appearance from reality, to penetrate disguises, or to refrain from leaping to conclusions, they are all indeed fools.

The play turns upon a misunderstanding between two characters: Willie Tatham, Grenham's son, and Margot Tatham, Willie's wife. Willie is forced to wear the disguise of guilt, while Margot assumes the disguise of innocence. When the play opens, Willie has agreed to let Lady Frinton use his house to give a dance. Willie is worried and lonely. His wife has gone on a trip to Egypt, and he has not heard from her for more than a week. At the dance, a former actress with whom Willie is acquainted, Kitty Lake, is sympathetic to him, and they exchange a consoling kiss. Margot arrives home unexpectedly at that very moment and assumes immediately that Willie and Kitty are having an affair. Margot is unforgiving and proposes to leave Willie, but her very intransigence arouses the suspicions of her father-in-law, Lord Grenham. In an attempt to save his son's marriage, he unearths a secret alliance that Margot has formed in Egypt and arranges a confrontation between her and the young man concerned. His plan fails, however, when the young man gallantly pretends not to know Margot. Margot's mask remains secure, but her own confidence in her behavior toward her husband is shaken. Their peccadilloes cancel each other out, and at the end they go away together, reconciled.

The slightness of the plot is bolstered by two other concurrent actions: one in which Lord Grenham's sister, Angela, is gradually humanized as she learns to discard the appearance of grim, repressive "virtue" and to appreciate her brother's more flexible attitude toward life; the other in which

Grenham is trapped into marriage with Lady Frinton by Margot, who, to revenge herself for his attempt to unmask her, places an announcement of their engagement in *The Times*. As in the main plot, changes are brought about in the circumstances of the characters as they are compelled to relinquish one set of attitudes for another.

Lonsdale's reputation for wit is not, on the whole, reinforced by the dialogue of this play. Lonsdale clearly intended Lord Grenham to be the main conduit of this quality, but at best he is able to rise to the sub-Wildean: "All my life I have found it very difficult to refuse a woman anything; except marriage." On the other hand, the dialogue generally is efficient, uncluttered, and has the rhythm, if not the content, of wit. Spoken, as it originally was, by first-rate light comedians, it seems to have persuaded audiences and critics alike that they had experienced the sensations of surprise and delight which true wit brings.

In 1925, two years after the premiere of *Aren't We All?*, Lonsdale's most successful nonmusical play was staged. *The Last of Mrs. Cheyney* is, in a sense, an anomalous play since it resurrects the atmosphere and many of the devices of nineteenth century society melodrama. The echoes of, for example, Oscar Wilde's *Lady Windermere's Fan* (pr. 1892) are very strong, particularly during the second-act climax, which involves a woman being trapped in compromising circumstances with a man of dubious reputation. Lonsdale, however, amusingly inverts the formula to create a comedy-drama with several well-placed *coups de théâtre*. The one which ends the first act is particularly effective. Mrs. Cheyney, apparently a wealthy widow from Australia, is holding a charity concert in the garden of her house. The concert is attended by various representatives of London society, including the upright Lord Elton, the disreputable Lord Dilling, and Mrs. Ebley, a woman who has grown rich on the attentions of other women's husbands. Lord Elton and Lord Dilling are both attracted to Mrs. Cheyney, but Elton's intentions are honorable whereas Dilling's are not. Rather unusually, Mrs. Cheyney's establishment seems to be staffed entirely by menservants; one of them, Charles the butler, strikes a chord in Dilling's memory. The butler is suspiciously gentlemanly, and Dilling suspects that they were at Oxford together. When the guests leave at the end of the concert, Mrs. Cheyney, who has represented herself as someone who neither smokes nor drinks nor swears, immediately lights a cigarette, burns her fingers on the match, and curses. Then, as she sits at the piano and begins to play, her menservants enter, sprawl on the furniture, and smoke. It becomes clear that they and Mrs. Cheyney are a gang of jewel thieves bent on relieving Mrs. Ebley of her pearls.

The play's second act builds to a similar bravura climax. It is set in Mrs. Ebley's house, where the characters from act 1 have assembled for the weekend. The plot to rob Mrs. Ebley is foiled by Lord Dilling, who, having recognized Charles as a jewel thief whom he had once encountered in Paris, switches bedrooms with Mrs. Ebley and catches Mrs. Cheyney as she comes in to steal the pearls. Dilling presents a proposition: Either Mrs. Cheyney can submit to him and remain undiscovered or he will ring the bell and turn her over to the police. Instead, Mrs. Cheyney rings the bell herself and, in front of Dilling, Elton, and the rest, hands back the pearls to Mrs. Ebley.

Act 3, adding a touch of Augustin Scribe and Victorien Sardou to the Wildean mix, revolves around a letter. Written by Elton to Mrs. Cheyney and containing a proposal of marriage, it also includes a number of painfully accurate pen portraits of the upper-class set in which Mrs. Cheyney has been moving and of which the stiff-necked Elton intensely disapproves. The possibility that Mrs. Cheyney might use this letter to cause a scandal prompts heavy bidding for its return. Elton writes Mrs. Cheyney a check for ten thousand pounds, and Mrs. Ebley promises to drop the charges of theft. Mrs. Cheyney accepts the check but then tears it up and informs them that she has already torn up the letter. The members of the house party, amazed by this, are even more amazed when they learn that it was she and not Dilling who rang the bell in Mrs. Ebley's bedroom. Their attitude toward her changes; they see her as someone with a sense of good sportsmanship, which is their equivalent of honor. Somewhat surprisingly, she is willing to be reabsorbed into the set which has shown itself so eager to reject her, and, as the play closes, she agrees to become Dilling's wife.

Lonsdale's two chief themes echo throughout this play. Mrs. Cheyney is clearly more interested in being accepted by society than in thieving from it. As she says to Charles, her butler and coconspirator, toward the end of the first act: "I'm sorry, but I didn't realise when I adopted this profession that the people I would have to take things from would be quite so nice." Even when they have proved themselves not "quite so nice," she is willing to forgive and be forgiven by them. On the other hand, the flaws of the play's three main representatives of high society are repeatedly exposed to the audience. Lord Elton is priggish and pompous; Lord Dilling is a wastrel and a womanizer; Mrs. Ebley exploits her appeal for men. At the climax of the play, the unmasking of Mrs. Cheyney is paralleled by the unmasking of society itself. Lonsdale's ambivalence is amply demonstrated.

The pleasures and perils of disguise are illustrated chiefly in the characters of Mrs. Cheyney and Charles, though William the footman, Jim the chauffeur, and George the page boy are also implicated in the masquerade. Mrs. Cheyney and Charles, however, unlike the latter three, who are lower-class "Cockney" types, are represented as people of grace, wit, and charm, educated people who might well have made their way into society by legitimate means but who have chosen a more adventurous course. At the same time, their actions are given a moral color which verges on Lincoln green, inasmuch as the people they rob deserve it, having in their turn, morally speaking, robbed others:

> CHARLES: I'm not trying to persuade you, my sweet, but there is this to be remembered, the pearls we want from Mrs. Ebley were taken by that lady, without a scruple, from the wives of the men who gave them to her.

Mrs. Cheyney is persuaded, and she goes on to play a bold and dangerous game, seemingly courting exposure and disaster but winning through to acceptance and marriage into the peerage.

The Last of Mrs. Cheyney is a very skillful theatrical piece, with cleverly placed reversals, recognitions, crises, and climaxes. It is an admirable mechanism, like a fine example of a Swiss clockmaker's art, and as such it can still be persuasive on the stage. Yet in *The Last of Mrs. Cheyney*, Lonsdale had not yet achieved as sure a grasp of his themes as he did in his next play, *On Approval*.

On Approval is in many respects the most economical of Lonsdale's comedies. It has only four characters, dispensing with the clutter of minor figures which in the earlier plays give substance and color to the milieu but contribute little to the action. The premise of the play is as self-consciously daring as that of Coward's *Private Lives*, to which it also bears a certain structural resemblance. The principal characters, Maria Wislak and the Duke of Bristol, are as monstrously egotistical as Coward's Eliot and Amanda, though they belong not so much to the smart set who honeymoon on the Riviera as to the landed gentry who grouse-shoot in Scotland. Like *Private Lives*, *On Approval* is a minuet of changing alliances. The action is initiated by the wealthy Maria, who decides that the pleasant but penniless Richard Halton may be a suitable candidate for her next husband. To try him out, she proposes to take him to her house in Scotland for a month. Her longtime enemy, the Duke of Bristol, decides that he will go, too, ostensibly to lend Richard moral support but actually to escape his creditors. The fourth member of the group is an attractive, good-natured pickle heiress, Helen Hayle, who follows in pursuit of the duke, with whom she is in love.

In the course of the action, Lonsdale leaves the audience in no doubt that the representatives of the ruling class are outrageously and comically tiresome. Not only do Maria and the duke berate and abuse each other incessantly, but also they treat the penniless Richard and Helen, the pickle-profiteer's daughter, like servants. The effect of this is to draw Richard and Helen closer together, and finally they conspire to sneak away in the only available automobile, just as a massive snowstorm is beginning—a snowstorm which threatens to trap the monstrous Maria and the appalling duke together for several weeks. As Richard says: "It's the kindest thing that has ever been done for them. Such hell as a month alone here together will make them the nicest people in the world." This denouement recalls that of *Private Lives*, in which Eliot and Amanda tiptoe out of the Paris apartment to which they have eloped, leaving their respective spouses, Victor and Sybil, quarreling violently. Because *Private Lives* appeared two years later than *On Approval*, it is more than probable that Coward learned something from Lonsdale about the construction of sophisticated drawing-room comedies.

Clearly, in *On Approval*, Lonsdale has resolved his conflict with respect to acceptance/rejection by society. In this play, it is the upwardly mobile who are the "nice" people, unequivocally; the established members of society may yet become "nice" but only through undergoing an ordeal of isolation in uncongenial company. There is no falsely sentimental juxtaposition of gentlemen and jewel thieves, or duchesses and ex-chorus girls, with Lonsdale judiciously trying to hold the balance; here he rightly identifies with the aspiring middle class and asserts his own niceness against the arrogance of the upper class.

Lonsdale's other perennial theme, of masks and unmasking, is also present, though in a subtler form than in *The Last of Mrs. Cheyney*. Maria Wislak takes Richard Halton "on approval" to find out if he is as pleasant and congenial as he appears to be. She decides that he is, but meanwhile Richard has found out that Maria is not as she has appeared to him for twenty years, "too good, too beautiful, too noble" for him; indeed, she is "one of the most unpleasant of God's creatures." Like Lady Mary Carlisle in *Monsieur Beaucaire*, Maria is deeply chagrined at this turn of events: "To think I brought the brute here to find out if I like him, and he has the audacity the moment I tell him I do, to tell me he doesn't like me!" Similarly, Helen sees through the Duke of Bristol's charm to the spoiled schoolboy underneath: "To make him a decent man he needs six months before the mast as a common sailor." The misunderstandings and deceits that complicate the lives of the four characters in *On Approval* are much more character-based than in the somewhat mechanically contrived *Aren't We All?* and *The Last of Mrs. Cheyney*.

The dialogue, too, is more distinctive, more deft and more plausible. Instead of the secondhand epigrams of Lord Grenham and Lord Dilling, there is the genuine crackle and tension of strong-willed people using language as a weapon to penetrate their opponents' armor of conceit and self-absorption. The play's witty lines cannot be taken out of context to survive as freestanding aphorisms; their humor depends entirely on the audience's understanding of the characters of Maria, the duke, Richard, and Helen, and of the conflicts between them.

On Approval is the high point of Lonsdale's achievement as a comic playwright. Though he continued to write sporadically for another quarter of a century and though none of the plays he wrote in that period (except

The Foreigners) lost money, he never quite repeated the artistic and popular success he reached with his comedies of the mid-1920's. A typical example of his later work is *Let Them Eat Cake*, which like many of Lonsdale's plays is a revision, or a renaming at least, of an earlier one. *On Approval*, for example, was a substantial revision of an early, unproduced work, "The Follies of the Foolish," and *Aren't We All?* was a reworking of *The Best People*. *Let Them Eat Cake* was first titled *Half a Loaf* (written in 1937); was produced in 1938 as *Once Is Enough*; reappeared as *Half a Loaf* at the Theatre Royal, Windsor, in 1958, four years after Lonsdale's death; and finally opened at the Cambridge Theatre, London, in 1959, as *Let Them Eat Cake*. In it, Lonsdale reverts to the pattern of earlier plays such as *Aren't We All?* Indeed, its theme of marital misunderstanding is not dissimilar, and its cast list is even more replete with titled characters, including the Duke and Duchess of Hampshire, Lord and Lady Plynne, Lord and Lady Whitehall, Lord Rayne, and Lady Bletchley. The main action involves Johnny, the Duke of Hampshire, who becomes infatuated with Liz Pleydell, the wife of his friend Charles, and Nancy, the Duchess of Hampshire, who attempts to save their marriage. Johnny is prepared to leave his wife and run away with Mrs. Pleydell to her orange plantation in South Africa. Nancy prevents them by the simple expedient of telling Mrs. Pleydell that she will not divorce Johnny, thereby rendering Mrs. Pleydell's social status, if she persists in going off to live with him, uncomfortably precarious. In the rather unconvincing denouement, Johnny realizes that Mrs. Pleydell's real object is not him, but his title, and that he has been suffering from the "temporary disease" of infatuation.

The main characters are even less attractive than those in *On Approval*, but in this case unintentionally so. There is also, as in *Aren't We All?* and *The Last of Mrs. Cheyney*, a superfluity of minor figures who have little function other than to provide a sort of living decor. Furthermore, the dialogue has the secondhand ring of reach-me-down epigrams, common in the earlier plays, as in this exchange:

> LADY BLETCHLEY: What actually is cirrhosis of the liver?
> REGGIE [LORD RAYNE]: A tribute nature pays to men who have completely conquered Teetotalism!

All in all, the play marks a regression in Lonsdale's technique: less economical and integrated than *On Approval* and less splendidly theatrical than *The Last of Mrs. Cheyney*.

Lonsdale's work, placed in historical perspective, occupies the midpoint in what might be called "the rise and fall of the drawing-room comedy," beginning not so much with Wilde as with Thomas William Robertson in the 1860's, continuing through such work in the late nineteenth and early twentieth centuries as Arthur Wing Pinero's *The Gay Lord Quex* (pr. 1899) and Maugham's *Lady Frederick* (pr. 1907), reaching a peak in the 1920's with *Private Lives* and *On Approval* and declining in the 1950's with such works as Terence Rattigan's *The Sleeping Prince* (pr. 1953), William Douglas Home's *The Reluctant Debutante* (pr. 1955), and Hugh and Margaret Williams' *The Grass Is Greener* (pr. 1958). The shock waves that John Osborne's *Look Back in Anger* (pr. 1956) sent reverberating through the British theater made it difficult for any playwright thereafter to practice the art of light badinage among the denizens of Mayfair and Belgravia with quite such unself-conscious insouciance.

Comedy seldom gets a fair hearing from literary critics and historians, and writers who specialize in comedy must often be content with only the most condescending of acknowledgments. To point to Aristophanes and Molière, to Congreve, W. S. Gilbert, and George Bernard Shaw, will give pause only temporarily to those who regard comic playwriting as an inferior vocation. Yet, if one weighs Lonsdale's work against the "serious" work of his British contemporaries, the comparison is not altogether in Lonsdale's disfavor. J. B. Priestley's time plays and expressionist experiments, the attempts of W. H. Auden, Christopher Isherwood, Ronald Duncan, T. S. Eliot, and Christopher Fry to revive poetic drama, the bourgeois realism of R. C. Sherriff, John Galsworthy, St. John Ervine, and John Van Druten seem no likelier to hold the attention of future audiences and readers than Lonsdale's best comedies. The only British playwrights of the first half of the twentieth century who clearly surpass him are not the "serious" playwrights but other writers of comedy: Sir James Barrie, Shaw, and Coward.

With all of his failing, his laziness, his self-plagiarism, his too-easy cynicism, and his occasional sentimentality, Lonsdale at his best possessed some distinct countervailing virtues, not least among them being a consummate sense of theater and a keen eye for the foibles of the upper class. Above all, his basic respect for human honesty and decency raised his most assured work to the level of critical comedy, an achievement that might very well have earned for him a nod of approval from both Aristophanes and Molière.

Other major works

SCREENPLAYS: *The Devil to Pay*, 1930; *Lovers Courageous*, 1932; *The Private Life of Don Juan*, 1934 (with Lajos Biro); *Forever and a Day*, 1943 (with Charles Bennett, C. S. Forester, John Van Druten, Christopher Isherwood, R. C. Sherriff, and others).

Bibliography

Donaldson, Frances. *Freddy*. Philadelphia: J. B. Lippincott, 1957. This biography was written by the playwright's daughter, herself an actress and author. She paints an affectionate portrait of her father, being careful to discuss the weaknesses as well as the virtues of his character. She tells the remarkable story of a young man who was a shopkeeper's son and who had little formal education but who, because of his talent and native wit, transformed himself into one of the most successful authors of high comedy and chroniclers of England's upper class during the 1920's. She also notes that when one of his plays was revived in the 1950's, critics such as Kenneth Tynan dismissed him as irrelevant.

Geisinger, Marian. *Plays, Players, and Playwrights.* Rev. ed. New York: Hart Publishing, 1975. A discussion of the actors and the plays in which they appeared, as well as the playwrights themselves. It is clear that despite Lonsdale's enormous popularity during the first quarter of the twentieth century, his reputation, unlike that of some contemporary writers of comedy, did not survive the times. Illustrations.

Nicoll, Allardyce. *English Drama.* Cambridge, England: Cambridge University Press, 1973. Nicoll believes that Lonsdale occupied the middle ground between W. Somerset Maugham and Noël Coward and was overshadowed by both. Lonsdale lacked Maugham's depth and Coward's cleverness, and although he enjoyed great success before and immediately after World War I, his lack of ideas soon dated him. Bibliography.

Reynolds, Ernest. *Modern English Drama.* London: George Harrap, 1949. This survey of the theater from 1900 discusses Lonsdale's achievements at the height of his career, when he was likened to an English Molière. Reynolds points with appreciation to the playwright's easy-flowing lines, amusing situations, and clever management of theatrical effects, giving him high praise for his "crook comedy," *The Last of Mrs. Cheyney,* produced in 1925. Illustrations, bibliography, and list of theaters.

Trewin, J. C. *Dramatists of Today.* London: Staples Press, 1953. This English critic devotes an entire chapter to Lonsdale, a playwright who considers men of title, specifically dukes, to be instruments for the manufacture of epigrams. Although Lonsdale began his career as a musical-comedy librettist, he soon graduated to the sphere of light comedy and for a number of years was ranked with such practitioners of the genre as Oscar Wilde and W. Somerset Maugham. Lonsdale had a gift for amusing dialogue and well-drawn characters rather than strong plots, and as audience taste changed, he grew less and less able to interest his public. In the rare cases when a play of his is revived, it is seen merely as a vehicle for a star performer. Illustrations, play lists, and bibliography.

Anthony Stephenson
(Updated by *Mildred C. Kuner*)

JOHN LYLY

Born: Canterbury(?), Kent, England; c. 1554
Died: London, England; November, 1606

Principal drama

Campaspe, wr. 1579-1580, pr., pb. 1584 (also known as *Alexander, Campaspe and Diogenes*); *Sapho and Phao*, pr., pb. 1584; *Galathea*, pr. c. 1585, pb. 1592; *Endymion, the Man in the Moon*, pr. 1588, pb. 1591; *Midas*, pr. c. 1589, pb. 1592; *Mother Bombie*, pr. c. 1589, pb. 1594; *Love's Metamorphosis*, pr. c. 1589, pb. 1601; *The Woman in the Moon*, pr. c. 1593, pb. 1597; *Dramatic Works*, 1858 (2 volumes; F. W. Fairholt, editor).

Other literary forms

John Lyly continues, unfortunately, to be most remembered for his early prose works, *Euphues, the Anatomy of Wit* (1578) and *Euphues and His England* (1580). These works uneasily combine the values of moralistic Humanism with the erotic subject matter and psychological potential of the Italian novella; these two elements are overlaid and indeed overwhelmed by the famous style, subsequently labeled "euphuism." Both Lyly's own contemporaries and scholars have also assigned Lyly the authorship of *Pap with an Hatchet* (1589), a turgid religious tract published anonymously in the course of the Martin Marprelate controversy.

Achievements

Twentieth century readings have led to recognition of John Lyly as more than a quaint writer. Since the initial work of Jonas Barish in 1956, Lyly's prose style has been more highly (though still variously) valued, and both Barish and, in 1962, G. K. Hunter helped to enhance appreciation of Lyly's plays. Lyly has been served by the freeing of Elizabethan drama criticism in modern times from its earlier compulsion to consider its material in the light of William Shakespeare. Lyly can be seen now as, at his best, a highly intelligent writer of comic psychological and philosophical allegory. He is important not merely for his historical position or for his constructive skill, but also for his insight—which is part of the general Renaissance insight into human personality, informed by the newly experienced classics, often expressed in a symbolic rather than a purely realistic mode.

Biography

Unsurprisingly for an Elizabethan, John Lyly's date of birth cannot be ascertained. From college records, it can be extrapolated back to some time in the early 1550's, probably between late 1553 and late 1554. Lyly was brought up, perhaps also born, in Canterbury, where his father was a cleric attached to the official service of the archbishops. Lyly's near ancestors and family included central figures in the tradition of Humanism in England.

In the early 1570's, John Lyly appears on the books of Magdalen College, Oxford. There is evidence that Lyly intended to pursue an academic career. On the other hand, some rather problematic testimony suggests that Lyly at Oxford was most noted for his interest in the fashionable life and recreations accessible to young men there. By the end of the 1570's, he had moved out of the academic setting and was living in London. His two Euphues books, which he wrote around this time, seem to reflect both an affinity for a Humanistically colored academic world and a certain distance from such a world. The two books were immediately immensely popular, and with their publication, Lyly's life rose clearly into a new orbit, around the court of Queen Elizabeth I.

Lyly became attached to the household of Edward de Vere, Earl of Oxford, an important courtier; Lyly may have been the earl's secretary. The connection led into another one, crucial to Lyly's creative life. Oxford patronized the troupes of choirboy actors that were based on the Chapel Royal and St. Paul's Cathedral. These troupes, carefully recruited and trained, entertained the court during the major winter holidays, such as New Year's, and also, from the 1570's on, performed for paying audiences at the indoor "private" theater of Blackfriars in London. The semicourtly, semiprofessional boys' theater was the highly specialized medium in which Lyly worked throughout the 1580's. Seven of his eight known plays were written for boys; six of the eight are heralded on the title pages of their quarto editions as having been performed before the queen.

Lyly's first play, *Campaspe*, had almost the same phenomenal early popularity as his fiction. Lyly clearly believed he was given reason during the 1580's to hope for regular employment under the queen. As the decade wore on, however, Lyly's court and theatrical career lost its promising rhythm.

The boys' companies' obstreperous participation in the Martin Marprelate controversy of 1588-1590 led to a ban on their productions throughout the 1590's, which all but shut down Lyly's theatrical work. His euphuistic style went rapidly from being in vogue to being the target of sophisticated ridicule. Although Lyly did serve in various parliaments throughout the 1590's, he never achieved the court office to which he aspired. At the time of his death in 1606, Lyly was burdened with a family whom he could not support and suits from his creditors which he failed to answer.

Analysis

Campaspe, John Lyly's first play, is closely related to the Euphues works in several respects, first of all in its Humanism. It shares with segments of the Euphues writings a typical Humanistic source, Plutarch. The work is to a large extent one of ethical counsel, specifically of counsel to the ruler. The boy actors produced the play before Queen Elizabeth, and much of it constitutes an image of wise conduct by an exemplary ruler from the past, Alexander the Great.

For critics such as Hunter and Peter Saccio, *Campaspe* is a major instance of lack of plot development or even sequence in Lyly's dramaturgy. Some scenes in the play, such as a meeting of Alexander with the philosophers of Athens, are detached set pieces not meant to advance any plot line, and involve characters who appear nowhere else in the play. Lyly regularly breaks the continuity of such actions as do develop in the play and thus denies the audience any steadily growing involvement with them. An action begun in one scene will not be resumed until several scenes later, after one's attention has been diverted and diverted again by different bits of other material. Characters' motives shift without explanation from one scene to another.

The point seems to be that Lyly's sense of construction is not based on the wholeness of a realistic action but, in this case, on a doctrinal picture. The interrelatedness of many of *Campaspe*'s scenes arises not from their placement in a plot but rather from their function as sections of the image of Alexander which the play is putting together. The scenes show the different characteristics (or characteristic modes of behavior) of Alexander as the good king: his benevolence toward the weak, his regard for the learned, and so on. Much of the play builds less by a process of sequential development, in which each new scene depends on previous ones for its full significance, than by additive composition, in which each scene is discrete, making its separate contribution to the total construction.

To the extent that *Campaspe* is more Humanistic picture than plot, it resembles the many images of model human figures in Renaissance literature such as Desiderius Erasmus' Christian knight in the *Enchiridion militis christiani* (1503), Baldassare Castiglione's *The Courtier* (1528), and Sir Thomas Elyot's *The Boke Named the Governour* (1531). Like much Humanistic writing, *Campaspe* is concerned with the function of the prince but also, as an important corollary, with the prince's relationship to his counselors (in Renaissance terms, to Humanistically educated subjects). *Campaspe*'s picture of Alexander is complemented by its picture of the Cynic Diogenes, an embodiment of an extreme claim for the virtuous counselor's status in the polity. One of Alexander's most exemplary decisions is his drafting of Diogenes for attachment to the court: Alexander wants to listen to a voice that speaks only for virtue, without regard for power.

In addition to these model figures, the Humanistic aspect of *Campaspe* involves sketches of moral tales. The prodigal-son narrative structure that critics have recognized in *Euphues, the Anatomy of Wit* also seems related to the rather minimal sustained sequence of actions in which Alexander does become directly involved: his experience of love for Campaspe, the realization that she loves the painter Apelles, and Alexander's final renunciation of her. Campaspe, humbly born, is clearly inappropriate as a match for Alexander; Hephastion moralizes upon Alexander's love for her as a tempting detour from the course of honor.

Campaspe's resemblance to the Euphues books involves factors besides Humanism. Much of the play is overlaid by a euphuistic style; the style sometimes works positively to give dialogue epigrammatic pointedness. The love of Apelles and Campaspe is a very different matter from that of Alexander, and one that can be related not to the Humanistic but to the novella pattern lying behind *Euphues, the Anatomy of Wit*. Apelles and Campaspe's scenes, though other kinds of scenes are interspersed between them, themselves follow a perfectly regular rhythm, in which scenes of dialogue alternate with soliloquies by the two lovers; dialogue and soliloquy were the major frameworks in which emotion could be explored in the Euphues books and the narrative tradition anterior to them. The love portrayed in the scenes is not a distraction from honor or serious matters; rather, it is personal feeling which seems to be central to the psychic lives of the two people involved, and it grows. Unlike the Humanistic picture scenes with their additive interrelation, the scenes of Apelles and Campaspe dramatize an intelligible development, through which the characters move continuously from the first sense of love toward more ample realization and expression of it.

As in the Euphues books, Humanism and this other narrative component coexist uneasily in *Campaspe*. The motif of Apelles and Campaspe's kind of love, virtually absent from the play's first two acts, weighs heavily in the last three, receiving about eight of their thirteen scenes. The large influx of romantic feeling produces an unbalancing shift in the whole mood of the play.

Along with the pictures of Alexander and Diogenes and the love story of Apelles and Campaspe, there is one further set of scenes in the play, which is of a kind different from anything in the Euphues books and which became increasingly important in Lyly's playwriting as it progressed. In *Campaspe*, there are only two or three scenes of high-spirited page comedy, in which servants of the play's major figures meet on some pretext, exchange jokes, mock their masters, and express unflagging appetites for food and drink. Such scenes sometimes culminate in the singing of drinking songs. It seems reasonable to relate this kind of material to two circumstances of the production of Lyly's plays. As court entertainment for holidays such as Christmas and Twelfth Night, Lyly's plays belonged to the Saturnalian context that C. L. Barber described in *Shakespeare's Festive Comedy* (1959), in which rule for the moment was to be made light of and appetite gratified even to excess. As plays performed by choirboys, Lyly's works gained dimensions when their comedy projected standard boys' appetites and smart-aleckism, and when they exploited the boys' musical talents. Among the other constituents of *Campaspe*, the festive, disrespectful page comedy attaches itself most strongly to the characterization of Diogenes, the disrespectful satirist, but the pages completely lack Diogenes' will to make moral judgments; their mockery is for the sake of having a good time. In fact, the page comedy seems extraneous both to the play's nobler Humanistic themes and, certainly, to Apelles and Campaspe's love.

Campaspe is a rich combination, but the continued lack of integration of the work's elements makes it a noticeably less impressive play than Lyly's more mature and mythic works. The play's proportion of success is connected with the appeal or impact of certain moments—bits of incisive dialogue such as that between Parmenio and Timoclea in the play's first scene, which, even more than the language of Diogenes, has the excitement of truth spoken to force; the last line, in which Alexander charmingly warns Hephestion that when he has no more worlds to conquer, then he may yet fall in love.

Sapho and Phao involved a new source for Lyly, Ovid, whose potential impact, however, was not fully realized until *Galathea*. Lyly was remarkably successful in adapting his source material to a generally Humanistic pattern. The Sappho of Ovid's *Heroides* (before A.D. 8), whose whole character is that of a passionate lover, becomes in Lyly's play the queen of Syracuse, controlling a court and herself conditioned by social and political duties and norms. Phao becomes a figure like Campaspe, an inferior love; the play ultimately dramatizes Sapho's taking control of erotic power (personified as Venus and Cupid), which had sought to rule her. The parallel between Queen Elizabeth's chastity and Sapho's is obvious; the triumphant establishment of the latter becomes clear praise of the former.

Roman mythography became a potent influence in Lyly's work in *Galathea*. Ovid was Lyly's source for this symbolic drama in which actions clearly have significance as they refer to an underlying dynamic pattern. Ovid's *Metamorphoses* (c. A.D. 8) comprise many incidents, through each and all of which the reader looks toward the underlying universal process of metamorphosis itself, the reality of change. Both *Galathea* and Lyly's later play, *Love's Metamorphosis*, consist of plots that are discontinuous—inconsequential if taken strictly on their own terms—but that imply a continuous line of allegorical meaning. This kind of writing clearly differs in several ways from the Humanistic modes that had more or less dominated Lyly's first two plays. It is truly dynamic, never static or additive as *Campaspe* was, even though the dynamic continuity does not appear on the literal plot level. It embodies truths (or visions) instead of encouraging conduct; thus, it presents human life in a psychological rather than a hortatory manner, concerning itself with growth and health rather than with virtue and vice. Lyly's Ovidian drama is not set in an arena of social or political action, a historical or pseudohistorical court or city. The plots of *Galathea* and *Love's Metamorphosis* occur in the pastoral world, which traditionally has had symbolic value. Setting and symbolic purpose also differentiate this drama from the more realistic novella.

Love appears in *Galathea* not as a temptation countervailed by honor, but as a psychic presence experienced and accepted differently at different stages in a process of human growth. In other words, the play is a vision of adolescence. It takes its name from its adolescent girl heroine and ultimately from the nymph in *Metamorphoses* 13 whose lover changes before her eyes. As the play opens, young virgins are exposed to rumors of an incomprehensible savage force bent on attacking them. The allegorical progression begins as the play moves into the next scene, in which a better-understood, less terrifying, clearly erotic power, Cupid, is incited to show his power over virgins who are more mature at least in understanding. Thereafter, as the play meanders engagingly back and forth between its two main plots, love is presented in guise after different guise, but changing fairly steadily in a determinate direction, appearing in embodiments that are less frightening: Cupid descends to the disguise of a shepherd, is captured, and exercises his nature in a disarmed (and less external) state, as love develops as an emotion Galathea and Phyllida feel within themselves.

As love becomes understood as more acceptable, it also becomes more accepted. Through the course of the play, Galathea, Phyllida, and Diana's nymphs all succumb and come to enjoy this new part of their beings. The process is happy in its result. Neptune, who has become a mediator, effects a resolution in which love's power is recognized, not repressed, but in which it can be incorporated into intact human personalities rather than destroying them. Galathea and Phyllida are ready for healthy, mature, emotional life. With lovely precision, the play leaves them just ready, just at the verge, still within a semi-sexual stage which Lyly (like Shakespeare) dramatizes as involvement with someone not fully identifiable as one's sexual complement. As in *Twelfth Night* and *As You Like It*, produced about five years later, girls disguise themselves as boys and are fallen in love with as such: Galathea and Phyllida fall in love with each other, each under the misapprehension that the other is a boy. One is left uncertain at the end of the play which of the two a generous Venus is about to metamorphose into a male, to make full sexual life for them possible.

The delighted, smooth comic feeling of the play's ending is a point around which Lyly manages to orient a remarkable number of elements. *Galathea* is typical of Lyly's work inasmuch as it is a hybrid of diverse constituents—Lyly's first fully successful work in that these elements are fully integrated and mutually responsive. There is a good deal of euphuism in the style, but now delight in its neat working-out of syntax and sound can be subsumed in delight at the economy of growth which the play symbolizes (instead of jarring against a Humanistic message). Like the euphuistic aspects, the festive servant boys' subplot can now work to expand and prepare the audience for the joy to which the main plots are leading. In mood, the comedy of Rafe, Robin, and Dick represents a distinctive modulation away from Lyly's norm for such scenes: Instead of Lyly's usually loud, rambunctious, prank-playing boys, *Galathea*'s boys are gulls, and the resulting humor is somewhat quieter and very much in keeping with the whole play's trend, which is to settle into a smile more than to explode in laughter. At the end of the play, Venus welcomes the boys into direct contact with the main action. They are to serve as entertainers, enhancing the joy of the forthcoming marriage—which is exactly the role they have been performing throughout the play.

Galathea is in some ways Lyly's most characteristic success; it involves tendencies that were important in many of his other works. Like Ovid's *Metamorphoses*, it achieves a smooth unity among a diversity of coequal factors. The play marks the beginning of a mature phase of not invariably but usually unified dramatic works.

Endymion dramatizes a Neoplatonic ascent through various levels of love and being to transcendent knowledge. Important details make the play's process congruent also with the general Christian concept of redemption.

The protagonist first appears caught in involvement with his immediate physical world, but also drawn by a reality beyond it. He loves Cynthia, with whom he is not yet in direct contact. The attraction seems bizarre and out of order, both to his friend Eumenides and to himself. Endymion's situation is complicated by his difficult and ambivalent relationship with Tellus. Low metaphysical status is represented here not only through the drama of Endymion's attitudes and problems, but also in the modes of description used: Cynthia at this point is, to all intents and purposes, the actual physical moon; Tellus is a very material, fecund earth goddess. Endymion's persistence on the earthly level appears in Tellus' power over him, which, however, has its limits. She cannot force Endymion's love back to herself, but she can hinder his rise. Through her agent Dipsas, she holds Endymion in sleep; he rests suspended, out of the worldly consciousness that has prevailed to this point in the play but unable to waken to the life which appears around his sleeping figure and which includes Cynthia as a directly present character.

As in *Galathea*, Lyly's allegorical line passes unbroken from one plot medium to another. As Endymion is sleeping, two surrogates, Corsites and Eumenides, act out the position that he occupies between two worlds. Both are deputized by Cynthia, Corsites to control Tellus, which he fails to do, thus continuing the dramatization of human weakness. Eumenides' mission is to find a way to help Endymion. He does so and reaches the height of purely human potential when, at some emotional cost, he puts aside the claims of human sexual love in favor of those of more purely spiritual friendship and of duty to Cynthia. The discovery he makes at this level is that further progress, in the form of the main protagonist's recovery from his trance, can come only through an act of condescension by Cynthia in the form of an act of love, a kiss. This is one of the points clearly suggestive of Christianity in the play, specifically of the Christian doctrine of human beings' need for God's loving gift of grace.

Cynthia's kiss arouses an Endymion who definitely has surpassed the passionate love in which he began. His altered language is noticeable, especially when one comes to this play from Lyly's earlier works. By the time *Endymion* was written, euphuism, certainly of the kind found in the early narratives, was receding as a factor in Lyly's writing. By the play's end, Endymion is speaking in relatively even, straightforward sentences, reflecting his arrival at a definitely rational frame of mind. No longer so committed to a set style, Lyly could make language flexibly project action.

Endymion's appearances as an old man toward his play's end have a clear philosophical association. He resembles the old Platonic lover described by Pietro Bembo in Castiglione's *The Courtier*. Like the old lover, Endymion is no longer interested in physical love; instead, he is happy with the position he has achieved as a purified attendant in Cynthia's immediate presence. Endymion's final metamorphosis, back into a young man (he has slept and aged for forty years), may imply a Christian step beyond a philosophical one, a putting off of the old man and entry into a new life of redemption. Cynthia herself emerges as a benevolent supernatural figure near the play's close.

As a final image of hierarchy, Cynthia in the last scene brings love to fulfillment for several couples: herself and Endymion on down through pairs representing less exalted levels. The lowest in the line is the impersonal mating instinct of Sir Tophas, who earlier had wanted Dipsas, but— now that she is unavailable—reaches for her servant Bagoa. The play's low comedy is one of its liveliest elements. Sir Tophas is a new feature in such writing by Lyly—a sustained, gradually developed, low-comic character. His place in the play is somewhat indeterminate until he forces himself on the other characters' attention in the last scene, as the lowest level from which the hierarchical structure they have elaborated rises.

Endymion is Lyly's most ambitious play. With its reach toward philosophy and religion, it embodies the continued expansiveness of Lyly's mind as well as the extent of his mature control.

Much of *Midas* is topical, political, and Humanistic. It is quite clear in the play, and accepted in the critical tradition, that discussion of an unsuccessful war by Midas' Phrygia against the island of Lesbos allegorically refers to Philip of Spain's attack on England with his Armada. Like its predecessors from *Sapho and Phao* on, *Midas* has its source in Ovid. The lighthearted Ovidian fables which provide *Midas'* plot coexist rather uneasily with much of the dialogue's serious moral tone. The Humanistic lessons delivered by Midas' counselors are not responsive to the developing Ovidian plot. They stand apart as set pieces and tend simply to be repeated in one debate scene after another, instead of changing in any way corresponding to plot changes. In several respects, *Midas* is a rather unsatisfying reversion to Lyly's early dramatic pattern.

Neither hortatory nor Ovidian, *Mother Bombie* is instead a very pure experiment in neoclassic secular comedy. It is witty New Comedy of clever servants helping young people to overcome obstacles raised by their selfish elders; its ultimate ancestor is the Roman comedy of Terence. Within Lyly's work, there is a connection not to the kinds of dramatic writing that dominate his other plays as wholes, but instead to the usually secondary element of page comedy. In tone and action, the play is fairly firmly and neatly unified, although it seems thinner in meaning and less inventive than Lyly's plays based on mythography.

Love's Metamorphosis is the most interesting of Lyly's later works, and probably his most underrated play. It is close to *Galathea* in several ways. As its title suggests, the whole play is Ovidian in feeling, although the main plots are actually not drawn from Ovid or from any other source. The play is a sequential allegory: It presents not only physical metamorphoses performed by the god Cupid but also, and much more important, like *Galathea*, changing visions of love (and of human relationships in general). The allegory is organized somewhat differently from that of *Galathea*. A distinct major vision is localized in each of the play's plots. The plot which gets first exposure, that of three amorous foresters' love for three nymphs, could be interpreted as a sane psychological critique of traditions of courtly love and Petrarchianism. The three lovers are met with refusals to love from the ladies to whom they are drawn. The ladies' refusals, instead of being idealized, are analyzed as various forms of sexual egotism. The ladies are punished by being metamorphosed into items of subhuman nature—a stone, a flower, a bird—symbolic of their different kinds of detachment from human involvement. Punishment in itself is not a solacing ending. The audience is left with a picture of one-sided adoration as a type of failed relationship.

On the other hand, instead of being an opposing figure who withdraws into himself and refuses contact (as the ladies themselves do to the foresters), Erisichthon emerges to attack the nymphs' own space, their sacred grove, and to prevent them from carrying out the activities proper to their natures. Relationships here are not exclusively erotic, but rather more well-rounded. The divinity to whom the maidens can appeal is Ceres, who suggests a broader (but less exalted, literally more down-to-earth) image of human experience than does the foresters' Cupid. Erisichthon is punished with famine, although again punishment is not resolution; he is brought before the audience later in the play, repentant of his actions but caught in punishment, unable to escape his actions' consequences.

The play's movement toward resolution begins when a third, clearly different vision of human relationships comes about, one that involves mutuality. Its protagonist, Protea, is constantly helping others and being helped by them. The pattern began in the character's past, when she yielded her virginity to Neptune and received his promise of future help in return. Neptune keeps faith, and Protea is saved through supernatural power in the various situations in which she finds herself during the play's course. At the same time, she is saving her father and her lover. She first avoids a relationship of pure (and not specifically erotic) dominance when she escapes from enslavement by a merchant. Then she destroys the alluring power of the selfish, isolated Siren over her lover Petulius. Thus, she has managed to eliminate from her life both of the dilemmas that the play's first two plots embody. Mutuality is allied to flexibility. Protea's name indicates her ability to change, and she defeats the bad versions of relationship through magical metamorphoses of her person. At the play's end, the vision associated with Protea expands over the play and redeems the other characters from their symbolic entrapment.

Although similar to *Galathea* as highly sophisticated psychological allegory, *Love's Metamorphosis* differs in tone. The play certainly remains a comedy, but it is a darker one than *Galathea* and allows at least as much awareness of difficulties and problems as any of Lyly's other works. The three ladies continue to resist love even in the play's last scene, long after (in the progress of the allegory) the benign concept of mutual, flexible interaction has become available. There is the suggestion of an egotism so profound that it cannot be brought into relationship to the external world except through coercion. *Love's Metamorphosis* does not include the page comedy which lightens up *Galathea* and tonally predicts a happy ending; one reaches the happy ending of *Love's Metamorphosis* with some feeling of relief, not through a play full of light or bland emotional ease. *Love's Metamorphosis* is also not very euphuistic. Instead of continuously providing symmetry, the play's language often conspicuously evades it. The description of the famine that will attack Erisichthon has some of the ruggedness and irregularity of seventeenth century "anti-Ciceronian" prose. The play in general experiments with asymmetry as a medium for its emotional, psychological conceptions.

The characterization of Protea involves a successful modulation for Lyly in the direction of genuine pathos. *Love's Metamorphosis* represents human beings' achievement of love against odds within themselves that must be taken seriously. Along with *Galathea* and *Endymion*, this is one of the works by which Lyly ought to be remembered.

A sense of the Elizabethan literary environment suggests one appropriate overall comment on Lyly's work. The 1580's, the decade of Lyly's principal achievements on the stage, were years of extraordinary literary ferment. Sir Philip Sidney and Edmund Spenser were decisively altering values in poetry. Almost doctrinaire neoclassic drama lingering from the 1560's gave way not only to Lyly but also to the violent tragedy of Thomas Kyd and Christopher Marlowe. Lyly's drama corresponds to its transitional, eclectic times: His work made use of change as a chance for variety, instead of suffering from it as disorienting or disintegrating. Juxtapositions of Lyly to Shakespeare are likely to be odious, but Lyly may not be harmed by the recognition that, like Shakespeare, he profited from his historical moment. Lyly, like Shakespeare, grew toward a capacity to merge diverse elements in his plays and to hold together in suspension tints of different kinds of awareness and experience—Humanistic and Neoplatonic, lightly comic and seriously problematic. In Lyly's earlier works, the multiplicity of available influences helps create disunified writing; later, it yields writing that is rich and experimental.

Linking this literary-historical pattern mechanically with the content of the work would be a mistake, in Lyly's case as much as in Shakespeare's. Still, Lyly's greatest works celebrate change and greet it as comic growth through which people become more fully human. *Galathea*, *Endymion*, and *Love's Metamorphosis* especially should still be enjoyed for their adult gentleness, consciousness, and openness.

Other major works

FICTION: *Euphues, the Anatomy of Wit*, 1578; *Euphues and His England*, 1580.

NONFICTION: *Pap with an Hatchet*, 1589.

MISCELLANEOUS: *The Complete Works of John Lyly*, 1902, 1967 (3 volumes; R. Warwick Bond, editor).

Bibliography

Hueppert, Joseph W. *John Lyly*. Boston: Twayne, 1975. This general review of Lyly's career contains a brief discussion of euphuism and the prose period preceding dramatic involvement. The plays are analyzed as belonging to Lyly's early, middle, or late periods of development, and the scholarship is organized into negative and positive sections. Concludes with comments on Lyly's critical reputation and influence.

Hunter, G. K. *John Lyly: The Humanist as Courtier*. Cambridge, Mass.: Harvard University Press, 1962. Lyly is accepted as a product of his time, a subject discussed in depth for its humanistic tendencies. Hunter analyzes Lyly's works in an effort to refute the assertion that Lyly has little aesthetic merit, only historical influence (as argued in John Dover Wilson's book below). He also discusses Lyly in connection with William Shakespeare. Complemented by an appendix on Lyly's songs.

_____. *Lyly and Peele.* London: Longmans, 1968. Considers the special nature of the plays performed in the small and intimate theaters, such as Blackfriars, where plays were acted by children. A brief study, largely on Lyly, analyzing five of his plays.

Saccio, Peter. *The Court Comedies of John Lyly: A Study in Allegorical Dramaturgy.* Princeton, N.J.: Princeton University Press, 1969. Contains an informative opening section on the staging requirements for plays presented at court. Saccio analyzes *Campaspe* and *Galathea* in great length in individual chapters and covers *Love's Metamorphosis*, *Sapho and Phao*, and *Endymion, the Man in the Moon* in briefer discussions. Includes an investigation of allegory and anagoge.

Weld, John. *Meaning in Comedy: Studies in Elizabethan Romantic Comedy.* Albany: State University of New York Press, 1975. Weld states that the political and moral satire in *Midas* resulted from government policies toward Spain. Sees the attitudes toward love as the keys to establishing meaning in other plays, for love takes on the role of the Vice in earlier drama, being the disruptive force upsetting kings and countries. Notes but no bibliography.

Wilson, John Dover. *John Lyly.* 1907. Reprint. New York: Haskell House, 1970. This older work by a notable scholar is intentionally limited to historical rather than aesthetic criticism of Lyly. Wilson traces Lyly's influence on English prose style, on the development of the novel of manners, and on English comedy. Considers Lyly's influence and his "dynamical value" to be great.

John F. McDiarmid
(Updated by *Howard L. Ford*)

CARSON McCULLERS

Born: Columbus, Georgia; February 19, 1917
Died: Nyack, New York; September 29, 1967

Principal drama
The Member of the Wedding, pr. 1950, pb. 1951 (adaptation of her novel); *The Square Root of Wonderful*, pr. 1957, pb. 1958.

Other literary forms
Carson McCullers will be remembered primarily as a writer of fiction who experimented, with varying degrees of success, in the genres of drama, poetry, and the essay. She was one of the foremost of the remarkable generation of Southern women writers that included, in addition to McCullers herself, Flannery O'Connor, Eudora Welty, and Katherine Anne Porter. With her fellow women writers, and with such Southern male writers as William Faulkner, Truman Capote, and Tennessee Williams, McCullers shares an uncanny talent for capturing the grotesque. Her fictional world is peopled with the freaks of society: the physically handicapped, the emotionally disturbed, the alienated, the disenfranchised. This preoccupation with the bizarre earned for her a major place in the literary tradition known as the "Southern Gothic," a phrase used to describe the writers mentioned above and others who use Gothic techniques and sensibilities in describing the South of the twentieth century.

Few have created a fictional South as successfully as has McCullers in her best fiction. Hers is a small-town South of mills and factories, of barren main streets lined with sad little shops and cafés, of intolerable summer heat and oppressive boredom. In her first and perhaps best novel, *The Heart Is a Lonely Hunter* (1940), she portrays a small Southern town from the points of view of five of its residents: Mick Kelly, the confused adolescent heroine; Doctor Copeland, an embittered black physician whose youthful idealism has been destroyed; Jake Blount, an alcoholic drifter with Marxist leanings; Biff Brannon, the sexually disturbed owner of the café, where much of the novel's action takes place; and John Singer, the deaf-mute whose kindness, patience, and humanity to the other characters provide the moral center of the novel.

The themes of *The Heart Is a Lonely Hunter* are ones that McCullers never completely abandoned in her subsequent fiction and drama: the loneliness and isolation inherent in the human condition; the impossibility of complete reciprocity in a love relationship; the social injustice of a racially segregated South; adolescence as a time of horrifying emotional and sexual confusion. In *Reflections in a Golden Eye* (1941), she explored sexual tension and jealousy among the denizens of a Southern army post. *The Mem-*

ber of the Wedding (1946), the novel which she later adapted into the successful play of the same title, treats the delicate symbiotic relationship between a lonely adolescent girl, her seven-year-old cousin, and a black domestic. *The Ballad of the Sad Café*, first published in *Harper's Bazaar* in 1943 and later in a collection of McCullers' short works, is justifiably called one of the finest pieces of short fiction in American literature. It deals with another bizarre triangle, this one involving a masculine, sexually frigid, small-town heiress; her cousin, a hunchback dwarf; and her former husband, a worthless ex-convict with an old score to settle.

The four works of fiction mentioned above guarantee McCullers a permanent place among American writers of the World War II and postwar era. She also published more than a dozen short stories, most of which are not specifically set in the South. The best of them—"Wunderkind" (1936) and "A Tree. A Rock. A Cloud." (1942), for example—are proficiently executed exercises that demonstrate the sure control and balance so crucial to McCullers' longer fiction.

McCullers also wrote critical essays that betray a deep emotional and technical understanding of imaginative literature. Her small body of poetry, heavily influenced by the seventeenth century Metaphysicals, is consistently interesting. After McCullers' death, her sister, Margarita G. Smith, collected her previously uncollected short fiction, her literary criticism, and her poetry and essays in *The Mortgaged Heart* (1971).

Achievements

McCullers' reputation as a playwright rests solely upon the phenomenal success of one play, *The Member of the Wedding*, which she based on her novel of the same title. Her only other play, *The Square Root of Wonderful*, was a critical and popular failure and a professional disappointment from which McCullers never quite recovered. The very critics and theatergoers who hailed McCullers as a brilliant innovator in 1950 turned their backs on her in 1958. Flawed and uneven as her theatrical career was, however, McCullers deserves a special place among modern American playwrights, not only for what she achieved but also for what she attempted. With her friend Tennessee Williams, she was one of the first American playwrights to parlay a fragile, moody, nearly static vision of human frailty into solid commercial theater.

No one was more surprised by the success of *The Member of the Wedding* than McCullers herself. She had seen but a handful of plays in her life when Williams, with whom she was spending the summer of 1946 on Nantucket, suggested that she turn her novel into a play. Excited by the idea of writing in a new and unfamiliar genre and intrigued by Williams' sense that the novel had strong dramatic possibilities, McCullers spent that June calmly and steadily composing a draft of the play. Across the dining room table from her sat Williams, who was working on *Summer and Smoke*—it was the only time either of them was able to work with anyone else in the room. Despite Williams' willingness to help, McCullers steadfastly rejected her friend's advice, following instead her own creative instincts.

Though all odds were against it, the play was an immediate success when it opened on Broadway in January, 1950. Audiences gave the cast standing ovations, and the critics almost unanimously praised the work's grace, beauty, and timing. In the spring, *The Member of the Wedding* won two Donaldson Awards—as the best play of the season and as the best first Broadway play by an author—and the New York Drama Critics Circle Award for Best Play. McCullers was named Best Playwright of the Year and given a gold medal by the Theatre Club. *The Member of the Wedding* ran for 501 performances and grossed more than one million dollars on Broadway before enjoying a successful national tour.

This great acclaim, remarkable enough for a more conventional drama, is even more remarkable when one considers that *The Member of the Wedding* is a "mood play," dependent upon emotion and feeling rather than upon a standard plot. All three acts take place on one deliberately confining set, and much of the play's significant action happens offstage, "between acts," as it were. Indeed, even while praising the play, reviewers questioned whether it was a genuine drama at all. Like Williams' *The Glass Menagerie* (pr. 1944) and Arthur Miller's *Death of a Salesman* (pr. 1949)— significantly, the only two plays Carson McCullers had seen produced on Broadway prior to writing her hit—*The Member of the Wedding* is a play that subordinates plot to characterization, action to the almost poetic accretion of psychic detail. That audiences would even sit through, let alone cheer, such a slow-moving piece of drama was a revelation to the theater world of 1950.

The success of *The Member of the Wedding* solved McCullers' chronic financial problems and earned for her a reputation as a gifted and innovative dramatist, but seven years of ill health and personal tragedy ensued before her next play, *The Square Root of Wonderful*, opened on Broadway in October, 1957. Plagued from the outset by personnel changes and by McCullers' incompetence at the kind of last-minute rewriting required by the theater, the play failed almost immediately. Neither McCullers nor director Jose Quintero could do anything to save it, and it closed after only forty-five performances. The disaster of *The Square Root of Wonderful* left McCullers severely depressed, so anxious had she been to repeat the triumph of *The Member of the Wedding*. Various physical ailments by then made it difficult for her to write at all, and she never again attempted writing for the theater.

Though McCullers' reputation as a playwright will never approach her reputation as a writer of fiction, it is her uniqueness in both genres that accounts for both her successes and her failures. Her first play succeeded because it defied conventions of plot and action; her second play failed in part because it too often mixed the modes of tragedy, comedy, and romance. It is no accident that three of her novels have been made into successful films, nor is it accidental that no less a playwright than Edward Albee adapted her novella *The Ballad of the Sad Café* for the stage. Carson McCullers' dramatic sense was in every way original, and both her hit play and her failure demand acceptance on their own terms, quite apart from the whims of current theatrical convention and popular tastes.

Biography

Carson McCullers' life was one beset by intolerable illnesses and complex personal relationships. The last twenty years of her life were spent in the shadow of constant physical pain, but, like her fellow Southerner Flannery O'Connor, she continued working in spite of her handicaps, seldom complaining. She was married twice to the same man, an emotional cripple who drained her financially and psychically and who ultimately killed himself. That she left behind her a magnificent body of work and any number of devoted friends when she died at the tragically young age of fifty is a testament to the courage with which overwhelming obstacles can be overcome.

McCullers knew at first hand the small-town South that figures so prominently in her best writing. As the eldest of the three children of Lamar and Marguerite (Waters) Smith, Lula Carson Smith spent a normal middle-class childhood in the racially segregated mill town of Columbus, Georgia. Her father, like Mr. Kelly in *The Heart Is a Lonely Hunter* and Mr. Addams in *The Member of the Wedding*, was a jeweler who spent much of his time at work. Her mother, a lively, cultured woman and a strong influence throughout McCullers' life, encouraged her daughter's intellectual and artistic pursuits. By the age of fourteen, Carson Smith had dropped the Lula from her name and had announced her intention to become a concert pianist. She was by then practicing the piano several hours a day and taking lessons from Mary Tucker, the wife of an army colonel stationed at nearby Fort Benning. Her complex relationship with the Tucker family, at once giving her a sense of belonging and of estrangement, was later to provide material for the triangle theme of *The Member of the Wedding*. Like her heroine Frankie Addams, McCullers was fond of writing plays, casting them with family and friends, and staging them in her living room.

By the time she was graduated from high school, McCullers had already privately decided to become a writer rather than a musician. Inspired by the Russian realists and by the plays of Eugene O'Neill, McCullers had already tried her hand at both drama and fiction. The seventeen-year-old McCullers set out for New York City in September, 1934, with vague plans both to study music at the Juilliard School of Music and to study creative writing at Columbia University. By February, 1935, she had enrolled at Columbia, and the following September she enrolled in Sylvia Chatfield Bates's writing class at New York University.

During the summer of 1935, while she was vacationing in Georgia, a mutual friend introduced her to James Reeves McCullers, an army corporal stationed at Fort Benning. Reeves McCullers, like Carson, was interested in a career in letters. That he had neither the motivation nor the talent that enabled Carson to become a successful author was to be the source of much friction between them and a contributing factor to Reeves's eventual mental collapse. In 1936, Reeves left the army to join Carson in New York, and in September of 1937, they were married in the Smith home in Columbus.

By this time, McCullers had begun to undergo the cycles of illness and creativity that would characterize the rest of her life. Fatigued by the hectic pace of New York, she was forced to return to Georgia from time to time for peace and quiet, but her writing career had also taken off. Whit Burnett, with whom she had worked at Columbia, had published her story "Wunderkind" in the December, 1936, issue of his magazine *Story*, and she had begun to outline the plot of what would become her first novel, *The Heart Is a Lonely Hunter*. In the spring of 1939, while she was living with Reeves in Fayetteville, North Carolina, "The Mute" (as the novel was then called) was accepted by Houghton Mifflin. By autumn, she had completed a second manuscript, "Army Post" (later published as *Reflections in a Golden Eye*).

McCullers had long before vowed that when she would become a famous author, she would make New York her home. Feeling stifled in the South, their marriage in trouble, the McCullerses moved to New York only a few days after the publication of *The Heart Is a Lonely Hunter*, in June, 1940. The move, however, did nothing to improve their relationship. Carson, a sudden celebrity, was being courted by the literary world and making distinguished friends, among them W. H. Auden; that summer, as recipient of a fellowship to the Bread Loaf Writers Conference in Middlebury, Vermont, she came to know Wallace Stegner, Louis Untermeyer, and Eudora Welty. It was not only Carson's increasing fame and Reeves's continued obscurity that placed stress on their relationship. Both were sexually naïve at the time of their marriage, and both were given to infatuations with members of their own sex. Though most of their homosexual relationships remained unconsummated, Carson's crush on the brilliant young Swiss emigrant Annemarie Clarac-Schwarzenbach was difficult for Reeves to tolerate. In September, 1940, Carson and Reeves separated. They were later divorced, only to remarry in 1945 when Reeves returned from action in World War II. For the rest of Reeves's life, they were to be alternately separated and reconciled. Their long and stormy relationship was ended only by Reeves's suicide in France in 1953.

When she separated from Reeves in the autumn of 1940, Carson accepted an invitation from her friend George Davis to move into a restored brownstone located in Brooklyn Heights. Upon establishing residence at 7 Middagh Street, she found herself in the midst of an unusual experiment in group housing; it later came to be known as February House. Besides her and Davis, the inhabitants included W. H. Auden, the striptease artist Gypsy Rose Lee, and, later, the composer Benjamin Britten and the writer Richard Wright and his family. McCullers made her home in this strange household intermittently for the next five years. When not traveling abroad, resting in Georgia, or spending time at Yaddo, the artists' colony in upstate New York, she played hostess in Brooklyn Heights to a distinguished group of celebrities from the literary and entertainment worlds, including Janet Flanner, Christopher Isherwood, Salvador Dalí, and Aaron Copland.

While in Georgia in February, 1941, McCullers suffered a stroke that left her partially blind and unable to walk for weeks. She would be victimized by such attacks for the rest of her life, and even after the first one, she never quite regained the kind of creative fervor of which she had once been capable. She was not to finish her next novel, *The Member of the Wedding*, until 1946, six years after she first started drafting it. Her final novel, *Clock Without Hands*, took her ten years to complete, not appearing until 1961. After 1947, as a result of the second severe stroke in a year, her left side was permanently paralyzed, and even the physical act of sitting at a typewriter was a challenge for her.

McCullers' Broadway career of the 1950's was, as has been noted, a source both of exhilaration and of disappointment for her. Nevertheless, her uneven career as a playwright brought her financial security, greater exposure than she had ever had before, and the fame she had craved since childhood. By the end of her life, she was an international literary celebrity, able to count among her friends the English poet Edith Sitwell and the Danish-born writer Isak Dinesen.

In 1958, severely depressed by Reeves's suicide in 1953, her mother's death in 1955, and the failure of her second play, McCullers sought professional psychiatric help from Dr. Mary Mercer, a therapist who was to care for McCullers until the author's death. Through the 1960's, McCullers was progressively less able and willing to leave the Nyack, New York, house that she had bought in 1951. She died there on September 29, 1967, of a cerebral hemorrhage.

Analysis

Like the novel from which it was adapted, *The Member of the Wedding*,

Carson McCullers' first play, is a masterpiece of timing, mood, and character delineation. Insofar as there is a plot, it can be summarized as follows: Somewhere in the South, twelve-year-old Frankie Addams, a rebellious loner and a tomboy, secretly longs to belong to a group. Rejected by the girls at school, having recently lost her best friend, Frankie has no one to talk to except Berenice Sadie Brown, the black woman who cooks for Frankie and her father, and a seven-year-old cousin, John Henry. When she discovers that her brother, Jarvis, is going to be married, Frankie decides to join him and his bride on their honeymoon and make her home with them in nearby Winter Hill, thus becoming once and for all a member—a member of the wedding. Though Berenice tries to make her come to her senses, Frankie persists in her plan and makes a scene during the ceremony, begging the couple to take her with them. When they refuse, an agonized Frankie vows to run away from home. Sticking her father's pistol into the suitcase that she has already packed for the honeymoon, Frankie does leave, but it is later disclosed that she has spent the night in the alley behind her father's store. Chastened and somewhat resigned, she returns home, admitting that she had thought of committing suicide but then had changed her mind.

By the end of the play, which takes place several months after the wedding, life has changed for all three main characters. John Henry has died of meningitis; Berenice has given notice to Mr. Addams; and Frankie, having largely outgrown the adolescent identity crisis of the previous summer, has acquired a best friend and a beau, both of whom she had earlier hated. While Frankie is undoubtedly much happier than she was at the beginning of the play, she has become a pretentious teenager, bereft of the poetry and passion of childhood. Berenice has lost not only John Henry but also her foster brother, Honey, who has hanged himself in jail. As the curtain falls on the third act, Berenice is alone onstage, quietly singing "His Eye Is on the Sparrow," the song that she had sung earlier to calm the tortured Frankie.

Most of the "action" of the play takes place offstage and is only later recounted through dialogue. The wedding and Frankie's tantrum occur in the living room of the Addams house, but the scene never moves from the kitchen: The audience is told about the wedding and about Frankie's disgrace by characters who move back and forth between the two rooms. Both Honey's and John Henry's deaths occur between scenes, as does Frankie's night in the alley. By thus deemphasizing dramatic action, McCullers is able to concentrate on the real issue of the play, the relationship among Frankie, Berenice, and John Henry. By confining the action to one set, the kitchen and backyard of the Addams residence, the author effectively forces the audience to empathize with Frankie's desperate boredom and sense of confinement (and, perhaps, with Berenice's position in society as a black domestic). For much of the play, the three main characters are seated at the kitchen table, and this lack of movement lends the work the sense of paralysis, of inertia, that McCullers learned from the plays of Anton Chekhov and applied to the South of her childhood.

Frankie Addams is one of the most memorable adolescents in literature, at the same time an embodiment of the frustrations and contradictions inherent in adolescence and a strongly individual character. She yearns to belong to a group even as she shouts obscenities and threats to the members of the neighborhood girls' club. She is both masculine and feminine, a tomboy with a boy's haircut and dirty elbows who chooses a painfully vampish gown for her brother's wedding. McCullers skillfully exploits alternately comic and tragic aspects of Frankie's character. The audience must laugh at her histrionic declarations ("I am sick unto death!") but must also experience a strong identification with her sense of vulnerability and isolation ("I feel just exactly like somebody has peeled all the skin off me"). Caught between childhood and womanhood, she is curious about both sexual and spiritual love. She claims to have been asked for a date by a soldier, only to wonder aloud "what you do on dates," and she is still capable of climbing into Berenice's lap to hear a lullaby. Frankie's body is fast maturing, but her emotions are slow in catching up.

Berenice Sadie Brown serves in the play as Frankie's main female role model (Frankie's own mother has died in childbirth), an embodiment of fully realized adult sexuality. As complex a character as Frankie, Berenice is much more than a servant: She is confessor, nurse, and storyteller. At forty-five, Berenice has been married four times but truly loved only her first husband—the remaining three she married in vain attempts to regain the bliss she enjoyed with Ludie Maxwell Freeman. Her search for love closely parallels Frankie's own, and despite their often antagonistic relationship, they share moments of spiritual harmony, as when they discuss the nature of love, a "thing known and not spoken."

Berenice also represents the position of the black in a segregated South; indeed, the issue of racism is very much present in *The Member of the Wedding* (as it is in *The Heart Is a Lonely Hunter* and *Clock Without Hands*), a fact that has often been overlooked by critics of both the novel and the play. Though she is the most influential adult in the world of the two white children, she is treated as a servant by the white adults. Berenice must deal not only with Frankie's growing pains but also with problems ultimately more grave: the funeral of an old black vegetable vendor and the arrest, imprisonment, and suicide of her foster brother, Honey. Both Berenice and T. T. Williams, her beau, behave noticeably differently around white adults, while Honey, in a sense representative of a new generation of Southern blacks, refuses even to call Mr. Addams "sir." He is eventually jailed for knifing a white bartender who will not serve him.

Honey's flight in the third act coincides with Frankie's own. Like Frankie, Honey is rebellious and frustrated, but unlike her, he is unable to find a place for himself in a hostile society. Death for Honey is preferable to confinement in the "nigger hole" or more "bowing and scraping" to white people.

If Honey's death in the third act symbolizes the end of Frankie the rebel, the death of John Henry represents the end of Frankie's childhood. Throughout the play, John Henry acts as a sort of idiot savant, uttering lines of great insight and demanding the plain truth from a hypocritical adult world. He asks Berenice why Mr. Addams has called Honey a nigger, and seems, ironically, incapable of understanding the nature of death. He is a link between Frankie and her childhood, a constant reminder of how recently she played with dolls (he gratefully accepts the doll that Jarvis has given Frankie as a gift after she rejects it). Frankie wants at once to be John Henry's playmate and to outgrow him. Though the transformed Frankie reacts coldly to John Henry's death, Berenice is devastated by it. She truly loved her "little boy," and she blames herself for having ignored his complaints of headaches in the first stages of his disease. John Henry dies a painful death, a victim who has done nothing to deserve his cruel fate.

The Member of the Wedding is a play about growing up, but it is also about the sacrifices that must be made before one can enter the adult world. Frankie is composed and even confident at the end of the play, but she has lost whatever sympathy she had for Berenice. Berenice is severely depressed by two deaths whose logic defies her. John Henry and Honey are dead, and the newlyweds are stationed in occupied Germany. When Berenice is left alone onstage at the end of the third act, holding John Henry's doll and singing a song whose truth the play has seriously questioned, the audience is forced to wonder with her whether the adult world of compromise and responsibility is worth entering.

McCullers stated in the author's preface to the published version of *The Square Root of Wonderful* that the lives and deaths of her mother and her husband in part compelled her to write the play. Marguerite Smith's grace, charm, and love of life emerge in the character of Mollie Lovejoy, while Phillip Lovejoy embodies all the tragic contradictions that led Reeves McCullers to alcoholism and suicide. Like so much of McCullers' work, the play concerns a love triangle: Mollie Lovejoy, who lives on an apple farm in suburban New York with her twelve-year-old son, Paris, has twice been married to Phillip Lovejoy, an alcoholic writer now confined to a sanatorium. As the play opens, Mollie has only recently met John Tucker, a no-nonsense architect who is determined to wed her. Complications arise when Phillip Lovejoy unexpectedly returns to the farm, intent on a reconciliation with Mollie. His mother and his spinster sister are also on the scene, having come to New York from the South to visit Mollie and Paris and to see Phillip's new play (ironically, a failure).

The relationship between Phillip and Mollie has been a stormy one. The sexual attraction between them remains strong, and they sleep together on the night of Phillip's return, much to the chagrin of John Tucker. Still, Mollie cannot forget the years of drunken abuse she suffered at Phillip's hands. Physical abuse she could tolerate, but she decided to divorce him finally when he humiliated her by telling her that she used clichés. Mollie is clearly in a dilemma. In one of the play's most successful scenes, she admits to Paris that she loves both John and Phillip.

Phillip's problems, however, are manifold and insoluble. Clearly, he wants a reunion with Mollie so that she will protect him, as she once did, from his own self-destructive tendencies. When he at length realizes that Mollie will not return to him and, perhaps more important, that he will never again be able to write, he commits suicide by driving his car into a pond. With Phillip's death, Mollie is free to leave the apple farm and move to New York, and there is every reason to believe that she will eventually marry John Tucker.

Despite its commercial and critical failure, the play is perhaps worthy of more attention than it has received. At its best, it is a meditation on the nature of love. Mollie Lovejoy has always conceived of love as a sort of magic spell that is divorced from logic and free will. Her love for Phillip has brought her as much humiliation as happiness. From John Tucker, she learns that love can also be a matter of choice among mature adults. He uses the language of mathematics in describing his view of love to Paris: For John, humiliation is the square root of sin, while love is the square root of wonderful. The minor characters also provide interesting commentaries on the nature of love. Sister Lovejoy, the spinster librarian, lives in a world of fictional lovers drawn from the pages of books. Mother Lovejoy, while often a comic character, is at base a loveless woman who has spent her life humiliating her daughter.

The play's weaknesses, however, are many. The sure sense of timing that characterizes *The Member of the Wedding* is largely absent from *The Square Root of Wonderful*. The shifts in mood are less subtle than in the earlier play, and tragedy often follows too closely on the heels of comedy. The superb early morning scene in which Phillip Lovejoy says goodbye to his son, for example, is too rapidly undercut by a comic scene between Mother and Sister Lovejoy as they discuss Phillip's death. This tragicomic mixture of modes that McCullers executes so well in *The Member of the Wedding* goes awry in *The Square Root of Wonderful*, in part because none of the characters—except, perhaps, Phillip Lovejoy—is carefully enough drawn to elicit an audience's sympathy.

McCullers' best work is set in the South, not in upstate New York farmhouses. Her best work is also fiercely individual, completely defiant of convention and popular tastes. *The Square Root of Wonderful* fails largely because its author, in her eagerness to produce a second Broadway triumph, allowed producers, directors, and script doctors to strip it of the brilliant idiosyncracies that make *The Member of the Wedding* an American classic.

Other major works

NOVELS: *The Heart Is a Lonely Hunter*, 1940; *Reflections in a Golden Eye*, 1941; *The Ballad of the Sad Café*, 1943 (novella); *The Member of the Wedding*, 1946; *Clock Without Hands*, 1961.

SHORT FICTION: *The Ballad of the Sad Café and Collected Short Stories*, 1952, 1955.

CHILDREN'S LITERATURE: *Sweet as a Pickle and Clean as a Pig*, 1964.

MISCELLANEOUS: *The Ballad of the Sad Café: The Novella and Stories of Carson McCullers*, 1951; *The Mortgaged Heart*, 1971 (short fiction, poetry, and essays; Margarita G. Smith, editor).

Bibliography

Carr, Virginia Spencer. *The Lonely Hunter.* Garden City, N.Y.: Doubleday, 1975. This detailed biography includes many interviews with McCullers' friends and with fellow writers. Carr uses letters that had not been published before. Complemented by genealogies, a detailed chronology, a bibliography, an index, and photographs.

Clark, Gerald. *Capote: A Biography.* New York: Simon & Schuster, 1988. Contains scattered, brief accounts of Capote's early friendship with, and later enmity toward, McCullers.

Cook, Richard M. *Carson McCullers.* New York: Frederick Ungar, 1975. Cook deals with McCullers' fiction thematically, an "almost naïve acceptance of the facts of life, . . . a refusal to judge." He ends the volume with a quotation from *The Ballad of the Sad Café*: "So who but God can be the final judge of this or any other love?" Contains a brief bibliography and an index.

Evans, Oliver. *The Ballad of Carson McCullers.* New York: Coward, McCann, 1966. In this critical biography, which includes McCullers' plays, Evans calls the playwright the "most controversial living writer" and analyzes the reasons. Evans believes that *The Ballad of the Sad Café* alone would have given McCullers a major reputation. He includes McCullers' outline of "The Mute," the original title of *The Heart Is a Lonely Hunter.* Brief index.

McDowell, Margaret M. *Carson McCullers.* Boston: Twayne, 1980. Part of Twayne's United States Authors series, this volume analyzes McCullers' fiction and drama. "Her exploitation of the grotesque for dramatic or comic effects or to emphasize the isolation of the human being" McDowell notes, "led her beyond realism to an experimentation with the gothic mode." Contains a brief chronology, a bibliography of works by and about McCullers, and an index.

Shapiro, Adrian M., Jackson R. Bryer, and Kathleen Field. *Carson McCullers: A Descriptive Listing and Annotated Bibliography of Criticism.* New York: Garland, 1980. Shapiro prepared the first section, a descriptive listing of McCullers' works. Bryer and Field did the second, an annotated bibliography of pieces about McCullers. The first section contains photographs of dust jackets of first editions, and gives publication information about all printings of her books. The second part includes books and scholarly articles about McCullers and reviews of her books and plays. Lengthy index.

Westling, Louise. *Sacred Groves and Ravaged Gardens: The Fiction of Eudora Welty, Carson McCullers, and Flannery O'Connor.* Athens: University of Georgia Press, 1985. This feminist analysis of the three Southern writers deals with what it means for a (white) woman to grow up in the South. Looking for what the three authors have in common, Westling discusses "their experience as women in a society which officially worshipped womanhood but in its imaginative life betrayed troubled, contradictory undercurrents." Discusses their differences, noting that "O'Connor had an almost constitutional aversion to Carson McCullers" but that there is evidence of a "real though unconscious debt."

J. D. Daubs
(Updated by *Katherine Lederer*)

DONAGH MacDONAGH

Born: Dublin, Ireland; November 22, 1912
Died: Dublin, Ireland; January 1, 1968

Principal drama

Happy as Larry, wr. 1941, pr., pb. 1946; *God's Gentry*, pr. 1951; *Step-in-the-Hollow*, pr. 1957, pb. 1959; *Lady Spider*, pb. 1980.

Other literary forms

In addition to writing plays, Donagh MacDonagh collaborated with A. J. Potter in a ballet, *Careless Love*, and an opera, *Patrick*, neither of which has been published. MacDonagh published two essays—one on his father, Thomas MacDonagh, in 1945, and one on James Joyce, in 1957—and was the author of several short stories. He often wrote new lyrics for old Irish ballads, some of which are collected in *The Hungry Grass* (1947) and *A Warning to Conquerors* (1968), two volumes of his poetry. With Lennox Robinson, MacDonagh coedited *The Oxford Book of Irish Verse* (1958) and, at the time of his death, was working on a dictionary of Dublin slang, which remains unfinished. The dictionary and the rest of MacDonagh's personal library and papers became the property of the Irish University Press.

Most important is MacDonagh's poetry, published in four volumes: *Twenty Poems* (1933), *Veterans and Other Poems* (1941), *The Hungry Grass*, and *A Warning to Conquerors*. Even his earliest poems are essentially dramatic and therefore foreshadow his later plays. Some, such as "Dublin Made Me" and "The Hungry Grass," are essentially mood pieces calculated to evoke in the reader precise feelings, such as patriotic allegiance to a proud, unbowed city or the nameless, all-encompassing fear of straying into a cursed area. Other poems are character sketches or dramatic dialogues apparently indebted to Alfred, Lord Tennyson.

Major themes of MacDonagh's drama also appear in his early poetry. In "Alleged Cruelty," for example, MacDonagh writes that we are all torn "with longings/ For something undefinable and wild," a recurrent thought in both the author's poems and his plays, often symbolized by the beauty of an unattainable woman. In contrast to such longings, our real lives, the poet asserts, are more like a horse, freighted with each passing year, endlessly running around the same track, or like "the changeless sound/ Of an engine running." This view leads MacDonagh to see past, present, and future as the same and therefore to accept and make the most of an inherently flawed world. Allied with this perception is a strong note of resignation, perhaps even fatalism, that creeps into MacDonagh's poetry from time to time, most notably in "The Veterans," one of his best poems. Like William Butler Yeats's "Easter 1916," "The Veterans" examines the famous

Easter Rising of 1916. For his part in this rebellion, Donagh MacDonagh's father, Thomas MacDonagh, was executed on May 3, 1916. Whereas Yeats questions the human cost of this Irish rebellion, MacDonagh, one generation later, questions its legacy. Domesticated by time and history, the Easter Rising has become "petrified" and academic, at best a shadowy memory of what it once was.

Two other themes are worth mentioning, one traditional and the other radically modern. Like the Elizabethan sonneteers, especially William Shakespeare, MacDonagh sometimes envisioned life as a struggle between love and the ravages of time. In his poems and some of his best plays, "Joy" and "the heart's extravagance" are offered as experiences that temporarily halt the inexorable corrosion of time. More contemporary is Mac-Donagh's recognition that culture, knowledge, and thought are all "varnish," under which lurks the primitive beast in all of us, from which springs "all wild desirable barbarities" and "time's rat teeth."

Achievements

Although MacDonagh was a poet, playwright, and scholar, a writer of ballads and short stories, the coauthor of a ballet and an opera, and a skillful and knowledgeable editor of Irish poetry, his real achievements are hard to gauge. This is true for two reasons. First, modern scholars have not yet focused sufficiently on the Irish playwrights and poets who followed William Butler Yeats, John Millington Synge, George Russell (Æ), and Sean O'Casey. Consequently, no complete history of modern Irish drama, no adequate bibliography, and few good anthologies exist. Indeed, many important plays of this period, at least one of which is by MacDonagh, remain unedited and unpublished. With the exception of a brief but trenchant study by Robert Hogan, the dean of modern Irish studies, no scholarly evaluations of MacDonagh have appeared. The second reason for the neglect of MacDonagh's work is more personal. His father, Thomas MacDonagh, has been the subject of numerous articles and two critical biographies, and the political and historical importance of the father has tended to overshadow the literary achievements of the son.

Some tentative judgments of Donagh MacDonagh, however, can be made. He was a better poet and playwright than his more famous father, and he, along with T. S. Eliot, deserves pride of place for attempting to resurrect poetic drama in the modern theater. In fact, MacDonagh's verse is more flexible and lively than Eliot's, and it has a much broader range, from ballad forms to rhyming couplets, from blank verse to colloquial Irish expressions, à la Synge. *Happy as Larry* is the best-known Irish verse play of recent memory, and some of MacDonagh's other plays, though almost completely unknown, are even better. His plays are notable for their deft characterization, whether sketched in detail or painted with a broad brush.

Fame largely eluded MacDonagh during his lifetime, although he was elected to the Irish Academy of Letters, saw his verse play *Happy as Larry* translated into twelve European languages, and gained great popularity as a broadcaster on Radio Éireann, where he sang and recited folk ballads and ballad operas, often his own, and where he explained the significance and importance of Irish songs and poetry to a large and enthusiastic listening audience. Selected by Lennox Robinson to help edit *The Oxford Book of Irish Verse*, MacDonagh also contributed a learned and insightful introduction to the collection.

Biography

Born in Dublin on November 22, 1912, Donagh MacDonagh made the most of a life that was singularly unlucky and troubled. His father, Thomas MacDonagh, the great Irish patriot, was executed when Donagh was only three years old, and shortly afterward the young boy contracted tuberculosis, a disease that greatly hampered him for the rest of his life. On July 9, 1917, only fifteen months after his father's death, Muriel MacDonagh, Donagh's mother, drowned while attempting to swim to an island off the shore of Skerries, an ocean resort close to Dublin. Thereafter, the custody of Donagh and his sister Barbara was contested for some time by the families of their father and mother, apparently in part because of a disagreement about whether the children should be reared as Catholics.

In time, Donagh was sent off to school, first to Belvedere College, where James Joyce had been a student some years earlier, and then to University College, Dublin, where he was part of a brilliant student generation that included such future notables as Niall Sheridan, Brian O'Nolan (who is best known under his pen names, Flann O'Brien and Myles na gCopaleen), Denis Devlin, Charles Donnelly—MacDonagh's close friend who died in 1937 during the Spanish Civil War—and Cyril Cusack, who later became an accomplished actor.

MacDonagh took both his bachelor of arts and master of arts degrees at University College, Dublin, and became a barrister in 1935. He practiced law until 1941, when he was named as a district justice for County Dublin, a post that required much traveling in the countryside.

At the time of his death on New Year's Day, 1968, MacDonagh was serving as a justice for the Dublin Metropolitan Courts. MacDonagh was twice married: His first wife drowned while she was taking a bath, and his second wife, who survived him, later choked to death on a chicken bone.

Analysis

Donagh MacDonagh's plays derive from three distinct sources. The first of these is the double heritage of the early Abbey Theatre: on the one hand, Yeats's romantic, poetic drama, and, on the other hand, the more realistic plays of Edward Martyn. All of MacDonagh's major works are comedies—even *Lady Spider* is technically a comedy—but in each one, the author offers a particular blend of realism and fantasy, with one or the other usually predominating. Another important source for MacDonagh's drama is his deep love of poetry and various verse forms. As a practicing poet, he attempted to revive the marriage of poetry and drama, experimenting with different types of verse that he thought were appropriate for and pleasing to theater audiences. The third source of MacDonagh's art is his great learning, above all his familiarity with Elizabethan and Jacobean drama, especially Shakespeare, and his scholar's interest in old Irish poetry and ballads and in various Irish dialects and slang.

All of these influences are present in MacDonagh's first published drama, *Happy as Larry*, his most popular and successful play. Technically accomplished, *Happy as Larry* has been described as "a ballad opera without music," and the definition is a good one. The rhythms of well-known Irish ballads and the use of homey Irish words and phrases provide a constant undercurrent of familiar patterns that make the verse easy to listen to or to read. MacDonagh employs short, medium, and long lines of verse, together with musical repetitions and refrains, to which he adds simplicity and clarity of diction. The result is a verse play of uncommon pleasure.

The plot of *Happy as Larry* is highly fanciful and melodramatic. Six tailors, one of whom is Larry's grandson, are located on the outer stage and introduce the story. Larry, a hard-drinking, fast-talking Irishman, happens upon a young woman of about twenty who is kneeling by the grave of Johnny, her recently deceased husband. She is fanning the dirt on Johnny's grave, for her late husband made her promise not to marry again until the clay on his grave is dry. Intrigued and amused, Larry invites the young widow home to have a cup of tea. Meanwhile, at Larry's house, the local Doctor is attempting to seduce Mrs. Larry. Soon after Larry and the widow arrive, Seamus, the pharmacist, enters with a vial of poison, ordered by the evil Doctor, who puts it in Larry's drink. Poor Larry dies from the poison, and the shocked and bereaved Mrs. Larry quickly plans a wake, during which the nefarious Doctor presses his suit. Soon Mrs. Larry weakens and agrees to marry the Doctor, even though her husband's corpse is not yet cold. Outraged, the six tailors, with the help of the three Fates, travel back in time to join the party at Larry's wake, where they decide to take a hand in events by using the Doctor's own poison against him. The unsuspecting Doctor toasts his future happiness and promptly dies. Seamus convinces Mrs. Larry to draw some blood from Larry's corpse in order to give the Doctor a transfusion which, according to the pharmacist, will bring the Doctor back to life. Mrs. Larry agrees but faints and dies when she sees Larry's blood. Incredibly, the blood she drains from Larry contains the poison that killed him, so Larry revives, believing that he is the victim of a monumental hangover. The young widow consoles Larry over the loss of his wife and talks him out of a life of debauchery and dissipation. The second tailor ends the play by telling the audience that Larry will marry the young widow and live happily ever after.

MacDonagh provides a cast of wonderfully drawn comic types to complement his fantastic plot. Mrs. Larry talks too much, bosses her poor husband around, and is somehow capable of delivering a highly metaphysical eulogy for her dead husband: "Empty on their racks the suits are hanging,/ Mere foolish cloth whose meaning was their wearer." Still, she is a loving and faithful wife until Larry's death. The Gravedigger, wholly superfluous to the plot, is right out of Shakespeare's *Hamlet*; he is a comic reductionist and a walking, talking memento mori whose every line is a reminder that death is both unpredictable and unconquerable. The young widow is the Gravedigger's opposite number, healthy and buxom, good-humored and witty, and convinced that she can conquer death—as, in a way, she does, by marrying again and refusing to be a widow for the rest of her life. Larry is the archetypal henpecked husband, decent enough and faithful to his wife, but not above a little flirting on the side.

The star of the show is MacDonagh's evil Doctor, a hilarious combination of Oil Can Harry and Groucho Marx. MacDonagh endows the Doctor with the spurious eloquence of a first-class rake and with the persuasive powers of John Donne. Arguing at one point that love is religion because God is love, the Doctor slyly turns to Mrs. Larry and croons, "Let us pray/ Together, Mrs. Larry." Later, this schemer touts the virtues of friendship to Mrs. Larry, arguing that since friendship transcends passion, his kiss should be allowed to linger. When the six tailors succeed in poisoning him, the audience is sure to cheer: He has been hoist with his own petard.

The Doctor's fellow in crime, the unctuous pharmacist, spotlights MacDonagh's major theme in the play. Seamus' presence in this comedy is a kind of learned joke: The Greek *pharmakos* means both remedy and poison, just as the word "drug" even today carries both a positive and a negative sense. Thus, infusing this delightful comedy is a vision of the world in which nearly everything cuts two ways, and in which rigid views, either of proper conduct or of the opposite sex, need to be broadened and softened. Except for the Doctor and his henchman Seamus, everyone in *Happy as Larry* is a mingled yarn—both good and bad together.

The play gently asks us to support a widow's right to remarry. According to custom, especially in Catholic Ireland, widows do better to honor the memory of their dead husbands by not remarrying—Mrs. Larry makes exactly this point to the young widow—yet such expectations are both unrealistic and cruel, as Mrs. Larry discovers in the course of the play. MacDonagh endorses the young widow's wish to marry again rather than follow the outdated suicide of Dido or the self-immolation of Indian wives, both mentioned at the start of the play.

Allied to the theme of remarriage is MacDonagh's attempt to adjust male attitudes toward women. Though written twenty years before the rebirth of feminism in the 1960's, the play poses a key question about Larry's two wives: Which is bad and which is good? The answer is that both are essentially good. The play approves of Mrs. Larry's wish for companionship after Larry's death, though it does not approve of the way the Doctor manipulates her, and Mrs. Larry's attempt to save the Doctor, though it fails, stems from the reasonable premise that it is better to save a life than to let someone die. Likewise, the lusty young widow's wish to dry her husband's grave quickly is rewarded at the end of the play when MacDonagh allows her to marry Larry.

The second tailor, Larry's grandson, begins as a misogynist—"Woman curses every plan"—but ends by praising the many virtues of the young widow and by wishing that his own son "may be as happy as Larry." Like the second tailor, the audience learns the need for tolerance and empathy in an imperfect world.

Step-in-the-Hollow, like *Happy as Larry*, is an experimental play. Local dialects and lively, contemporary turns of phrase energize this comedy, which, again like its predecessor, contains a wide variety of verse forms. In both technique and construction, however, *Step-in-the-Hollow* is superior to *Happy as Larry* and was a great success when it premiered at the Gaiety Theatre, Dublin, on March 11, 1957. Parts of the play are written in rhyming couplets, a difficult and demanding form that MacDonagh uses with great skill and to good effect. The verse is flexible enough for the actors to avoid the singsong monotony that can vitiate a long series of couplets, and MacDonagh also employs the couplet form wisely: to highlight important moments in the play, and as a device to underscore the character of Julia O'Sullivan, the local harridan who threatens to destroy Justice Redmond O'Hanlon, the title character.

The play is so well constructed that it moves along with great speed, full of interest and crackling with life and vitality. MacDonagh deftly uses the first act to introduce the main complications one by one. First, the audience learns that a government inspector is on his way to evaluate the courtroom procedures of Justice O'Hanlon. Then Julia O'Sullivan appears, with her daughter, aptly named Teazie, in tow, demanding that the Justice try Crilly Duffy, a local boy, for compromising her daughter's virtue. Throughout, the reactions of the Justice's cohorts—Molly, the Sergeant, and the Clerk—establish their essential characters for the audience, while MacDonagh holds back the main antagonists, Justice Redmond O'Hanlon and Sean O'Fenetic, the government inspector. When the Judge finally enters, MacDonagh adds a third complication: An old man, much like Redmond O'Hanlon, was in Teazie's room before Crilly Duffy entered.

Act 2 consists of two short scenes in which the case of O'Sullivan versus Duffy is argued and almost resolved. With the Inspector watching every move, Justice O'Hanlon tries as hard as he can to prevent the truth from being discovered, but Julia O'Sullivan discovers that O'Hanlon, not Duffy, is the real villain and storms into the courtroom to accuse the Justice. Overcome with emotion and gin, she builds to a climax at great length, allowing O'Hanlon to adjourn the court and whisk away the Inspector before Julia can name the man who compromised her little Teazie.

Act 3 belongs wholly to Molly Nolan, who conceives and executes a plan that saves the Justice, the Sergeant, and the Clerk, while ensuring her own future as the heir of Redmond O'Hanlon and the new wife of the Inspector. Skillful, effective, and satisfying, the conclusion to *Step-in-the-Hollow* is both unexpected and delightful.

The twin themes of this play are love and justice. The symbol of playful, worldly love is Sandro Botticelli's *The Birth of Venus*, prominently displayed in Justice Redmond O'Hanlon's apartment, the location for acts 1 and 3. During the play, MacDonagh examines different kinds of love: the May-December infatuation of the Justice for Teazie; the young love of Crilly and Teazie, who are to be married by the end of the play; the romantic, yet imprudent, love of the Sergeant for Molly; the lascivious love of the Justice for Molly; the liquor-induced love of the Clerk for Molly; and, finally, the birth of the Inspector's love for Molly, which she both induces and accepts in act 3.

In some ways, Molly is an unlikely heroine—as clever and resourceful as Shakespeare's comic heroines, which she clearly resembles, but much less chaste. She took a tumble in the hay with the Sergeant once, and the full extent of her duties for the Justice clearly exceed those of a paid housekeeper. Moreover, Molly is no starry-eyed, empty-headed girl, such as Teazie; rather, she wants respectability and a good fortune, as well as the passion of first love, all of which the Inspector finally provides. Molly is not above asking, "What's in it for me?" and her mixture of love and prudence wins the day for herself and for others.

Molly's attitude toward love is highly practical, not extreme. The need for a practical, reasonable approach to justice is the play's complementary theme. Justice Redmond O'Hanlon and Inspector Sean O'Fenetic represent radical attitudes toward the law, neither of which can be accepted. Once a good scholar and student of the law, Justice O'Hanlon has been worn down by thirty years on the bench and has become the very embodiment of the Seven Deadly Sins that justice seeks to prevent and punish. On the other hand, the God-fearing Inspector, sworn to temperance, is an essentially innocent and sterile advocate of governmental rules and regulations that often hinder instead of promote the impartial administration of justice. Molly, rather than the Justice or the Inspector, leads the audience to a better understanding of justice and the law. She puts the Inspector in the same compromising position in which Crilly Duffy found Justice Redmond O'Hanlon. The point is simple and clear: Let him who is without sin cast the first stone. Thus, mercy and forgiveness, and a second chance, are the better parts of justice.

As in his other plays, MacDonagh's characters are exceptionally well drawn—from the gin-soaked Julia O'Sullivan and the voyeuristic Mary Margaret Allen to the inhibited Inspector, who, with Molly's help, discovers at the end of the play that he has always been afraid of women. Above all, there is Justice Redmond O'Hanlon, an authentic triumph of the literary imagination. Old in years yet young at heart, limping after his last exploit with Teazie yet still chasing after women, this fat Justice is a liar, a cheat, and a scoundrel, but his cleverness and humor are endearing qualities that help him retain audience sympathy. He derives from Sir John Falstaff, as does the basic conflict of *Step-in-the-Hollow*: The clash between the Inspector and the Justice is an Irish version of the contest between the Lord Chief Justice and Falstaff in Shakespeare's *Henry IV, Part II*. Moreover, some of the pathos and melancholy of Shakespeare's work creep into MacDonagh's play: Justice O'Hanlon's startling admission, "An old man knows what's lost," echoes Falstaff's frank confession in *Henry IV, Part II*, "I am old, I am old."

In part, however, O'Hanlon is an alter ego of the author himself, who also spent many years on the bench in Ireland. Though obvious differences exist between the playwright and his creation, a Justice who quotes T. S. Eliot and who displays above his bench the harp of Ireland, the symbol of old Irish poetry and music, shares something with MacDonagh. One suspects, for example, that O'Hanlon's wish to replace the rules of evidence with common sense echoes the wish of his creator, and the Justice's view that the law seems bent on mystifying common people may also have been shared by MacDonagh.

The Justice provides a sobering counterpoint to an otherwise happy ending. As the curtain is about to fall, O'Hanlon stands alone, looking out the window at Molly and the Inspector as they leave to get married. To grow old, the Justice muses, is to gain money, place, and power but to lose forever carefree youth and the chance to be in love again. "I can't complain" is O'Hanlon's last line, but the audience knows better.

Lady Spider is MacDonagh's most daring and ambitious play, in which he offers his version of the Deirdre legend that has obsessed Irish poets and playwrights for more than one hundred years. The tragedy of Deirdre is to the Irish imagination as Homer's *Iliad* is to the English, and it is fair to say that MacDonagh handles the love of Deirdre and Naoise much as Shakespeare treats the story of Troilus and Cressida; *Lady Spider* minimizes romance and fantasy by pushing comedy to the limits of realism. In short,

MacDonagh demythologizes myth by making it modern, psychological, and political. The result is as brilliant as it is unsettling, a fable for modern times.

The story of Deirdre is part of the Red Branch Cycle of ancient Irish tales. During the reign of Conor, King of Ulster, a female child named Deirdre is born who, according to prophecy, will bring down the House of Usna and Emain Macha, the palace of King Conor. Conor refuses to kill the child; instead, he sends her into the wilderness to be brought up by Leabharcham, a nurse. Deirdre, whose name means "alarm" or "troubler," grows up to be so desirable that Conor intends to marry her, but she meets Naoise, a son of the House of Usna, and runs away with him and his two brothers, Ardan and Ainnle. After a few years, Conor sends Fergus to convince the lovers that all is forgiven. They accept Conor's offer to return to Ireland, whereupon the still lovesick king uses stealth and guile to kill Naoise and his brothers once they arrive at his palace. Three variant endings exist: Deirdre immediately kills herself, she quickly dies of sorrow, or Conor keeps her for a year, after which she commits suicide.

Three great Irish plays before MacDonagh's were based on the Deirdre legend, and each in its own way interprets Deirdre as a romantic symbol of female heroism and as a model of support, inspiration, and companionship for the Irish hero. In his *Deirdre* (1902), Æ depicts the heroine as the incarnation of the ancient Irish gods, who will one day return to validate the sacrifice of Deirdre and Naoise, made immortal by their escape into death. Images of sleep, dreams, and vision help establish a mystical context in which the world of myth and magic, not the everyday world, is the deepest reality and the most true. Yeats's *Deirdre* (pr. 1906) is an exercise in concentrated poetic imagery that accentuates the passion of the lovers and invites them to live forever in the Byzantium of art. The greatest of these three plays is Synge's *Deirdre of the Sorrows* (pr. 1910), written in simple, direct prose with a peasant dialect. Synge's version establishes a sympathetic connection between the lovers and nature; the lovers triumph over age and the mutability of earthly love by choosing the timeless immortality of death.

Just as Shakespeare wrote his *Troilus and Cressida* with Geoffrey Chaucer and Homer in mind, so MacDonagh composed his play as both a contribution to and a comment on the great plays that preceded his. He deromanticizes the story by using the technique of inversion. Unlike Æ, MacDonagh refers to no gods who wait in the wings, and mysticism gives way to a hard-nosed, deeply flawed world. Unlike Yeats, MacDonagh refuses to glorify the passion of Deirdre and Naoise; in fact, he purposefully degrades it into a sexual obsession that Deirdre must overcome. Like Synge, MacDonagh fills his play with nature imagery, but the effect is very different. Images of nature, animals, and food in *Lady Spider* accentuate the bestial side of man and his subjugation to appetites of all kinds. The blank verse that contains these images is tough, lean, and elemental, stunningly beautiful in its starkness.

The central purpose of *Lady Spider* is to criticize earlier versions of the Deirdre legend and to recover the basic meaning of the myth, which proves to be startlingly modern. This purpose may be seen by examining closely the way in which MacDonagh changes a scene that first appears in Synge's play. Synge invented the character of Owen, a grotesque peasant who values nothing but Deirdre's love. MacDonagh replaces Owen with Art, a Scottish king who promises Deirdre "honey words" and "truth," and who wishes to take her to the Palace of Art, the home of "sweet poetry," where all the bards and harpers will sing of Deirdre. She is singularly unimpressed with Art and threatens to cut out his tongue, the traditional punishment for poets who lie.

Literally, this exchange emphasizes Deirdre's desirability—wherever she goes, men lust after her. The scene also foreshadows the real reason that Conor wants her back in Ireland: Like King Art, King Conor is a lustful, unprincipled old man, as drawn to Deirdre as any young man. Symbolically, however, the ugly little Scottish king represents literary art, which has tried to appropriate Deirdre for its own purposes, oblivious to the beauty of the original myth. As MacDonagh sees it, Æ, Yeats, Synge, and many others are guilty of attempted rape, of forcing the legend into wholly alien significance. Soon after Deirdre first meets Art, he is killed while attempting to flee and lies sprawling in the middle of the stage at the end of act 2. This is poetic justice, so to speak, and the end, MacDonagh implies, of all of this romantic Deirdre nonsense in Irish art.

As this short explication illustrates, *Lady Spider* is richly artistic, despite its attitude toward art and poetry, and its characters are superbly realized. Naoise, Deirdre's lover, is the playboy of the Western world, cynical about women and sex and unable to get enough of either, a sort of Hotspur without young Percy's charm. Naoise is full of empty idealism and self-interest but unable to develop into anything better. His rival Conor is shrewder and more intelligent but has grown old without wisdom. A superb manipulator of men, he is in turn manipulated by his own glands, which make him as lecherous as a monkey. Buffeted between these two men, Deirdre is a quintessentially modern woman, blamed for being the source of all trouble yet in reality the victim of men's appetites and of her own.

Deirdre's development is the center of interest in the play. At first, MacDonagh's Deirdre dreams romantically about men. It is love she wants, but in Naoise she gets animal lust that makes her his sexual thrall. Desperate, she puts Naoise under *geasa*—magical bonds that are supposed to force consent—in an attempt to make Naoise marry her. After the couple flees to Scotland, Deirdre hardens with time, still sexually captivated by her lover but increasingly aware of his faults, especially his promiscuity. Lured back to Ireland, Deirdre has outgrown Naoise, both mentally and physically, and she has frank admiration for the way in which Conor outwits and outmanipulates her and Naoise, causing the death of the latter. Seeing that manipulation is the necessary means to any end in this brutal, political world, Deirdre resolves to become Conor's wife, not out of love or even pity but to torment him with his sexual inadequacy, thereby becoming his master, driving him to despair, and securing his crown for her son, who is safe in Scotland. Deirdre's final goal will elude her, for the audience knows in advance that she will be the one to commit suicide.

The world of *Lady Spider* turns on negatives, on false hopes and Pyrrhic victories. MacDonagh has revealed the modern world in an ancient mirror, and it is a world in which all value has drained away, a world in which love is reduced to sex, in which supernature is replaced by nature, in which wisdom gives way to craft and guile, and in which human virtues are supplanted by animal appetites. This kind of world cannot support real tragedy, and so Deirdre remains alive at the play's end—doomed but denied the dignity of death. Paradoxically, however, the play itself is captivating, possessed of a hard, gemlike brilliance that simply overpowers the audience with the force of MacDonagh's vision. For all of these reasons, *Lady Spider* is the best of the Deirdre plays.

Yet it may not be MacDonagh's best play. Surprisingly, *God's Gentry* remained unpublished despite the fact that Robert Hogan, one of the few scholars to have seen it acted, calls *God's Gentry* "a much more colorful and theatrical show than *Happy as Larry*." The exact opposite of *Lady Spider*, *God's Gentry* pushes romance and fantasy to their limits in a story about a band of tinkers who invoke the help of an Irish god to turn County Mayo upside down. Tinkers and gentry trade places for a year until the god's power wears off. According to Hogan, *God's Gentry* is a perfectly delightful play, full of "dancing, singing, spectacle, and high spirits." It remains for some enterprising scholar to edit and publish this play—and other inaccessible or unpublished plays by MacDonagh—so that this neglected modern playwright can begin to receive the critical attention and the wide audience that he deserves.

Other major works

POETRY: *Twenty Poems*, 1933; *Veterans and Other Poems*, 1941; *The Hungry Grass*, 1947; *A Warning to Conquerors*, 1968.

ANTHOLOGY: *The Oxford Book of Irish Verse*, 1958 (editor, with Lennox Robinson).

Bibliography
Browne, E. Martin, ed. Introduction to *Four Modern Verse Plays*. Har-

mondsworth, Middlesex, England: Penguin Books, 1957. One of the plays selected is MacDonagh's *Happy as Larry*. Browne discusses the play's particular sense of poetic drama in terms that provide a useful approach not only to the work in question but also to MacDonagh's distinctive language and dramaturgy. The discussion also draws attention to differences between MacDonagh and other modern writers of verse plays.

Hogan, Robert. *After the Irish Renaissance: A Critical History of the Irish Drama Since "The Plough and the Stars."* Minneapolis: University of Minnesota Press, 1967. MacDonagh's background and career are described in the context of experimentation in verse drama by the generation of Irish playwrights who immediately succeeded William Butler Yeats. All MacDonagh's important plays are examined, and their distinctive poetic origins and attainments are assessed. Contains bibliographical information concerning the plays.

MacDonagh, Donagh. "The Death-watch Beetle." *Drama*, no. 12 (February, 1949): 4-7. MacDonagh provides a succinct account of the rise, and what he considers the imminent fall, of the Abbey Theatre. His views are revealing in the light of his own status as a playwright, the orientation and tone of his plays, and the production of his works by companies other than the Abbey.

Norstedt, Johann A. *Thomas MacDonagh: A Critical Biography.* Charlottesville: University Press of Virginia, 1980. A biography of Donagh MacDonagh's poet-patriot father, which is essential reading for a sense of MacDonagh's background and his work's relationship to his illustrious heritage. Includes limited information relevant to an evaluation of MacDonagh's work for the theater. Also contains a full bibliography.

Wickstrom, Gordon M. "Introduction to *Lady Spider.*" *Journal of Irish Literature* 9, no. 3 (1980): 4-82. A first publication of MacDonagh's least-known work, based on the well-known Irish legend of Deirdre. The work's place in the canon of plays dealing with the Deirdre legend is evaluated, thereby providing a brief, instructive introduction to MacDonagh's dramatic imagination. The text comes complete with editorial annotations.

Edmund M. Taft
(Updated by *George O'Brien*)

JOHN McGRATH

Born: Birkenhead, Cheshire, England; June 1, 1935

Principal drama
Events While Guarding the Bofors Gun, pr., pb. 1966; *Bakke's Night of Fame*, pr. 1968, pb. 1973; *Random Happenings in the Hebrides*, pr. 1970, pb. 1972; *Trees in the Wind*, pr. 1971; *Fish in the Sea*, pr. 1972, pb. 1977 (music by Mark Brown); *The Cheviot, the Stag, and the Black, Black Oil*, pr., pb 1973 (revised edition pb. 1975, 1981); *Little Red Hen*, pr. 1975, pb. 1977; *Yobbo Nowt*, pr. 1975, pb. 1978 (music by Brown); *Joe's Drum*, pr., pb. 1979; *Swings and Roundabouts*, pr. 1980, pb. 1981; *Blood Red Roses*, pr. 1980, pb. 1981; *Behold the Sun*, pr. 1985 (opera libretto; music by Alexander Goehr); *Mairi Mhor: The Woman from Skye*, pr. 1987; *Border Warfare*, pr. 1989; *Waiting for Dolphins*, pr. 1992.

Other literary forms
John McGrath has written dozens of scripts for television and film. *Z-Cars* (1962), which he cowrote with Troy Kennedy Martin, was one of the most popular series in the 1962 television season, and his *Diary of a Young Man* ran a six-part television series in 1964. His films include *Billion Dollar Brain* (1967), *The Bofors Gun* (1968), and *The Dressmaker* (1988, shown again in 1992 on public television). Films have been made for television of several of his major plays—*The Cheviot, the Stag, and the Black, Black Oil* (1974), *Blood Red Roses* (1985), and *Border Warfare* (1989). His nonfiction works include *The Bone Won't Break: On Theatre and Hope in Hard Times* (1990).

Achievements
Known as a socialist playwright, McGrath writes mainly for working-class audiences in rural and industrial-urban Great Britain. The key influences on his work begin with the approaches of the Unity Theatre of the 1930's, the Workers Theatre Movement formed in 1924, and the early Theatre Workshop of the 1950's, which combine popular tastes as defined by working-class culture with political themes. Furthermore, McGrath deeply admires the revolutionary theater of Vsevolod Meyerhold and Erwin Piscator, and films with a social conscience such as those produced by Jean Renoir and Sergei Eisenstein. Many of McGrath's plays employ skitlike agitprop techniques that feature humor, the songs and satire of the music-hall tradition, and folk, rock, and carnival music. Even so, the plays make new, challenging demands on their audiences with the serious underpinnings of ideological and ethical issues that endorse a revolutionary rather than a reformist perspective.

Biography

Although his father was a middle-class secondary-school teacher, John McGrath identified with the working classes through his Irish Catholic immigrant grandparents and, especially, his paternal grandfather, who worked as a boilermaker in the Birkenhead yards. McGrath was reared in Merseyside (near Liverpool) until World War II, when the family was evacuated to a working-class district in North Wales, returning to Merseyside in 1951.

From 1953 to 1955, McGrath fulfilled his National Service as a gunner, bombardier, then artillery officer in the British army, which sent him to Germany and Egypt. His officer status helped to qualify him in 1955 as a student at the University of Oxford, where he took a Dip.Ed. in directing and writing in 1959.

McGrath gave up a promising career in commercial theater and the popular media to commit his talents to alternative groups. After being associated with the Royal Court Theatre and the Script Department at the British Broadcasting Corporation (BBC) from 1959 to 1965, he lent his energies briefly to Centre 42, the Writers' Action Group, and Everyman Theatre in Liverpool. One of the crucial turning points for McGrath was in 1968, when he went to Paris and was deeply influenced by the para-revolutionary fever during the May strike, when students joined nine million workers to shut down the French system.

In 1962, McGrath married Elizabeth MacLennan, a gifted actress who was also a 1959 graduate of the University of Oxford. To make their own statement about mainstream theater, McGrath and MacLennan helped to found the 7:84 Theatre Company in 1971 (known as 7:84), the name being a reminder that 7 percent of the population in Great Britain at that time owned 84 percent of the wealth. For seventeen years, the company played to packed houses, particularly in the Highlands of Scotland and around England. Moreover, McGrath's innovations in working-class theater inspired a new generation of political theater in Great Britain; many of the original members served as catalysts for other companies, such as the Belt and Braces Roadshow and the Monstrous Regiment.

In 1982, 7:84 began a series of revivals written by earlier playwrights called the Clydebilt Season. These shows, exploring the heritage of popular culture, complemented McGrath's own plays, which filled out the greater part of each new season. Despite 7:84's successful track record, or perhaps because of it, the conservative government of Margaret Thatcher, in 1985, withdrew the Arts Council grants for 7:84, England. In 1988, McGrath resigned as artistic director of the Scottish branch of 7:84 in response to fatal cuts announced by the Scottish Arts Council, and the company effectively died. After leaving 7:84, McGrath wrote for Wildcat, in Glasgow, and Freeway Films, a company that he founded in the late 1980's.

In 1979, McGrath became a Judith E. Wilson Fellow, a guest lecturer at the University of Cambridge. His lectures became the basis for *A Good Night Out: Popular Theatre: Audience, Class, and Form* (1981), a seminal work on the theory of working-class theater as a political forum. He returned to the University of Cambridge a decade later to discuss the problem of government subsidy for oppositional theater, a problem resulting from a clash in tastes between those who fund working-class theater and those who enjoy it. The lectures were published as *The Bone Won't Break: On Theatre and Hope in Hard Times.*

Analysis

John McGrath's works, numbering more than forty plays, roughly fall into three periods—the plays written before he began to define working-class theater for the contemporary stage, the plays of the 7:84 years that applied his theories, and his direction in theater since the collapse of state-run socialism in the Soviet Union and Eastern Europe.

His earliest works feature lone, rebellious men who openly oppose middle-class institutions that stand for moneyed success, dehumanizing deference, and conformity. Though these rebels are able to define the system of values that they reject, they provide few practical solutions that might alleviate oppression of the individual spirit. While positive about their own values and their attack on society, these loners never form adequate relationships, particularly with allies in causes that might help them create change, so their dissent remains fixed at a certain level. Being authentic— that is, living by their own principles—is more important to these men than joining others, lest they are forced to compromise. They have, therefore, a commitment largely to themselves and their own dissent. Nevertheless, they are compelling figures for the moral integrity that they articulate and the intensity of their resistance to mainstream values.

McGrath's early heroes in *Random Happenings in the Hebrides*, *Events While Guarding the Bofors Gun*, and *Bakke's Night of Fame* are thus best understood through the values of French existentialism, which influenced McGrath at the time. As an inmate on death row awaiting imminent execution, Bakke, in *Bakke's Night of Fame*, insists on defining his own humanity. He does this by drawing attention to himself as an individual unlike his predecessors on death row. He goads the attending priest, who tries to deal with him as yet another penitent parishioner, into consciously acknowledging Bakke as a person like any other, with contradictions, desires, fears, and whims. Bakke similarly toys with the guards and needles the executioner into catering to his mercurial moods. It is Bakke's way of struggling against the limitations of life itself and the humiliation of his fate. Teasing the priest into trying to guess whether he was guilty of his crime, Bakke attacks the traditional Christian notion of morality that judges human guilt.

It is never established whether Bakke committed a murder—some of the time he seems guilty and at other times he seems innocent—but the question of culpability is not important. Bakke wants to make it clear that he is a testament to the infinite mystery of human liberty. At the center of his being he has an inchoate but irreducible potential that gives him a freedom to assert his own autonomy. Whatever his fate, he attains dignity by virtue of his inviolable freedom to define himself as a human being and to amend that definition with each new act. The priest fails to grasp what Bakke is trying to teach him about life. He sees Bakke's patter as mere play-acting. Of course, that is what people around Hamlet accused him of doing too, and Bakke teases the priest with echoes from William Shakespeare that suggest that Bakke, like the Prince of Denmark, is conscious of being able to shape life's boundaries through each crucial decision and act.

For McGrath, *Bakke's Night of Fame* also provides an opportunity to protest the inhumanity of capital punishment, an issue that materializes the abstract nature of Bakke's struggle. Bakke insists on confronting his executioner and asking about the executioner's children, who might themselves have to face a death sentence some day. He is trying to force the person who will kill him to put a face on the man he will soon electrocute. Bakke makes no equivocation about capital punishment as an act of murder and the human life that is at stake.

By contrast, McGrath's plays written during the 7:84 period deemphasize individualism. Their protagonists are likely to be female as well as male, and they stress solutions to topical issues of economic and social injustice through communal interests. Convinced that the sources of the working-class struggle could not be readily visualized and fully understood through the surface reality of everyday situations, McGrath rejected naturalism or realism as choices for dramatic forms. To reveal the underlying economic forces that are normally suppressed in the dominant culture, McGrath draws on Brechtian forms of art that attempt to force the audience to contemplate and question what they see. Specifically, his strategy is to draw on very stylized scenery and dialogue—often exaggerated, cartoonlike, and humorous—which creates some distance between stage and audience, inhibiting identification with the characters and situations.

McGrath wisely chose, however, not to adopt the full measure of audience alienation but to develop a modified form of Brechtian theater that would have a wide appeal among his audiences and still achieve the effect of revealing the hidden forces of capitalism, corporate monopoly, power, and greed. Noting that art's appeal is not universal and that most standards for art are determined by middle-class tastes, McGrath set out to discover what characterizes working-class entertainment in particular. He determined, above all, that he must be direct in his message for the working classes—that it must not be embedded in artistic form—and that he should use plenty of variety with comedy, music, and moment-by-moment change of effect. Working-class audiences like a fast pace, with a variety of emotion and rhythms defined by laughs, silence, song, and tears. He also decided to employ topical subject matter especially linked to local concerns and to work informally with the audiences using plenty of give-and-take with the crowds. Audiences are sometimes asked to join the actors on the stage with dancing and singing, as one of several ways audiences participated in 7:84's shows.

The best-known play of this period—already a classic in its own right— is *The Cheviot, the Stag, and the Black, Black Oil.* The play protests the appropriation of Scotland's land over the centuries for raising sheep, hunting grouse, and exploiting oil reserves. It begins with the tragedy of the Clearances, a period in the 1800's when the crofters (tenant farmers) were thrown off their land at the whim of the large landholders, who wanted the land for recreation or income. So many of these people were burned out, chased to the sea, and put on ships for Canada that their number today is a mere fraction of what it once was. After repeated torture and harassment by the authorities, whole villages disappeared. Throughout *The Cheviot, the Stag, and the Black, Black Oil* are a parade of crofters who tell their stories with poignancy and humor, and their version of history contrasts with the aristocrats who, by their own words, reveal profit motive and callousness. This history of the Clearances finds its analogue at the end of the play with the displacement of Scots in the Shetlands and Orkney islands by North Sea oil development. Since the cost of living has become too high for local inhabitants, they have had to sell out to developers.

The Cheviot, the Stag, and the Black, Black Oil was enormously popular on tour largely because it expressed the concerns of people in the Highlands, but also because it successfully employed the techniques that McGrath had earlier identified as characteristic of working-class theater. The scenery was a giant pop-up book, all the music—both rock and Highland fiddle tunes—was live, and the play drew on the Gaelic *Ceilidh* as a paradigm, a folk party with whiskey, storytelling, Scottish poetry, local music, and general entertainment.

With plays such as *The Cheviot, the Stag, and the Black, Black Oil*, McGrath found his voice in the issues defined by Scottish history, especially in celebration of folk heroes who protest colonization by outsiders and decry mistakes made by the Scots themselves, who have, in effect, relinquished control over their own affairs. These plays—among them *Little Red Hen*, *Joe's Drum*, and *Mairi Mhor*—point the way to *Border Warfare*, a work of epic proportions that brings together many of the themes of McGrath's earlier historic drama with themes on the nationalist cause. In this play, Scotland is the primeval land corrupted by cross-border raids between England and Scotland, diminished by foreign rule, and ennobled only by the contemporary hope of devolution (transfer) of power from the

British parliament. All the key points of Scottish history concerning home rule are here—the battles over Northumbria, the clan rivalry that allowed the English an early foothold in Scotland, the scheming of King James I of Scotland and Mary Queen of Scots, the Union of 1707 that legalized absorption of the Scottish parliament by England, and the political infighting during the nineteenth century that has kept devolution almost within reach, but not quite. Once again, the play uses a combination of folk and contemporary music, stylized scenery, and a pageantlike structure that calls forth spokespeople from each generation. Despite the size of the production, *Border Warfare* was mounted without government subsidy.

Waiting for Dolphins possibly marks a third shift in McGrath's writings, since it is aimed more at middle-class leftists who feel alienated and isolated by the breakup of the world's largest Marxist government, the Soviet Union. With remarkable honesty, the play faces up to the destruction and mistakes of the Left and, with humor and acerbic commentary, takes on the demonization of socialism by reaffirming the leftist belief in a more just system. Its protagonist is Reynalda, a member of one of "the best English radical, non-conforming intellectual families," who runs a bed-and-breakfast place in North Wales and wonders how she will get along with her capitalist guests. While she reviews the contours of her activist years, she wonders what her response should become to the loss of socialist values. As an analogue, she recalls the dolphins she had once seen frolicking near Cyprus. They represent all that hangs delicately in the balance for both the environment and socialism. If future decisions do not consider their contribution to the world, they could become extinct. Her only recourse is to wait for the dolphins to resurface.

Waiting for Dolphins is an important departure for McGrath because it once again features an individual voice and addresses a new audience without the trappings of big production values. It turns to a more realistic dramatic form with well-developed characterization that invites audience sympathy and identification.

Other major works

NONFICTION: *A Good Night Out: Popular Theatre—Audience, Class, and Form*, 1981; *The Bone Won't Break: On Theatre and Hope in Hard Times*, 1990.

SCREENPLAYS: *Billion Dollar Brain*, 1967; *The Bofors Gun*, 1968; *The Virgin Soldiers*, 1969; *The Reckoning*, 1970; *The Dressmaker*, 1988.

TELEPLAYS: *Z-Cars*, 1962 (with Troy Kennedy Martin); *Diary of a Young Man*, 1964; *The Day of Ragnarok*, 1965; *Mo*, 1965; *Shotgun*, 1966; *Diary of a Nobody*, 1966; *Orkney*, 1971; *Bouncing Boy*, 1972, 1974; *The Cheviot, the Stag, and the Black, Black Oil*, 1974, *Once upon a Union*, 1977; *The Adventures of Frank*, 1980; *Blood Red Roses*, 1985; *Border Warfare*, 1989.

TELEVISION DOCUMENTARIES: *The Entertainers*, 1964; *Sweetwater Memories*, 1984.

Bibliography

Cherns, Penny, and Paddy Broughton. "John McGrath's *Trees in the Wind* at the Northcott Theatre, Exeter." *Theatre Quarterly* 19 (September/October, 1975): 89-100. Although describing the workings of an early production, this article offers real insight into the 7:84 Theatre Company's rehearsal process and the special mix of ideology and theater that shapes the plays.

Craig, Sandy. "Unmasking the Lie." *In Dreams and Deconstructions: Alternative Theatre in Britain.* Ambergate: Amber Lane Press, 1980. A spirited account of the revolution in British theater beginning in 1968. Craig's discussion, which describes the whole range of theater in Great Britain, situates McGrath's work in the continuum between commercial and subsidized theater.

Itzin, Catherine. *Stages in the Revolution: Political Theatre in Britain Since 1968.* London: Eyre Methuen, 1980. An invaluable handbook that documents the work of the most important political writers and theater companies between 1968 and 1980. Arranged in chronological order, this book explains the sequence of events that shaped alternative theater and suggests a line of influence among the most creative people in theater at that time. Accurate and complete.

McGrath, John. "The Theory and Practice of Political Theatre." *Theatre Quarterly* 35 (Autumn, 1979): 43-54. McGrath's own article is the best theoretical discussion of 7:84's goals and ambitions. McGrath explains these theories simply and elegantly.

MacLennan, Elizabeth. *The Moon Belongs to Everyone: Making Theatre with 7:84.* London: Methuen, 1990. Heartwarming and informative, this book records the commitment and will of an entire family to the fulfillment of a dream. Especially valuable are MacLennan's details about the history of the 7:84 Theatre Company and the battle to keep it afloat financially once the Conservative government had targeted it for cuts. Most memorable are MacLennan's accounts of caring for the family while handling their many crises through many months on the road.

Page, Malcolm. "John McGrath: NTQ Checklist Number One." *New Theatre Quarterly* 4 (November, 1985): 400-416. This bibliography is the place to begin serious research on McGrath and the 7:84 Theatre Company. It includes not only a brief chronology of McGrath's career and an annotated list of his plays up to 1985 but also an impressive catalog of the major articles written about McGrath and select reviews of his plays.

Van Erven, Eugene. *Radical People's Theatre.* Bloomington: Indiana University Press, 1988. Covers popular theater around the world and uses the

7:84 Theatre Company to represent Great Britain. Especially good at providing a larger context for the theater company's politics and practices.

Reade W. Dornan

EDUARDO MACHADO

Born: Havana, Cuba; June 11, 1953

Principal drama

Worms, pr. 1981; *Rosario and the Gypsies*, pr. 1982 (one-act musical; book and lyrics by Machado, music by Rick Vartoreila); *The Modern Ladies of Guanabacoa*, pr., pb. 1983; *There's Still Time to Dance in the Streets of Rio*, pr. 1983; *Broken Eggs*, pr., pb. 1984; *Fabiola*, pr. 1985, pb. 1991; *When It's Over*, pr. 1987 (with Geraldine Sherman); *Why to Refuse*, pr. 1987 (one act); *A Burning Beach*, pr. 1988; *Don Juan in New York*, pr. 1988 (two-act musical); *Once Removed*, pr., pb. 1988; *Wishing You Well*, pr. 1988 (one-act musical); *Cabaret Bambu*, pr. 1989 (one-act musical); *The Day You Love Me*, pr. 1989 (translation of the play by José Ignacio Cabrujas); *Related Retreats*, pr. 1990; *Stevie Wants to Play the Blues*, pr. 1990 (two-act musical); *The Floating Island Plays*, pb. 1991 (includes *The Modern Ladies of Guanabacoa*, *Fabiola*, *In the Eye of the Hurricane*, and *Broken Eggs*); *In the Eye of the Hurricane*, pr., pb. 1991; *1979*, pr. 1991; *Breathing It In*, pr. 1993.

Other literary forms

Eduardo Machado is known primarily for his plays.

Achievements

Machado is in the vanguard of a generation of playwrights who, having immigrated with their families from various countries of Latin America, give voice to the experience of Latino displacement in North America. His best-known works are family dramas that chronicle the experiences of well-to-do Cubans as they awake to their betrayal by Fidel Castro's revolution, prepare for an exodus from the homeland, arrive in and adjust to the "new world," and reach their ultimate destinies. Machado dramatizes outward from the microcosmic domestic world to encompass the historical sweep of great social movements. His plays capture onstage the critical point at which momentous political events intersect with and influence intimate family crises. In so doing, he breaks iconoclastically with traditional dramatic form, attempting to lift naturalistic situations to a level of heightened theatrical poetry that may be called symphonic tragicomedy, synthesizing innovations of such precursors as Anton Chekhov, Federico García Lorca, and María Irene Fornés. Machado has received three National Endowment for the Arts Fellowships for playwriting (1981, 1983, 1986), a Rockefeller Foundation Fellowship (1985), and a Dorothy Chandler Pavilion Viva Los Artistas Award (1992).

Biography

Eduardo Machado was born in Havana, Cuba, on June 11, 1953, the son of Othon Eduardo and Gilda (Hernandez) Machado. He was reared in the coastal town of Cojimar, in a large villa full of various relatives. His family members were of the class of landed businesspeople, and his father lived a life of leisure while residing in Cuba. Later, after immigrating to the United States, his father became an accountant. His grandfather owned a bus company. Machado attended a Catholic boys' school in Guanabacoa, six miles from home, until the age of eight, when his family, fearing the radical social changes that Castro was implementing, sent him and his four-year-old brother to live with an aunt and uncle in Miami, Florida. Despite the boys' inability to speak English, they were immediately enrolled in an English-speaking public school. One year later, their parents followed them to Florida, and they soon resettled in Canoga Park, California, located in the San Fernando Valley, close to Los Angeles. He attended Van Nuys High School, then college for about four months, before going on to acting school.

Machado came to playwriting indirectly, first indulging an interest in acting, although at the age of twenty he managed a stage production of García Lorca's *La casa de Bernarda Alba* (pr., pb. 1945; *The House of Bernarda Alba*, 1947) at C. Bernard Jackson's Inner City Cultural Center in Los Angeles. His interest in acting led him to roles in plays by Fernando Arrabal, Bertolt Brecht, Franz Xaver Kroetz, and John Steppling at the Beverly Hills Playhouse, the Ensemble Studio Theatre, and the Padua Hills Playwrights Festival. It was at the latter that he first met Fornés, who was giving workshops in playwriting. He first became her assistant for her production of her own play *Fefu and Her Friends* (pr. 1977). Intuiting Machado's interest in playwriting, Fornés invited him to participate in a workshop. Fornés, also an expatriate Cuban, became the single most influential force on his writing style and philosophy of theater. Machado followed her to New York, where he performed in her play *A Visit*, in 1982.

Machado started writing in 1980, and his first play, *Worms*, was given a reading at Ensemble Studio Theatre West in 1981. His subsequent plays were staged Off-Off-Broadway and in regional productions in rapid succession, appearing in such theaters as Ensemble Studio Theatre, Theatre for the New City, Duo Theatre, Downtown Arts Company, and the American Place in New York; the Long Wharf Theatre in New Haven; the Mark Taper Forum and the Los Angeles Theatre Center in Los Angeles; the Actors Theatre of Louisville; the New Mexico Repertory; Stage One in Dallas; and the Magic Theatre in San Francisco. Several works were also mounted in Spanish translation at the Repertorio Español.

Machado married a Jewish social worker in 1972 at the age of nineteen and was divorced in 1989. His parents were divorced when Machado was twenty-one, and his father remarried soon after, an unusual occurrence among conservative Cubans. Machado lived bicoastally for many years but after his divorce settled in New York City. He is a flamboyant figure who likes grand public gestures; an example is when he noisily submitted his resignation from Ensemble Studio Theatre in protest against its proclivity for naturalism. His plays *Broken Eggs*, *Fabiola*, *In the Eye of the Hurricane*, and *The Modern Ladies of Guanabacoa* were published together by Theatre Communications Group under the title *The Floating Island Plays.*

Analysis

The four plays that form the Floating Island series represent the core of Eduardo Machado's oeuvre. These four plays depict the sequence of events that led members of the Cuban upper classes from complacent hegemony in their native land to exile and displacement in the United States. They depict key incidents in the lives of disparate members of the Marquez/Ripoll/Hernandez clan as they attempt to adapt to the cataclysmal changes that rain down on Cuba. It may be surmised that these families represent persons about whom Machado heard through family mythology (and whom he then embroidered) and family members whom he actually knew. Some characters, such as Oscar in *Broken Eggs*, could have been drawn from Machado himself.

The first play of the Floating Island series, *The Modern Ladies of Guanabacoa*, chronicles the Ripoll family in the years 1928 through 1931. While showing the romantic and sexual intrigues that beset the family, especially the leitmotif of sexual infidelity, Machado depicts in the background the first seeds of the social dissolution that would bear fruit in the later plays. Manuela, the young lady of the house, is being courted by Oscar Hernandez, a young man from a socially inferior household. Having survived a seven-year engagement with a fiancé who died, she is now considered "used goods" and undesirable by men of her station. Once Oscar and Manuela have fulfilled the proper steps of courtship and are married, Oscar wastes no time parlaying investments of his in-laws' money into a successful bus company, of which he becomes the head and through which he succeeds in displacing and marginalizing Manuela's brothers, the rightful heirs to the fortune, both of whom lack Oscar's drive and will. In an echo of Chekhovian drama, Oscar, like the merchant Lopakhin in *Vishnyovy sad* (pr., pb. 1904; *The Cherry Orchard*, 1908), benefits from the decadence of the upper classes and hoists himself up the social scale at their expense.

Ripoll, Sr., Arturo, is a prosperous merchant who is prodigally using up the family fortune and his respectable name in a long-term, flaunted romantic liaison. In the play's climax, he is shot offstage, probably by his mistress' enraged husband. Oscar takes advantage of this turn of events to gain control of the family fortune and take a mistress for himself even as his wife, Manuela, is expecting a baby. Arturo's and Oscar's accepted adultery is juxtaposed with that of Adelita, Manuela's sister-in-law, who is viciously censured by the family for her infidelity to Ernesto. The prevailing sexual double standard for men and women in Cuban society is also reflected in the smaller daily rituals and mores among the Ripolls. Even as Manuela is straining to be more modern (and more American) by smoking, wearing low-cut dresses, and cutting her hair short, she and her mother still wait hand and foot on her two weak, pampered brothers, Ernesto and Mario. Whereas Maria Josefa, the family matriarch, agrees not to notice or mention her husband's unfaithfulness, all the family members complain vociferously about Adelita's conduct. In fact, the play is a compendium of the ceremonies that form their life together and to which they all cling as known safe reality—ceremonies of courtship, adultery, eating, social hierarchy, and skin color. The Ripolls have a way of rating suitors according to the amount of Spanish as opposed to mulatto and Indian blood reflected in an individual's skin color. It is significant that Oscar, who gains economic ascendancy in the end, has a darker skin than the Ripolls, who boast of their Basque, European heritage.

The dialogue of *The Modern Ladies of Guanabacoa* is written in a typical Machado rhythm—short percussive lines that are reminiscent of Fornés. His scenes often turn, as do those of Chekhov, on secrets that remain unspoken even as the characters weave a verbal skein of inessentials—food, servants, styles, and etiquette. Every so often a character will burst out with an unmediated, coarse exclamation that expresses the feelings that lurk at a primitive level and that the proper surface of discourse is meant to hold in check.

Fabiola, the next play of the series, switches over to the Marquez family. Sonia Hernandez, a major character in *Fabiola* and presumably the daughter of Oscar and Manuela, the characters from *The Modern Ladies of Guanabacoa* (who do not appear in *Fabiola*), has married into the Marquez family. *Fabiola* gives the impression of greater passage of time, spanning the years 1955 to 1967, and is divided into six scenes. It encompasses the years of Castro's rise to power through his takeover and eventual embracing of Soviet-style Communism. The Marquez family, prosperous factory owners, at first enthusiastically back Castro with money and strategy, since he promises to stand up to the North American giant that has made of Cuba a puppet under Fulgencio Batista. Although they cheer when Castro takes Havana, they never count on having to make further sacrifices for the revolution. Castro's gradual conversion to Communism ultimately forces them to flee Cuba in small groups, and in the last scene, they are made to vacate their home altogether and hand it over to the government.

In typical Machado fashion, the political action erupts onto the main action at first mutedly, as the lady of the house, Cusa, a sworn expert in the coming revolution, intently follows Castro's progress over the radio. Octavio, a cousin, intrudes at one moment, with his fingernails mutilated following a torture session by Batista's thugs. Ultimately, Castro's *milicianos* swarm through the house, triumphantly ordering about their social superiors. Machado furthermore epitomizes the brewing social transformation in the person of Sara, a servant. Sara is humiliated in the first act by a sister-in-law, Clara, a figure reminiscent of Natasha from Chekhov's *Tri sestry* (pr., pb. 1901; *Three Sisters*, 1920), who spits in the loyal servant's face. This same servant joins the revolution and, in a tense scene in the second act, refuses to aid the family, much to their surprise, since they had always considered her a family member and were blissfully oblivious to the inequities implicit in the master-servant arrangement.

In the play's foreground, once again, is a web of interpersonal conflicts among family members. Most prominent is the covert sexual relationship between the two Marquez brothers, Osvaldo and Pedro. Pedro's wife, Fabiola, has died before the curtain rises, and her body has mysteriously vanished from the crypt. Pedro, in reaction, is drinking heavily and enters a downhill spiral, which ends only in the play's denouement, his suicide. He proposes to his married brother Osvaldo that they pick up where they left off with the sexual play in which they engaged when they were children. Osvaldo at first eludes him but then succumbs, and they have a protracted liaison, ending only with Osvaldo's immigration to the United States, his absence leaving Pedro bereft and serving as a catalyst for his total disintegration.

The brothers' incestuous relationship is played off against the other characters of the play: their father, Alfredo, who, like Arturo in *The Modern Ladies of Guanabacoa*, is having a long-term illicit relationship; their mother, Cusa, who takes refuge in politics and superstition; their high-spirited sister Miriam, who is enduring the clumsy wooing of the stiff Raulito and who ultimately consents to marry him against her better judgment; and Sonya, Osvaldo's wife, whose struggle is essentially intrapersonal, as she longs unrequitedly to fulfill herself intellectually and make an impact on the world. Sonya suffers both from the marginality of living in Cuba and from the sense of her own uselessness in relation to a world in turmoil. She recalls, yet again, the Chekhovian archetype of the frustrated aristocrat who yearns for a self-significance never to be achieved.

Machado symphonically juggles the mosaic of characters, combining and recombining their encounters in brief two- and three-character scenes. The first act essentially focuses on the two Marquez brothers, whose cat-and-mouse game of attraction is repeatedly interrupted by intrusions from others but then is ultimately consummated as the curtain falls. Again, Machado's characters are aware of, but avoid discussing, the major issues that preoccupy them all: Osvaldo and Pedro's illicit relationship, one that everyone apparently knows about but that no one will openly discuss; Alfredo's kept woman; the growing dread of the family's exclusion from Cuban life; and Pedro's alcoholism and incipient disintegration. All these issues are swept under the carpet in a froth of music, dancing, fun, frolic, and, in the case of Cusa, political fanaticism.

The figure of Fabiola, the dead woman whose body at first disappears and then stubbornly refuses to decompose, stands for the dying aristocracy. She is decadence incarnate, and she literally haunts the house, causing records to start and curtains to flutter and preoccupying Pedro and all the others.

The action of *In the Eye of the Hurricane*, the third play in the series, is contemporaneous with that of *Fabiola*, occurring in the aftermath of Castro's rise to power. Built on a leaner, more linear crisis-drama structure than the sprawling, intricate *Fabiola*, it returns to the Hernandez and Ripoll families, now at the time of the Castro uprising. Oscar Hernandez is head of the prospering bus company and is assisted by his wife, Manuela. Oscar has long ago deprived Manuela's brother, Mario, of his portion of the family wealth, and the latter now lives a dependent and subservient life with them. Maria Josefa, Mario and Manuela's mother, a severe woman and the repository of all the old values and manners, lives with them as well. The first act hinges on two unspeakable secrets that pierce the surface and dominate the action of the second act: The first is a letter that has arrived informing the family that Castro is planning to confiscate their buses, and the second is the news that Maria Josefa is dying. The play opens with Manuela speaking of safety as something to which to cling for dear life. Her mother rejoins that feeling safe is "the first step to violence and death." Defiant and in denial, the family goes on as though nothing un-usual were in the wind; indeed, the spoiled daughter of the house, Sonia, is picking out a fancy sportscar at the very moment the *milicianos* appear with the confiscation order.

The two strands, the confiscation of the buses and the death of Maria Josefa, intersect in a curious fashion at the play's climax. This particular scene admirably illustrates Machado's tragicomic, ironic method at its most typical. Manuela and Oscar instruct their entourage to lie down in front of the buses to prevent Castro's men from taking the vehicles. Their unswerv-ing certainty that they will save their property begins to crumble as many bus drivers disobey their orders and go out on their normal routes, only to have their buses swiped out from under them. Those who remain on the premises do an about-face and refuse to lie down in front of the buses, with the exception of one loyal employee, Fulgencio, who caves in at the first sign of trouble. The crowd that the family called together to protest the *milicianos'* confiscation turns instead on the Hernandez family, who had oppressed them for decades, and chant rhythmically for the *milicianos* to go ahead and take the buses. In heroic desperation, Manuela and Oscar lie down in front of their buses, but the *milicianos* put them into reverse, a direction that the two had not anticipated, and drive them off, leaving their owners farcically lying on the ground.

Manuela tries to throw a lit cigarette into the motor of one departing bus but is restrained by Mario, who betrays his hated brother-in-law and shows himself fully prepared to go to work for Castro. Mario uses the social upheaval as an opportunity to correct the injustice perpetrated within the family. During the scene's greatest intensity, the old lady, Maria Josefa, comes back to life, again symbolic of the indomitable spirit of these proud, tenacious people. This crucial scene presents an occasion to reveal the family's courage and foolishness, their arrogance and blindness to the false premises on which their economic ascendancy rests.

The fourth play of the Floating Island series, *Broken Eggs*, is the most unremittingly comedic. Set in 1979 in Los Angeles, it shows what has become of the clan once transplanted to North America. The occasion is the wedding of Lizette, the young Americanized daughter, who is trying to leave her Latin roots behind her by marrying the scion of a Jewish family, the Rifkins. The setting is a waiting room of a "wedding mill," offstage so to speak from the main action—the wedding and banquet proper.

The family structure and traditional roles have now totally crumbled. Osvaldo (the same character from *Fabiola*, now middle-aged) has done the unthinkable: He was divorced from his wife, Sonya. He is now married to an Argentine woman whom they all hate. Their son, Oscar, is a homosexual and a cocaine addict. Osvaldo's sister Miriam, also from *Fabiola*, is a freewheeling alcoholic. Sonya's mother, Manuela, is stolidly and ineffectually still holding the line of the old traditions, just as her predecessor, Maria Josefa of *The Modern Ladies of Guanabacoa* did fifty years earlier, but with even less success. Looking back on the trajectory of all four plays, it is clear that once the "modern ladies" started smoking, the family's ultimate debacle was inevitably laid out for it.

Sonya's ultimately futile attempt to win back her wayward husband constitutes the main action of *Broken Eggs*. In the meantime, the comic preparations for the wedding and the way they go dizzyingly awry rip across the stage in a parade of quick scenic encounters. Whatever should not happen does: The Argentine wife shows up and the Cuban family members taunt her, to their in-laws' consternation; they get drunk and high respectively and hurl home truths at one another; and, as comic debacle, they run out of wedding cake and scurry to cut smaller pieces and give away their own slices to the Rifkins. *Broken Eggs*, the title of which represents the fate of the family victimized by the revolution and the saying "You can't make an omelette without breaking a few eggs," dramatizes the final gasp of the Cuban dynasty's grandeur and the varied choices the family members have made in California—assimilation, dissolution, and clutching the final vestiges of a dead tradition.

Though not part of the Floating Island series, *Once Removed* is very much in keeping with Machado's theme of displaced Cubans. This work depicts a Cuban family summarily wrenched from their dignified existence in their homeland and dropped in an anonymous motel room in Hialeah, a place best known (as they ruefully remark) for dog races. *Once Removed* differs from the Floating Island plays chiefly for its pronounced boulevard tendencies. More than the other Machado plays, it is a well-made, Broadway-style comedy, full of one-liners about the Spam (canned meat) that the family is forced to ingest in a thousand different forms.

Also about Cuba, but a Cuba of the more remote past—the end of the nineteenth century—is *A Burning Beach*. It allegorically depicts the point in history during the Spanish-American War at which Cuba was wrested from Spain's domination and placed under American puppet rule. A jaunty American woman, Constance Buchanan, niece of one "Theodore" (who is meant to represent Theodore Roosevelt, hero of San Juan Hill), arrives at the home of a wealthy Cuban family. Although ostensibly a guest, she quickly shifts into business mode, figuratively seducing Ofelia, the maiden-lady who is also the head of the house, and negotiating for the family's profitable sugar plantation. Constance succeeds in gaining hegemony, although the interracial son of the family, Juan, encounters the apparition of the liberator José Martí on the beach and swears to regain Cuba for Cubans. *A Burning Beach* is entirely schematic in its austere treatment of historical metaphor, and so it is a stylistic departure for Machado.

Machado leaves his immigrant theme behind with such major works as *Stevie Wants to Play the Blues*, a musical about a female singer who transforms herself into a man, and *Don Juan in New York*, which is chiefly about sexual ambivalence in the age of acquired immune deficiency syndrome (AIDS). The latter play, a work that is operatic in scope and amplitude, centers on D. J. (Don Juan), an experimental-film maker, as a retrospective of his work is planned and executed. Apparently bisexual, D. J. is torn between a female singer-celebrity, Flora, and his trashy male lover, Steve. His conflict is enacted against the backdrop of the AIDS epidemic: D. J.'s good friend, Paul, a female impersonator, has taken refuge in the guise of Carol Channing and is preparing first for a concert of Channing's songs and subsequently for a successful suicide, as he eludes the depredations of AIDS. The baroque action is further complicated by actual film clips from D. J.'s creations and by passionate songs performed by two mysterious figures, Abuelo and Mujer, representatives of the world of traditional heterosexual love for which the classic Don Juan was known.

Machado has called *Stevie Wants to Play the Blues* a "gender-bender," a genre in which he examines premises about sexuality and takes the characters through surprising and unconventional revelations about their gender identifications. Other plays in which he toys with the notion of sexual identity are *Related Retreats,* about the lives of writers at an arts colony under the tutelage of a female guru, and *Breathing It In*, about a motley band of lost souls who congregate around a male/female guru couple who espouse the individual's embracing the woman-nature within. It at once satirizes cults such as Werner Erhard's individual, social transformation technique (EST) and the women's liberation movement of the 1970's and 1980's, and concocts a string of variations on sexual transformation among its characters.

Machado has most articulately woven a latter-day Chekhovian theater out of his and his family's experience of the Cuban Revolution. He has explored its dimensions in various styles. His forays into other subjects, such as AIDS and sexual ambivalence, are equally evocative. Machado succeeds in giving events of epic sweep a human face, without reducing their scale, and in daring to strive for fresh dramatic solutions to equally virgin thematic ground.

Bibliography

Feingold, Michael. "Hersterics." Review of *Breathing It In. The Village Voice* (February 16, 1993): 97. Comparing this play with *Five Women Wearing the Same Dress* (pr. 1993) by Alan Ball, Feingold writes that "'Machado's text, which veers from sharply intelligent debate to the rankest drivel, alternately delves into abstract ideas and wallows in sensual impulses." He criticizes what he calls Machado's "uncertainty of tone" and compares this work unfavorably with the earlier Floating Island plays.

_____. Review of *The Modern Ladies of Guanabacoa. The Village Voice* (February 1, 1983): 95-96. Discusses the play as a fusion of "domestic travails as fused with politics" in which Machado "uses the position of women as a locus for examining the whole social structure."

Henry, William A., III. "Visions from the Past: Emerging Playwrights Trade Anger for Dialogue." *Time*, July 11, 1988, 82-83. Part of an extensive, multipart section entitled "Hispanic Culture Breaks Out of the Barrio." Selects María Irene Fornés, Carlos Morton, Reinaldo Pavod, Milcha Sanchez Scott, and Machado as examples of the new wave of mainstream-bound Latino playwrights and designates Machado as "perhaps the most gifted" of the group. Quotes him as saying, "I was the first Hispanic playwright in America to write about upper-class people," a fact he blames for his difficulty in being performed by Hispanic theaters. Includes a flashy photograph of Machado.

Machado, Eduardo. "Addressing a Cultural Chasm." Interview by Robert Koehler. *Los Angeles Times*. January 28, 1989, pp. 7-8. In this interview,

Machado explains why Latin immigrant theater cannot be linear in the same way as "Anglo, capitalist" plays.

Madison, Cathy. "Writing Home." *American Theatre*, October, 1991, 36-40. An interview with Machado and other emerging American playwrights, including Suzan-Lori Parks, Christopher Durang, Ping Chong, and Migdalia Cruz. Contains a photograph of Machado.

Mirabella, Alan. "Write Where He Belongs." *New York Daily News*, November 6, 1988, p. 5. Interweaves interview and accounts of upcoming productions of *A Burning Beach*, directed by Rene Buch, at the American Place Theatre, and *Don Juan in New York*, directed by David Willinger, at Theatre for the New City. A full-page article with a photographic montage of Machado's earlier productions.

Rich, Frank. Review of *Once Removed. The New York Times*, December 7, 1992, p. 53. A favorable review of John Tillinger's production at the Long Wharf Theatre in New Haven. Calls this play his most polished one, replete with "wit and assurance," and compares Machado to Terrence McNally.

David Willinger

ARCHIBALD MacLEISH

Born: Glencoe, Illinois; May 7, 1892
Died: Boston, Massachusetts; April 20, 1982

Principal drama

The Pot of Earth, pb. 1925; *Nobodaddy: A Play*, pb. 1926; *Panic: A Play in Verse*, pr., pb. 1935; *The Fall of the City: A Verse Play for Radio*, pr., pb. 1937; *Air Raid: A Verse Play for Radio*, pr., pb. 1938; *The Trojan Horse: A Play*, pr. 1952 (broadcast), pb. 1952, pr. 1953 (staged); *This Music Crept by Me upon the Waters*, pr., pb. 1953 (one act); *J.B.: A Play in Verse*, pr., pb. 1958; *Herakles: A Play in Verse*, pr. 1965, pb. 1967; *Scratch*, pr., pb. 1971 (inspired by Stephen Vincent Benét's short story "The Devil and Daniel Webster"); *Six Plays*, pb. 1980.

Other literary forms

Critics concerned with the achievements of Archibald MacLeish unite in warning literary taxonomists against differentiating between his work as poet and as dramatist, for with only one exception, all his plays are composed in verse. Nevertheless, his poetic dramas form a group that can be considered separately from his poetry. Indeed, MacLeish's output in both genres is considerable; of the three Pulitzer Prizes he received, two were awarded for his poems.

As early as 1917, MacLeish published his collection of verse *Tower of Ivory*, bringing together his undergraduate efforts from his years at Yale, detached poems derivative in both tone and technique of the powerful nineteenth century British Romantic lyric tradition. The volume is significant, however, for introducing MacLeish's ubiquitous artistic themes: human beings' relation to God and the reality of human existence. No more of his poetry appeared until 1924, when *The Happy Marriage* was published. Here, MacLeish appears more influenced by the Metaphysical poets of the seventeenth century, and here he experimented with a number of more complex verse forms as well as with the difficulties inherent in paradox. Two other works of the 1920's, *The Pot of Earth* and *Nobodaddy*, have been included variously in discussions of either MacLeish's poetry or drama. In truth, they are embryonic verse plays, despite the author's reference to them as poems; since they prefigure and resemble his fully developed plays, they should be included with that genre.

After continued exclusive attention to poetry, especially during his sojourn in France, MacLeish received his first major recognition as a poet for *Conquistador* (1932), a powerful lyric and descriptive epic in free terza rima form. Chronicling the heroic exploits of Hernando Cortés, as seen through the eyes of a Spanish soldier, the narrative poem was awarded the

1933 Pulitzer Prize for poetry. MacLeish had personally visited Mexico in 1929, retracing by mule and on foot the route of the sixteenth century Spanish explorer and conqueror of Montezuma's Aztec empire. The poem expresses the ultimate hollowness of heroism, as both adversaries, Cortés and Montezuma, fall victim to corruption. Only the majestic landscape remains, the scene of monumental waste and loss.

Yet another facet of MacLeish's talent became evident in 1934, for then the poet was librettist for a ballet, *Union Pacific*, celebrating the completion of the transcontinental railroad in 1869. A resounding critical and artistic success, the ballet was performed in New York and on extensive tours in both the United States and Europe by the Ballet Russe de Monte Carlo company, providing the rapidly maturing writer with his first experience on the professional stage.

Escapism into a more joyous and optimistic past was not, however, MacLeish's primary artistic thrust in the increasingly troubled 1930's, a decade which marked the poet's increased concern with social and political issues and his recognition of both the rapidly developing crisis in Europe and the infiltration into the United States of foreign ideologies, particularly Marxism. To give voice to his fears for America's ability to withstand these threats, MacLeish turned to prose, and by the time of World War II, he had published a number of volumes of patriotic political essays; among the most influential was *A Time to Speak* (1941), followed by *A Time to Act* in 1943.

Since the early days of Franklin D. Roosevelt's New Deal, MacLeish had been an editor of *Fortune* magazine, using that journalistic forum to express his views on contemporary issues. Wartime public service claimed most of his creative energies, and it was not until 1948 that his next collection of poetry, *Actfive and Other Poems*, appeared. Although written as a play in three scenes and using the language of stagecraft, "Actfive" is usually considered a poem, one expressing disillusionment with American politics in action, for MacLeish had believed very strongly in Roosevelt's idealistic program for economic and social reforms.

In 1950, the first of MacLeish's two theoretical analyses of poetry appeared, *Poetry and Opinion*, followed eleven years later by *Poetry and Experience* (1961). In these essay collections, MacLeish expanded on his theories of "private" and "public" poetic worlds, extending his classroom work as a professor at Harvard to a larger reading audience. As if being a literary essayist, poet, playwright, and journalist were not challenge enough, MacLeish at this time in his career also wrote several screenplays and television scripts and innumerable contributions to periodicals both in the United States and abroad. In 1966, he won an Academy Award for Best Feature Documentary for his 1965 screenplay *The Eleanor Roosevelt Story*.

Achievements

Throughout his long and distinguished career, MacLeish's seemingly un-limited energies were spent in an amazingly broad range of activities directed at the reconciliation of literature and public service, far more so than any other modern American poet. He was an indefatigable lecturer in halls and on university campuses throughout the United States, exemplify-ing his informing belief that artists cannot indulge themselves by retreating exclusively to a private "tower of ivory" (the title of his first poetry collec-tion), but must use their "gifts" (the title of his first published poem) by addressing themselves to current public issues in the larger world in which they all live.

In both his prose and poetry, MacLeish drew on his wide-ranging intel-lectual and aesthetic resources to recast the American legacy of myth, his-tory, and folklore into powerful and moving parables for troubled times. The British critic John Wain has observed that "MacLeish . . . has certainly made it a central part of his business to 'manipulate a continuous parallel' between the immemorial and the modern." This tendency is most evident in MacLeish's verse drama, and it is here that his achievement in twentieth century American literature is most significant. Until the appearance of *J.B.*, there had been little work of any importance in this genre, and the success of this monumental epic of philosophic rationalism encouraged oth-ers to explore new possibilities for poetic drama.

The popularity and critical acclaim earned by MacLeish's exemplary *J.B.* proves that he not only mastered the techniques of stagecraft, but also, and more important, created a responsive, humanistic, yet classically theatrical work that speaks to common experience while at the same time engaging each member of his audience personally. In an age geared to mass audi-ences and noncontroversial, often mindless yet commercially successful pro-ductions, MacLeish's courage in refusing to compromise his beliefs and val-ues is remarkable in itself.

Biography

The son of upper-middle-class parents, Archibald MacLeish was born in 1892 in Glencoe, Illinois, where he attended grammar school. His father, a Scotchman, was a prosperous department-store executive whose wealth allowed his son the privilege of a preparatory-school education at Hotch-kiss School before his entrance into Yale University, where he took a B.A. degree in 1915. His mother, his father's third wife, was graduated from and taught at Vassar College and, before the birth of the poet, was president of Rockford College in Illinois. The young MacLeish was active in both lit-erary and athletic groups at Yale, and was elected to Phi Beta Kappa his junior year.

He enlisted for military duty in World War I, entering as a private in an army hospital unit and serving as a volunteer ambulance driver. After transferral to the artillery, he saw active duty at the front in France; he was discharged in 1918 with the rank of captain. In 1916, he married his childhood sweetheart, Ada Hitchcock, a singer. Four children were born to the couple, although one son died in childhood. After the war, he returned to Harvard Law School, which he had attended briefly before his military service. He taught government there for a year after he was graduated first in his class in 1919. Although avidly concerned with his developing poetic career, he practiced three years with a prestigious law firm in Boston.

By 1923, MacLeish had decided to give up the law, despite his election as a member of the firm. With his wife and children, he left for a five-year sojourn in France and Persia, and there he cultivated his artistic taste and talents by steeping himself in French literary culture. He also associated with the coterie of American expatriates then in Paris, among them Gertrude Stein, Ezra Pound, and Ernest Hemingway. MacLeish, however, had no intention of leaving his homeland permanently, and in 1929, he and his family returned, settling in the small New England village of Conway, Massachusetts, where the poet lived as a "gentleman farmer" for the rest of his life.

During these formative years abroad, the years MacLeish considered "the beginning of my more or less adult life," he matured rapidly as a poet and began to gain an audience for his work as well as critical acclaim. To support his family after his return, he joined the editorial board of *Fortune*, a new business magazine, work which brought him into intimate contact with influential leaders of business and government. This position provided him with a sense of focus for his increasingly liberal views concerning the destiny of the United States during the New Deal years of the Great Depression and the eve of global war.

In 1939, after holding office as the first curator of the Neiman Collection of Contemporary Journalism at Harvard, MacLeish accepted his first position in public life, serving as Librarian of Congress until 1944. During the early war years, he also was a director of various branches of governmental information services, and spoke and wrote effectively about the crucial issues of the day. In 1944-1945, he served as Assistant Secretary of State. After the war, he was one of the founders of the United Nations Educational Scientific and Cultural Organization (UNESCO) and, in 1946, was chairman of the American delegation at its first conference in Paris.

In 1949, MacLeish accepted an appointment as Boylston Professor of Rhetoric and Oratory at Harvard, holding this honored position until his retirement in 1962. In 1953, he received for *Collected Poems, 1917-1952* his second Pulitzer Prize for Poetry, and he was elected president of the American Academy of Arts and Letters. In 1959, he received another Pulitzer Prize for his verse drama *J.B.*, and in 1963, was named Simpson Lecturer at Amherst College, remaining there for four years.

Less than a month before his ninetieth birthday, MacLeish died in a Boston hospital. Even in the final months of his life, he was actively engaged in both writing and granting interviews, continuing to express both his unquenchable passion for art and his concern for justice.

Analysis

A critic observed in 1910 that "we cannot expect a rebirth of the poetic drama until our poets turn playwrights"; such an extended generic transition is obvious in the career of Archibald MacLeish. After publishing two early volumes of verse, he wrote two embryonic verse plays in the mid-1920's, *The Pot of Earth* and *Nobodaddy*, works often regarded as long poems. MacLeish himself included *The Pot of Earth* in his first anthology, *Poems, 1924-1933* (1933). All of this creative output resulted from his five-year sojourn in Paris.

Its title taken from William Blake's derisory name for the Old Testament God of vengeance and mystery, *Nobodaddy* was written before *The Pot of Earth* but published a year after it. A short philosophical verse play in three acts, sometimes classed as a poetic essay or closet drama, *Nobodaddy* treats the Genesis story of the first family and prefigures MacLeish's use in *J.B.* of modernized Old Testament material to illuminate universal human dilemmas. In *Nobodaddy*, Cain and Abel struggle as adversaries, representing the conflict between the independent mind and the dogma of orthodoxy, a theme to which the poet would return in *J.B.*, three decades later.

The Pot of Earth is also significant as a precursor of *J.B.*, for here too MacLeish used ancient myth as a vehicle for suggesting a reinterpretation of values—in this case Sir James Frazer's description, in *The Golden Bough*, of fertility rites in the garden of Adonis as a metaphor for the disillusionment of a representative human being. In a series of dramatic scenes, an anonymous modern young girl realizes the lack of meaning and lack of free will in her existence as she, like the mythic symbolic plants, rapidly grows to sexual maturity, marries, reproduces, and dies, sacrificed in the endless pattern of ruthless natural forces directed by an indifferent and invisible Gardener, a figure previously evoked in *Nobodaddy*. Technically, *The Pot of Earth* offers evidence of MacLeish's mastery of a variety of verse patterns and other techniques of prosody such as complex assonance and alliteration, and has often been compared to T. S. Eliot's *The Waste Land*, which was published three years earlier. The two works do resemble each other in their mythic basis, although MacLeish's work is far more conservative stylistically; each emphasizes, in a manner typical of the 1920's, the transience of life.

Returning to poetry, including *Conquistador*, MacLeish did not attempt drama for another decade, when *Panic* appeared. Together with two half-hour radio scripts provoked by MacLeish's concern for the seeming indifference of Americans toward the threatening world crisis, these plays were his only dramatic work until 1952, and they demonstrate the poet's exploration of the "underlying reality" beneath surface events. Shortly before his death, MacLeish recalled that he had "never seen anything that even remotely approached the misery and anguish and horror of the Great Depression"; this dark epoch in America's history was the background for *Panic*, his first play performed in a theater.

As in all of his poetry and prose during this period, MacLeish's theme in *Panic* is a warning against mindless acceptance of authoritarianism, and a reminder of the threat to personal freedom in time of crisis. Here, the protagonist, McGafferty, a powerful and wealthy New York industrialist and financier, finds himself at the height of the American financial crisis, in February, 1933, elevated beyond his leadership abilities by the blind fear of those who look to him as their savior. These people, including his bank colleagues and the poor unemployed, perish; in the end, in the classical tradition, McGafferty perishes helplessly along with them. The play, which has been seen as a hybrid—both Aristotelian tragedy and proletarian drama—drew heavily on the then voguish expressionist techniques. MacLeish was encouraged by the play's acceptance: When both workers and the unemployed responded enthusiastically, MacLeish stated, "Now I have found my audience."

This period piece of the Depression is highly significant in MacLeish's dramaturgic development, for in *Panic*, he experimented with a new verse form, accentual meter, responsive to the contemporary American speech rhythms. He continued to use this form, and not the popular blank verse, in all of his subsequent plays, with one exception, the prose *Scratch*. Briefly, accentual meter is a type of sprung rhythm; rather than counting syllables, one counts the number of stresses or accented syllables in a line. MacLeish's choice was a combination of five-accent lines (but unlimited syllables) and three-beat lines, both to underline conflict inherent in his plots and to avoid monotony.

MacLeish's two vivid half-hour radio dramas in verse, *The Fall of the City* and *Air Raid*, followed his next poetry collection. Along with *Panic*, all three of his verse plays of the 1930's were evidence of his "public" poetry, generalizations of philosophical truths about human behavior focused on timely political issues. In the radio plays, which featured a collective protagonist, the seductive dangers of rampant totalitarianism as well as isolationism were presented by expressionist techniques. *The Fall of the City*, broadcast on the Columbia Broadcasting System (CBS) in 1937, included in its published version a foreword in which the playwright remarked upon the effectiveness of radio for the presentation of verse drama to attract large audiences, claiming that "the imagination works better through the ear than through the eye." Here, MacLeish recalls that poetry is meant primarily to be heard, and thereby to stimulate the undistracted "word-excited imagination" into evocation of the depicted action. The advent of television eclipsed radio presentations of this sort, however, and MacLeish's advocacy came to little, as graphically visualized action rapidly captured popular taste.

In MacLeish's play *The Fall of the City*, the disembodied voice of an Announcer (as in classic Expressionism, the characters lack personal names) objectively and dispassionately describes the collapse and destruction of a metropolis. A demoralized and terrified population has mindlessly refused to defend itself against the attack of the Conqueror, who promised a strong leadership for which they are willing to sacrifice personal freedom ("Freedom's for fools: Force is the certainty!"). The more digressive *Air Raid* does not exemplify the unity of place evident in the other radio drama, and therefore lacks the total immediacy and impact so vivid there but gains its effect by its topicality: Two years prior to *Air Raid*'s presentation on CBS, the ancient Basque town of Guernica had been destroyed by Nazi planes in a cruel demonstration of the blitzkrieg strategy of modern warfare. Again, in this play, MacLeish employed a callous and impersonal Announcer to describe the attack, underlining the grave dangers inherent in refusal by Americans to denounce this massacre of the innocent and the vulnerability of those who refuse to protect themselves against aggression. Ruthless and impersonal technical "progress" is thereby measured ironically against its price in human suffering. Together, these two verse plays, *The Fall of the City* and *Air Raid*, constitute American radio's major contribution to dramatic literature.

Not until the 1950's did MacLeish turn again to poetic drama. In six years, three plays appeared—*The Trojan Horse*, *This Music Crept by Me upon the Waters*, and his masterpiece in the genre, *J.B.*—each increasingly more complex both poetically and dramaturgically than anything he had previously attempted. *The Trojan Horse* continued MacLeish's indictment of mindless collective consent to self-destructive fear, in this case generated by the accusations of Joseph McCarthy. Recognizing that in the age of television, poetic drama written for radio was all but moribund, MacLeish indicated that his new one-act play would be performed on the stage, without scenery or other elements of stagecraft that might detract from the impact of the spoken word, as well as on radio. Indeed, the play was presented in both forms, broadcast by BBC radio and included in a double bill with *This Music Crept by Me upon the Waters* by the Poets' Theatre in Cambridge, Massachusetts.

The Trojan Horse continued MacLeish's use of mythology as a vehicle for social criticism. Here he varied somewhat his use of accentual meter, combining a verse line of three accents with blank verse. MacLeish continued his expressionist technique of de-emphasis on individual characters by using nameless type characters, thereby focusing on the theme rather than on fully rounded characterization.

MacLeish's other one-act verse drama of this period, *This Music Crept by Me upon the Waters* (the title is from William Shakespeare's *The Tempest*), uses the more conventional pattern of ten named cast characters to focus on an American proclivity to spoil whatever dreams and plans one has for achieving happiness. Because of the large cast, emphasis is on conversation, much in the manner of Eliot's *The Cocktail Party*. Living on a contemporary paradisiacal Caribbean island, a group has gathered for dinner and falls into a discussion of what might constitute the good life— peace, order, simplicity—but each speaker reveals an inability to sustain such an idyllic existence. MacLeish implies that such idlers dream of the prelapsarian Edenic state without the willingness to assume the efforts that would earn it; in their despair, the antithesis of Job's fortitude, they inevitably "fumble happiness."

MacLeish's major achievement in poetic drama, *J.B.*, fulfilled his own exhortation to poets to discover a metaphor for the truth they were moved to communicate. In the poetry of the Old Testament Book of Job, Mac-Leish found a metaphor for the eternal human dilemma: human beings' compulsion to know the meaning and cause of their afflictions and to be able to justify the works of God.

From one point of view, *J.B.* is two plays: the original script (the basis of the popular published version) produced at Yale University in April, 1958, and the revision that was produced and directed by Elia Kazan on Broadway in December of that year. The original is far more austere and poetic, although critics generally agree that the verse in *J.B.* does not represent MacLeish's finest poetry. When the drama was mounted for New York, a largely rewritten version developed during rehearsals, one which not only altered the play's structure (from eleven continuing scenes to two acts with an intermission) but also introduced new characters (such as the roustabouts), deleted others, and altered the roles of still others. Dramatically effective episodes of stage business were also developed in the Kazan production. Many of these changes resulted in little more than clarification for the stage of MacLeish's original ideas, but in the play's final scene, the entire philosophic resolution is altered by a shift in the protagonist's rationalization of his ordeal. In the New York version, as he is reunited with his wife, Sarah, he recognizes the value of his experience and affirms an almost Shelleyan belief in the strength and efficacy of love as a requisite for survival. In the original script, the play ends with Sarah's conviction that eventually the couple will achieve knowledge ("Blow on the coal of the heart and we'll know. . . . We'll know. . . ."). In the Kazan version, however, J.B. refutes her claim ("We can never *know*"), proclaiming that only by his suffering has he learned that one can "still live . . . still love."

Structurally also, *J.B.* is two plays, for the trials of the protagonist, the wealthy, powerful, and satisfied industrialist and banker, J.B., form a play within a play. J.B.'s story is framed by the drama of Zuss and Nickles, who appear to be "two broken-down actors" (MacLeish's own description of them) reduced to hawking balloons and popcorn at "a side show of some kind." As Zuss gradually assumes the role of a god (Zeus), metamorphosing into the imposing God of the biblical Job, Nickles assumes the role of the taunting Satan (Old Nick); together these two characters function as a Greek chorus, commenting upon and participating in the trials of J.B. (Job).

MacLeish himself pointed out yet another aspect of duality in *J.B.*: He saw his accomplishment as the construction of "a modern play inside the ancient majesty of the Book of Job," rather than as a distinct freestanding reconstruction, for he admitted the questions he probed in the play were "too large" to be handled without the strong undergirding structure of the biblical story. Thus, many of the original situations and characters appear in MacLeish's modernization: the specific details of Job's suffering (loss of fortune and family, as well as his physical afflictions), and the parade of his comforters, the ostensibly supportive Bildad, Eliphaz, and Zophar, who jargonize respectively Marxist, Freudian, and theological arguments that leave J.B., like his earlier counterpart, suffering even more acutely.

The original version of *J.B.* opens with a prologue: The elderly actors Zuss and Nickles are inspired to play an impromptu dialogue between "God in Job" and Satan, and they wear appropriate masks to facilitate their performance under the circus tent. By nature, Zuss is reluctant to attempt such a lofty role, but during the repartee with the cynical wit Nickles, he eventually assumes a highly orthodox religious posture which only goads his adversary to more audacious taunts. As they prepare for their "performance," they realize the need for someone to play Job, but foresee no difficulty, for, as Nickles observes, "Job is everywhere we go."

Now that the casting is complete, with Zuss as God and Nickles as "opposite to God," and mindful of the "they" who are the originals, the two actors gradually and unconsciously assume the actualities behind the roles they are playing. In effect, their play becomes the Book of Job. The satanic Nickles accuses God of being a creator who "fumbles Job" by giving him a mind that could "learn to wish" and be concerned with justice. As they continue, they discover that their masks have transformed them into the characters they have assumed; Nickles asks, "You really think I'm playing?" and from the darkness comes "A Distant Voice" that affirms their transformation into more than two seedy actors. The prologue ends with the voice beneath the Godmask speaking the words from the Bible that ask of Satan when he seeks a subject for his test of power "Hast thou considered my servant Job?" and the two begin their rivalry for supremacy over a contemporary counterpart.

Scene 1 follows with a joyful Thanksgiving dinner under way at J.B.'s house, where the family considers their good fortune ("we have so much!"). J.B. asserts seriously that "never . . . have I doubted God was on my side, was good to me," although his prescient wife, Sarah, is frightened: "It's not so simple as all that," for "God rewards and God can punish," because He is just, and J.B. agrees that indeed "a man can count on Him." Scene 2 returns to Zuss and Nickles, now controlled by their assumed roles, who rejoice that in the complacent J.B. they have found their "pigeon," and gloat that he will soon find out "what the world is like" as he becomes God's "victim of the spinning joke!"

In scenes 3 and 4, callous messengers come to the home of J.B. to tell him and his wife of the deaths of three of their five children in senseless accidents. In scene 5, Zuss and Nickles, who have been silently watching, return to centerstage to prophesy that J.B. is learning God's purpose for him—to suffer. The light on them fades as another messenger enters to report that J.B.'s youngest daughter has been abducted, sexually abused, and murdered by a psychopath, and Zuss and Nickles allude to the universality of their dramatized actions by recognizing that actually J.B. "isn't in the play at all," but is "where we all are—in our suffering."

Zuss and Nickles peer down in scene 6 as J.B. discovers that a bomb has destroyed his bank, taking with it his fortune as well as killing his last child. By now, Sarah is rebellious and hysterical and shrieks that God not only gives but also takes and "Kills! Kills! Kills! Kills!" Despite everything, J.B. continues to bless "the name of the Lord." In scene 7, Zuss and Nickles review the trials of J.B. and ridicule his endurance and refusal to despair. Zuss, as God, feels that he has triumphed over Nickles in J.B.'s test, but Satan refuses to concede, even though J.B.'s acceptance is "the way it ends" in the Bible. The two decide to continue his trials.

Scene 8 reveals that a worldwide nuclear holocaust has destroyed all but a few pitiful survivors, a rag-clad J.B. and his wife among them. His skin is blistered by the fire, the modern counterpart of Job's boils, but even now J.B. refuses to join Sarah in condemning God as their enemy, although he agonizes over why God is continuing their persecution. Sarah refuses to accept her husband's adamant defense of God as just, and she vows to leave him, seeing his position as a betrayal of the innocence of their children. When he responds that he has "no choice but to be guilty," she challenges him to "curse God and die," and runs from him. Now totally alone, J.B. pleads "Show me my guilt, O God!" but experiences only an agonizing silence, just as Adam and Eve did after their Edenic transgression in *Nobodaddy*. Nickles, who has been watching, decides that this is the time to bring to J.B. the "cold comforters" who also appeared in the Book of

Job, those dogmatists "who justify the ways of God to Job by making Job responsible."

The three appear in scene 9, with the same names as their biblical counterparts. When J.B. asks "My God! What have I done?" (to justify such suffering), Bildad, a Marxist, cries, "Screw your justice!" and praises collectivism as the ultimate solution to man's pain ("One man's suffering won't count"). J.B. insists that guilt matters, or all else is meaningless, but Bildad rants that "guilt is a sociological accident." The Freudian Eliphaz sees guilt as "a psychophenomenal situation," inciting Zophar, a religionist, to proclaim his belief that "All mankind are guilty always!," thereby negating any place for individual will in the matter. J.B. chides them all for squabbling and for mocking his misery, asserting that only in his suffering could he have found affirmation of his identity, by knowing it was "I that acted, I that chose."

J.B. again cries, "What have I done?" but there is still no answer from Heaven. Suddenly he hears the Distant Voice in a whirlwind; it rebukes and humiliates him for his arrogance in challenging God, and in the familiar biblical catechism reminds J.B. of His many powers and accomplishments. The three glib comforters depart as J.B. is accused of desiring to instruct God. Not answered, only silenced, the humbled J.B. nevertheless proclaims that his eye has now seen God, and that because of this experience, "I abhor myself . . . and repent. . . ."

As scene 10 opens, Nickles and Zuss decide that they have had enough; Zuss is particularly distressed because, as Nickles observes, although he won the argument and was right about J.B., "being magnificent and being right don't go together in this universe." Together they ridicule what they see as J.B.'s impotence, because he has "misconceived the part" and because he has given in and whimpered before the omnipotent voice of God. Outraged by his refusal to despair and by his utter subjection to God's will, the two old actors prepare to resume their circus jobs but recall that there is one more scene "no matter who plays Job or how he plays it," the restoration of his fortunes. Zuss reminds Nickles that when he is released from his suffering, J.B./Job will again assume his life, just as those of all generations do, so Nickles confronts J.B. directly to inform him of the resolution of his fate; signs of his deliverance appear, for J.B.'s blistered skin is healed and Sarah returns.

In the final lyric reconciliation scene, a new beginning from the ashes of destruction is evident as Sarah convinces J.B. that indeed there is no justice in the world, but there is nevertheless conjugal love, which, if strong enough, can triumph over heavenly tyranny. Even if God does not love, J.B. asserts, His existence suffices. In a final declaration, Sarah prophesies that when the heart is warmed by love, despite the loss of religious and societal support, "we'll see where we are" and "we'll know." They have no assurance of the truth of this claim yet no alternative but to accept its challenging promise, affirming, in MacLeish's words, "the worth of life in spite of life."

J.B. ran for 364 performances on Broadway. In its published form (the original version), it became a best-seller and was translated into several foreign languages. Some critics faulted MacLeish's attempt to portray modern people "in terms of a cosmic myth," while others pointed to excessive rhetoric. Although critical interpretations differed, all agreed that MacLeish's controversial modern morality play was a rarity on the American stage—a religious poetic drama that was a commercial and artistic success.

MacLeish followed the triumph of *J.B.* with another verse play, *Herakles*, in 1965, and with the prose *Scratch* in 1971, in addition to the short *The Secret of Freedom* (1960), which was published together with two poetic radio dramas of the 1930's, *The Fall of the City* and *Air Raid*. *Herakles* ran for fourteen performances at the University of Michigan theater, and *Scratch* ran for four in New York. *The Secret of Freedom* was written for television and was televised by the National Broadcasting Company (NBC).

Returning to Greek heroic myth and to Euripides for inspiration, MacLeish sought in *Herakles* to achieve the moral resonance of *J.B.* In this new parable, a monomaniacal American physicist is awarded the Nobel Prize for his Promethean achievement in finding new sources of energy but fails both as a humanist and as a husband and father in his mad pursuit of even greater glory and accomplishment. Like the labors of Herakles, Professor Hoadley's work benefits humankind, but he is an irresponsible individual and is forced to recognize the limits of his humanity. Less lyric than the original version of *J.B.*, *Herakles* is more tragically realistic in its portrayal of yet another victim of the sin of excessive pride. Whereas the essentially passive Job endured seemingly endless, meaningless suffering, the anti-Job Hoadley is a dynamic achiever, willing to sacrifice everything for the palpable rewards of his efforts.

In *Scratch*, a drama suggested by Stephen Vincent Benét's popular short story "The Devil and Daniel Webster," MacLeish once again warned against the willingness to sacrifice personal freedom in exchange for controlled lives of comfort and stifling "law and order." Although relevant to the turmoil of the 1960's, *Scratch* was an artistic failure, dismissed by critics as ambiguous, too abstract, talky, and even tedious and incomprehensible. MacLeish never attempted full-length theatrical drama again. *The Great American Fourth of July Parade* (1975) was his final, somewhat nostalgic return to the form he had so ardently defended and so skillfully practiced.

Other major works

POETRY: *Songs for a Summer's Day*, 1915; *Tower of Ivory*, 1917; *The Happy Marriage*, 1924; *Streets in the Moon*, 1926; *The Hamlet of A. Mac-*

Leish, 1928; *Einstein*, 1929; *New Found Land: Fourteen Poems*, 1930; *Conquistador*, 1932; *Poems, 1924-1933*, 1933; *Frescoes for Mr. Rockefeller's City*, 1933; *Public Speech*, 1936; *Land of the Free*, 1938; *America Was Promises*, 1939; *Brave New World*, 1948; *Actfive and Other Poems*, 1948; *Collected Poems, 1917-1952*, 1952; *New Poems, 1951-1952*, 1952; *Songs for Eve*, 1954; *The Collected Poems of Archibald MacLeish*, 1962; *The Wild Old Wicked Man and Other Poems*, 1968; *The Human Season: Selected Poems, 1926-1972*, 1972; *New and Collected Poems, 1917-1976*, 1976; *On the Beaches of the Moon*, 1978; *Collected Poems, 1917-1982*, 1985.

NONFICTION: *Housing America*, 1932; *Jews in America*, 1936; *Background of War*, 1937; *The Irresponsibles: A Declaration*, 1940; *The American Cause*, 1941; *A Time to Speak: The Selected Prose of Archibald MacLeish*, 1941; *American Opinion and the War*, 1942; *A Time to Act: Selected Addresses*, 1943; *Poetry and Opinion: The "Pisan Cantos" of Ezra Pound*, 1950; *Freedom Is the Right to Choose: An Inquiry into the Battle for the American Future*, 1951; *Poetry and Experience*, 1961; *The Dialogues of Archibald MacLeish and Mark Van Doren*, 1964; *The Eleanor Roosevelt Story*, 1965; *A Continuing Journey*, 1968; *The Great American Frustration*, 1968; *Champion of a Cause: Essays and Addresses on Librarianship*, 1971; *Riders on the Earth: Essays and Reminiscences*, 1978; *Letters of Archibald MacLeish: 1907-1982*, 1983 (R. H. Winnick, editor); *Reflections*, 1986 (Bernard A. Drabeck and Helen E. Ellis, editors).

SCREENPLAYS: *Grandma Moses*, 1950; *The Eleanor Roosevelt Story*, 1965.
TELEPLAY: *The Secret of Freedom*, 1960.

RADIO PLAYS: *The States of Talking*, 1941; *The American Story: Ten Radio Scripts*, 1944; *The Great American Fourth of July Parade: A Verse Play for Radio*, 1975.

Bibliography

Aaron, Daniel. *Writers on the Left.* New York: Harcourt, Brace & World, 1962. This book is a social chronicle of the left wing from 1912 to the early 1940's. It describes the response of a select group of American writers to the idea of communism and deals with particular issues and events that helped to shape their opinions. The discussion of MacLeish focuses on the author as the "darling of communism" during the Spanish Civil War.

Donaldson, Scott. *Archibald MacLeish: An American Life.* Boston: Houghton Mifflin, 1992. This exceptionally well-written biography has as its sources not only MacLeish's published poetry, essays, and plays but also his notebooks and journals. It is based on new accounts, articles, reviews, and letters from friends. The essence of the man, according to the author, was his multiplicity. His life was driven by two powerful and sometimes conflicting goals: He wanted to write great poetry, and he wanted to advance great causes. The kernel of his emotional life is embedded in his poems, which is why this biography is both a life story and a selected anthology. Numerous illustrations and a bibliography.

Gassner, John. *Theatre at the Crossroads.* New York: Holt, Rinehart and Winston, 1960. An assessment of mid-twentieth century theater as viewed from the vantage point of Broadway and Off-Broadway stage productions since World War II. Begins with a series of essays offering perspectives on the emergence of modern drama. Concludes with discussions of specific productions from 1950 to 1960. MacLeish's play *J. B.* is discussed in this latter section of the book. For the general reader.

MacLeish, Archibald. *Reflections.* Edited by Bernard A. Drabeck and Helen E. Ellis. Amherst: University of Massachusetts Press, 1986. This thoughtful biography is based on a collection of interviews with MacLeish conducted during the six years before the author's death. It is a "spoken" biography rather than a written autobiography and is filled with fascinating anecdotes and insights. It covers MacLeish's association with world figures in literature, art, and politics. Also chronicles the Paris years, the 1930's, MacLeish in government, the Harvard years, and the later years. Contains illustrations and an afterword.

Weales, Gerald C. *American Drama Since World War II.* New York: Harcourt, Brace & World, 1962. A critical description of the American plays produced between the years 1945 and 1960. In the section devoted to MacLeish, the author discusses MacLeish's plays as experiments using poetic form. Provides a general overview of the subject and specific insights on MacLeish's drama.

Maryhelen C. Harmon
(Updated by *Genevieve Slomski*)

TERRENCE McNALLY

Born: St. Petersburg, Florida; November 3, 1939

Principal drama

The Lady of the Camellias, pr. 1963 (adaptation of a play by Giles Cooper, based on the novel of Alexandre Dumas, *fils*); *And Things That Go Bump in the Night*, pr. 1964, pb. 1966 (originally as *This Side of the Door*, pr. 1962); *Next*, pr. 1967, pb. 1969 (one act); *Tour*, pr. 1967, pb. 1968 (one act); *Botticelli*, pr. 1968 (televised), pb. 1969, pr. 1971 (staged, one act); *¡Cuba Si!*, pr. 1968, pb. 1969 (one act); *Noon*, pr. 1968, pb. 1969 (one act); *Sweet Eros*, pr. 1968, pb. 1969 (one act); *Witness*, pr. 1968, pb. 1969 (one act); *Bringing It All Back Home*, pr. 1969, pb. 1970 (one act); *Where Has Tommy Flowers Gone?*, pr. 1971, pb. 1972; *Bad Habits: Ravenswood and Dunelawn*, pr. 1971, pb. 1974 (two one-acts); *Let It Bleed*, pr. 1972; *Whiskey*, pr., pb. 1973 (one act); *The Ritz*, pr. 1975 (staged), pr. 1976 (screenplay), pb. 1976 (as *The Tubs*, pr. 1974); *Broadway, Broadway*, pr. 1978 (revised as *It's Only a Play*, pr. 1982, pb. 1986); *The Rink*, pr. 1984, pb. 1985 (musical; book written by McNally, music by Fred Ebb, lyrics by John Kander); *The Lisbon Traviata*, pr. 1985, pb. 1986; *Frankie and Johnny in the Clair de Lune*, pr., pb. 1987; *Lips Together, Teeth Apart*, pr. 1991, pb. 1992.

Other literary forms

In addition to his stage plays, Terrence McNally has written scripts and revised play scripts for screen, television, and radio. His teleplays include *Botticelli*, *The Five Forty-eight* (1979, adapted from a John Cheever story), and *André's Mother* (1990). Among his screenplays are *The Ritz* and *Frankie and Johnny* (1991). McNally has also contributed several articles and interviews to *The Dramatists Guild Quarterly*.

Achievements

Throughout his career, experimenting freely with style and technique, McNally has revealed a chameleon-like ability to adopt new comic guises. His earliest works, such as *And Things That Go Bump in the Night* and *Next*, reflect the influence of the Theater of the Absurd in their trenchant, black-humor ridiculing of a variety of social values and institutions. Moving toward a more sympathetic engagement in the plight of his characters, McNally has gradually muted his comic vision, producing plays such as *The Lisbon Traviata* and *Frankie and Johnny in the Clair de Lune*, which, though witty, are far more lyrical, sensitive, and forgiving.

McNally has been awarded two Guggenheim Fellowships and won an

Obie Award (for *Bad Habits* in 1974) and an Emmy Award (for the teleplay *André's Mother* in 1991). He is a member of the American Academy of Arts and Letters and in 1981 became vice president of the Dramatists Guild.

Biography

Terrence McNally was born in St. Petersburg, Florida, in 1939, but he grew up in Corpus Christi, Texas, where he received his early education. His parents, both from New York, prompted his enthusiasm for theater by taking him to see both plays and musicals. In 1956, he entered Columbia University, where he took courses in writing and collaborated on variety shows. He completed his B.A. in English, Phi Beta Kappa, in 1960, and was named an Evans Traveling Fellow. With the fellowship, McNally went to Mexico, where he wrote a one-act play and sent it to the Actors' Studio in New York. It piqued the interest of Molly Kazan, who appointed him stage manager there. Through his association with the Kazans, McNally was hired as tutor to John Steinbeck's teenage sons, and in 1961 and 1962, he toured the world with the Steinbeck family.

Back in New York, McNally won an award for a one-act play, which, with revisions, would become *And Things That Go Bump in the Night*. In 1964, he received a grant for staging *And Things That Go Bump in the Night* at the Tyrone Guthrie Theatre in Minneapolis. The notoriety that surrounded the production induced producer Theodore Mann to try a New York staging in 1965, but it was met with extremely hostile reviews and closed within two weeks. The disheartened McNally briefly dropped playwriting and took up journalism, but prompted by theater friends, he returned to begin a prolific period in which he wrote several one-act plays produced either Off-Broadway or on public television. The best known, *Next*, ran for more than seven hundred performances and secured McNally's reputation as a talented writer of trenchant satire. Critics were generally less receptive to McNally's full-length plays, and the failure of *Broadway, Broadway* in 1979 sent the playwright into new creative doldrums. It was five years before he returned to the Broadway stage with the musical *The Rink*, for which he wrote the book. Although received tepidly by critics, the work had a fairly long run, with large audiences.

With *The Lisbon Traviata* and *It's Only a Play*, McNally showed that he was back in high gear as a playwright and that he was capable of garnering important critical acclaim. The two plays were followed by *Frankie and Johnny in the Clair de Lune*, later revised for the screen, and by the Emmy-winning teleplay *André's Mother* and the play *Lips Together, Teeth Apart*, also a highly regarded work. An ardent theater activist with a passionate belief in New York's Off-Broadway theaters, McNally has been an articulate spokesperson for experimental theater, and in *The Dramatists*

Guild Quarterly he has been a forceful proponent for that movement. He settled in Greenwich Village, spending, however, much of his time at his summer home on Long Island.

Analysis

Terrence McNally's earliest plays, influenced by both avant-garde theater and Cold War anxieties, offer savage criticism of society. Called by Harold Clurman "one of the most adept practitioners of the comedy of insult," McNally lashes out at various targets with an angry-young-man malice made palatable by his acerbic wit and solid stranglehold on a sense of the absurd.

Two prevalent, related themes that mark his early pieces are the dysfunction of the family and the alienation of the individual. His first major play, *And Things That Go Bump in the Night*, deals with a bizarre family living in a basement, exiled from normal society. An absurdist farce à la Samuel Beckett's *Fin de partie* (pr., pb. 1957; *Endgame*, pr., pb. 1958) and Arthur Kopit's *Oh, Dad, Poor Dad, Mamma's Hung You in the Closet and I'm Feelin' So Sad* (pr., pb. 1960), the work is a devastating critique on the perversion of values forced on human beings by modern exigencies. The plot, a series of sadomasochistic exercises accompanied by shrieks of fear and outrage, involves the ritual destruction of Clarence, the play's only "normal" character. He becomes a hapless victim in the sadistic and seemingly pointless games adroitly played by the "opera queen" Ruby and her children, Sigfrid and Lakme. Caring no more for their own kin, this trio mocks Grandfa, the grandfather who is about to be trundled off to an asylum for the insane. Love has simply degenerated into perverse carnality, care into apathy, respect into derision. What remains are childish fears, such as the dread of the dark or solitude, that suggest an awful entropy in the human soul. There is no hope for humankind in this play's apocalyptic vision, but there may be some sort of retributive justice, symbolized by the persistent "thump" that grows in volume and frequency as the play draws to an end.

Although hostile to the play, critics did identify McNally as a disciple of black comedy. The family members are, after all, outrageously humorous in their grotesque fashion. The play is perplexing, however, in part because of the playwright's technique. It is a crazy quilt made up of non sequiturs, arcane references, foreign phrases, musical oddments, and disconnected and, at times, obtuse behavior. Stung into clarifying his vision by the play's poor reception, and after flirting with a career change, McNally began bringing his satire into sharper focus. In 1968, he had six plays in production, all one-acts Off-Broadway or teleplays on public television. In all of them, he takes a jaundiced look at dehumanizing and alienating aspects of American life. A favorite target is the Vietnam War and its eroding influence on values, a topic he treats in several works.

The best-known example is *Next*, a one-act spoof about a middle-aged theater manager, Marion Cheever, who has been sent a draft notice by accident. The two-character play takes place at an induction center, during a humiliating physical examination conducted by a tough, no-nonsense female, Sergeant Tech. Cheever, who has no desire to be drafted into the army, tries to wheedle out of his situation, but his tormentor carries on with all the inexorable indifference of a federal meat inspector. Forced to strip, Cheever, ashamed of his plump body, wraps himself in the American flag, and despite his desire to evade the draft, is upset when he fails the ludicrous psychological portion of the examination and is ruled unfit. When the ritual is over, Cheever burlesques it in a monologue in which he apes Sergeant Tech and with increasing stridency attacks the dehumanizing way in which society sets its standards.

Another example, *Bringing It All Back Home*, focuses on a dysfunctional family unable to grieve for the son killed in Vietnam and sent home in a wooden crate conveniently deposited in their living room. The dead soldier's sister and brother, engaged in a fierce sibling rivalry, verbally abuse each other, while their inept parents console themselves with inane observations, including the bromide that their son's death was quick and painless, even though a mine "tore his stomach right open." Selfish and vindictive, the nameless son and daughter excoriate each other while whining about their need for sex and drugs. The brother accuses his sister of being a slut; she accuses him of being a homosexual and a drug addict. The father offers simplistic parental advice, lecturing his son on becoming a manly adult through self-discipline and learning to bowl. Meanwhile, he pets his daughter in an obvious display of repressed incest, and when left alone, makes obscene telephone calls to total strangers. His wife, perpetually under a hair dryer, is unable to surface and listen to the conversation. All seem to treat the son's death with stupefying indifference. At one point, that son pops up in his crate to protest, confiding that, contrary to what his family claims, his death "hurt like hell." Matters come to a head of sorts when a television crew shows up to tape a human interest segment for the news. Interviewed by Miss Horne, a "black troublemaker" who asks penetrating questions about the son's death, none of the family members can give a better answer than those provided by the worst self-serving apologists for the war. They are sorry human specimens, devoid of understanding, and numbed to uncaring by overexposure to daily horrors.

In several of his plays of the late 1960's and early 1970's, McNally attacks such distressing complacency and insensitivity to human misery. *Sweet Eros* and *Witness*, produced as companion pieces on the same bill, both stress human beings' need to assume personal responsibility for action and passivity alike. Both are troubling allegories.

In *Sweet Eros*, a man abducts a girl, strips her, ties her to a chair, and then proceeds to tell her his life story. Although personable and glib, he has a massive ego and is principally interested in justifying his narcissism. At first, the girl struggles with moral outrage, but in the end, she becomes docile, finding it easier and safer to acquiesce before madness than to fight it. She symbolizes a society that indicts itself by entering into a silent partnership with evil.

Similarly, in *Witness*, another victim is tied to a chair, this time a salesman captured by a young man planning to kill the president of the United States. The would-be assassin wants a witness who can later testify to his sanity. Also invited to witness the act are a window washer and a female neighbor, neither of whom finds it the least bit odd that the bound and gagged salesman sits in their midst. Neither of them wishes to take any responsibility for what is planned, partly because, as the window washer complains, too much freedom has left them without any rules or moral imperatives. He thinks that shooting the president is all right in a doing-your-own-thing sort of way. In contrast, the young man plans the death of the president because he wants to demonstrate that such an act is futile, that it can change nothing.

In two other one-acts, *Ravenswood* and *Dunelawn*, joined together as *Bad Habits*, McNally mocks two ways in which authority, represented by staff members at two contrasting sanatoriums, has dealt with asocial behavior. At Ravenswood, Dr. Jason Pepper encourages his patients to do whatever they want, even if it is demonstrably bad for them, while at Dunelawn, Dr. Toynbee and his two nurses drug unruly patients into silent stupors. As microcosms, the two sanatoriums suggest alternative ways in which governments have dealt with modern neuroses. At Ravenswood, Dr. Pepper panders to his patients' desires, even encouraging aggressive and aberrant behavior, whereas at Dunelawn, the patients are kept in wheelchairs and straitjackets and, if unruly, are drugged into docility. Neither solution to human problems is satisfying, though the therapy used at Ravenswood seems to promote at least an ephemeral happiness.

Ravenswood and *Dunelawn* reflect both the characteristic strengths and weaknesses of McNally's early satirical farces in the absurdist mode. While much of the dialogue is humorous, the characters tend to be caricatures. Some are even reminiscent of cartoon characters. For example, Bruno, the groundskeeper in *Dunelawn*, is a variation on the cartoon Neanderthal at large in the modern world, as his "hubba hubba" tag phrase suggests. Both plays also have structural problems. They tend to dwindle away, more like skits than organic, complete pieces, which is a fault found even with *Next*, the playwright's most successful one-act.

McNally was well aware of the limitations and was sensitive to the criticism. He credits Elaine May, whose *Adaptation* (pr. 1969) was once staged with *Next*, with helping him rethink his ideas about character. She encouraged him to "write people instead of symbols." Aware, too, that short one-acts were too restrictive for developing characters to their full potential, McNally turned increasing attention to writing full-length plays, including *Where Has Tommy Flowers Gone?*, which some consider his best early play.

As critics have noted, the action of *Where Has Tommy Flowers Gone?* reflects the influence of Bertolt Brecht's epic theater. Using several episodic flashbacks, it chronicles the experiences that have shaped Tommy into an anarchist bent on destroying various art centers. Like other McNally antiheros, Tommy is an alienated but engaging young man drawn to violence as a last recourse in a stagnating, suffocating, and insensitive world. His story is presented in a stage collage, using pyrotechnics, photographic images, music, asides, and "news" vignettes to piece it all together. Tommy is drawn in the tradition of the picaresque rogue, part con artist, part pariah, wounded by an indifferent or hostile world. His personal hero is Holden Caulfield, from J. D. Salinger's novel, *The Catcher in the Rye* (1951). Like Holden, he sees the system as phony and is determined to destroy even the most noble and benign aspects of it, its art. As he wanders, he gathers a family of misfits around him, almost in a sacrilegious parody of an American ideal. An old drifter-actor, Ben Delight, who is full of self-aggrandizing lies, becomes his surrogate father, while Nedda, a girl encountered on his sexually promiscuous rampage, becomes a substitute wife. There is also Arnold, an ugly dog, that, loyal until Tommy's death, at curtain is led off on a new master's leash. The play's techniques sufficiently distance the audience to keep the whole mélange comical and innocuous. Although Tommy's outrageous romp involves wanton destruction, flimflam tricks, and petty thievery, it elicits neither sympathy nor condemnation, only laughter. McNally tries to make one think in the aftermath of that laughter, and to that end, as Brecht does, he constantly reminds his audience that what is before it is, after all, merely a fantasy.

Another energetic piece, free of polemic design, is *The Ritz*, wherein McNally demonstrates his mastery of high-speed, offbeat farce. It is set in a New York steam bath catering exclusively to homosexuals, where the pudgy protagonist, Gaetano Proclo, has sought refuge from his brother-in-law, Carmine Vespucci, who is out to kill him. As it turns out, Proclo has been set up by Vespucci, whose machinations have deliberately drawn Proclo to the place, an establishment owned and operated by Vespucci. Pursued by Michael Brick, a detective hired by Vespucci to hunt him down, Proclo dexterously but narrowly evades a series of comic disasters. Besides Brick, he is pursued by a homosexual "chubby chaser" whose taste in partners runs to the obese; a talentless female singer, Googie Gomez, who has it in her head that he is a producer; and, finally, his wife and Vespucci himself, who is hell bent on deceiving his sister into believing that her husband is a homosexual. It is a high-spirited, if silly, contrived plot, full of mistaken identities, misencounters, door-slamming and bed-hopping razzle-dazzle—pure nonsense with all hints of playwright as angry-young-man-with-a-message leached out of it. With it, the entertainer in McNally seems to score a total victory over the social critic.

For a time, McNally had difficulty following up *The Ritz* with a play that fulfilled its promise of future pieces crafted with an untroubled and detached comic vision. The poor reception of *Broadway, Broadway* and its first revival in 1982 as *It's Only a Play* dispirited the writer, sending his career into a temporary tailspin. His book for the musical *The Rink* was also panned as dated, lacking in both "bite" and "originality." McNally was obviously struggling to free himself of Cold War and free-speech demons that by the 1980's critics were dismissing as clichés.

Success came in 1985 with *The Lisbon Traviata* and a revival of *It's Only a Play*, both produced Off-Broadway by the Manhattan Theatre Club. The former play, revived in a critically acclaimed production of 1989, focuses on four homosexual men, two of whom, Stephen and Mike, are at a breakup point in their relationship. The demise of their "marriage" occurs in the second act, which in mood turns the play on end. The first act which is uproarious, gives way to an acrimonious and sad conclusion.

The play opens in the apartment of Stephen's friend, Mendy, where Stephen has taken refuge because at home Mike is entertaining his new friend, Paul, in what Stephen hopes will be a one-night stand. Stephen and Mendy are opera buffs and devoted fans of the great diva Maria Callas, and they spend the evening bantering about opera lore. The crisis in Stephen's life is divulged almost offhandedly when Mendy pleads with him to return home to retrieve a recording of Callas as Violetta in Giuseppe Verdi's *La traviata* (1853). Stephen refuses, covering his anxieties with what for Mendy is a maddening insensitivity to Mendy's need to hear the legendary, Lisbon performance. In tormenting the desperate Mendy, Stephen reveals a keen verbal wit and seems totally in control of his emotions. That mask, however, comes off in the second act when he confronts Mike, who is moving out on him. It is now Stephen who is desperate and must do the pleading. His wit, though still with him, becomes sadly deficient, even hollow. It only angers Mike, who, before he leaves, punches Stephen to the floor and, at curtain, leaves him abandoned and miserable.

McNally, himself an opera enthusiast, uses music of great passion in ironic counterpoint to the glib, "bitchy" wit of Mendy and Stephen, and although the playwright himself claims that his play is about "people with great passions," those passions at first seem to be sublimated in music; in the second act, however, Stephen's passion finally erupts in the futile confrontation with Mike. Stephen, who seems to need music as a continuous presence in his life, arrives home and immediately turns on the stereo receiver, tuning to a classical music station. When Mike appears, Stephen offers to put on music that Mike will like, something that will appeal to Mike's pedestrian tastes. Mike, as if to assert his total independence from Stephen, first tunes in a rock station, then later turns off the stereo. In the silence, Stephen is emotionally naked and extremely vulnerable.

In *It's Only a Play*, McNally ignores conventional advice against writing plays about the theater. Reflecting some of his own frustrations with the "system," epitomized by Broadway theaters and New York reviewers, he uses his talent for acerbic dialogue to puncture holes in its various pretensions and, in the process, creates an uproarious play with a simple premise. The piece is set in an upstairs bedroom in the town house of a wealthy woman who has just made her debut as a play producer and is now hosting an opening-night party. Most of the characters who parade in and out of the room are in some way connected with the play. The tension mounts as the moment of truth, the verdict of the reviewers, approaches. Unlike the offstage, famous guests who flit in and out of the party downstairs, those upstairs are short on talent and experience. They are, however, long on anxiety and ego. Included are the playwright Peter Austin, whose hopes for a second success will be crushed; James Wicker, a frantic actor whose television series gets cancelled; Frank Finger, a director, who, lucky but talentless, wants to salve his conscience with a flop; Julia Budder, the hostess; Virginia Noyes, a fading starlet; and Ira Drew, a minor critic and closet dramatist writing under the pseudonym "Caroline Comstock." Gus Washington, a streetwise black man who wants to be an actor and who is providing temporary help for the party, and Emma, an outspoken taxi driver, complete the *dramatis personae*. Offstage, in the bathroom, there is also Torch, a feisty dog that intimidates the unwary who attempt to use the facilities.

First-act hopes run high, as the initial reviews are favorable, but in the second act, reality in the form of a devastating review in *The Times* hits the hopefuls like acid sleet on a picnic. At the end, while the rest take new heart and excitedly plan to put another play into production, Peter Austin is left to his sullen self to ponder the fickleness of fortune and friends. Both witty and vitriolic, the play is merciless in its depiction of the New York theater scene. The back-stabbing and name-dropping, threaded together with insincere flattery and a bravado that masks the characters' insecurities, are not that much of an exaggeration. McNally himself claims that the play comes as close to being a documentary as anything he ever wrote. It is, for all of its comic energy, a devastating indictment of a world that can be both fickle and cruel.

In two later plays, *Frankie and Johnny in the Clair de Lune* and *Lips Together, Teeth Apart*, McNally demonstrates that his comedy can never be pigeonholed. The first of these is an erotic rhapsody on heterosexual love. Though just as witty, it is far more lyrical than any of McNally's earlier plays. It has only the two characters named in the title and focuses on Johnny's efforts to parlay his relationship with Frankie into something more than a one-night stand. She, worldly-wise, resists, but by the end of the play, which is left inconclusive (a McNally characteristic), she seems, if not resigned to her fate, certainly more receptive to it. Johnny is the one with the old-fashioned notions about marriage and family. He verges on an anachronism, particularly in his unwavering insistence that fate has drawn them together. His mounting possessiveness annoys Frankie, who is not willing to leap into the commitment fire without a long, hard look. She meets his persistence with hurtful retorts that Johnny, always resourceful, deflects. In its comic duel, the play thus offers an ironic reversal of the relationship of the ballad characters of the same name.

Frankie and Johnny are unusual creations for McNally, whose focus in many plays is on a well-educated and culturally elite class, with mostly upstream sexual preferences. Frankie and Johnny are relative nobodies, born and reared in Allentown, Pennsylvania, but now living failed dreams in the Big Apple as coworkers in a short-order restaurant. Culture remains in the background of this two-part fugue on love.

In *Lips Together, Teeth Apart*, McNally sets the scene in Fire Island, a predominantly homosexual resort. John and Chloe Haddock and Sam and Sally Truman, two married couples, are celebrating the Fourth of July at a beach house, formerly the property of Sally's gay brother who has died of acquired immune deficiency syndrome (AIDS). Against a background of a suicidal drowning, and fireworks and music from neighborhood parties, the characters try to work out their complex emotional problems. Chloe and Sam, who are brother and sister, know that John and Sally have had an affair, and they must sort through its implications for their friendships and marriages. Sally, meanwhile, deeply troubled by her brother's death, is trying to cope with the fact that he was homosexual and had a black lover. She is also determined to discourage any renewal of her brief affair with John, who presses with an urgency arising from the knowledge that he has an inoperable cancer of the esophagus.

Although the characters try to suppress their feelings, passions do flare up, erupting at one point in a fist fight between John and Sam. Their fears and anxieties are, however, buffered by the witty dialogue and some comic aspects of the situation. For example, all four are intimidated by the fact that on both sides of the house, in taller, more imposing beach houses, gay parties are in progress, and they have ridiculous fears about what their neighbors may assume about their sexual orientation. They also avoid the swimming pool, from the suspicion, Sally charges, that the water is infected with the AIDS virus.

The unhappiness of the situation comes in time-released doses. For example, knowledge of John's cancer is not disclosed to Sam and Sally until late in the third and final act. The pain is also blunted by McNally's technique of revealing the inner thoughts of his characters in quiet, unemotional asides to the audience that modulate what is otherwise often humorous dialogue. As in *The Lisbon Traviata*, in *Lips Together, Teeth Apart*, McNally elicits both laughter and compassion and puts them into a delicate comic alignment, a trick requiring a special kind of theatrical magic.

In his later works, McNally has revealed an increasing sympathy for his characters without sacrificing his acerbic wit, and although he has increased his comic range, there remains in all of his work a residual sense of the absurd. Time, however, may prove unkind to the playwright. Critics have carped about his topicality and use of arcane references and in-jokes that could quickly date some of his plays. For example, *It's Only a Play* could share the fate of some sparkling comedies of another era, a play such as Moss Hart and George S. Kaufman's *The Man Who Came to Dinner* (pr., pb. 1939), which now reads like a radio-era museum piece. McNally has cheerfully made his peace with what he is—a New York playwright—and admits to a provincial snobbery that may cost him recognition and acclaim in other theatrical climes. His sure sense of the comic, however, especially an offbeat variety, cannot be faulted. He is a profoundly humorous writer who has mastered his craft.

Other major works

SCREENPLAY: *Frankie and Johnny*, 1991.

TELEPLAYS: *Last Gasps*, 1969; *The Five Forty-eight*, 1979 (from a story by John Cheever); *Mama Malone*, 1983 (series); *André's Mother*, 1990.

Bibliography

Albee, Edward. "Edward Albee in Conversation with Terrence McNally." Interview by Terrence McNally. *The Dramatists Guild Quarterly* 22 (Summer, 1985): 12-23. As vice president of the Dramatists Guild, McNally has conducted interviews with fellow playwrights. This important example chronicles Albee's career with important parallels to McNally's own, with an emphasis on the new playwrights of the early 1960's.

Barnes, Clive. "Making the Most of *Ritz* Steam Bath." Review of *The Ritz*. *The New York Times*, January 21, 1975, p. 40. In this review of *The Ritz*, Barnes notes McNally's ability to write an engaging and zany farce based on situation. An even-tempered assessment by an important theater critic.

De Sousa, Geraldo U. "Terrence McNally." In *American Playwrights Since 1945: A Guide to Scholarship, Criticism, and Performance*, edited by

Philip C. Kolin. New York: Greenwood Press, 1989. This valuable aid to further study contains a brief assessment of McNally's reputation, a production history of his plays, a survey of secondary sources, a comprehensive bibliography through 1987, and suggested research opportunities. It is highly recommended as a guide to secondary sources.

Gussow, Mel. "Agony and Ecstasy of an Opera Addiction." Review of *The Lisbon Traviata*. *The New York Times*, June 7, 1989, p. C21. A review of the revised, nonviolent version of *The Lisbon Traviata*, this article offers a mixed appraisal of McNally's work and typifies the critical reception that the playwright garnered during the 1980's. Gussow relates the play to the influence of opera on McNally's life and art.

Hewes, Henry. " 'Ello, Tommy." Review of *And Things That Go Bump in the Night*. *Saturday Review* 49 (May 15, 1965): 24. This piece is uncharacteristic of early critical assessments of McNally's work. It praises the playwright's talent and his willingness to tackle difficult themes. Hewes was one of the first to recognize McNally's great potential.

John W. Fiero

DAVID MAMET

Born: Chicago, Illinois; November 30, 1947

Principal drama

Camel, pr. 1968; *Lakeboat*, pr. 1970, pr. 1980 (revised), pb. 1981; *Duck Variations*, pr. 1972, pb. 1977; *Sexual Perversity in Chicago*, pr. 1974, pb. 1977; *Squirrels*, pr. 1974, pb. 1982; *American Buffalo*, pr. 1975, pb. 1977; *Reunion*, pr. 1976, pb. 1979; *A Life in the Theatre*, pr., pb. 1977; *The Revenge of the Space Pandas*, pr. 1977, pb. 1978 (one act; children's play); *The Water Engine*, pr. 1977, pb. 1978; *Dark Pony*, pr. 1977, pb. 1979; *The Woods*, pr. 1977, pb. 1979; *Mr. Happiness*, pr., pb. 1978; *Lone Canoe*, pr. 1979 (music and lyrics by Alaric Jans); *The Sanctity of Marriage*, pr. 1979; *Donny March*, pr. 1981; *The Poet and the Rent*, pr. 1981; *A Sermon*, pr. 1981; *Short Plays and Monologues*, pb. 1981; *Edmond*, pr. 1982, pb. 1983; *Glengarry Glen Ross*, pr. 1983, pb. 1984; *The Disappearance of the Jews*, pr. 1983, pb. 1987 (one act); *Red River*, pr. 1983 (adaptation of a play by Pierre Laville); *Goldberg Street: Short Plays and Monologues*, pb. 1985; *The Shawl*, pr., pb. 1985 (includes *Prairie du Chien*); *A Collection of Dramatic Sketches and Monologues*, pb. 1985; *Vint*, pr. 1985 (adaptation of a story by Anton Chekhov); *The Cherry Orchard*, pr., pb. 1986 (adaptation of Chekhov's play); *Three Children's Plays*, pb. 1986; *Three Jewish Plays*, pb. 1987; *Speed-the-Plow*, pr., pb. 1988; *Uncle Vanya*, pr., pb. 1988 (adaptation of Chekhov's play); *Bobby Gould in Hell*, pr. 1989, pb. 1991 (one act); *Three Sisters*, pr., pb. 1990 (adaptation of Chekhov's play); *Oh Hell: Two One-Act Plays*, pb. 1991; *Oleanna*, pr. 1992, pb. 1993.

Other literary forms

David Mamet has enjoyed some success in reworking older classics. For example, *Red River*, his stage adaptation of a play by Pierre Laville, and *Vint*, his adaptation of a story by Anton Chekhov, are two minor pieces that reveal his emerging skill as a crafter of others' works; his adaptations of Chekhov's *The Cherry Orchard*, *Uncle Vanya*, and *Three Sisters* all received favorable reviews. While first and foremost a theatrician, Mamet has also gained respect for his work in other literary forms. Perhaps Mamet's most popular contributions come from Hollywood. His screenplays—*The Postman Always Rings Twice* (1981), *The Verdict* (1982), *The Untouchables* (1985), *House of Games* (1987), *Things Change* (1988), *We're No Angels* (1989), *Homicide* (1991), and *Glengarry Glen Ross* (1992)—have been praised for their intriguing plots and monologues of cruelty. Most scholars point to *House of Games*, with its ritualized forms of expiation, and

Glengarry Glen Ross, with its dazzling repartee, as his best work in film. Finally, Mamet demonstrates his skill as an essayist in *Writing in Restaurants* (1986), a collection of essays that best spells out the playwright's theory of dramatic art as well as his sense of cultural poetics.

Achievements

Mamet, winner of a Pulitzer Prize in 1984 (for his play *Glengarry Glen Ross*), two Obie Awards (1976, 1983), and two New York Drama Critics Circle Awards (1977, 1986) among many others, is regarded as a major voice in American drama and cinema. He animates his stage through language, a poetic idiolect that explores the relationship between public issue and private desires—and the effects of this relationship on the individual's spirit. He is known for his wit and comedy, but beyond the streetwise dialogues lie more problematic concerns. The typical Mamet play presents the near-complete separation of the individual from genuine relationships. Mamet replicates human commitments and desires in demythicized forms: commodity fetishism, sexual negotiations and exploitations, botched crimes, physical assaults, fraudulent business transactions enacted by petty thieves masquerading as business associates, and human relationships whose only shared feature is the presence of sex and the absence of love. Although he varies his plays in terms of plots and themes, Mamet seems at his best when critiquing what he believes is a business ethic that has led to the corruption of both the social contract and his heroes' moral values. Mamet's major achievements, then, concern his use of language, his social examination of professional and private betrayals and alienation, and his ability to capture the anxieties of the individual—whether he or she is a small-time thief, a working-class person, or a Hollywood executive.

Biography

Born on the South Side of Chicago on November 30, 1947, David Alan Mamet became interested in the theater as a teenager. He worked at the Hull House Theatre and at Second City, one of Chicago's richest improvisational performance sites at the time, experiences that he recognized as having exerted an important influence on his language, characterizations, and plot structures. His mother, Lenore Silver, was a schoolteacher, his father, Bernard Mamet, a labor lawyer and minor semanticist, and though the parents' intellectual awareness of language plainly influenced their son, their divorce seems to have affected the young Mamet even more greatly. Exiled to what Mamet saw as a sterile suburb of Chicago—Olympia Fields—his geographical move seemed all the more complicated because of his familial dislocations. His stepfather apparently (Mamet revealed in a 1992 essay entitled "The Rake") physically and psychologically abused the Mamet family, and it seems as if the world of the theater offered the playwright some form of reprieve and, later, recognition from a tension-filled youth. As a boy, Mamet also acted on television, an opportunity made possible by his uncle, who was the director of broadcasting for the Chicago Board of Rabbis. Mamet often was cast as a Jewish boy plagued by religious self-doubt and concerns.

After graduating from Francis Parker, a private school in downtown Chicago, Mamet attended Goddard College in Plainfield, Vermont, where he majored in theater and literature. At Goddard, he wrote his first play, *Camel*, which fulfilled his thesis requirement for graduation and was staged at the college in 1968. During his junior year (1968-1969), Mamet moved from Plainfield to New York City, where he studied acting at the Neighborhood Playhouse with Sanford Meisner, one of the founding members of the Group Theatre in the 1930's. While his talents as an actor were minimal at best, Mamet's attention to idiolect and its cadence was greatly enhanced by Meisner. After earning his B.A. in literature in 1969, he worked in a truck factory, a canning plant, and a real estate office, and he labored as an office cleaner, a window washer, and a taxi driver. He also became a drama teacher for a year at the Marlboro College (1970-1971) and, after working at more odd jobs, returned to Goddard College as artist-in-residence (1971-1973); while at Goddard, he formed a group of actors that soon moved to Chicago as the St. Nicholas Theatre Company, for which he served as artistic director. Soon, Mamet's plays became regular fare within the burgeoning theater world in Chicago. Such small but influential theaters as the Body Politic, the Organic Theatre, and then the more established Goodman Theatre presented *Sexual Perversity in Chicago* and *American Buffalo*. In 1974, Mamet became a faculty member on the Illinois Arts Council and a year later a visiting lecturer at the University of Chicago; in 1976-1977, he became a Teaching Fellow at the Yale School of Drama.

Thus, the mid-1970's were pivotal years for the playwright. In 1975, *American Buffalo* opened at the Goodman Theatre and soon moved to the St. Nicholas Theatre; the play won a Joseph Jefferson Award for Outstanding Production, as did *Sexual Perversity in Chicago* that same year. Moreover, Mamet in 1975 finally saw his work staged in New York City: *Sexual Perversity* and *Duck Variations* opened at the St. Clement's Theatre and, in 1976, moved to the Off-Broadway Cherry Lane Theatre. In 1976, *American Buffalo* opened at the St. Clement's Theatre and Mamet won an Obie Award for *Sexual Perversity in Chicago* and *American Buffalo*. No less than nine Mamet plays appeared in 1977 in theaters in New Haven, New York, Chicago, and, among other cities, London. *American Buffalo*, for which Mamet received the New York Drama Critics Circle Award, premiered on Broadway in 1977, starring Robert Duvall. In 1980, Al Pacino starred in a revival of *American Buffalo* in New Haven. Such successes confirmed Mamet's reputation as a new and vital theatrical voice in the United States.

Mamet has written more than thirty plays, a number of sketches, poetry, essays, children's plays, several important Chekhov adaptations, a book concerning film directing, and more than a dozen screenplays. He has also garnered many awards, including a Pulitzer Prize for *Glengarry Glen Ross* in 1986. Mamet in the 1990's has been honored for his brilliant use of language and characterizations that capture important aspects of American cultural poetics. His play *Oleanna*, which opened at the Orpheum Theatre in New York City in October, 1992, and features William H. Macy and Mamet's wife, British-born Rebecca Pidgeon, has only added to the dramatist's reputation for staging serious plays about serious matters.

Analysis

David Mamet is an ethicist. From his initial plays—*Camel, Lakeboat*—to those pivotal works that first brought him notoriety—*Sexual Perversity in Chicago, American Buffalo*—and from *Glengarry Glen Ross* to *Oleanna*, Mamet explores a delicate moral balance between private self-interests and larger public issues that shape modern culture. Indeed, Mamet is at his best when critiquing the tensions between his heroes' sense of public responsibility and their definition of private liberties. Throughout his theater, Mamet presents a dialectic that, on the one hand, recognizes the individual's right to pursue vigorously entrepreneurial interests, but that, on the other, acknowledges that in an ideal world, such private interests should, but do not, exist in equipoise with a civic sense and moral duty. This underlying tension produces in Mamet's protagonists divided loyalties. Such tension also gives his theater its particular unity of vision and ambivalent intensity. Mamet has often mentioned that his views of the social contract have been greatly influenced by Thorstein Veblen's *The Theory of the Leisure Class* (1899), and such indebtedness in part accounts for Mamet's preoccupation with business as a sacramental world. Veblen's work, like Mamet's, underscores human action and response in terms of "pecuniary emulation," imperialist ownership, primitive sexual roles as first seen in ancient tribal communities, questions of honor, invidious comparisons, and the relationship between self-worth and wealth. Mamet is a theatrician of the ethical precisely because his characters, plots, and themes map out a predatory world in which only the fittest, and surely the greediest, might survive. Hence, Mamet's plays all are concerned with charting the moral relationship between the public issues of the nation and the private anxieties of its citizens.

Mamet seems at his best when dramatizing the way in which public issues, usually in the form of business transactions, permeate the individual's private sensibilities. "Business," for Mamet, becomes an expansive concept, including not only one's public, professional vocation but also one's private, personal existence—the problematic "business" of living itself. Under the guise of healthy competition and the right to pursue a contemporary version of the myth of the American Dream, Mamet's heroes too often conveniently twist such business savvy to suit their own selfish needs. Further, this examination of "business" suggests, for Mamet, that people live in a Macbethean world, where "fair is foul and foul is fair," where sharp business practice too often leads to corruption, where deception and stealing are simply regarded as being competitive within the American business world.

Mamet believes in the powers of the imagination and art to liberate, to create a liberal humanism. This is exactly what John in *A Life in the Theatre* or Karen in *Speed-the-Plow* believe. Such an attitude, however, clearly does not make sense, Mamet also implies throughout his theater, because there is little or no place for such romantic impulses in a hurly-burly business world. What makes Mamet's heroes so theatrically engaging to watch concerns an invisible inner drama, a subtextual crisis that haunts them: Underneath the character's hard-boiled, enameled public bravado lies a figure plagued with self-doubt and insecurities. If Mamet's heroes try to come to some higher consciousness, as do Don in *American Buffalo*, Aaronow in *Glengarry Glen Ross*, and Karen in *Speed-the-Plow*, such valiant impulses to come to awareness are not ultimately to be realized. Many of Mamet's best characters—Bernie in *Sexual Perversity in Chicago* or Teach in *American Buffalo*—simply seem unwilling or unable to understand what Mamet believes are the regenerative powers implicit in self-awareness and self-responsibility. Some of his characters—most of the men in *Lakeboat*, for example—do not seem to understand that any form of transcendent consciousness even exists as a possibility. Perhaps this explains why many Mamet heroes lack the capacity to celebrate any experience external to the self. Instead, typical Mamet heroes seem motivated only in sexual and financial terms, blinding themselves to the larger personal or societal implications of their exploits. To be sure, some Mamet characters exude a deeper awareness, as do the Father and Daughter in *Dark Pony*, Aaronow in *Glengarry Glen Ross*, or Karen in *Speed-the-Plow*. Others, moreover, come tantalizingly close to understanding their own essential self and the reason for their existence in a world of diminished possibilities; Lang in *The Water Engine* and Edmond in *Edmond* possess some degree of self-awareness, ineffectual as such awareness turns out to be for them.

Mamet's works, however, show a grimly deterministic theater in which his heroes are victims. Their victimization stems from outer forces—a ruthless business associate, an opportunistic executive, a petty thief—as well as from inner forces: the failure of self-reliance, the exaggerated claim that proves false, and characters' obsession with money that they will never see and with relationships that will never be fulfilling. Thus, throughout

his career, Mamet investigates the relatedness of one's job, sense of fulfillment, and morality. The problem facing his characters, however, is that
they struggle (and usually fail) to take responsibility, choosing instead to
avoid honest communication or anything that might lead to an authentic
encounter. Instead, Mamet's heroes often commit ethically perverse deeds
that only further contribute to their own marginalization. In their efforts
not to confuse public and private issues, Mamet's characters ironically distort the social contract to such an extent that humane values, communication, and love are reduced to barely felt forces.

Three early Mamet plays prefigure the issues discussed above. *Duck
Variations* concerns Emil Varec and George S. Aronovitz, two men in their
sixties sitting on a park bench, whose reflections and constant duologues
reveal their attempt to come to terms with their own insignificance in the
world. Built on numerous episodes, the play shows that the two men come
too close to talking about their own finiteness, and so both replace honest
conversation with banal talk, their way of avoiding their fear of death. In
another early play, *Lakeboat*, Mamet presents life aboard the *T. Harrison*,
a ship traveling through the Great Lakes. The men are leading death-in-life
existences because their jobs have reduced their lives to deadening routines
and habits. Built around fragments of conversation, the play presents ordinary men—Joe, Fred, and Fireman—leading desperate lives. To fill the
void, they engage in endless talks that lead to no epiphany; like the ship,
they simply sail through their lives. *Sexual Perversity in Chicago* presents
thirty-four scenes dealing with sex. The play opens in a singles' bar, where
Bernard tells his friend Danny, in graphic detail, about his recent sexual
encounter with a woman. Their conversations are carnivalesque dialogues
filled with obscenities and dirty jokes. Deb and Joan, the central females
in the drama, seem little better off, as Bernard's sexist remarks are
matched by Joan's hostile response to Danny. Clearly in this play, Mamet
outlines a world in which eros has been defleshed and a fundamental and
anxiety-producing loneliness dominates. Near the end of the play, Danny
and Bernard stare at women on the beach, and when one does not respond
to Danny's coarse remarks, he screams obscenities, which outline the intensity of his frustration and his inability to deal with loss. Sexual encounters, devoid of any genuine love, account for the title and theme of this
important work.

These three earlier plays stand as examples of Mamet's interest in portraying people whose lives have almost been reduced to nothingness, a
motif that he continues to refine in *American Buffalo*, *Glengarry Glen
Ross*, *Speed-the-Plow*, and *Oleanna*, plays that most theatergoers and
critics believe represent his best work.

American Buffalo concerns small-time thieves who find a buffalo nickel
in Don's junk shop (where the play unwinds), motivating them to rob the

man from whom Don supposedly purchased the coin. Don orchestrates the robbery plans, which the younger Bob, who eats sugar, soda, and drugs, will try to accomplish. Teach, a nervous man with a swagger, insists that he, a man, do the job; Teach cannot believe that Don would let Bob, a boy, try such a robbery. A long honor-among-thieves conversation ensues in which Teach's lines brilliantly reflect Mamet's vision, a vision suggesting the extent to which ethics have been devalued and stealing has been elevated to the status of good business savvy. Free enterprise, Teach lectures Don, gives one the freedom "[t]o embark on Any . . . Course that he sees fit. . . . In order to secure his honest chance to make a profit." He quickly adds that this does not make him "a Commie" and that the "country's *founded* on this, Don. You know this." The robbery never takes place, but near midnight, Bob returns with another buffalo nickel. Don seems embarrassed, and Teach becomes agitated, hitting the boy several times. Bob reveals that he bought the coveted nickel, made up the story about a rich coin collector, and suggested the burglary. Suddenly, whatever friendships exist among the men temporarily evaporate: Teach attacks Bob and trashes the entire junk shop. A precarious friendship, however, still remains. The play ends when Teach regains his composure and readies himself to take the injured Bob to the hospital; Bob and Don exchange apologies, and the curtain falls. If the characters do not realize how much they have buffaloed one another, the audience certainly does.

Glengarry Glen Ross extends Mamet's preoccupation with business as a sacramental world. The play dramatizes the high-pressure real estate profession as seen through the plight of small-time salesmen. Greed lies at the center of the play, for the characters' directing force in life is to secure sale "leads" and clients to "close" deals, and to rise to the top of the "board," the chart announcing which man in the sales force wins the ultimate prize—the Cadillac. The losers will simply be fired. *Glengarry Glen Ross*, like *The Water Engine*, *Mr. Happiness*, and *American Buffalo*, relies on the myth of the American Dream as its ideological backdrop. The title refers to Florida swamps, not the Scottish Highlands, which indicates just how much the playwright wishes to make experience ironic in this drama. Whereas the characters in *Lakeboat*, *Reunion*, and even *The Shawl* lead lives of quiet desperation, those in *Glengarry Glen Ross* scream out two hours of obscenity-laced dialogue. Levene may be the most desperate, for his business failures of late lead him to crime: Through a Pinteresque unfolding of events, viewers learn that he robs his own office to secure precious sales "leads." Moss is the most ruthless, masterminding the robbery while Aaronow simply seems bewildered by his cohorts' cheating. Williamson is the office manager, whose lack of sales experience and pettiness earn him the scorn of all. Ricky Roma, however, is different.

Roma emerges as the star of the sales team. He also appears as the most complex. Youthful, handsome, Roma exudes a certain panache that sets him apart from the others. Whereas the others talk about their past conquests and how, with luck (and deception), they will rise to the top of the sales board, Roma produces. If Levene and Moss radiate a frenetic pursuit of customers, Roma appears soft edged. Roma, indeed, nearly succeeds in swindling an unsuspecting customer, James Lingk, who nearly gets locked into buying suspect real estate. Ironically, Williamson reveals to Lingk the truth, and Roma loses his prized commission when Lingk cancels the deal. When Roma hears this, he screams obscenities at Williamson and adds: "You just cost me *six thousand dollars.* (*Pause.*) Six thousand dollars. And one Cadillac." More than losing a sale, Roma loses what ethical perspective, if any, he possesses. Roma, of course, cannot comprehend this. Like Levene and Moss, Roma has no conscience, no sense of the boundaries of business ethics. Like the characters throughout Mamet's theater, Roma and his colleagues distort language and action to justify their work. The play ends with Levene's arrest; Mamet suggests that, after Levene's and perhaps Moss's arrests, life will go on, business as usual.

Speed-the-Plow extends Mamet's business plays. Set in Hollywood, the play centers on Bobby Gould, the recently promoted head of production for a Hollywood film company, and Charlie Fox, a friend who shows him a "buddy prison" film script. They sense a hit because of a macho star who will fill the lead role. In a dialogue that by now is regarded as vintage Mamet, the two celebrate their future fame and money (that surely will be certified by casting the macho star in the film) through a litany of obscenities. The plot thickens when they have to read a serious novel for cinematic possibilities, and when a temporary secretary, Karen, enters and Charlie bets five hundred dollars to see if Bobby can seduce her. Karen, however, preaches the truth to Bobby ("Is it a good film?" she asks), who decides to replace the "buddy prison" script with a film based on a novel on radiation. An outraged Charlie verbally and physically assaults Bobby when he hears this and rages at Karen. After Karen says that she would not have gone to bed with Bobby, Charlie throws Karen out, and he and Bobby become friends again and produce the banal "buddy" film. A lack of trust animates this play in which these Hollywood men are the spiritual kin of the men in *American Buffalo* and *Glengarry Glen Ross.*

Mamet's theater, in sum, repeatedly returns to broader social questions about communication and community. To be sure, not every Mamet drama includes verbal tirades and physical if not psychological violence. *Duck Variations*, *A Life in the Theatre*, *Reunion*, *The Woods*, and *The Shawl*—to cite plays spanning much of Mamet's career—appear as relatively quiet, meditative works whose plots and themes seem more interiorized. On the other hand, the playwright seems most comfortable, and at the height of his aesthetic power, when he replicates anger and betrayal, mystery and assault, and when he deepens social satire into private loss. From *Sexual Perversity in Chicago* through at least *Speed-the-Plow*, relationships are as ephemeral as they are unsatisfying, and a brutalizing language seems to be an attempt by his heroes to mask, unsuccessfully, their primal insecurities. There are no villains in his theater—only individuals whose world of diminished possibilities and banalities define and confine them. The detectable optimism found throughout much of *Writing in Restaurants*, a collection of essays that Mamet published in 1986 concerning his theory of art, seldom manifests itself in his theater. In a Mamet play, "things change" (to use the title of a Mamet screenplay), or perhaps things do not change, his characters remaining ossified spirits, divided against the self and the other, against home and their outer world. Mamet *is* a theatrician of the ethical. His characters, sets, and overall situations, however, map out a predatory world in which genuine communication and authentic love remain distant forces. Hence, Barker's lines in *The Water Engine* ratify, Mamet suggests, the gulf between idea and reality: "And now we leave the Hall of Science, the hub of our Century of Progress Exposition. Science, yes, the greatest force for Good and Evil we possess. The Concrete Poetry of Humankind. Our thoughts, our dreams, our aspirations rendered into practical and useful forms. Our science is our self." Such practicality, for Mamet, prefigures a kind of spiritual death on both a cultural as well as an individual level.

Oleanna, a play that in part concerns sexual harassment, represents the playwright's response to the Anita F. Hill-Clarence Thomas controversy. In act 1, a male college professor, John, and a female student, Carol, are in his office, she there because of difficulties in understanding his class. John, who is under tenure review, offers to help. The complacent professor, who is happily married and is negotiating a deal on a house, listens as she confesses, "I don't *understand.* I don't understand what anything means . . . and I walk around. From morning til night: with this one thought in my head. I'm *stupid.*" He offers Carol some advice and a consoling hand. While the audience senses an impending catastrophe, act 1 gives little hint at—depending on one's point of view—just how distorted the interpretation of the seemingly innocuous events of the first act will become.

The hurly-burly of act 2, however, makes for sparkling drama. Carol registers a complaint, accusing the professor of sexism, classism, and sexual harassment. He calls her back to the office in a failed attempt to clear up any misunderstandings. For John, she is dealing with "accusations"; for Carol, he has to face "facts." A campus support group helps Carol, and the play presents her growing sense of power and John's loss of control over events for which he may or may not be responsible. By the final scene, John loses more than the house and tenure. The college suspends him, and he may be facing charges of rape. Reduced to a groveling, pathetic figure, John appears in stark contrast to the suddenly articulate and holier-than-thou Carol.

In *Oleanna*, Mamet returns to a world in which the gaps between words and deeds remain. The play is theatrically powerful precisely because its author never fills in such gaps. Instead, theatergoers might ask: Is Carol framing John? Are her accusations legitimate? Is Carol simply the first to have the courage to challenge a patronizing and, perhaps, womanizing male teacher? Is John so much a part of an inherently misogynistic world that he seems blithely unaware that his well-meaning actions are in fact highly sexist? Mamet invites viewers to respond to these and many other questions (issues of censorship, political correctness, battles of the sexes, representations of women in theater, and so on). Thus, this 1992 play continues Mamet's exploration of a world that remains a battleground of the sexes, where primal feelings of trust and rational human discourse between women and men remain problematic at best—if not impossible. The title of the play, taken from a folk song, alludes to a nineteenth century escapist vision of utopia. *Oleanna* reminds the audience of the impossibility of such vision.

It seems appropriate to close the essay with a consideration of two other Mamet plays: *Reunion*, a play whose title might better read as "disunion," and *Edmond.* In the first, Bernie tells Carol that, although he comes from a broken home, he is "a happy man" who works at "a good job," but his uneasiness remains, particularly when one sees the contemporary world in which he and Carol live: "It's a . . . jungle out there. And you got to learn the rules because *nobody's* going to learn them for you." Thus, true knowledge about the soul and the universe can, in Mamet's world, only be purchased, as the almost poetic lines continue: "Always the price. Whatever it is. And you gotta know it and be prepared to pay it if you don't want it to pass you by." Out of such everyday as well as sensory experiences, Mamet implies throughout his canon, emerge no epiphanies. Rather, his characters merely internalize the messy inconclusiveness of their misspent lives, without the reassurances of some higher consciousness. In the other play, *Edmond*, Edmond is a racist, sexist, homophobic who leaves his "safe" marriage and embarks on an urban quest to find meaning to his fragmented world. Encountering violence, murder, sexual frustration, and so on, he winds up in jail, sodomized by his black cell mate. If Edmond learns anything from his quest, it is that he accepts his own plight as an acquiescent victim in the jail cell. He becomes the compliant mate with his cell mate.

Mamet's following observation from *Writing in Restaurants* is hardly surprising: "As the Stoics said, either gods exist or they do not exist. If they exist, then, no doubt, things are unfolding as they should; if they do *not* exist, then why should we be reluctant to depart a world in which there are no gods?" This comment stands as the metaphysical question Mamet raises, and refuses to resolve, in his theater. The resolutions, whatever they may be, are left for the audience to ponder.

Other major works

POETRY: *The Hero Pony*, 1990.

NONFICTION: *Writing in Restaurants*, 1986; *Some Freaks*, 1989; *On Directing Film*, 1991; *The Cabin: Reminiscence and Diversions*, 1992.

SCREENPLAYS: *The Postman Always Rings Twice*, 1981 (adapted from the novel by James M. Cain); *The Verdict*, 1982 (based on the novel by Barry Reed); *The Untouchables*, 1985; *House of Games*, 1987; *Things Change*, 1988; *We're No Angels*, 1989; *Homicide*, 1991; *Glengarry Glen Ross*, 1992 (adapted from his play); *Hoffa*, 1992.

TELEPLAY: *Five Television Plays*, 1990.

RADIO PLAYS: *Prairie du Chien*, 1978; *Cross Patch*, 1985; *Goldberg Street*, 1985.

CHILDREN'S LITERATURE: *The Owl*, 1987; *Warm and Cold*, 1988 (with Donald Sultan).

Bibliography

Bigsby, C. W. E. *A Critical Introduction to Twentieth-Century American Drama: Beyond Broadway.* Vol. 3. Cambridge, England: Cambridge University Press, 1985. Bigsby devotes pages 251 to 290 to Mamet, whom he considers "a poet of loss." His analyses are as sensitive as they are challenging, and they are compulsory reading for anyone interested in Mamet. Includes a bibliography.

_____. *David Mamet.* London: Methuen, 1985. This first book-length study of Mamet is essential reading. Bigsby examines twelve plays and sees Mamet as "a moralist lamenting the collapse of public forum and private purpose, exposing a dessicated world in which the cadences of despair predominate." Contains a brief bibliography.

Carroll, Dennis. *David Mamet.* New York: St. Martin's Press, 1987. Carroll's discussions of Mamet's language are excellent, and he considers the plays in terms of business, sex, learning, and communion. This slender volume also contains a useful bibliography and chronology.

Dean, Anne. *David Mamet: Language as Dramatic Action.* Rutherford, N.J.: Fairleigh Dickinson University Press, 1990. Language describes, prescribes, defines, and confines Mamet's characters, Dean suggests in this perceptive study.

Kane, Leslie, ed. *David Mamet: A Casebook.* New York: Garland, 1992. Kane has edited the first collection of critical essays on Mamet. The volume contains Kane's introduction, her two interviews, and her bibliography in addition to twelve essays by Ruby Cohn, Dennis Carroll, Steven H. Gale, Deborah R. Geis, Ann C. Hall, Christopher C. Hudgins, Michael Hinden, Pascale Hubert-Leiber, Matthew C. Roudané, Henry I. Schvey, and Hersh Zeifman. This 310-page volume, which contains a detailed annotated bibliography, an excellent chronology, and a thorough index, is an exemplary addition to Mamet scholarship.

Schlueter, June. "David Mamet." In *American Dramatists: Contemporai Authors Bibliographic Series*, edited by Matthew C. Roudané. Vol. : Detroit: Gale Research, 1989. Schlueter's bibliographic essay surveys th major primary and secondary items on Mamet. This extremely thoroug account includes production history as well. A crucial addition for scholars and students.

Matthew C. Roudané

CHRISTOPHER MARLOWE

Born: Canterbury, England; February 6, 1564
Died: Deptford, England; May 30, 1593

Principal drama

Dido, Queen of Carthage, pr. c. 1586-1587, pb. 1594 (with Thomas Nashe); *Tamburlaine the Great, Part I*, pr. c. 1587, pb. 1590; (commonly known as *Tamburlaine*); *Tamburlaine the Great, Part II*, pr. 1587, pb. 1590; *Doctor Faustus*, pr. c. 1588, pb. 1604; *The Jew of Malta*, pr. c. 1589, pb. 1633; *Edward II*, pr. c. 1592, pb. 1594; *The Massacre at Paris*, pr. 1593, pb. 1594 (?).

Other literary forms

Christopher Marlowe translated Lucan's *Pharsalia* (1600) and Ovid's *Elegies* (*Amores*, 1595-1600) while still attending Cambridge (c. 1584-1587). The renderings of the *Elegies* are notable for their imaginative liveliness and rhetorical strength. They provide as well the earliest examples of the heroic couplet in English. *Hero and Leander* (1598), a long, erotic poem composed before 1593, is also indebted to Ovid. It is the best narrative of a group that includes William Shakespeare's *Venus and Adonis* (1593) and John Marston's *Metamorphosis of Pygmalion's Image* (1598). The vogue for these Ovidian epyllions lasted for more than a decade, and Marlowe's reputation as a poet was confirmed on the basis of his contribution. He completed only the first two sestiads before his death, after which George Chapman continued and finished the poem. Marlowe's brilliant heroic couplets create a world, in Eugene Ruoff's words, of "moonlight and mushrooms"; his lovers are the idealized figures of pastoral, chanting lush and sensual hymns or laments. A sophisticated narrator—viewed by most critics as representing Marlowe's satiric viewpoint—manages to balance the sentimentalism of the lovers, giving the poem an ironic quality that is sustained throughout. This tone, however, is not a feature of Marlowe's famous lyric, "The Passionate Shepherd to His Love." First published in an anthology entitled *The Passionate Pilgrim* (1599), the poem is a beautiful evocation of the attractions of the pastoral world, a place where "melodious birds sing madrigals." Technically called an "invitation," "The Passionate Shepherd to His Love" became an extremely popular idyll and was often imitated or parodied by other writers. One of the most intriguing responses, "The Nymph's Reply," was composed by Sir Walter Raleigh and published in *The Passionate Pilgrim*. Its worldly, skeptical attitude offers a contrast to the exuberance of Marlowe's lyric. Without a doubt, this pastoral piece, along with *Hero and Leander*, would have ensured Marlowe's reputation as a major literary figure even if he had never written a work intended for the stage.

Achievements

It is difficult to overestimate the poetic and dramatic achievement of Marlowe. Although his career was short (about six years), Marlowe wrote plays that appealed to an emerging popular audience and that strongly influenced other dramatists. The heroes of the plays have been called "overreachers" and "apostates," figures whom many critics believe reveal the defiance and cynicism of Marlowe himself. In addition to introducing these controversial, larger-than-life protagonists, Marlowe was also instrumental in fusing the elements of classical—and especially Senecan—drama and native morality plays, thereby establishing a style that would be followed by many subsequent playwrights. *Doctor Faustus* is the prime example of Marlowe's talent for combining classical satire and a conventional Elizabethan theme of man in a middle state, torn between the angel and the beast. The vitality of *Doctor Faustus*, *Tamburlaine the Great*, and Marlowe's other works can be traced as well to his facility for writing powerful yet musical blank verse. Indeed, so regular and forceful is his style that his verse has been described as "Marlowe's mighty line," and his achievement in blank verse no doubt influenced Shakespeare. It is apparent in such plays as *Richard II*, *The Merchant of Venice*, and *Othello* that Shakespeare was also inspired by certain of Marlowe's themes and plots.

Marlowe did not possess a patriotic spirit; his heroes are not Prince Hals but rather men similar to Shakespeare's Richard III. Yet he was sensitive to the range of passion in human nature. Many of Marlowe's characters reflect a true-to-life, even psychological complexity that preceding English playwrights had been incapable of demonstrating. Doctor Faustus' fear on the night he will lose his soul is beautifully portrayed in the memorable Latin line, adapted from Ovid's *Amores*, "O lente, lente currite noctis equi!" ("O slowly, slowly, run you horses of the night"). Barabas, villain-hero of *The Jew of Malta*, displays almost the same intensity of feeling as he rhapsodizes over his gold, his "infinite riches in a little room." Over the short span of his career, Marlowe moved away from the extravagant declamatory style of *Tamburlaine the Great* to a blank verse—notably in *Edward II*—that echoed the rhythm of elevated speech. It is difficult to predict what further advances there would have been in his style had he lived as long as Shakespeare. It is doubtful, however, that he would have changed so radically as to achieve universal popularity. His vision was satiric and therefore narrow; the themes and characters that he chose to write about lacked widespread appeal. Nevertheless, "Kit" Marlowe transformed the English stage from a platform for allegorical interludes or homespun slapstick into a forum for exploring the most controversial of human and social issues. Marlowe also established the poetic medium— vigorous blank verse—that would prove to be the dominant form of dramatic expression until the close of the theaters.

Biography

Christopher Marlowe was born in Canterbury, England, in February, 1564. His father was a respected member of the tanners' and shoemakers' guild. Marlowe attended the King's School of Canterbury in 1579 and 1580, leaving in 1581 to study at Corpus Christi College, Cambridge. He was the recipient of a scholarship funded by Matthew Parker, Archbishop of Canterbury; as a foundation scholar, Marlowe was expected to prepare for a post in the Church. In 1584, he took his bachelor of arts degree, after which he continued to hold his scholarship while studying for his master of arts degree. It appears that he would not have been granted his degree in 1587 except for the intervention of the queen's Privy Council. This body declared that Marlowe had done the government some service—probably as a spy in Reims, home of exiled English Catholics—and ordered that he be granted his M.A. at the "next commencement." Marlowe had no doubt been writing poetry while at Cambridge, and he probably decided to make his way in this profession in London. It is certain that he was there in 1589, because he was a resident of Newgate Prison during that year. He and a man named Thomas Watson were jailed for having murdered another man, although it appears that Watson actually did the killing. Three years later, in 1592, Marlowe was again in trouble with the law, being placed under a peace bond by two London constables. Clearly, the young writer and scholar did not move in the best of social circles, even though his patron was Thomas Walsingham and Sir Walter Raleigh was his close friend. One of Marlowe's colleagues, a man with whom he once shared a room, was Thomas Kyd, who in May of 1593 was arrested, charged with atheism, and tortured. Kyd accused Marlowe of atheism, claiming that the heretical documents found in their room belonged to the latter. The Privy Council sent out an order for Marlowe's arrest (he was staying at the Walsingham estate), but instead of imprisoning him, the Council simply required that he report every day until the hearing.

That hearing never took place: Marlowe died within two weeks after his detainment. On May 30, after a bout of drinking at a tavern in Deptford, Marlowe quarreled with a companion named Ingram Frizer, who settled the account by stabbing the playwright. Those who believed the charge of atheism brought against him saw Marlowe's end as an example of God's justice. Others, however, speculated on the possibility that he was the victim of an assassination plot, spawned to eliminate a spy who may have known too much. This theory seems fanciful, but it had many contemporary adherents; the details surrounding the murder do not adequately explain the facts. Whatever the cause, Marlowe's death marked the tragic end of a meteoric career on the public stage. As an innovator—and rebel—he challenged his fellow playwrights to achieve greater heights of creativity while he himself left behind a rich legacy of plays and poems.

Analysis

Christopher Marlowe probably began writing plays while he was a student at Cambridge. *Dido, Queen of Carthage*, which appeared in quarto form in 1594, was composed in collaboration with Thomas Nashe and was first performed by the children's company at the Chapel Royal. How much Nashe actually had to do with the work is conjectural; he may have only edited it for publication. The tragedy shows little evidence, however, of the playwright's later genius. It is closely tied to Vergil's *Aeneid*, with much of its blank verse qualifying as direct translation from the Latin. The characters are wooden and the action highly stylized, the result of an attempt to translate the material of epic into drama. The play impresses mainly through the force of its imagery.

Sections of Marlowe's first popular theater success, *Tamburlaine the Great, Part I*, were probably sketched at Cambridge as well. First produced around 1587 (probably at an innyard), this exotic, bombastic piece won for its author considerable fame. His name was quickly cataloged with other so-called University Wits—men such as Robert Greene, John Lyly, and George Peele, whose dramas dominated the Elizabethan stage in the late 1580's. Marlowe's great dramatic epic was roughly based on the career of Timur Lenk (1336-1405), a Mongolian fighter who had led an army that defeated the Turks at Ankara in 1402. The defeat meant the salvation of Europe, an event that doubtless stimulated Marlowe's ironic vision. The playwright could have found the account of the audacious Scythian's career in many Latin and Italian sources, but his interest may have been first aroused after reading George Whetstone's *The English Mirror* (1586).

Tamburlaine emerges as an Olympian figure in Marlowe's hands. He begins as a lowly shepherd whose physical courage and captivating, defiant rhetoric take him to victories over apparently superior opponents. Although episodic, the plot does achieve a degree of tension as each successive opponent proves more difficult to overcome. Tamburlaine's first victim is a hereditary king named Mycetes, who underrates his adversary's strength and persuasiveness. The lieutenant who is sent to capture the upstart is suddenly and decisively won over to the rebel's side. Tamburlaine next outwits Cosroe, Mycetes' brother, who thinks he can use this untutored fighter to consolidate his own power. As the "bloody and insatiate Tamburlaine" kills him, Cosroe curses the turn of Fortune's Wheel that has cast him down. Even so, Marlowe believes not in the capricious goddess as the chief ruler of men but in a kind of Machiavellian system directed by the will of his larger-than-life hero.

A major test of Tamburlaine's will comes in his confrontation with Bajazeth, Emperor of the Turks. Before the battle between the two warriors, there is a boasting bout between their two mistresses, Zenocrate and Zabina. The former, daughter to the Soldan of Egypt and in love with

Tamburlaine, praises her beloved's strength and his destined glory. Both women also pray for the victory of their men, parallel actions that invite a comparison between the pairs of lovers. When Tamburlaine defeats Bajazeth, he takes the crown from Zabina's head and gives it to his queen—and "conqueror." Marlowe thereby demonstrates that the play qualifies as a monumental love story as well. Bajazeth is bound up and later thrown into a cage with his defeated queen; this contraption is then towed across the stage as part of Tamburlaine's victory procession. Before the final siege of Damascus, the city that houses Zenocrate's father, the Soldan, Tamburlaine unveils a magnificent banquet. During the festivities, he releases Bajazeth from his cage in order to use him as a footstool from which he will step onto his throne. This audacious touch of spectacle verifies Marlowe's aim of shocking his audience and displays contempt for the pride of rulers.

In the midst of this banquet, Tamburlaine orders his lieutenants to "hang our bloody colors by Damascus,/ Reflexing hues of blood upon their heads,/ While they walk quivering on their walls,/ Half dead for fear before they feel my wrath!" These threatening, boastful words are followed quickly by a change of colors to black, which signifies Tamburlaine's intention to destroy the city. He underscores this purpose by condemning four virgins, supplicants sent to assuage his anger, to their deaths on the spears of his horsemen. The destruction of the city soon follows, although the Soldan and the King of Arabia (to whom Zenocrate is still betrothed) lead out an army to do battle with their oppressor. While this battle takes place offstage, Bajazeth and Zabina are rolled in to deliver curses against their torturers. Wild from hunger and despair, Bajazeth asks his queen to fetch him something to drink; while she is away, he brains himself against the bars of the cage. Zabina, returning from her errand, finds her husband's battered corpse and follows his lead. The horror of this double suicide no doubt satisfied the popular audience's appetite for gore, an appetite that Marlowe fed lavishly in this play.

The finale of the first part depicts Tamburlaine's victory over the Soldan, who is spared because the victor plans to crown Zenocrate Queen of Persia. Meanwhile, her betrothed, the King of Arabia, dies from battle wounds; his death causes little conflict, however, in Zenocrate, who follows Tamburlaine as if he were indeed her conqueror, too. Now the lowly shepherd-turned-king declares a truce, buries his noble opponents with solemn rites, and prepares to marry his beloved in pomp and splendor. He appears to stand atop Fortune's Wheel, a startling example of the Machiavellian man of iron will to whom no leader or law is sacrosanct. There is little sense here that Tamburlaine is intended as an example of pride going before a fall. He has achieved stunning victories over foes who are as immoral as he is; most of them, including Bajazeth, emerge as fools who miscalculate or underrate Tamburlaine with fearful consequences. No doubt the popularity of the play is traceable to this fact and to the truth that most people nurture an amoral desire for fame or power that this hero fulfills with startling success.

Part II shows Tamburlaine continuing on his road to conquest, securely characterizing himself as the Scourge of God. As the play opens, Sigismund, Christian King of Hungary, and the pagan monarch Orcanes agree to a truce. This ceremony strikes one as ironic, as pagans and Christians swallow their pride in order to challenge and defeat the half-god who threatens them. In the meantime, Tamburlaine proudly surveys the fruits of Zenocrate's womb: three sons through whom he hopes to win immortality. One of the brood, however, is weak and unattracted by war; Calyphas seems devoted to his mother and to the blandishments of peace. His effeminate nature foreshadows Tamburlaine's decline and fall, revealing that his empire cannot survive his own death. Even though his two other sons exhibit natures cruel enough to match their father's, the flawed seed has obviously been planted.

The hastily forged truce is suddenly broken when Sigismund tears the document and turns his forces on Orcanes. Though Marlowe appears to be attacking the integrity of Christianity, he was in fact appealing to his audience's anti-Catholic sentiments. When Sigismund is wounded and dies, moreover, Orcanes announces that Christ has won a victory in defeating one so treacherous as Sigismund. While these events transpire on the battlefield, another death is about to take place in Tamburlaine's tent. Zenocrate has been in failing health, and her imminent death causes her husband to contemplate joining her. That he should entertain such a gesture at the height of his power confirms the depth of his love for Zenocrate. Her imploring words—"Live still, my lord! O, let my sovereign live!"—manage to stay his hand, but his pent-up rage cannot be restrained at her death. Shifting from a figure of gentleness and compassion in a moment's time, Tamburlaine orders the town in which she dies to be burned to the ground.

With the defeat of Sigismund, Orcanes emerges as a kingmaker, leading the grand procession at which Callapine, the avenging son of Bajazeth, vows to use his new crown as the means to conquer the lowly Scythian. This scene is succeeded by another ceremonial pageant, this one led by the mournful Tamburlaine and his sons carrying the coffin of Zenocrate. Her body will remain with the company wherever they go in battle. Determined to teach his sons the arts of war, Tamburlaine commences a lesson in besieging a fort. When Calyphas balks, afraid of wounding or death, an angry father lances his own arm and orders his sons to dip their hands in his blood. All of them comply, although Calyphas is moved to pity at this horrid sight. With this ritual, Marlowe underscores the tribal nature of his hero's family but at the same time implies that the letting of blood by Tamburlaine will not necessarily cure the "defect" in it.

The central battle in the second part pits Tamburlaine and his sons against Callapine and his crowned kings before Aleppo. In a preliminary verbal skirmish, Tamburlaine belittles Almeda, a traitor, who cowers behind Callapine's back when invited to take his crown. The scene is serio-comic as Almeda proves himself a coward before his kingly followers; his weakness is meant to parallel that of Calyphas, Tamburlaine's son. The latter remains behind in a tent playing cards while his two brothers earn martial honors on the battlefield. When they and their father enter, trailing the conquered Turkish monarchs behind them, Tamburlaine seizes his weakling son and stabs him. Among the many scenes of bloodshed Marlowe presents in the play, this is probably the most shocking and repulsive. Although he cites his role as God's scourge and this deed as "war's justice," Tamburlaine here reveals a self-destructive side of his nature that has not been evident before.

The audience does not have long to ponder the murder; the scene of horror is quickly followed by one of pageantry. Trebizon and Soria, two pagan kings, enter the stage drawing a chariot with Tamburlaine holding the reins. This spectacle is accompanied by the superhero's disdaining words: "Holla, ye pamper'd jades of Asia!/ What can ye draw but twenty miles a day,/ And have so proud a chariot at your heels,/ And such a coachman as great Tamburlaine?" The monarch-prisoners hurl curses at their captors as, like Bajazeth and Zabina, they are taunted unmercifully. Tamburlaine's soldiers are rewarded with Turkish concubines, after which the royal train heads toward Babylon for yet another bloody siege.

Before the walls of this ancient city, Tamburlaine calls upon its governor to yield. (The scene recalls the negotiations before the walls of Damascus in Part I.) When he refuses, the lieutenants Techelles and Theridamas lead their soldiers in scaling the city's walls. The victory is quickly won, and Tamburlaine, dressed in black and driving his chariot, proudly announces the city's defeat. A quaking governor promises Tamburlaine abundant treasure if he will spare his life, but the conqueror disdains such bribes and has his victim hanged in chains from the walls. Theridamas shoots the governor while Tamburlaine proceeds to burn Muhammadan books in an open pit. Defying Mahomet to avenge his sacrilege if he has any power, Tamburlaine suddenly feels "distempered"; he recovers quickly, however, when he hears of Callapine's army advancing. Does Marlowe mean to imply that his hero's unexpected illness is punishment for his act of defiance? Although such an explicit moral lesson seems uncharacteristic, the connection between the two events appears to be more than a passing one.

The weakened Tamburlaine manages a final victory over Bajazeth's son, after which he produces a map that represents the extent of his conquests. With a trembling finger, he also directs his sons' attention to the remaining countries that they will be expected to conquer. Giving his crown to Theridamas (who later bestows it on Amyras) and turning his chariot over to his sons, Tamburlaine then calls for Zenocrate's hearse, beside which he stretches out to die. Before the mighty general's body is carried off, Amyras delivers the fitting eulogy: "Meet heaven and earth, and here let all things end,/ For earth hath spent the pride of all her fruit,/ And heaven consum'd his choicest living fire:/ Let earth and heaven his timeless death deplore,/ For both their worths will equal him no more." The death of the Scourge of Heaven follows no particular event; its suddenness only serves to underscore Tamburlaine's mortality. The audience is reminded of Alexander's demise in the midst of his glory. Because the chariot becomes such a dominant prop in the second part, Marlow may have likewise meant to suggest a parallel between his hero and Phaëthon, who in his pride fell from Jove's chariot because he could not control its course. Whatever the interpretation of this hero's fall, there can be little doubt that his mighty feats and his Senecan bombast made him an extremely popular—and awesome—figure on the Elizabethan stage.

For his next play, *The Jew of Malta*, Marlowe also chose an antihero who poses a threat to the orderly rule of European society. As Tamburlaine had ruled by martial strength, Barabas (named to recall the thief whose place on the Cross was taken by Christ) hopes to dominate the world by his wealth. Although Marlowe depicts him as a grasping, evil man (to the delight of the anti-Semitic Elizabethan audience), Barabas holds one's interest as Richard III does—by the resourcefulness of his scheming. Just as Tamburlaine's audacity appeals to an unconscious desire for power, so Barabas' scorn for Christian morality probably appealed to the audience's wish to defy authority. He is not portrayed, however, as a sympathetic character, even though in the early stages of the play, the behavior of his Christian opponents toward him reveals their hypocrisy. Faced with a threat from the powerful Turkish fleet, Ferneze, the Maltese governor, turns to Barabas for help in raising tribute money. While three of his colleagues agree to give up half of their estates and consent to baptism, Barabas refuses this arrangement, miscalculating the power and determination of the governor. Accompanied by a chorus of anti-Semitic remarks by the knights, Ferenze announces that he has already sent men to seize Barabas' property. He also declares that he intends to transform the Jew's mansion into a nunnery; this news further enrages Barabas, who curses them: "Take it to you, i' th' Devil's name." This scene highlights the hypocrisy of the Maltese; it also reveals the extent of Barabas' hatred for those among whom he has lived and worked. The audience has learned from the prologue spoken by Machiavel that the hero is one of his disciples and soon realizes that the subsequent action will show him "practicing" on his enemies.

When his daughter Abigail comes to recount angrily the takeover of their house, Barabas counsels patience, reminding her that he has hidden a fortune beneath its floorboards. In order to recover the money, he spawns a daring plan that requires his daughter to take vows as a means of entering the newly founded nunnery. In a heavily theatrical confrontation staged by Barabas, father accuses daughter of deserting him and their religion, while in an aside he tells her where to find the money. As Abigail is hurried into the mansion, she is spied by two young men, Mathias and Lodowick, both of whom fall in love with her—a rivalry that Barabas will later turn to his advantage. Later that night, Abigail appears on a balcony with Barabas' bags in her hands; she throws these down to him as he sees her and shouts: "O girl! O gold! O beauty! O my bliss!" This outburst illustrates the Jew's seriocomic nature, as he employs such impassioned speech to praise his gold. Eight years later, Shakespeare incorporated this trait into his characterization of Shylock in *The Merchant of Venice*.

In the square the next day, Barabas begins to practice in earnest against Ferneze. Ferneze's son Lodowick expresses his love for Abigail and is invited by Barabas to supper for a meeting with his "jewel." This dinner will prove Lodowick's undoing, as Barabas tells the audience in an aside. The Jew then proceeds to purchase the slave Ithamore, who will serve his master's will no matter what the command. In order to test the fellow, Barabas lists a remarkable catalog of evil deeds—including poisoning wells in nunneries—that he has supposedly committed. Ithamore responds by declaring himself in a league of villainy with the Jew: "We are villains both!—Both circumcised, we hate Christians both!" The slave aids his master by taking a forged challenge from Lodowick to Mathias, with whom Abigail is truly in love, even though her father has forced her to display affection for Lodowick. When the rivals meet to engage in a duel, Barabas is positioned above them, watching with pleasure as they kill each other.

Now, however, Ithamore and Abigail, whom he has told of the feigned challenge, know the extent of Barabas' treachery. In melodramatic fashion, the Jew decides that his daughter must die or she will reveal his deed; to kill her, he has Ithamore prepare a poisoned pot of rice to be "enjoyed" by all the nuns. To secure Ithamore's loyalty, Barabas promises him the whole of his inheritance, and he seems to adopt him as his son. The audience, however, knows from another aside that Barabas intends to kill his slave as well when the time is right. Ithamore does his master's bidding, but before Abigail dies, she gives proof of her father's guilt to Friar Bernardine (depicted as a lustful clown), who vows to confront the Jew with it, accompanied by Friar Jacomo. Barabas outwits these two fellows, assuring them that he wishes to be converted; as he did with Lodowick and Mathias, he starts the two men quarreling with each other. By means of a clever ruse devised with the aid of Ithamore, he also eliminates these potential enemies. As each of his schemes proves successful, Barabas celebrates more openly and melodramatically. In this play, unlike *Tamburlaine the Great*, the audience senses that the hero-villain will soon go too far, tripping up on some unforeseen obstacle. The audience is meant to experience this sense of impending doom, especially after the murder of the innocent Abigail, who converted to Christianity before her death. This deed establishes a parallel between Barabas and the biblical Herod, another murderer of innocents.

Meanwhile, Ithamore, aided by a pimp and his whore, tries to blackmail his master to feed the whore's expensive tastes. Barabas resolves to kill them all. Disguised as a French musician, he comes to the party at which Ithamore and the others are drunkenly planning to destroy the Jew. Barabas plays and sings, then tosses to the revelers a bouquet that he has dusted with poison. They smell it and they go ahead boldly in their plan to expose the Jew's actions. Before they die, they manage to tell Ferneze of Barabas' treachery; he and the others are led offstage, from where an officer quickly comes to tell of *all* of their deaths. The audience quickly learns, however, that Barabas has taken a sleeping potion and thus has deceived his enemies. Now intent upon revenge, he joins forces with the besieging Turks, showing them a way into the city through a hidden tunnel.

With a suddenness of movement that imitates the Wheel of Fortune, Ferneze is defeated and Barabas is appointed governor of the island by the Turks. Rather than torturing and killing the former governor, as might be expected, Barabas offers to return his power and destroy the Turks if Ferneze will pay him, which Ferneze agrees to do. The Jew then invites Calymath to a feast in celebration of their great victory. Hard at work in the hall, Barabas constructs an elaborate trap that he plans to spring on Calymath with Ferneze's help. When the moment arrives, however, the Maltese governor cuts a rope that causes Barabas to fall into the trap, a large cauldron filled with boiling liquid. Ferneze then arrests the Turkish leader, telling him that his troops have been surprised and killed in the monastery where they were housed. Amid the shouts and curses of the Jew—"Damn'd Christians, dogs, and Turkish infidels!"—the play ends in triumph for the Maltese citizens.

The Jew of Malta ends in the defeat of Machiavellian plotting. Even though he is a scheming villain throughout most of the action, however, Barabas might also be considered a near-tragic figure if one regards him as a man who degenerates in reaction to the evil done to him. In part, this reaction must follow from the behavior of Ferneze and Calymath; neither is morally superior to Barabas. He must honestly be described as the Elizabethan stereotype of a Jew, given to melodrama and sardonic humor. The audience feels no sympathy for him in his death, only a kind of relief that his destructive will has been defeated by someone capable of outwitting him. Although he finally overreaches himself, Barabas emerges as a totally fascinating villain, matched only by Shakespeare's Iago and Richard III.

In *The Massacre at Paris*, Marlowe depicts the episodic adventures of another antihero, the Guise, who is distinguishable from his predecessors only in representing the power of the Papacy. The character is based on a historical figure who was assassinated in 1588; the action recounts the infamous Saint Bartholomew's Day debacle of 1572, when hundreds of Huguenots were murdered by Catholic forces. The succession of victims, whom the Guise orders murdered ostensibly to please the Church, makes the audience recoil from the character and his motives. Lacking any comic element in his nature, he qualifies as a parodied Machiavel intent on disrupting the reign of Henry III, a lecherous and inept leader. The Guise's soliloquies show him to be in quest of an "earthly crown," which he believes he deserves because of his superior will and intelligence. What makes him different from Tamburlaine is his inability to control his passions and the behavior of those closest to him. In critical situations, his rhetoric fails him. His wife's affair with the king's favorite cuckolds the Guise; Henry delights in making the sign of the horns at him in public. Enraged at being made a figure of public ridicule, he arranges to kill his rival, an act that all but ensures his fall.

The man who stands in opposition to both the Guise and Henry III is King Henry of Navarre. Although his speeches lack the fire and melodrama that mark the Guise's outbursts, Navarre champions a Catholicism that is anticlerical, even fundamentalist. He also defends the principle of king and country, which the Guise and Henry seem to have forgotten in their quest for power. To prove his antipapal views, Navarre joins forces with Queen Elizabeth in an alliance the rightness of which Marlowe underscores by having a dying Henry III embrace it. This bit of manipulation has led some critics to argue that with this play, Marlowe was returning to his own Christian faith and was rejecting the amoral position taken by Tamburlaine. It is dangerous, however, to infer an author's beliefs from those held by his characters; there is no corroborating evidence in this case. There can be little doubt that Navarre is intended to be seen as a heroic character unlike any encountered in the other plays. If he is not Prince Hal, he is certainly Bolingbroke, a man who acts on principle and proves effective.

Even though the confrontation between Navarre and the Guise has about it all the elements of exciting drama, *The Massacre at Paris* is ultimately disappointing. The Guise's philosophy of seeking out perilous situations in order to test his strength of will does hold one's attention for a while, but the play offers none of the heroic bombast of a Tamburlaine or witty audacity of a Barabas. There is a great deal of bloodshed on the stage and off, but there is no clear purpose for the murders, no sense in which they forward some particular end in the plot. To complicate matters, the text that has survived is garbled; no amount of reconstructing can account for the missing links. While Marlowe may have been attempting a new dramatic design (some textual critics suggest that the original version was twice as long), *The Massacre at Paris* in its present form cannot be regarded as achieving the degree of pathos necessary to call it a successful tragedy.

In *Edward II*, however, such pathos can be found in the fateful careers of two men whose wills and hearts are sorely tested. Edward is presented as a man who is required to rule as king even though his weak nature disqualifies him from the task. As misfortune hounds him, he acquires humility and insight, which help to give him a more sympathetic personality than he had at the play's opening. He progresses toward self-understanding, and this transformation distinguishes him from more static characters such as Tamburlaine and Barabas. On the other hand, Mortimer, a man like Navarre who starts out professing deep concern for the destiny of his country, gradually loses the audience's sympathy as he becomes driven by ambition for the crown. This pattern of characterization charges *Edward II* with pathos of the kind Shakespeare would achieve in his tragedy *Richard II*, which was based on Marlowe's play and appeared a year after it.

Like Shakespeare, Marlowe turned to Raphael Holinshed's *Chronicles* (1577) to find the source material for *Edward II*. While earlier playwrights had attempted to transform the stuff of chronicle history into drama, Marlowe was the first to forge a dramatic design that is coherent and progressive. He presents a single theme—the struggle between Edward and his nobles—modulating it by means of the hero's victories and defeats. When Edward is finally overcome and the crown falls to his heir, he pursues Mortimer and his deceitful queen until revenge is won. In an ending unlike those of Marlowe's earlier plays, the accession of Edward III brings with it the promise of happier, more prosperous days. This exuberance at the close is a far cry from the condition of the state when the action begins. Gaveston, Edward's minion, seeks to divide his lover from the nobles not only for sexual reasons. He shows that he is ambitious and disdainful of his superiors. In an opening-scene confrontation (which Gaveston overhears), Edward defies the lords, announcing his intention to appoint Gaveston Lord High-Chamberlain. Edward's brother Kent at first supports him, telling the king to cut off the heads of those who challenge his authority. Yet by the close of the scene, when Edward has alienated the lords, the commons, and the bishops, Kent begins to wonder openly about his brother's ability to rule.

Mortimer, a man possessed by brashness, stands as the chief opponent to the king. He is begged by Queen Isabella not to move against the crown, even though she has been displaced by Gaveston. Mortimer is not alone in his opposition to the king's behavior; the Archbishop of Canterbury joins the peers in composing a document that officially banishes Gaveston. Although Edward rages against this rebellious act, he soon realizes that to resist might well lead to his own deposing. He is trapped because he has placed love for his minion above his concern for England. It is significant in this regard that Gaveston is both low-born and a Frenchman, which qualified him as a true villain in the eyes of Elizabethan Englishmen. Before the two men part, expressing vows that sound like those of heterosexual lovers, Edward turns to Isabella, accusing her (at Gaveston's prompting) of being involved in an affair with Mortimer. Tortured by her husband's harsh, and for the moment untrue, words, Isabella approaches the lords and, with Mortimer's aid, convinces them to rescind the banishment order. Edward rejoices, suddenly announcing plans to marry Gaveston to his niece; his enthusiasm is not shared by Mortimer and his father, who see this as another move to entrench Gaveston in royal favor. The minion's success also breeds Machiavellian ambition in younger courtiers, the audience learns from a short interlude involving Young Spencer and Baldock. This mirroring technique, by which lesser characters are observed copying the traits of the central figures, serves Marlowe's moral or instructive purposes in other plays as well.

When Gaveston returns in triumph, he expresses contempt for the "base, leaden earls" who greet him with a mocking recital of his newly acquired titles. Lancaster, then Mortimer and others, draw their swords and threaten Gaveston, an action that prompts Edward to order Mortimer from his court. A shouting match follows, sides are taken, and the earls set about planning how they will murder Gaveston. Fuel is added to the fire when Edward childishly refuses to ransom Mortimer's uncle, who has been captured by the Scots. (One can see in this episode parallels with the Hotspur-Henry IV quarrel in Shakespeare's *Henry IV, Part I*.) Rejecting his brother Kent's sound advice to seek a truce with the lords, Edward declares his intention to be revenged on them all, plotting openly with Gaveston to be rid of his enemies. By allowing himself to be driven by anger, Edward exhibits his political naïveté: His threat against Mortimer also alienates the people, to whom he is a hero. Furthermore, as Marlowe makes clear, the lords frequently express their desire to expel the king's favorite, not the king. It is important to realize that the playwright does not present the homosexual affair in an exploitative way; rather, he wants the audience to understand how Edward's blind defense of his "friendship" makes it easy for his enemies to rally to the cause.

The lords finally decide to move openly against Gaveston, whose whereabouts Isabella reluctantly reveals. Isabella's position has been made increasingly difficult by the king's claim that she and young Mortimer are lovers. Now her action seems to confirm Edward's suspicions, even though she affirms her love for the king and her son. When Gaveston is overtaken by his enemies—one of whom compares him to Helen of Troy—he is accused of being a common thief then given over to Warwick's custody, an act that assures his death. Rather than solving the country's problems, however, the removal of Gaveston exacerbates them. Edward quickly embraces the support of Young Spencer and Baldock, his new favorites, while continuing to ignore the incursions of Scots marauders and of the French King Valois, who has invaded Normandy. Marlowe here paints a vivid picture of the collapse of the body politic from internal and external forces. Yet when the inevitable civil war breaks out, Edward wins, proceeding quickly to take revenge against those "traitors" who opposed him. In his rage, however, he makes another mistake; rather than killing Mortimer, he imprisons him in the Tower, where his ambition (or *virtu*) has an opportunity to flower. With the aid of Edward's disgruntled brother Kent, Mortimer escapes to France to seek aid—along with Isabella—to restore England to her former health. It now appears that Isabella and Mortimer have joined forces to place Prince Edward on the throne. Yet as they leave the French court with promises of support, the queen and the young climber appear to have their own interests, not those of the kingdom, at heart.

Not surprisingly, Edward is easily defeated in a second encounter with the lords, bolstered as they are by the troops of Mortimer and Isabella. Isabella immediately proclaims Prince Edward the new "warden" of the realm, then turns the question of Edward's fate over to the lords. It is at this point that Marlowe begins portraying the deposed king in a more sympathetic light. When he is captured by Leicester, Edward, along with Young Spencer and Baldock, is disguised and begging sanctuary from an abbot. In these perilous straits, he still refuses to denounce his friendship with obvious parasites. As the Bishop of Winchester asks for his crown, deeming the act for "England's good," Edward suddenly refuses to take it from his head, accusing Isabella and Mortimer of outright rebellion. What makes Edward such a pitiful figure here is his inability to comprehend his part in creating the circumstances of his fall. He regards himself as a wronged innocent surrounded by wolfish traitors; this self-blindness prevents him from acting wisely and in the country's best interests. Although he lacks the spiritual dimensions of Shakespeare's *King Lear*, his jealous possession of the crown represents the same childlike faith in the object, not in the qualities which it represents. This attitude and the behavior that it engenders—a self-dramatizing resignation—lead to Edward's death.

References to the Wheel of Fortune fill the final scenes of *Edward II*. Mortimer and Isabella appear to have reached the Wheel's top, as both actively plot Edward's death. Isabella emerges, however, as a mother determined to see her son ascend the throne, while Mortimer clearly plots to seize power for himself. He determines that the deposed king must die, but he will act through subordinates rather than directly. Mortimer's tactics represent the victory of Machiavellianism, as he proceeds to rule through plotting and hypocrisy. He has Prince Edward crowned, declaring himself to be protector, then sends Lightborn and Matrevis to murder Edward. In a sad yet gruesome scene, the disheveled Edward is murdered in his jail bed when Lightborn places a table on top of him and jumps up and down on it. This horrible deed is quickly answered by Edward III, who arrests Mortimer, has him hanged and beheaded, and then places the head on his father's hearse. Isabella is sent to the Tower as the new king demonstrates the traits of strength and decisiveness that assure England's future glory. Edward III is a monarch who, like Shakespeare's Henry V, restores not only peace but also the values of patriotism and justice, which are necessary to the peaceful progress of the state.

In *Edward II*, Marlowe scores several successes. He creates a coherent play out of strands of historical material, lending pathos and poetic strength to the main character. He explores the depths of human emotions and depicts skillfully the ambiguous personalities of figures such as Isabella with consummate talent. He also reveals the effects of Machiavellianism in a personage, Mortimer, whose nature is more believable, less stereotyped, than those of Barabas or the Guise. These advances in dramaturgy not only lent tragic potency to *Edward II* but also prepared the way for Marlowe's most spectacular tragic achievement, *Doctor Faustus*.

A major obstacle in the path of critics of Marlowe's most popular melodrama, however, is the state of the text. Not published until eleven years after the playwright's death, the play was modified by "doctors" who were paid to add certain effects and delete others. To complicate matters further, an enlarged quarto edition was published in 1616; this version features alterations that suggest it may have been printed from the promptbook. Today's text is largely the work of Sir Walter Greg, who attempted a reconstruction of the play based on the extant quartos. The tragedy bears some resemblance to English morality interludes dealing with damnation and salvation. By selecting the Faustus myth, however, Marlowe was committed to portraying a story of damnation alone, with a hero who realizes too late the terrible consequences of selling his soul to the Devil. Indeed, the most impressive aspect of *Doctor Faustus* is its incisive treatment of the protagonist's tortured state of mind, which could easily be construed as an object lesson to sinners in the Elizabethan audience. Yet Marlowe was not preparing an interlude for the edification and instruction of simpleminded rustics. He was a daring, provocative artist exploring the character of a man who was legendary for his intellectual curiosity, for his intense desire to break the bonds of human knowledge and experience. As Irving Ribner so persuasively puts it (in his introduction to *The Complete Plays of Christopher Marlowe*, 1963): "*Doctor Faustus* is not a Christian morality play because it contains no affirmation of the goodness or justice of the religious system it portrays." This statement indicates how intimately related Doctor Faustus is to Tamburlaine, another Marlovian hero whose desire for knowledge and power sent him on a spectacular quest. While Tamburlaine, however, is able to win the prize—if only for a brief time—Doctor Faustus in fact falls from the position of social and spiritual prominence he holds at the play's opening. He is a victim of a system he chooses to defy; in that act of defiance, he begins almost immediately to deteriorate into a fool. The stages of that decline are carefully, ironically traced by Marlowe, who seems to want the audience to regard his hero's striving as a futile gesture. The play's ending, with Faustus being led away by devils who torture and then dismember him, offers no optimistic vision to the audience. *Doctor Faustus* thus stands as Marlowe's most pessimistic play, a tragedy that instructs its spectators in the dangers and ultimate limitations of the human imagination.

The play's opening (after an induction by a Senecan Chorus) finds Faustus in his study rejecting the orthodox or conventional disciplines and hungering for the demigod status of a magician. Even though he is cautioned against incurring God's anger by the Good Angel, Faustus invites two magicians, Valdes and Cornelius, to dine with him. In an effective bit of mirroring, Marlowe invents a servant named Wagner, who mimics the behavior of his master by behaving condescendingly toward two scholars who have come to warn Faustus about practicing the "damn'd art." One is struck throughout the play by the concern shown for the hero by his friends.

When Doctor Faustus manages to cast a spell and call up his servant Mephostophilis, the audience should quickly realize that he has made a bad bargain. Lucifer's messenger tells him directly that he desires the magician's soul and that Faustus will possess only the power the devils choose to give him. Unfortunately, Faustus' pride blinds him to the reality of the contract, which he signs with his own blood. He must forfeit his soul after twenty-four years of magic. In a humorous parallel scene, Wagner, too, calls up spirits and purchases the services of a clown, the burlesque counterpart of Mephostophilis. The slapstick underplot makes clear the ironic point: The servants control their masters and not vice versa.

While the Good Angel urges Faustus to repent, he instead boldly defies God and mocks the existence of Hell. His haughtiness begins to weaken, however, when second thoughts about the contract start to plague him. Supposing himself to be beyond salvation, Faustus instead turns to Mephostophilis for answers to questions about the creation of man and the world. In place of answers, Mephostophilis offers evasions and sideshows, such as the procession of the Seven Deadly Sins. Again a comic scene echoes the main action as Robin the Clown steals his master's conjuring books and invites Dick to turn invisible with him, in which state they plan to visit the tavern and drink all they wish without paying. References to bills and non-payment throw into relief the predicament of the hero, whose "bill" must be paid with his life. When the audience next encounters Faustus, he is in fact supposed to be invisible as he visits a papal banquet, where he daringly strikes the pope and plays sophomoric tricks on the cardinals. The appeal of such anti-Catholic skits to a Protestant audience is obvious; Marlowe reinforces that point when he has Faustus help rescue the rival Pope Bruno from imprisonment. Yet even though he succeeds in puncturing the vanity of Rome, Faustus also reveals himself to be a second-rate showman rather than the demigod he had hoped to become. Marlowe accomplishes this effect by depicting his hero first in the papal setting; then in Emperor Charles' court, placing the cuckold's horns on the heads of three courtiers; and finally in a tavern, where he tricks a horse-courser into believing he has pulled off Faustus' leg

This foolery has been heavily criticized by commentators as nothing more than an attempt to divert the mechanicals. Some have argued that the scenes involving Robin and the other clowns were in fact added by subsequent playwrights. There can be little doubt, however, that many of these scenes are intended to underscore the hero's decline and to foreshadow later events. The horse-courser's pulling off of Faustus' "leg" and the subsequent purchase of a mare that turns out to be a bale of hay foreshadow the hero's final dismemberment and comment on the bad bargain that Faustus has made with Lucifer. As in plays such as Shakespeare's *Henry IV, Part I*, burlesque business in the underplot of *Doctor Faustus* provides a more informal way of appreciating the thematic significance of the main action.

Marlowe also exhibits his expertise in using conventions of the Elizabethan stage to reinforce his main themes. At the court of Emperor Charles, Faustus creates a dumb show that depicts Alexander defeating Darius, then giving the defeated king's crown to his paramour. (While this action is taking place, Mephostophilis places the cuckold's horns on the head of Benvolio, one of the courtiers who has challenged Faustus' authority.) The dumb show celebrates the victory of a great warrior and is obviously intended as an elaborate compliment to the Emperor. Yet it also suggests how distant Faustus himself is from the noble stature of an Alexander; instead of performing great deeds—his original purpose—he can function only in the medium's role. This identity is reinforced in the climactic scene of the play, when Faustus requires Mephostophilis to conjure up Helen of Troy. She crosses the stage quickly, leaving Faustus unsatisfied. He is then approached by an old man who urges him to repent before it is too late. Stricken by these words and by his conscience, Faustus nearly commits suicide with a dagger that the invisible Mephostophilis conveniently places in his hand. The old man returns to stop him, but when he leaves the stage, Mephostophilis materializes and berates Faustus for his desperate attempt. Now believing himself beyond redemption and driven by desire, the magician calls again for Helen of Troy, whom he praises, kisses, and then leads away.

Several commentators believe this act of intercourse with a spirit (a succuba) damns Faustus unequivocally. His soul has become so corrupted as a result that it shares the demoniac spirit with the other devils. Marlowe, however, clearly wants his audience to believe that Faustus could save himself at any time should he decide to repent and ask forgiveness. The dilemma he faces is that he is torn between despair and faint hope; he never manages to decide on a course of action and take it. This depiction of man as a battleground for the forces of good and evil looks back to the morality plays and ahead to plays of psychological complexity such as Shakespeare's *Hamlet*. In the case of Doctor Faustus, the failure to repent allows Lucifer, Mephostophilis, and other devils to conjure up yet another vision, this time of a horror-filled Hell. Left alone on the stage, Faustus makes a pitiful attempt to slow the passage of time—"O, lente, lente, currite noctis equi!"—but now his magic has left him. This speech highlights one of the play's chief ironies: Twenty-four years have passed as quickly as twenty-four hours, the last one ticking away toward Faustus' doom. When the scholars who were Faustus' friends next enter, they find only his limbs, the grim remains of a man who thought himself to be a god. Hell turns out to be no fable for the damned hero.

Doctor Faustus certainly qualifies as Marlowe's major artistic and popular success. Its hero belongs with Marlowe's others by virtue of his defiance and his compelling rhetorical style. Taken as a whole, Marlowe's canon represents a crucial step forward in the development of Elizabethan dramaturgy. Without him, there could not have been a Shakespeare or a John Webster, both of whom learned something of the art of popular melodrama from this master. It is lamentable that Marlowe's early death deprived audiences and subsequent critics of more examples of his poetic drama, drama that stirs both the heart and the mind.

Other major works

POETRY: *Hero and Leander*, 1598 (completed by Chapman); "The Passionate Shepherd to His Love," 1599 (in *The Passionate Pilgrim*).

TRANSLATIONS: *Elegies*, 1595-1600 (of Ovid's *Amores*); *Pharsalia*, 1600 (of Lucan's *Pharsalia*).

Bibliography

Bloom, Harold, ed. *Christopher Marlowe.* New York: Chelsea House, 1986. Though only one essay (Lawrence Danson's) offers an overview of Marlowe's entire career, the remaining twelve collect the work of a number of notable scholars: Harry Levin on *Edward II*, David Bevington on *The Jew of Malta*, David Daiches on *Tamburlaine*, and Cleanth Brooks and A. Bartlett Giamatti (both on *Doctor Faustus*). Bloom's introduction focuses on *The Jew of Malta.*

Friedenreich, Kenneth. *Christopher Marlowe: An Annotated Bibliography of Criticism Since 1950.* Metuchen, N.J.: Scarecrow Press, 1979. An opening essay surveys early criticism, and 581 citations describe books and articles about Marlowe. Arranged and indexed so that one may isolate the work of a particular critic, general studies of Marlowe, or material on individual plays and poems.

Friedenreich, Kenneth, Roma Gill, and Constance B. Kuriyama, eds. *"A Poet and a Filthy Play-Maker": New Essays on Christopher Marlowe.* New York: AMS Press, 1988. Twenty-four essays take various approaches on wide-ranging topics, such as Marlowe's relation to his literary peers, his dramatic language, his nondramatic works, and interpretations of specific plays.

Knoll, Robert E. *Christopher Marlowe.* New York: Twayne, 1969. A fine introductory study of Marlowe's plays, Knoll's book provides an excellent chapter on the structure (what Knoll calls a "statement and variation" approach) of *Doctor Faustus.* His work includes a chronology, a biographical chapter, and an annotated bibliography.

Levin, Harry. *The Overreacher: A Study of Christopher Marlowe.* Cambridge, Mass.: Harvard University Press, 1952. If one were to read only one book on Marlowe, Levin's seminal work would be an ideal choice. He defines in jargon-free language the Marlovian hero's rebellious, larger-than-life dimensions and shows how with Marlowe, Renaissance tragedy, unlike didactic medieval tragedy, focused on the pride of protagonists rather than on their fall.

Ribner, Irving, ed. *Christopher Marlowe's "Dr. Faustus": Text and Major Criticism.* New York: Odyssey Press, 1966. An edition of the play with notes for the student and general reader, the book includes an excellent sampling of diverse critical opinions (including a section from Richard B. Sewall's book mentioned below) about many aspects of Marlowe's art. Ribner also issued editions of Marlowe's other plays with accompanying interpretive essays. Any of his books would be a helpful source for the reader exploring a single play in depth.

Sewall, Richard B. *The Vision of Tragedy.* 1959. 3d ed. New York: Paragon House, 1990. An enlarged third edition of the famous work first published in 1959 on the development of tragedy as a genre. The chapter on *Doctor Faustus*, in which Sewall describes the play as the first "Christian tragedy" and identifies its subject as the divided soul, has become a basic part of an understanding of the contributions of Renaissance drama. Sewall's other chapters discuss selected tragedies from the Book of Job to *Death of a Salesman* (pr., pb. 1949).

Robert F. Willson, Jr.
(Updated by *Glenn Hopp*)

JOHN MARSTON

Born: Near Coventry, England; October 7, 1576 (baptized)
Died: London, England; June 25, 1634

Principal drama

Histriomastix: Or, The Player Whipt, pr. 1599, pb. 1610; *Antonio and Mellida*, pr. 1599, pb. 1602; *Antonio's Revenge*, pr. 1599, pb. 1602; *Jack Drum's Entertainment*, pr. 1600, pb. 1601; *What You Will*, pr. 1601, pb. 1607; *The Dutch Courtesan*, pr. c. 1603-1604, pb. 1605; *The Malcontent*, pr., pb. 1604; *Parasitaster: Or, The Fawn*, pr. 1604, pb. 1606 (commonly known as *The Fawn*); *Eastward Ho!*, pr., pb. 1605 (with George Chapman and Ben Jonson); *The Wonder of Women: Or, The Tragedie of Sophonisba*, pr., pb. 1606 (commonly known as *Sophonisba*); *The Insatiate Countess*, pr. c. 1610, pb. 1613 (completed by William Barksted); *The Plays of John Marston*, pb. 1934-1939 (3 volumes; H. Harvey Wood, editor).

Other literary forms

John Marston's satiric bent is apparent in his first publications: *The Metamorphosis of Pigmalion's Image and Certaine Satyres* (1598) and *The Scourge of Villanie* (1598). Indeed, the Pigmalion poem, ostensibly in the Ovidian amatory mode fashionable in the 1590's, is most interesting and effective as a satiric commentary on the very tradition that it purports to embrace. Underlying the familiar romantic paradigm of the sculptor's infatuation with his creation is the portrayal of an artist beset by what Marston calls a "fond dotage," a form of insanity. Pigmalion's inability to separate shade from substance is an obvious target for the unremitting satire that informs nearly all of Marston's work. Moreover, the poem's lurching oscillations between the genres of erotic epyllion and verse satire point to the stylistic confusion that mars several of Marston's plays.

Certaine Satyres and *The Scourge of Villanie* broaden the field of satire to include an entire world of corruption and decay, of dissolving social ties and religious values. Emotionally forceful, if not always structurally coherent, the satires parade a motley cast of characters representative of the assorted vices and foibles of fallen man. This dramatization of moral states, as well as an overriding obsession with sexual depravity and hypocrisy, carries over into Marston's plays.

Achievements

A ceaseless experimenter, Marston invested a variety of dramatic forms with the satiric, even mordant, worldview that originated in the late 1590's and came to define Jacobean drama. To study Marston, therefore, is to study the structural varieties of Elizabethan and Jacobean drama: the morality play in *Histriomastix*, revenge conventions in the Antonio plays, romantic comedy in *Jack Drum's Entertainment*, tragicomedy in *The Malcontent*, classical tragedy in *Sophonisba*. Marston's recurring dramatic strategy pits individual integrity against worldly corruption under hysterically theatrical conditions. His protagonists are often conscious role players, gambling for survival in a world not of their making, which they bitterly condemn. Fascinated by theatrical artifice, by shadings of illusion and reality, and by the interplay between actor and role, Marston speaks to the twentieth century as clearly as he did to his own. Despite the relatively infrequent performance of his plays, even in his own day, Marston's influence upon his contemporaries was profound, his uniquely strident voice echoing through the plays of John Webster, Cyril Tourneur, and John Ford, among others. A judicious assessment of his achievement must at least acknowledge, with Una Ellis-Fermor's *The Jacobean Drama* (1936, 1958), that Marston passed "on to the hands of masters the vision he himself could not express, transmitting to them images, phrases, situations which just fail in his hands of becoming poetry and with them become inevitable and immortal."

Biography

John Marston, the son of a prominent and prosperous lawyer, was christened on October 7, 1576. The exact date and place of his birth are unknown, although he surely passed his youth in Coventry, where his father, a distinguished member of the Middle Temple, was town steward from 1588 until his death in 1599. Little is known of Marston's early life until he matriculated at Brasenose College, Oxford, in 1592. Completing his bachelor of arts degree in 1594, he assumed residence in London at the Middle Temple, sharing his father's chambers and beginning to study law. That Marston would never practice law was apparent by 1599, when his father cautioned him "to foregoe his delighte in playes, vayne studdyes, and fooleryes." A resigned yet plaintive note creeps into the final version of his father's will, when, leaving his law books to his son, the dying man recalls his hope "that my sonne would have proffetted in the studdye of the lawe wherein I bestowed my uttermost indevor but man proposeth and God disposeth." Marston nevertheless continued to live in the Middle Temple, a not uncommon practice at a time when fewer than fifteen percent of the residents actually embraced law as a profession. No better place for witty companionship, lively debate, and satiric mockery could have been found; the influence of Middle Temple life was to shape Marston's entire literary output.

That output, as well as its early cessation, was perhaps regulated by the religious and political climate of the era. The bishops' ban on satiric and erotic poems in 1599 may have prompted Marston's shift to playwriting in the same year. In 1605, Jonson and Chapman were jailed for their jibes in

Eastward Ho! against James I and the Scots, although the offending material might as easily have been Marston's. When the king, insulted by attacks against him in two plays, one of which may have been Marston's *The Fawn*, closed all London theaters in March, 1608, he vowed that the offending playwrights should "never play more but should first begg their bred and he wold have his vow performed." This time Marston could not avoid the punishment he had luckily escaped in 1605; he was committed to Newgate Prison. He wrote no plays thereafter.

From the time of his 1606 marriage to Mary, daughter of the Reverend William Wilkes, one of King James's favorite chaplains, Marston had given up his Middle Temple lodgings to reside at the Wiltshire living of his father-in-law. Whether it was that churchman's influence, the fear of the king's wrath, or the natural evolution of a moral habit of mind that led Marston into holy orders is unclear. In any event, the playwright severed his theatrical connections in 1608 by selling his shares in the Blackfriars Theatre. He was ordained as a deacon in September, 1609, and as an Anglican priest later that year, on Christmas Eve. Thereafter, Marston surfaced from his provincial clerical duties only briefly in 1633 to demand the withdrawal of an unauthorized collection of six of his plays. Marston died in London on June 25, 1634; his epitaph, *Oblivioni Sacrum*, recalls his early dedication "To Everlasting Oblivion" from *The Scourge of Villanie.* By the time of his death, Marston had long since put behind him that "delighte in plays, vayne studdyes and fooleryes" of which his father had despaired.

Analysis

John Marston's entire dramatic career can be read as an attempt to adapt the materials of Renaissance formal satire to the stage. While his output reveals no neat gradations of development, it falls conveniently into two general divisions: those plays from *Histriomastix* through *What You Will*, crowded into the years between 1599 and 1601, and those that followed, ending with Marston's retirement from the theater. Perhaps the 1601-1604 hiatus constituted a period of artistic reflection and consolidation for Marston; in any event, the later plays seem clearly more successful in their integration of satiric materials and dramatic form.

Whatever their relative success as dramatic vehicles, Marston's plays characteristically advance his moral vision by means of a potent mixture of satiric denunciation and exaggerated theatricality; the grotesque savagery of his early imagery was remarkable even in an age when harsh rhetoric was the norm. While Marston's satirists never lose their hard-edged scorn, they are gradually transformed from irresponsible railers lashing out at anyone or anything that angers them into responsible critics of men and manners. Marston's targets are legion, but they all inhabit the world of city or court, "of perverted or wasted work, ruins and catacombs, instruments of torture and monuments of folly," as Northrop Frye describes the typical satiric world in *The Anatomy of Criticism* (1957).

The crucial task for Marston the dramatist is to find appropriate modes of theatrical expression for his essentially mordant worldview. Since no single attitude is proof against the rapacious onslaughts of human wickedness, the playwright is forced into constant shifts of rhetoric and tone. These, in turn, produce a drama of wrenching extremes in which tragedy is forever collapsing into melodrama and comedy into farce. At the heart of the drama is usually found Marston's mouthpiece, a satiric commentator living painfully in a fallen world whose vices he condemns and whose values he rejects. Often disguised, the satirist proceeds by seeming to embrace, even to prompt, the very crimes and foibles which he savagely denounces. His disguise symbolizes the chasm between being and seeming wherein lies the hypocrisy to be discovered and exposed; moreover, it allows the fitful starts and stops, the aesthetic and moral twists embodied in the deliberate theatricality of Marston's seriocomic vision.

The dangerously insecure and deceptive worldview of the plays invites the growing misanthropy of Marston's satire. Feelings of guilt and revulsion define bodily functions and poison sensual delights. Una Ellis-Fermor argues in *The Jacobean Drama*:

> There proves, upon analysis, to be an almost overwhelming preponderance of images from the body and its functions, sometimes normal but more often images of disease, deformation or maiming; these make up more than a third of the total imagery of one play [*Antonio and Mellida*] and give a clue, if not to Marston's conscious thought, at least to his unconscious preoccupations.

Dramatic action takes place in a nightmare world of brutal lust and violent intrigue where darkness cloaks venal and shameful deeds. Women, once incidental factors in man's degeneracy, increasingly become repositories of perverted desire, culminating in the animalistic Francischina of *The Dutch Courtesan*. Social intercourse consists mainly of manipulations and betrayals from which Marston's dramatic persona finds refuge only in the impassive self-containment of stoicism. When neither stoicism nor withdrawal can protect Sophonisba from the spreading stain of worldly corruption, Marston's last heroine elects the only remaining moral refuge: suicide. It is an ironically apt solution to the problem of acting in a depraved world, and it highlights the central theme of Marston's plays: the moral cost of living in such a world.

Marston's early plays experiment with various dramatic forms: the morality play in *Histriomastix*, romantic comedy in *Jack Drum's Entertainment*, the revenge play in *Antonio's Revenge*. Chiefly interesting as attempts to find appropriate vehicles for satiric commentary, they contain many of the theatrical ingredients but little of the dramatic power of Marston's masterpiece, *The Malcontent*.

The Malcontent depicts the morally debilitated world of *What You Will* and the Antonio plays; here, however, the characters are neither the mere labels for the commonplace ideas of *What You Will* nor the tenuous projections of the satiric background of the Antonio plays. In the central figure of Malevole-Altofronto, Marston has created the perfect objective correlative for his worldview. That view is embedded in the structure of *The Malcontent*, which continues and amalgamates *Antonio and Mellida* and *Antonio's Revenge*. Eddying between comedy and tragedy, *The Malcontent* employs all the Senecan sordidness, theatrical self-consciousness, and satiric commentary of its predecessors. Ostensibly, *The Malcontent* is a revenge play at the heart of which Altofronto, deposed Duke of Genoa, assumes the disguise of Malevole in order to regain his dukedom from the usurper Pietro, who, in turn, is the tool by which the scheming Mendoza advances his own ducal ambitions. Unlike the typical revenge play, which culminates in the hero's bloody reprisals, *The Malcontent* achieves a fragile harmony based upon the hero's modified goals, for this revenger seeks to reform rather than to destroy. Undeniably bitter at his dispossession, Altofronto is nevertheless driven as much by the will to rejuvenate his enemies as to reclaim his rule. A victim of deception and intrigue, Altofronto must learn to deceive his deceivers. The mask of Malevole becomes a strategy for survival in the ridiculous yet hazardous world created by fallen man. That world is defined by the sexual corruption of Aurelia, Pietro's unfaithful wife; of Ferneze, her lustful lover, who competes with Mendoza for her favor; of Biancha, who distributes her favors wholesale; and of Maquerelle, the overripe procuress, no less than by the sinister plotting of Pietro and Mendoza.

Altofronto's mask is so firmly in place from the outset that a considerable portion of the first act transpires before Malevole reveals his true identity to the "constant lord," Celso. By this time, he has already tortured Pietro by disclosing Aurelia's adultery with Mendoza. Liberated by the traditional role of the malcontent, Malevole will continue to castigate the corruption which he exposes. Malevole shapes the play even as he is shaped by its demands: It is in the service of reform that he spotlights human vice and folly. The essentially passive satirist, periodically intruding into other characters' stories, now emerges as the hero of the play whose still biting commentary is crucial to its action. When Malevole, who has been hired by Mendoza to solicit Altofronto's "widow," Maria, and to murder Pietro, reveals the depth of Mendoza's perfidy to the horrified Pietro, the latter disguises himself as a hermit and returns to court to announce his own death. Mendoza now moves swiftly to consolidate his rule, banishing Aurelia, sending Malevole off to urge his case to the imprisoned Maria, and hiring the hermit to poison Malevole, who in turn is ordered to poison the hermit. Forced into a horrified recognition of the depraved world that he has helped create, Pietro is not even permitted the solace of Aurelia's sincere repentance before Malevole's savage castigation of earth as "the very muckhill on which the sublunarie orbs cast their excrement" and man as "the slime of this dongue-pit." This episode at court and its aftermath typify Malevole's practice of moral surgery: positioning characters first to confront their own depravity, then to repent of it, and finally to excise it. Malevole's manipulations fittingly culminate in the court masque that ends the play. Ordered by Mendoza to celebrate his accession to power, the masque becomes the vehicle of his undoing. The masquers reveal themselves as Mendoza's apparent murder victims and Malevole, again Altofronto, reclaims Maria and his dukedom. Such characters as Pietro, Aurelia, and Ferneze, truly contrite and repentant, are freely pardoned; others, such as Maquerelle and the knavish old courtier, Bilioso, are banished from court. Mendoza, reduced to cravenly begging for his life, is contemptuously, and literally, kicked out.

Altofronto's intricate role-playing and manipulations have brought concord out of discord. By consciously delimiting his revenge, by constantly pointing to the absurdity of human action, and by the consummate theatricality not only of his gestures but also of his double role, he transforms the revenge play into a vehicle for social conciliation.

In *The Dutch Courtesan,* Marston abandons the satiric furor and Italianate intrigues of *The Malcontent* for exuberant comedy. While its dramatic material is undeniably lighter, *The Dutch Courtesan* is equally successful in its depiction and analysis of human nature. The play's moral center is Freevill, who plans one last visit to Francischina, the courtesan of the title, before settling down to married life with the angelic Beatrice. Outraged by Freevill's loose conduct, Malheureux goes along in order to admonish Francischina and dissuade his friend. A chilly, puritanical, and inexperienced young man, Malheureux is jolted from his moral complacency at first sight of the courtesan, whom he immediately longs to possess. When Francischina demands Freevill's murder as the price of her favors, the distressed Malheureux confesses his plight to his friend. Concluding that only strong medicine can restore Malheureux to his senses, Freevill concocts a bizarre plot. The friends stage a quarrel, after which Freevill goes into hiding. Claiming Francischina's favors as his promised reward for killing Freevill, Malheureux is deceived when she betrays him to the law. Meanwhile, Freevill has vanished, and with him, the corroborating evidence of the hoax. Condemned to hang, Malheureux is saved only at the gallows by Freevill, who justifies his friend's anguish as the price that must be paid for moral enlightenment.

The Dutch Courtesan is a comic morality play whose end is psychological and social, rather than religious, salvation. It proceeds by establishing a dialectic between love and lust, defined at the outset by Freevill, who sees no moral inconsistency between his former lust for Francischina and his present love for Beatrice. Whoring, no less than marriage, is a valid expression of man's nature. This Malheureux denies, arguing for a rigid line of demarcation between virtue and vice and thereby against the reality of the human condition. A "snowy" man of cloistered virtue, Malheureux must be brought face-to-face with an exemplum of his folly in the alluring person of Francischina. Undeniably a good man, as evidenced by his refusal to betray Freevill at Francischina's behest, Malheureux must be brought to the foot of the scaffold to attain self-knowledge. Regarding himself as above passion, he becomes "passion's slave"; proffering himself as Freevill's moral tutor, he becomes his moral pupil. One of Marston's most effective characterizations, he mirrors the playwright's moral torment. Regarding lust as the deadliest sin, his imagination nevertheless dwells on the loose sexuality he abhors. Shocked by the moral degeneracy of the beautiful Francischina, he eddies between frantic desire and consuming guilt. In this drama of initiation, Malheureux, like his creator, must learn to recognize and control his natural desires, not to annihilate them.

These lessons are farcically reinforced in a brilliant subplot that features Cocledemoy's gulling of the affected pseudo-Puritans, the Mulligrubs. By causing Mulligrub's false arrest for thievery and effecting his victim's release only at the point of execution, Cocledemoy, like Freevill, exposes and cauterizes moral absolutism. This subplot, combined with Tysefew's bantering wooing of Beatrice's sister, Crispinella, also functions to preserve the play's light tone.

By introducing a purely comic subplot, by inflating Malheureux's rhetoric, by layering Francischina's diatribes with a thick Dutch accent, and by establishing Freevill's beneficent control of the action, Marston invokes a world of comic absurdity as he dissipates its potential tragedy. A perceptive study in sexual psychology, *The Dutch Courtesan* balances and expands its author's moral vision.

The Fawn, Marston's frothiest comedy, recapitulates that vision and its modes of achievement. Like *The Dutch Courtesan*, it treats the perverted natural instincts resulting from repressed or misdirected sexuality; it also employs a double plot no less sophisticated than its predecessor's. Like *The Malcontent*, it is set in an Italian court corroded by folly and flattery; its hero is a disguised duke bent on reform. *The Fawn*'s lighter tone stems primarily from its unthreatened duke and its more farcical than sinister court intrigues.

Hercules, Duke of Ferrara, appears at the court of Gonzago, Duke of Urbin, disguised as Faunus, the consummate flattering courtier and a member of his son Tiberio's retinue. Tiberio's ostensible mission is to negotiate the marriage of Gonzago's fifteen-year-old daughter, Dulcimel, to his sixty-four-year-old father. Actually, Duke Hercules hopes that Dulcimel's charms will arouse his unnaturally aloof son to woo the girl for himself; to ensure that end, he monitors the action as Faunus. Because Dulcimel immediately falls in love with Tiberio and sets out to awaken the young man's latent feelings, Faunus is freed to deal with the corruption and hypocrisy of the court; nearly half the play is devoted to providing him with appropriate occasions to practice the art of flattery on the unsuspecting courtiers. Lulled into freely confessing their follies, Faunus' victims indirectly satirize themselves. Since vanity rather than Machiavellian intrigue marks Urbin's court, Faunus contents himself with exposing grotesqueries rather than reviling corruption. The stuff of satire—Nymphadora's claim to be the world's great lover, Herod's assertion of superiority, Dosso's impotence and his wife Garbetza's adultery with his brother, Zuccone's jealousy of his estimable wife Zoya—takes the form of sexual foibles. That these sins are merely skin-deep allows Marston to turn his satiric commentator from savage railer to witty practitioner of the courtly games he plans to expose. Moreover, the sexual waywardness of the minor characters functions as an implicit comment upon the sexual backwardness of Tiberio. The double plot of *The Fawn* therefore proceeds along parallel tracks, Faunus dealing with sexual excess, Dulcimel with sexual indifference. Successful resolution depends upon the ability of Faunus and Dulcimel to awaken Gonzago to the folly around him—his own as well as his court's.

Gonzago, Duke of Urbin, is one of Marston's most inspired comic creations. Delighting in words and garrulous in conversation, he imagines himself the consummate rhetorician. His several long-winded speeches, studded with odd bits of classical lore, are designed to bolster his self-image of a learned man of ripe wisdom; instead, they reveal him as an unknowing self-flatterer and, therefore, as a potential gull. Dulcimel plays upon her father's vanity to promote the very affair he would frustrate, using him as a go-between to inform the slow Tiberio of her interest. Shamelessly flattered by his daughter, Gonzago becomes her unwitting instrument; "hee shall direct the Prince the meanes the very way to my bed." Through four acts, Dulcimel, like Faunus, wields the weapon of flattery. "Dulcimel is not conducting an experiment in moral reformation through her flattery, but in the fifth act the Fawne exploits her work and draws the duke into the web in which he has trapped the rest of his victims," notes Philip Finkelpearl in *John Marston of the Middle Temple* (1969).

The final act is played on a two-level stage: Tiberio climbs a "tree" to join Dulcimel above, while Hercules remains below. The marriage of the young lovers presumably coincides with the several judgments rendered by Cupid's Parliament. Symbolic of healthy and natural love, the union of Dulcimel and Tiberio implicitly condemns the courtiers, who have violated

Cupid's laws. Paraded before the court and arraigned upon Faunus' evidence, they are exposed and released. Finally, Gonzago is indicted for his pretensions to wisdom and, more serious, for his attempts to obstruct life's natural flow. "What a slumber have I been in," cries the duke, whose court promises to be healthier hereafter.

In its comic characterizations, in its tonal consistency, and in its technical assurance, *The Fawn* is a masterly achievement. Marston's fusion of satiric force and content, apparent in *The Malcontent* and *The Dutch Courtesan*, is no less perfect in *The Fawn*.

Sophonisba is Marston's attempt at high Roman tragedy. Full of high moral sentiment expressed in consistently lofty verse, it impressed T. S. Eliot as Marston's best play. Its purpose, implicit in its alternate title, *The Wonder of Women*, is to portray human perfection in the person of its heroine, Sophonisba. To evoke her ideal virtue, Marston employs his characteristic tactic of pitting individual honor and integrity against a corrupt world. It is in the altered relationship between character and context, however, that *Sophonisba* embodies Marston's tragic design. Earlier protagonists manipulated adversaries and events; Sophonisba is victimized by them. A Malevole or a Hercules recognized surrounding evil, satirically castigated it, and finally dispersed or reformed it. Sophonisba, no less perceptive, can only reaffirm her virtue in a world whose evil she cannot alter and can evade only by suicide. The wildly chaotic settings for court intrigues have yielded to a harder, more frightening world of realpolitik.

Before the end of the second act, the main characters and the political world they inhabit are sharply defined. A note of discord is struck early, when the news that Carthage has been invaded disrupts the nuptials of Sophonisba and the famed Carthaginian general Massinissa. When she selflessly postpones marital consummation in the face of her husband's martial duty, she elicits the first of his many expressions of awe at her character: "Wondrous creature, even fit for Gods, not men . . . a pattern/ Of what can be in woman." Much of the remainder of the play consists of tableaux that present repeated assaults upon Sophonisba's unassailable virtue, each designed to spotlight her moral grandeur. In similar fashion, political evil surfaces in the scene immediately following Massinissa's departure for battle. No sooner does he leave than the senators of Carthage plot to betray him and Sophonisba for an alliance with the powerful Syphax. Their treachery backfires when Syphax, driven by lust for Sophonisba, who had earlier rejected him, deserts his army in his frenzy to reach her. Syphax's forces defeated, Massinissa and Sophonisba are reunited. Their happiness is, however, as illusory as it is brief. Syphax, his lust frustrated by Sophonisba's virtue and his prestige tarnished by Massinissa's victory in single combat, conceives a final act of vengeance. Arguing, ironically, that Sophonisba's virtues of loyalty to Carthage and constancy to Massinissa will tempt the latter to break his oath of allegiance to Rome, Syphax convinces the Roman general Scipio to demand that she be delivered up to Roman captivity. Confounded by the excruciating choice of betraying his allies or his wife, Massinissa crumbles. No such dilemma exists for Sophonisba, whose immediate decision to commit suicide implicitly condemns her husband's failure to do so. A good and courageous man, albeit Sophonisba's moral inferior, Massinissa is reduced to mixing the poisoned wine for her supremely stoic gesture. Eulogizing her—"O glory ripe for heaven"—he measures her distance from ordinary mortals.

The meaning of Sophonisba's suicide transcends its dramatic function of saving Massinissa by eliminating his moral dilemma. For Marston's heroine, suicide is a welcome escape from "an abhord life" of Roman captivity; it has become virtue's only possible response to the world's depravity. For the playwright, her death creates a dramatic impasse. An obsessive moralist from the outset of his literary career, Marston found in satiric comedy the means of exposing, castigating, and reforming evil. Abandoning satire for pure tragedy, he traps Sophonisba in a world of omnipresent evil which she can recognize but not alter. Thus, the final outcome of the struggle of individual integrity against the corrupt world is martyrdom. After *Sophonisba*, Marston's eventual desertion of the stage for the pulpit may have been the only viable extension of that struggle.

Other major works

POETRY: *The Metamorphosis of Pigmalion's Image and Certaine Satyres*, 1598; *The Scourge of Villanie*, 1598.

Bibliography

Caputi, Anthony. *John Marston, Satirist.* Ithaca, N.Y.: Cornell University Press, 1961. By treating Marston primarily as a satirist, Caputi's book demonstrates the unity of thought between Marston's verse satires and his drama, both comic and tragic. Caputi offers important background information on the companies that performed Marston's plays, though sometimes overemphasizing their importance for interpreting Marston's drama.

Finkelpearl, Philip J. *John Marston of the Middle Temple.* Cambridge, Mass.: Harvard University Press, 1969. Primarily a literary biography, this book stresses Marston's experience in London's Middle Temple (the Tudor equivalent of a modern law school) and its effect on his drama. The book's focus is not unbalanced, but it is not general enough to be a first resort for readers seeking an introduction to Marston.

Gibbons, Brian. *Jacobean City Comedy: A Study of Satiric Plays By Jonson, Marston, and Middleton.* London: Hart-Davies, 1968. Though not limited to Marston, as its title suggests, this book places Marston's satiric plays in the context of other ones involved in the "War of the Theatres." Gibbons offers facts and historical commentary, which create a social backdrop for Marston's plays and demonstrate how Marston lampooned his culture.

Ingram, R. W. *John Marston*. Boston: Twayne, 1978. The best introduction to Marston available, this general book covers all of his works, including the nondramatic. Its analysis of the plays, however, is thorough and integrates earlier criticism. Its annotated bibliography evaluates selected books and articles, including general sources on the period and on the genre of satire.

Tucker, Kenneth. *John Marston: A Reference Guide*. Boston: G. K. Hall, 1985. The most complete annotated bibliography available for Marston, listing, in chronological order, all significant studies of Marston's work from his time to 1985. The exhaustive nature of this work may make its use limited in most libraries, including as it does obscure journals, and books and articles in many languages.

Lawrence S. Friedman
(Revised by *John R. Holmes*)

EDWARD MARTYN

Born: Masonbrook, Ireland; January 31, 1859
Died: Dublin, Ireland; December 5, 1923

Principal drama
The Heather Field, wr. c. 1893, pr., pb. 1899; *Maeve*, pb. 1899, pr. 1900; *An Enchanted Sea*, pb. 1902, pr. 1904; *The Place-Hunters*, pb. 1902; *The Tale of a Town*, pb. 1902, pr. 1905; *Romulus and Remus*, pb. 1907; *Grangecolman*, pr., pb. 1912; *The Dream Physician*, pr., pb. 1914.

Other literary forms
Edward Martyn is known exclusively as a playwright, although he also published a novel, *Morgante the Lesser* (1890), under the pseudonym "Sirius." The novel's combination of wit and scatology makes Martyn a remote relation of Jonathan Swift and François Rabelais, and as a shaggy-dog story, it owes a debt to Laurence Sterne. In addition, the novel belongs to a rich Gaelic and Anglo-Irish tradition of satires on learning. Its interest is confined exclusively to literary history, however, thanks to its turgid style and flaccid pace. Perhaps its most surprising aspect is its authorship. Nothing in the rigorous Ibsenite realism of his major plays, or in the ascetic idealism of his private life, would lead one to suspect that Martyn ever perpetrated a work which might well be ascribed to Alfred Jarry.

Achievements
Martyn has a permanent, if minor, place in the history of the Irish Literary Revival. As this cultural phenomenon undertook no less than to change, or indeed to review, the mind of a nation, a minor contribution to it should not necessarily be considered negligible. William Butler Yeats, in one of his summaries of Martyn's achievements, dismissively mentions Martyn merely as one of Lady Augusta Gregory's neighbors who "paid for our first performances" (those, that is, of the Irish Literary Theatre, the company, which, in 1904, became the Abbey Theatre). In fact, Martyn was a founding member of the Irish Literary Theatre, and his play *The Heather Field* was the company's second production. Moreover, Martyn brought to the company a set of theatrical ideals, heavily influenced by the drama of Henrik Ibsen, which offered an alternative to Yeats's concept of "peasant drama." This alternative remained underdeveloped, and partly as a result, Martyn's playwriting career stagnated. In *The Heather Field*, however, Martyn demonstrated, intriguingly but embryonically, how his approach could have spoken in realistic terms about contemporary Irish idealism.

Far from being merely the nascent Irish theater's well-disposed financier, Martyn was as committed to the Revival as was any of its other initiators.

Despite more lasting contributions to other spheres of Irish culture and the fact that he was, by temperament, better equipped to be a critic than an artist, Martyn's position in the anterooms of fame is assured. He gave significant impetus to one of the twentieth century's most distinctive theatrical undertakings.

Biography

Edward Martyn was born to an illustrious family of Irish Catholic aristocrats at Masonbrook, near Loughrea, County Galway, on January 31, 1859. His father died the following year, and Edward and his brother were reared in the Martyn family home, Tulira Castle (which he subsequently inherited).

When Martyn was eight years old, the family moved to Dublin, where Martyn briefly attended Belvedere College. A further move, to London, led to his enrollment, in 1870, at Beaumont College, Windsor (like Belvedere, a prominent Jesuit school). Completing his secondary education in 1876, Martyn—in an unusual move for a Catholic—entered Christ Church College, Oxford, in 1877. There he had an undistinguished career and left, without taking his degree, in 1879, though not before falling under the influence of the aesthetic philosophy of Walter Pater.

The following year found Martyn in Paris, in the company of his cousin and subsequent nemesis, the Irish novelist George Moore. Paris gave him access to such contemporary artistic movements as Symbolism and Impressionism (Martyn had an important collection of Impressionist paintings, notably of works by Edgar Degas). Extensive travel in Europe put him in touch with other important cultural developments, such as Wagnerism and Hellenism. The latter proved an important enthusiasm on Martyn's return to Tulira Castle, and he divided his time between Tulira and London artistic circles, in which he cultivated the acquaintance of, among others, Arthur Symons and Aubrey Beardsley.

In 1885, however, Martyn underwent a spiritual crisis of some severity, resulting in the replacement of virtually all the modern tastes which he had formed with a more pious and ascetic regimen. The most important survivors of this reevaluation were the drama of Ibsen and the music of Giovanni Palestrina. It is tempting, with this crisis in mind, to view Martyn's contribution to the Irish Literary Theatre as, in part, rehabilitative. The crisis certainly contributed to the scathing attitude, and essentially inchoate argument, of his pseudonymous novel, *Morgante the Lesser*.

The Irish Literary Theatre was founded by Yeats, Martyn, and Lady Gregory in 1899, and in its early days, Martyn, as well as Yeats, was its principal playwright. By 1902, however, Martyn had resigned from the venture, partly because of artistic differences with Yeats, but partly also because of the arrival of George Moore. (Moore was later to subject Martyn to merciless satire in his three-volume memoir of those years, *Hail and Fare-well*, 1911-1914—treatment to which Martyn eventually responded in kind in *The Dream Physician*.)

The matter at issue between Moore and Martyn was the latter's play *The Tale of a Town*. In response to Yeats's criticism of it, Moore revised the piece, which was then staged under the title *The Bending of the Bough* (pr. 1900). After resigning from the Irish Literary Theatre, Martyn continued his playwriting career. He directed a large share of his energies to other areas of Irish culture, however, particularly to music.

In 1902, after protracted negotiations, the Palestrina Choir was established at the Pro-Cathedral, Dublin. The choir was exclusively Martyn's idea, and at the time of its inauguration he referred to it as "the chief interest of my life." This interest reflected an unorthodox approach to bringing art to the people. A unique expression of the Irish Literary Revival's ethos, the choir was financed almost exclusively by Martyn. As a result of this venture's success, Martyn devoted further time and money to beautifying provincial churches with tapestries, stained glass, and similar ornamentation.

After his break with Yeats and Moore, Martyn also developed a strong interest in, and commitment to, the Gaelic League, an organization devoted to the restoration of the Irish language. Martyn believed Irish to be second only to Greek among the world's languages; as a practical expression of his commitment, he set about rehabilitating traditional Irish music. He was instrumental in organizing an annual outlet for amateur performers called Feis Ceoil (music festival). At one of these, a tenor named James Joyce performed. Perhaps the most substantial expression of Martyn's involvement with the non-Yeatsian Revival was his presidency of Sinn Féin (the Revival's political manifestation) from 1904 to 1908.

In 1906, Martyn helped establish the Theatre of Ireland. Its principles were identical to those of the more successful Irish Theatre, which Martyn founded in 1914, assisted by Thomas MacDonagh and Joseph Plunkett, both of whom were executed for their parts in the Easter Rising of 1916. These principles echo Martyn's lifelong admiration of drama which was intellectual in theme and which availed itself of contemporary European dramaturgical models. Despite numerous vicissitudes, the Irish Theatre managed to remain open until 1920.

Martyn's activities on behalf of the Irish Theatre marked the end of his public life. He died in Dublin on December 5, 1923, a lonely and neglected figure. He was unmarried.

Analysis

Edward Martyn made his name as a dramatist with *The Heather Field*, and his subsequent works comprise a series of not very startling variations on that play. Without being autobiographical, *The Heather Field* draws on important features of Martyn's life. It is set in the wild country of the author's native western Ireland. The action takes place in the context of the Land War, as the struggle between peasants and landlords over conditions of tenure was called. The play is not absolutely contemporaneous with the events it relates; the Land War was at its height from the late 1870's to the mid-1880's and had simmered down considerably by the turn of the century. Nevertheless, the play's references to events still fresh in the minds of an Irish audience emphasize Martyn's rejection of prehistoric material as the vehicle of his vision and have something in common with the belief of James Joyce (another Ibsenite) that art may be won from the life of one's own unpromising times. This belief is implicit in all of Martyn's plays. Regardless of whether one accepts that the handling of the belief conforms to the tenets of realism, the plays' intellectual bases are firmly grounded in realism.

In addition, the protagonist of *The Heather Field*, Carden Tyrrell, is a landlord, as Martyn himself was. He is given a surname whose Irish associations are as notable in their own right as is the name Martyn. Tyrrell is provided with one of Martyn's own formative experiences, that of hearing exalted song from the choir of Cologne Cathedral. Tyrrell is also an "improving" landlord—that is, one who takes an interest in his property (which a great number of Irish landlords did not). In fact, the play contains an unexamined paradox concerning Tyrrell's social commitments: He makes every effort to reclaim land and enlarge his holdings, yet he is notably unsympathetic to the causes of the Land War. This paradox is subsumed under the more divisive and irreconcilable aspects of Tyrrell's case. Martyn is less interested in his protagonist's social situation than in his psychological condition. It should be noted, however, that *The Heather Field* is an important step forward in the representation of typical Irish types not as figures of fun but as serious embodiments of predicaments experienced by the majority of conscious humanity. By remaining faithful to conditions with which he was intimately familiar, Martyn helped to enlarge the stock of Irish dramatic characters; by dignifying stereotypes, he offered the basis for a new dramatic perspective on Irish life.

The plot of *The Heather Field* is somewhat spare. Tyrrell conceives an overweening ambition to reclaim the wild, infertile areas of his demesne. To this end, he has risked his fortune draining the heather field of the title. This project is, ostensibly, a success: Productive grass has evidently supplanted pretty, barren heathland. As a result, Tyrrell is determined to go forward and put the whole of his property in financial jeopardy in order to expand his reclamation scheme. Barry Ussher, a friend and neighbor, attempts to dissuade Tyrrell from his rash ambition, but to no avail. Moreover, Tyrrell's wife, Grace (like most of Martyn's protagonists, Tyrrell is unsuitably married, a fate which the author himself assiduously avoided), is aggressively opposed to the scheme, so much so that she attempts to have her husband certified as insane. Only the timely intervention of Barry Ussher thwarts such a development, Tyrrell being so engrossed in his dream of fertility that he cannot perceive Grace's tactics or defend himself against the two doctors summoned to the house to carry out Grace's design. As events reveal, however, official certification of insanity becomes a formality. In the third act, spring has come round again and with it the triumph of heather over grass. The result is that Tyrrell, refusing to accept that nature has declined to answer his needs, loses his mind; he cannot tell past from present, or anything else about himself and the real world which has frustrated his dreams.

Establishing a theme that was to recur in Martyn's work, *The Heather Field* is a critique of idealism—or perhaps of idealism in a solipsistic formulation. Tyrrell does not recognize that his ambition is flawed on practical grounds. He cannot accept the fact that the world will not necessarily accommodate the needs he foists on it. His indifference to society, both in the polite sense of the word and in the historical sense, throws him back on his own psychic resources, which wilt under the pressure. Tyrrell's isolation is subjectively crucial and objectively crippling: The belief that the reclamation scheme is the signature of his integrity leads inevitably to his disintegration; as practical dramatic evidence of his situation, Tyrrell seems to exist in the play in order to contest what everyone else says to him rather than adjust to it. The only relaxation of this intransigent manner occurs in exchanges with his young son, Kit, who is being reared as a child of nature. These exchanges ironically portray the child as father to the man: the child's genuine, naïve wonder of the same state of mind—a pursuit of the natural which requires the face of nature to be redrawn.

One of the rewards of *The Heather Field*, therefore, is in identifying the protagonist's problems from an intellectual standpoint. In terms of its theatrical dynamics, however, the play is less satisfactory. The dialogue is written in prose of a rather leaden variety, and the scenes are conceived as set pieces in an argument rather than as occasions in a man's life. These drawbacks are nevertheless redeemed by the strength of Tyrrell's commitment to his ideal: It does, after all, cost him everything. The audience's involvement with his fate is sustained by the persuasiveness with which the ideal is conveyed: It is clear that for Tyrrell, the heather field and the dream of rehabilitation which it duplicitously facilitates offer the possibility of beauty, renewal, and completeness. It is an alternative to history, both personal (his marriage) and social (the Land War). Tyrrell claims to hear voices when he is out in the field, the voices of a German choir, the definitive experience of beauty which he received in his formative years, and it is these voices he welcomes when nature fails and madness overwhelms him.

The author's unsparing revelation of his protagonist's irreconcilable tensions gives the play its dramatic strength and also lends to it a cultural significance of which Martyn may have only been incidentally aware: The play is a fascinating and idiosyncratic example of a distinctively Irish genre, comprising works, in a variety of literary forms, which deal with the decline of the Big House, the generic term for the homes of the landed gentry.

As noted, Martyn's other plays repeat the themes of *The Heather Field*, but whereas *The Heather Field* contains a degree of tacit sympathy for Tyrrell (if only because all the other characters are narrower in spirit than he is), the critique of idealism in later plays is rather more bitter. In fact, what causes subsequent works to have destructive endings is not idealism of the characters as such, but its frustration.

Grangecolman is a case in point. The action is set in the Colman family home, a large old house outside Dublin, and the plot is concerned with the hauntings of an irrecoverable past. This theme is conveyed with a symbolic explicitness that borders on the obtuse and that, at the same time, leaves the intellectual burden of the play vague and generalized.

The household consists of old Michael Colman, the last of his line, his daughter Catherine, and her ne'er-do-well husband, Lucius Devlin. Michael is an antiquarian, a pursuit which in the Irish literature of the generation before Martyn's epitomized impotent reclusiveness. Catherine, who, with her husband, espouses the contemporary feminism, is a doctor, but her career has been blighted because of Lucius' irresponsible financial speculations. To assist him with his research, Michael hires young Clare Farquhar. Her grace and energy have a restorative effect on the old man's morale. This development, in turn, arouses Catherine's hostility.

Early in the play, the notion of the house's decline is introduced. Incursions, by thieves from the outside and ghosts from within, are feared; Miss Farquhar, handling a revolver, promises to deal with intruders of whatever kind. The audience soon learns, however, of the depth of Catherine's jealousy of Clare, whose vitality and resolve are at odds with Catherine's self-abnegating temperament. Catherine's hostility erupts in her peremptory dismissal of Clare from her duties.

Ignorant of this development, Michael proposes marriage to Clare, a step which Catherine naturally opposes, using the occasion to voice the ideals of feminism and independence, which, for all of her enthusiasm for them, have evidently driven her into a dead end. Leaving the scene in an agitated state, she later returns, impersonating the family ghost. Clare takes the revolver and kills her.

Undoubtedly the plot's Gothic machinery gets in the way of the play's intellectual brooding. Nevertheless, there is no escaping the ideological impasse to which Catherine's idealism has led. Once again, the world resists the pressure placed by the mind upon it, with catastrophic results for the mind's proprietor. The contrived nature of the scenario diminishes the play's surface plausibility, while at the same time drawing attention to the situation's latent incoherence. In the dialogue, Martyn shows himself to be as tone-deaf as ever to the rhythms of human speech, but the consistency of the play's gloom and pessimism in a sense works to sanction its short-comings. It seems remarkable that a committed Catholic such as Martyn continued to write plays which implicitly deny the possibility of faith. The depiction of conditions that are apparently beyond redemption—a promi-nent feature throughout Martyn's work—is given its most funereal presen-tation in *Grangecolman*, a play which, in the hands of a more adept play-wright, would have fully realized itself as a plainsong dirge for the past, present, and future; for cultural recuperation, social commitment, and per-sonal vanity.

In his last play, *The Dream Physician*, Martyn resorted to an unchar-acteristic mode which perhaps he should have cultivated—namely, satire. (*The Tale of a Town* is the other major dramatic example of Martyn's sa-tiric powers.) The basic framework of the plot is no more than a pretext for the author to have the last word about the role of Yeats and George Moore (particularly the latter) in the Irish Literary Revival. The surgery which exposes these luminaries' pretensions in act 4 is wholly out of keep-ing with the play's stilted pace, but the results are hilarious. Moore is pre-sented as the fraudulent, malicious, self-seeking George Augustus Moon, while Yeats is caricatured as Beau Brummell, whose self-appointed destiny is to save the soul of his people with the aid of a banjo.

The plot concerns Shane Lester, who has betrayed his Anglo-Irish origins by becoming president of, and later member of Parliament for, an Irish nationalist group. His wife, Audrey, a social butterfly, cannot forgive Shane for this shift in allegiance, and she and her husband have a violent fight, during the course of which Audrey believes that she has killed him. Nothing will expunge this fantasy—the dream of the title. Audrey is con-fined to bed in a semicatatonic state, despite Shane's numerous entreating visits. A nurse, Sister Farnan, is engaged to care for Audrey, and it is she who suggests that the patient will snap out of her dream if confronted with a reality to which she cannot possibly assent. This reality is provided by the antics of Moon and company, and exposure to it has the desired therapeu-tic effect: The play ends with Audrey and Shane reconciled. Moon's pos-turing makes him the dream physician; the imbalance resulting from his pre-tensions make it impossible to take seriously what he represents. By virtue of experiencing that impossibility, Audrey is restored to a reality which she can take seriously, her husband's.

Clearly, however, *The Dream Physician* is itself imbalanced, formally and thematically. Martyn was unable to work out a unified relationship between the more general theme of Shane's idealism, embodied in his nationalist leanings, and the more local and personal bouts of character assassination, which have little or nothing to do directly with Shane. This failure places the play in danger of being a unique example of a hopelessly implausible genre, the revenge farce. After the sobriety of most of its predecessors, however, it is pleasant to encounter a spirited Edward Martyn. The caricatures of Moore and Yeats show all the signs of being an insider's work. Less successful are the cartoons of Lady Gregory (Sister Farnan) and James Joyce. Joyce was allegedly the model for Otho, Audrey's insufferable brother, who finally comes to life when he denounces Moon because his beloved, Moon's grandniece, "a woman of genius" who signs her poetic effusions "La Mayonaise" (Mayo was George Moore's native county), proves to be nonexistent.

The uncharacteristic note on which Martyn's playwriting career ended is perhaps symptomatic. Inspired by the most impressive contemporary models and fortified by the principles derived from them, Martyn had perhaps too clear an intellectual formula for his work, and an insufficiently coherent aesthetic approach. Adherence to his formula made the work repetitive, two-dimensional, and lacking in vitality. Like so many of his protagonists, Martyn failed to live up to the promise of his ideals. Yet those ideals, particularly in their eschewal of sentimentality, and the works which attempt to articulate them, provide an important perspective from which to view the theatrical accomplishments of his contemporaries.

Other major work
NOVEL: *Morgante the Lesser*, 1890 (as Sirius).

Bibliography
Courtney, Marie Therese. *Edward Martyn and the Irish Theatre.* New York: Vantage Press, 1956. A detailed portrait of Martyn in the context of Irish theatrical history. Courtney examines his involvement in the establishment of a national theater movement from both a biographical and an artistic point of view and assesses the eventual effect of that involvement on Martyn. All Martyn's dramatic works are thoroughly evaluated.

Gwynn, Denis. *Edward Martyn and the Irish Revival.* London: Jonathan Cape, 1930. An early and still valuable attempt to describe Martyn's role in the Irish Literary Revival. Much of the focus is on Martyn's contributions to the development of Irish drama. The study, however, also contains information on his other cultural commitments, with the result that an overall sense of Martyn's cultural context emerges.

Hogan, Robert, and James Kilroy. *The Irish Literary Theatre, 1899-1901.* Atlantic Highlands, N.J.: Humanities Press, 1975. Contains a considerable amount of detailed information regarding Martyn's involvement in the events that led to the eventual formation of Ireland's national theater. Includes accounts of the production and reception of Martyn's plays. The volume also provides extensive scholarly support for the study of the formative period of modern Irish theater.

Setterquist, Jan. *Edward Martyn.* Vol. 2 in *Ibsen and the Beginnings of Anglo-Irish Drama.* 2 vols. Reprint. New York: Gordian Press, 1974. The impact of Henrik Ibsen's revolution in the social and critical role of the drama on the fledgling Irish theater is examined. Martyn's complicated attitude toward Ibsen's example is central to this study's argument, and Martyn's plays are also seen in the context of the Ibsenite dimension of the contemporary Irish drama.

Yeats, W. B. "Dramatis Personae, 1896-1902." In *Autobiographies.* London: Macmillan, 1956. A primary source on Martyn's social background, cultural interests, and contributions to the Irish Literary Revival. In particular, Martyn's personality is vividly conveyed, and his artistic temperament is subjected to keen scrutiny. Not all Yeats's statements, however, should be taken at face value.

George O'Brien

JOHN MASEFIELD

Born: Ledbury, Herefordshire, England; June 1, 1878
Died: Near Abingdon, England; May 12, 1967

Principal drama

The Campden Wonder, pr. 1907, pb. 1909 (one act); *The Tragedy of Nan*, pr. 1908, pb. 1909; *Mrs. Harrison*, pb. 1909 (one act); *The Tragedy of Pompey the Great*, pr., pb. 1910; *The Witch*, pr. 1911 (adaptation of a Norwegian play); *Philip the King*, pr. 1914 (one act); *The Faithful*, pr., pb. 1915; *The Sweeps of Ninety-eight*, pr., pb. 1916; *Good Friday: A Dramatic Poem*, pb. 1916, pr. 1917; *The Locked Chest*, pb. 1916, pr. 1920 (one act); *Esther*, pr. 1921 (adaptation of Jean Racine's play); *Melloney Holtspur: Or, The Pangs of Love*, pb. 1922, pr. 1923; *A King's Daughter: A Tragedy in Verse*, pr. 1923; *Tristan and Isolt: A Play in Verse*, pr. 1923, pb. 1927; *The Trial of Jesus*, pb. 1925, pr. 1927; *The Coming of Christ*, pb. 1928; *Easter: A Play for Singers*, pr. 1929; *End and Beginnings*, pb. 1933; *A Play of St. George*, pb. 1948.

Other literary forms

John Masefield is noted for his lyric and narrative poetry, and because of poems such as "Sea Fever" and "Cargoes," he will continue to be read. For more than sixty years, however, he was prolific in many other genres as well. Between 1902 and 1966, Masefield wrote more than forty volumes of poetry or verse plays and more than twenty novels, in addition to short stories, essays, reviews, biographies, historical works, addresses, and prefaces, totaling about fifty books in all. Masefield's first book of verse was *Salt-Water Ballads* (1902); his narrative poem, *The Everlasting Mercy*, (1911), caused a sensation with its realistic diction. Masefield wrote eight other book-length narrative poems, the most important being *The Window in the Bye Street* (1912), *The Daffodil Fields* (1913), *Reynard the Fox* (1919), *Right Royal* (1920), and *King Cole* (1921). As his sea poems and ballads are about the life of the common sailor, his narrative verse tells about the lot of the rural folk of the Malvern Hills in his native Herefordshire.

Masefield's fiction is varied and uneven; his most popular and successful novels were his books about the sea and strange lands, written in the vein of Joseph Conrad and Robert Louis Stevenson—tales such as *Captain Margaret* (1908), *The Bird of Dawning* (1933), and *Victorious Troy* (1935). While not a great critic, Masefield was a thoroughly professional man of letters who turned out well-focused articles and reviews by the hundreds, as well as book-length studies. In the field of history, Masefield gave accounts of World War I debacles in *Gallipoli* (1916) and *The Battle of the Somme* (1919); he told the story of the evacuation of Dunkirk in *The Nine*

Days Wonder (1941). In addition, Masefield wrote about maritime history in *Sea Life in Nelson's Time* (1905), *On the Spanish Main* (1906), and *The Conway from Her Foundation to the Present Day* (1933). Masefield's autobiographical works include *In the Mill* (1941), *New Chum* (1944), *So Long to Learn* (1952), and *Grace Before Ploughing* (1966).

Achievements

Masefield's plays have lost much of their appeal for stage audiences, but some of his dramatic work, such as that written about the common people, has a vitality to recommend it, particularly his most successful play, *The Tragedy of Nan*, which reveals Masefield's ability to tell a vivid story in dramatic terms. It is not likely that any of his plays will become standard reading in drama courses, nor are any likely to be revived for production, yet Masefield should be commended for trying to infuse the English commercial theater in the early twentieth century with dramatic works of serious artistic intent. In the years after World War I, Masefield largely abandoned this ambition; the postwar plays were the products of an avocation rather than a true vocation. Though some of these plays were staged by local amateur dramatic clubs, Masefield wrote them primarily for his own edification and for the entertainment of his family and friends.

Although Masefield was writing plays after George Bernard Shaw, Henrik Ibsen, August Strindberg, and Anton Chekhov had established the dimensions of early modern drama, his dramatic values have the conventionalities of Victorian theater. Despite their conventional manner, his plays never appealed to a wide popular audience, nor, for the most part, did they satisfy the critics. Masefield's endeavors as a playwright did, however, enhance his reputation in Georgian literary circles, and his mastering of the dramatic conventions enabled him to write novels with well-constructed plots and carefully focused characterizations.

Whatever the merits of his drama, it is for his achievements as a poet that Masefield will be remembered: His tenure as England's poet laureate, from 1930 until his death in 1967, was one of the longer ones.

Biography

John Edward Masefield was born on June 1, 1878, in the small town of Ledbury in rural Herefordshire, England; he was the son of George Edward and Carol Parker Masefield. Masefield's father, a fairly successful solicitor, died at the age of forty-nine following a period of mental disorder that may have been caused by the death of Masefield's mother, who died from complications following childbirth in 1885. Thus left an orphan when he was only six years old, Masefield was taken in by his aunt and uncle, who reared him in pleasant circumstances in a Victorian country house called The Priory. There, young Masefield learned to love the waters, woods, and flowers of Herefordshire, and from his aunt's teaching he acquired a love for literature, particularly the narrative poems of Henry Wadsworth Longfellow. In 1888, Masefield was sent to the King's School in Warwick as a boarding student. Homesick and unhappy at Warwick, Masefield ran away from school, and though he was to return, it was obvious that this experience with formal education was not to produce the desired results. Masefield was allowed to join the merchant navy, leaving home at thirteen and enlisting as a midshipman; he was posted to the H. M. S. *Conway*, a famous training ship. During his days as apprentice seaman, he took long voyages to South America and around Cape Horn, but the ardors of a sailor's life were not to his liking, and he jumped ship in New York, giving up his berth as sixth officer on the White Star liner *Adriatie*. The young Masefield's disgraceful behavior caused his uncle to disinherit him, and Masefield was forced to take whatever work he could find. For some time, he lived a nearly vagrant life in Greenwich Village, where he started to write poetry seriously. Masefield remained in New York for two years before returning to London in 1897, where he took a post as a bank clerk, a position he held for three years, during which time he started to publish some of his own verse and to meet some of the London literati, becoming acquainted with William Butler Yeats, Lady Augusta Gregory, and John Millington Synge, along with others whom he came to know during regular gatherings in Bloomsbury. Masefield's first book of poems, *Salt-Water Ballads*, was published in 1902 and enjoyed immediate success, becoming popular with the public and critics alike.

Masefield met Constance Crommelin in 1903, and they were married the same year, when he was twenty-five years old and his bride was thirty-five. Despite the difference in their ages, the marriage seems to have been as happy as most. Masefield acquired a job as an editor and settled in Greenwich with his wife and baby daughter. In 1904, Masefield received an offer to write for the *Manchester Guardian*, but newspaper writing deflected him from his main interest at this period—writing plays. He managed to turn out a series of dramas, despite the demands of producing reviews and articles for the *Manchester Guardian* seven days a week. Although most of Masefield's early dramatic writings were left unfinished or destroyed, he completed and produced his first play, *The Campden Wonder*, in 1907. In addition to writing another six plays in the years before World War I, he also produced novels, stories, sketches, his first long verse narratives, and more ballads and poems, although he considered himself to be primarily a playwright. In 1910, about the time of the birth of his son Lewis, he become involved with Elizabeth Robins, an American actress and leader of the suffragettes. Although she was nearly fifty and he was only thirty-one, he became totally enamored of her; for her part, she accepted Masefield's attentions with reservation, and their affair was conducted under the guise of an imaginary mother-son relationship, he calling her "mother" and she addressing him as her "little son." Most of Masefield's ardor went into his letters; he often wrote her as many as two a day. Their actual meetings were confined primarily to rendezvous at the British Museum, where "mother" and "son" would tour the galleries. Finally, Robins, having tired of Masefield's filial pose and the maternal role imposed on her, called off the relationship.

After a period of desolation caused by Robins' withdrawal, Masefield moved his family to an old manor house in the Berkshire hills. It was at this time that he wrote the long narrative poem *The Everlasting Mercy*, which established his fame as the premier poet of the Georgian period.

Masefield's life as a literary country squire was disrupted by the start of World War I. Although he tried to enlist in the army, Masefield was not able to join a combat branch because of his poor medical record, but he was accepted for service in the British Red Cross, going to France in 1914 with the British Expeditionary Force; later, in 1915, he was posted to the Dardanelles, where he participated in the debacle at Gallipoli. Because of his literary reputation, he was relieved of his duties as a field officer and sent by the Red Cross to promote the war effort with two lecture tours of the United States.

As the war ended, Masefield moved his residence again, settling at Boar's Hill, near Oxford. His neighbors there included Gilbert Murray, Sir Arthur Evans, and Robert Bridges, and Masefield became the landlord for a young war-poet, Robert Graves, to whom he leased a cottage on his property. Masefield also became a friend to Edmund Blunden, another war-scarred writer who was returning to Oxford to be a professor of poetry. The two young veterans saw Masefield as a mentor who, like them, was opposed to modernists such as Ezra Pound, T. S. Eliot, and Edith Sitwell, and stood, like them, rooted in the native English tradition.

The postwar years were good ones for Masefield. He was the originator of annual verse recitals called the Oxford Recitations and devoted himself to writing plays again as well as history books about the war. He founded a local amateur theatrical company in 1919 that put on the plays of Euripides, William Shakespeare, and John Galsworthy. The Hill Players, as they were called, performed in a theater called the Music Room from 1922 until 1932, staging several experimental plays by young, unknown playwrights as well as some of Yeats's later plays and Masefield's own *Tristan and Isolt* and *The Trial of Jesus*. In effect, Masefield had created his own private theater, where he could try out his plays without worrying about commercial success. He could give young dramatists a vehicle for their plays and could cast his friends and family in the parts.

At the end of the decade, Masefield was named poet laureate, and in 1930, he moved from Boar's Hill to Pinbury Park, near Cirencester in

Gloucestershire. There, Masefield lived in a grand house with great rows of oak trees, playing his part as a public figure with quiet dignity, but, as before, another world war disturbed his serene life.

Masefield once again offered his services to the nation and, during the dark days of the early war years, produced an inspiring story of the escape of the British Army from the beaches of Dunkirk. Personal grief came to him in this war: His son Lewis was killed in action in the African desert while serving with the Royal Ambulance Corps. The aging Masefield never fully recovered from the heartbreak caused by his son's death. In the years after the war, his life was given over to letter writing, by which he kept up a wide range of friendships, and to completing his sequence of autobiographical works. His official duties as poet laureate kept him occupied in cultural affairs, promoting the Royal Academy of Dramatic Art and serving as president of the National Book League. In the autumn of 1959, Mrs. Masefield became ill, and she died in 1960 at the age of ninety-three. Masefield's life became increasingly reclusive, but he continued to write; among the works required by his office were poems upon the deaths of T. S. Eliot and President John F. Kennedy. Indeed, Masefield's energy as a writer seemed inexhaustible, and he produced his last book, *In Glad Thanksgiving* (1967), when he was eighty-eight years old. On May 12, 1967, he died and was cremated; his ashes were placed in the Poets' Corner of Westminster Abbey, though he had requested that they should be scattered in the winds and waters of his native downs.

Analysis

Very early in his career as a writer, John Masefield developed an interest in playwriting. His deep study of Shakespeare and his personal association with Yeats, Lady Gregory, and Synge instilled in Masefield a desire to revive the English drama as his friends were attempting to rekindle the drama of Ireland by infusing it with the vitality of mythic and folk elements. Masefield saw what could be done with folk materials in plays such as Synge's *Riders to the Sea* (pb. 1903) and *In the Shadow of the Glen* (pr. 1903); his own first play, *The Campden Wonder*, is a one-act drama in the expressionistic-symbolic mode of Yeats, to whom it was dedicated. Using the colloquial idiom, it deals with a brutal story that Masefield had heard about a hanging in Chipping Campden of three innocent people. This first effort was followed by several more one-act plays: *Mrs. Harrison*, a sequel to *The Campden Wonder* and also an exercise in sustained naturalism; *The Sweeps of Ninety-eight*, an amusing comedy with a historical background concerning the outwitting of the British Navy by an Irish rebel in 1798; and another short play, *The Locked Chest*, which is a suspenseful drama about a clever wife who tricks her confused husband.

Good Friday, also written during this period, is a morality play in rhymed verse. Its subject is the Passion of Christ, and Masefield employs an austere style in imitation of the cycle plays of medieval drama, but his modern idiomatic phrases are somewhat out of keeping with the spirit of the original. Nevertheless, the play contains a moving account of the Crucifixion, simple and vivid in its effects:

> We were alone on the accursed hill
> And we were still, not even the dice clicked
> On to the stone . . .
> And now and then the hangers gave a groan,
> Up in the dark, three shapes with arms outspread.

Overall, in the period between 1907 and 1916, Masefield finished ten plays. During this decade, he produced some of his most important dramatic works, including longer, full-length plays such as *The Tragedy of Nan*, *The Tragedy of Pompey the Great*, *Philip the King*, and *The Faithful*.

The first of these, *The Tragedy of Nan*, was produced at the New Royalty Theatre under the direction of Harley Granville-Barker; it had a long and successful stage run in repertory theaters in England and abroad. Based on a true "country tragedy" of the early nineteenth century, it is a play with the capacity to move audiences. The poignant plot details the plight of Nan Hardwick, an orphaned charity girl whose father is hanged for stealing sheep. She is taken in by a stingy uncle whose family is unkind to her, but her life is made bearable by the attention paid her by Dick Gurvil, a local youth of uncertain moral fiber who has plans to marry Nan. Her chances for happiness are destroyed when her mean-spirited aunt, who wants him for a husband to one of her own daughters, reveals to Dick that Nan is a murderer's daughter. Fearful that he cannot expect a dowry from Nan and that he will be disinherited by his own father, he breaks off their engagement and marries one of Nan's cousins. Nan realizes the defective character of her lover, but her pain and humiliation at losing him are nevertheless acute. In an ironic turn of events, it is discovered that her father was the victim of a miscarriage of justice: He was innocent of the charges, and she is paid a large sum of money in compensation for his death. Her former fiancé realizes that she is a richer prize than the cousin, so he turns to her again with a proposal of marriage. In a fury at his duplicity and temerity, Nan stabs him in the heart with a bread knife, saying that he must be killed to keep him from preying on any more innocent women. She then throws herself in the Severn River, closing the play on a note of unrelieved tragedy.

Although a summary of the play makes it appear like a study in naturalism, it is, in fact, less so than Masefield's early plays; nevertheless, some contemporary drama critics indicted the drama for its use of dialect, vicious characters, and commonplace scenes to tell an ugly story. In general, *The*

Tragedy of Nan seems most to echo Thomas Hardy's novel *Tess of the D'Urbervilles* (1891): Both are rustic melodramas that feature pure, beautiful country girls who are the playthings of cruel fate. Like Hardy's Tess, Nan is truly a tragic protagonist, and her death induces the proper feeling of catharsis in the audience.

Masefield followed *The Tragedy of Nan* with *The Tragedy of Pompey the Great*, which was written during the winter of 1908-1909 and produced for the stage in 1910, opening at the Aldwych Theatre in London under the direction of Harcourt Williams. Masefield began this history play as a one-act drama in which he tried to dramatize the life of the ill-fated Roman general as it was depicted in Sir Thomas North's translation (1579) of Plutarch' *Parallel Lives* (105-115). The events of the story required a fuller treatment, however, and Masefield expanded his play into a complete three-act drama. The tragic career of Pompey, who goes down to defeat with brave dignity in his struggle with Caesar, embodies a theme often found in Masefield's work: the idea that the greatest victories are those of the spirit. Masefield draws Pompey's character in more complimentary terms than history does, making him into a magnanimous, peace-loving general.

As a play, *The Tragedy of Pompey the Great* has some arresting scenes, with battles on land and sea which provide an opportunity for striking stage effects, but as Aristotle reminds us in *The Poetics*, spectacle is the lowest artistic ingredient of the drama. The main weakness of this play, though, is its lack of dramatic tension. Masefield idealizes Pompey as a highly principled aristocratic leader who opposes Caesar's mob appeal and egalitarian policies. Masefield's Pompey, much like Shakespeare's Brutus, is motivated by a patriotic desire to preserve the ideals of republican Rome. Unfortunately, Caesar is not among the *dramatis personae* of Masefield's play; as a result, there is no dramatic tension between Pompey and a worthy antagonist. Instead, there is only an extended exposition of Pompey's character. Pompey's tentative idealism is no match for the single-minded Caesar's ambition; his efforts at compromise and his rational appeals to avert civil war are not successful, and strife breaks out with seeming inevitabilty. In this respect, some reviewers saw the play as an effort by Masefield to warn audiences of the threat to peace which international tensions posed in the period just before the outbreak of World War I.

One of Masefield's next plays, *The Faithful*, a total departure from any of his previous dramatic works, reflects the vogue for Oriental culture that swept England and France during the early years of the twentieth century. Using Japanese rather than Roman history as his subject, Masefield— inspired perhaps by Yeats's adaptations of Nō plays—tried a more experimental form of drama in *The Faithful*. The play opened at the Birmingham Repertory Theatre in 1915 and ran until 1918. After the end of the war, it had a run of more than forty performances on Broadway, where it enjoyed a critical rather than a commercial success. The play is about the forty-seven rōnin, whose tragic story Masefield at first planned to tell in a verse narrative because he could not envision a dramatic structure for the story. Inspired in part by Granville-Barker's productions of Shakespeare's *Twelfth Night* and *The Winter's Tale*, which, Masefield said, "showed me more clearly than any stage productions known to me the power and sweep of Shakespeare's constructions . . . ," he created a play of considerable lyric eloquence—a play that has all the blood and gore of a Jacobean tragedy, presented with a ritualistic air that mutes the violence and that invests the action with a timeless quality.

The action, set in medieval Japan, revolves around a revenge plot. The play's villain is an upstart tyrant named Kira, a newly rich daimyo, or feudal lord, who causes the death of a young rival, Asano. In the conflict that results, Asano's followers try to avenge their leader, but the rebels are routed and their families are scourged by the ruthless Kira. Finally, however, the tide turns, and Kira is executed by one of Asano's followers, the heroic Kurano. The curtain comes down with all the survivors preparing to commit hara-kiri. The pseudo-Japanese quality of the drama annoyed some of the play's critics, who questioned its historical and cultural credibility, but Masefield should be given credit for his attempted synthesis of Western and Oriental dramatic modes. All in all, *The Faithful* is an interesting example of the impact of Japanese theater on the dramatic arts in England.

Only a few of Masefield's post-World War I plays attracted any serious critical attention. One that did was a fantasy melodrama entitled *Melloney Holtspur*, a seriocomic ghost story about the way in which the peccadilloes of a past generation are passed on to the present. Written in the spirit of the supernaturalism of Sir James Barrie, the play was praised for its upbeat treatment of such solemn themes as ancestral sins and atonement. In addition, Masefield translated Jean Racine's play *Berenice*; he also adapted Racine's *Esther*. Masefield's last effort at playwriting was *A Play of St. George*; this drama in verse and prose, which was never staged, treats the famous legend of England's patron saint.

Masefield was always more the poet than the dramatist. His plays nevertheless retain historical interest, both as expressions of his many-sided talent and as reflections of diverse trends in British drama of the late nineteenth and the early twentieth century.

Other major works

NOVELS: *Captain Margaret*, 1908; *Multitude and Solitude*, 1909; *Lost Endeavour*, 1910; *The Taking of Helen*, 1923; *Sard Harker*, 1924; *Odtaa*, 1926; *The Hawbucks*, 1929; *The Bird of Dawning*, 1933; *Victorious Troy*, 1935; *Basilissa*, 1940.

SHORT FICTION: *A Mainsail Haul*, 1905; *A Tarpaulin Muster*, 1907.

POETRY: *Salt-Water Ballads*, 1902; *Ballads*, 1903; *The Everlasting Mercy*, 1911; *The Window in the Bye Street*, 1912; *The Story of a Round-house and Other Poems*, 1912; *Dauber: A Poem*, 1913; *The Daffodil Fields*, 1913; *Philip the King and Other Poems*, 1914; *The Cold Cotswolds*, 1917; *Rosas*, 1918; *A Poem and Two Plays*, 1919; *Reynard the Fox: Or, The Ghost Heath Run*, 1919; *Enslaved and Other Poems*, 1920; *Right Royal*, 1920; *King Cole*, 1921; *The Dream*, 1922; *Sonnets of Good Cheer to the Lena Ashwell Players*, 1926; *Midsummer Night and Other Tales in Verse*, 1928; *Ode to Harvard*, 1937; *Some Verses to Some Germans*, 1939; *Gautama the Enlightened and Other Verse*, 1941; *Natalie and Masie Pavilastukay: Two Tales in Verse*, 1942; *Wonderings (Between One and Six Years)*, 1943; *I Want! I Want!*, 1944; *On the Hill*, 1949; *Poems*, 1953; *The Bluebells and Other Verse*, 1961; *Old Raiger and Other Verse*, 1964; *In Glad Thanksgiving*, 1967.

NONFICTION: *Sea Life in Nelson's Time*, 1905; *On the Spanish Main*, 1906; *Shakespeare*, 1911; *Gallipoli*, 1916; *The Battle of the Somme*, 1919; *Chaucer*, 1931; *The Conway from Her Foundation to the Present Day*, 1933; *The Nine Days Wonder*, 1941; *In the Mill*, 1941; *New Chum*, 1944; *So Long to Learn*, 1952; *Grace Before Ploughing: Fragments of Autobiography*, 1966; *The Letters of John Masefield*, 1979.

TRANSLATION: *Berenice*, 1922 (of Jean Racine's play).

MISCELLANEOUS: *A Book of Sorts: Selections from the Verse and Prose*, 1947.

Bibliography

Babington-Smith, Constance. *John Masefield: A Life.* Oxford, England: Oxford University Press, 1978. This full biography was prepared with the active cooperation of Masefield's family and friends. The circumstances of individual plays are discussed but little critical evaluation is attempted. Complemented by a select list of books by Masefield and an index.

Drew, Fraser. *John Masefield's England: A Study of the National Themes in His Work.* Rutherford, N.J.: Fairleigh Dickinson University Press, 1973. As the title suggests, this work looks at the specific qualities of Masefield's "Englishness" through the corpus of his work—probably the first attempt to do this systematically. Bibliography and index.

Dwyer, June. *John Masefield.* New York: Frederick Ungar, 1987. This volume forms one in the useful Literature and Life series, and as such it covers the whole corpus of Masefield's work. One of the more recent attempts to reassess and reevaluate Masefield. Includes a bibliography and an index.

Hamilton, William H. *John Masefield: A Critical Study.* Port Washington, N.Y.: Kennikat Press, 1969. One of the many attempts to assess Masefield's work and chart his progress. This useful book is supplemented by an appendix and an index.

McDonald, Jan. *The New Drama, 1900-1914.* Basingstoke, England: Macmillan, 1986. A chapter on Masefield's *The Campden Wonder* and *The Tragedy of Nan* sets Masefield within the context of the Court Theatre and Harley Granville-Barker but sees him as somewhat atypical of the other "new dramatists." The chapter argues that these two early plays show evidence of a power and originality of style that could have befitted English drama had Masefield developed them. Bibliography and index.

Nicoll, Allerdyce. *English Drama, 1900-1930: The Beginnings of the Modern Period.* Cambridge, England: Cambridge University Press, 1973. Nicoll argues that Masefield lacked any clear dramatic vision or direction and was too restless to become a significant playwright. She traces the Irish influence on him in particular. Contains a full list of plays with first performances and an index.

Sternlicht, Sanford. *John Masefield.* Boston: Twayne, 1977. This volume, one of Twayne's English Authors series, covers both life and works in a clear, well-focused way. It contains a bibliography and an index.

Hallman B. Bryant
(Updated by *David Barratt*)

PHILIP MASSINGER

Born: Salisbury, England; November 24, 1583 (baptized)
Died: London, England; March 18, 1640

Principal drama

The Fatal Dowry, pr. c. 1616-1619, pb. 1632 (with Nathaniel Field); *Sir John van Olden Barnavelt*, pr. 1619, pb. 1883 (with John Fletcher); *The Custom of the Country*, pr. c. 1619-1620, pb. 1647 (with Fletcher); *The Little French Lawyer*, pr. c. 1619-1623, pb. 1647 (with Fletcher); *The Virgin Martyr*, pr. c. 1620, pb. 1622 (with Thomas Dekker); *The False One*, pr. c. 1620, pb. 1647 (with Fletcher); *The Double Marriage*, pr. c. 1621, pb. 1647 (with Fletcher); *The Maid of Honor*, pr. c. 1621, pb. 1632; *The Unnatural Combat*, pr. c. 1621, pb. 1639; *The Duke of Milan*, pr. c. 1621-1622, pb. 1623; *A New Way to Pay Old Debts*, pr. 1621-1622(?), pb. 1633; *The Beggar's Bush*, pr. before 1622, pb. 1647 (with Fletcher); *The Prophetess*, pr. 1622, pb. 1647 (with Fletcher); *The Bondman*, pr. 1623, pb. 1624; *The Renegado: Or, The Gentleman of Venice*, pr. 1624, pb. 1630; *The Parliament of Love*, pr. 1624, pb. 1805; *The Elder Brother*, pr. 1625(?), pb. 1637 (with Fletcher); *The Roman Actor*, pr. 1626, pb. 1629; *The Great Duke of France*, pr. 1627(?), pb. 1636; *The Picture*, pr. 1629, pb. 1630; *Believe as You List*, pr. 1631, pb. 1849; *The Emperor of the East*, pr. 1631, pb. 1632; *The City Madam*, pr. 1632(?), pb. 1658; *The Guardian*, pr. 1633, pb. 1655; *A Very Woman: Or, The Prince of Tarent*, pr. 1634, pb. 1655; *The Bashful Lover*, pr. 1636, pb. 1655; *The Dramatic Works of Thomas Dekker*, pb. 1953-1961 (4 volumes, Fredson Bowers, editor; includes collaborations with Dekker); *The Dramatic Works in the Beaumont and Fletcher Canon*, pb. 1966-1976 (4 volumes, Bowers, editor; includes collaborations with Fletcher); *Selected Plays of Philip Massinger*, pb. 1978 (Colin Gibson, editor).

Other literary forms

Philip Massinger wrote a few commemorative poems, commendations of other playwrights, and dedicatory epistles in verse and prose. These have been collected by Donald Lawless in a 1968 monograph, *The Poems of Philip Massinger with Critical Notes*. Massinger's reputation, however, rests firmly on his plays.

Achievements

Massinger's missing plays are the stuff of legend: An eighteenth century book dealer, Joseph Warburton, bought and stacked away in a closet an undetermined number of Massinger manuscripts, which his cook mistook for scrap and used, sheet by sheet, to line pie plates and start fires. What outlived the cook is a body of competently, sometimes brilliantly, plotted plays which are variations on three or four themes and character types.

In the past, critics such as Arthur Symons and Ronald Bayne have complained that Massinger's works offer no new insights into the relationship between human beings and society, no existential questions about the right and wrong of a character's course. They found his thinking conventional and his heroines smug. Later critics, such as Mark Mugglio and A. P. Hogan, attempted to rescue Massinger from such charges by arguing that he was subtly challenging the very assumptions his plays seem to support.

In fact, Massinger's plays do make conventional assumptions about art, society, and human motives. Art teaches pleasantly; society naturally forms a hierarchy in which those of good blood, well educated, rule over those of less exalted natures. Humans act from love, greed, ambition, or simple fellowship. Working from these assumptions, Massinger dramatizes the unsuccessful attempts of citizens who wish to rise above their natural stations. He twits the younger generation for its impatience; he upholds loyalty as an almost ultimate value, and he polishes with loving care his portraits of the loyal and the innocent, the gruff and the greedy.

Though he does not challenge his culture's values, Massinger can still fascinate and delight a modern audience for three reasons. First, he fills his scenes with accurate observations of daily details. He savors the dodges by which a shrewd merchant secures a mortgage, the puff pastries and sherry sauces which a good chef can concoct, the pearl necklaces and tavern reckonings upon which social status so often depends. Even in his most serious plays, one finds him lavishing stage time on the petty rituals and daily clutter which make men feel comfortably at home in the middle class. Through Massinger, one becomes intimate with the Renaissance Everyman, a hearty and surprisingly broad-minded figure.

Second, Massinger composes good, though not memorable, poetry and satisfying plots. His characters can dependably explain themselves and can use the common stock of images. Having apprenticed himself to such masters of double and triple plots as Thomas Dekker and John Fletcher, Massinger could weave most pleasing tapestries of contrasting threads. The saint's sweetness shows grandly against a background of sinners; the jealous man's frenzy, against the loyal anger of his wife.

Third, Massinger had an apparently lifelong fascination with the way that passion attacks reason. He continually examines the "something snapped" movement of a character's mind. In a Massinger character, passion's attack can numb the will as suddenly as the wasp's sting paralyzes the spider. Like Robert Burton in his *The Anatomy of Melancholy* (1621), Massinger concentrates sometimes on symptoms, sometimes on causes, sometimes on cures for the victims of jealousy or of "heroical love." His impassioned characters may be enrapt by Providence (as in *The Virgin Martyr*) or entrapped by their own possessive natures (as in *A New Way to Pay Old*

Debts) or by the lure of other characters (as in *The Maid of Honor*); whatever the causes, they act with a compulsiveness and are cured, if they are cured at all, by mechanisms that call into question the notion of free will perhaps more strongly than their creator intended.

Biography

Philip Massinger was baptized on November 24, 1583, at Salisbury, England, the son of Arthur and Anne Crompton Massinger. His father, "an honest gentleman and a loving man," served as trusted retainer to the powerful Henry Herbert, Earl of Pembroke. As Pembroke's retainer, Arthur Massinger held various minor political offices, sat three times in Parliament, and handled many of the earl's financial affairs. Massinger's mother came from a similarly professional family, but one whose political connections were smudged by more or less open Roman Catholicism. (Young Massinger may well have grown up Catholic; he treats Papists sympathetically, and their doctrines underlie at least three of his plays.) Early editors speculated that Massinger was reared as a page in a Pembroke household, where he could become familiar with the routines of gentry life. At the age of eighteen, he entered Oxford University, his father's alma mater. Though he may have stayed there until Arthur's death around 1606, he left without a degree.

Massinger's whereabouts after leaving Oxford are conjectural; probably he worked as an actor. By 1613 he was certainly scriptwriting in London, collaborating with other scriptwriters for hungry London audiences. Since playwriting paid very little, Massinger lived for some time on the fringes of poverty. In two letters, he seeks cash advances "without which we cannot be bailed" from prison for debt. Like a modern young screenwriter, he joined forces with one or another of the more established writers—Thomas Dekker, Nathaniel Field, Robert Dabourne—and worked for several of London's major production companies. Though Massinger wrote tragedies, tragicomedies, and comedies throughout his career, there was a general drift toward lighter plays as his career advanced.

By 1617, Massinger had begun what became his most fruitful writing partnership—with John Fletcher, who had succeeded William Shakespeare as chief writer for the King's Men, a highly acclaimed acting company. Massinger and Fletcher worked together on at least a dozen (and perhaps as many as nineteen) plays, mostly tragicomedies. In 1625, when Fletcher died in the great London plague, Massinger succeeded him as the company's chief writer; from then until his own sudden death in March, 1640, Massinger wrote almost exclusively for the King's Men.

Analysis

It is in Philip Massinger's studies of passion, whether the conclusion is tragic or comic, that one sees most clearly both his strengths and his limitations—both his famous seriousness as a dramatist and teacher, and the problems critics find with his use of conventions. Four plays particularly illustrate Massinger's "anatomy" of passion and will: *The Virgin Martyr*, *The Maid of Honor*, *The Picture*, and *A New Way to Pay Old Debts*.

In *The Virgin Martyr*, Massinger collaborated with Dekker to produce a hagiography with a decidedly Romish coloring. Massinger believed in ritual, ceremony, order, and in the power of prayer to change determinations. With a certainty bordering on superstition, he believed that those who adhere to a set body of moral codes will have an almost magical effect on their world.

Dorothea, the virgin martyr, has such an effect. She adheres to Christian dogma and practices the virtues of generosity, compassion, self-control, and rational argument. She gladly accepts martyrdom as payment for three benefits: heaven for herself; conversion of Antoninus, the young Roman who loves her; and a gift of fruit and flowers for Theophilus, her prosecutor. At her dying request, "A holy fire/ yields a comfortable heat" in Antoninus; soon thereafter, Theophilus, receiving his miraculous bouquet, sets about becoming Rome's next Christian martyr. Thus, prayer's power triumphs—perhaps over the free will of the converts.

Yet *The Virgin Martyr*, contrary to what the title leads us to expect, is not entirely Dorothea's story; her self-control in the face of physical torment is merely the simplest of several versions of self-control tested. Massinger gives as much attention to Antoninus, the governor's son, and Artemia, the emperor's daughter. Antoninus passionately loves Dorothea, yet when Artemia chooses him for her consort, he cannot safely refuse. He temporizes, then rushes off to pursue Dorothea again. The Christian virgin, completely occupied with prayer and good works, shows no interest in a pagan lover. She would rather feed the poor and instruct the ignorant.

Antoninus does not love Dorothea for her virtue—he simply loves her, irrationally. Of Artemia's proposal, he complains, "When I am scorched/ With fire, can flames in any other quench me?/ What is her love to me, greatness, or empire,/ That am slave to another?" That Dorothea's love brings him "assured destruction" bothers him not a whit, and when he attempts to color his passion with reason, the attempt largely fails.

Artemia, like Antoninus, covers passion with reasonable answers, yet ultimately, the pagan princess exercises a self-control that makes her admirable. Given her choice of husband, she bypasses kings and follows her affection for Antoninus; when she finds that he loves Dorothea, she impulsively wants him dead. She orders his execution but soon relents. Regaining control, she gives up her interest in him, "That all may know, when the cause wills, I can/ Command my own desires." At the play's end, she chooses a more appropriate husband, the Emperor Maximinus, grounding love and affection to him on a clearly rational basis.

The question of will is examined from two other perspectives as well—those of Theophilus' daughters and of Dorothea's servants. The daughters, at the play's start, have newly renounced their Christianity and returned to their father's pagan gods. Tortures and reasoning had not worked, but the knowledge that their father chose his cultural convictions over even paternal feelings brought the girls back to Jove's altar. Massinger casts their conversion from Christianity in convincing psychological terms; their father's will has overwhelmed them. (Later, Dorothea uses reason to bring them back to Christ.)

The other perspective is that of Dorothea's two reprobate servants, Hircius and Spungius, who provide a not very comic commentary on their mistress' intellectualism. Drunkard and whoremaster respectively, they squander, with mechanical predictability, money entrusted to them for the poor. They embrace Christianity or paganism, depending on which sect puts the readiest cash into their hands. They claim no will at all. As Spungius says, "The thread of my life is drawn through the needle of necessity, whose eye, looking upon my lousy breeches, cries out it cannot mend them." Derogatory comparisons and flat punch lines give these characters some cleverness but no will. Their conversations counterpoint Dorothea's rational control.

Several of the themes and characters of *The Virgin Martyr* turn up in later Massinger works. *The Unnatural Combat*, for example, is the study of a father's incestuous passion for his daughter. Malefort, the father, habitually does as he pleases; he has dispatched prisoners of war, disregarded friendship, done away with one wife to make room for a second. Massinger has his audience learn these things gradually as he builds a picture of an effective military leader, but one whose power comes from utterly undisciplined appetites. Malefort gradually loses the sympathy of the audience until, halfway through the play, he kills his own son in a duel. His saving grace has been his care for his daughter. Now he suddenly realizes that he wants the girl incestuously, and the habit of taking what he wants—of unbridled, undisciplined will—is so strong in him that his real and painful struggle to give her up is doomed to fail.

The Malefort character resembles that of Theophilus in *The Virgin Martyr* and has even stronger resemblance to the Duke of Milan in the play of that title. There, the possessive will of Duke Sforza demands that, should he die, his chaste and innocent wife be killed, lest she someday enjoy a second love. Sforza's possessive will, like Malefort's, derives from his habitual and public indulgence of his appetite for Marcelia, and, like Malefort's, it is fatal. Domitian and his wife in *The Roman Actor* share the same lack of disciplined will.

The willful will-lessness Massinger portrays in these characters is op-

posed in the likes of Dorothea and Artemia. Massinger is particularly interested in the influence of such characters on others. In *The Renegado*, for
example, the stalwart Christian hero converts the equally stalwart pagan
heroine by having a Jesuit sprinkle her with holy water as she passes by, a
rapid-transit baptism. In this case, the ritual itself effects the change in
will. (Such a belief in ritual's power to summon up prevenient grace served
as a kind of watershed in the early seventeenth century, separating Papists
from Anglicans. Thus, critics tend to think Massinger was a Catholic.) In a
humanized, toned-down form, Massinger's interest in the way wills fixate,
interact, and change informs three of his mature works, *A New Way to Pay
Old Debts*, *The Picture*, and *The Maid of Honor*. These three plays are
vintage Massinger; all three deserve close study.

In *A New Way to Pay Old Debts*, Massinger packs the *deus ex machina*
in mothballs and stores it backstage along with the thunderbolts and heavenly flowers. The play, often considered his masterpiece, depends on
human goodwill and gets most of its energy from one man's bad will. *A
New Way to Pay Old Debts* transfers the single-minded bad man of *The
Unnatural Combat* to the world of London city comedy, reshaping him into
a Sir Giles Overreach, a character based on the real-life monopolist Sir
Giles Mompesson. Sir Giles moves so firmly over Massinger's stage that,
despite a highly conventional comic plot, the play almost loses its status as
comedy.

A New Way to Pay Old Debts contains all the conventions of Jacobean
double-plot comedy. In one of its plots, Frank Wellborn, Overreach's
nephew, schemes to regain the land his uncle has deceitfully appropriated.
In the other plot, Wellborn's younger friend, Tom Allworth, schemes to
win Overreach's daughter Margaret. Each plotter uses a similar device.
Wellborn asks Widow Allworth, Tom's mother, to pretend that she is
infatuated with him; Overreach jumps to furnish Wellborn with riches as
bait to catch the wealthy lady. Allworth asks Lord Lovell, his employer, to
pretend that he is infatuated with Margaret Overreach. Her father jumps
to furnish Margaret with riches, a marriage contract, and all things necessary for eloping with a lord. Thus, Wellborn regains his wealth and Tom
Allworth gets Margaret. To complete the symmetry of the plots, Widow
Allworth and Lord Lovell become a loving couple.

The play is rich in imagery; a gang of butlers and chefs at the Allworth
house, with names such as Furnace and Order, keep up a running account
of the way various schemers use food and fancy dress as weapons in their
battle of wits. Among Overreach's retainers is a crooked, pathetically thin
judge whose perpetual hunger mirrors the insatiable appetites of his master. The vignettes of taverners and tailors clamoring for payment and the
scenes of banqueting and muted bits of courtship would make the play a
good one even without its gargantuan villain. Yet for most audiences, the

play belongs to Sir Giles—and he goes mad.

The role, like that of Shylock in Shakespeare's *The Merchant of Venice* (pr. c. 1596-1597), is a rich one. Sir Giles has more land, more money, more luxuries, and more dreams than any other two characters combined. A commoner by birth, he has parlayed small sums into huge fortunes. Early in the play, he gives detailed instructions for ruining a neighbor and appropriating his land—beginning with cutting his fences, firing his barns, and trampling his grain; moving on through protracted lawsuits and phony writs; and concluding with the forced sale of the land for a fraction of its worth. Bitter against those who claim aristocratic status from birth, Overreach relishes the knowledge that his servants are the widows of gentlemen he has ruined, that his daughter wears elaborately jeweled dresses, that his home far outshines those of the gentry.

Yet despite this bitterness, Sir Giles wants more than anything else to see his daughter married to a nobleman, to call her "right honorable" and bounce young lordlings on his knee. To achieve that aim, he virtually orders the girl to prostitute herself to Lord Lovell so that a marriage between them will be necessary. He oversees preparations for her courtship with a vigor and a compulsiveness that almost win the sympathy of modern democratic audiences, whatever their original effect may have been. When he finds that his plans have failed—that she has eloped not with a lord but with a dependent page—he goes mad.

Critics disagree on whether Massinger intended Sir Giles's ambition to gain the sympathy it does. Certainly, Massinger did not believe that usurers should cheat the poor or that citizens and lords should intermarry. He does, however, structure the play's last scene so that Sir Giles, at last sure of his goal, receives one irreversible blow after another. When Wellborn counsels the "true valor" of repentance after the penultimate revelation, Sir Giles replies, "Patience, the beggar's virtue/ Shall find no harbour here." Though he has competently manipulated people throughout his career and has adopted patience when it suited his purpose, the anger he has hidden earlier has cut a deep underground channel in him, and now it floods out in murderous fury. When others prevent his carrying out his threats, his mind snaps. In his frenzy, he cries out one last lucid line before drowning in hallucinations: "Why, is not the whole world/ Included in myself?" It is a question Massinger's tragic protagonists—Malefort or Sforza—might have asked, one that Sigmund Freud would have found revealing.

In *A New Way to Pay Old Debts*, Massinger examines human will in the context of greed and social ambition. In *The Picture*, the context is jealousy and trust. The play teaches that loyalty begets loyalty, while mistrust begets mistrust. When soldier Mathias goes to Hungary to seek fortune as a mercenary, he leaves behind his lovely wife, Sophia. He secretly takes with him, however, a magic picture of her, a likeness that will turn yellow if

she is sexually tempted and black if she is unfaithful to him. Mathias soldiers so well that meek King Ladislaus and his gorgeous wife Honoria
stand indebted to him. His boasts about his wife, however, arouse
Honoria's envy. Like the spoiled and willful villains of Massinger's early
tragedies, she decides to destroy what stands in her light, namely the constant love of Mathias and his wife. She sends goatish courtiers off to seduce
Sophia and offers herself to Mathias. In a series of parallel scenes,
Mathias, strengthened by the Picture, resists Honoria while his wife resists
Ubaldo and Ricardo. The courtiers (and her husband's long delay in
returning home) eventually convince Sophia that her husband is unfaithful;
in jealous anger, she decides that she, too, will embrace wantonness. As
the lines of the Picture turn yellow and begin to blacken, Mathias, in
anger, gives in to the queen's kisses. Conscience, religion, and "love to
goodness for itself," however, soon recall Sophia from her wayward
schemes. As the Picture correspondingly regains its natural colors, Mathias
finds it easy to lecture the queen on the value of married love.

The Picture trumpets Massinger's theme of will. Honoria has been badly
spoiled. Her husband proclaims himself her slave, gives her charge of the
treasury, and knocks timidly at her bedroom door at night, unsure of
admission, while dependable observers voice authorial comments on such
submissiveness. Willfulness reigns so supremely in Honoria that she sees
Mathias and Sophia's loyalty as something else for her to overcome. "I
thought one amorous glance of mine could bring all hearts to my subjection," she complains. "I cannot sit down so with mine honour." Accustomed
to having her way, she no longer questions whether her way is just.

It takes the Picture, indirectly, to save her. A day's journey from the palace waits a good woman, one capable of doubt and anger but essentially
honorable. While Honoria and Mathias circle each other like amateur
wrestlers looking for a headlock, Sophia manages her household in Bohe-
mia. As the match in Hungary gets tougher, she loses her sense of humor,
punishing servants for pranks. When she succeeds in bringing her suspicions and fears under control and chooses "goodness for itself," the long-
distance reformations begin: First Mathias chooses chastity, then Honoria
learns humility, and Ladislaus gains in fortitude.

This growth in the characters' virtue comes through a magic totem, just
as Theophilus' conversion had come from flowers and the pagan princess'
Christianity had come through a sprinkle of water. The problem of *deus ex
machina* has thus surfaced again, yet in *The Picture* Massinger backs away
from superstition. Sophia is outraged to learn that her husband relies on a
picture instead of doing, as she has, the very hard work of trusting one's
spouse. Her sense of humor becomes astringent: She will teach the courtiers a lesson, so she pretends to make assignations, robs them of their
clothes, dresses them in women's garb and sets them to work spinning

wool. She will teach Mathias, too, so she disorders the house for his home-coming, ignores his royal guests, and pretends to have become promiscuous. In the play's final scene, it takes the entire cast's pleading to keep Sophia from entering a convent.

Sophia's lessons work. The lecherous courtiers renounce womanizing. Her pretense rouses an almost murderous wrath in her husband; when he is made aware how unjust and unstable his jealousy makes him, he learns to value trust. The royal Hungarians also find a better marital balance. Sophia's actions produce these effects directly, not through flowers or thunderbolts. Her will is strong enough to affect the other characters' wills, in a purely human way.

The anatomy of will shapes *The Maid of Honor* as fully as it does *The Picture*, yet the test cases differ. Sophia and Mathias, Honoria and Ladislaus, have to learn to control but not ignore their jealousies. In *The Maid of Honor*, the test case is the oath. Almost every character in the play makes and wants to break an oath, yet for Massinger oath-breaking inevitably signals a disordered will. (Massinger rarely questions whether a conventionally condemned action is right or wrong but rather whether the character has will enough to choose the course assumed right. In his better plays, such as this one, even the very good characters are capable of moral failure.)

The title character, Camiola, is a lovely, charmingly honest young maid. She cherishes oaths; being naturally inclined to "deal in certainties," she likes having things spelled out, contracted. She believes in the social order that has produced her. When the king's brother, Bertaldo, sends eye beams toward her, she tells him she loves him but denies his passionate suit. "Reason, like a tyrant," forbids a match between his royal blood and even the richest and fairest of citizens, which she grants herself to be. Besides, she is convinced that "when what is vow'd to heaven is dispens'd with/ To serve out ends on earth, a curse must follow," and Bertaldo, as a Knight of Malta, has vowed lifelong celibacy. Thus, at the play's start, she sacrifices her love.

Such a sacrifice, however, is not easily made. Like any self-confident, honest, and infatuated young woman, Camiola sees in his "sweet presence/ Courtship and loving language" evidence that Bertaldo possesses "so clear a mind, . . . furnished with Harmonious faculties moulded from Heaven." She proclaims that her passion for Bertaldo rests on his solid virtues, on "the judgment of my soul." (In fact, her catalog of his virtues relies heavily on the superficial.) Because she is rich and charming, she has had little need for or practice in renunciations. When he leaves, she is sure her sun has set forever. Her passions fight so fiercely against reason that she first takes to her bed, then tries to recover by amusing herself with the vain suit of a fop, Signior Sylli, himself a prodigious breaker of oaths.

Bertaldo, frustrated, embarks on a time-honored cure for the constellation of feelings that Robert Burton called "heroical love." He goes to war: An ally of Sicily has invaded the kingdom of Duchess Aurelia and is in need of assistance. The war is patently unjust, as even the ally's ambassador admits, but Bertaldo needs a fight, and his brother, King Roberto, allows him to go. In fighting against the duchess, Bertaldo is breaking yet another of his knightly oaths, to protect the innocent. Back in Sicily, his brother the king sends an ambassador of his own to Duchess Aurelia. His mission: to swear falsely that Bertaldo is fighting without the king's consent. Most of the play's characters see promises as convenient ways to get what they want. They use oaths willfully. Fulgentio, the king's favorite, for example, uses them to turn the king against his brother, and, when Camiola scorns him, he swears to tell "every man in every place" that she is a strumpet.

Because Camiola is strong-willed rather than willful, she keeps her resolutions even when they are inconvenient. Yet once, temporarily, she falters. She has refused Bertaldo on two counts—the difference in their social classes and his vow. When, in the course of battle, he is captured and refused ransom by his brother, she gladly sends fifty thousand gold crowns to redeem him. Buying him from slavery, she believes, makes her his social equal and thus frees her to marry him. In her exuberance at finding a way around the problem of class, she apparently forgets his vow. She sends off a betrothal contract with the ransom money. She employs as messenger a man who, she knows, loves her loyally from a distance. Anticipating Bertaldo's gratitude, she lives a dance of glee, daydreaming their future together.

In a play about the importance of vows, Philip Massinger, moralist, will not let a heroine, no matter how charming, build a happy future on broken promises. Bertaldo does sign the betrothal agreement but almost immediately finds himself the object of another infatuation. The normally level-headed Duchess Aurelia, like Camiola, sees his courtly bearing as proof of a wise and noble nature. Forgetting past offenses, she offers him marriage, a dukedom, and a papal dispensation from his vow of celibacy. Bertaldo, like the spoiled Honoria, has few scruples. He accepts and returns home in triumph, doubly promised.

Massinger's conclusion owes much to Shakespeare's *All's Well That Ends Well* (pr. c. 1602-1603). Bertaldo, like Bertram, is publicly exposed. The duchess shakes off her infatuation and Camiola wins fair title to the now repentant man. Then, in a plot twist destined to perplex readers for centuries, Camiola abandons the court, abandons Bertaldo—whom she now pities as a weakling—and marries herself to the Church as a nun.

Massinger may have intended Camiola's decision as a comic resolution, but several things qualify the reaction audiences have to it. Though she has proved strong-willed and loyal, Camiola is very young. She has misjudged Bertaldo's character through her own inexperience. She has a flair for drama that needs careful control. She choreographs the entire last scene of the play, from exposing Bertaldo to taking the veil, deliberately arranging events to "deserve men's praise, and wonder too," and she does so immediately upon learning of his betrayal. Thus, the will, which has guided her throughout the play in delightfully good-hearted ways, shows itself even in the act of renouncing itself.

The shaping and testing of will is certainly not Massinger's only theme, but its development in several of his major plays amply illustrates both his talents and his limitations. Whether the will is tested by the demands of religion, the lure of lucre, the icy grip of jealousy, or the sweetness of an infatuation, Massinger manages to stir the theme deep into a play, to arrange characters and events to illustrate it. If he did not challenge the social or psychological conventions of his day as John Webster or John Ford did, he did make dramatically vivid and sometimes convincing cases for the wisdom of those conventional attitudes.

Other major works

POETRY: *The Poems of Philip Massinger with Critical Notes*, 1968 (Donald Lawless, editor).

MISCELLANEOUS: *The Plays and Poems of Philip Massinger*, 1976 (5 volumes; Philip Edwards and Colin Gibson, editors).

Bibliography

Adler, Doris. *Philip Massinger*. Boston: Twayne, 1987. Adler briefly comments on the life, then analyzes the plays in historical and dramatic contexts. Promotes Massinger as a political analyst concerned with the dangers to England represented by corrupt Stuart courts, especially by such men as Robert Carr and George Villiers—and also Sir William Davenant, who was promulgating values at court that the poet could not accept. Owes some debt to the authoritative introduction by Philip Edwards and Colin Gibson for *The Plays and Poems of Philip Massinger*.

Ball, Robert Hamilton. *The Amazing Career of Sir Giles Overreach*. Princeton, N.J.: Princeton University Press, 1939. Provides a stage history of *A New Way to Pay Old Debts* in Great Britain and America and an examination of the play as drama performed in the theater. Explains the reasons for its popularity and what this should contribute to criticism of the play. Includes commentary on the actors playing the lead role, a lengthy bibliography, a valuable index, and numerous illustrations.

Cruickshank, A. H. *Philip Massinger*. New York: Frederick A. Stokes, 1920. The first and for years the only full-length study in English of Massinger's life and works. Exhibits some historical documents concerning Massinger and provides significant commentary on the playwright's style as well as his borrowings and the literary influences on him. Pays attention to the collaborative works.

Evenhuis, Francis D. *Massinger's Imagery*. Salzburg, Austria: Institut für Englische Sprache und Literatur, Universität Salzburg, 1973. Compares Massinger's imagery with that of others, particularly two predecessors, Christopher Marlowe and William Shakespeare, and a major contemporary and collaborator, John Fletcher. The imagery is approached through types—decorative, humorous, violent, and others—and through subject matter—arts, the body, and nature.

Howard, Douglas, ed. *Philip Massinger: A Critical Reassessment*. Cambridge, England: Cambridge University Press, 1985. Contains valuable essays by eight scholars, with an appendix by Anne Barton on "Massinger's distinctive voice." Topics include the collaboration with John Fletcher, charity and social order, and Massinger's theatrical language. Plays treated in depth include *The Maid of Honor*, *The City Madam*, and *A New Way to Pay Old Debts*. Howard's own essay, "Massinger's Political Tragedies," contains useful information concerning Massinger's art and thought in *The Roman Actor* and *Believe as You List*.

Elizabeth Spalding Otten
(Updated by *Howard L. Ford*)

W. SOMERSET MAUGHAM

Born: Paris, France; January 25, 1874
Died: Saint-Jean-Cap-Ferrat, France; December 16, 1965

Principal drama

A Man of Honor, wr. 1898-1899, pr., pb. 1903; *Loaves and Fishes*, wr. 1903, pr. 1911, pb. 1924; *Lady Frederick*, pr. 1907, pb. 1912; *Jack Straw*, pr. 1908, pb. 1911; *Mrs. Dot*, pr. 1908, pb. 1912; *The Explorer*, pr. 1908, pb. 1912; *The Noble Spaniard*, pr. 1909, pb. 1953; *Penelope*, pr. 1909, pb. 1912; *Smith*, pr. 1909, pb. 1913; *Landed Gentry*, pr. 1910 (as *Grace*), pb. 1913; *The Tenth Man*, pr. 1910, pb. 1913; *The Land of Promise*, pr. 1913, pb. 1913, 1922; *Caroline*, pr. 1916, pb. 1923 (as *The Unattainable*); *Our Betters*, pr. 1917, pb. 1923; *Caesar's Wife*, pr. 1919, pb. 1922; *Home and Beauty*, pr. 1919, pb. 1923 (also as *Too Many Husbands*); *The Unknown*, pr., pb. 1920; *The Circle*, pr., pb. 1921; *East of Suez*, pr., pb. 1922; *The Constant Wife*, pr., pb. 1926; *The Letter*, pr., pb. 1927; *The Sacred Flame*, pr., pb. 1928; *The Breadwinner*, pr., pb. 1930; *The Collected Plays of W. Somerset Maugham*, pr. 1931, 1952 (3 volumes, including 18 plays); *For Services Rendered*, pr., pb. 1932; *Sheppey*, pr., pb. 1933.

Other literary forms

W. Somerset Maugham was a celebrated writer of novels and short stories. In addition, he published ten important books of travel, autobiography, criticism, and miscellaneous essays. He was a constant contributor to periodicals, and he furnished prefaces, stories, and chapters to more than two dozen anthologies and books by other writers. Many of his works have been translated into foreign languages.

Maugham's novels began with a story of London slum life, *Liza of Lambeth* (1897), and closed with *Catalina: A Romance* (1948), a love story of no great importance. Of the eighteen novels published between these two, at least five are of major importance: *Mrs. Craddock* (1902), *Of Human Bondage* (1915), *The Moon and Sixpence* (1919), *Cakes and Ale: Or, The Skeleton in the Cupboard* (1930), and *The Razor's Edge* (1944).

Of the collections of short stories, only the three volumes of *The Complete Short Stories* (1951) need be mentioned here. The publishing history of the individual stories is extremely intricate. An excellent detailing is provided in Raymond Toole Stott's *Maughamiana: The Writings of W. Somerset Maugham* (1950). Stott traces the publishing history of Maugham's short stories from "Don Sebastian," which appeared in *Cosmopolis* magazine in October, 1898, through the publication of "Mr. Know-All" in the April 16, 1949, issue of *Everybody's Weekly*. Of special value is Stott's tracing of the stories which appeared in *Nash's Magazine, Cosmopolitan, Hearst's International Magazine,* and *Good Housekeeping* from November, 1920, to March, 1947. Maugham's stories that were written in French and published in three French periodicals receive separate treatment.

Maugham's travel books include *The Land of the Blessed Virgin: Sketches and Impressions in Andalusia* (1905), *On a Chinese Screen* (1922), *The Gentleman in the Parlour: A Record of a Journey from Rangoon to Haiphong* (1930), and *Don Fernando* (1935). Literary criticism and autobiography are curiously mixed in *The Summing Up* (1938) and *A Writer's Notebook* (1949), later printed together as *The Partial View* (1954). The autobiographical *Strictly Personal* (1941) details Maugham's flight from France in World War II. *The Writer's Point of View* (1951) is a lecture to aspiring writers delivered to the National Book League in London. Other essays and criticism are to be found in *The Vagrant Mood: Six Essays* (1952), *Ten Novels and Their Authors* (1954), and *Points of View* (1958). All of these books may be said to be both frank and secretive. In his works, Maugham expresses himself freely on many public and some private subjects, but he guards his innermost privacy carefully.

Achievements

That Maugham was one of the more successful English writers of the first half of the twentieth century is clear enough, even though the fact is sometimes obscured by that preliminary rising and falling of popular and academic estimation which accompanies the settling of a writer into his place in history. Early criticism tended to portray Maugham's plays as cynical, shallow, and witty, after the manner of Restoration comedy and of Oscar Wilde. Appreciation of Maugham's broader and more serious themes— poverty, social injustice, the possibilities inherent in the relationships between the sexes, privilege versus responsibility, and the ultimate nature of human good and evil—has emerged gradually over three-quarters of a century and has established that Maugham the playwright was a thoughtful observer and critic of life.

Maugham's reputation as a serious dramatist seems likely to continue growing as scholars and critics reconsider his plays, and the success of revivals indicates that at least some of the plays will be part of the living repertoire of English drama for some time to come.

Biography

William Somerset Maugham was born in the British Embassy in Paris, which ensured his British citizenship. He passed his early life in France and, although he was staunchly English, he never lost his attachment to France, living and vacationing there whenever he could and, in the end, dying in his longtime home, the Villa Mauresque on Saint-Jean-Cap-Ferrat.

Maugham was born into a "legal" family: His father, Robert Ormond Maugham, was a solicitor for the British Embassy in Paris; his grandfather was reputedly one of the founders of the Law Society in England; and Maugham's brother Frederick Herbert Maugham, First Viscount Maugham of Hartfield, was an outstanding lawyer, politician, and writer. His mother, Edith Mary Snell Maugham, a woman of great beauty and sensitivity, was socialite of some note in Paris. Her death at forty-one (January 13, 188. was a shock from which Maugham never fully recovered. Her portra stood at his bedside for the rest of his life. Edith Maugham bore six sor in all. Among those who survived to adulthood, Henry Neville Maugham was an unsuccessful writer who committed suicide in 1904, while Charles Ormond Maugham went into the law and eventually headed the family law firm in Paris.

In 1884, Maugham was uprooted from his Parisian home and was sent to live with his uncle, the Reverend Henry MacDonald Maugham, vicar of Whitstable, Kent, and his aristocratic German wife. While his older brothers were romping their way through Dover College, young Maugham was enrolled in the famous King's School in Canterbury. There, the stuttering youngster had a very hard time of it until he left behind what was, in his opinion, the brutal staff of the lower forms. In later life, he became one of the school's chief benefactors and established a library there which bears his name.

In 1890, Maugham was sent to the Riviera to recover from lung disease, a complaint which plagued him in one form or another periodically throughout his life. There he discovered French literature, an influence which was to be lasting. In *The Summing Up*, Maugham declared that it was the fiction of Guy de Maupassant which most influenced him when he set about becoming a writer.

In 1891, Maugham left the King's School and persuaded his uncle to send him to Heidelberg, where he acquired a lasting taste for philosophy from Kuno Fischer, attended his first play, and became much involved with the students' informal discussions of drama.

From 1892 to 1895, Maugham studied medicine at St. Thomas's Hospital in London, gaining much experience of life in the wards, in the clinic, and as an obstetrical clerk in the Lambeth district of London, then a slum of incredible squalor. The first fruit of his medical experience was the novel *Liza of Lambeth*, the success of which so encouraged Maugham that he turned down the offer of an assistantship at St. Thomas's. He decided later that this had been a great mistake, since it robbed him of a further chance to study human nature under stress and at its most primitive. Abandoning medicine, except for his wartime tour in the ambulance corps, Maugham began his writing career in earnest. He also began his lifelong habit of travel.

In the next several years, Maugham traveled in Spain and Italy, saw his first full-length play, *A Man of Honor*, performed by the Imperial Theatre Stage Society in 1903 (an error, he ultimately concluded, because it labeled his work as "intellectual" and frightened off the commercial managers), and even tried his hand at editing. After finding editing uncongenial, he established residency in Paris.

The year 1907 was a gala one for Maugham. After years of struggle, he had determined in 1903 to write plays with the deliberate goal of producing "surefire" commercial successes. *Lady Frederick*, his first attempt under the program, languished for several years before being produced at the Court Theatre, but within the year, four of Maugham's plays were running simultaneously in London: *Lady Frederick, Jack Straw, Mrs. Dot*, and *The Explorer*. All but the last were resounding commercial successes. This triumph freed Maugham from nagging money worries, and he would never again be forced to resume them.

A series of commercially successful but artistically mediocre plays followed, with only *Smith, Loaves and Fishes*, and *The Land of Promise* having some pretense to addressing serious themes, namely social caste and religious hypocrisy.

In 1913, Maugham began having an affair with Syrie Wellcome, a married woman. The alliance was quite open, and it was accepted by Maugham's set. The outbreak of World War I found Maugham signing up for ambulance service, an occupation he found to be physically rigorous but oddly free from responsibility in that he was under orders and thus free from personal decision-making. In 1915, through Syrie, with whom he was sharing an apartment in Rome and whom he was to marry that same year, he transferred to the intelligence branch of the British forces and was sent as a spy to Lucerne and Geneva, Switzerland. The Swiss police were at once suspicious, and he found that writing was necessary for a cover. In August, he published his great novel, *Of Human Bondage*, which he had begun in 1911 and in which autobiography and imaginative invention were so intertwined that he observed in his later life that he could not distinguish one from the other.

In 1916, Maugham went to the South Seas for his health, his always weak lungs having given way to bronchitis during the rugged Swiss winter. It is an open question whether he was also traveling on an intelligence assignment. His companion was Gerald Haxton, a dashing American whom Maugham had met in the ambulance service and who was to be his special friend for years to come. The trip gave Maugham the material for his short story "Miss Sadie Thompson" (better known under the later title "Rain") as well as for his novel *The Moon and Sixpence*, about the art and career of Paul Gauguin.

The Russian Revolution was well under way when Maugham, in 1917, was posted to Saint Petersburg to keep the Kerensky government in the war. Maugham seems not to have fully realized the preposterousness of the mission and later suggested that, had he been sent earlier, he might have had a chance of success. Once again, his lungs gave way, this time with tuberculosis, and he entered Banchory Sanitorium in Scotland. He found the hospital a perfect place in which to relax and write, in spite of the bitter cold, which, according to the medical theories of the time, had to be freely admitted into the sickroom along with the fresh air.

During 1919, Maugham determined to enter upon unlimited travels. *The Moon and Sixpence* having been seen through the press, he visited the South Seas again and toured the Far East, the United States, Europe, and North Africa. Meanwhile, he kept up a regular flood of publication of all kinds.

In 1927, Syrie and Maugham were divorced. The parting was not friendly, and Maugham observed at her death in 1955 only that he was at last free of alimony payments. In 1928, Maugham bought the charming Villa Mauresque on Saint-Jean-Cap-Ferrat, west of Nice, France, which remained his home for the rest of his life except for the period of World War II. In the same year, *Ashenden: Or, The British Agent* was published, and in 1930, *Cakes and Ale*, one of Maugham's best works, appeared.

In 1933, Maugham announced his retirement from playwriting, stating quite simply that he had lost touch with the public and had no desire to resume the contact, since it would require him to master the tastes of a new generation of theatergoers, which was a drudgery he was not willing to undertake.

After a visit to the West Indies in 1936 and another to India in 1938, Maugham was dislocated by World War II. No friend of the Germans, he found it prudent to put his treasured art in the care of French friends and flee Nice to escape probable arrest. London proved incompatible, and he weathered the war in South Carolina and Massachusetts.

In 1944, *The Razor's Edge*, Maugham's mystic novel, which expresses his deep belief that human kindness is the central fact of life, was published. To Maugham's grief, Gerald Haxton died the same year.

From the war years onward, Maugham's interest in film deepened, climaxing, a few years after his return to Villa Mauresque, with the filming of *Quartet* (1949). *Trio* (1950) and *Encore* (1951) followed, along with a new interest in television as a medium.

Honors came to the aging author: In 1952, Oxford University awarded Maugham a doctorate, and two years later, the Garrick Club made him a Companion of Honor. In 1959, Maugham made his final visit to the Far East. In 1962, he published *Looking Back*. From that point on, he lived a rather solitary and antisocial life until he died on December 16, 1965, at Saint-Jean-Cap-Ferrat.

Analysis

An examination of the body of W. Somerset Maugham's plays must begin with a paradox: Maugham, who claimed that he could write nothing that was not based on his personal experience or upon his observation of the experience and personality of others, came, as a playwright, as close as it is possible to come to the impersonality of T. S. Eliot's objective correlative, the evoking of emotion by dispassionately presenting objects or situations without comment. Maugham achieved that aesthetic distance which makes his plays independent of whatever personal experience triggered them. It is hardly surprising, in an age devoted to the public confession and to the propagandizing of whole programs of social theory, that Maugham's aloofness was mistaken for cruelty, cynicism, failure of nerve and of sensitivity, vacuousness, and simple avarice and mendacity. Indeed, Maugham's assiduous cultivation of several public identities to mask his basic kindliness, his bisexuality, and his serious concern for the human condition, with its struggle for freedom in the face of the deterministic pressures which beset it from all directions (not the least of which were the conventions which condemned women to a demeaning social role) has hindered a full appreciation of his artistic achievement in drama.

Maugham's statements about his own plays have tended to blur his intentions further rather than clarifying them. In *The Summing Up*, in one of his clearer statements about his comedies, Maugham wrote that they followed the Restoration tradition in being dramas of conversation, not of action. Unfortunately, he added that the comedies treat the follies and vices of the fashionable with "indulgent cynicism." In the preface to the first volume of *The Collected Plays of W. Somerset Maugham*, which includes eighteen plays by which Maugham wished to be known, he further muddied the waters by declaring that the purpose of drama is solely to please and delight, that playwriting is merely "a graceful accomplishment" and "the most ephemeral of all the arts." He followed this by denying that plays are, in fact, art at all, since they must appeal to the common denominator of the audience's passion and not to the intellect of its individual members. Thus, he argued, the theater of ideas is possible only on the most elementary level, a notion he also discussed in *The Summing Up*. Yet, in *The Summing Up*, he also argued that an art which exists only to give pleasure is no art at all, or at least is of little consequence. Art, he asserted, if it is to be considered one of the most important aspects of life, must teach "humility, tolerance, wisdom, and magnanimity." Proper art, he added, leads not to beauty but to right action. Perhaps it is irony, perhaps it is only the mask of humility slipping a bit, but Maugham concluded the discussion by remarking that the most effective sermon the artist preaches is the one he has no notion that he is preaching. One suspects that he knew well enough the sermons in his plays. In the best of them, the audience never suspects the presence of the playwright in the pulpit and takes Maugham's ideas for their own.

Lady Frederick, by far Maugham's best play before *Our Betters*, was one of the famous "four at one time" plays of his early triumph. Maugham had decided that the way to a playhouse manager's heart was through interesting an actress in her part, and he wrote *Lady Frederick* with this scheme in mind. His formula was to present the average woman's ideal, a heroine who is a good-hearted, titled adventuress, a "wanton of impeccable virtue" who gets her way in everything. The managers saw his point, but neither an American nor a British actress would touch a part which called for her to appear onstage neither dressed for the day nor with her hair arranged nor with her makeup on. Not until 1907, when Otho Stuart, manager of the Royal Court Theatre, unexpectedly needed a stopgap play, did *Lady Frederick* get produced. It was a smash hit; just how Stuart persuaded an actress to take the part is not clear. The previously rejected *Jack Straw* (written in 1905), *Mrs. Dot* (written in 1904), and *The Explorer* (written in 1899) joined *Lady Frederick* on the stage in 1908; all but *The Explorer* enjoyed good runs.

Lady Frederick, potboiler or no, is good theater, a combination of bedroom and drawing-room comedy shot through with the witty repartee that makes comparison with Wilde as inevitable as it is misleading. The essentially trifling game of sorting out partners is played against a background of the romantic and decadent habits of the upper classes. Two scenes in particular fit Maugham's theory of "big scenes" comedy. In one, Lady Frederick, whose great talent is to charm whomever she pleases, turns away the wrath of an unpaid dressmaker by treating her as a social equal. In the second, Lady Frederick invites her stripling suitor, "Charlie," the Marquess of Mereston, to her dressing room, where she treats him to the dubious spectacle of a middle-aged woman transforming herself from a morning fright into the artificially youthful charmer who had infatuated him. The scene was an impressive, if shocking, success.

Our Betters, produced nearly a decade later, is much superior to *Lady Frederick* in technique and impact. While it deals with an infinitely small segment of humanity—wealthy, title-hunting American women and their foreign husbands and gigolos—it offers universal insights concerning sexuality, idleness, ignorance, and egocentric indifference.

Pearl, Lady Grayston, heads a set of self-exiled American women. Her lover, who financially backs her social climbing, is a gross, not quite brutal, extremely wealthy American businessman. Into this environment of false values and sensual abandon wanders Bessie Saunders, Pearl's younger sister. She and her rejected suitor, Fleming Harvey, act as commentators on the action, as she gradually comes to see the corruption of this imitation European society which at first attracts her. Pearl, who is caught *flagrante delicto* with an English adventurer, brazenly brings her set to heel again through a series of shabby tricks. Only Bessie and Fleming escape, after Bessie makes a scathing denunciation of the uselessness of the women who are now neither Americans nor the aristocrats they pathetically ape. Interspersed with this intrigue are scenes in which the misery of people who marry for false reasons and the hopelessness of women who have been brought up to no purpose is examined. On the whole, the play denounces the human waste produced by a frivolous, even a vicious, civilization that puts wealth and leisure into the hands of people who have neither the responsibility, the education, nor the instincts to employ it creatively.

Home and Beauty, which was produced in the United States as *Too Many Husbands*, is an example of Maugham's romping farce. The play revolves around a selfish young chit whose first husband was reported killed in World War I and who married his best friend shortly thereafter; she has had a child by each. When the first husband shows up from the dead, there is surprisingly little conflict. Stage irony develops as it becomes clear that neither man is keen to become the official husband, and a *ménage à trois* creaks along until the wife, to their untold relief, decides to divorce them both. If there is social commentary at all, it is aimed at the antiquated English divorce laws, which are ruthlessly parodied in the last act.

The Constant Wife is a nearly perfect example of drawing-room comedy, but it is also clearly a play of ideas. It reverses the plot of William Shakespeare's *The Taming of the Shrew* (pr. c. 1593) in that the wife tames the philandering husband and makes him agree to her "sauce for the gander" fling with her lover before settling down to a marriage of equals. It also works with the theme of the "new woman," a staple from Henrik Ibsen and George Bernard Shaw. The point is that a wife is in honor bound to be faithful to her husband so long as she is financially dependent upon him, the more so since wealth, servants, and modern conveniences have robbed her of all meaningful domestic functions. Financially independent, however, she is free to love where she chooses. While the play inevitably suggests Ibsen's *A Doll's House* (pr. 1879), it is notably different in that Constance achieves her independence before making her gesture of defiance. The gesture may seem somewhat tawdry, but it is more satisfying than kissing and making up would be.

The Breadwinner is another study of marriage conventions. A husband-father revolts from his conventional role of the taken-for-granted provider and from the meaningless life thrust upon him as a stockbroker. His children grown and his wife provided for, he simply leaves to lead his own life in America without a twinge of conscience. The picture of the parasitic wife and the egocentric, unloving children is a devastating commentary upon the "lives of quiet desperation" led by most men. The husband points up his plight as a taken-for-granted provider when he observes that people are quite able to accept other people's sacrifices without feeling much pain, in spite of their protestations to the contrary.

For Services Rendered, one of Maugham's last four plays—plays written, he said, to "suit himself"—is perhaps his bitterest. In it, he examines the plight of one war veteran who is blind and another who will be financially ruined by the indifference of people who profited from his sacrifices and who could help him if they would. The play closes on a mad scene in which a daughter dances and sings patriotic songs while her father mouths the most blithering platitudes about home and family.

St. John Ervine disliked the play, arguing that the Ardsleys were made unnecessarily spineless simply to serve the needs of the satire. Even so, he declared it to be "a moving and sincere tragedy, with moments of great beauty." John Fielden was yet more perceptive: He saw that, through the focus of a nation's self-serving disregard for the welfare of its returned soldiers, Maugham was making a point against a larger attitude that allows people to "bravely make light of the suffering of others."

Sheppey, Maugham's last play, is a sort of morality play, fantasy, and allegory combined; it turns on the question of what would happen to an ordinary person who accidentally became enormously wealthy and decided to dispose of that wealth on strictly Christian principles. The answer is that the world would follow his family in declaring him mad. John Fielden rejected the play as weak, while Desmond MacCarthy found Sheppey a highly sympathetic character in whom theatergoers could take refuge from the otherwise too bitter satire. He saw it as a mark of Maugham's skill that he could make Sheppey sympathetic without sentimentalizing him. Richard Ward paid a high compliment indeed in declaring that, while *Sheppey* was far from Maugham's best play, none better achieved the purpose of art, the expression of spiritual reality in material terms.

The Circle is generally considered to be Maugham's masterpiece. It combines the often brutal wit of drawing-room comedy with drama of ideas. Once more, the upper classes and their marriage habits are the target of satire. The aftermath of the elopement of a married woman, who is willing to give up child, reputation, position, and security for the companionship of the man she loves, is placed under microscopic observation. Some thirty years after the elopement, she returns to her son's country house with her lover and encounters, unexpectedly, the man who is still legally her husband. Age has not been kind to the wife, a former beauty, or to her lover, a politician of great promise gone to seed, and worse, in self-imposed exile. In contrast, the husband has aged well, though beneath his façade of cleverness and self-satisfaction lurks a selfish bitterness. The abandoned son is himself a rising politician; his wife is bored with him and is planning an elopement in her turn. Attempts are made to dissuade her. First her father-in-law and then the mother-in-law and her lover cut to ribbons the notion of romantic love, painting a picture of the slow horror of a life in adulterous exile. The knowledge that their class code ties them together more inescapably than marriage laws rankles both of the aging lovers. Yet, even after seeing what silly, shallow, unhappy people their lives have made them—the mother-in-law, a painted harridan, and her lover, a testy, bridge-playing drunk—the daughter-in-law decides to elope and does so with the aid of the older couple. The play closes with their knowing laughter coupled with the blind laughter of the now twice-duped father-in-law.

The Circle, then, examines English marriage laws, the codes of love in upper-level social circles, and, very quietly, the notion that women will achieve equality with men only when they can earn their living exactly as men do. Meanwhile, they are condemned to a degrading marriage or to a romantic flight to a situation which is at least equally degrading. The circle is Fortune's wheel—there is no getting off it, and eventually it smashes its riders.

Maugham's comedy, then, follows the classical tactic of ridiculing humankind's vices and follies and, in doing so, combines obvious pleasure with more or less subtle teaching. The plays, insofar as they treat universal subjects, will remain viable, in spite of Maugham's own predictions, because his theatrical techniques are solid as well as unusually skillful. That they still play well more than a half century later makes the case.

Other major works

NOVELS: *Liza of Lambeth*, 1897; *The Making of a Saint*, 1898; *The Hero*, 1901; *Mrs. Craddock*, 1902; *The Merry-Go-Round*, 1904; *The Bishop's Apron: A Study in the Origins of a Great Family*, 1906; *The Explorer*, 1907; *The Magician*, 1908; *Of Human Bondage*, 1915; *The Moon and Sixpence*, 1919; *The Painted Veil*, 1925; *Cakes and Ale: Or, The Skeleton in the Cupboard*, 1930; *The Book-Bag*, 1932; *The Narrow Corner*, 1932; *Theatre*, 1937; *Christmas Holiday*, 1939; *Up at the Villa*, 1941; *The Hour Before Dawn*, 1942; *The Razor's Edge*, 1944; *Then and Now*, 1946; *Catalina: A Romance*, 1948; *Selected Novels*, 1953.

SHORT FICTION: *Orientations*, 1899; *The Trembling of a Leaf: Little Stories of the South Sea Islands*, 1921; *The Casuarina Tree: Six Stories*, 1926; *Ashenden: Or, The British Agent*, 1928; *Six Stories Written in the First Person Singular*, 1931; *Ah King: Six Stories*, 1933; *East and West: The Collected Short Stories*, 1934; *Cosmopolitans*, 1936; *The Favorite Short Stories of W. Somerset Maugham*, 1937; *The Round Dozen*, 1939; *The Mixture as Before: Short Stories*, 1940; *Creatures of Circumstances: Short Stories*, 1947; *East of Suez: Great Stories of the Tropics*, 1948; *Here and There: Selected Short Stories*, 1948; *The Complete Short Stories*, 1951; *The World Over*, 1952; *Seventeen Lost Stories*, 1969.

NONFICTION: *The Land of the Blessed Virgin: Sketches and Impressions in*

Andalusia, 1905; *On a Chinese Screen*, 1922; *The Gentleman in the Parlour: A Record of a Journey from Rangoon to Haiphong*, 1930; *Don Fernando*, 1935; *The Summing Up*, 1938; *Books and You*, 1940; *France at War*, 1940; *Strictly Personal*, 1941; *Great Novelists and Their Novels*, 1948; *A Writer's Notebook*, 1949; *The Writer's Point of View*, 1951; *The Vagrant Mood: Six Essays*, 1952; *The Partial View*, 1954 (includes *The Summing Up* and *A Writer's Notebook*); *Ten Novels and Their Authors*, 1954 (revision of *Great Novelists and Their Novels*); *The Travel Books*, 1955; *Points of View*, 1958; *Looking Back*, 1962; *Purely for My Pleasure*, 1962; *Selected Prefaces and Introductions*, 1963.

SCREENPLAY: *Trio*, 1950 (with R. C. Sherriff and Noel Langley).

Bibliography

Calder, Robert. *Willie.* London: Heinemann, 1989. Through interviews with friends of Maugham and through letters made available for the first time (and published here), Calder offers the most informed account of the playwright and novelist. Contains an excellent discussion of Maugham's early life in Paris and the strong influence of French literature on his writing style. Also contains a detailed study of his experiences as a doctor, which contributed to his development. Photographs, bibliography, index.

Curtis, Anthony, and John Whitehead, eds. *W. Somerset Maugham.* London: Routledge & Kegan Paul, 1987. This book offers reprints of reviews of Maugham's plays, novels, short stories, and essays from 1897 to 1965. Many distinguished names appear as critics of his work; among them are Virginia Woolf, Max Beerbohm, Theodore Dreiser, Katherine Mansfield, Rebecca West, D. H. Lawrence, and Evelyn Waugh. A treasure trove of critical information. Bibliography and index.

Kronenberger, Louis. *The Thread of Laughter.* New York: Alfred A. Knopf, 1952. One of the United States' most distinguished drama critics is the author of this study on comedy. The book is divided into seventeen chapters devoted to playwrights from Ben Jonson to Maugham. The latter is seen as the direct heir of such representatives of the comedy of manners as William Congreve, Richard Brinsley Sheridan, and Oscar Wilde. With Maugham's best-known play, *The Circle*, Kronenberger believes that the genre comes to the end of the line.

Mander, Raymond, and Joe Mitchenson. *Theatrical Companion to Maugham.* London: Rockliff, 1955. A pictorial record of the first performances and revivals of Maugham's plays. It contains synopses of the plots, the names of the performers appearing in the productions, first-night reviews, and notes on the adaptations of the plays into films. Also includes an appreciation of Maugham's theater by the British circle J. C. Trewin. Many marvelous photographs and an index.

Raphael, Frederic. *Somerset Maugham and His World.* New York: Charles

Scribner's Sons, 1977. Raphael, himself a well-known playwright, has effectively woven together Maugham's biography and creative output. Raphael also draws a vivid picture of Edwardian and Georgian times. As each page contains period photographs of persons, places, and things, the effect is that of thumbing through a rare, old family album. Index.

Sanders, Charles, ed. *W. Somerset Maugham.* De Kalb: Northern Illinois University Press, 1970. An annotated bibliography of all the writings about Maugham. The extent of his popularity is made clear: The critics cited come from every part of the globe. He is especially esteemed by Indian and Japanese scholars. An essential source book.

Whitehead, John. *Maugham: A Reappraisal.* London: Vision Press, 1987. Whitehead studies Maugham from his beginnings as a late Victorian writer to the close of his literary career, showing how he retained his public for almost sixty years. Whitehead gives Maugham high marks for three novels, four plays, and a number of short stories, and he pays tribute to his underestimated skill as an essayist, concluding that the "baggage with which Maugham set out for the future was not, after all, as slender as he feared."

B. G. Knepper
(Updated by Mildred C. Kuner)

MARK MEDOFF

Born: Mount Carmel, Illinois; March 18, 1940

Principal drama

The Wager, pr. 1967, pb. 1975; *Doing a Good One for the Red Man*, pr. 1969, pb. 1974; *The Froegle Dictum*, pr. 1971, pb. 1974; *The War on Tatem*, pr. 1972, pb. 1974; *The Kramer*, pr. 1972, pb. 1976; *When You Comin' Back, Red Ryder?*, pr. 1973, pb. 1974; *The Odyssey of Jeremy Jack*, pr., pb. 1974 (with Carleene Johnson); *The Ultimate Grammar of Life*, pr., pb. 1974; *The Halloween Bandit*, pr. 1976; *The Disintegration of Aaron Weiss*, pr. 1977 (radio play); *Children of a Lesser God*, pr. 1979, pb. 1980; *The Hands of Its Enemy*, pr. 1984; *The Majestic Kid*, pr. 1985, pb. 1989; *The Heart Outright*, pr. 1986, pb. 1989; *Big Mary*, pb. 1989; *The Hero Trilogy*, pb. 1989; *Stumps*, pr. 1989; *Stefanie Hero*, pr. 1990.

Other literary forms

In addition to his plays, Mark Medoff wrote the screenplays for the films *Children of a Lesser God* (with Hesper Anderson, 1986), *Clara's Heart* (1988), *The Majestic Kid* (1988), and *City of Joy* (1992). A story he wrote is anthologized in *Prize College Stories* (1963), and his first novel, *Dreams of Long Lasting*, appeared in 1992.

Achievements

Although some of his early works found their way to the Off-Broadway circuit, Medoff's real achievement rests with his Tony Award–winning *Children of a Lesser God*, the first major play since *The Miracle Worker* to depict deafness onstage, but unique in that the play was written to be played by a deaf actress, Phyllis Frelich. Written in a stunning dramaturgical style, in which the speeches are signed in American Sign Language, Medoff explores not only the love story of the two protagonists but also the hidden assumptions about "being different" that can result in prejudices in the "normal" person.

The 1980 Tony Award was added to the Drama Desk Award and the Outer Critics Circle Award that same year; it was Medoff's second Outer Critics Circle Award, the first coming from *When You Comin' Back, Red Ryder?*, which also won an Obie Award and the Jefferson Award. A Guggenheim Fellowship in 1974-1975 allowed Medoff to pursue his writing while holding a faculty position at New Mexico State University. The film version of his play has also garnered many awards, including the Academy Award for Best Actress.

Biography

Mark Howard Medoff was born to educated parents (his father a physician and his mother a psychologist) and was educated at the University of Miami and at Stanford University. Intending to undertake a writing career, he gradually moved toward teaching, and found unexpected rewards. While pursuing his professional playwriting career, he advanced in academia, chairing the Department of Drama at New Mexico State University, a position which would allow him to mount college productions of his work before attempting professional productions in the regional or New York market.

Medoff's relationship with Phyllis Frelich and her husband, Robert Steinberg, began in 1977, when Medoff promised Frelich, an accomplished deaf actress, to write a play for her. The resulting three-year collaboration moved to Broadway after Steinberg and Frelich helped Medoff refine the play's ideas into a finished script. John Rubenstein replaced Steinberg for the Broadway run, winning a Tony for his work, as did Frelich. After a long hiatus, during which Medoff wrote and rewrote his next two works, *The Hands of Its Enemy* was performed Off-Broadway to mixed reviews, with Phyllis Frelich again cast as a deaf person and with Steinberg as her interpreter. *The Heart Outright* received a workshop production at the American Southwest Theatre Company, where Medoff served as artistic director from 1984 to 1987.

The Hero Trilogy, consisting of *When You Comin' Back, Red Ryder?*, *The Heart Outright*, and *The Majestic Kid*, was published in 1989, with an introduction by the author. His film work includes *Clara's Heart* (1988), and *City of Joy* (1992), as well as the screen version of his own play, *The Majestic Kid* (1988). He has received many awards, including the Media Award of the President's Committee on Employment of the Handicapped and an Oscar Award nomination for Best Screenplay for *Children of a Lesser God* in 1987.

Analysis

Because of his practice of carefully rewriting every detail of his work and testing it in readings and workshops, and because his academic duties limit his writing time to the mornings, Medoff has only a modest number of plays to his credit. While some theatrical stylization is also present (as in his early *The War on Tatem*, in which a narrator helps the audience through several years of a young man's experiences, or in *Children of a Lesser God*, in which time is condensed by eliminating blackouts and other theatrical devices, allowing characters to move in and out of the stage frame at will), Medoff stays with realistic plots and psychologically believable characters. While on the surface Medoff deals with a variety of topics, placing his plays in quite different locales and social settings (a college dormitory room, a restaurant, a home for the deaf, a rehearsal stage, and the like), certain themes gradually emerge in Medoff's work as concerns which are central to the playwright's artistic vision and as recurring motifs important to understanding the larger ideas of his plays. Three major concerns can be discerned: the journey to self-realization; violence as an event which precipitates that journey; and the relation of language to meaning, in its ability to obfuscate as well as its limitations for full communication. Deafness is a built-in metaphor for all Medoff's themes, in that the deaf person must suffer not only the handicap but also the prejudices of the hearing public, who perceive deaf persons as somehow less than whole, as if the inability to speak the oral language somehow precludes their experiencing the same emotions and having the same thoughts as the hearing. This violence done to the deaf makes them highly sensitive to the limitations of all communication.

Thematically, there seems to be an underlying sense of incipient violence in many of Medoff's plays. The early one-act play titled *The War on Tatem*, far from a fully mature work, begins the exploration of a theme which seems to follow Medoff from play to play in steadily more sophisticated form. The "war" is a gang war in Miami Beach, between adolescents who do not even know the function of a gang, but know only that they must "fight it out" for some sort of vague control over an even vaguer territory. Here is the primeval impulse toward winning and keeping a territory; the young boys make a comedy of an inclination that becomes deadly serious a few years later in urban areas and that carries with it the seeds of nationalism and war. Tough-guy King Myron sends his challenge to Louis Dunbar via messenger. Louis, the leader of a sorry group of youngsters known as the Tatem Perch, knows that a showdown is inevitable, but he avoids it as long as he can, with glibness and clever talk. When, however, Myron picks on Louis's little brother, Louis sees that it is time for action. He gets a bloody nose for his trouble, but the lesson is learned and a reputation is saved. Most important, Louis comes to know things about himself that he carries with him into adult life and, as twenty-year-old narrator, explains in retrospect to the audience.

From this modest beginning, Medoff continued to explore the basic human trait of avoidance of violence. His notion is clearest in the two early full-length works that made their way to New York: *The Wager* and *When You Comin' Back, Red Ryder?* In *The Wager*, for example, two college men, Ward and Leeds, lounge in their dormitory room discussing the possibility of seducing Honor, the wife of a neighbor, Ron. Very early, and for no immediately explainable purpose, Leeds carries a revolver, an image which shadows the play as it moves toward its climax, exaggerated in a second-act scene in which Honor's husband brandishes a machine gun. The play moves within the possibilities of violence; Leeds is described in a stage direction: "A dangerous explosiveness rages beneath his very cool exterior." The sense is that underneath the complex patina of social conventions lies the ever-present possibility of physical violence, which exposes all the hypocrisy behind which normal personalities hide from raw forces. The "dance" of word games, double entendres, subtle reverse psychological ploys, and the like is interrupted by the unequivocal burst of energy implied in the violent act.

If the undercurrent of violence can be seen in *The Wager*, it bursts to the surface in *When You Comin' Back, Red Ryder?*, a play which explores more directly and visually the question of bravery and cowardice in the face of danger. Teddy, a dangerous man who is making his way across the country by his wits, confronts the self-protective and falsely safe inhabitants of a run-down wayside restaurant. At stake—besides the very expensive violin held "hostage" by Teddy throughout the play—is the presence or absence of bravery in the face of violence: Stephen, a frightened young man, is forced into humiliating acts before his girlfriend, Angel, and in the process discovers his own manliness. Teddy is not so much a real threat as he is the embodiment of all the threats to one's comfortable mental existence, a challenger not simply to the body but also to protective attitudes and self-deceit. Nor is Teddy a simpleminded brute; his cruelty is calculated and clever, and it stems from a rudimentary but accurate understanding of how humans act toward one another. He instinctively senses the affection of Angel for Stephen, and forces Stephen to "look bad" in front of her.

The violence he does to the married couple Richard and Clarisse, who have stopped for breakfast, is parallel to the Stephen-Angel plot: Richard is forced by Teddy to choose his wife's humiliation over the dollar value of the violin; when he turns his back on Clarisse, the false values of their marriage are exposed. It should be remembered, however, that Richard has been shot (a flesh wound) by this time and that Teddy still holds the gun, so the choice is not as simple as the wife chooses to interpret it. The dilemma, however, does seem to expose the duplicity and thinness of the marriage. Thus, Teddy, without destroying the violin, destroys the marriage. Ironically, after Teddy's departure, Richard himself destroys the violin in anger and as a gesture of what he has lost. Like Stephen, however, Clarisse is freed by the violence of the events to identify herself, finally, as a whole person no longer burdened with the falseness that the marriage forced on her. Thus, Medoff's plays explore how honest the characters are with themselves, given a situation which forces them to back away from all the façades and face who they really are behind the masks of social acceptability. While on the surface the plays are about violence, they are in fact about the realizations that come from the introduction of violence to an otherwise false and superficial life. Acting as a catalyst for the reaction that lies dormant within the human personality, violence, like agitation in a test tube, begins the chain reaction that results in a satisfaction, a neutralizing, of the disparate "chemicals" of the human personality.

Working alongside the themes of violence in Medoff's plays are his concerns with the manipulation of language to achieve the characters' ends. In every play, the dialogue hinges on wordplay: vague references, subtle and obscure distinctions in the language, a preciseness on the part of one character in order to intimidate another, less verbally accomplished person. Some of the battles are entirely verbal for a large part of the play. In *The War on Tatem*, for example, Louis does everything that he can, verbally, to avoid and then to ameliorate the actual fight, and he succeeds until his brother, less verbal and less cowardly, gets Louis to act on his principles with something besides words. The entire conflict of *The Wager* centers on Ward's ignorance of the subtleties of the (often unspoken) dialogue between Leeds and Honor. A typical line, showing how Leeds can manage the language to suit his ends, is: "You think I'm cleverer than you think I am, when in fact you think I'm cleverer than I am. And that's one of the reasons why I'm king and you clean the stables." Leeds, too, is possibly hiding something from himself. Hints of homosexuality or impotence are sprinkled through the play, and his ultimate discovery may be that his attraction to Honor may finally bring his sexual preferences to the surface. In *Children of a Lesser God*, the entire action revolves around the question of whether Sarah is somehow obligated to learn to read lips or whether she has a right to stay within her own range of expression and expect others to enter into it. The mode of communication becomes the arena of conflict not only for Sarah and James but for Sarah and the "real" world of the hearing as well.

Finally, the single most important aspect of Medoff's plays is the discovery by the protagonist of his or her own identity, a discovery often precipitated by the introduction of the possibility of violence. All of his plays are really moments when the search for self is intensified by circumstances. *Children of a Lesser God* is not merely James's play, in which he discovers that deaf people are whole people; it is, most important, a journey taken by Sarah into articulating a truth for herself, one which has lain embedded in her anger and defensive attitudes. When she tells James about the "joining" that they can never have, she is telling herself for the first time as well. The whole "speech" to the panel is in fact her manifesto for her future, and she comes to it only after her relationship with deafness is replaced by her relationship with James. It is no coincidence that James's last name is Leeds, the name of the character in *The Wager*, since in both cases a man hurries to assumptions about a woman, who must during the course of the action set him straight about those assumptions. Honor and Sarah are alike, too, in that they both are clearheaded about their defense systems against humanity but must discover who they are during the play itself. They both become more satisfied with themselves after the male (in both cases Leeds, a name which takes on significance in the abstract) helps them through the complexities of self-argument.

Continuing the themes of self-awareness and the difficulties of verbal communication, in Medoff's next play, *The Hands of Its Enemy*, it is a stage director who guides a woman on her journey to self-realization. The title refers to the existential saying "Life is in the hands of its enemies." Here, the play-within-a-play form is employed as a device for exploring the ways that a novice playwright (a deaf woman, played by Frelich in New York) hides the truth from herself about a violent incident in her past. As the rehearsals progress on her autobiographical play, the director admonishes her for writing a "little revenge play" instead of a "large play about domestic violence." The playwright has written a play about a wife's revenge on her husband, instead of about the pain and violence of her own experience. This self-disguise of one's real anguish is central to all Medoff's plays. He sees his characters as exposing themselves *to* themselves in the course of the play.

As Medoff's body of work grows and his dramaturgical skills become more refined, the recurring themes of self-realization, violence as catalyst, and the properties of language continue to identify his creative style. Given his habits of careful attention to detail and his obsession with drafts and workshops, the positive critical reception of his first plays in New York, and his opportunities for regional tryouts of all new work, Medoff is in a good position to continue a playwriting career offering high-quality drama to the American theatergoing public. His talent for detecting the larger ideas of American cultural conflict bracketed inside the personal dramas of his protagonists has not yet exhausted its possibilities. This potential, if realized, along with his outstanding canon, puts him in the company of David Mamet, Sam Shepard, and Lanford Wilson, the best of contemporary American playwrights.

Other major works

SCREENPLAYS: *Children of a Lesser God*, 1986 (with Hesper Anderson); *Clara's Heart*, 1988; *The Majestic Kid*, 1988; *City of Joy*, 1992.
NOVEL: *Dreams of Long Lasting*, 1992.

Bibliography

Barnes, Clive. "*Children of a Lesser God* Flows Like a Symphony." Review of *Children of a Lesser God. Post* (New York), March 31, 1980. "Barnes states that in any season this play would be a major event, a play of great importance, absorbing and interesting, full of love, understanding and passion." Finds it to be "a play that opens new concepts of the way of a man with a woman, and even new thoughts on the means and matter of human communication."

Erben, Rudolf. "The Western Holdup Play: The Pilgrimage Continues." *Western American Literature* 23 (February, 1989): 311-322. A study of "hold-up" plays, among them *The Petrified Forest*, the 1935 Robert E. Sherwood play, which introduced the genre. *When You Comin' Back, Red Ryder?* is almost a sequel to the Sherwood play; like Mantee, "Teddy is a mixture between cowboy and gangster." Stephen's and Angel's sexual reunion, ten years later, is the subject of *The Heart Outright.* The genre is an offshoot of the "Lifeboat or Snowbound" dramatic convention.

Holden, Stephen. "Mark Medoff Tells of Softness in a Macho World." *The New York Times*, May 21, 1989, p. A68. A penetrating analysis of *The Heart Outright*, "a psychological melodrama in which Stephen's fighting spirit is severely tested and found wanting." Holden believes that the "themes of machismo and cowardice in American life" are not fully explored, and the central character is "a gentle soul in a barbaric Cowboys and Indians environment [who] merely wants to do the decent thing."

Kerr, Walter. "The Stage: *Children of a Lesser God.*" Review of *Children of a Lesser God. The New York Times*, March 31, 1980, p. C11. A favorable but reserved review of the Longacre Theater opening on Broadway. Cites the provocative opening of the play, a misdirection by the character, around whom the play is built. "We remain eager to know what last barriers can be broken down," Kerr states, but "as the committed couple begins to run into difficulties, so does the dramatist."

Medoff, Mark. *The Hero Trilogy.* Salt Lake City: Gibbs Smith, 1989. A collection of *When You Comin' Back, Red Ryder?*, *The Heart Outright*, and *The Majestic Kid*, with individual introductions to each play, plus an introductory autobiographical essay, "Adios, Old West," in which Medoff remarks on his relationship to Western heroes, his views of women, film directors, and other matters.

Thomas J. Taylor

HENRY MEDWALL

Born: England; fl. 1486-1500
Died: Unknown; after 1501

Principal drama
Fulgens and Lucres, pr. c. 1497, pb. c. 1513-1519; *Nature*, pr. c. 1500, pb. c. 1530; *The Plays of Henry Medwall*, pb. 1980.

Other literary forms
Henry Medwall is known only for his two plays.

Achievements
Medwall was the first vernacular dramatist in English, and he wrote two of the most significant plays in the history of English drama. *Fulgens and Lucres*, the first vernacular play to be printed in England, is also the first to show influence of classical antiquity, the first on an entirely secular theme, the first in which a woman is the central character, the first—aside from the Wakefield Master's *The Second Shepherds' Play* (fifteenth century)—to incorporate an extensive secondary plot, and the first English romantic comedy. *Nature*, a Humanist morality play, is notable for its lively characterizations of the Vices, its allusions to contemporary London, and the excellence of its verse.

Biography
Henry Medwall's London origins are reflected in his works' occasional references to the unsavory haunts of his native Southwark. He probably came from a family involved in the cloth trade. From 1475 to 1480, he attended Eton as a king's scholar and proceeded to King's College, Cambridge, where he studied for three years. His precipitate departure, without his taking a fellowship, may have been a result of the shift in political power on the accession of Richard III. He continued to dine occasionally at King's and more than once was present at theatrical performances there on feast days. In London, he entered legal service, either with John Morton, Bishop of Ely, later Archbishop of Canterbury and Chancellor of England, or with Oliver Kyng, both of whom were prominent in government after Henry VII's accession in 1485. He was definitely in Morton's employ by 1490, when he was ordained to minor orders of acolyte and dean. In 1491, Cambridge granted him the degree of master of civil law. In 1492, he received a benefice, the living of Balinghem near Calais, which he held in absentia. A grant of another living, in Norfolk, was never ratified.

Morton, who became a cardinal in 1493, died in 1500, after which Medwall's career seems to have ended. After he resigned his living in 1501, nothing further is known of him. There is no indication on the title page of *Fulgens and Lucres* as to whether he was still alive; the description of him as "late chaplayne to . . . John Morton" may merely refer to the ending of his appointment.

The extent of Medwall's ecclesiastical employment, since he never took full orders, is uncertain. His chief legal occupation was as notary public, and he seems to have reached a position with Morton of considerable power and trust, for he was the keeper of important records after Morton's death. His attachment to Morton's household, where Thomas More was in youthful service, and the printing of his two plays by John and William Rastell, suggest that he was associated with the circle of John Rastell and John Heywood.

Analysis

Henry Medwall's plays reflect the aristocratic, Humanistic, social, and political preoccupations of their audience, as well as the physical conditions under which they were performed. Drawing on diverse dramatic and intellectual influences, they achieve remarkable unity and focus and succeed in their purpose of combining entertainment and instruction. Although the dearth of extant plays from this period makes it difficult to judge the extent of Medwall's innovativeness, it is possible to appreciate his dramatic genius in its own right and at the same time to use his plays as an index to the progress of dramatic form and to theatrical conditions in the court drama of his time.

Both plays were probably written for performance in the Great Hall at Lambeth Palace, the residence of Medwall's patron, Cardinal Morton, at banquets during winter festivals. The audience (aside from the servants) was aristocratic and intellectual and included, if passing references in both plays are to be credited, women as well as men. The situation was an intimate one, with the dining audience seated at tables on three sides of the hall and the play taking place in the center of the floor, down the length of the hall, with entrances through the two doors in the screen at the end opposite the high table (possibly raised) where sat the host with his chief guests. The play took place, therefore, in the midst of the audience, and Medwall shows his genius in adapting and exploiting this close relationship to manipulate the relationship between reality and illusion and to provide humor.

In *Fulgens and Lucres*, Medwall makes a virtue of the physical closeness which renders illusion impossible. The play begins as two characters, differentiated only by the speech prefixes "A" and "B," step forward, apparently from the audience, to anticipate the coming performance and summarize the plot. When the rival suitors of the main plot enter, A and B take service with them and proceed thereafter to shift in and out of the play, discussing its moral and intellectual argument and mediating between it and the audience. Medwall uses A and B to guide his audience's response to the play's moral theme.

The main plot is based on Buonaccorso da Montemagno's treatise *De Vera Nobilitate* (c. 1428), translated into English by John Tiptoft, Earl of Worcester, about 1460 and printed by Caxton in 1481. Lucres, daughter of the Roman senator Fulgens, is sought in marriage by Cornelius Flavius, a dissolute aristocrat, and Gayus Flaminius, a virtuous commoner. Her father leaves the choice to her, and she urges the suitors to plead their respective cases in a debate, intending to choose the suitor who proves himself more noble. In the source, this debate takes place before the senate, and no decision is rendered, though the outcome points to Gayus. Limitations of cast size and considerations of dramatic interest and focus led Medwall to have Lucres herself be the audience and judge of the debaters, thus providing English drama with its first heroine. Her decision in favor of Gayus is announced in the play.

The play considers a moral question: the source of true nobility. This was a particularly topical matter because Henry VII's government restrained the power of the old nobility and promoted accomplished commoners, such as Morton, to high office. The emergence of this new class encouraged a strong interest in Humanism, which emphasized innate virtue. Because Medwall's audience must have included both old and new nobility, he took pains to avoid offending either. He distanced the argument by setting it in ancient Rome, and the brunt of his criticism is directed not at Cornelius' inherited nobility but at his abuse of it by indulgence in ostentation and pride, theft, murder, riot, and sloth. Lucres makes it clear that honor with inherited nobility is preferable to honor without it, but when the ideal is unavailable, as in this case, honorable poverty is preferable to dishonorable nobility. Her insistence that her decision applies to her case alone and is not to be taken as a general rule provides a critically neutral setting for exploring the question. Finally, that A and B disagree with her conclusion admits the possibility of disagreement, although Medwall has steered the audience toward agreeing with Lucres by characterizing her as intelligent and virtuous and placing the opposite opinion in the mouths of A and B, who are scurrilous rogues without honor or nobility.

It may be no coincidence that virtually the first subplot in an English play originated in a household where young Thomas More, as a page of fourteen, used to get up and improvise merry parts for himself during the Christmas plays, as his son-in-law and biographer William Roper tells us. Whether More's antics inspired in Medwall the idea for A and B or whether More may even have played one of them is unknown. In any event, their shifting character and status allow Medwall to control the audience. The illusion of their improvisation makes A and B seem more "real," and their comic confusions therefore achieve a sense of spontaneity, while being carefully controlled by the author.

A and B provide a comic parallel to the main plot and prepare for the coming debate by prefiguring it. As servants of Gayus and Cornelius, they become rivals for the affections of Lucres' serving maid Joan, who puts them to a test as Lucres has done with her suitors: They must show their relative merits. This they proceed to do in a song contest, a wrestling match, and a mock tournament, which seems to involve beating buttocks with blunt spears (perhaps mops or brooms), with the competitors' hands tied. Joan, comically apostrophized as "flower of the frying pan," is the "lady" honored by the joust. Like Lucres, she exercises control over the two suitors, eventually rejecting both. While the elevated tone of the main plot allows no outlet for expression of the physical side of love, A and B's scatological jokes in their wooing of Joan fill this need and express the license appropriate to Christmas revelry.

In structure, the play falls into two parts. The division was probably occasioned by the exigencies of the dining situation. As A points out at the end of the first part, the members of the audience "have not fully dyned." The first part of the play has been presented between courses of the mid-day dinner, and at the end of it, A directs the usher to fill the diners' glasses with the best wine, at the request of the "master of the fest" (probably Morton). When the play resumes, it is evidently still the same day, for A refers to the earlier part as taking place "today." Medwall builds this social requirement into the structure of the play by applying the break to the suitors' needs as well: They need time to prepare their speeches. The play is given a natural time scheme: Lucres has appointed the suitors "to be here/ Sone, in the evynyng aboute suppere" to receive her decision.

As the first part presented diversions in song, wrestling, mock tournament, and bawdy jest, the second—the text of which, because of this diversion, is shorter—includes a mummers' dance. As the comic wooing and mock tournament farcically prefigure the suitors' debate, the dance prefigures it romantically (Cornelius offers it as a wooing device). These actions recall the wooing contest of courtly love poetry. By these means, and by the suspense created with the interval, attention is directed to the debate as the climactic event of the play. The intelligentsia, many trained in law, were accustomed to regarding public disputation as entertaining and diverting. The debate itself seems to draw on two earlier traditions: the medieval *demande d'amour* and the classical *controversia*. Medieval love literature often poses a question about love—for example, whether a rich or a wise suitor is preferable—and the question is followed by a debate. The *controversia* was an exercise in pleading by students of oratory and came to be a rhetorical showpiece for the entertainment of lawyers, in which two disputants argued each side of a philosophical question, with the choice (as in *Fulgens and Lucres'* source) left to the audience. In the play, Lucres rounds off the argument by revealing her choice to B, while conflict is avoided by her not being seen to reveal it to the suitors: She intends to write to them. This avoidance of conflict should not be regarded as a dramatic flaw, since conflict would distract the audience from the play's main purpose of reaching a resolution to the problem of choice in an exemplum framed to illustrate a moral question.

The conclusion, the choice of Gayus, has been well prepared for in advance by the characterizations and relations of the characters to one another. Cornelius' excess in sartorial ostentation, which exemplifies pride, is revealed in the first part by B. In the second part, B has to rebuke Cornelius for not behaving according to his rank in waiting on the mummers instead of letting them wait on him; this characterizes him as somewhat foolish. Cornelius is undercut in that his message to Lucres is given bawdy signification by B's mistaking of words. Gayus, on the other hand, is portrayed as modest and direct, kind and considerate. In the debate, Cornelius offers Lucres a life of idleness. Gayus' speech expresses his piety and his military and political activity, and he promises Lucres moderate but sufficient wealth and harmony of disposition. The characters' relationships are subtly demonstrated: Cornelius appeals to Lucres' father, and he later approaches her indirectly again in the courtly form of wooing with mummers. Gayus, on the other hand, has a sensitive scene with Lucres herself early in the play and expresses his love to her directly.

Medwall takes and incorporates into the structure of his play traditional Christmas games and entertainments: mummings and disguisings, song and dance, wrestling, jousting, and debate. There is the parody and the sense of topsy-turveydom characteristic of Christmas revelry in the parodied tournament: apparent in the use of a kitchen wench as its lady, in Cornelius' subservience to the mummers, and in A and B's occasional cheekiness to their noble audience. A and B draw on the seasonal tradition of the Lord of Misrule as leaders of the Christmas games. The inclusion of these elements illustrates A's elucidation of dramatic theory at the beginning of the second part, where he mentions that "Dyvers toyes" are mingled with the substance of the play "To styre folke to myrthe and game/ And to do them solace," so that all the spectators will be pleased, both those that like serious and those that like comic matter. B expresses at the end of the play its other purpose:

> Not onely to make folke myrth and game,
> But that suche as be gentilmen of name
>   May be somwhat movyd
> By this example for to eschew
> The wey of vyce and favour vertue;
>   For syn is to be reprovyd

> More in them, for the degre,
> Than in other parsons such as be
>   Of pour kyn and birth.
> This was the cause principall,
> And also for to do with all
>   This company some myrth.

He then brings the audience into the play by inviting them to rewrite it if they wish.

The play's purpose, then, is to entertain the audience and also to teach them, by leading them to participate in exploring the moral question so that the ideal of virtue mingled with nobility—hinted at but not realized in the play itself—may reach fruition in them. The shifting relationship of reality and illusion attains this conclusion: The lesson of the play may be taken into the real life of the spectators.

Fulgens and Lucres was probably performed by a small, professional company of four men, with two boys to play Lucres and Joan, unless one boy doubled the two female roles (they do not appear together). That Fulgens appears only at the beginning suggests that the actor playing him had to double as Gayus. It is not known whether this troupe of actors, or the dancers, were permanently attached to Morton's household. The musicians probably were members of the household. Costume, judging from the description of Cornelius' elaborate clothing and the engraving of a well-dressed medieval man and woman which Rastell selected for the title page, was contemporary and, along with the jokes, the place references, and the characters of A and B, would have added topicality to the moral. The dominant verse form is rhyme royal, but there is a colloquial fluency in the comic sections achieved through the rhythm, the division of stanzas between speakers, and the use of slang and colloquial expressions. It has been suggested, because there is a Spanish dance and a line of Flemish in the mumming section, that the play was written in 1497 to honor a visit of the Spanish and Flemish ambassadors, but this is very tenuous, and the tone is better suited to a less formal occasion. There is no evidence permitting closer dating.

Though there is no evidence of *Nature*'s having been composed later than *Fulgens and Lucres*, it was published later. *Fulgens and Lucres* was published by John Rastell, who, in printing what appears to be the first vernacular play in English, embarked on a daring venture. *Nature* was published some twenty years later by his son, William Rastell. It is in line with the native English morality play, which patterns man's journey through life from his birth into the world as its ruler, through his succumbing to sin, to his salvation through contrition, confession, and adoption of virtue. A conflict for the mastery of his soul is carried on between personified virtues and vices. Man, whose personal attributes they represent, is passive between them, though in *Nature* he is not lacking in characterization. In *Nature*, the Virtues and Vices prepare an offstage battle, but the audience does not see them in conflict with each other. There is a dramatic cause for this in that man's backsliding after virtue has won him over gives the play its structure, and a theatrical cause in that the actors probably doubled as Vices and Virtues. Medwall innovatively conceives of the relationship of humanity to its attendant virtues and vices as that of a ruler in relation to his courtiers: He uses a political metaphor to symbolize the human state as the Virtues and Vices offer themselves as attendants to Man sitting on his throne.

There are two concurrent structural patterns in *Nature*, as in other moralities of the period, a structure foreshadowing that of William Shakespeare's *Henry IV* (pr. c. 1597-1598). Over the course of the play, there is a progression through the ages of man, from birth through maturity to old age. The cycle of temptation, fall, and redemption, however, is repeated, as it may be in the life of a man. It appears once in the first half, at the end of which man suddenly repents, without apparent motivation, and again in the second, when age has made sin impossible.

The opening of the play, in which Nature, a medieval deity, after a long speech on natural order, sends Man to the World with Reason on one side and Sensuality on the other, advising him to take Reason as his chief guide, is based on John Lydgate's poem *Reson and Sensualyte* (c. 1430). Medwall takes this as his starting point, his vantage point from which to explore dramatically the age-old conflict of the Vices and Virtues. In so doing, he makes sin the result of unreason: Man banishes Reason and thus becomes prey to the Vices. The play proceeds from this point more compactly and clearly in its allegory and its line of action than the poem does.

The play was apparently performed in the same setting as *Fulgens and Lucres*, the Great Hall, with its entrance doors through which the actors come and go, and the winter fire. Unlike *Fulgens and Lucres*, however, the first half occurs at night, with the second apparently taking place on another day. The time scheme, which encompasses the whole life of man, is telescoped. The opening is more ceremonial than that of *Fulgens and Lucres*: The World enters with Worldly Affection, who carries the garments man is to don, and sits down silent. Then Nature, accompanied by Man, Reason, Sensuality, and Innocencye, enters, sits, and begins to speak. Nature advises man and sends him on his journey to the World (actually from one end of the hall to the other), where he is dressed and ascends the World's throne. He begins as a pious ruler, submissive and grateful to God. In selecting his court, however, he dismisses Reason and Innocencye, retaining as advisers Worldly Affection and Sensuality. The Deadly Dins, beginning with Pride and Bodily Lust in the first half and all the others in the second half, find easy access. They are disguised, in traditional fashion, as Virtues: Pride as Worship, Lechery as Love, Wrath as Manhood, Gluttony as Good Fellowship, Sloth as Ease, Envy as Disdain, and Covetousness as Worldly Policy.

Vice is most clearly exemplified in the character of Pride, who is dominant among the Vices. The chief manifestation of sin, as in *Fulgens and Lucres*, is sumptuous dress. Man's first assumption of apparel is not essentially sinful; it signifies the conferring of rulership and majesty. At the same time, however, it signals temptation. Pride, who is dressed in garments exactly echoing those of Cornelius, will purvey to Man far better garments. During the play's first half, these are in the making, and in the second half, Man's wearing of them signals a descent into deeper sin. Sumptuous dress is culpable not only because it indicates personal vanity and addiction to changing foreign fashion, but also because it supports the exploitation of the poor. As with Cornelius, it signifies poor stewardship of worldly goods. Medwall thus expresses support for Henry VII's policies against livery and maintenance and in favor of fiscal moderation.

Like *Fulgens and Lucres, Nature* is a didactic play, giving advice not only to men generally but specifically to the ruling class. Like Medwall's other play, it is also varied with mirthful elements, though it does not contain extensive subsidiary entertainments. Particularly diverting are the vividly salacious descriptions of Man as a haunter of the stews, where, as a tavern customer, he consorts with the whore Margery in the first part, and in the second, jests with Sensuality and Bodily Lust about Margery, who has missed him so much during his temporary sojourn with Reason that she has joined a "convent," the Green Friars, where entrance is free to all men. The characterization of the Vices, especially in the second half, provides diversion as well as the chief dramatic interest. They muster troops for a battle against Reason. Medwall has made their defeat and desertion of Man dramatically powerful in showing that it has an internal cause, springing from their own characteristic weaknesses. After mastering Man, they defeat themselves and each other and desert the field. Bodily Lust is disinclined to go anywhere near blows and bloodshed. Gluttony comes in, like Falstaff in Shakespeare's *Henry IV*, with a bottle and a cheese as his sword and buckler and expresses his intention of keeping out of the way of gunshot. Sloth is afraid and feigns sickness. Wrath storms off in a rage, though he does not actually desert. Envy, resenting Pride's ostentatious appearance, sends him off in a dudgeon with a false report that Man has taken away his office.

With the disappearance of the Vices, the dramatic aspect of the play ends. Man, by reason of age, can no longer sin actively; the Vices have gone to seek a new master. He can approach only Covetousness to wait on him, but Covetousness is busy with churchmen. Reason leads Man to be addressed by the Virtues in turn and encourages him to continue in the path of virtue, and the play ends as "they syng some goodly ballet," this harmony contrasting with the discord of the Vices.

Again, the basic verse form is rhyme royal, but the play is remarkable in containing the first example of prose speech in English drama, an aside by Pride to Sensuality. The language of the Vices is dynamic and colloquial, that of the Virtues formal and measured. In several places, notably Nature's opening speech, the verse rises to heights of quite notable poetry. Metrical ease and rhythmic unobtrusiveness are among Medwall's virtues. A rather interesting feature of the original printed text is the marking of caesuras, which seem to designate pauses for the actor, so it is possible to gain some idea of the pacing and rhythm of speech. The more colloquial speeches have fewer of these and seem therefore to have been spoken rapidly.

The setting is contemporary London, with its peculiarly urban haunts of vice, and again the costume, judging from Pride's apparel, is contemporary. The Vices talk familiarly to the audience, as do A and B (who exhibit some characteristics of the morality Vices), insulting them and asking them for favors, and there are references to the hall setting and furniture. The cast is larger than that of *Fulgens and Lucres*, requiring at least eight or nine players. That Innocencye is addressed as both a boy and a woman may suggest that he was played by a boy dressed as a woman. He could have doubled as Pride's son Garcius.

Until the twentieth century, Medwall's reputation was low, and it was believed to have been poor in his own day, because of a fabricated account by John Payne Collier of Henry VIII's walking out in boredom on *The Finding of Truth*, a supposed play by Medwall. The discovery in 1919 of the sole surviving copy of *Fulgens and Lucres*, and the exposure of the fabrication, led to recognition of his significance. *Nature*, which has been known to specialists since the beginning of the seventeenth century, has been, until recently, somewhat in the shade critically because of the bias against morality plays. The success of performed moralities, however, and an increasing tolerance of religion and ribaldry on the stage have allowed it, too, to be given its critical due. Medwall is now appreciated for his dramatic flair, his linguistic vitality and rhythmic ease, structural tightness, vivid characterization, good jokes, and especially for the way in which he controls his material, shaping traditional elements to his central purpose while giving them fresh life, and guiding the responses of his audience to his moral themes and to his humor.

Bibliography

Bevington, David. *Tudor Drama and Politics: A Critical Approach to Topical Meaning.* Cambridge, Mass.: Harvard University Press, 1968. Sees *Fulgens and Lucres* as a commentary on the political divisions in Henry

VIII's court, where the old aristocracy, represented by Publius Cornelius, strove for power with the "new men," represented by Gaius Flaminius. Considers *Nature* also as a political play, its attack of Pride being a condemnation of the old nobility.

Medwall, Henry, and M. E. Moeslein. *The Plays of Henry Medwall: A Critical Edition.* New York: Garland, 1981. The section on Medwall's life is dotted with general information about Tudor England that is not immediately or definitely applicable to the dramatist. Contains a consideration of the language, style, and versification in the plays, a discussion of Medwall's literary reputation, and a separate introductory section for each play with extensive commentary. Lengthy and in the main valuable, but with extraneous comments. Includes an appendix for life records and illustrations. Unattractive format.

Nelson, Alan H., ed. *The Plays of Henry Medwall.* Totowa, N.J.: Rowman & Littlefield, 1980. Contains a substantial amount of material on Medwall's life, including connections with the powerful cardinal John Morton and the young Thomas More. Offers interesting comments on the morality play technique and the language of Medwall's two surviving plays. Includes a listing of documents pertaining to Medwall's life, texts of both plays with notes and a glossary, and illustrations.

Reed, A. W. *The Beginnings of the English Secular and Romantic Drama.* London: De La Mare Press, 1922. This brief study is totally absorbed into the much longer Reed study listed below. Presents important biographical information on Medwall and refutes the argument that plays assigned to Medwall were written by William Cornyshe. Discussion of *Fulgens and Lucres* as England's first romantic drama.

_____. *Early Tudor Drama: Medwall, the Rastells, Heywood, and the More Circle.* London: Methuen, 1926. Establishes Medwall's place at the very beginning of the new drama developing just before 1500. Discusses Medwall's relationship with Cardinal John Morton and possible connections with Thomas More. Presents information on Medwall's association with John Rastell, himself a playwright, who printed *Fulgens and Lucres*, and whose son William printed *Nature.*

Whall, Helen M. *To Instruct and Delight: Didactic Method in Five Tudor Dramas.* New York: Garland, 1988. Sees *Nature* as a failure (too instructive and insufficiently delightful) and *Fulgens and Lucres* as a success: (highly didactic; marvelously entertaining, and almost perfect). Medwall's source for his best play is viewed as a product of Renaissance rhetoric, oratory and debate, and Medwall's best play is found to be gently persuasive, with its concepts of true nobility presented with diplomacy and good humor.

Arthur Kincaid
(Updated by *Howard L. Ford*)

THOMAS MIDDLETON

Born: London, England; April 18, 1580 (baptized)
Died: London, England; July, 1627

Principal drama

The Honest Whore, Part I, pr., pb. 1604 (with Thomas Dekker); *The Family of Love*, pr. c. 1604-1607, pb. 1608; *The Phoenix*, pr. 1604, pb. 1607; *Your Five Gallants*, pr. 1604-1607, pb. 1608; *A Trick to Catch the Old One*, pr. c. 1605-1606, pb. 1608; *A Mad World, My Masters*, pr. c. 1606, pb. 1608; *Michaelmas Term*, pr. c. 1606, pb. 1607; *The Roaring Girl: Or, Moll Cutpurse*, pr. c. 1610, pb. 1611 (with Dekker); *The Witch*, pr. c. 1610, pb. 1778; *A Chaste Maid in Cheapside*, pr. 1611, pb. 1630; *No Wit, No Help Like a Woman's*, pr. c. 1613-1627, pb. 1657; *More Dissemblers Besides Women*, pr. c. 1615, ph 1657; *A Fair Quarrel*, pr. c. 1615-1617, pb. 1617 (with William Rowley); *The Widow*, pr. c. 1616, pb. 1652 (with Ben Jonson and John Fletcher?); *The Major of Queenborough*, pr. c. 1616-1620, pb. 1661 (with Rowley); *The Old Law: Or, A New Way to Please You*, pr. c. 1618, pb. 1656 (with Rowley and Philip Massinger); *Anything for a Quiet Life*, pr. c. 1621, pb. 1662 (with John Webster?); *Women Beware Women*, pr. c. 1621-1627, pb. 1657; *The Changeling*, pr. 1622, pb. 1653 (with Rowley); *A Game at Chess*, pr. 1624, pb. 1625; *The Selected Plays of Thomas Middleton*, pb. 1978.

Other literary forms

Thomas Middleton's nondramatic work includes a number of youthful, less accomplished works. He produced *The Wisdom of Solomon, Paraphrased* (1597), a poem based on the Book of Solomon; *Micro-cynicon* (1599), a volume of satiric poems; *The Ghost of Lucrece* (1600), a narrative poem; and *The Black Book* (1604) and *Father Hubburd's Tales* (1604), two satiric pamphlets, the latter of which includes poetry. Through the rest of his career, the main body of Middleton's writing that was not for the theater consisted of the lavish public or court entertainments known as masques, pageants, or shows. Middleton was the author of at least seven Lord Mayors' shows—huge allegorical spectacles honoring the city, performed outdoors using expensive sets and costumes. In 1604, he collaborated with Thomas Dekker and Ben Jonson on a coronation pageant, *The Magnificent Entertainment Given to King James*, and in 1625 he was in charge of a pageant to welcome Charles I to London after King James's death. Between 1604 and 1625, he wrote at least six other masques and entertainments for the court and for important occasions.

Achievements

Like most of the dramatists of his day, Middleton lived as a practicing man of the theater without apparent concern for claiming literary stature. As with William Shakespeare (but in contrast to Jonson), the evidence suggests that he cared little about having his works published. Apparently the success he sought was that of the playwright whose works were performed, not read. Yet his works do have stature, both in reading and in performance. He created a number of interesting and insightful comedies, several substantial tragicomedies, and the most fascinating political satire of the age. Four of his comedies are frequently described as masterpieces, and two of his tragedies are considered great works. The four comedies, all dating from the first half of his career (1604-1613), are *A Chaste Maid in Cheapside*, *A Mad World, My Masters*, *The Roaring Girl*, and *A Trick to Catch the Old One*. The two tragedies, both written later (1620-1627), are *The Changeling* and *Women Beware Women*. (To these might be added *The Revenger's Tragedy* of 1606-1607, generally attributed to Cyril Tourneur but believed by some critics to be Middleton's work.) Middleton is judged by some to be the third great playwright, after Shakespeare and Jonson, in a period notable for its abundance of gifted dramatists.

Biography

Very little is known about Thomas Middleton's life except what can be determined from legal and theater records. Middleton's father was a bricklayer but also a gentleman who acquired a sizable estate by buying London property. Middleton was born in 1580, and when he was five, his father died, leaving an estate of more than three hundred pounds to his wife. She then wisely placed the estate in trust to three advisers to protect herself and her children from fortune hunters. Soon, she married Thomas Harvey, an adventurer who had just returned from Sir Walter Raleigh's expedition to colonize Roanoke Island. Apparently, marrying Middleton's mother was also a business venture and apparently Harvey did not know about the trust; as a result, between 1587 and 1599 there was constant litigation as Harvey attempted to gain control of his wife's fortune. From the age of seven on, young Middleton was in the midst of an ugly family situation that undoubtedly encouraged his later bent for satire.

At eighteen, Middleton entered Oxford, where he studied for at least two years but left without taking a degree. By 1601, he had left Oxford for his new love, the theater, and in the following year was receiving payment from Philip Henslowe, the theater owner, for collaborations with Dekker and John Webster. About this time, Middleton married Mary Marbeck, the sister of an actor.

At first, Middleton was writing for the Lord Admiral's Men, but beginning in 1603 he began writing primarily for Paul's Boys and the Children of the Chapel Royal, two companies of professional "child" actors (actors in their early and middle teens). For the private indoor theater called the

Blackfriars, which served a well-to-do, sophisticated audience, Middleton wrote a number of his most satiric, and successful, city comedies. During the years when Jonson wrote *Volpone* (pr. 1605) and when Shakespeare was approaching the end of his career, Middleton became established as one of the leading English playwrights.

Soon, Middleton was working more for the adult companies, especially the Prince's Men and the Lady Elizabeth's Men. He came to associate more with Dekker and Webster and with William Rowley and to write a broader type of comedy. Middleton suffered from indebtedness and had to struggle through lawsuits. By 1609, he was living at Newington Butts because it was close to the theater district, and he apparently lived there until his death. Beginning about 1613, Middleton turned increasingly to writing and producing Lord Mayors' shows, and this led in 1620 to his appointment as city chronologer, by which time he was probably fairly well-to-do. During this period, he tried his hand at several tragicomedies, a genre made popular by Francis Beaumont and John Fletcher. Finally, in the 1620's came his two great tragedies, *The Changeling* and *Women Beware Women*.

In 1624, *A Game at Chess*, probably Middleton's last play, created a huge scandal. At the time, anger toward Catholic Spain was especially high in England, and Middleton provided a focus for this sentiment. His play is an elaborate allegory in which a game of chess reflects the contemporary international situation. The play was a phenomenal success, drawing capacity crowds for nine days in succession, an unusually long run for the theater in that era. Finally, because of protests by the Spanish ambassador over the play's seditious nature, the Privy Council ordered the play closed down and, according to one report, had Middleton imprisoned. In any case, he was soon involved with overseeing the printing of the play, which was also very successful. Although *A Game at Chess* was probably very lucrative for Middleton, he left very little behind for his widow when he died three years later, at the age of forty-seven. Her death followed two weeks after his own.

Analysis

As is the case with many writers of the Elizabethan and Jacobean stage, Thomas Middleton's canon has never been definitively established. For several reasons, it is extremely difficult to determine what is his work: The concrete evidence is scanty; many plays were published in pirated editions; and Middleton frequently collaborated in writing his plays. Many critics do not believe that Middleton has a distinct style; indeed, T. S. Eliot, in an essay highly praising Middleton as an artist, went so far as to say that he felt no sense of a distinct personality unifying the plays: To Eliot, Middleton was simply a name connecting a number of works.

Although the controversy surrounding Middleton's authorship has not been resolved, the critical consensus is that there are stylistic and thematic patterns connecting those plays which are definitely by Middleton. In fact, the Victorians had already perceived a pattern in Middleton's plays: To them, Middleton's viewpoint was immoral. Modern criticism consistently rejects this reading but acknowledges that Middleton's subject matter was frequently low and often shocking and was presented with little apparent value judgment by the author. Middleton's comedies, usually set in the city and usually antiromantic, are pictures of lust, greed, and ambition. They are frequently called "realistic," and the term applies well in one sense. The modern reader must not expect consistent realism or naturalism in the modern sense, for, like all plays of the period, Middleton's plays employ many nonrealistic conventions. Still, they are realistic in that they are filled with the language and behavior of the least elegant characters of London— with the bravado of grocers and the gabble of grocers' wives, with the slang of whores and the cant of thieves, and with the equally unrefined attitudes and language of various gentlemen and gentlewomen, who are also hungry for gold and glamour. In all of this uproar, Middleton is remarkably detached; authorial judgments are made, but they are implied through subtle ironies rather than directly stated.

Middleton worked at first with a comedy of humors in the tradition of Roman comedy and under the immediate influence of Jonson. In these early comedies, he developed an increasing interest in character, in the psychology of human behavior and particularly the psyche's response to sin. Often, Middleton's characters undergo startling but carefully prepared-for conversions as their sins overwhelm them. Also, he became fascinated with presenting contemporary London life from a woman's point of view: Middleton often placed female characters at the center of his plays. Consistent with his psychological interest, Middleton from the beginning stood apart from his characters, allowing them to speak and act with little authorial intrusion. Irony is an increasingly persistent effect in these plays, and it is often gained through the aside and the soliloquy. With these conventions, Middleton reveals inner fears and desires, often in conflict with a character's public pose. Middleton's detached, ironic stance and his intense psychological interest are even more apparent in the tragedies later in his career. In these plays in the tradition of Shakespeare, Webster, and John Ford, he continued to use sin and retribution, particularly sexual degradation, as major themes. As in his earlier plays, he typically blended prose with blank verse, a verse that is never ornate but that rises to eloquence when the scene demands it.

Written in collaboration by Middleton and Dekker, *The Roaring Girl* centers on a real-life London woman who was named Moll Frith. Moll was reputed to be a prostitute, bawd, and thief, but the playwrights present her as a woman of great spirit and virtue whose reputation is maligned by a petty, convention-bound society. In the play, as in real life, Moll dresses in men's clothes, smokes a pipe, and wears a sword; this unconventionality, the play suggests, leads to her spotted reputation. She is a roaring girl—a brash woman-about-town—but beneath this lack of femininity is a courageous, high-principled woman. Moll intervenes in the main plots and is involved in skirmishes with many of the characters, consistently displaying her ability to stand up for the oppressed and mistreated, most eloquently when they are women.

The main plot of *The Roaring Girl* involves a young man, Sebastian Wengrave, and a young woman, Mary Fitzallard, in love with each other but prevented from marrying because Sebastian's father, Sir Alexander Wengrave, wants a well-to-do daughter-in-law. Sebastian plots to outwit his father: He will pretend to be in love with the infamous Moll, and when his small-minded father learns this, he will agree to the union with Mary simply to get rid of Moll. The plan temporarily backfires, however, because Sir Alexander at first reacts by employing a false-witted humor character named Ralph Trapdoor, "honest Ralph," to tempt Moll to theft and have her executed. Moll resists his temptations and instead exposes Trapdoor as a coward, ultimately eliciting a confession and an apology from him; she is also instrumental in helping Sebastian win Mary and even in bringing on a complete conversion of his father, who eventually sees Moll with the eyes of true judgment rather than through his willful prejudices.

Accompanying the main plot are two parallel stories of couples whose marriages are tested by callous gallants. One of these men, Laxton, leads on Mrs. Gallipot until she tricks her supremely gullible husband into giving thirty pounds to him. Ultimately, however, she becomes disgusted with her would-be seducer and denounces him to her husband, whose eyes are finally opened. Similarly, a "gentleman" named Goshawk tries to seduce Mrs. Openwork; her husband, however, is far shrewder than Gallipot. He outmaneuvers Goshawk, and together husband and wife expose Goshawk's lechery. In both of these plots, marriage survives its attackers, but the differences between the marriages are equally important. Given Gallipot's blindness and Mrs. Gallipot's lechery, their marriage survives largely because Laxton prefers money to sex. The Openworks' marriage, on the other hand, survives because of the intelligence and integrity of the marriage partners.

A major motif in *The Roaring Girl* is the reversal of gender stereotyping. Moll wears masculine clothes; Mary disguises herself in men's clothes; Mrs. Gallipot speaks scornfully of her "apron" husband; and Moll several times overcomes male antagonists by means of her sword and the manly art of bullying. These reversals of sex roles are one of the means of uniting the many elements of the play: They reveal that appearances count for little, that the reality of a person's character shows up only through certain kinds of trials. Such trials or tests are quite frequent in the play. For example, Openwork tests Goshawk's integrity, Goshawk tests Mrs. Openwork's virtue, and Laxton tests Mrs. Gallipot's. Moll's honesty is tried by Sir Alexander through Trapdoor, and Moll herself tests the courage and integrity of many characters. The play overturns conventional assumptions that men have a monopoly on courage and that all women are the daughters of Eve. Instead, the play implies that men and women must be judged carefully and on their individual merits. Throughout the play, Moll stands as a lively, unconventional, attractive woman—an ancestor of the Shavian heroine. She is the one shining example of integrity in the play and one of the great creations of the period.

In contrast to *The Roaring Girl*, which was coauthored by Middleton and Dekker, *A Chaste Maid in Cheapside* was written by Middleton alone. Also, in contrast to the eponymous protagonist of *The Roaring Girl*, the "chaste maid" of the title is a minor character. The play focuses instead on several men—Allwit, Sir Walter Whorehound, and Yellowhammer—who embody the values of London's Cheapside district (an area notorious for its unchaste women—and men). The play is admirable for its complex interweaving of many plots and for Middleton's detached stance, which creates such effective satire.

Yellowhammer, a goldsmith, and his wife, Maudlin, have two children: One is sweet, silent Moll, the chaste maid of the title, and the other is Tim, a foolish young man who is overly impressed with himself for having done well in Latin at Cambridge. The parents' overriding concern is to "sell" their children to prosperous spouses. They plan to have Moll marry Sir Walter Whorehound (in spite of his last name), and they hope to marry Tim to Sir Walter's "niece" (even though, as they eventually learn, she is actually his cast-off whore). In the meantime, Allwit (a play on the term "wittol," a willing cuckold) has been living comfortably without working because he and his wife have been quite willing for wealthy Sir Walter to "keep" Mistress Allwit as his mistress. In fact, Allwit is quite content that Sir Walter has fathered all of Mistress Allwit's children. The central conflict in the play develops when Allwit learns that Sir Walter might marry Moll: Allwit must prevent this if he and his wife are to remain in Sir Walter's keep.

A romantic plot runs through the play: Moll and a penniless young gentleman, Touchwood Junior, want to marry, but her greedy father opposes the plan. Another plot involves Touchwood Senior, who is so sexually potent that his wife (and many other women as well) are continually bearing his children. As a result, he and his wife have agreed that they must separate for a time because of the expense of increasing the size of their family. Finally, a related plot involves Sir Oliver Kix and his lady, relatives of Sir

Walter, who are miserable because they are childless.

The ways the plots develop and are resolved reveal their related purposes. Touchwood Senior generously fathers a child for Sir Oliver. This of course resembles the Allwit/Sir Walter arrangement but with the important exception that Sir Oliver has no idea that he is a cuckold. Because Sir Oliver and Lady Kix now have an heir, they take the place of their relative, Sir Walter, in line for the family fortune and thus ruin his chances to win Moll. Meanwhile, however, Sir Walter and Touchwood Junior have a sword fight because of Moll, in which Sir Walter is seriously wounded. Thinking that he is dying, Sir Walter undergoes a kind of deathbed conversion and delivers an angry sermon to Allwit, who callously throws his former benefactor out. Then, in a burlesque of a tragicomic ending, the characters assemble for what they believe is the funeral of Touchwood Junior (dead from the sword fight) and of Moll (dead of grief), but in the middle of the ceremony both characters arise from their coffins and reveal that they are married.

In the outcome of the play, a rough poetic justice operates. Touchwood Junior wins Moll, and Tim Yellowhammer finds himself married to Sir Walter's "niece," who is almost what he deserves. Although Sir Walter has repented and become a sort of moral spokesman, his rejection by Moll and his loss of fortune are a suitable penance for his earlier lechery. On the other hand, the treatment of Allwit violates the pattern. Throughout the play, he has served as a remarkably detached commentator on morals and manners. For example, in one sharply satiric scene he delivers the author's cutting observations about the hypocrisy of the Puritan women when they come to the christening of the Allwit's child. This uncomfortable intimacy between the audience and such a character complicates the audience's judgment of him and at least disconcerts the audience as they condemn him. Ultimately, Allwit is left with a comfortable home and has begun to play the role he will adopt thereafter—that of the hypocritically "moral" citizen. At this point Middleton chooses realism over a too-simplistic moralism: Although comedy demands a degree of poetic justice, life reminds one that degenerate behavior often goes unpunished.

Middleton's greatest and most frequently read play is *The Changeling*. Coming near the end of an extraordinary period in English drama, it is often described as the last great English tragedy. The play's psychological realism makes it particularly appealing to the modern temperament. *The Changeling* was written in collaboration with William Rowley, and scholars generally agreed that Rowley wrote almost all of the subplot, while Middleton wrote almost all of the main plot and was responsible for the unity of the whole.

Set in Spain, *The Changeling* centers on a young woman, Beatrice, who falls in love with one young man, Alsemero, whom she first meets five days after she has become betrothed to another man, Alonzo. Beatrice believes that fate has been unfair to her in causing her to find true love five days too late. She is desperate to break off the engagement to Alonzo but feels bound to it because of her father's insistence and because she would be dishonoring her vow. To resolve this dilemma, she exploits De Flores, a poor gentleman employed as a servant to her father. Beatrice finds De Flores physically repulsive, but De Flores is passionately attracted to her. Noticing this, Beatrice flatters him into thinking that she finds him handsome and then easily persuades him to kill Alonzo. All along, she blindly assumes that payment in gold will satisfy him; she fails to see that De Flores (whose name suggests "deflower") expects to have her as his reward.

For his own part, De Flores, having seen that Beatrice can cold-bloodedly arrange her fiancé's murder, understandably assumes that she will no longer have scruples about yielding her virginity to him. This radical, but psychologically plausible, misunderstanding creates considerable tension until De Flores must finally state the payment that will satisfy him. Beatrice is shocked that he would "murder her honor," at which De Flores points to her moral blindness: "Push, you forget yourself!/ A woman dipped in blood, and talk of modesty?" De Flores reminds her that she is now "the deed's creature," that her moral innocence is gone now that she has commissioned a murder. Beatrice first becomes furious and then kneels and implores him to spare her, but he stands triumphant over her, grandly declaring, "Can you weep fate from its determined purpose?/ So soon may you weep me."

Alsemero and Beatrice are soon married, but Alsemero, largely because he is obsessed with being sure of his wife's purity, proposes to administer a virginity test. Since she has been seduced by De Flores, Beatrice is able to pass the test only by deception. She realizes that she will fail the next test, her wedding night, and she plots to have her maid Diaphanta take her place in the wedding bed for a few hours. Diaphanta stays too long; she is awakened by a fire in the house, started by De Flores, who kills her in the ensuing confusion. At this point, Beatrice recognizes that she has come to love De Flores, revealing, in the psychological terms of the play, that she has been reduced to his level. Finally, Alsemero discovers Beatrice and De Flores together and confronts her as a whore. As the confessions at last come out, De Flores kills Beatrice and then himself, and her husband and father are left with the horror of what has happened.

The subplot of *The Changeling* takes place in an insane asylum, where Alibius, who runs the madhouse, jealously keeps his wife, Isabella, closely guarded. Two inmates who are merely feigning madness, Antonio and Franciscus, and Lollio, Alibius' subordinate, all try to seduce Isabella. Although she has more of a motive for unfaithfulness than does Beatrice, she remains loyal to her vows and eventually shames her husband into treating her better. This subplot works as a comic contrast to the main action of the tragedy. Lollio unsuccessfully tries to use Isabella's apparent unfaithfulness to blackmail her into yielding to his lust, and the scene in which this occurs is pointedly placed between the two private meetings between Beatrice and De Flores. On several occasions, the madmen in the asylum run across the stage shouting out their dangerously uncontrolled desires, provoking their keepers to use the whip on them. This image of uncontrolled human appetite held in check reflects on the main plot: Beatrice and De Flores—and, arguably, Alsemero, because of his failure to honor Beatrice's betrothal—fail to check their own libidinous desires.

The main plot of *The Changeling* was based on a moralistic narrative by John Reynolds called *The Triumphs of God's Revenge Against the Crying and Execrable Sin of Willful and Premeditated Murder* (1621); Middleton's version makes changes that soften the harsh judgment of the original. In the source story, Beatrice is continuously self-possessed, but in the play she is pictured as distracted, out of control, moved by an overwhelming fate. She frequently allows this fate, operating through her willful temperament, to distort her sense of morality. Through a heavy use of the soliloquy and the aside, Middleton reveals the intense inner struggles and desires of his characters, particularly Beatrice and De Flores. Ultimately, Beatrice is disgusted with her sinful behavior, even though, in contrast to many of the great figures of Shakespearean tragedy, she is not fully enlightened about her errors at the end; a part of her tragedy lies in her moral blindness. De Flores, by contrast, gains less sympathy but, like Shakespeare's Macbeth, more stature by always behaving with his eyes open.

As in *The Changeling*, the characters in *Women Beware Women* are obsessed with lust; like Beatrice, they become totally degraded because of it. Also as in *The Changeling*, two plots borrowed from two distinct sources are woven together ingeniously, each one commenting on the other. The main plot deals with a marriage that at first seems wholesome, perhaps even romantic. Leantio, a Florentine businessman, has married a Venetian woman, Bianca, who appears not to regret having given up family riches for love. When he leaves her with his mother as her chaperone, the Duke of Florence sees the beautiful, foreign Bianca and desires her. In order to pander to their sovereign, a brother and sister, Hippolito and Livia, plot to bring the two women to their house so that the duke can seduce Bianca. While Livia distracts Leantio's mother with a game of chess, Hippolito conducts Bianca on a tour of the house. Hippolito suddenly presents the duke to Bianca and leaves her alone with him. Bianca halfheartedly resists the duke but soon yields to his passionate wooing and his promises of wealth. While this is occurring, the chess game below provides brilliant ironic commentary on the seduction above. When Leantio returns, Bianca treats him scornfully and openly flaunts her new lover. Leantio strikes back by becoming the lover of Livia, who has developed a sudden passion for him.

The subplot presents the relationship between Hippolito and his niece Isabella, who at first seem to have a pure, loving friendship. When Hippolito tries to seduce his niece, however, Isabella rejects him in horror. As in the main plot, Livia intercedes to help her brother by telling Isabella a lie—that she is not really a blood relative of Hippolito. Relieved of the threat of incest, Isabella can now express her love for Hippolito. Thus far, Isabella is essentially an innocent victim, but she is not so innocent when she agrees to go ahead with an arranged marriage in order to cover her love affair. She is betrothed to a coarse, stupid man, the ward of a character named Guardiano.

Both plots revolve around women who appear to be virtuous but who quickly reveal their frailty. Isabella at first appears to be a foil to Bianca, but she is scarcely her moral superior. In both plots, Livia schemes to destroy a woman in order to please her brother. Eventually, Hippolito learns about Livia's relationship with Leantio and, strangely, defends her honor by fighting and killing him. In anguish, Livia retaliates by revealing Hippolito's relationship with his niece, and this brings on the series of revenges in the denouement. During a masque to celebrate the wedding of the duke to Bianca, fictitious violence turns out to be real revenge and suicide. At the end, death comes to Isabella, Guardiano, Livia, Hippolito, the duke, and Bianca.

As a summary of its plot suggests, *Women Beware Women* is a play of almost unrelieved horror and baseness. The play's only decent character, the cardinal, appears late in the action as a commentator on this baseness. Several of the main characters highlight their moral confusion by adopting moral poses in the midst of their depravity; Isabella's marriage with Guardiano's ward is an example of this defense mechanism, as is Hippolito's concern for his sister's honor even though at the time he is knowingly committing incest. Similarly, the lecherous duke deludes himself that he will become a virtuous person simply by marrying Bianca. At the center of the intrigue stands Livia, outwardly a good-humored, sociable woman but underneath a vastly dangerous person because of her extraordinary indifference to moral standards. Hippolito, as he dies, has some sense of what the tragedy has been about: "Lust and forgetfulness has [*sic*] been amongst us,/ And we are brought to nothing." Through this and other reminders near the end, and above all through the many ironies of the play, audiences are able to see the tremendous waste of healthy instincts destroyed by lust and ambition.

There is something particularly modern about Middleton's attitude toward his material; perhaps it is a moral relativism. This modernity shows up in his persistent exploration of the psyche's complexity and in the ironies through which this complexity is expressed. His characters cannot be dismissed or summarized easily—a disturbing fact to previous ages looking for more decisive, discriminating judgments. Yet to the modern age, this is the highest kind of morality, and for that reason, Middleton's reputation will probably endure.

Other major works

POETRY: *The Wisdom of Solomon, Paraphrased*, 1597; *Micro-cynicon*, 1599; *The Ghost of Lucrece*, 1600.

MISCELLANEOUS: *The Magnificent Entertainment Given to King James*, 1604 (with Thomas Dekker and Ben Jonson); *The Black Book*, 1604; *Father Hubburd's Tales*, 1604 (includes poetry); *Sir Robert Sherley*, 1609; *The Works of Thomas Middleton*, 1885-1886 (8 volumes; A. H. Bullen, editor).

Bibliography

Barker, Richard Hindry. *Thomas Middleton*. New York: Columbia University Press, 1958. Barker begins with a twenty-five-page account of Middleton's life and then devotes chapters to the early and later comedies, the tragicomedies, and the later tragedies. He boldly ascribes *The Revenger's Tragedy* to Middleton and gives it a separate chapter. The fifty pages of annotations of Middleton's works are excellent.

Brittin, Norman A. *Thomas Middleton*. New York: Twayne, 1972. This volume in the Twayne series presents in a chronology and an introduction what little is known of Middleton's life, then marches through the generally accepted canon. The final chapter outlines the critical response to Middleton, and the annotated secondary bibliography is a good guide.

Farr, Dorothy M. *Thomas Middleton and the Drama of Realism: A Study of Some Representative Plays*. Edinburgh, Scotland: Oliver & Boyd, 1973. Farr divides her study into an analysis of the early comedies, then devotes individual chapters to *A Fair Quarrel*, *The Changeling*, *Women Beware Women*, and *A Game at Chess*, stressing this last work's historical references. An appendix departs from most scholars' research in suggesting that *Women Beware Women* may have been written in 1623 or 1624.

Heinemann, Margot. *Puritanism and Theatre: Thomas Middleton and Opposition Drama Under the Early Stuarts*. New York: Cambridge University Press, 1980. Heinemann considers a series of problems: Why do Middleton's tragedies differ in tone from others of the period? Why did his work change so much over his career? How could *A Game at Chess* have been staged in the midst of a political crisis? Heinemann finds the answers in the plays' political settings.

Holmes, David M. *The Art of Thomas Middleton: A Critical Study*. Oxford, England: Clarendon Press, 1970. Holmes denies that there is no moral purpose in Middleton's work. The early work of 1601-1605 is studied under the heading "An Interest in Sin," that of 1606-1615 under "An

Interest in Character," and the period of 1616-1620 is analyzed under "Variations on Themes." A chapter on the last plays, five appendices, and a bibliography complete this scholarly study.

Rowe, George E., Jr. *Thomas Middleton and the New Comedy Tradition.* Lincoln: University of Nebraska Press, 1979. Rowe argues the thesis that "Middleton's plays systematically undermine New Comedy conventions in order to criticize the assumptions and values which lie behind them and, ultimately, to reject the explanation of existence which the form embodies." The ensuing probing is enlightening about both New Comedy and Middleton's plays.

Schoenbaum, Samuel. *Middleton's Tragedies: A Critical Study.* New York: Columbia University Press, 1955. Schoenbaum studies problems of the canon, looking at Middleton's handling of his sources and analyzing the conventions in which Middleton was working. Schoenbaum includes *The Revenger's Tragedy* and *The Second Maiden's Tragedy* as Middleton's and argues for "a moral order which seems so clearly to underlie the action of the plays."

Elliott A. Denniston
(Updated by *Frank Day*)

ARTHUR MILLER

Born: New York, New York; October 17, 1915

Principal drama

The Man Who Had All the Luck, pr. 1944, pb. 1989; *All My Sons*, pr., pb. 1947; *Death of a Salesman*, pr., pb. 1949; *An Enemy of the People*, pr. 1950, pb. 1951 (adaptation of Henrik Ibsen's play); *The Crucible*, pr., pb. 1953; *A Memory of Two Mondays*, pr., pb. 1955; *A View from the Bridge*, pr., pb. 1955 (one act version); *A View from the Bridge*, pr. 1956, pb. 1957 (two-act version); *Collected Plays*, pb. 1957 (includes *All My Sons*, *Death of a Salesman*, *The Crucible*, *A Memory of Two Mondays*, *A View from the Bridge*); *After the Fall*, pr., pb. 1964; *Incident at Vichy*, pr. 1964, pb. 1965; *The Price*, pr., pb. 1968; *The Creation of the World and Other Business*, pr. 1972, pb. 1973; *The American Clock*, pr. 1980, pb. 1982; *Arthur Miller's Collected Plays, Volume II*, pb. 1981 (includes *The Misfits*, *After the Fall*, *Incident at Vichy*, *The Price*, *The Creation of the World and Other Business*, *Playing for Time*); *The Archbishop's Ceiling*, pr., pb. 1984; *Two-Way Mirror*, pb. 1984; *Danger: Memory!*, pb. 1986, pr. 1988; *The Ride Down Mt. Morgan*, pr. 1991; *Last Yankee*, pr. 1993.

Other literary forms

Although Arthur Miller's major reputation is as a playwright, he has published reportage, *Situation Normal* (1944); a novel, *Focus* (1945); a novelized revision of his screenplay *The Misfits* (both 1961); a screenplay entitled *Everybody Wins* (1990); a collection of short stories, *I Don't Need You Any More* (1967); three book-length photo essays in collaboration with his wife, Inge Morath: *In Russia* (1969), *In the Country* (1977), and *Chinese Encounters* (1979); and one television drama, aired in 1980, *Playing for Time*. Most studies of Miller's career neglect his nondramatic writing, even though he has demonstrated an impressive command of the short-story form and has proved himself remarkably adept at blending reportage, autobiography, and dramatic reflection in his later essay-length books, such as *"Salesman" in Beijing* (1984) and *Spain* (1987). All the important themes of his plays are explored in his nondramatic work, which also contains considerable comment on the nature of drama. *The Theater Essays of Arthur Miller* (1978), edited by Robert A. Martin, and *Conversations with Arthur Miller* (1987), edited by Matthew C. Roudané, are essential to an understanding of Miller's theory of drama, his career in the theater, his political views, and his work as a whole; as is his autobiography, *Timebends* (1987).

Achievements

Arthur Miller has been acclaimed as America's most distinguished dramatist since the death in 1953 of Eugene O'Neill, the father of modern American drama. Some critics have favored Tennessee Williams over Miller, and the quality of both playwrights' work has been high enough to rank them equally. Because of Miller's direct engagement with the political issues of his day and with the theoretical concerns of contemporary drama, he has often been treated as one of the most significant spokesmen of his generation of writers. Not only is his national reputation secure, but also his international renown is growing; indeed, at this moment, his reputation abroad may be greater than at home, where a number of academic critics have reassessed his career negatively. His plays continue to be performed all over the world, and his place in the American college curriculum seems secured.

Unlike O'Neill, Miller will endure not as a great innovator in dramatic form but as a superb synthesizer of diverse dramatic styles and movements in the service of his capacious understanding that a play ought to embody a delicate balance between the individual and society, between the singular personality and the polity, and between the separate and the collective elements of life. Miller is a self-described writer of social plays who is always vitally concerned with the interpenetration of individual and mass psychology. He builds upon the realist tradition of Henrik Ibsen in his exploration of the individual's conflict with society, but Miller also borrows Symbolist and Expressionist techniques from Bertolt Brecht and others, for his plays are organized on the assumption that while there is something like an objective reality that can be comprehended, there is also a subjective reality for each person that makes life in its entirety problematic and ambiguous. Thus, all attempts to interpret his work from either an exclusively political or an exclusively psychological standpoint fail, because Miller rightly regards his plays as indissoluble amalgamations of the inner and outer realities of his characters and their communities. His achievements as a dramatist have been recognized with numerous awards, including Tony Awards in 1947, 1949, and 1953 for, respectively, *All My Sons*, *Death of a Salesman*, and *The Crucible*. In 1984, he was honored with the John F. Kennedy Award for Lifetime Achievement.

Biography

Arthur Miller grew up in New York City with an older brother and a younger sister. His father was a prosperous businessman until the Crash of 1929, after which the family suffered through the Depression, a period that had a major impact on Miller's sense of himself, his family, and his society, and one that figures prominently in many of his dramas, essays, and stories. During the Depression, Miller drove trucks, unloaded cargoes, waited on tables, and worked as a clerk in a warehouse. These jobs brought him close to the kind of working-class characters who appear in his plays. His observation of his father's fall from financial security and of the way the people immediately around him had to struggle for even a modicum of dignity placed Miller in a position to probe individuals' tenuous hold on their place in society.

Although Miller had been a poor student in school, he was inspired by Fyodor Dostoevski's implacable questioning of individual impulses and societal rules in *The Brothers Karamazov* (1879-1880), and eventually he was able to persuade the University of Michigan to admit him. Almost immediately he began to write plays that were to receive several Hopwood awards. If Miller was not exactly a Marxist during his college years (1934-1938), he was certainly a radical insofar as he believed that American society had to be made over, to be made fair to the masses of people who had been ruined by the Depression.

His early student plays contain sympathetic portrayals of student militants and union organizers as well as compassionate characterizations of small businessmen and other professional people caught in the economic and political tyranny of capitalism. In the fall of 1938, after his graduation from the University of Michigan with a bachelor of arts degree in English language and literature, Miller joined the Federal Theatre Project in New York City, for which he wrote numerous radio plays and scripts until 1943. Some of these works express his irrepressible interest in social and political issues.

From Miller's earliest student plays to *Death of a Salesman*, there is an evolution in his treatment of individuals in conflict with their society, a gradual realization of conflicts within individuals that both mirror the larger conflicts in society and define a core of singularity in the characters themselves. Undoubtedly, Miller's intense involvement in public affairs in the 1940's and 1950's—his support of various liberal and radical causes and his subsequent testimony about his political commitments before the House Committee on Un-American Activities in 1956 are two examples—reflected and reinforced his need to write social plays.

Miller's marriage to Marilyn Monroe in 1956, far from being the perplexing and amusing sideshow the press made of it, had a significant impact on his writing, not only by encouraging him to focus on female characters in ways he had not done before but also by stimulating him to enlarge on and reconsider the theme of innocence that he had adumbrated in earlier plays. After his divorce from Monroe in 1960, he wrote some of his finest plays and continued to participate in local, national, and international affairs— including two terms as international president of PEN, the worldwide writers' organization. He was a delegate to the Democratic conventions of 1968 and 1972. Miller married Inge Morath, a photojournalist, in 1962, and the couple collaborated on several travel books. After serving as a lecturer at the University of Michigan in the mid-1970's, Miller retired to a large Connecticut estate, where he continued to write and where he indulged in such hobbies as carpentry and gardening.

Analysis

A back injury prevented Arthur Miller from serving in the armed forces during World War II, but in characteristic fashion, he became involved in the war effort by gathering material for a screenplay, "The Story of GI Joe," that was never filmed but instead became the basis of his book *Situation Normal*, in which he reported on army camps in the United States and on soldiers' attitudes toward the war in which they were preparing to fight. For the most part, the soldiers had no great interest in the democratic principles for which Miller believed the war was fought, but he elevated one war hero, Watson, to a representative position as a figure whose intensely avowed loyalty to his company represents the democratic solidarity many others cannot articulate. Miller admitted candidly the skepticism of Watson's company commander, who doubted Watson's wholehearted commitment to rejoin his fellow soldiers in one of the most dangerous theaters of the war: "The company pride that made him do the great things he did do is gone now and he is left unattached, an individual," who yearns for—yet probably fears—returning to men he knows he will never see again. Thus, *Situation Normal* was transformed into the drama of how Miller's innocent convictions about the war were challenged by psychological and social complexities; indeed, the book is informed by a crisis of conviction that Miller did not fully recognize until the writing of *After the Fall* and *Incident at Vichy*.

Even in an early play, *The Man Who Had All the Luck*—Miller's first Broadway production—there is some awareness of the dangers inherent in the innocent attitude of characters such as David Frieber, who insists that the world conform to what his employer, Shory, calls "the awards of some cloudy court of justice." At twenty, Frieber is still a child, Shory suggests, and Frieber admits that he does not know what he is supposed to be. He believes that he must somehow earn everything that comes to him. That good fortune and the complex interplay of societal forces he cannot control also contribute significantly to his success is an idea that disturbs him. In his quest to become self-made, he withdraws from society, from his family, and ultimately from himself; in the midst of his guilty obsession with the fact that others have aided him, he is unable to see that he has already demonstrated his resourcefulness. In his delusion that he can measure himself, he gives up everything he owns and starts a new business. Frieber's lunacy seems somewhat forced—much too strident, making it all too obvious that Miller has a point to prove. Moreover, Frieber's quasi-philosophical declamations disturb what is otherwise rather well-executed midwestern dialogue.

Miller comes even closer to fluent dialogue and carefully crafted dramatic structure in *All My Sons*, his first Broadway success and the first play he deemed mature enough to include in his *Collected Plays* of 1957. Critics have long admired the playwright's suspenseful handling of the Keller family's burden: the father's permitting defective parts to remain in warplanes that subsequently crash. Not only does Joe Keller fail to recognize his social responsibility, but also he allows his business partner to take the blame and serve the prison term for the crime. Gradually, events combine to strip Keller of his rationalizations. He argues that he never believed that the cracked engine heads would be installed and that he never admitted his mistake because it would have driven him out of business at the age of sixty-one, when he would not have another chance to "make something" for his family, his highest priority. "If there's something bigger than that I'll put a bullet in my head!" he exclaims. He also claims that other businessmen behaved no differently during the war and that Larry, his son who died flying a warplane, would have approved of his actions: "He understood the way the world is made. He listened to me," Keller contends. He maintains these arguments, however, as a man who has clearly been challenged by his surviving son, Chris, who questions his father's very humanity when the full truth of Joe's irresponsibility is exposed: "What the hell are you? You're not even an animal, no animal kills his own, what are you?" Joe Keller's tough, resilient character crumbles quickly after Larry's former fiancée, Ann, discloses Larry's last letter, in which he expresses his intention to crash his plane in shame over his father's culpability. The play turns somewhat melodramatic with Joe's reversal of viewpoint, his discovery of his social responsibility, and his human loss in the deaths of the young fliers. His statement, "They were all my sons," depends heavily on Larry's self-abnegating idealism and on other contrived plot devices, as Leonard Moss instructively points out. Miller resorts to the theatrical trick of the last-minute revelation rather than relying on character development. Nevertheless, the logic of destroying Joe's innocent disregard of the world at large—he is not so much deeply cynical as he is profoundly unaware of the ties that must hold society together—is compelling, especially because he cries for moral direction. "What do I do? he asks his wife, Kate, thus strengthening Chris's imperative that his father reckon the consequences of his terrible moral oversight. If audiences are still gripped by the final events of *All My Sons*, it is because the play's early scenes convincingly dramatize familiar aspects of family and community, with characters who know one another very well, who are quick to respond to the nuances of conversation and to what is unspoken but clearly implied.

What disables Miller's plays before *Death of a Salesman* is not so much an inadequate understanding of dramatic form; rather, both his dramatic and nondramatic prose lack artistic tact. He tends to overstate social problems, to give otherwise inarticulate characters such as Lawrence Newman in the novel *Focus* an inappropriately self-conscious language that is meant to identify their cumulative awareness of societal sickness—in Newman's case, of anti-Semitism. Like so much of Miller's writing, however, *Focus* transcends its faults because of its author's incisive portrayal of events that relentlessly push Newman to the brink of self-knowledge.

In *Death of a Salesman*—originally entitled "The Inside of His Head"— Miller brilliantly solves the problem of revealing his main character's inner discord, rendering Willy Loman as solid as the society in which he tries to sell himself. Indeed, many critics believe that Miller has never surpassed his achievement in this play, which stands as his breakthrough work, distinguished by an extremely long Broadway run, by many revivals, and by many theater awards, including the Pulitzer Prize in 1949. *Death of a Salesman* seems destined to remain an American classic and a standard text in American classrooms.

Willy Loman desperately wants to believe that he has succeeded, that he is "well liked" as a great salesman, a fine father, and a devoted husband. That he has not really attracted the admiration and popularity at which he has aimed is evident, however, in the weariness that belabors him from the beginning of the play. At the age of sixty-three, nearing retirement, Willy dreads confronting the conclusion that his life has gone offtrack, just like the automobile he cannot keep from driving off the road. His mind wanders because he has lost control: He has trouble keeping up with the bills; he feels hemmed in at home by huge, towering apartment buildings; his sales are slipping drastically; and his sons have thwarted his hope for their success.

Earlier in his career, Miller might have made a good but unremarkable play out of Willy's dilemma, a drama about how American society has misled him and stuffed him with unrealizable dreams until a conflict between social structures and individual desires becomes inevitable. Instead, Miller learned from the mistakes in his earlier plays not to divide individual and social realities too neatly or too simply, so that in *Death of a Salesman*, he created a great play that is not merely about a victim of society.

Willy is not easily categorized; he is both simple and complex. On the one hand, he has all the modern conveniences that stamp him as a product of society; on the other hand, he is not content to be simply another social component. As he tells Linda, his wife, who tries to soothe his sense of failure, "some people accomplish something." "A man has got to add up to something," he assures his brother, Uncle Ben. Willy resists the idea that his life has been processed for him—like the processed American cheese he angrily rejects for Swiss, his favorite. Still, he wonders, "How can they whip cheese?" and thus he can be diverted from self-scrutiny to the trivialities of postwar consumer society. Willy worries that he talks too much, that he is fat and unattractive, but he also brags about his persuasive abilities, his knack for knowing how to please people. Similarly, he alternately regards his son Biff as a bum and as having "greatness"; Willy's automobile is alternately the finest of its kind and a piece of junk. Willy is a mass of contradictions who asks why he is "always being contradicted." He has never been able to sort himself out, to be certain of his course in life. He is insulted when his friend Charley offers him a job, because the job offer and Charley's self-assured demeanor—he keeps asking Willy when will he grow up—remind Willy of Uncle Ben, a man who is "utterly certain of his destiny," who once extended to Willy a tremendous opportunity in Alaska, an opportunity Willy rejected with regret in favor of a salesman's career. He lives with the might-have-been of the past as though it were his present and even confuses Charley with Ben; as a result, scenes from Willy's past and present follow—and indeed pursue—one another successively in a fuguelike fashion that shows his awareness of his failure to progress.

There is a grandeur in Willy's dreams of success; his self-deceptions are derived from his genuine perceptions of life's great possibilities, which are like the big sales he has always hoped to make. This is why Linda abets his penchant for self-aggrandizement. She knows that he has not been a successful salesman, but she tempers his faults: "You don't talk too much, you're just lively." At the same time, she is utterly believable as a housewife who has to know how much money her husband has brought home from work. After Willy exaggerates his sales from one trip, Linda quietly but firmly brings him back to reality by simply asking, "How much did you do?"—a question that becomes more pointed if the actress playing the role delicately emphasizes the word "did."

When the play is read aloud, there is an uncanny power in some of its simplest and seemingly pedestrian lines, lines that capture the nuances and innuendos of colloquial language. This subtly effective dialogue is enhanced by a powerful use of human gesture that distinguishes *Death of a Salesman* as a completely realizable stage drama. Toward the end of the play, for example, after Biff, "at the peak of his fury," bluntly tells Willy, "Pop, I'm nothing!" Biff relents, breaks down, sobs, and holds on to Willy, "who dumbly fumbles for Biff's face." This brief intimate encounter encapsulates everything that can be learned about Willy and Biff and about the play's import, for the son renounces the father's ridiculous belief in the son's superiority even as the son clings to the father for support. While Biff rejects Willy, he embraces him and has to explain himself to Willy, who is "astonished" and at first does not know how to interpret his son's holding on to him. Willy does not understand why Biff is crying. Willy has always been blind to Biff's needs, has always "fumbled" their relationship, yet—as so often—Willy transforms Biff's words of rejection into an affirmation. The Biff who leans on him is the son who "likes me!" Willy exclaims, after their close but momentary contact. This fleeting instance of family solidarity, however, cannot overcome the abiding family conflicts and misunderstandings, epitomized by Willy's delusion that the insurance money accrued from his suicide will finally make him the good provider, the furtherer of his son's magnificent future.

Miller followed *Death of a Salesman* with his 1951 adaptation of Henrik Ibsen's *An Enemy of the People* (1882). Miller transforms Ibsen's language into American idioms and shortens the play to emphasize the impact of Dr. Stockmann's confrontation with his community, which will not acknowledge its polluted water, its own moral and political corruption. Stockmann's battle against public opinion clearly foreshadows John Proctor's struggle with his society's self-inflicted evil in *The Crucible*. *The Crucible* is far more complex than Miller's adaptation of Ibsen's play, however, because Proctor is much more complicated than Stockmann, and the motivations of the Puritans are not as easily fathomed as those of Stockmann's townspeople, who are primarily worried about their economic welfare. Even so, *An Enemy of the People* prefigures the fundamental questions raised in *The Crucible* about the value of human dignity and individuality and the kind of justice one can expect from a majority culture, especially when that culture begins to doubt its own coherence.

With incisive historical summaries, Miller, in *The Crucible*, characterizes the community of Salem, Massachusetts, in 1692, which has been beset by property disputes, by a slackening in religious fervor, and by an increasing lack of trust among its citizens. Rather than face their inner turmoil, certain of Salem's citizens search for scapegoats, for persons who can take on the society's sense of defeat and frustration, who can be punished, and who can carry away by means of their execution the society's burden of guilt. In short, the Puritans seek signs of the Devil and Devil-worship in their midst in order to dissolve their own dissension. Although John Proctor, like Stockmann, speaks against his community's blindness to the true causes of its corruption, he does not share to the same degree Stockmann's naïveté, youthful outrage at injustice, and virtually pure innocence as a dissident. On the contrary, Proctor eventually opposes the witch-hunt, because he accepts his own part in having made that hysterical clamor for scapegoats possible. He knows that he has not acted quickly enough to expose Abigail, the chief instigator of the witch-hunt, because he has feared his own exposure as an adulterer. What finally exercises his conscience is not simply that he had previously given way to his lust for Abigail but that he had deluded himself into thinking he no longer cared for her and had even reprimanded his wife, Elizabeth, for failing to forgive him. Elizabeth is unbending but not without cause, for she intuits her husband's tender feelings toward Abigail and suspects that he refuses to know his own mind. Proctor almost relinquishes his good name by confessing to witchery, until he realizes that however deep his guilt and responsibility may be for the community's corruption, he cannot surrender his integrity, his cherished individuality. Like Willy Loman, Proctor reaffirms his own name—"I am John Proctor!"—and prefers his own crucible to his society's severe test of him for its redemption.

The Crucible is not only Proctor's play, however, and as important as its moral and political implications are—it was first received as a parable on McCarthyism and the 1950's hysteria over Communism in America—it deserves analysis as a dramatic whole in the same way that *Death of a Salesman* does. In Miller's superb creation of scenes that require a company of carefully choreographed actors and actresses, he is able to dramatize an entire society and to show the interplay of individual and group psychology. Proctor would not be regarded as such a powerful personality were it not for the full panoply of personalities out of which he emerges. In this respect, *The Crucible* has a finer equilibrium as a social play than does *Death of a Salesman*, which is inescapably dominated by Willy Loman's consciousness. Miller's accomplished use of the Puritans' formal idioms suggests their rigid judgments of one another. Perhaps he even exaggerates the archaisms of their language in order to stress the gravity of their worldview, although at the same time, he dramatizes a childishness in their readiness to credit the workings of witchcraft. There is a great deal of humor, for example, in one of the play's early scenes, in which Mrs. Putnam's energetic entrance explodes the seriousness of reports that the Reverend Parris' child, Betty, has been bewitched. Mrs. Putnam, every bit as excited as a child, immediately glances at Betty and wonders, "How high did she fly, how high?" The simple, naïve directness of these words catches the audience up in a kind of enthusiasm for the marvelous that will soon infect Abigail and her female followers as well as the whole society of Salem. By varying his speakers' styles to conform to the precise demands of each dramatic situation, Miller wins the audience's absolute confidence in the psychological reality of his characters.

Miller's excursion into the Puritan past was followed by the writing of two one-act plays, *A Memory of Two Mondays* and *A View from the Bridge* (later revised as a two-act play), both of which he regarded as having arisen from his personal experience, although it took him some time to discover the autobiographical elements of the latter play. *A Memory of Two Mondays* covers the Depression period before Miller's admission to the University of Michigan, and the play centers on the discrepancy between human needs and work requirements. Kenneth, the most melancholy character in the play, also has the greatest feeling for life and for its poetry. In the end, however, he has forgotten the poems he recites to Bert, the only character who escapes the tedium of the automobile parts warehouse, who will read the great books and save enough money to go to college. The other characters remain very much imprisoned in their everyday lives. Bert's leavetaking is hardly noticed, even though he lingers in obvious need of making more out of his friendships at the warehouse than others are willing to acknowledge. Earlier, he and Kenneth had washed the windows of the warehouse to get a clear look at the world in which they were situated; now Kenneth is a drunk and Bert must stand apart, like his author, remembering the meaning of what others have already forgotten because of the demands of their jobs. Although *A Memory of Two Mondays* is one of Miller's minor achievements, it is also one of his most perfectly executed dramas in that the impulse to rescue significance from Bert's departure is sensitively qualified by the consciousness of human loss.

Miller's one-act version of *A View from the Bridge* is also a memory play—in this case based on a story he had heard and pondered for several years. Eddie Carbone, a longshoreman, is driven to violate the most sacred ties of trust that bind his community by his compulsion to possess his niece, Catherine—a compulsion that he denies and displaces by conceiving an unreasoning dislike for his wife's young relative, Rodolpho, an illegal immigrant whom Eddie has agreed to harbor. Eddie implies that Rodolpho is a homosexual, an unnatural man who will marry Catherine merely to make his stay in the country legal. Eddie's desperate need to have Catherine becomes so uncontrollable that, when she and Rodolpho make plans to marry, he informs on Rodolpho and his brother, Marco, who are apprehended in circumstances that expose Eddie to his neighborhood as an informer. In Marco's view, Eddie must be confronted with his subhuman behavior. In words reminiscent of Chris's charge in *All My Sons* that his father is not human, Marco calls Eddie an animal who must abase himself. "You go on your knees to me!" Marco commands Eddie, while Eddie expects Marco to give him back his "good name." They fight, and Eddie dies, stabbed by Marco with the former's own knife. In a sense, Eddie has stabbed himself; the play has shown all along that Eddie's mortal wound has been self-inflicted.

Eddie's cry for self-respect recalls similar pleas by Willy Loman and John Proctor, and the concern in *A View from the Bridge* with informing and betrayal of friendships and blood ties echoes themes from Miller's student plays through *The Crucible*, foreshadowing not only his own refusal to "name names" in his testimony before the House Committee on Un-American Activities but also Quentin's fundamental exploration of many different kinds of betrayal in *After the Fall*. Yet Miller first wrote *A View from the Bridge* as if he were aloof from its central story, as if it were a parable that he did not understand. He even provides a narrator, Alfieri, an attorney who ruminates over the significance of the story as Miller admits he had done in writing the play.

The one-act version of *A View from the Bridge* seems aloof from the audience as well. There is very little attempt to probe the characters' psychology, so that what Miller gains in dramatic force by presenting events swiftly and starkly, he loses in the audience's inability to empathize with circumscribed characters. Miller acknowledges these faults and notes that the two-act version more fully develops his characters' psychology, particularly that of Eddie's wife, Beatrice. Catherine, too, is a much-improved character in the two-act version. She tentatively expresses her divided feelings about Eddie, whereas in the one-act version, she is far less self-searching, almost woodenly immune to his passion. In the two-act, she desires to appease Eddie's growing fears of her approaching adulthood. She loves him for his devotion to her, but her childlike behavior, as Beatrice points out to her, only encourages his possessiveness. Thus, Catherine tries gradually to separate herself from Eddie so that she can attain full maturity. As a result, Eddie's rigid refusal to admit his perverse passion for Catherine, even when Beatrice confronts him with it, makes him singularly willful and more particularly responsible for his tragedy than is the case in the one-act version, in which all the characters, except Alfieri, are rather helplessly impelled by events. In this respect, Rodolpho is a more credible suitor for Catherine in the two-act version, since he is somewhat more commanding (she pleads with him, "I don't know anything, teach me, Rodolpho, hold me") in capturing her love and therefore a stronger counterweight to Eddie's authority.

A View from the Bridge in two acts still does not overcome all the play's weaknesses. For example, Alfieri, like many narrators in drama, seems somewhat intrusive in his use of elevated language to wrest an overarching meaning from characters and events, even though he is an active participant in some fine scenes. Nevertheless, the play is as beautifully written and moving as any of Miller's major works, and its main character is almost as powerfully drawn as Willy Loman and John Proctor, who, like Eddie Carbone, will not "settle for half"—will not be content with less than their lives' joy. Because of an ample sense of self, they allow themselves, in Alfieri's words, "to be wholly known."

Miller arrived at an impasse upon his completion of the two-act version of *A View from the Bridge*, which was successfully produced in England in 1956, and he did not have another new work staged until 1964. Various explanations have been offered for this long gap in his dramatic production— including his marriage to Marilyn Monroe, the attendant publicity that interfered with his working life, and the trying and time-consuming process of defending his political activities. Of crucial importance, however, seems to have been his feeling that what he had been working for in his plays had not been sufficiently understood by his public. At any rate, he wrote several plays that did not satisfy him, a number of short stories, and a screenplay, *The Misfits*, that was subsequently revised as a novel. He may have turned to other literary forms from a belief that he had temporarily exhausted what had been an evolving sense of dramatic structure. Nondramatic prose seems to have permitted him to explore certain themes and narrative viewpoints that he had not been able to incorporate fully in *A View from the Bridge*, for his next produced play, *After the Fall*, successfully fuses narrative and dramatic discourse in the figure of its central character, Quentin, who constantly forces the audience into the explicit position of auditors rather than into the intermittent role of eavesdroppers addressed by a narrator as in *A View from the Bridge*.

How does one live in a world beset by death? This question is relentlessly probed in *After the Fall*, with its concentration-camp tower serving as one of the central metaphors for the human betrayal of life. As was so often true in the camps, the characters in *After the Fall* are divided against themselves. Not only can kind men kill, but also intelligent men can act like idiots, and Maggie—innocent in so many ways—is horribly transformed into a hater of life. Quentin, who is Maggie's momentary stay against confusion, witnesses "things falling apart" and wonders, "Were they ever whole?" He proves to be incapable of protecting Maggie, so concerned is he with his own survival. In the very act of saving her from her pills—from her death—he defends himself by strangling her, suffocating her just as surely as the pills would have done. He discovers the limits of his own love for her, and Maggie sees his human incapacity for unconditional love as a betrayal, just as Quentin interprets the limitations of his mother's love as a betrayal of him. Thus, for Maggie, Quentin comes at "the end of a long, long line" of men who have degraded her, betrayed her, killed her. He is, in other words, an accomplice in the general evil of the world, and therefore his presence as an "accomplice" in the ultimate evil that is the concentration camp is not altogether unfitting. He has been his mother's accomplice in the degradation of his father and an accomplice in the death of his friend, Lou, who sensed that Quentin could not wholeheartedly defend his reputation and that he was not, in fact, a true friend. Quentin craves his own safety, and he feels the guilt of the survivor as the concentration-camp tower "blazes into life."

Maggie has no identity to hold back, no reserves of self to compensate for her disappointment in Quentin. She thinks of herself as "nothing" and hopes to please everyone by becoming "all love." (The metaphor's abstractness virtually ensures her inability to develop a defined self.) Ironically, her generosity eats her up—people eat her up—because she does not possess the normal defenses of a separate ego. Maggie requires from Quentin the same selflessness she represents. She wants him to look at her "out of [his] *self."* Quentin has abetted her by acting more like a child than an adult. Like William Faulkner's Quentin Compson in *The Sound and the Fury* (1929), Miller's Quentin is an idealist and something of a Puritan; he romanticizes Maggie's innocence and believes that she must be saved from herself and from a corrupt world. In some ways, he seems as thoroughly innocent as Quentin Compson's brother Benjy, an idiot—the word itself is applied to Miller's protagonist more than once, and it recurs obsessively as he recalls how others have employed the term to deny and attack one another. No more than Benjy or Maggie can Quentin accept the separateness of the adult world of his mother, his friends, and his wives.

These failures of love, of human connection, force Quentin to reexamine the moments of hopefulness that recur, one might say, idiotically—for no apparently sensible reason—throughout the play. From the concentration-camp tower, and upon "the mountain of skulls" where no one can be "innocent again," Quentin observes the "fallen Maggie," who once seemed like a proof of victory, and he realizes that his brothers both died in and built the camp, that Maggie's fall is his fall, and that without that fall he would have no hope, for hope in the real world is "not in some garden of wax fruit and painted trees, that lie of Eden," but in the knowledge of human destructiveness, of human idiocy, which will not go away and so must be taken to heart. In the full knowledge of his failures, Quentin embraces his life at the end of the play, whereas Maggie is seen rising from the floor "webbed in with her demons, trying to awake." Her partial consciousness reflects her inability to take full responsibility for her life, to see that she was not simply a victim but in charge of her emotions. The hardest thing Quentin must do is reverse the force of the play's dominant metaphor, making the idiot serve not as a rejection of the broken, fragmented facts of life but as an acceptance of the flawed face of all people. That reversal of rejection is accomplished by saying hello to Holga, his third partner in life, who has provided the dream—the metaphor, in truth—of how lives such as Quentin's ("Why do I make such stupid statements!") and Maggie's ("I'm a joke that brings in money") can tentatively approach redemption.

After the Fall sometimes suffers from a vagueness of rhetoric and from overstatement, so that Quentin's confessions overwhelm the dramatic action and diminish the substantiality of other characters. Miller restrains Quentin's verbosity in the revised stage version quoted here (printed in 1964, the same year as the production of the original stage version, available in *Collected Plays, Volume II*). A television adaptation (1974) removes nearly all of Quentin's verbiage, but in none of these versions is Miller entirely successful in balancing Quentin's subjective and objective realities. Edward Murray argues, for example, that not all scenes are consistently staged "in the mind, thought, and memory of Quentin," as the play would have it.

Hence it is difficult to find a "warrant," a certifiable viewpoint, for some of the play's action. In *Death of a Salesman*, on the contrary, the audience is compelled to move in and out of Willy's mind and is thereby able to comprehend his reality both subjectively and objectively. In part, Murray's objection may be met by carefully following Quentin's struggle to *know* his past, not simply to repossess it as Willy does. How does one achieve a viewpoint, Quentin asks, when there is no objective basis on which to recreate one's past? In the disagreements over Quentin's motives (some critics emphasize his self-criticism, others his self-exculpation), Miller adumbrates an ambiguity of viewpoint explored more successfully in *The Price*.

Some reviewers of the first production of *Incident at Vichy* mistook it as a message play and faulted Miller not only for his didacticism but also for teaching a lesson already learned about Nazism and man's inhumanity to man. It is a very talky drama, and given the various arguments advanced, it is easy to regard the characters as representative figures rather than as whole personalities. That that is not the case, however, is evident in the play's refusal to locate a winning argument, a resolution of the crisis of conviction besetting each character as his most cherished opinions are found wanting, are exposed as contradictory and self-serving. Even Leduc, who does a large amount of the debunking, discovers that he is not free of self-aggrandizing illusions. The Major reveals Leduc's privileged sense of himself, and Von Berg forces upon him a pass to freedom, which he must take at the cost of another's imprisonment. Von Berg's self-abnegating act of love for another man—although a moving statement of his belief that there are people in the world who would sacrifice themselves rather than permit evil to be done to others—is not dramatized as a final answer to the self-interested pleas of the other characters, however, and it does not cause the reversal of belief Miller coerced from Joe Keller after his son Larry's suicide in *All My Sons*. On the contrary, Von Berg is faced at the end of the play with an uncomprehending Major, a man who scorns gestures of self-sacrifice, except insofar as he is "an idealist" who ironically sacrifices himself for the perpetuation of the totalitarian system he serves. For all the characters, then, Vichy France during World War II is a place of detention where their self-justifications are demolished as they await their turns in the examination room, in which their release or their final fate in the concentration camps will be determined. Like Quentin, they are all vulnerable to the suspicion that they have not lived in "good faith." In other words, it is their questionable integrity, not their shaky ideas, that is ultimately at stake. *Incident at Vichy* is Miller's most existential play, in the sense that there is no exit from the dilemmas it portrays, no consoling truths to which characters can cling permanently; instead, there are only approximations of the truth, certain accurate perceptions, but there is nothing like the requiem, the coda, the summing up to be found in *Death of a Salesman*, *The Crucible*, and *A View from the Bridge*.

In *The Price*, Miller combines the best features of *After the Fall* and *Incident at Vichy*. Once again, the issue of coming to others in "good faith" is paramount, as Esther realizes in characterizing the surprise appearance of her husband Victor's brother, Walter. Walter returns to their boyhood apartment, where Victor is selling the family possessions because the building has been condemned. Walter has not seen his brother in sixteen years and wants to explain to him why he chose such an independent course, why he failed to support their father as Victor had done, to the detriment of his career. The immensely successful Walter feels stymied by the past and suggests that he and Victor took "seemingly different roads out of the same trap" created by their father's pose of helplessness after the failure of his business in the Crash of 1929. While Victor chose to "invent" a life of self-sacrifice, Walter chose to adopt a career of self-advancement. "We're like two halves of the same guy," Walter insists. His point is well-taken in terms of Miller's dramatic development, for Victor and Walter are also opposite sides of Quentin, whose family background is somewhat similar to theirs and who engages in similar debates with himself concerning the calls of self-denial and self-preferment; indeed, like Quentin, Victor and Walter are having what is essentially an argument with themselves in front of auditors (Esther and the furniture dealer, Gregory Solomon). Because Walter and Victor can go over the same ground of the past, their recollections are both arguable and utterly convincing as parallel but divergent interpretations. Thus, the audience responds to one character's point of view in the context of the other's and follows precisely the process by which these characters form their histories. Walter excuses himself by showing that in objective terms his father was not helpless; he had four thousand dollars he asked Walter to invest for him. Walter rejects the vision of family harmony that Victor worked so steadily to maintain; there was no love between their mother and father, only a business arrangement, as Walter brutally reveals with vivid memories of how their mother failed to support their father in his terrible need. Victor dismisses Walter's narrowly conceived interpretation of his father and their family. "A system broke down," he reminds Walter, referring to the Crash, "did I invent that?" Victor fights against Walter's simplification of their father's psychology. Embedded in Victor's words is an echo of Miller's original title for *Death of a Salesman*: "What about the inside of his head? The man was ashamed to go into the street!"

In the dialogue between these "archetypal brothers," as Neil Carson calls them, the nature of individual psychology and social reality, which Miller explores in all of his plays, is debated, and nowhere is that exploration more finely balanced, more convincingly conceived, than in *The Price*, where the two brothers—for all of their representativeness—steadfastly remain individual and irreconcilable. Moreover, the other two characters,

Esther and Solomon (a kibitzer who is Miller's funniest and wisest creation), are just as credibly presented, as they mediate between the hard positions held by Victor and Walter. Esther is one of Miller's most complex female characters, as her lyric memory at the end of the play demonstrates, for her wistful words richly embody all the wonderful promise of a life gone sour, just as Solomon's last actions—he is listening to a "laughing record" from the 1920's, "sprawling in the chair, laughing with tears in his eyes, howling helplessly to the air"—recall all the characters' hilarious and painful memories, leaving the audience perfectly poised in this drama of life's alternative expressions.

The Creation of the World and Other Business—with its archetypal brothers (Cain and Abel), its battle between God and Lucifer (who stand as the alternatives between which Adam and Eve must choose), its feel for human beings in a state of natural but problematic innocence, and its grappling with injustice—is an inevitable outgrowth of themes Miller has pursued throughout his career. When the play first appeared, however, it startled reviewers with its departure from Miller's realistic, domestic settings. They did not receive it favorably, and the play failed in its initial Broadway production, which is unfortunate, because it contains some of Miller's shrewdest writing and a surprisingly innovative rendition of the Edenic myth. The play's humor saves it from becoming a ponderous retelling of the familiar biblical account. The wide-ranging use of idiomatic expressions in English, Yiddish, and French mixed with the English of the Authorized Version of the Bible sets up a fascinating juxtaposition between the traditional story and the contemporary language that gives the whole play an uncanny freshness and irreverence. God calls Adam and Eve "my two idiotic darlings," and the profoundly comic nature of their moral and sexual education gradually acquires credibility. Would not the experience of being the first man and woman constitute the first comedy as well as the first tragedy? This is the question Miller appears to have posed for himself in this play, for Adam and Eve do not know what to do. Not having a history of feelings about God, about humanity, and about their sexuality, they must discover their sentiments about all of these things, and Lucifer would like to show them the shortcuts, to rationalize life, to avoid conflict before it begins. In order to follow him, however, Adam and Eve must accept the primacy of intellect over love.

Several of Miller's later plays, including *The American Clock, The Archbishop's Ceiling*, and *Danger, Memory!*, proved far more successful in London than in New York, a fact the playwright attributed at one point to the discomfort his American producers felt in dealing with "psychopolitical themes." Deeply cognizant of the dangers of social coercion and excessive conformity, Miller continued to hunger for the sense of community which he described in one of his books of photo essays, *In Russia*:

No one who goes to the theater in Russia can fail to be struck by the audience. . . . It is as though there were still a sort of community in this country, for the feeling transcends mere admiration for professionals doing their work well. It is as though art were a communal utterance, a kind of speech which everyone present is delivering together.

Other major works

NOVELS: *Focus*, 1945; *The Misfits*, 1961.

SHORT FICTION: *I Don't Need You Any More*, 1967.

NONFICTION: *Situation Normal*, 1944; *In Russia*, 1969 (photo essay with Inge Morath); *In the Country*, 1977 (photo essay with Morath); *The Theater Essays of Arthur Miller*, 1978 (Robert A. Martin, editor); *Chinese Encounters*, 1979 (photo essay with Morath); *"Salesman" in Beijing*, 1984; *Conversations with Arthur Miller*, 1987 (Matthew C. Roudané, editor); *Spain*, 1987; *Timebends: A Life*, 1987; *Arthur Miller and Company*, 1990 (edited by Christopher Bigsby).

SCREENPLAYS: *The Misfits*, 1961; *Everybody Wins*, 1990.

TELEPLAY: *Playing for Time*, 1980.

Bibliography

Bigsby, C. W. E. *File on Miller.* New York: Methuen, 1987. Contains a detailed, up-to-date chronology, synopses of the major and minor plays and of the drama on television and radio, and excerpts from nonfiction writing, with each section accompanied by critical commentary. Also includes a comprehensive bibliography of Miller's essays, interviews, and secondary sources (collections of essays, articles, chapters in books, and book-length studies).

Bloom, Harold, ed. *Arthur Miller.* New York: Chelsea House, 1987. This volume consists of essays on Miller's major drama from *All My Sons* to *The American Clock*, a brief introduction discussing Miller's significance, a chronology, an up-to-date bibliography, and an index. Includes important early essays (Raymond Williams and Tom F. Driver on the playwright's strengths and weaknesses) and later criticism by Neil Carson, C. W. E. Bigsby, and E. Miller Buddick.

_____, ed. *Arthur Miller's "Death of a Salesman."* New York: Chelsea House, 1988. Contains critical discussions published between 1963 and 1987, a chronology of Miller's life, a comprehensive bibliography of books and articles, and an index. In spite of reservations about Miller's importance as a writer, Bloom explains in his introduction how the play "achieves true aesthetic dignity" and discusses the particular merits of the essays in this collection.

Koon, Helene Wickham, ed. *Twentieth Century Interpretations of "Death of a Salesman."* Englewood Cliffs, N.J.: Prentice-Hall, 1983. These essays from the 1960's and 1970's emphasize the play's cultural significance, its status as a modern classic, and its style and point of view. The introduction provides a brief biography, a discussion of Miller's major themes, the play's relationship to classical tragedy, and his manipulation of time. Includes a brief bibliography and chronology of events in Miller's life and times.

Schleuter, June, and James K. Flanagan. *Arthur Miller.* New York: Frederick Ungar, 1987. Contains a comprehensive narrative chronology, a thorough first chapter on Miller's literature and life to 1985, chapter length discussions of his major plays (including *The Archbishop's Ceiling*), and a concluding chapter on his later one-act plays. Extensive notes, bibliography of Miller's work in all genres, select secondary bibliography of books and articles, and index.

Carl Rollyson